THE RISE AND FALL
OF
AMERICAN HUMOR

THE
RISE and FALL
OF
AMERICAN
HUMOR

JESSE BIER

Holt, Rinehart and Winston

NEW YORK   CHICAGO   SAN FRANCISCO

Grateful acknowledgment is made to the following publishers, authors, and agents who
have so generously granted permission to reprint from their publications:

Doubleday & Company, Inc., New York, New York, for excerpts from *Archy and
Mehitabel* by Don Marquis, copyright © 1927 by Doubleday & Company, Inc.; the
illustration by George Herriman from *The Lives and Times of Archy and Mehitabel* by
Don Marquis, copyright © 1927 by Doubleday and Company, Inc.

Gershwin Publishing Corporation, New York, New York, for excerpts from "It
Ain't Necessarily So" by George and Ira Gershwin, copyright © 1935 by Gershwin
Publishing Corporation, copyright renewed. Published jointly in the United States by
Gershwin Publishing Corporation and New Dawn Music Corporation.

Hamish Hamilton Ltd., London, England, for excerpts from *Vintage Thurber* by
James Thurber, copyright © 1963 by Hamish Hamilton, London.

Harms, Inc., New York, New York, for excerpts from "Anything Goes" by Cole
Porter, copyright © 1934 by Harms, Inc.

Harper & Row, Publishers, Incorporated, New York, New York, for excerpts and
illustration by Gluyas Williams from *Inside Benchley* by Robert Benchley, copyright © 1942 by Harper & Row, Publishers, Incorporated.

Harper & Row Publishers, Incorporated, New York, New York, for "Letter to the
Gas Company" (Hartford, Feb. 12, 1891) by S. L. Clemens from *Mark Twain's
Notebook,* edited by Albert Bigelow Paine, copyright © 1935 by The Mark Twain
Company and for excerpts from *Pudd'nhead Wilson* by Mark Twain, copyright © 1922
by The Mark Twain Company.

Holt, Rinehart and Winston, Inc., New York, New York, for excerpts from *Complete
Poems of Robert Frost,* copyright © 1923 by Holt, Rinehart and Winston, Inc., copyright © 1936, 1951 by Robert Frost, copyright © 1964 by Lesley Frost Ballantine.

Alfred A. Knopf, Inc., New York, New York, for excerpts from *The Prince of Wales
and Other Famous Americans,* by Miguel Covarrubias, copyright © 1925 by Alfred
A. Knopf, Inc., and renewed © 1953 by Miguel Covarrubias.

Little, Brown and Company, Publishers, Boston, Massachusetts, for excerpts from the
poem "To A Small Boy Standing On My Shoes While I Am Wearing Them" as it
appeared in *The Face is Familiar* by Ogden Nash, copyright © 1931 by Ogden Nash,
and for excerpts from the poem "Bankers Are Just Like Anybody Else, Except Richer"
from *Verses from 1929 On* by Ogden Nash, copyright © 1935 by Ogden Nash; originally
appeared in *The New Yorker.*

The Macmillan Company New York, New York, Mr. M. B. Yeats and Macmillan
and Company, Ltd., London, England, for excerpts from the poem "The Gyres" by W.
B. Yeats in *Collected Poems of W. B. Yeats,* copyright © 1956 by The Macmillan
Company, New York and copyright © 1950 by Macmillan and Company Ltd., London.

Random House, Inc., New York, New York, for excerpts from *The Reivers* by
William Faulkner, copyright © 1962 by William Faulkner.

Mrs. Helen Thurber, for excerpts from "University Days" in *My Life and Hard Times,*
copyright © 1933, 1961 by James Thurber, published by Harper and Row Publishers,
Incorporated, and originally printed in *The New Yorker;* excerpts from "The Greatest
Man in the World" in *The Middle-Aged Man on the Flying Trapeze,* copyright © 1935
by James Thurber, copyright © 1963 by Helen W. Thurber and Rosemary Thurber
Sauers, published by Harper and Row and originally printed in *The New Yorker;* fables
from *Fables for our Time,* copyright © 1940 by James Thurber, published by Harper
and Row and originally printed in *The New Yorker;* fables from *Further Fables for
our Time,* copyright © 1956 by James Thurber, published by Simon and Schuster;
illustration "What have you done with Dr. Millmoss?" from *The Thurber Carnival,*
copyright © 1945 by James Thurber, published by Harper and Row and originally
printed in *The New Yorker.*

DESIGNER: VINCENT TORRE

8655458

Printed in the United States of America

For my father,
and to my mother and brothers

CONTENTS

PREFACE ix

Introduction 1

I   Early American Humor 32

II   "Southwestern" Humor 52

III   "Literary Comedians":
The Civil War and Reconstruction 77

IV   Mark Twain 117

V   Intercentury Humor 162

VI   Interwar Humor 208

VII   Modern American Humor 285

VIII   Humor in Selected Major American Writers 360

IX   American and Foreign Humor 415

X   Conclusion 454

BIBLIOGRAPHY 479

INDEX 491

PREFACE

As FAR as tone is concerned, I hold with Josh Billings: if a man is wrong, he can't be too conservative; if he's right, he can't be too radical. One might as well say what he has to say strongly or not at all and commit rather than omit himself. If he remains unfathomable he ought to be sentenced with his own crime, obscurity. My own intentions are to be as clear and forthright as possible, setting my views before an educated but restive audience. I make no concessions to illiteracy in what follows and all concessions to directness. There is an ostentation of coyness, which I wish to avoid—although that is not a reason to be perverse.

This is a critical book. I hope it is also a truthful one. I find no necessary contradiction between the two. All that is required is a strict order of priority. A reader is willing to indulge almost any declaration of opinion but is never well disposed toward even slightly incorrect facts. That is because opinion may be right, half-right, or mostly wrong but still claim interest. But being dishonest is like being gravid: either you are or you aren't, and time will soon tell. For my own part, I hope that my critical views are not urged upon the reader out of the same motive that activated the seriocomic Jewish father of a wayward daughter. Lavishly and abruptly he increased her dowry to a duped prospect, confessing finally that his daughter was "just a little bit" pregnant. I should like to believe that my own manner suggests nothing more than reasonable conviction. I hope time will show that my facts are accurate, that I have not ignored inconvenient ones, and that I have not made up any information to suit my purposes.

Because I do not wish to say something about everything and thus nothing very much or very new, my procedure is selective. Nonetheless, I believe that the authors and performers chosen are, by and large, standard or otherwise significant. Such connections as I may draw between them are generally verifiable. But sometimes they are presumptive guesses that seem to me strong enough, but they may be taken or left alone.

The "periods" designated are quite arbitrary. Although I shall treat popular forms and mass media as well as more formal literature, I have turned to the broadest literary-historical divisions as simple convenience. We may reflect that all of American literature is itself a subspecies of English-speaking literature and, in turn, of western world expression. A narrow refinement of periods and genres within this field may strike some people, especially foreign observers, as an altogether amusing pedantic pastime. I should think so, too.

It may be deplorably informal procedure to refer to popular texts and editions when I allude to titles at all and not to exotica the general reader cannot put his hands on. But this review is designed only secondarily for scholars. Therefore, I use terms like "humor" and "comedy" interchangeably and no doubt blur special distinctions among a host of other literary definitions. Mostly these distinctions are totally unnecessary to my purpose, and though I worry a few, like punning, I spend little time on others like the formal difference between "black" and "sick" humor. I hope only that the major terms of my own discussion are, at last, sufficiently clear.

Footnotes accompanying the text are contrapuntal rather than essential references. They are informative or perhaps entertaining divagations, but always extra considerations. I have reduced them to a minimum so that they do not function as another book in themselves. As to bibliographic references, I shall not generally interrupt my coverage to give all sources and full citations in the body of the text. Nor shall I do so in the footnotes either. But every important author, editor, scholar and critic to whose work I refer will be duly listed in the Bibliography at the back of the book.

Critical and judgmentive as the work is, yet I prefer not to think of my views as intensely or even predominantly personal. No author ought to labor under the delusion that he has subdued all his own inclinations or demurrals. But he need not make a virtue of the defect and thereby settle on taste as final arbiter. My remarks on such modern figures as Salinger, Bellow, Gover, or Heller, for example, seem to me to err on the side of severe objectivity and do not reveal my own admirations. I believe this may be true further back in time, as in judgments on Bierce and even Poe. And something of the reverse may be the case for my consistently favorable adversions, in historical context, to Artemus Ward. As far as the matter has been in my control, my preferences and exceptions have been treated as the irrelevancies they ought to be. There is no getting away from the central interests that organization itself creates, but I hope that such emphasis is somewhat closer to the truths of the subject than to my own feelings.

One prime factor guides the investigation of all the periods and figures we shall consider. That is to have preserved the complication of the subject. To do so is to reconcile our study with all that we appreciate of ordinary psychology and, at the very least, to make it serve the latitudinarian spirit of comedy itself. That aim supersedes any important argument I pursue, including the one that governs the title of the book, and all other leading theories which I adopt, and even my placement of humor among literary modes. These pragmatical concepts may be right or wrong in themselves, either illuminations or indiscretions. But they are indefensible if they lead to a swift and easy understanding. Any expedient simplification of the ins-and-outs of national or even regional expression would be the very worst of devaluations. That is no less true in a country regularly given to general and compulsive formulations and to urging them upon us from every side.

Certainly there is something amusing in a serious treatment of humor. We may find it easier to be reconciled to the situation, however, if we remember that there is usually something serious going on in almost all effective humor itself. At all events, I shall not assume the role of comic commentator or comedian myself—not primarily, in any case, and only if temptations are overwhelming, and never for long. But if the reader is struck by any particular illustration or analysis, he need not hesitate to laugh. It is the one allowable distraction.

I reserve a note of extenuation only about the past, for all I have perpetrated during the last three years upon the unsuspecting heads of students, twice in Montana and once in Pennsylvania. Those early lectures and classroom explorations of the subject, I feel obliged to say, were naïve impostures disguised only by a certain stridency of the vocal cords. It was professorial hazard. I wish these now anonymous students, all of them very patient and some of them even helpful to me though in no way responsible for my errors, the best of fortune and compensatory careers, and I thank them.

My gratitude also to Professors Warren Carrier and Harry Garvin, chairmen of the English Departments at the University of Montana and Bucknell University respectively. Professor Garvin extended every facility for my work while I was Visiting Lecturer at Bucknell. And at my home university in Montana, Professor Carrier's cooperation was frequently sacrificial, an indulgence outweighed only by his own considerable and educated interest in the topic.

As to all those other commentators and scholars both named and unnamed in the discussion that follows, my indebtedness goes without saying. There are pioneers among them, and invaluable compilers, venturesome theorists and astute critics. Always indispensable to my views, they form by now a community strong enough to absorb or withstand anything I may say.

J.B.

Missoula, Montana
January 1967

THE RISE AND FALL

OF

AMERICAN HUMOR

Introduction

"DROWND them kittens!" Shillaber's comic heroine, Mrs. Partington, calls out to her nephew. But she has an afterthought. "Stop a minute. . . . I'll take the chill off the water."

She is actually a prim but kindly old lady. Her career now appears dated and ineffectual, existing in a sidestream of benevolent, mild, and harmless American whimsicality. And yet there are these deflections to cruelty and grotesquerie. Meanwhile, the rest of authentic American humor is as we shall find it: caustic, wild, savage. All of our comic expression may be placed along a continuum from irreverence to outright shock.

The general impulse of our humor is to enjoy life's conquest over all particular systems of values. The paradox of pluralistic American life is that our special history has furnished our humor simultaneously with both its targets and weaponry. One consequence of pluralism is a desperate conformity, of value or status or aspiration, in order to hold our society together at any given time. The other consequence is to safeguard enrichment and to oppose fanaticism by encouraging all dissent and even attack. Humor has accepted that challenge with alternate glee and rage, and it has pushed its peculiarly heightened prerogatives in America to the furthest limits.

Our humor, for instance, employs a great number of nonsense jokes and stories. The phenomenon is like that of "witty" music, of melodic lines that are funny because they do not develop. Such humor lies in our frustrated expectations. "The highest part of this mountain," lectures Artemus Ward, "is the top." We are thwarted, the way we are in watching the fizzled firework. A good deal of American humor has its point in not rocketing to glory. But we cannot fully relate the point to purely psychological theories that explain our laughter as a discharge of pent-up tension. There is a philosophical activity, equally reflexive. In America we laugh at a visible progress disappearing before our eyes; we laugh at our assumption of utter and sequent control, at our subsequent and real diminishment.

And we laugh harder, and need to in the United States, where pretense and rhetoric and sentimental shibboleth have been more solidified than elsewhere. When Fred Allen's Senator Claghorn declares, "Ah stand four-square. Sixteen, that is," we laugh at more than the deflated politician. We also laugh at what the particular devices, literalism and circularity, imply for us psychically: the humor of nonadvancement in a nation committed to "progress" everywhere. Indeed, undisguised thematic counterparts of the same nature occur in almost every comedian's repertoire of jokes. Even benign Will Rogers becomes explicit: "America—a nation that flourished 1900–1942, conceived many odd inventions for getting somewhere, but could think of nothing to do when they got there."

The greatest part of American waggery and comic attitude exists in a magnetic field, and we miss the force of the whole if we separate devices and objects of the humor from potent undersetting. Moreover, this field force of what we may call antitheticism in American humor has repercussions for general theories of humor that, up to now, have not taken the American demonstration into adequate consideration. In any event, it promotes generalizations of its own, some of them unexpected.

Our humor criticizes all verities and cozy securities, consistently idealized as these have been in America. Its voice is the voice of hard, fresh truth, as the long and popular tradition of the cartoon shows. Moreover, this urge to tell the whole truth lies behind the function of so much cruelty in our humor. This may be the cruelty of Shillaber's drowned cats, where it is rather gratuitous. Or we may find it in Erskine Caldwell's episode of the grandmother who is repeatedly run over by an old Ford car in the gravel driveway, where it is a requirement. Against a nauseatingly prettified ideal of American life, humorists set their cruelty as a particular redressment of reality. The fact that they can go too far is a commentary on the intrinsic difficulties of the approach, as seen often in the extremes of black humor, and also on the proportions which false idealizations of character and prettifications of life have assumed in America.

A leading approach, in these respects, has been that of mockery. The famous Jewish sense of humor has had particular success in the United States. Here is Groucho Marx on Horatio Algerism. "When I came to this country, I didn't have a nickel in my pocket. Now I have a nickel in my pocket." Literalism here serves a comic mockery that would have been intolerable in Hitlerite Germany. There, as John Mander has pointed out, Jewish cabaret humorists became prime enemies of a state dedicated to a self-exaltation so insanely serious that, indeed, only comic ridicule could have successfully withstood or destroyed it. There was a method, then, in the madness of anti-Semitism. Artificial mythmakers know their enemies everywhere. But that pluralism which has led America to similar messianic positions or to a host of social and psychological tyrannies of the mind has also savingly kept open its lines of reactive or subversive attack. Which is to point out how necessary freedom is to humor, a fact that is no less true because it is a commonplace.

But insights into the antithetical nature of American humor must not lead us to define all the humor itself as simple in function. As a matter of fact, since much of the American mentality itself battens on simplifications—on clichés, on shibboleths, on proverbs, on slogans, on formulas—an equal amount of our humor is in the service of unholy complication. That is not unique in the world either, although a surprising number of European theoreticians ignore the point and attack humor itself as a genre of gross simplification. They need only attend one of their own circuses and watch the impresario clown push the grand piano across the stage to the lightweight stool. This is not only reversalism but complication, more often than not an inherent characteristic of comedy. Indeed, the greater part of American literary, journalistic, and cinematic comedy is humor that makes simple events or situations unforeseeably complex.

The observation, for instance, accounts for the whole career of Rube Goldberg. His cartoon work involves the comedy of wild and unnecessary though ingenious complication. Here are the details for his "automatic" device for keeping screen doors closed:

> House flies (A), seeing open door, fly on porch. Spider (B) descends to catch them and frightens potato bug (C), which jumps from hammer (D), allowing it to drop on pancake turner (E), which tosses pancake into pan (F). Weight of pancake causes pan to tilt and pull cord (G), which starts mechanical soldier (H) walking. Soldier walks to edge of table and catches his head in noose (I), thereby hanging himself. Weight in noose causes string to pull lever and push shoe against bowling ball (J), throwing it into hands of circus monkey (K), who is expert bowler. Monkey throws ball at bowling pins painted on screen door, thereby closing it with a bang.

It is to the point, of course, that at any juncture of levers, strings, shoes, or rolling balls, Goldberg could have simplified and still been funny enough. But his task was always to pack as much as the cartoon space and comic imagination allowed. The very essence of the comedy was complexity.[1]

Likewise, when Laurel and Hardy appear in their first two-reeler simply to sell Christmas trees to a Scotsman on Vine Street, the chaotic mayhem that follows is a product of pure complication. Not to be denied on their first call, they insist on calling him back to the door, and he finally whisks out a pair of shears and clips their samples. The graduated mayhem builds from there. A simple confrontation turns into a complicated comic war.

Inadvertent humor provides final confirmation. Here is a scene of Ernest Hemingway's partisan group sitting down to eat:

> "There are no plates," Anselmo said. "Use your own knife." The girl had leaned four forks, *tines down,* against the sides of an iron dish.

It is true that in *For Whom the Bell Tolls* Hemingway is aiming for a particularly significant sense of experience for Robert Jordan.

---

[1] Frequently the nature of a movie gag by W. C. Fields is sheer complication. A man enters a stationery store and asks for a 2¢ stamp, choosing the one in the middle of a huge sheet which Fields places on the counter. Fields gives the stamp to him with the corners of 8 other stamps surrounding it—costing Fields 16¢.

The work is altogether serious, and we are seriously involved, even at this moment. But Hemingway introduces, as I have italicized the detail, an unintentionally funny complication. That is why he is notoriously easy to parody. It is sufficient to our purposes, however, to show how unnecessary complication may disrupt a serious and even powerful work or an absorbing scene, because it is inherently funny.[2]

One is led to conclude that overt American humor is filled with more complication than the humor of other nations. In fact, English and Italian film makers of the post-World War II period learned that lesson from our example, apparently after we forgot it. In any event, the role of complication in successful American humor is primary. Its ultimate function is to complicate our idealized simple modes of customary thought.

But there is a humor of the obvious, too. The overflowing washing machine is a simple cinematic scene, where there is hardly any complication, only inevitability: the sure advance of the suds into the living room in a vast tide of catastrophic foam. But in every use of minimal complication, there is always the hypnotic comic power of disaster, *that* supreme antithetical deflation of smooth-going American living.

If the exception to the rule confirms a yet larger rule, still the lesser rule holds in great part. The humor of exaggeration and tall tales employs techniques of frustration and complication. We might consider all nonsense humor in this connection, especially the American tendency to *non sequiturs,* first epitomized by Artemus Ward. "I knew a man from Oregon once who didn't have a tooth in his head, and that man could play the drums better than anyone I ever met."

This is depthless humor, but effective in the United States. Most foreigners denigrate it out of hand. That is because it exists in a general background field which they, as outsiders, cannot fully detect.

Such observers may miss the force of another trait of our humor as well. It is that element of antic, absurd, comic freedom best

---

[2] We often encounter variations of the phrase, "It's so complicated, it makes you laugh," applied to all fields of advanced investigation—musicology, biophysics, economics, or whatever. Over and beyond the nervous reflex of incomprehension, there is intrinsic amusement in complexity itself.

exemplified by our movie cartoons. Tom and Jerry are freed of a thousand deaths, exempt from all physical laws and even the worst consequences of unmitigable catastrophe. The largely European theories of comedy as discharge of tension will not quite serve. For the tension itself is annihilated in the wild antics of these movie cartoons and other cinematic comedy. We are liberated from consequence as well as judgment and, indeed, from all biologic purpose itself, even that of discharge. All counter-pressures themselves are blown away in obedience to no rules at all. In our comic heritage there are indigenous sources for these phenomena, such as our frontier comedy, especially the Bunyan and Crockett humor of unbounded extravagance. Other elements and explanations are involved, of course, like the psychic realism of aggression operative under all the fantasy, or of wish-fulfillment, particularly that of immortality. But in any event, social and physical terms of existence are not merely reversed or upset but annihilated in the American contribution, which is an explosion rather than a simple discharge. And what that suggests, as a kind of ultimate comic freedom, is a commentary on the general repressiveness against which American humor is set. Needless to say, in these connections, theories of comic proportion, like Molière's, are not directly applicable to the subject.

The question of comic freedom is related to an even more distinctive feature of American humor, what we may call comic momentum. In a situation or joke of this kind, we are the witnesses and victims not of a sudden change in direction, or even of surprise,[3] but of the sheer momentum involved in going the whole distance. The comic matter goes out of control, as in the vignette where, as a milliner, Groucho Marx tries to sell a hat to Madeleine Carroll on the radio program of the thirties, "The Circle":

CARROLL: This is a lovely five-dollar hat. How much were you asking?
MARX: I was asking fifteen. I'll settle for fourteen.
CARROLL: I'll give you six.
MARX: Make it thirteen.

[3] Surprise has been grossly exaggerated as an indisputable or unique characteristic of comedy. The humor of George Ade, for instance, as Mencken was first to point out, contains virtually no element of surprise at all.

She says seven, and he says twelve, and she moves to eight. Marx
quotes eleven, and she nine. "Ten," he declares, and she cries,
"Eleven." He shouts nine, and she twelve. Eight, he insists, and
she answers thirteen. "Seven," he bargains doggedly. "Fourteen."
His tone rises at, "Six," and there is the slightest pause.

> CARROLL: Fifteen!
> MARX: Five! *Sold.* There, you'll have to get up early in the
> morning to put one over on me!

We do not have what Koestler has defined as bisociation here, the
sudden intervention of another plane of meaning. There is an
unstoppable momentum of thought or reflex. It characterizes not
only such jokes but a great deal of our movie comedy, as in the
custard-pie crescendo portrayed on the American screen. It is
another consequence of extreme psychic freedom, a distinctive
native technique that only the French approximate on occasion.
Inclusive theories of humor must make room for it.

They must also account for another striking American characteristic. That is what we can name comic pertinence, the comic
recall to relevance, as in Josh Billings. "The hawk is a carnivorous
animal—and a chickenivorous one, every chance it gets." Often
the comedy resides in the simple recall to truth, funny only because we have pretentiously hidden or conveniently forgotten it, as
when Mark Twain refers to "Authors' Readings, that kind of
crime."

Sometimes what is comic, especially in America, where all sorts
of interests are at work to conceal all sorts of truth, is the merest
statement of truth, without any colorful or hyperbolic style whatsoever. Perhaps this again is a subtle question of comic momentum
as applied to ordinary facts. They are supposed to remain in a
state of rest; pushing them along a steady line of implication is
amusing in itself. Ask the average man, for instance, to remember
the architecture of old banks, some of which he can still see in
old-fashioned neighborhoods, crenelated, fortress-like, designed
visibly to protect and defend his money, which he had deposited
there specifically for safekeeping. Then point out the new design
of our banks, with their open, fluid driveways around an outside
booth, which in a credit age facilitates the public's taking rather

than leaving of money. Our audience smiles. But not at our figure of speech, for there is no comic metaphor at all, only the literal, drawn-out truth. If they do not suffer concealment or disguise, facts suffer a kind of inertia in the United States, and giving them a certain natural movement makes for humor.

American comedy is voracious, deflationary, skeptical, cynical, pessimistic, blasphemous, and black, not by turns or accident but in an inevitable sliding scale of function. Its spirit is realistic. Its realism often serves the fiercer hostilities, and the principal risk it takes is to be too highly charged for its own good. It has characteristically taken that risk. In doing so, it has scored phenomenal successes in just hitting a certain line of exposé and comic criticism. Only in contemporary times does it go over that line with a full force, for reasons which we shall examine in concluding chapters.

A list of its leading modes and devices—nonsense, confusionism, reversal, anticlimax, antiproverbialism, undercutting—indicates the predominately negative, penetrative tendencies throughout its history. As such, it is not merely allied with the movement of Realism in American literature and culture, but is part and parcel of it. American humorists have consistently given their minority realist report on American life. It is no coincidence either that a great many of our comics have risen from the lower class, from frontier or immigrant quarters, conditioned to disabusement and resilient clarity. Furthermore, humorists, as in the Local Color movement, spearheaded Realism itself, and figures like Bret Harte and Mark Twain are pertinent in this connection. Moreover, in their advanced use of real speech and dialect (as in the early "southwest" humorists), in all their antirhetorical devices, and in their combativeness, they foreran the Realists by a full generation. They have gone on to pace the Realist movement in a great range of techniques, and they have regularly contributed subject matter others pick up later, such as the frank cruelty and sexuality of George Washington Harris, the political satire of the earlier Seba Smith, and the excoriations of the later Finley Peter Dunne. Struck by such features, the commentator, T. L. Masson, has even made the claim that humorists as gentle as George Ade surpass standard Realists like Theodore Dreiser and Sinclair Lewis in sheer accuracy and consistency of performance, and famous critics like Howells and Mencken have said as much.

In any case, the alliance between American humor and formal Realism is as close as the alliance between American humor and general truthtelling, and the fact counts heavily. There is a strong mutual animus to counter the standard American pronouncements and formulas. On the whole, the element of corrective is far less optimistic in America than in most quarters of Europe. The Civil War and its aftermath appear to signal a decisive turn to corrosive acid and nascent savagery for their own sake. The "literary comedians" of the epoch register not only temporary virulence but a cynicism and contempt which persist afterward. The climactic war resolved too little of the social and moral past and only added northern rapacity and the sins of industrial conquest to a bloody ledger. Probably Professor Leo Marx's statement about "the bitterness present almost everywhere in American humor" rises especially from postbellum morale. It applies to Mark Twain's backward look to the 1840's, sweet humorous nostalgia turned acidic even in *Huckleberry Finn*.

Twain himself signals best the mounting pressures on one's sense of humor in America, where the comedian suffers from too rich a field and too many targets that blunt the comic assault and convert it to frustrated anger. "If I could keep my faculty for humor uppermost," he told Dunne, "I'd laugh the dogs out of the country. But I can't. I get too mad."

Certainly the earliest humorists, including Franklin, are traditionally "corrective," aligning themselves with society against foolish deviators from custom and sense. But the course of American humor is a rapid and accelerating realignment with the nonconformists, the maladjusted even, the hypercritical antagonists of social code and self-deception. Retrenchments from sharp commentary and virulent humor, as in Kin Hubbard or Will Rogers, are secondary and temporary phenomena, though explicable and even inevitable, as we shall see. They afford the briefest rural respite from that surge to the pith and force of our modern cosmopolitism humor, itself an equally inevitable outgrowth of the latter quarter of the nineteenth century. The subsequent excesses of black or sick humor are the results of both a later sociopolitical development and a built-in tendency of our traditional comedy.[4] Just so long as a national identity is basically unattained and unnatural absolutisms continue, American humor will appear vengefully antithetical and will have to resist a certain over-all momentum that characterizes the whole American genre.

With certain reservations, the redefinition of "comedy" by the British scholar, L. J. Potts, is the best we have in modern times. It is the most satisfactory way of bounding humor as a whole, though we must modify it by other theories and by American practice.

Potts places comedy midway between tragedy and satire or invective. His implication is that tragedy thoroughly heightens meaning and that satire maliciously destroys it, but that comedy chooses a mean between these extremes. As a mode of social ridicule, however, satire may be genuinely comic itself, and Potts's use of the term is imprecise. Moreover, his equation of tragedy with total elevation (and, as it were, with the greatest sense) and of satiric farce or invective diatribe with total reductionism (or no sense at all) forces us to equate humor with partial sense. Such a characterization means that we must overlook or otherwise account for nonsense humor, as in the old vaudeville joke that Max Eastman recalls:

COMEDIAN: Didn't I meet you in Buffalo?
STRAIGHT MAN: I've never been to Buffalo.
COMEDIAN: Neither have I. It must have been two other fellows.

Or we must give up the humor of wild American extravagance, which in its way is the humor of exaggerated sense, as in the typical frontier anecdote of a man so tall he had to stand on a ladder to shave himself.

Indeed, most American humor demonstrates the fullest mockery of received sense and expectations. Our shaggy-dog stories provide a famous case in point. Our iconoclastic humorists who, with

[4] The banana-peel practical joke, particularly favored in America, indicates the readiness of antithetic laughter in the United States, the utter and unfailing release of predisposed feeling; the greater the pomposity of the victim as a social figure, of course, the more relevant and effective the comedy. The observation would be banal except that the course of recent sick humor moves in an opposite direction for sadism's sake.

Mencken, fling their dead cats into sanctuaries of communal "sense," invite the strongest consideration. In fact, the greatest number of our devices and targets argue a prima facie case for the denigrative function of our comedy.

And more damaging to Potts's view is Michael Wharton's recent contention that tragedy and satire are essentially alike because they are basically serious and that comedy and farce must be placed together because of their derogatory but characteristic fun. We can amalgamate Wharton's objection with Potts's generalization, however, and conclude the over-all argument in Potts's favor. Humor, and humorous satire and farce, can be placed between tragic—and, let us also say, sentimental—exaltation and heightened sense, on the one side, and invective and diatribic revulsion and utter reductionism, on the other. In other words, the humorous and human are located between the divine and the subhuman. Comic realism is situated between transcendence and annihilation, between transfiguration and black despair, between bland illusionism and the rage of the sickest humor that is no humor at all, between the highest and the lowest, between rival extremisms of thought, between equally unreal fanaticisms. And, by virtue of American example, humor shades over both the upper and lower borders, into Chaplinesque transfiguration or sentimentality and into the sick jokes of the Ginger Man. Its modern drift, however, is somewhat less toward nebulous light than to nether blackness.

These are governing considerations in our placement of American humor. By and large, they hold and serve a general purpose. Other theories apply only in part or not at all.

"Humor" derives from the Medieval concept of *humeurs*, wherein an imbalance of bodily fluids creates eccentricity. On the other hand, "to amuse" originates from the French *à muser*, "to think." And the writer Arthur Koestler reminds us that "wit" is traceable to the Old English *witan* or "understanding." There is no denying the coexistence of wild eccentricity and profound understanding in the American performance. But the insight is rather more academical than strictly useful.

With all rigid class theories of comedy, from Plato through Mazzoni to Renaissance and neoclassical critics, we have little to do. The place of comedy rose so swiftly from underground status, its movement from low to middle and high class so accelerated in the United States that it has seemed always generally authorized by the whole of society. Indeed, Washington Irving's full commitment to it blurs sociological distinctions very early in America.

One of Aristotle's perceptions, however, is especially instructive. He distinguished high comedy from low comedy and contended that high comedy was closer to tragedy than to low comedy. In his most poignant work, Chaplin is the American proof. And both the thesis and its latter-day proof prompt us to believe that the buffer territory of comedy is greater than either of the genres it separates. In the metaphorical geography of literature and entertainment, Alsace-Lorraine bulks larger than Germany and France.

Medieval and Renaissance scholastic definitions[5] insist upon differences of "grand" and "familiar" style, harping upon the use of prose or vernacular as the stylistic decorum for comedy. But the masterful use of the native vernacular—the American language, as Mencken finally dignified it in his study—in the work of Mark Twain and his successors showed it an instrument of powerful subtlety and eloquence. The familiar, lower style has had a sublimity earlier theorists could not imagine for it.

But we cannot be led to concede, as early Italian critics maintained without opposition, that comedy is exclusively democratic in ideology. The stubborn careers of Twain, Bierce, Mencken, Lardner, and others in the United States dispel a perfectly reasonable logic that the facts do not quite support.

Except for Hazlitt, English theorists tend to fight internecine critical wars on the subject of humor or specific stages of it, their positions largely unavailing to us. Meredith and Lamb, for instance, elaborate theories to destroy or rescue Restoration comedy. It is principally a matter of taste. And Meredith's standard view of the "corrective" function of humor has seemed largely irrelevant to American practice. More to the purpose is a growing perception from Shaftesbury through Lamb and Spencer about the free comic spirit that works a revenge on social constraints.

---

[5] Auerbach, in *Mimesis,* has refuted classical and medieval categorizations, recalling the Biblical sublimity given to low style and subject, particularly in the New Testament. This "impurity" of expression fell into long disuse, until the comedy of Cervantes and then the neotragedy of Stendhal.

There have been numerous critical arguments, by Karl Marx and others, that point to a fundamental historic progression, as in Greek culture, from elevated tragic drama to a later stage of decadent comedy. Grandeur becomes grandiosity. It ends in a pratfall. Using similar perspective but with a different judgment, Dürrenmatt, the Swiss writer, maintains that whereas tragedy naïvely overcomes all distance in order to make myths present to us, later and healthier comedy creates distance.

Such theories are formulated, for one reason or another, to give comedy the final word. The fact of the matter is that tragedy and comedy are two consistently different but often contemporaneous views of the human condition. Because certain commentators of the nineteenth and twentieth centuries have needed correlative and selective theories of history or class supersedence, comedy has been made into a climactic or final literary and cultural form. Or because ours tries to be a comic age, we tend to resolve distinctions in comedy's favor.

We do so more and more by calling attention to its realistic, objective, and relativistic features, referring to similar implications of modern physics, psychology, and art for appropriate support. All this is true enough. We ought to recall, however, that comedy no more cancels out the possibilities of tragedy than does tragedy the possibilities of comedy. Moreover, whatever threatens one, threatens both, as in mid-twentieth century. Nevertheless, the commitment to comedy in our time, with all its overindulgences, helps clarify distinctions as never before.

Brecht, for instance, points tellingly to a certain subjectivity in all tragedy. He means that the tragic mode is anthropomorphic. It rationalizes "divine" laws and seeks to make a supernal or a grandly human order out of chaos. With comedy, he suggests, it is the other way around. Fulfillment or transcendence count more than survival for the typical tragic protagonist, who may achieve or surpass himself through ultimate self-recognition alone. Survival and self-justification count far more heavily in comedy, and more and more so in a world of increasing complexity, paradox, or out-and-out contradiction. The distinction can be seen especially well in the gradations of tragicomedy, the forte of the mature Chaplin; we may contrast *The Great Dictator* and *Monsieur Verdoux*.

At all events, tragedy is the mode of human dignification. Bradley sounded the definitive modern note when he spoke of the "heightened awareness of the greatness of man" in tragedy. In his very lamentations for the decline of tragedy, Krutch has excoriated our lack of faith in that same greatness. And settling for less, Dobrée has written of the "glorification of man's power to endure." These are representative voices. We may weep in tragedy, but we are consoled and uplifted. We, too, with the heroes, come to high recognitions. We understand that the defeat which culminates a tragic work is, by and large, just. It asserts, as Frye maintains, a "universal moral order," which the very fall of the hero confirms. The point comes back to Nietzsche's *Birth of Tragedy* (1872); "tragic wisdom is joyful," not cathartic even but tonic. And all of our modern insight is compacted into Yeats's couplet from "The Gyres":

> Hector is dead and there's a light in Troy;
> We that look on but laugh in tragic joy.

Comedy proves itself the exact obverse of tragedy. Like the fairy tale, comedy does not mainly rationalize experience. Its happy ending is a disguise for the opposite effect, as the unhappy ending of tragedy is. What constitutes the comic experience is very often even terrifying just before the end, the bulk of events prior to the conclusion a veritable succession of defeats. In this sense the Frenchman, Lucien Fabre (1889–1952), was correct in describing comedy as dismay followed or rescued by a happy resolution; and this dismay is not the kind easily or convincingly subject to a justified, conclusive order of any real sort, least of all the kind that magnifies our human capacities. Brecht is right, then, to think that in so far as we impose order or assume heights of significance, our tragedy is subjective and egocentric. Making the opposite case, the history of American humor provides a long argument for the disorder of objective reality.

Our humor depicts a pronouncedly varied and recalcitrant human nature. All deep metaphysical issues apart, it steadily becomes the mode of the times, because the times cannot accept a magnification of man. In this sense, comedy is not even especially deflationary in function, only noninflationary and honest. In a country like ours, where the attempt to erect pseudomyths of optimism and opportunity, for instance, has been extraordinary, antithetic comedy has been necessarily stronger than elsewhere, predictably destructive and more and more fierce, by a principle of reaction. The indicative American joke defining optimists and pessimists has nothing to do with the proverbial half a glass of water, whether it is half full or half empty. It sets no objective riddles but sides with gleeful derogation.

> Optimist (waking, throwing off covers, flinging back the drapes and opening the window): Good morning, God!
>
> Pessimist (with wearily lidded eyes, dragging himself from bed, sidling to window and peering out): Good God! morning.

In that intrigue of our unconscious, Pollyanna and Horatio Alger call forth demons of reversal and ridicule. American humor makes an early and abiding alliance with the forces of realism and reality. Its approach cannot help being, by degrees, skeptical, cynical, misanthropic, and then brutal.

In this light, the thinking of Spencer, Freud, Koestler, Bergson, and others seems more pertinent to us, even if not always meeting certain of our objections. Discussions of psychological incongruity, of laughter as release, or explosion, of energy, of feeling catching up belatedly with understanding, of superiority—all are provocative.[6] Such psychological theories are invariably by-products of larger philosophical positions, however, functioning selectively to prove other general theorems of human nature, and they must be tested with impartial austerity by the pragmatist. For instance, Bergson laughs at people when they behave mechanically like things. But we wonder, with the journalist, Weightman, if Bergson laughs at things, puppets perhaps, when they behave like people. We must pick and choose what applies to the evidence even in the comprehensive criticism of this greatest of all theorists. When Bergson speaks of a certain "anesthesia of the heart," we hear the note of relevance. It comes from critical forebears, too, of course; Bain, like Shaftesbury and Lamb, speaks of comedy as deliverance from emotional and moral constraints; Renouvier adds a deliverance from rationality itself; Penjon speculates on a

---

[6] The theorists do not necessarily agree with one another, however. Kant and Spencer, for example, suggested that all laughter, not only that of nonsense humor, parodies human logic and makes fun of reason. But Bergson always saw reason vindicated by laughter.

sudden surging of a sense of freedom as essential to humor; L. W. Kline, very close to Bergson, sees comedy as an evolutionary tool of growing human perspective on life; and Horace Kallen thinks of laughter as a necessary vestige of our predatory nature, the destructiveness necessary to survival and ascent. We accept the culminative Bergsonian view of the primitive efficiency of laughter. But the opposition of the natural and the mechanical in Bergson's theories seems pedantic and, worse, irrelevant.

Freud is closer to us. Wit's[7] resistance to authority is consistent with the local evidence. A joke is a circumvention allowing the expression of hostility after all. Freud, cut off from the American experience and weighed down by the pressure of European Victorianism, is too cautious in his estimate of the explicitness of a great deal of humor, especially in the United States. In addition, his interests and those of his followers seem over-clinical and hair-splitting, as Freudians earnestly define the difference between humor ("nonhostile jest under stressful situation") and wit ("hostile retort in the absence of objective stress"). Still, Freudian theories of aggression, escapism, and compensation are pertinent. Some conjunction of the social Bergsonian insights and the Freudian psychology, fully consistent with the evidence, best serves our purpose. We take what is true and helpful, as we reject all a priori concepts and irrelevencies.

For much the same reasons, we are wary of the wholesale theories of practitioners of comic literature themselves. What they say may be so general that it gives us little to work with, like Molière's remarks about comedy's assault upon our lack of proportion (*passer la mesure*). Or they give us wholly arbitrary impressions, like Twain's unsound distinctions between American, British and French funny stories. American theorists, quite apart from their intentions, may give us insights into the rising respectability or maturation of American humor itself. But the theories in themselves, from Josh Billings through Bret Harte and Mark Twain to James Thurber, W. C. Fields, and E. B. White, are either innocuous or particularist. They may point out, in passing, the "caustic" quality of our native style, or the interminable leg-

---

7 "Tendency" wit, in Freud, as opposed to a harmless, childish exhibitionist wit. But, as in "harmless" nonsense wit, we believe certain antithetical tendencies operate in the secondary humor also.

pulling that goes on, or the ominous character of our comedy, or the dangerous terror and pain it deals in, or the truth it hotly strives for. But they argue from the experience of special careers, which must be surveyed and judged as part of a large development.

There *is* a type of wandering and even pointless story, as Twain knew and practiced it. But the rambling technique or slow pace is not really representative of our general performance. On the contrary, one is struck by the relative speed of our humor. Our usual jokes are quick and pointed. Our best film comedies move extremely fast. Our newspaper and magazine cartoons have generally run to single-lined captions, instead of the virtual British paragraph or interlocutions of *Punch,* or they do without captions entirely. It is our speed that typifies us and, in current times, even influences foreign example.

And, on the whole, there is a surprisingly high verbal capacity in our humor. For a people who are renowned for their lack of conversation, who may be garrulous but rarely pithy or eloquent, and whose literary heroes are characters like Hemingway's inexpressive Nick Adams and whose cinematic heroes are voiceless western types or Marlon Brandos, we produce a highly articulate humor. The monologue, for example is a favorite and essential device. It permeates the humor of our southwest, of almost all our tall tales, of Twain, Bierce, Dunne, Will Rogers, Benchley, and our mass-media comics.

We are, likewise, marvelously adept at original metaphor.

"his eyes glared like two dogwood blossoms." (Mike Hooter)

"a-goin' down his throat just like a snake treadin' through a wet sausage gut." (G. W. Harris)

"one of your lively men . . . all right angles and activity." (N. P. Willis)

"a senator. Like a balloon, the higher he rises, the smaller he looks." (G. P. Prentice)

And we are continuously combinative, experimental, and neologistic: "outdacious," "sogadoguler," "copacetic," "heebie-jeebies," "gobbledegook," etc.

We are also notoriously given to the pun, outrageous heirs of Shakespeare. "If you're insulted," Groucho Marx quips, "you can leave in a taxi. If that's not fast enough, you can leave in a huff. If that's *too* fast, you can leave in a minute and a huff." The problem here is not to disentangle punning from other literalism or from comic momentum, for it is a truism that two or more techniques are frequently braided together for greater effect. The separate devices are usually discernible anyway. The problem is whether, when we isolate it, the punning is witty or not. In Groucho Marx's epithetical vein, for instance, there is the American tendency to build to a doubled hostile climax, and that effect alone is close to wit's social antagonism or characteristic sting. But this feature obscures the proper question.

Punning itself, which *is* a lower form of humor, is mere sound effect, the result of simple association or simultaneity. There are degrees of puns, of course. In the revelation that Santa Claus's Helpers are "Subordinate Clauses," we are slightly amused by the applicability of a grammatical term to the bureaucracy of the North Pole, but there is no further effect for us. On the other hand, we are grateful for more than the clever transliteration in "One man's Mede is another man's Persian," because in addition to the ingenious sound effects there is a covert assault upon over-educated affectation in the first of the two terms.

Wit, when it includes punning, is a satiric play on sound and sense together. "I've been as sick as a spy. I've had a code in my nose," is a modern approximation, since to its play upon the sniffler's nasalized mispronunciation it adds its sense of satire on extravagant Bondian contrivances. It comes close to what the French refer to as *équivoque*, a conceptual matter. A noticeable shift occurs in punning, but wit deepens. Artemus Ward claimed great personal success when he visited England, where he "rolled them in the aisles—the British Isles." But Thoreau makes witty fun out of the parade and militant fireworks and Mexican War hoopla in his hometown, *Concord*. In one case there is an associational leap and the slimmest coherence,[8] in the other a satiric play on sense and utmost coherence.

[8] The very lowest form of sound-effect punning is that in which only one of two terms has any truth at all: A bicycle cannot stand up because it is . . . two-tired. The concept of fatigue, "too tired," is inapplicable, and we have been merely fooled; but "aisles," in the joke about Ward, was as active a term as "isles" and a higher, though not witful, pun.

By and large our wit, which appears on occasion, is not our strongest trait. We are given inordinately to the pun, where the epithetical setting often conceals its true nature. Of course, now and then, a particular pun in itself is a subtle and imaginative triumph in American humor. But we are not the most sophisticated of peoples usually, and these transcendences are rare. In these connections, the distinction between wit and sheer malapropism need not detain us. The difference is between a knowing and unknowing play on words. Terry Southern's "prevert" is malapropistic in *Dr. Strangelove.* And so, for "eunuch," is John O'Hara's "unique" in *Appointment in Samarra,* though it certainly verges.

If our humor is inclined to speed and demonstrates a high verbal energy, it also includes other persistent devices. Comic literalism, for instance, occurs everywhere. It characterizes the greatest number of our quips, particularly effective when combined with reversalism. "I've been getting so nervous reading about cigarettes and cancer that I've had to stop . . . reading." Or it is put to characteristic service of overcomplication.

NORTHERN MONTANA RANCHER: I hope the land I just bought on the Highline border is actually in the States.
SURVEYOR: We just checked. It is.
RANCHER: Good! I can't stand the thought of one of those Canadian winters.

We are also prone to anticlimax and undercutting. Anticlimax refers to "periodic" comic disqualification, operating in final words:

"Ar-rmed on'y with a small thirty-two which I used in th' West to shoot th' fleet prairie dog. . . ." (Finley Peter Dunne)

Or it may be accompanied by an anticipatory signal, Sut Lovingood's technique.

". . . he tried tu shoot hissef wif a onloaded hoe-handle." (George Washington Harris)

Undercutting, less frequent in our comedy, is simply initial disqualification, as again provided by Dunne.

"A Spanish gin'ral. . . . Give him a typewriter and set him to wurruk. . . ."

Now and then the two devices may be combined: "If I had some eggs, we'd eat ham and eggs, if I had some ham." The extra com-

plication, a technical subtlety here, consists in the interchanged
order of terms.

Both anticlimax and undercutting are special compactions of
the whole technique of deflation which, contrarily, may be viewed
as more lengthy and elaborate disqualification. By one means or
another, our comedy abounds in deflationism. That includes the
comic catalogue. Mr. Dooley's relentless impersonation of Teddy
Roosevelt illustrates the matter:

> "these brave men had seen me with me trusty rifle shootin' down th'
> buffalo, th' elk, th' moose, th' grizzly bear, th' mountain goat . . .
> th' silver man, an' other ferocious beasts in thim parts . . . On
> th' transport goin' to Cubia . . . I wud stand beside wan iv these
> r-rough men threaten' him as a akel, which he was in ivrything
> but birth, education, rank an' courage, an . . . we wud . . . quote
> th' bible fr'm Walt Whitman."

The reference to Whitman, by the way, reminds us of the poet's
own humorlessness, and is focused for us precisely. We are accustomed to expect a concluding humorous deflation in his dis-
tended poetic catalogues, and we supply it ourselves when he
persists in not giving it to us.

My phrase is fortuitous, because it reminds us of the question
of comic paradox, which is *not* one of our usual modes, however.
We are not given to it as a technique and must leave the mode
to people like the British. The cultural contrast, in turn, prompts
a remark on the whole field of comparative humor, which we
shall touch upon subsequently. We may observe for now that,
along with our speed, our concreteness is a distinctive feature
of American comic style. A stripped-down Lend-lease locomotive
during World War II was lowered to the docks at Liverpool and
promptly named by the English, "Austerity." When the Americans
subsequently arrived in England and took over some equipment,
they renamed one of these locomotives, "Gypsy Rose Lee."

We shall consider other distinctions of American technique,
our ultimately rampant antiproverbialism, for example, throughout our survey. But we may mention a special idiosyncrasy here
before concluding our introduction on ruling American techniques. That has to do with our frequent self-consciousness. The
factor is of the essence for contributors like Benchley, Thurber,
Jules Feiffer, and others. It underlies the phenomenon of crucial

hesitation in our cinematic comedy. I do not refer only to the influential "double take," but to that moment of queer semitruce in the middle of a fight in film after film of Laurel and Hardy, the Marx Brothers, or Chaplin. We have the prolonged comic stare of mutual self-consciousness before mayhem is resumed. A moment of utter and saving recognition flickers . . . and dies. The device may be moralized. Suffice it to say, it is a special American trait. It can also be pressed too far and break an illusion or otherwise distract us, a more recent and regrettable failing of American humor. But, at its best, it is a native device of piquant and high effectiveness.

The targets of American humor are as manifold as examples of human self-interest, self-importance, and hypocrisy are anywhere. Singled out especially in the United States is a semiofficial system of prettifications and general soft-headedness, bigotry sometimes, complacency often, and conformism always: the indigenous mentality of the native middle class. The pieties of religion suffer steady attack, as do even the greater sanctities of American politics. But two particular targets claim introductory notation. One of them, women, entails an attitude purified of all ambiguity. The other, the confidence man, brings along reactions that are consistently impure and bedeviling.

The sociologist and anthropologist, George P. Murdock, tells us that there is never a joking relationship between a man and his mother-in-law in any culture of the world. No such generalization holds for women and their fathers-in-law. We must conclude that any relationship of matriarchal cast or undertone produces hostility. This is true for any culture that allows women to threaten men's position—from on high, as it were. That has evidently been the situation in the United States, for a variety of reasons. The result has been a rampant misogyny in all of our humor. No one needs to be instructed about how well this subject of American humor is an index to the life at large in the country.[9] In all countries a certain tension between the sexes is,

---

[9] And yet there is a residual and tawdry joke upon women in the land of momism and insurgent feminism: the servant class of women disappears only to be replaced by housewives who ceaselessly tend machines inside

of course, universal, naturally latent, and on occasion active. But
the misogyny and the hostility between the sexes provided by
American evidence are volatile and often fierce.

Their emergence occurs early, their career is consecutive, and
their culminations are extreme in America. Women's extravagance
and general disabilities are subjects of our earliest—eighteenth-
century—*Farmer's Almanacs*. Shrewishness is focused for us
(though not quite fairly) in our first celebrated short story,
Irving's "Rip Van Winkle." Feminine weakness, fearfulness, or
dissembling appear in the humor of the southwest, as in Baldwin's
stories of Simon Suggs and in George Washington Harris' yarns.
The female prerogatives of change and perversity are memorialized in Lowell's famous poem, "The Courtin'." In the rest of the
literary comedians of the late nineteenth century, from Josh
Billings on, there is continuous masculine criticism and attack,
by turns gentle, condescending, irritated, and sharp. It gets sharper
in Finley Peter Dunne and corrosive in Ambrose Bierce. It
continues unmistakably through the twenties and receives
apotheosis in the work of James Thurber, the archetypical general
of the war in his "The Battle Between the Sexes." His story, "The
Secret Life of Walter Mitty," is practically folklore now, and the
enemy is a pitiless harridan. Female characters will not gather nuts
in artistic patterns or see the unicorn in the garden; they are made
to suffer cruel, grim fates. And women who want to take over
completely, as Mrs. Ulgine Barrows does in "The Catbird Seat,"
are harrowed terribly by the comic avenger. One would have
thought that Thurber had exhausted possibilities, but the theme
resurges, as in the popular monologues of Alan King, where it is
generally the whole vitriolic point of his stand-up comedy. Nowhere else as in the humor of the United States is there such a
consistent tradition of charged and recharged antagonism between
the sexes. In no period whatsoever of our comic literature is
misogyny lacking or its force unclear.

Our attitude toward the confidence man, however, has been
fraught with ambivalence from the start. The early Yankee peddler, Sam Slick, is at once patronized and admired—by the author

and outside the home; women become higher class menials as constant
chauffeurs, etc. for their own families; and women are shamelessly under-
paid in their relentlessly secondary role within our economy.

and by the public. Our indeterminacy or doubleness of mind attends a gallery of con men throughout our history. From Haliburton's character through Poe's "diddlers," Melville's *Confidence Man*, even the Duke and Dauphin of Twain, to the sly underdogs of Joel Chandler Harris, we are never clear. The indecision extends into the present century in the work of Ring Lardner and, certainly, Sinclair Lewis. The movies and modern literature and our jokes and cartoons continue our fascination with the type and our dilemma of value. As far back as Haliburton, we cannot be certain of where the precise target is, the overly shrewd, slick character himself or his gullible, materialistic clients and victims.

When the matter occurs in other cultures, the field of attention and the target seems a good deal more exact, as in the Spanish Sephardic stories of Jorá. In one old tale, for instance, Jorá collects damaged pots and pans from a village for mending. He returns later with the repaired pieces plus a few extras, diminutive pots and pans that he gives away as bonuses. He explains that the originals had "babies." The bonuses are laughingly but greedily accepted, so that on his next tour his business is prodigious indeed. Now, however, he returns doleful and empty-handed, walking in a slow dirge down the main street. Unfortunately, he explains to the populace at last, all of the new batch have "died" this time. Well, directions and attitudes are clear. The target is the con man's audience, which has every consequence of the joke coming to it. There are no final doubts or presuppositions that unsettle the whole situation. And that is largely true in the European history of the subject all the way through Hasek's *The Good Soldier Schweik* and Mann's *Felix Krull*.

But the trickster himself, in America, has always been as reprehensible as he has been clever or admirable. And his victims tend to be pitiful objects of poetic justice. It is we ourselves who are fundamentally perplexed and "duplicitous" in the matter. The issue, however, is not one of mere hypocrisy but long-standing psychic dilemma.

Aligned with the Realist movement, liberal humorists have tended to see the landscape filled with all sorts of confidence men, sanctimonious frauds who are enemies of plain folk. Because the social confusion of America has proved a thorough host to con men, they seem the aptest targets for exposé and abuse. And so our comic literature shows a long line of political, religious, and especially commercial frauds. At the same time, however, these figures are portrayed with their fingers on the pulse of an indulgent, foolish, and ill-motivated audience that positively invites chicanery. As a result, the con men are also welcomed as unofficial castigators of the public. And there is a kind of esthetic involved, so that we admire exactitude and skill, too. P. T. Barnum's sign, put up at an exit to keep the crowds flowing through a small exhibition hall, "This Way to the Grand Egress," is rascally but delicious imposture. And when the Duke and Dauphin are at last tarred and feathered we are, with Huck, almost more sorry than vengeful at this climax to such a long and dedicated career of conning the public that asked for it.

We do not know how to mediate between sympathy and judgmentiveness in the matter. Furthermore, our probity wars with self-interest. We do not know where to place our allegiance. That is because we both love and hate our systemless system. The ambiguity permeates our very language, so that to be "shrewd" or "smart" is to be condemned and admired at the same time, and "to be taken (in)" calls for consolation and ridicule equally.

One is not surprised, then, to find this ambivalence discharging itself violently where the economic system itself, responsible for most of the dilemma, is in comic question. The agrarian southerners, early and late, are anticapitalist. And on the eve of total northern industrial victory, we find Artemus Ward uncharacteristically scathing. At the turn of the century, the progressivist Dunne recognized our imperialism for what it was. Bierce is uncompromising and fanatical in the matter:

Piracy, n. Commerce without its folly-swaddles, just as God made it.

Even the mild Will Rogers turns to stringencies as well as to good nature on the subject, as in his quip during the Depression:

The country is prosperous on the whole. But how much prosperity is there in a hole?

And there is no doubt that, in affluent postwar America, black humorists turn to darker and darker effects in confronting a split but potent way of life that drives them to a rage otherwise reasonless. But the irony is that in their brutal depredations upon that way of life they often engage in an enormous confidence game of their own.

All in all, we may view the signal hostility between the sexes, the ambivalence before the con man, and the antagonism toward the broad socioeconomic complex as the strongest instances of the antithetical nature of our comedy. They are especially American themes in the frequency and high charge of their appearance.

There is, of course, an underlying drift of such comedy as ours, from deflation to demolition, from negativity to nihilism. We have said that humor in general may shade off into upper and lower levels of sentimentalism and invective respectively. A predominantly antithetical humor is weighted to nether regions in particular. We may trace it not only through a steady history of cruelty and grotesquerie in our performance, culminating in sick humor, but in a certain amorality and immoralism embedded in the orthodox humor itself.

Baldwin and Longstreet and G. W. Harris are themselves quite drawn to the white trash they portray in dim interiors of geography and mind. Bill Nye's gentle amoralism is unsettling, and the immoralism of Locke's Petroleum Nasby is not only grisly but deeply frightening. Indeed, all through American humor our delight turns to disconcertion just as often as our discomposure turns to laughter. We tend, on the whole, to permit ourselves a continuous comic outlawry of sorts, an utter freedom or license that we decide to enjoy no matter what the cost. In the now classic comic literature of Thurber, the villainesses of "The Catbird Seat" and "The Unicorn in the Garden" are mercilessly packed off to insane asylums, and the archetypical Lindbergh hero in "The Greatest Man in the World" is gratefully shoved out of the ninth floor of a skyscraper for the good of the country. The thick spools of our cinematic consciousness reel off sequences of Harpo Marx in his unashamed, uninhibited, and rapacious pursuit of girls. And Chaplin, after all, bounces in and out of jail in film after film.

Indeed, Chaplin's tramp owes much, as Professor Seelye has shown, to the history of the clown tramp in America, a figure who has always parodied the very basis of our life, our pioneer and pragmatic American energies. Even more deeply than that, comedy wreaks havoc not only with particular values but with the very principle of value itself. "We'll *never* come out!" shout the Marx Brothers, intricately barricading themselves from gangsters in *The Big Store*. After hearing what they think is an answering shot outside the door, "We're coming!" they decide. We laugh not only at the quick reversal in such humor, but at the instantaneous exhaustion of any self-respect or ideals at all. Principles are swiftly recognized as pretenses, reversal is not really reversal but exposé, and the very assumption of value is parodied to the bare bone. The humor is instinctive and joyously amoral. Just this side of some invisible tactical line of judgment, such humor is healthy and saving. Across that line, in the blackest of humor, it passes out of the realm of our strict concern, a symptom of psychopathology instead of an exercise in salvation.

But there is a way other than the descent to psychotic humor or diatribe for comedy to turn unsalvational. That is, simply, by showing it to be unavailing, for all of its putative moral or psychic freedom. And that penultimate stage of decline is best shown in our twentieth-century literature, where Hemingway provides the clearest example in book after book. His novelistic heroes like Jake Barnes, Lieutenant Henry, and Robert Jordan can laugh sardonically or even good-naturedly, but not savingly. No comic banter, no American jocularity will protect them in the end. The same is true of characters in O'Hara, like Julian English of *Appointment in Samarra*, whose sense of humor is automatic and quite real but ineffectual. And this is wistfully true of more updated and reckless literary heroes.

And, finally, another American type of comic protagonist, who never seems to learn from untoward experience, calls on our attention. Benchley will lecture himself into trap after trap and go on lecturing, or get tangled in ironing boards and keep coming back to his disastrous domestic rounds. In *City Lights*, Chaplin will never be skeptical enough toward his drunken millionaire friend, who keeps throwing him out into the gutter the morning after. And a modern literary prototype like Bellow's Augie March never essentially profits from a wild and checkered career. And so the last principle or end of conduct, basic recognition or self-recognition, goes by the board, and Americans do that best, most eloquently, darkly, and truly of all.

There is, of course, a drift in the other direction, too, less pronounced but more than occasional. There are those who ascend to apostasy and silence. If Twain persists in his latter career, Bierce simply and literally and completely disappears. If Thurber follows his logic, Sinclair Lewis renounces himself, and Lardner and Benchley shut up. There is a certain percentage of failed nerve.

The supreme instance, perhaps, occurs in our movies, where a superb talent like Frank Capra's quails before its own true visions. In a crescendo of original motion pictures, from *It Happened One Night* and *Mr. Deeds Goes to Town* to *Meet John Doe*, Capra moved to that ledge of genius that hangs over the void. Then he shrank back. He knew how little availing his arbitrary O. Henry-like comic coincidences and fairy-tale conversions would be to him, and he failed to proceed out of fear that no other device would indeed save his stories. He retreated from the hard realistic comedy he had been pursuing and turned to inconsequentia and remakes. This softening or quitting is an accentuated threat in America. It occurs again in the short, astringent career of Preston Sturges, in a way that never would occur to the Swedish Ingmar Bergman. And, of course, it happens to Chaplin, in *Limelight, A King at New York,* and *A Countess from Hong Kong,* though one hesitates to indict old age. In the full tide of talent, the diminuendo is a frequent enough American development, and, while not confined to Hollywood, is seen most clearly there.

It is a sort of voluntary failure of nerve, as if the alternative were not lofty genius but suicide. For particular writers or directors, the interior defense of comedy or comic satire has failed, and perhaps they know best what is good for them. They shrink from lonely eminence and band together for a conspiracy of sentimentalism or the comforts of combined rage. Or they quit entirely. Our judgment is clinical on the point rather than editorial, a description of part of the past and, hopefully, not a prophecy.

All of which, however, recommends not balance only, or courage, but genius. And that cannot be ordered or predicted. Or perhaps it can. In a population expansion such as ours, there are bound to be the counterparts of all the greatness we have had, in comedy as elsewhere. Given the slightest favorable circumstances, they will surpass their models rather than exceed themselves. It is a statistical probability. All we need is an actual set of circumstances or morale approximating that of our best periods.

What were those periods? They were the Jacksonian period, the Civil War and postbellum period, and the decade of the 1930's. On the basis of the second and third periods, one would conclude that times of national disaster best encourage humor, when it may be needed to protect us deeply. But the greatest number of "literary comedians," including Mark Twain, flourished after the Civil War, and figures of the Jacksonian period defy the easy formula anyway.

There is another generalization we may try. These periods happen to correspond to our most successfully purposeful stages of national development: our crucial expansion and democratization under Jackson, our maintenance of union under Lincoln and our economic consolidation immediately afterward, and our redefinition of sociopolitical national character under Franklin Roosevelt. An overquick logic would have suggested that fecund periods of American humor correspond to times of abnormally high conformism and subjectivity, perhaps, or to times of grave doubt. But practically speaking, something close to the opposite seems true. A spirit of confidence and objectivity allows the maximum comic criticism. What is operative in these periods is a profound security or assurance felt in the pursuit of national goals, an undeniably insurgent or resurgent feeling of power or of oncoming victory. There is the sense of open possibilities, of renewal. If we apply these observations to individual people about us, personal psychology seems to confirm our wider speculations. There are some people almost without any sense of humor at any time; they are always highly subjective, unsure persons in their daily life. Theoreticians like Hazlitt ("only very sensible . . . people . . . laugh freely at their own absurdities") and practitioners like Al Capp ("The more secure a man feels, the more ready he is to laugh") have called attention to the fundamental disposition necessary to comedy. Objectivity and confidence are the major psychic conditions for a sense of humor, on any level.[10]

The conditions of decline in our humor of the post-World War II period tend to certify the case. Affluence and international leadership do not alone generate a sense of purpose sufficient to counteract languor, disaffection, and insecurity. We have been engaged in a protracted Cold War and two hot wars impossible to win, a vast and ungrateful holding action merely; we have experienced politics of McCarthy fanaticism and then of mere caution and then of balked progressivism; we have entered a period of fundamental racial crisis in this time. For any or all of these reasons, we are in a mood that is anything but assured and highly objective. What catalyst new visions or "great societies" will afford, after the supreme shock of an assassinated young president and of murdered hopes, remains to be seen.

It is doubtful that humor itself can ever contribute decisively to the circumstances that nourish it. These circumstances are a product of a seething conjunction of factors and often perverse ruling psychology in no way predictable but always determining. Comedy seizes its grand opportunity but does not create it, although there may be the barest reciprocal relation. In any case, those governing circumstances or cultural interchanges do not appear cyclical. That, at least, keeps us expectant.

We have, then, a general profile of American humor. It is filled with skepticism, cruelty, and derogation, a means of perspective

---

[10] Bergson defines the comic butt as an "unconscious" person. Freud's clinical observation is even more explicit: "those who are least repressed laugh easiest, those most repressed not at all." And Erich Fromm tells the classic psychiatrist's story of humorless narcissism: a woman calls up her doctor, wanting to come to his office that same day, but is told that he has not the free time and cannot see her until the next day; her answer is, "But, Doctor, I live only five minutes from your office." Levine and Redlich, in a special experiment reported in *Psychoanalytic Quarterly,* describe the failure of women in marital difficulty to recognize the idea in Thurber's cartoon of a house formed like a harridan head for the homecoming husband or even, after having it pointed out, to appreciate the point at all. One may add that making or even appreciating a pun necessitates a double or multiple comic and objective consciousness; single-minded and subjective people are incapable of both the wittier and lower expressions of the device.

between exaltation and destruction. Its prime function is anti-thetical,[11] superlatively so in the United States. As a genre of deflation, its chief risk is extreme misanthrophy and nihilism, though it may abruptly surrender itself also to sentimentalism. Its principal spirit is either that of controlled hostility or mockery. It may parody any and all progressive logic and even, on occasion, all sense. But fundamentally it drives for the truth behind the big and little stultifying lies of our national life. Its blasphemy has been a counteractive both to our made-up myths and to all the forces of obvious and subtle conformism. Its intrinsic effect of overcomplication is accentuated in a country where people tend to oversimplify and idealize experience and to rest upon formulas of conduct. It reinstates disaster as a principle of life, and is often fixed upon the grotesque for the same reason.

It is both a product and exultation of freedom. It seeks to distance itself as widely as possible from its objects of criticism in order to disengage our loyalties and explode its own energies. It is given to extravagant momentum and wild exemption from physical and moral law as techniques to these ends.

It often relies on mere pertinence alone for effect, and is closely allied to the realistic movement in American literature for purposes of exposé and denigration. But in its pluralism and openness, it displays no exclusive democratic favoritism, though its impulse is democratically irreverent and combative and its style is popular and concrete. Its expression, after certain positivistic beginnings, also tends to antiproverbialism, the tactic of anticlimax, and the strategy of reversal.

It is more negative than corrective. Iconoclasm and despair threaten its realistic function in the United States more than self-betrayal does. And its drastic honesty calls for a ceaseless joy in technique and a discriminatory, objective practice to keep it from psychopathology. It may need the strongest support now, including international cross-influences, in order to maintain its speed, distance, and verbal capacity and to expand comic characterization and thematic content. It may have to exercise itself in the broadest experimental devices in order to recapture its

[11] And it is unformulaic; this is what primarily distinguishes it from serious protest literature, revolutionary manifestoes, and programatical realism.

sustained talent at comic monologue, rich metaphor, and triumphant literalism. It ought in part to revitalize itself from the
example of comic flexibility in its major writers. In any event, it
must be accorded all of its traditional targets, including all the
old idolatries and new sanctities and including the country itself.

All that we require of it is a stability of function and nerve,
so that it does not either sweetly abandon itself or pass darkly
out of the realm of our hearing. For its function is more necessary
to us than to others. The fact that we tend to survey or study it
nowadays, brooding upon it perhaps, gives us qualms, however.
The phenomenon is not altogether natural and is a counterpart
of specific self-consciousness in recent humor, as it is also a consequence of an absorbedly critical age.

But no humor, even in sharp decline, ever disappears. Moreover, there are clear-headed arguments for the resurgence of
American humor. There are also arguments for its intrinsic place
in American literature and in our very consciousness, so that it
may be inherent in us, as a people. Manifold and devious as life
itself, and reflexive in Americans, it accepts no final pronouncements.

I

Early American Humor

IN THAT inordinate rescue of Americana from every nook and cranny accessible to us, it is no surprise that too much is made of our earliest humor. Learning that some of the Pilgrims had comic impulses, that the colonial period was not devoid of jokes, or that the years of the new republic were not swathed in solemnity gives us no license to rhapsodize an era. The fact is that our initial excursions into humor were largely weak and immature, a fit subject only for federal writers of the lean thirties, professional folklorists, and indefatigable students of "American civilization." Our earliest examples of humor are indecisive and confused, highly derivative and labored, severely topical, and otherwise inexpert. Even a period of tentative effort has certain highlights, of course, and contains particular features and combinations that deserve unmanufactured interest. But the era as a whole invites a governing candor.

The insecure shifts of protagonal role, from comic butt to social critic, illustrates the flaccid execution of the time. Franklin's Poor Richard is the only character who manages a stable transformation, from the fool he was in the earliest Almanac versions to the epigrammatical wise man he becomes later on. The feat is an exception. We cannot ever be sure how to view Haliburton's

Yankee peddler, Sam Slick; is he a developing character at all; where should we place our allegiance between his easy chicanery and his gullible and materialistic clientele? We are struck, further-more, by a veritable strategy of inconstancy in Seba Smith's later portrait of the amateur politician, Jack Downing, whose striped costume was probably the very adumbration of Uncle Sam. This particular derivation of our venerable national image in the figure of the clown provides an exact commentary not only on our early confused exploration of a comic genre but on the question of self-definition fundamentally allied to a comic sense. Smith's Downing is alternately a wise, shrewd observer of the Jacksonian political scene and the butt sometimes of his own naïveté and other times of his cynicism, and we can never be sure which is which. Similarly, in the celebrated play, *The Contrast*, Royall Tyler is never quite certain of his own valuation of the stage Yankee character who victoriously appears in it, as either a superb bumpkin or our hero.

This indecisiveness of comic portraiture is best seen in key pieces of Washington Irving (1783–1859), ostensibly the surest writer of the period. Actually, his treatment of Rip Van Winkle is highly ambiguous, for he makes Rip both the lazy parasitic butt of the termagant wife and the townspeople in the famous story and also the wizened hero of an extravaganza. The tale is other-wise precious to us, as our first putative fiction, but it is riddled thematically and psychologically as well, no matter what depth analysis we have subsequently brought to a story of male meno-pause. There is a similar failure of comic portrait and strategic sense in Irving's characterization of that other legendary hero, Ichabod Crane, in "The Legend of Sleepy Hollow." Avaricious as he is, the Yankee is climactically punished for his covert greed and absurd expectations. He turns pathetic and sympathetic, however, as the object of Brom Weber's cruel insensitivity and as the butt of the practical joke of the frightening pumpkin head. He is also victimized by a rather disproportionate hostility of the Dutch community. No more than anyone else in his time could Irving manage a steady comic control or master his intentions. The initial undercutting of Rip Van Winkle as village hero and the later overcapitalization of a wistful Ichabod Crane demonstrate tellingly the confusion and indecisiveness of our early comic sense.

And that comic sense was highly derivative, too. It was predominantly British. Almost all the overt satire and humor of Franklin (1706–1790) came to him directly from recognizable English sources. "The Titan Leeds Hoax," aimed to put his astrological rival out of business, he culled from Jonathan Swift's "Bickerstaff Papers." He not only modeled his satiric approach on Swift's "A Modest Proposal" but copied its tactics of ferocious literalism in his own "Sale of the Hessians"; its inhuman proposition, the Prussian King's insistence that more mercenaries be allowed or encouraged to die from battle wounds and assorted illnesses in order to finance his forthcoming opera season, is put forward in a cool Swiftian reversal of values designed to inflame the colonists who have "intercepted" the letter to the Hessian commander. It is well enough done, but it is not Franklin. These later transpositions of Swift are akin to his earlier thralldom to Addison and Steele. If the most prestigious of early American humorists was a man of many parts, they were not generally his own.

Need we be reminded either of Irving's whole effort in Knickerbocker's *A History of New York?* The work, our first comic "hit," consisted of mock heroical technique and stylistic circumlocutions borrowed from highfalutin British comic tradition, but it delighted the sophisticated New York audience that an American could do it at all. Neither should we forget all of the traceable European sources behind Irving's domesticated tales, including the German analogues he appropriated for his Hudson River fables. And if Hugh Brackenridge (1748–1816) had not Smollett's example at his elbow, in the rogue-like conception and the technique of comic contrasts and the imitative style of British parallel sentence structure, his novel *Modern Chivalry* (1815) could never have been written, though we would not reckon the loss irreparable. It is safe to say that without assiduously followed models from abroad there would have been no sustained comic writing, or any other kind, worth even a glance. That is not unnatural for a new people and citizenry not yet culturally independent. By the same token, however, these facts need not be taken so much for granted that they become lost upon us.

Such prevailing circumstances underscore other matters, like the low incidence of antiproverbialism in our earliest period. We were not sufficiently advanced at the time to turn truisms comically around. There is some aphoristic skepticism, as in Franklin's gibe: "Three may keep a secret . . . if two of them are dead." But generally a penny saved *is* a penny earned, and if we get to bed early all the rest will follow. We were in need of an epigrammatical positivism, unsettled, dynamic, formative, and psychologically unsure of ourselves as we were. Hence Poor Richard's phenomenally popular maxims and also that flow of aphorisms which issued everywhere in Franklin's writings. Even in his dialogue with "The Gout" epigrammatical Franklin is answered in his own terms, as if the id were in the service of the superego.

> FRANKLIN: I am convinced now of the justness of Poor Richard's remark, that "Our debts and our sins are always greater than we think for."
> GOUT: So it is. You philosophers are sages in your maxims, and fools in your conduct.

Irving is given to the same practice.

> . . . [Rip] would rather starve on a penny than work for a pound.
> . . . he was fain to . . . take to the outside of the house—the only side, which, in truth, belongs to a henpecked husband.
> Times grew worse . . . a tart temper never mellows with age, and a sharp tongue is the only edged tool that grows keener with constant use.

And so is Haliburton (1796–1865: a Canadian to whom we grant hospitality because of his great use of and influence upon downeast speech and humor).

> Politics make a man as crooked as a pack does a peddlar. Not that they are so awful heavy either, but it teaches a man to stoop in the long run.

The practice is incessant, pervasive, and probably compulsive. One is led to the critical commonplace that only a formative or immature stage of culture needs to be so certain of itself in its unalterably straightforward proverbial wisdom. Americans persist in a type of smart-alecky humor, however, and we may guess that the "wisecrack" descends indirectly from the earlier reflex.

Probably the wise guy is a descendant of the wise man, questions of legitimacy aside; both are simple epigrammatists. But an epithetical mode intervenes between the two, and the wisecracker of vaudeville, comic drama, radio, movies, and TV has had his lease on fictive life perpetually renewed because of a later tradition of aggression and epithetical ingenuity. In our first stage, however, we wanted only the compacted innocuous wisdom of straight-lined proverbialism. It was a frank question of our earliest and simplest needs.

That need and practice continued past Franklin and through Irving and Cooper and Haliburton's *The Clockmaker* (1837) to mid-century. In fact, it has never fully vanished, and is with us yet as journalistic filler and subpoetic magazine verse. Its strongest incorporation, however, came in the work of both Emerson and Thoreau, who at their best lent sophisticated and often subtle treatment to the tradition. Nonetheless, even the major literary figures often labored the technique. A certain overexpository single-mindedness is the latent threat in this mode, even for men of talent and genius.

Indeed the threat is clear in the greatest part of all the period's humor. The work of Benjamin Shillaber (1814–1890) is the quintessence of the heavy-handedness that persists to a late date.

> She had a great reverence for this same almanac, and we cannot refrain from speaking of an incident in connection with it. She put implicit faith in its predictions, and the weather-table stood like a guide board to direct her on her meteorological march through the year. One year, however, everything went wrong. Storms took place that were not mentioned, and those mentioned never occurred. The moon's phases were all out of joint, and the good dame sat up all one cold night to watch for an advertised eclipse that didn't come off. For a long time she tried to vindicate her favorite, but at last, when a "windy day" predicted proved as mild a one as ever the sun shone on, her faith wavered, to be entirely overthrown by a cold north-easterly storm that had been set down for "pleasant." A timely discovery, that Ike had put a last year's almanac instead of the true one, alone saved the credit of that mathematical standard of natural law. (*Life and Sayings of Mrs. Partington,* 1854)

The anticlimax is prolonged, the comic strategy is overexpository, and particular tactics are self-conscious, so that the whole of it is malformed and unfunny. It is an index to the feeblest but prevailing mode of our overt humor up through mid-century, downeast especially but apparent everywhere.

All the same, despite our academic and in a sense teleologic interest, certain matters invite natural attention. A strong democratic quality, for instance, emerges pervasively in this period, the south excepted. Humor centers and highlights the common man. He rises in general favor—and in his own estate. Poor Richard winds up neither mentally nor financially impoverished, furnishing us with the famous anthology, *The Way to Wealth,* a philosophic as well as economic handbook. The common man speaks, at the last, with his own eclectic authority. As for Franklin himself, his very life provided the nation with a humorous epitomization of the rags-to-riches theme, invidious only because it was true. Graphically, the runaway boy became an electrical Prometheus and homespun Socrates to the world. His career was a kind of legitimate hyperbole welcomed by the French especially and celebrated by his countrymen. The victorious comic hero in his own right, Franklin held values that were nonetheless real for being self-publicized, and they were enshrined in the national consciousness.

There is a steady emergence of democratic types in the north and west. Only Brackenridge thoroughly denigrates the Irish retainer, Teague O'Regan, in *Modern Chivalry,* relentlessly keeping him the lowly comic butt of his pseudoepic, an attitude held over from Old World patronization and literary abuse. Everywhere else the rise of democratic characters is indisputable and forthright. The frontiersman is glamorized in his simple if sometimes extravagant primitivism. The historical Davy Crockett is transformed into a living legend subsequent to the rise of Jacksonian democracy. He is dignified as a whimsical political philosopher by pro-Jackson newspapers before his defection and then, of course, celebrated by the opposition. In either case the development is indicative, as of course is the Presidency of Jackson himself.

Leading entertainment in the latter part of the epoch was blackface minstrelsy. The phenomenon has been singled out rightly as a sort of minority group production, imposing a semblance of unity and mutual good will upon our social chaos. Frequently, in point of fact, the "Jim Crow" character was clever rather than foolish, and unexpected sallies of apt political satire came from the mixed democratic line of banjo strummers and jokesters. In other traveling theatrical groups, parodists of Shakespeare were especially in favor. They entertained with travesties that coarsened the Bard, reducing him for popular American confrontation. An undeniable anti-intellectualism is the hallmark of an extreme common sense, and in our humor it contributes to an irreverence no more intimidated by master dramatists than by Presidents. Or by brigadier generals and university professors: Seba Smith's Jack Downing, ex-officio member of the Kitchen Cabinet, accepts a "Doctor of Wars" degree from Harvard.

The figure of Jack Downing demands two pertinent clarifications. Created by Seba Smith (1792–1868), his character was later appropriated by C. A. Davis for Whig attacks on Jackson. In Smith's editions (1831 and 1833 especially) of his peregrinations, Downing is confusedly both the comic fool and sage observer, but in neither case is he ever used to expose Jackson himself, only the world of political chicanery to which the President is an honest exception. Davis, in *Letters to Dwight* (1834), makes Downing over into a complete nincompoop for the Whig papers, never an ambiguous comic rogue but a stupid partisan of a ruinous Jackson. Smith himself was influenced by the scandalous new character of Davis' Downing to the extent that at a later date (1859) he viewed Downing as a far less tolerant and easygoing person than his own earlier versions had shown him. So that there were, finally, at least two Downings, or two views of him, as there were of Crockett. In both instances, however, he was vigorously in character as the common man.

But if in a fashion Davis overcame Smith, in another regard Smith earned an enduring victory from the outset. One consistent facet of the different political and moral characterizations of Jack Downing is paramount and reveals the underlying democratic insurgencies breaking through even the conservative exploitation of him. He speaks in colloquial New Englandese, a democratic dialect indispensable to his character, insistent, appealing, and probably undermining much of the obverse effect Davis was

after. If Smith subsequently had to assume some low-level cor-
rosiveness after Davis' plagiaristic use of Downing, Davis always
had to imitate Smith's superlative accuracy of regional and deflationary speech, which he was constrained even to perfect. The
common man might be comically manipulated, but he had to be
heard by now, he had to be heard.

By all odds the most interesting development of the period,
and its greatest distinction in American humor, lies in the burgeoning of tall-tale humor. Here are the roots of our most extravagant supernaturalism, comic grotesquerie, and fantasy.

Certainly Max Eastman's insight into the phenomenon is worth-
while. The question, as he phrases it, is not that our most
primitive humor was exaggerated but that our primitive exaggerations were humorous. Extravagant incident, incredible character, and violent action have assumed serious forms almost
everywhere else, as in the epical sense of the Greeks and the
heroical sagas of the North. But in backwoods native America
mythic tendencies were surprisingly, persistently humorous.

It is quite true that the humorous exaggerations of the earliest
explorers and colonists represent European whimsy. And a later
infusion of Baron Munchausen, as Professor Willard Thorp has
suggested, might have affected our imagination. Still, the subsequent manner, the specific content and tone, and the pervasiveness of this comic mode became distinctively and durably American. In early Carolinian writing there are descriptions of horn
snakes that roll like a hoop or launch themselves like spears. Franklin brings himself to speak waggishly of sheep whose tails are so
heavy that they must be trailed in little carts behind them. But
these early indications of the mode represent playful animal lore
that might have disappeared later on or are simply lighthearted
afterthoughts not fundamental to the psyche. They do not account sufficiently as sources for an entire, swelling stream. They
remain genetic indications and not explanations of a special, whole
tendency.

What answers Eastman's point is the reductionist function of
this mode. We cannot accept the convenient hypothesis of giantism as an explanation for the phenomenon. Saying that the great

American landscape encouraged the tall tale is much like saying that passionate writing must occur in the equatorial belts or that tragic heights may be achieved only in Switzerland. Not that geography goes for nothing, by any means, but it scarcely has such an exclusive and simple effect. Our critical attitude may indeed be influenced by the very latitude of mind comedy itself is derived from, but that is a welcome transference from the subject matter. We learn by comic instruction that what seems logical may not be exactly true. Or that there may be other logics. All the truth we can be relatively sure of is that certified by a broad, consistent, holistic view. In the pragmatic case of American humor, that means the following.

What was empirically there, or *believed* to be really there before us, was a huge, wild, and fantastical New World, awesome and horripilating, the sheer native plenitude and obliterating scale of which had to be reduced at the earliest psychological convenience. For this task, extravagant but reductionist humor was the necessary device. However violent the Homeric Greeks were, we may conclude that they were more comfortable and at home on their peninsula than we were, set all at once upon this wide continent, and that they could psychologically afford heroic heightening and epical cast. (The Greek god Pan, from which we derive "pan-ic," was not a frightening god, except occasionally to unwary travelers, but a god of fertility and merriment.) On these immense and alien shores, through these ceaseless forests, by these lonely great rivers, under these varied climatic winds, blocked by mountains or malaria, beset by beasts and surrounded by Indians, nothing would do on the frontiers but to employ two standard tall-tale techniques for psychic respite or defense.

The first entailed a gross exaggeration of the conditions of frontier life in order to diminish them, upon actual contact, to what they simply were, large enough but confrontable when reduced from what was preternaturally imagined. That imagination worked like a mithridatic cure for what lay ahead of the psyche, exaggerative in order to tolerate subsequent realities pioneers dared not fully acknowledge otherwise. Quite contrary to the theory of the magnification of our powers correlative to the size of the continent, the truest function of this humor showed that the country had to be reduced to be lived with. A land where

Crockett could make the sun and earth move when they were frozen stuck and could put a piece of sunrise in his pocket was not so awesome anymore. The explanation is as feasible and coherent as its rival, and it is more consonant with other effects of the genre, both contemporary and late, according crucially with the deflating and assaultive function of American humor as a whole.

In the second case, if one took to bragging enough of his own powers, with that boyish impulse to exercise a competence not yet fully in being and therefore comically overstated, he might dispel any leftover fear. Along the dark apprehensive paths of early America, we blew our own loud horns, as it were, rather than merely whistled, trudging past cemeteries of disappeared explorers, starved hunters, trapped trappers and bushwhacked frontiersmen. Against physical difficulties and antagonists, the boasting was inclined to be athletic and pugnacious. But the braggadocio that James Kirke Paulding (1778–1860) uses in *The Lion of the West* (1830) is rooted obviously and naturally enough in a basic inferiority under all the extravagance.

. . . a feller I once hit a sledge hammer lick over the head—a rale "sogdolloger." He disappeared altogether; all they could ever find of him was a little grease spot in the corner.

And let us recall that the most sustained exaggerative storyteller of them all, the rustic narrator that T. B. Thorpe (1815–1878) employs in "The Big Bear of Arkansas" (1841) has just been to New Orleans, where he was discomfited by the city. In telling his wild tale on board the river boat, he is compensating in a triumphantly comic though thoroughly predictable fashion.

In either event, we equalized ourselves to the American frontier experience by a devious process of comic magnification which sought ultimate reduction of conditions and opposition. We heightened and supernaturalized dangers and powers in order to deflate apprehensions. If a fair amount of tall-tale jokes persist in America, they come perforce as conditioned reflex to lingering and new intimidations by the vast land itself still, out west, or by the overwhelming pressures of an urban and unruly culture and an alienating, accelerative technology.

The crucial argument against the simplified theory of giantism, which Constance Rourke elaborated in her prestigious book, *American Humor,* is this. Men of real confidence never feel compelled to show off. If one does, he *needs* to, and that need may come from any characteristic in him except confidence. When, for instance, we arrive at the quicksand pit in old Ohio and see a hat upon the surface and lift it and find a man under it[1] who laughs hugely and says he's got a good horse under him, we may accept his comic boast that he will make it, though we wonder about the horse. But no trained rider on a strong, sure-footed mount along a fine turnpike on a glorious day needs to boast or exercise himself in any way. Giants in the earth are desperate men or comedians, and their extravagant claims are manifest defense mechanisms.

Rourke seeks to confirm her argument, at the last, by an appeal to hyperbolic western oratory in the period. The Kentuckian cries, "Who can restrain himself to mere facts?" But this is subsidiary and loosely related evidence, more correctly illustrating the comic freedom of our purely verbal comedy, and is part of a satiric portrait of a fast and loose politician anyway.

The fundamental apprehension rather than overblown assurance at the base of the tall tale is no better illustrated than in a modern version. In variations of the Grand Central Station joke the subject of our anxiety is the machine and, under all the coincident and flamboyant detail, our updated fear of annihilated humanity.

A New York commuter arrives ealier than usual for his train home at Grand Central Station one evening. Restively he buys a newspaper, then a package of cigarettes while waiting for his schedule. Perhaps he walks in impatient nonchalance in the throng or decides on an additional stick of gum from a vending machine. But he spies a fortune scale and decides to insert a coin in it. The penny goes in, the machine click-click-clicks, and the ticket comes out. It reads: "You are five feet ten, white, weigh 175 pounds and are going to take the 6:08 to Westport, Connecticut."

[1] Later on, similarly, signs reading "Man Lost" were placed in the appalling mud streets of mid-century Chicago, where the humor functioned in a more topical way to poke fun at local conditions. Under those circumstances we need not altogether give up our theories of apprehension. (See Marjorie Tallman [*sic*], *Dictionary of American Folklore.* Philosophical Library, New York, 1959, p. 187.)

Astonished, he ambles fecklessly back and forth before the scale. Just then, one of his passers-by is a tall, bronze-faced man with an Indian headdress, probably a performer in the closed-out circus at Madison Square Garden.

"Excuse me," our man asks, absorbed but inspired. "Are you in a hurry, or could I ask you for a moment's help?"

"Sure."

"Well, would you mind if I took your weight here?"

Surprised but amiable, the other agrees. The penny goes in, the machine click-click-clicks, and the ticket comes out. It reads, "You are six feet one, a full-blooded Cherokee, weigh 198 pounds, and are going to take the Union Pacific to Oklahoma City."

"Are you six feet one?" asks the commuter, trembling.

"That's right."

"A Cherokee?"

"Yes."

"You're going to Oklahoma City?"

"Sure."

"And what about your weight?"

The other nods. He smiles and starts off.

"Wait!" The commuter sounds a victorious note. "Just another minute?" he pleads.

"All right."

"May I?" The commuter deftly lifts the other's headdress from his head and puts it on his own. With it on, he mounts the scale. The penny goes in, the machine click-click-clicks, and the ticket comes out. It reads, "You are five feet ten, white, weigh 175 pounds and have fooled around with that Indian so long you have missed the 6:08 to Westport."

If we could survive the hoop and spear snakes of presettled Carolina, maybe we could also the rattlers and water moccasins. If we could come through the quicksands of Ohio, maybe we could survive the Overland Route. And if we can withstand the omniscient scales of our urban imagination, perhaps we may mitigate the computers. We seek to head off supreme threats to our existence on old and new frontiers through the reduction provided by our comic supernaturalism and fantasy.

There is a coalescence of necessary exaggeration with sheer outlandishness in much of this humor. As a matter of fact, the appearance of an outlander, as subject or observer, is a frequent insertion in the extravagant American story, so that the outré and incongruous go together. Polyglot and mobile from the outset, our society has given warrant to such extravagance and incongruity. A further consequence, as Rourke has rightly seen, is the competitive character of much of this comic invention, which accounts for much of the excess upon excess of fancy in our ring-tailed roarers and exotic half-alligators and half-men of frontier tavern exchanges and their physical and verbal wrestling matches. But insufficiency explains the phenomenon of verbal competition as well as braggadocio; there is no contradiction between the two. In all probability the motive of competition not only generally reinforced boastful exaggeration but led directly to the introduction of outlandish types as a prime American resource of further comic extravagance. The element of social absurdity in our tall-tale jokes cannot be underestimated. That culminative production, the minstrel show, was a tall-tale joke in itself, assembling coon-hatted and overly fringed frontiersmen, white comedians putting on black face, drawling Yankees, and so on in formless and outlandish mixture.

The bizarre confrontation of the races, with the western Indian as a special supernumerary, is a part of the continuing development of the genre, straight through its nineteenth-century codifications in legends and writers like Mark Twain, until an advanced modern stage where the outré and satiric come together. This variation of the modern tall tale, however, does not exist for itself alone but serves ulterior purposes. It makes sophisticated fun of primitive powers but at the same time deflates a certain modish cynicism, which is the modern snobbery.

During hectic days of World War II, a Northern Pacific train bound from Chicago to Seattle is sidetracked at Missoula, Montana, to allow a troop train through. A Chicago executive finds himself on the railroad platform, stranded for an hour or two in the Montana town. He purchases a paper or magazine from the newsstand and asks the newsman what he might do for distraction.

"Well, there's the state university," he is told, "and a Forest Service Headquarters and down town and—oh yes, you could start with Indian Sam, he's on the platform here. He's got the greatest memory in the West, maybe in the world."

The big city man smiles, but the newsman challenges his skepticism and leaves his stand to take him over to Indian Sam.

"Go ahead, ask him something, anything."

"Oh well," the Chicagoan is indulgent, "all right." He turns to Sam. "What did you have for breakfast on July 18, 1937?"

"Eggs," says Indian Sam.

"See," says the executive, "a pat answer! I thought so. Never mind," he wrestles free of the protesting newsman, "I'll see the rest of the town."

It is a minor incident for him and fades from his mind, and he subsequently joins his train for Seattle, where he spends a week on west coast business. Coming back, however, he has the natural misfortune in those days of Pacific military build-up to be delayed again, also at the Missoula terminus. As his train pulls in slowly, he recognizes the place and catches sight of Indian Sam. Out of a companionable reflex, at least, he steps from his car and greets the Indian, "How!"

"Scrambled," says Sam.

But this is sophisticated double effectism, the impure product. Its object is still deflation, and it contains features of extravagance and supernaturalism, pointed coincidence, and outlandish social incongruities that are recognizable. But the social function has usurped the genre, and satire has overtaken the psychological motive. This is, in fact, a progressive and natural development, to be expected. We must reserve surprise not for its occurrence but for the viability of the pure thing which, in the Grand Central Station tale, suggests an arrested or regressive state of American consciousness. Many of us are no more at home in the dislocating modern setting than we were in the chaotic wilderness, and our purest comic reaction to our experience is as deep as it is broad.

Factors of cruelty and nihilism also inform the tall-tale tradition from the outset, as they do the other modes of early humor. There are exceptions like the relatively mild Bunyan tales,[2] where the

[2] Paul Bunyan is a purely mythical character of American folklore, though perhaps derived from a legendary French Canadian figure, "Bon Jean." Almost always Bunyan appears merely gigantesque, representing the need for an outsized indestructible hero who was not destructive himself . . . except in his role as a cataclysmic agent who formed western landmarks. It is to our previous point that the legendary figure reduced the landscape to his size; his motives, moreover, were often trivial and his exploits were in general grossly comic. In one instance Bunyan grimly chastises his bedeviling son, but this is an exception to his characteristic activity. Generally no man or domestic beast is ever harmed.

loggers deal with things and not animals and find themselves working with instead of against other men, having perhaps no need to overcome with cruelty. But in the predatory, fugitive, combative lies and wiles of most frontier characters, like the keelboatman, Mike Fink (based on an authentic figure, like Crockett, and legendized through popular literature between 1770–1823), comic gusto becomes exuberant sadism and cruel punishment, picturesque but excessive.

"Get in there and lie down,'" was the command to Peg, topped off with one of Mike's very choicest oaths. "Now, *Mr.* Fink"—she always mistered him when his blood was up—"what have I done? I don't know, I'm sure—"

"Get in there and lie down, or I'll shoot you," with another oath, and drawing up his rifle to his shoulder. Poor Peg obeyed, and crawled into the leaf pile, and Mike covered her up with the combustibles. He then took a flour barrel and split the staves into fine pieces, and lighted them at the fire on board the boat, all the time watching the leaf pile, and swearing he would shoot Peg if she moved. So soon as his splinters began to blaze he took them in his hand and deliberately set fire, in four different places, to the leaves that surrounded his wife. In an instant the whole mass was on fire, aided by a fresh wind which was blowing at the time, while Mike was quietly standing by enjoying the fun. Peg, through fear of Mike, stood it as long as she could; but it soon became too hot, and she made a run for the river, her hair and clothing all on fire. In a few seconds she reached the water and plunged in, rejoiced to know she had escaped both fire and rifle so well. "There," said Mike, "that'll larn you to be winkin' at them fellers on t'other boat."

These elements of humor operate far from the frontier as well. When we hear Mrs. Partington's injunction to drown them cats in warmed water, we are not sure if we have changed regions or texts at all, moving from western folklore to the prim and conventional New England humor of B. F. Shillaber. A grim and sharp grotesquerie interfuses the humor of the period, making no distinction among modes.

Even the impeccable Washington Irving provides us enthusiastically with a shudder, Gothic or comic, we cannot tell for sure, in his story, "Adventure of the German Student." The poor, lonely, foreign student in revolutionary Paris meets and befriends a beautiful woman near a public scaffold. He leads her home and after their night together discovers in the harrowing light of the following morning that he had hallucinated a lover guillotined the previous day. The incident has an unimpeachable source.

"And is this really a fact?" said the inquisitive gentleman.
"A fact not to be doubted," replied the other. "I had it from the best authority. The student told it me himself. I saw him in a madhouse in Paris."

Whether or not Irving's story is a mere exercise in the macabre, its upshot is a grotesque joke, a hard one on the protagonist twice over.

Two incorrigible subjects make at least an appearance in this formative period of American humor. One is the question of the confidence man, as embodied in the characterization of Sam Slick and, for all we know, epitomized in the true character of Benjamin Franklin. Are we to admire Sam Slick's independent wit played upon his public or condemn his overshrewd psychology; are we to accept Franklin's pragmatic social formulae for success or despise a cynicism put to public service at the same time it served himself? In all their ambiguity, both the fictional and real con men—more real when fictional, perhaps, and more fictional when real—will be followed by a long line of con men as traders or profiteers, fraudulent political and military heroes, religious demagogues, literary impersonators, and general impostors. Our bafflement with the type in the subsequent development, at the hands of the southwesterners, or Poe, Lowell, Joel Chandler Harris, Mark Twain, Sinclair Lewis, Groucho Marx, and William Faulkner, will be the same as it is in this stage. Interest falls not on the character per se but on the bases of our judgment of him. Does Sam Slick acquit himself if he is slick *enough?* If he is frank enough, does Franklin earn our unmitigated praise? And if, later, P. T. Barnum is clever enough in painting his exit sign, "This Way to the Grand Egress," taking educated advantage of his overflow exhibition crowds, is he our prototypical entrepreneurial hero or not? The questions are bound up both with the success ethos and the principle of comic survivalism in our history, and are, in a sense, unanswerable at the last. But the issue first arises clearly in this period.

So does the subject of misogyny. Franklin's earliest versions of Poor Richard show the man in active hostility to his wife. Indeed, the biography of Franklin himself is germane. His life is composed like the model romance it is, and in the course of it the famous entrance into Philadelphia is a comic interlude, and Deborah Read is there to laugh at him. Franklin's later vindication of himself, by jilting and then marrying her (so that we are left to judge which punishment is worse), gives us a precious masculine archetype in the war between the sexes. Still, the battle lines are not yet quite declared, nor are they culminatively and literally drawn for us as they will be by Thurber. There are only these early indications and harassments, including Irving's debonair treatment of Dame Van Winkle, whose shrewishness is the result and not the cause of Rip's monumental laziness. The matter remains a secondary one in this early phase,[3] as if the battle is not joined chiefly because we did not yet know the precise array of opposing forces.

Of several repetitive comic devices, one in particular calls attention to itself, and that is the use of the masquerade. Irving, of course, assumes it when he periodically takes the narrative mask of an old man or historiographer. Seba Smith's and C. A. Davis' impersonations of Jack Downing are elaborate masquerades. And we must not overlook the obvious blackface and braggart masks worn in our minstrel and exaggerational humor.

In such a matter Franklin again provides at once the most subtle and flagrant example. In *The Comic Tradition in America*, Kenneth Lynn points out that the man disguises himself in life and literature as a moderate, ideally disciplined, and consistent person. The real Franklin was not so unappetitive, thrifty, conservative or mechanical a human being. The image of prudence systematized beyond belief, Franklin was a revolutionary, after all. Either he is winking at some of us, or he is hoodwinking all of us. There are endless disconcertments that occur during his

[3] Later indications, placed here with Shillaber's work for convenience's sake, include books of Frances Whitcher, 1814–1852 (*The Widow Bedott Papers*, etc.) and Marietta Holley, 1836–1926 (*Samantha at Saratoga*, etc.), notable as women's delicate but definite portrayals of warfare between the sexes. Both Whitcher and Holley were greatly popular writers.

most serious counsel in the *Autobiography,* and we are not certain if he is frowning or smiling under all his incessant effort at countenance. He trundles his wheelbarrow of newsprint down the cobblestone streets at six o'clock of a Philadelphia morning, for instance, making every attempt in his noisy occupation to bring solid citizenry to glance at him through their shuttered windows— making every attempt, so long as he *was* busy, "to avoid all appearances to the contrary." This is the essence of the man. Accordingly, we are never sure of the true face he puts on any matter. And then the basic question becomes one of how serious he ever is in his personal campaigns or lifelong whimsicality, and our suspicions convert his *Autobiography* into possibly the most covert and sustained joke in our literature.

After the masquerade, the most noteworthy technical feature of the period is experimentation in language. In the tradition of what we may call Crockettry (because of the widespread appearance of contemporary "Crockett Almanacs" capitalizing on his popularity), neologisms are especially prevalent, though cloying.

> When he was alive, it was most beautiful to hear his scream coming through the forest; it would turn and twist itself into some of the most splendiferous knots, and then untie itself . . . (Crockett)
> So he looked up at me slantindicular and I looked down on him slanchwise. . . . Mister, says he, I'm the best man—if I ain't I wish I may be tetoticiously exflunctified! I can whip my weight in wild-Cats . . . (Nimrod Wildfire)
> after the critters got into a somniferous snore, Sal got into an all-lightnin' of a temper, and . . . with a suddenachous jerk that made the entire woods tremble, pulled the entire lot . . . (Sal Fink)

And there are Downingisms, like "conniption fit." But poetic assonance is a by-product. The linguistic experimenting remains generally primitive and self-conscious although healthy, as we seek a national expression through comic manipulation.

There is a certain amount of distinctive American concreteness in the period, a more fundamental and promising consideration.

> Thar's a great rejoicin among the bears of Kaintuck, and the alligators of the Mississippi rolls up thar shining ribs to the sun, and has grown so fat and lazy that they will hardly move out of the way for a steamboat. The rattlesnakes come out of thar holes and frolic

within ten foot of the clearings, and the foxes goes to sleep in the goose-pens. ("Death of Crockett")

And we recall Franklin's undoubted talent throughout his proverbs of rephrasing the old British abstractions. His tactic in revising "Take Care of the Main Chance, and the Main Chance will take Care of thee" to "Keep thy Shop, and thy Shop will keep thee" accounts probably for his whole success in journalism, a series of signal transpositions in the native grain.

And there is the related and indisputable attempt at dialect. It underlies the obvious doggerel and jokes of Negro minstrelsy and our first renderings of western regional speech. It aids Haliburton, though, as Professor Willard Thorp has suggested, his whole employment of New England speech for Sam Slick is condescending and weak. But there is also expert and telling use of regional and colloquial language, as the rural characters speak it in the early *Farmer's Almanacs* (from 1793). And Jack Downing, especially under Seba Smith's guidance, speaks naturally and unmistakably.

Still, these are highlights. Most of the verbal performance itself is inferior and overextended, like the cute malapropistic punning of Shillaber.

> . . . troubled in the old country by certain unpleasant and often-occurring reminders of indebtedness, yclept "bills," which were always, like a summer night, falling due, and certain urgently-pressing importunities, the which, added to a faith that was not too popular, by any means, at last induced him to warily scrape together such small means as he could, and incontinently retire from metropolitan embarrassment to the comparative quiet of an emigrant's life, where he might encounter nothing more annoying than the howling of wolves, or the yelling of savages,—sweet music both when contrasted with the horror comprised in the words "PAY THAT BILL!" which had long distressed him. Here the voice of the dunner was done, . . . (*Life and Sayings of Mrs. Partington*)

The effort is overdrawn, belabored, and vapid, and we are reminded again of the salient facts of the period. By and large the humor is immature, imitative, unsure of itself, and groping. Our interests in it are sometimes teleologic, almost always clinical, and only here and there caught up by fascinations with mode or early technique.

We see little comic bravery as yet. Although it was feared that Benjamin Franklin might crack a joke at the Constitutional Convention, like his earlier quip about hanging together or separately, he never did, and he was, in fact, finally devout. Philip Freneau[4] (1752–1832), the "poet of the American Revolution" and later satirical partisan journalist for the anti-Federalists, had his exceptional audacities, especially in attacking Hamilton. Washington was moved to mild epithet in referring to him as "that rascal Freneau." His Addisonian "characters" ("Tom Slander," "Christopher Clodhopper") and his Hudibrastic and Popean verse, however, remorselessly betray his lack of originality. And his romantical divagations, "The Indian Burying Ground," "To a Caty-did," etc., are sentimental embarrassments.

Irreverence was not yet a prevailing or consistent attribute of our humor. When it occurred, it was like a bloom against a largely artificial background or painted forest. "Brethren," goes a frontier rebuff to religious zeal, "thar ain't a bit of use in prayin' for rain as long as the wind is in the west." This is the sign of original comic pertinence to come, the deflationary and irreverent and outspoken comic voice. But such authenticity and strong comic realism are in only slight evidence before mid-century in the United States, except, oddly and originally and deviously, in the south.

----

[4] He is not to be confused with John Fenno (1751–1798), the Federalist journalist. When Robert Benchley, over a century later, spoofed the comic confusions of early American history and politics, he had all he could do not to get too close to the actual facts. His situation would have been perilous in this instance. Freneau published the *National Gazette* on Jefferson's side, while Fenno founded the *Gazette of the United States*, later changed to *United States Gazette* by his son, against Jefferson. The anti-Federalist party of Freneau's cause became the Democratic Republicans and then Democrats, and the Federalists of Fenno's persuasion disappeared as a political force after the election of Monroe, their position ultimately occupied in our history by the Republicans, who had been de-hyphenated from the Democrats as early as 1803. The rest is almost clear. The strict-constructionist Democrats became split into conservative and liberal sectional groups, the liberals finally predominating; and the later liberal Republicans, by virtue of comic inevitability, became in modern times the conservative political party. The difficulties of comic distance and sustained humor have been early and abiding ones in American history. The Fenno newspaper, by the way, finally became the *North American and United States Gazette*, suggesting a slight degree of megalomania; for his part, Freneau gave up editing and partisanship altogether and spent his last years at sea.

II

Southwestern Humor

What we still call "southwestern" humor is the ante-bellum humor of our southeastern states during the period of the 1840's and 1850's. From its very beginnings there was a certain veil of mock heroical British humor placed upon it, but the special covert comedy of this section and time became rapidly distinctive, and it constitutes one of the most surprising and forthright developments we have. The writing of A. B. Longstreet (1790–1870), J. J. Hooper (1815–1862), Joseph Baldwin (1815–1864), W. T. Thompson (1812–1882), T. B. Thorpe (1815–1878), George Washington Harris (1814–1869), H. C. Lewis (1825–1850), and others is doubtlessly uneven work. At its best, however, it displays those original and compound talents that preceding and contemporary humor crucially withheld.

It is a kind of underground humor, finding its way to W. T. Porter's *New York Spirit of the Times,* an organ lonesomely and almost fanatically dedicated to broad, earthy writing. Porter's associate editor and successor, George Wilkes, was highly reactive to the "stale, didactic, pompous, bloodless" literature spelled with capitals all around him, and he provided an enthusiastic outlet for work he considered at least vital. Originally a sporting magazine, the *Spirit of the Times* virtually placed itself at the disposal of southern humorists, many of whose stories could be classified as outdoor athletic pranks and contests. With Porter's and Wilkes' encouragement principally, a growing number of writers soon found themselves with enough published material, up in New York and then locally, to put together between covers, and a spate of books saw print though not quite universal praise. The general atmosphere never permitted their attempt any real status—not until Mark Twain, who was heavily indebted to his southwestern predecessors, rose to fame. We are now everywhere rescuing major and minor lights of this comic literature, a body of work we no longer qualify by any patronization. Experts and students want, furthermore, to avoid considering it as a coterie literature (although they form clubs like "The Sut Society"). Indeed the danger now, under the predominant force of the retrospective study of Twain, is to exaggerate our discoveries of the period. These are natural compensatory claims for previous neglect.

Still, the realistic techniques and the content of this humor are unquestionably enterprising, vigorous, and unique. A native, southern, oral tradition, maintained by the camaraderie of coach travel and tavern talk, was synchronized with the growing influence of popular journalism, and both factors of regional life put a premium on concrete, realistic speech, especially in the dialogue of lower-class comic characters. Here is Hooper, for example, in "Simon Suggs attends a Camp-Meeting."

". . . that brother spoke a word that struck me kleen to the heart, and run all over me, like fire in dry grass——"

"*I-I-I* can bring 'em!" cried the preacher alluded to, in a tone of exultation—"Lord thou knows ef thy servant can't stir 'em up, nobody else needn't try—but the glory aint mine! I'm a poor worrum of the dust," he added, with ill-managed affectation.

"And so from that I felt somethin' a-pullin' me inside——"

"Grace! grace! nothin' but grace!" exclaimed one; meaning that "grace" had been operating in the Captain's gastric region.

"And then," continued Suggs, "I wanted to git off, but they hilt me, and bimbeby I felt so missuble, I had to go yonder"—pointing to the mourner's seat—"and when I lay down thar it got wuss and wuss, and 'peared like somethin' was a-mashin' down on my back——"

"That was his load o' sin," said one of the brethren—"never mind, it'll tumble off presently, see ef it don't" and he shook his head professionally and knowingly.

"And it kept a-gittin heavier and heavier, ontwell it looked like

THE RISE AND FALL OF AMERICAN HUMOR

it might be a four year old steer, or a big pine log, or somethin'
of that sort——"

"Glory to my soul," shouted Mrs. Dobbs, "it's the sweetest talk I
ever hearn. . . ."

And Longstreet, for his part, will not boggle at some profanity, a
brave achievement for the time, as in "The Gander Pulling."

"Come here, Neddy Prator," said he, with a triumphant smile;
"let your Uncle Johnny put his potato stealer [hand] into that hat,
and tickle the chins of them *are* shiners a little! Oh you little shining
sons o' bitches! walk into your Mas' Johnny's pocket, and jingle. . . ."

It comes as a surprise that the realistic expression is there at all.
But it is not quite perfected, and for two principal reasons. In
the first place, the effort is somewhat experimental at this time,
and there are lapses in speech and character. They occur even
under a master hand, like T. B. Thorpe's, in "The Big Bear of
Arkansas."

". . . at this they laughed harder than ever, and asked me if I
lived in the woods, and didn't know what game was? At this I
rather think I laughed. 'Yes,' I roared, and says, 'Strangers, if you'd
asked me how we got our meat in Arkansaw, I'd a told you at
once, and given you a list of varmints that would make a caravan,
beginning with the bar, and ending off with the cat; that's meat
though, not game.' Game, *indeed* that's what the city folks call
it . . . ."

The connectives I italicize are those which upset the tone and
they represent Thorpe, not his narrator. Similarly in the excerpt

"Having completed every thing *to my satisfaction,* I started at sunrise, and *to my great joy,* I discovered from the way the dogs run,
that they were near him. . . ."

the obtrusions are clear. And in an admixture like the following
in the same piece, the concluding verbal, after accurate collo-
quialisms, makes for an unintended effect:

"'Twould astonish you to know how big he was: I made a bed-
spread of his skin, and the way it used to cover my *bar* [bear]
mattress, and several feet on each side *to tuck up,* would have *delighted* you."

In the second place, a ruling desperation not to contaminate
aristocratic elegance intrudes on almost all work. There is a

rigorous, self-conscious attempt to keep the vulgarly realistic
style in its place. The writers form a clear group in their joint
efforts to differentiate as sharply as possible between lowborn
comic protagonists and those amused and affected narrators who
are actually surrogates of the authors. Longstreet, especially, risks
an absurd inflation in this way in "The Turf."

> "Come," said my friend . . . , "let us go to the turf."
> "No," said I, "I take no interest in its amusements."
> "Nor do I," rejoined he; "but I visit it to acquire knowledge of the
> human character, as it exhibits itself in the various scenes of life,
> and with the hope of turning the knowledge thus acquired to some
> good account. I am the more desirous that you should accompany
> me," continued he, "because, as one pair of eyes and ears cannot
> catch all that passes within a scene so spacious, I shall lose many
> instructing, interesting, or amusing incidents without the assistance
> of a friend; and therefore I wish to enlist your services."

The highfalutin quality appears as a shocking contradiction to
Longstreet's declared purposes of graphic realism in speech and
customs. But we are to understand that, like his peers, he meant
strictly to confine his realism to where he thought it exclusively
belonged. He maintains such severe proprieties of characterization
and style, however, that we suspect his rigid control: the stronger
the fences such writers build about themselves, the stronger the
urge to be utterly free. Only one character in this body of comic
literature is an exception to desperate, arbitrary linguistic man-
agement, and he is Thompson's Major Jones. An uneducated but
valid squire of the middle state, a redneck taking to a lace collar,
he is too valuable a sociologic type for Thompson to falsify in the
standard manner.

The equivocal condescension or prejudice of these writers toward their protagonists suggests in reality a profound and rebellious identification with them. But leaving aside consideration of
subtle psychology and sociologic inversion for the present, we are
left with a striking omission in this humor of the old south, the
deep south in so many unconscious ways. If these writers turn
their ambivalent patronization or contempt inveterately against
the lower white class, they never do against Negroes. That is not
due to high-mindedness; rather, we may say, it is due to such a
stratospheric superiority that their bigotry could never admit the

Negro into their consciousness as a human being. Tandy reminds us that Negroes were slaves, after all, and slaves have never been considered as fit literary subjects. All of which makes casual literary references to accidentally or otherwise killed Negroes no less heartless, of course. But in their conscious thinking, at all events, these writers were so much disengaged from the question that such incidents were the merest gratuities, not to be thought of as strong humor, cruel comic release, or anything else. Meanwhile, like Tolstoy who could never forgive Greek antiquity its slavery, most of us are helpless to overlook the sin of our south, where the defect never seems compensated by any agrarian vitality or neoclassical wisdom of its own. Be that as it may, to understand those southern terms of life—which, just a generation later, Mark Twain spares no less than we do—we have to meet those terms squarely and with momentary critical toleration. Negroes were simply so functional and irrelevant, as part of the landscape and inscape, that they could never receive any real attention, not even that outré or morbid amusement which was bestowed upon lower-class whites. To explain is not finally to excuse; but in this context it is perhaps forgivable to observe that the Negro down south was considered simply . . . beyond the pale. Meanwhile, heavy condescension of the rural type of white was rife in this literature, often directed at even the yeomen of the countryside.

> I had made the intended disposition of my business, and was on the eve of my departure for the city of my residence, when I was induced to remain a day longer by an invitation from the squire to attend a dance at his house on the following day. Having learned from my landlord that I would probably "be expected at the frolic" about the hour of 10 in the forenoon, and being desirous of seeing all that passed upon the occasion, I went over about an hour before the time. (Longstreet's "The Dance")

The brunt of comic derogation, however, is borne by rogues and ignoramuses, giving us the humor of provincial slapstick and naïve misapprehension. Although the literate creators seem inspired in their invention almost in spite of themselves, they strive nonetheless, or all the more, to avoid any possible confusion between their own elegant manner and the low subject matter. The whole of Baldwin's *Flush Times of Alabama and Mississippi,* says

Kenneth Lynn, is written in a fashion that deliberately "marks off the author from his material, thereby defining his superiority." And Johnson J. Hooper, in his ostensible treatment of Simon Suggs, is ceaselessly antidemocratic. But because they are all lured by their characters and material in the first place and because part of their comic performance is in itself a holding action, the southwestern writers had at least to grant the emergence of tawdry Jacksonian types in the south as elsewhere. What we have seen, therefore, as the rise of the common man everywhere else is true here also. The only difference was that the southwestern humorists kept their hidden fascinations under urgent control.

They were overtly overcome in one regard, their allowances of sexual realism. We feel the force of certain released enthusiasms in a number of these writers, like a grateful seduction. In following Suggs through his camp meeting, for example, Hooper enjoys frank innuendo.

> ". . . Brother Fant, fetch up that youngster in the blue coat! I see the Lord's a-workin' upon him! Fetch him along—glory—yes!—hold to him!"
> "Keep the thing warm!" roared a sensual seeming man, of stout mould and florid countenance, who was exhorting among a bevy of young women, upon whim he was lavishing caresses. "Keep the thing warm, breethring!—come to the Lord, honey!" he added, as he vigorously hugged one of the damsels he sought to save.

The passage stands in ebullient comparison with Hawthorne's masterful but overdelicate treatment of the Reverend Dimmesdale and his virginal parishioners in *The Scarlet Letter*. A little later during the camp-meeting scene, Hooper proceeds to surpass himself in symbolic vocabulary.

> "Gl-o-ree!" yelled a huge, greasy negro woman, as in a fit of the jerks, she threw herself convulsively from her feet, and fell "like a thousand of brick," across a diminutive old man in a little round hat, who was speaking consolation to one of the mourners.
> "Good Lord, have mercy!" ejaculated the little man earnestly and unaffectedly, as he strove to crawl from under the sable mass which was crushing him.

And George Washington Harris is a direct enough compatriot in "Parson John Bullen's Lizards."

". . . Passuns ginerly hev a pow'ful strong holt on wimen; but, hoss, I tell yu thar ain't many ove em kin run stark nakid over an' thru a crowd ove three hundred wimen an' not injure thar karacters *sum*. Enyhow, hits a kind ove show they'd ruther see one at a time, an' pick the passun at that."

Sut adds about the parson, "His tex wer, 'Nakid I cum intu the world, an' nakid I'm gwine outen hit, ef I'm spard ontil then.' He sed nakidness warnt much ove a sin, purtickerly ove dark nights." Furthermore, Harris has a punning good time with the word "seed," a past tense for vision and a present one for fornication. And, finally, in "Mrs. Yardley's Quilting" he allows Sut Lovingood all the explicitness he wants.

". . . Es I swung my eyes over the crowd, George, I thought quiltins, managed in a morril an' sensibil way, truly good things—good fur free drinking, good fur free eatin, good fur free huggin, good fur free dancin, good fur free fitin, an' goodest ove all fur poperlatin a country fas' . . . . One holesum quiltin am wuf three old pray' meetins on the poperlashun pint, purtickerly ef hits hilt in the dark ove the moon, an' runs intu the night a few hours, an' April ur May am the time chosen."

In these particular respects, no matter what our general view may be of their split or downright personalities, the humorists of the southwest were not merely spearheading the realistic movement; they were scouting so far in front as to be some decades ahead of other vanguards.

Second only to the striking comic realism of this humor, under whatever conscious or unconscious auspices it is bred, is the emphasis on cruelty and violence. Lynn has noticed the special and continuing connection between cruelty and laughter in the United States.

. . . nowhere is the connection more evident than in American humor. Efforts have been made to explain away this fact by assigning the coarseness and violence of our comic tradition to the grotesque taste of the frontiersman, now happily a thing of the past. But the sadism of the animated cartoons, in which laughter is evoked by the electrocution, flagellation, or mangling of animals dressed up as human beings, is proof enough that as a people we still retain our peculiar sense of fun; and the fact that the most important literary outlet for southwestern humor in the nineteenth century was a magazine published and sold in New York City suggests that the appetite for cruel comedy was never confined to the frontier. (*The Comic Tradition in America*, p. 94)

Nowhere is the phenomenon more stark than in the sadism and apparent meaninglessness of so much of it in the southwest.

A. B. Longstreet is a prime case in point. Like George Washington Harris, he was very short in stature, physically weak, and perhaps deformed. He would seem to plead for orthodox psychoanalysis. Lynn entertains the additional idea of Longstreet's need, as a virulent States Righter, for an expression of pent-up frustration and emotional release. Traditionalists would counter that the political position is another exacerbated effect, rather than cause, of Longstreet's psychology. But Lynn's perception of a social element in the neurosis is germane, although he stops too short. For it is too much for us to believe that Longstreet and Harris shared particular characterological defects coincident, in turn, with purely personal trauma in all the others of this period, including Poe. But we may defer comprehensive suggestions while we take the measure of Longstreet's particular example.

In his work the cruel violence is so manifestly enjoyed for its own sake and so easily eruptive at any given moment that we can only marvel at its queer high spirits. Excerpts from "The Fight" are indicative.

"Look yonder!" cried the west. "Didn't I tell you so? He hit the ground so hard it jarred his nose off. Now ain't he a pretty man as he stands? He shall have my sister Sal, just for his pretty looks. I want to get in the breed of them sort o' men, to drive ugly out of my kinfolks."

I looked, and saw that Bob had entirely lost his left ear and a large piece from his left cheek. His right eye was a little discolored, and the blood flowed profusely from his wounds.

Bill presented a hideous spectacle. About a third of his nose, at the lower extremity, was bit off, and his face was so swelled and bruised that it was difficult to discover in it anything of the human visage, much more the fine features which he carried into the ring.

. . . . .

. . . it became obvious that Bill wanted the room which Bob's finger occupied for breathing. He would therefore, probably, in a short time, have let it go, had not Bob anticipated his politeness by jerking away his hand and making him a present of the finger.

All the way through his book, *Georgia Scenes*, Longstreet exercises his telltale prerogative, always willing to deflect to details.

> Whenever either of them came round, the gander's neck was sure of a severe wrench. Many a half pint of Jamaica was staked upon them, besides other things. The poor gander withstood many a strong pull before his wailings ceased. At length, however, they were hushed by Odum. Odum, it was thought, would bear away the head; . . . .

And it is Longstreet, in "The Turf," who gives us the incident of the Negro rider killed in a horse race and then extends himself typically to overhear a callous spectator's remark, which he does not discountenance in any way.

> They entered upon the third mile in this way, when, at the first turn of the course from the judges' stand, Eclipse fell and killed his rider. . . .
> "I declare," said Mrs. Blue, as her carriage wheeled off, "had it not been for that little accident, the sport would have been delightful."

But more pertinent is Longstreet's steady focus on some central perversity. The climactic revelation in "The Horse Swap" is lingered over for comic highlight.

> The old man removed the saddle, but the blanket stuck fast. He attempted to raise it, and Bullet bowed himself, switched his tail, danced a little, and gave signs of biting.
> "Don't hurt him, old man," said Blossom, archly; "take it off easy. I am, perhaps, a leetle of the best man at a horse-swap that ever catched a coon."
> Peter continued to pull at the blanket more and more roughly, and Bullet became more and more *cavortish,* insomuch that, when the blanket came off, he had reached the *kicking* point in good earnest.
> The removal of the blanket disclosed a sore on Bullet's back that seemed to have defied all medical skill. It measured six full inches in length and four in breadth, and had as many features as Bullet had motions.

It is true that the narrator is "sickened" at the sight, but the crowd laughs and then doubly so when everyone discovers that Blossom's exchange for Bullet is a blind and deaf horse. The merriment is general. Moreover, Longstreet is not only a type of sadist but a nihilist too, and the conjunction is as fascinating as it is unnerving. The barbarous fisticuffs which he overhears in "Georgia Theatrics," for example, turn out to be no fight at all, only the private dramaturgy of a boy engaged in loud, play-active fantasies of his future prowess. And the actual combatants of "The Fight," after really vicious eye gouging, senselessly become friends again at the end. So that Longstreet's last joke of all resides in the complete meaninglessness of his cruelest violence. But we never find the man himself philosophically bitter, which would be understandable no matter what his inner compulsions or professed documentary intention. We confront more than insensibility in him. We face a dissociation of southern personality.

Hooper also has his moments of opaque cruelty toward animals and Negroes. And in "Simon Suggs, Jr., Esq., of Rackinsack—Arkansaw," Baldwin is titillated in the passive, standard way by almost charming eruptions of sharp violence: "so soon as the matter of the killing a member on the floor of the house, by the speaker, with a Bowie knife, was disposed of by a resolution of mild censure, for impudent precipitancy, Simon Suggs, Jr., Esquire was elected solicitor for the Rackinsack district." It is characteristic bravura. And in "The Big Bear of Arkansas" Thorpe's penchant for sadistic details reinforces Longstreet, making the whole matter generic.

> "I recollect one perty morning in particular, of putting an old fellow on the stretch, and considering the weight he carried, he run well. But the dogs soon tired him down, and when I came up with him wasn't he in a beautiful sweat—I might say fever; and then to see his tongue sticking out of his mouth a feet, and his sides sinking and opening like a bellows, and his cheeks so fat he couldn't look cross. In this fix I blazed at him, ..."

As for meaninglessness, G. W. Harris provides a patent if despairing rationalization about universal evil for Sut Lovingood in "Rare Ripe Garden Seed."

> "Whar thar ain't enuf feed, big childer roots littil childer outen the troff, an' gobbils up thar part. Jis 'so the yeath over: bishops eats

elders, elders eats common peopil; they eats sich cattil es me, I eats
possums, possums eats chickins, chickins swallers wums, an' wums
am content to eat dus, an' the dus am the aind ove hit all. . . ."

Do Longstreet, Harris, Hooper, Baldwin, Thorpe, and others
revel in a senseless violence and cavorting evil as part of their
stark comic apprehension of self-interest and the world's way?
Or do they elaborate their anecdotes to extremes out of peculiar
need and from a surfeit of local aggression? The point is moot,
perhaps, but in any case their performance and their need appear
to be communal. That collective quality of what is probably our
first movement of sick humor forces us to explanations somewhere in the matrix of social psychology. And when we link these
figures legitimately with Poe, the whole group stands as an early
indication of the deepest sources of American humor. I do not
mean to obscure their sense of excess but to take the abnormal-
ities as a heightened measure of the normal. Aside from their influence, a considerable one on later southerners, they furnish a
meaningful insight into the nature and perversion of antithetic
comedy in America.

It is a commonplace by now in the literary criticism of Poe to
see him as more than a case history. Despite Dr. Marie Bonaparte's exhaustive psychoanalysis of Poe, most of the world has
adopted the other French view, descended from Baudelaire, that
Poe's antisocial impulses were a measure not of his own limita-
tions but of bourgeois society's. In this manner he has become the
Romantic hero of *symboliste* poets and all *revoltés* since. His partisans have at least reopened the debate about the assumptions
of neo-Freudian psychology of adjustment (which Freud himself
always left open). The question is, of course, how does one adapt
to a wrong environment? Only an incorrigible individualist, artist,
or comedian, perhaps, would dare postulate a wrong environment. The healthier creative individualists and artists consciously
seek to mediate social change and adjustment; others, functioning unconsciously, are driven to perpetual and tyrannical rebellion. What has happened in the long and signal history of
Poe's reputation is that symbolists and their heirs abroad and at
home supply their fullest consciousness to make up for what is
lacking in their unconscious model. For our part, we can critically
place the southwesterners as alter egos of the Virginian Poe—

who read and appreciated Longstreet, by the way—a combined group in a psychic revolt they did not fathom.

With whatever defects and neuroses some of them might have been especially afflicted, they partook of a rebellion deeper and broader than they knew. In or out of their playful moods, they were always more serious than they were sensationalistic or merely antic. With Poe, these southern writers were the first informal school to protest a growing nineteenth-century prettification of life, most absurdly idealized in the south. In their reinstatement of realism and cruelty, they overextended themselves, a perennial difficulty in the United States, solved only by comic genius from time to time. But the basic drift of their fierce and extravagant humor and their identification with their rogue heroes are clear and suggestive enough. These men took so much joy in wild rectification of values that they did more than demonstrate irreverence, they insisted upon it. And the wellspring of their energies was more than a simple irreverence, it was contempt and covert hostility for a veritable system of falsifications, of which "moonlight and magnolias" of the old slavocracy remains the apotheosis in our history. Southern manners were an efflorescence of corruption beneath. Gentility was a flowering pretense, stemming from violent control. The very consistency and degree of comic excess and nihilism are a precise gauge of the pressures upon and within these humorists.

But they were split men and had to live an interior life in a nether world. Poe's choice of that world was sometimes a comic one but generally the horrific fantasyland we are more aware of ... although, as we shall glimpse later, that land also bordered frequently on terrain of grim comedy. The southwesterners could exteriorize themselves more easily and comically with a ready-made, rowdy frontier close by. The actual backwoods were indeed rough and tumble, as Tocqueville had learned.

> In the new states of the southwest the citizens generally take justice into their own hands and murders are of frequent occurrence. This arises from the rude manners and ignorance of the inhabitants of these deserts . . . . (*Democracy in America*, 1848)

But there is, in southwestern writing, an extra, zealous dwelling upon or enlargement of rude Georgia, rough Alabama, coarse

Mississippi, lewd Louisiana, and lawless Arkansas. Together, the writers reveal no simple though happy documentary interest in this landscape. They were too grateful to it. They participated in and enjoyed the experience too much and too perversely for us to ignore the whole fact. That speaks volumes about them as a strategic group in American humor. And about the prevailing genteel lies and repressions they sought to escape or undermine. For such violation Poe created substitutes of himself to suffer exquisite and memorable Gothic terrors, while his countrymen in the sub-literature of the time wrote themselves out with an exuberant and grotesque comedy. For the "heresies" that he only dimly understood, Poe condemned himself to the deepest pit of introverted mind beneath that inescapable social symbol of the castrating pendulum. Somewhat less self-flagellant and guilty, his counterparts fled imaginatively and some of them literally to the southwestern countryside, which they, too, would have had to invent, in all its rowdy violence, if it had not been there.

For all that they fundamentally had in common, these men varied a good deal in the exercise of their talents. There is an extensive range to their interests and treatments in this area of southwestern humor, all the way from the comparative mildness of Thompson to the brutality in Longstreet and G. W. Harris and the grotesqueness of the "Louisiana Swamp Doctor," H. C. Lewis. The latter was particularly fond of gross interne anecdotes, like the substitution of a dead baby fresh from the dissection room for a delectable piglet at dinner. Like Longstreet, Lewis could suddenly and disconcertingly turn serious and even eloquent, or else all at once satirical or abnormally insensitive, displaying that extra dissociated sensibility and pathology we have noticed before and eventuating in his probable suicide by drowning. He also called himself "Madison Tensas," through his twin pseudonyms distancing himself two removes, as it were, from gruesome subject matter he would not sponsor directly. Curiously, however, as the least squeamish member of the group, he yet understood enough technically to move through his most macabre passages as quickly as possible. The evidence of his work prompts us to believe that he might have grown rapidly away from his colleagues in a developed tactical sense and forsaken his protective devices had he not died so early—at twenty-five. But, like Poe again, he may have actually composed his own death as final resolution.

Of all of them, George Washington Harris probably looms largest in sheer talent. He is the one who rescues the surest-handed successes from his material, as in *Happenings in Tennessee*. For he calculates closely how near he can come to specific effects of grotesque violence, which Longstreet infallibly enters upon, and then he skips them. Lewis was approaching some such solution, with even more dangerous subject matter. Later on, Faulkner learned that device of the close narrative leap, in stories of tragic as well as comic violence, doubtless from Harris. For such material, this single tactic is the work of artistry. And Harris had the additional virtue, as does Faulkner, too, of achieving the utmost comic complication and momentum from the simplest prank. In that regard alone, he was a born humorist.

In this southwestern literature, the flourishing rogue type is a variation of the confidence man. In Longstreet's old horseswappers, he is a local, countrified Sam Slick. In Hooper's Simon Suggs (1846) and Baldwin's Simon Suggs, Jr. (1853)—Baldwin, the southern counterpart of C. A. Davis, at least acknowledged his lineage from Hooper, the southern Seba Smith—he is an evangelical and military fraud. In Baldwin's other portraits, like those of Bolus and Jim T., he is a figure of superlative deceit in law and politics. In all cases what compounds the author's normal southern ambivalence is a total American confusion of values and aims. But once again the starkness of their approach is instructive for a whole view of the subject in American humor.

Hooper, for instance, clearly intends to provide a mock campaign biography of Simon Suggs, modeled after and parodying Kindall's biography of Jackson. But, just as clearly, the character proceeds to run away with Hooper's initial conception and pedestrian aims. In the end the author is himself fascinated by his downright but also engaging rogue, who is a superlatively inventive opportunist. There is, of course, that protective gulf between author and character. But the distance does not mitigate Hooper's own gay bewilderment at a deceitful object lesson, who becomes a comic hero despite all of Hooper's first intentions.

Later, Harris' Sut Lovingood (1858–1861, and in book collection, 1867) causes his creator similar troubles of identity and auctorial relationship. Sut is eventually brought into association with Lincoln, which is meant to be like the invidious associations that Downing and Suggs supposedly bore to Jackson. But no more than in previous cases, especially Suggs', does topical malice hold steady as Harris' governing motive. Lovingood grows and grows in perverse vitality. His main characteristic is deceptiveness; he trades on personal confidences to instigate local mayhem, either for the sake of private revenge or for general practical-joking delight (hence the ironical surname, Lovingood). His inventiveness is so varied and his enjoyment so pure that Harris often identifies himself with him and uses him to purposes that transcend basic political animus.

Similarly, throughout his numerous portraits of the species in his collection, *Flush Times,* Joseph Baldwin is unsure of his creations. Although it would seem to be the safest of all literary dodges, he is in thematic and psychological trouble at once when he allows Simon Suggs, Jr., his early and supreme victory in cheating his father at cards, as in the story, "Simon Suggs, Jr., Esq., of Rackinsack—Arkansaw."

> Just as the deal commenced, after one of the most brilliant shuffles the senior had ever made, Simon carelessly laid down his tortoise-shell snuff-box on the table; and the father, affecting nonchalance, and inclining his head towards the box, in order to peep under as the cards were being dealt, took a pinch of snuff; the titillating restorative was strongly adulterated with cayenne pepper; the old fogy was compelled to sneeze; and just as he recovered from the concussion, the first object that met his eye was a Jack turning in Simon's hand. A struggle seemed to be going on in the old man's breast between a feeling of pride in his son and a sense of his individual loss.

Baldwin's own admiration is strong, and his perverse loyalty is never really dissipated by subsequent cluckings of censure throughout the narrative. Further along in his book, when he sketches Bolus' triumphant mendacity, he can rely on no literary dodge or short circuit of psychology whatsoever, and he grants his character the justification of pure talent: "The truth was too small for him." For all of Baldwin's patronizing asides, there is

what Professor Walter Blair, in *Native American Humor*, analyzes
as a certain huge enjoyment Baldwin derives from his characters.
Furthermore, in the study of Jim T., in "The Bench and the Bar,"
Baldwin's own lawyer's heart swells at the brashness and pseudo-
competence of Jim's legal vocabulary.

> ". . . Is that endorsed on the writ? No, sir. Don't you know the
> statute requires the cause of action to be endorsed on the *capias ad
> respondendum*? I mean to see whether an action for a malicious
> suit wouldn't lie for this; and shall move to strike out all these counts
> as multifarious and incongruous and heterogeneous." . . . "Now,"
> said A., "Jim, hold on—all I want is a fair trial—if you will let me go
> to the jury, I'll strike out these common counts." "Well," said Jim,
> "*I will this time,* as it is you; but let this be a warning to you, A.,
> how you get to suing my clients on promiscuous, and fictitious, and
> pretensed causes of action."

This particular example of the confidence technique opens up
the process of con man activity broadly for us. What the type
characteristically and deeply does is to turn the prevailing means-
to-an-end against the end itself, limited or hypocritical as the end
is. Jim T.'s spurious legalisms subvert the law; there is never any
question of justice.

The study of such con men is an exposé of the whole social
process, and it is no accident that these comic protagonists are
generally cast in a role commensurate to ruling enterprise or
value at a given time: the military, the religious, the legal, or the
commercial. The terms of the situation being what they are, the
audience reacts with a splendid puzzlement, not knowing which
side it is on, although for the most cogent effect the author ought
to know his own position as consciously as possible. For the
essential comedy resides in a halving of means and ends and then
proceeds to reduction of the ends themselves, and for that purpose the author needs an overview for his greatest effectiveness.

In the best work of Mark Twain, Sinclair Lewis, or Ring
Lardner, for instance, such an understanding is the governing
factor in the most successful work. The objective of such humor,
essentially satiric, is a frank critique of society, achieved through
the use of a character who confidentially epitomizes self-interest
in taking advantage of blatantly contradictory or masked values.
But when, as in the southwesterners, the authors themselves are

drawn into the confusion, then the thrust is toward a chaotic immorality instead of toward an ultimate misanthropy. Not that the latter ought to be actually sought as a resting place either, but it is a more logical and, so to speak, purer direction, at least, I mean, in the American experience.

Still, talent cannot be denied to the southwesterners in these respects either. Thackeray praised their characterization and general treatment, particularly in Hooper and Baldwin. He may have been additionally delighted, or flattered, by some of the imitative narrative style, but that is by the by.[1] There is a fund of interest in the work that pays a compound interest for the reading.

And apart from the appeal of its own richness, the period directly subsidizes not only Mark Twain a little later in the nineteenth century but Faulkner and Caldwell, for example, in the twentieth. The social and sexual realism of the latter day, the cruel violence of explosive humor, the studies of ignorant white trash and local con men are all direct levies upon the former age, especially on G. W. Harris, whose hero, "Sut," suggests the mnemonic south as enduring inspiration.

What we saw previously in the content of sexual realism confirms a certain ideal of male superiority among these writers. That is consistent with other things we know about the old south, but the empiric evidence from this group is pointed and obvious enough. What Hooper allows Suggs as camp-meeting indulgence is suggestive in all ways, including wayward feminine psychology. And Harris gives full force to Sut's raw exposés of devious feline hypocrisy in those coy, aphrodisiac country gals who attend "Mrs. Yardley's Quilting."

"Did yu ever notis, George, at all soshul getherings, when the he's begin tu gather, that the young she's begin tu tickil one anuther an' the old maids swell thar tails, roach up thar backs, an' sharpen thar nails ontu the bed-posts an' door jams, an' spit an' groan sorter like cats a' courtin? Dus hit mean *rale* rath, ur is hit a dare

[1] On the other hand, Thomas Hardy, in a description of a military band during *The Trumpet Major,* probably cribbed from Longstreet's "The Militia Company Drill."

tu the he's, sorter kivered up wif the outside signs ove danger?
I honestly b'leve that the young shes' ticklin means, 'Cum an' take
this job often our hans.'"

He adds later, knowingly:

"I dus know one thing tu a certainty: that is, when the he's take
hold the ticklin quits, an 'ef you gits one ove the old maids out tu
hersef, then she subsides an' is the smoofes, saft thing yu ever seed,
an' dam ef you can't hear her purr, jis' es plain!"

In fact, a few comic pieces came to be written on the subject
exclusively and not incidentally. Robb, for instance, helps draw
the battle lines in "His Excuse for Being a Bachelor."

"What is a cussed sight wusser than his gittin' Sofy war the fact,
that he *borrowed that calf the night before from Dick Harkley!*
Arter the varmint got Sofy hitched, he told the joke all over the
settle*ment*, and the boys never seed me arterwards that they didn't
b-a-h at me fur lettin' a *calf* cut me out of a gal's affections. I'd a
shot Jake, but I thort it war a free country, and the gal had a
right to her choice without bein' made a widder, so I jest sold out
and travelled; I've allays thort sence then, boys, that *wimin* wur a
good deal like *licker,* ef you love 'em too hard thar sure to throw
you some way."

This is gentle misogyny, but insistent and recollected in the
cozy and permissive company of the "boys." When placed with
the ambiguous condemnation of the con man and the deeper
hostilities to the culture, it reinforces a latent but charged antitheticism.

A few particularities of comic technique deserve special attention. Southwestern humor inaugurates a mode of combative
verbal exchange in American comedy. The extravagant frontier
narrator of Thorpe's "The Big Bear of Arkansas," both a southern
and western type, exchanges intermittently with his urbane
steamboat audience in a spirit of hostility which is at once put
on and real. Longstreet, too, furnishes passages of country wit
designed to illustrate local aggressive charm, as in "The Shooting
Match."

"I didn't know," said I, "but that you were going to meet the huntsmen, or going to your stand."

"Ah, sure enough," rejoined he, "that *mout* be a bee, as the old woman said when she killed a wasp. It seems to me I ought to know you."

"Well, if you *ought*, why *don't* you?"

"What *mout* your name be?"

"It *might* be anything," said I. . . .

"Well, what *is* it then?"

"It *is* Hall," said I; "but you know it might as well have been anything else."

"Pretty digging!" said he. "I find you're not the fool I took you to be; so here's to a better acquaintance with you."

"With all my heart," returned I; "but you must be as clever as I've been, and give me your name."

"To be sure I will, my old coon; take it, take it, and welcome. Anything else about me you'd like to have?"

"No," said I, "there's nothing else about you worth having."

The special device of the violent and elongated personal epithet also makes its initial American appearance in this mode. It is at the same time an experimental transcription of regional speech and a raiding of Shakespeare. Accordingly, perhaps, it lacks originality in its separate elements, though it contributes energy as a whole:

"Who do you call an impudent hussy, you nasty good-for-nothing, snaggle-toothed gaub of fat, you?" (Longstreet)

"Warnt that rale low down, wolf mean? Thet durned infunnel, hipercritical, pot-bellied, scaley-hided, whiskey-wastin, stinkin ole groun'-hog." (G. W. Harris)

This is a vein that surfaces in later minstrel and burlesque theater, vaudeville interludes of the 1920's, and radio of the 1930's (the "feuds" of W. C. Fields and Charlie McCarthy, Jack Benny and Fred Allen, etc.). With the passing of that comic forthrightness in radio and the scant amount of it in the successive medium, the vein has gone back underground generally.

Comic metaphor may not be an inheritance mainly of south-western humor, but it is a strong element of the comedy, and here there is original invention.[2] There is speed, too. In fact, the

[2] And a heavy, almost exclusive reliance on concrete imagery from nature.

fast southwestern comic metaphor may be considered an astonishingly rapid and compact tall tale.

> "Thar war the passun, his legs fast to the critter's flanx, arms lockt round his neck, face as pale as a rabbit's belly, and the white flag streemin' far behind—and thar war Mam, fust on one side, then on t'other, her new caliker swelled up round her like a bear with the dropsy. . . ." (Madison Tensas, "A Tight Race Considerin'")

There is orthodox tall-tale technique also, where the extra refinement lies in imperturbability, a southern contribution.

> " 'Lord,' said I, 'them ar "cedar stumps" is beets, and them ar "Indian mounds" ar tater hills.' As I expected, the crop was overgrown and useless: the sile is too rich, *and planting in Arkansaw is dangerous.* I had a good-sized sow killed in that same bottom land. The old thief stole an ear of corn, and took it down where she slept at night to eat. Well, she left a grain or two on the ground, and lay down on them: before morning the corn shot up, and the percussion killed her dead. I don't plant any more; natur intended Arkansaw for a hunting ground, and I go according to natur." (T. B. Thorpe, "The Big Bear of Arkansas")

The complement to this technique and tone, infrequently used in the rest of American humor, is understatement; characteristically, the manner is deliberately ill-concealed, and so it is hyperbole anyway: Sut's phrase, "es restless as a cockroach in a hot skillet."

These writers are particularly adept at anticlimax. In "Simon Becomes Captain," Hooper provides example: "Early in May of the year of grace—and excessive bank issues—1836, the Creek war . . ." But G. W. Harris is a special master.

> "Ove all the durn'd misfortinit weddins ever since ole Adam married that heifer, what wer so fon' ove talkin tu snaix, an' eatin appils, down ontil now, that one ove Sicily's an Clapshaw's wer the worst one fur noise, disappinment, skeer, breakin things, hurtin, trubbil, vexashun ove spirrit, an' gineral swellen." ("Sicily Burns's Wedding")
> ". . . fur I say that eny man who wud waste a quart ove even mean sperrits, fur the chance ove knockin a poor ornary devil like me down wif the bottil, is a bigger fool nur ole Squire Mackmullen, an' he tried tu shoot hissef wif a onloaded hoe-handle." ("Parson John Bullen's Lizards")

One may classify Harris' stroke otherwise, of course, as an example
of unprogressive comic redundancy or as anti-climax joined to
undercutting. The latter device is also a special favorite of
Longstreet and is somewhat more presumptive as a device in
"The Fight."

> His height was just five feet nothing; and his average weight in
> blackberry season, ninety-five.

As to the imitative half of their style during those assumptions
of the mock heroic voice, these writers may be derivative and
affected, but there are levels of competence. In "Ovid Bolus,
Esquire" Baldwin can be as good at it as Franklin was in adapting
Addison or Swift.

> I have had a hard time of it in endeavoring to assign to Bolus
> his leading vice; I have given up the task in despair; but I have
> essayed to designate that one which gave him, in the end, most
> celebrity. I am aware that it is invidious to make comparisons, and
> to give pre-eminence to one over other rival qualities and gifts,
> where all have high claims to distinction: but, then, the stern justice
> of criticism, in this case, requires a discrimination, which, to be
> intelligible and definite, must be relative and comparative. I, there-
> fore, take the responsibility of saying, after due reflection, that in
> my opinion, Bolus's reputation stood higher for lying than for any
> thing else; and in thus assigning pre-eminence to this poetic property,
> I do it without any desire to derogate from other brilliant char-
> acteristics belonging to the same general category, which have
> drawn the wondering notice of the world.

He is probably the best of the lot in this language, even as he is
a strenuous show off. At any rate, he is much better, as these
things go, than his nearest rival, Longstreet.

We are all the more surprised, however, that it is the highfalutin Longstreet who sometimes attacks the whole periphrastic
style, taking an antioratorical position in his infrequent but unmistakable satire.

> "*Mr. President*—Let the bias of jurisprudence predominate, and
> how is it possible (considering it merely as extending to those
> impulses which may with propriety be termed a *bias*), how is it
> possible for a government to exist whose object is the public good!
> The marble-hearted marauder might seize the throne of civil

authority, and hurl into thraldom the votaries of rational liberty.
Virtue, justice, and all the nobler principles of human nature would
wither away under the pestilential breath of political faction, and
an unnerved constitution be left to the sport of demagogue and
parasite. Crash after crash would be heard in quick succession, as the
strong pillars of the republic give way, and Despotism would shout
in hellish triumph amid the crumbling ruins. Anarchy would wave
her bloody sceptre over the devoted land, and the bloodhounds of
civil war would lap the crimson gore of our most worthy citizens.
The shrieks of women and the screams of children would be drowned
amid the clash of swords and the cannon's peal: and Liberty,
mantling her face from the horrid scene, would spread her golden-
tinted pinions, and wing her flight to some far-distant land, never
again to revisit our peaceful shores.   ("The Debating Society")

The confidence man is infiltrating aristocratic halls of Southern
debate just as insidiously as he is penetrating the raw and im-
pressionable frontiers, and Longstreet descries him wherever he
turns up. Perennially schizophrenic as Longstreet is, he acknowledges and attacks the abuse in himself (for the particular
character who speaks so culpably is named "Longworth"). The
rest of the group may sense the grave threat of southern rhetoric
all about them and now and then, in a removed setting, expose
corrupted expression. But on occasion Longstreet can disengage
the subject of con men from style and attack high style *per se* as
a deceit. In these moments, lucid or demonic, he does not merely
manipulate wry irreverence but mounts an effectual and total
assault. Humor is a dangerous weapon, a treacherous sacerdotal
instrument; it pricks a deific Calhoun as infallibly as it does a
battle-scarred Jackson. And all glorious archetypes are hemo-
philiac.

At any rate, the existence of two opposed styles in the same
literature and the divided attitude of a figure like Longstreet are
technical signals of the inherent conflict we have traced elsewhere.
Constantly they move back and forth, as a whole group, from a
dignifying and self-vindicating mode of expression to a renunciatory and repudiative one. Since it is the second mode that is
effortless and indigenous, what are we to conclude about where
their wild comic hearts were set?

Jeanette Tandy's discussion of southwestern technique, in

Crackerbox Philosophers in American Humor and Satire, avoids
these questions. Like Rourke and other liberal scholarly pioneers
of the last generation, Tandy is a celebrant of and searcher for
indubitable virtues and novelties. Knowing ahead of time what
she is looking for in sectional and folk humor to buoy up another
age, she discovers what she wants to. But her commitments do
not automatically invalidate all that she sees. She maintains, for
instance, that southwestern humor originated two American
comic character types, the amoral white rogue and the good "bad"
boy. Half of what she says is true enough; Simon Suggs represents
the former and he is the clear ancestor of Faulkner's Flem Snopes.
But Sut Lovingood is not a true instance of the latter type (nor
young enough), despite her strong claim and Faulkner's willing
admiration of Sut's "self-honesty." Undoubtedly the hints for a
lower-class and alienated "bad-boy" hero are there and will be
seized upon later in all their implicit possibilities, especially by
Mark Twain. But, strictly speaking, that is a later and distinct
development. We may add, however, to Tandy's search for
originality in the southwestern performance another innovation
of comic storytelling. That is the framework device which these
writers employ so steadily, a kind of anecdotal interview or meeting or traveler's observation, the semidocumentary report that is a
substitute for the old epistolary technique. It will have a prolonged
impact as a technique.

The last positive device of the southwestern humorists is the
use of the nom de plume, to which we have alluded in other
connections. It serves to mask the narrator-author, so that we dare
not identify the one with the other. Despite the fact that our
modern audacity is equal to the occasion, we must note the
masquerade as the emphatic technique it was: Longstreet as
"Hall," Lewis as "Madison Tensas,"[3] etc. (Sut calls his interviewer
and amanuensis "George," however.) In addition to the pseudonymic device, a few of the writers irregularly but conscientiously put on the aristocratic mask of ultrapropriety.[4] I refer to
Longstreet when he chooses to be didactic and moralistic, as

[3] Pronounced: Tin-saw. There may be a regional pun, surgical or otherwise, involved.

[4] Also the mask of age (and experience), H. C. Lewis's unfailing
device.

in his intermittent animadversions on alcoholism, a further warranty of the man—but a deep disguise.

Conspicuous for its absence is the device of comic aphorism, proverbial or antiproverbial. Except for minor sallies in Baldwin, Harris, and Robb, the period stands alone in American humor in its rejection of the technique. It is as if this tightly knit agrarian society had no body of capsulized wisdom either to call upon or to turn back on itself. Or did the enormous fact of slavery inhibit it thoroughly in this respect, cutting it off from its past more deeply than even our most acerbic social critics and antiproverbialists have felt themselves cut off at other times and other places in the nation? It appears that, one way or another, the involutions of southern life in the antebellum period denied the southwestern humorists profoundly negative as well as positive choices. They were crucially impoverished here, though vital and rich elsewhere, where they were, practically speaking, on their own.

Certainly, the essential southwestern contribution resulted from an overlay of radical frontier humor grafted upon the most conservative of bases. Perhaps the very force required to keep both together, satisfactorily or unevenly, comes from some reserve of comic energy that naturally flows toward incongruities, which would explain the relative outpouring of the humor. But such theorizing is fanciful and abstract. More to the point is some such psychological understanding as we have broached, especially when we join it to the effects of concrete social conditions in the life of most of these writers. Disinherited or otherwise thrown upon borders, journeying to landscapes otherwise familiar to themselves as interiors, they held desperately to old graces or values as they simultaneously joined the hurly-burly of the nation. The literal backgrounds of several of these writers, Baldwin, H. C. Lewis, and G. W. Harris, for example, are checkered ones. They have histories of varied, successive jobs and colorful demicareers. In this way, they are quite similar to the majority of "literary comedians" who next arrive upon the scene, heralds themselves of Twain and Harte and all the journeymen journalists. Perhaps an enforced but profound reflex of personal enterprise and motility lies behind much of our best American humor. An essential venturesomeness, coming also from a national expansion that was both physical and moral, may be a key to the greatest part of our comic audacities and explosiveness, wherever we find them.

III

"Literary Comedians": The Civil War and Reconstruction

99 THE GENERATION of war and reconstruction constitutes one of the richest and most diversified periods of American humor. This is our first era of full comic consciousness, permeating the national mind as never before. It was embodied, with other leading traits, by the President who became the American saint. It accounted for exclusive professional careers in humor. It attracted mass appeal. And it made its first claims, as in local color stories, to literary significance.

There is no question that the Civil War and the aftermath were the major causes of the accelerated outburst. Somehow, in our own strange mythology, Mars wrested a comic Pandora's Box from a unique underworld and opened it so that we have been both harried and diverted ever since. But that is too convenient a figure of speech. There is no rule of historical perversity or irony that says discord will unlock comedy. Our first vitalities of comic realism and jocund extravagance were actuated by expansionism. So the preservation of the union, as well as the end of cherished illusions, allowed victorious and truthtelling demons into the threshold of our consciousness. The bitterness of the struggle, the victory of centralization, the punishment of the south, and the triumph of northern capitalism irrevocably opened our mind, or deepened it, we may say, to the point where it incorporated the critical comic view as a permanent accession to its ego. In the now manifold targets of attack, in rampant styles, in the explosive growth of varied comic devices and their multiple combinations and in the insurgent development of comic irreverence and antitheticism, the period represents our first true efflorescence.

But it flowers in a thicket of thorns. We may speak, for instance, of Lincoln's undeniable sense of humor, but it is quite another thing to characterize him as essentially joyous, as a man whose sympathetic comic protections were adequate defenses. We may also be too quick to notice a certain positivism in the proverbial wit and general comedy of some leading figures in the period or to single out their sheer vigor and redemptive whimsicality. The underlying motive force through this humor—including Lincoln himself, and James Russell Lowell (1819–1891), Charles Farrar Browne ("Artemus Ward," 1834–1867), David Ross Locke ("Petroleum V. Nasby," 1833–1888), Henry W. Shaw ("Josh Billings," 1818–1885), Harriet Beecher Stowe (1811–1896), Robert H. Newell (1836–1901), and R. J. Burdette (1844–1914) in the north, George Horatio Derby ("Phoenix," 1823–1861), Bret Harte (1836–1902), and Bill Nye (1850–1896) in the west, and Charles Henry Smith ("Bill Arp," 1826–1903) and Joel Chandler Harris (1848–1908) in the south—is something other than geniality and social positivism. Its character is compounded of unequal parts of sad comprehension, disillusion, pessimism, and cynical amorality. It may start as a humor of regional partisanship, but it ends as generalized comic skepticism and hostile critique.

Certainly the partisan energies of the war itself manufactured a corrosive acid almost on order, as for Lowell's pen and Locke's. What follows in most humorists, however, is a prolonged tone of general skepticism, derived not from temporary vitriol alone but from a now opened well of doubt and pessimism which, we are forced to conclude, had always been there. If comedians come critically into their own, they do so vengefully and at length, and more than military enemies ask for attack. After the debacle of war, for example, the consistent onslaughts upon political and economic corruption and the subversions of industrial capitalism make the antithetical nature of American humor enduringly clear. Thus Henry Shaw in *Josh Billings, His Sayings,* 1866:

> It haz bin obsarved, "that corporashuns hain't got enny souls." There is excepshuns tew this rule, for i kno ov several that hav got the meanest kind uv souls.

Shaw also provides good illustration for the generalized mood of the period. Comparatively mild as he is, he practically exudes the skeptical spirit of the times, that pessimism we own now, almost dearly, in our awakening. About the lion and lamb bedding together, he remarks: "i am still betting on the lion." His cynicism is hyperactive.

> The furst law of natur iz tu steal; the sekund law iz tu hide, and the third iz tu—steal agin.

He writes about the draft in this manner:

> Alayens aint liable for the draft, espeshila if tha cum from the city of Ireland, and hav bin in the habit, for the laste 5 years, ov voting the democratic ticket.
> Againly: Widder-wimmin, and their only son iz exempt, provided the widder's husband haz alreddy sarved two years in the war, and is willing to go again . . . Moral Karakter aint required, the government furnishes thet, and rashuns.

His cynicism is less extravagant but just as steady in the postwar years.

> Yung man, mark yure goose up hi, 2/3 of the world hav no idea ov value, only by the price that iz put onter things.

And his wry hopelessness calls for comic attention.

> Snakes are innocent, but they hav got a bad reputashun, and all the innocence in the world won't cure a bad reputashun.

Of course we have the anonymous comic ironies and soldiering cynicisms of war like "hurry up and wait" and other sallies, which Crane's informal research led him to render so accurately a generation later in *The Red Badge of Courage* (1895). But there is a total mood that outlasts crisis itself. The attitude, as seen in Henry Shaw, is firmly entrenched in a veritable battle of American values, where popular cynicism now skirmishes with traditional optimism. This holds true in all regions. In the conquered south, Sut Lovingood's moments of dark philosophizing become general. Smith's Bill Arp has more than a temporary case of the blues, as the saying might go, when he speaks for the vanquished: "Looks like there is always sumthum preyin on sumthum, nothin is safe in this subloonary world." The attitude is a signal one in the south, touched with an embittered irony sometimes, as in "Bill Arp Addresses Artemus Ward."

> Didn't our four fathers fite, bleed, and die about a little tax on tea, when not one in a thousan drunk it? Becaus they sukseeded, wasn't it glory? But if they hadn't, I spose it would have been treesan. . . .

A little later, in the case of Joel Chandler Harris (no relation to G. W. Harris), we face at once the most fetching and deep-leveled cynical inversions in the entire period and perhaps in the whole of American humor. He achieves his fame by turning traditional values inside out for a regional but dubious triumph, the true character of which he does not fully measure. The violent Uncle Remus tales are given a duplicitous framework of gentle and charming interlocution between the boy and the old Negro retainer, and the fables themselves engagingly teach the wildest chicanery. The stories propound a cynical ethic of success at any cost, placing the rabbit (the wily, unreconstructed south) against the fox (the predatory north), allowing Brer Rabbit any means to the end of survival. There is no question of giving even lip service to an older code, acknowledging that outwitting, cheating, or tricking are bad form. The rule is: Don't be outwitted, cheated, or tricked. And this con-man defensiveness is easily converted into defensive aggression; he laughs last who outwits best. The Negro dialect is but a supreme ruse, as a superficial device one of the great implicit jokes in the history of American humor. The blackface mask and voice were taken in earnest by the south, and Uncle Remus' partisanship for the rabbit, who joyously and cunningly outtricks his oppressors, was Harris' own.

If might does not make right, guile does, as the Negro learned for whatever good it might have done him. Like the Freudian dream work, the frequent mechanics of humor are bizarre displacement and witful substitution, and the motive is wish fulfillment. Thus a history of American comedy turns comic itself,

tracing the spiral-like inversions of value; our insights flash from
brackets within parentheses set in digressionary passages more
in context than the text. We see the enslaving south twice enslaved
itself, first by the vindictive north and then by Negro psychology,
whose subversiveness it uses to be free of the other. Further, the
Negro, later in Faulkner, as in actual experience, will have to
appropriate the old imperturbability of the white south to aid
him in a resurgence of his own from southern reconquest. If the
re-emergence of white supremacy comes in great part from the
seriocomic lesson of Negro psychology, the endurance of the
Negroes is relearned in equal part from the example of deviousness and flexibility in the reorganized southern psyche. In the
end, it is a matter of which resiliency will win—and a comic dumb
show beneath directs a violent drama above. It is the American
subtlety under all the overt American action and mayhem.

Meanwhile, with our normal modern sensibilities, we tend to be
amused and gratified at the spectacle of literal black slaves and ex-
slaves seizing any psychologic means to their end. But we do not
grant the ex-slave owners the same means to their renewed ends,
and are scandalized when we penetrate the heavy disguise of
Harris and the enormous but unconscious deception of his
cynicism. If we are also partly amused, that is because we seek
general, annihilatory laughter as a way to explode the con-man
confusion that stems from Harris' brilliant added inspiration,
probably suggested to him by previous southwest example.

But the north was not without its newly prevalent ethic or non-
ethic of success. Artemus Ward's blatant cynicism becomes a
kind of national aphorism, though Browne's aim was direct exposé: "You scratch my back and Ile scratch your back." Connivance at any cost and at the expense of any person is the target
that figures in Browne's most critical humor, more realistic than
extravagant by now, as exemplified in *Artemus Ward: His
Travels* (1865).

> "Say, Bill, wot you done with that air sorrel mare of yourn?"
> "Sold her," said William with a smile of satisfaction.
> "Wot'd you git?"
> "Hund'd an' fifty dollars, cash deown!"
> "Show! Hund'd an' fifty for that kickin' spavin'd critter? Who'd
> you sell her to?"

"Sold her to mother!"

"Wot!" exclaimed brother No. 1, "did you railly sell that kickin' spavin'd critter to mother? Wall, you *air* a shrewd one!"

The difference between Shaw and Browne, on one side, and Joel Chandler Harris, on the other, lies in their overview. But our attention is directed in either case to a pervasive amoralism abroad in the land, which furnishes capital for either humorous exposé or propaganda. And so we dare conclude again that humor, like literature in general, is an index to mentality, probably the swiftest register of changing value in the recesses of national mind.

In his depths, Joel Chandler Harris takes a basically antithetical position toward inherited and mouthed values: "Proudness in a man don't count none if his head is cold." In the Aesopian guise of the freed slave, he sets himself against the old southern code of gentility, honor, and pride and against northern victory and rapacity. As for Charles Henry Smith, the attitude of his Bill Arp is unreconstructed antagonism, although he generally avoids being mordant. For the rest of the literary comedians, north and west, their position, whatever their diverse motivation and disparities of tone might be, is one of fundamentally adverse criticism: satiric exposé, ludicrous parody, or aggressive attack. They come into the open, respect no shibboleths, and may be roused at once. Josh Billings speaks representatively in *His Sayings* (1866).

Manifest destiny is the science ov going tew the devil. . . . I may be rong in this centiment, but that iz the way it strikes me, and I am so put together that when enny think strikes me i immejiately strike back.

The group develops multiple techniques for striking at increased targets. In "A Romance," Artemus Ward is savage in his onslaught on profiteering capitalism and cant.

". . . You spurned me from your door. But I did not despair. I secured a contract for furnishing the Army of the—with beef—"

"Yes, yes!" eagerly exclaimed the old man.

"—and I bought up all the disabled cavalry horses I could find—"

"I see! I see!" cried the old man. "And good beef they make, too."

"They do! they do! and the profits are immense."

"I should say so!"

"And now, sir, I claim your daughter's fair hand!"

"Boy, she is yours. But hold! Look me in the eye. Throughout all this have you been loyal?"

"To the core!" cried William Barker.

"And," continued the old man, in a voice husky with emotion, "are you in favor of a vigorous prosecution of the war?"

"I am, I am!"

"Then, boy, take her!"

Peg-legged "Birdofredum Sawin" is Lowell's instrument for a travesty of contemporary politics, in antiheroic couplets:

> There aint no kin' o' quality in can'dates, it's said,
> So useful as a wooden leg,—except a wooden head;

Whether the target is the beginnings of American adventurism or imperialism, rank excesses of the northern industrial juggernaut, or seamy politics in general,[1] the forces of humor are in open and varied array for counterattack. Behind their targets is the obvious frequent image of the self-serving hypocrite in commerce and national affairs, whose motives of self-interest and exhibitionism are under basic assault. Thus, at one point, Artemus Ward suggests that showmen ought to enter politics heavily, equating play actors and politicians and anticipating by a century the literal situation in post-Hollywood California, where realism and extravagance come superlatively together in all good sunny time. But although politics is the most convenient field of attack, the irreverence and hostility of the literary comedians for certain solidified types of Americans and for just about all sacrosanctities are clear and emphatic.

Least of all is religion sacred. Artemus Ward's onslaught on "The Shakers" is really nonsectarian and most comprehensive when he aims at the root concept of chosen-ness:

[1] The political cartoonists, Nast and Keppler foremost, form a bridge between this period and the intercentury group. The virulence of their partisan attack, as in Nast's cartoon of party bosses delineated as vultures in "Let Us Prey," is a noteworthy episode in American caricature and invective.

The Sperret, as they called it, then moved a short fat Shaker to say a few remarks. He sed they was Shakers and all was ekal. They was the purest and seleckest peple on the yearth. Other peple was sinful as they could be, but Shakers was all right. Shakers was all goin kerslap to the Promist Land, and nobody wa'nt goin to stand at the gate to bar 'em out; if they did they'd git run over.

Josh Billings pokes it relentlessly in *His Sayings*, although his deeper target is human nature.

What will it proffit a man, if he gain the whole world and loze his own soul? I answer, nothing: but there are cases, whare there wouldn't be enny loss tew speek ov.

His gibes at Christian culture may not be vicious but they are telling:

Heathins are alwus kind tew hosses; it iz only among Christian people, that a hoss haz tew trot 3 mile heats, in a hot da, for $2500 in kounterfit munny.

Even Edward Eggleston indulges little satires, on Protestant affectation and sectarian rivalry; in *The Hoosier Schoolmaster* he tries to locate the difference, for example, between "Methodists and Christians." And in "The Brakeman at Church," Burdette supplies his long clever railway allegory, only slightly more parochial, though much more literalistic, than Hawthorne's "The Celestial Railway."

"I went to church yesterday."

"Yes!" I said, with that interested inflection that asks for more. "And what church did you attend?"

"Which do you guess?" he asked.

"Some union mission church?" I hazarded.

"Naw," he said, "I don't like to run on those branch roads very much. . . ."

"Episcopal?" I guessed.

"Limited express," he said, "all palace cars and $2 extra for a seat; fast time and stop at the big stations. Nice line, but too exhaustive for a brakeman. . . ."

"Universalist?" I guessed.

"Broad gauge," said the brakeman; "does too much complimentary business. Everybody travels on a pass. Conductor doesn't get a fare once in fifty miles. Stops at all flag stations and won't run into anything but a union depot. No smoking car on the train. Train orders are rather vague, though, and the train-men don't get along well with the passengers. . . ."

"Presbyterian?" I asked.

"Narrow gauge, eh?" said the brakeman: "pretty track, straight as a rule, tunnel right through the mountain rather than go around it, spirit-level grade, passengers have to show their tickets before they get on the train. Mighty strict road, but the cars are a little narrow, have to sit one in a seat and no room in the aisle to dance. Then there's no stop-over tickets allowed, got to go straight through to the station you're ticketed for, or you can't get on at all. When the car's full, no extra coaches, cars built at the shops to hold just so many, and nobody else allowed on. But you don't hear of an accident on that road, it's run right up to the rules."

"Maybe you joined the Free Thinkers?" I said.

"Scrub road," said the brakeman: "dirt road bed, and no ballast, no time card and no train dispatcher. All trains run wild, and every engineer make his own time just as he pleases. Smoke if you want to; kind of go-as-you-please road. Too many side tracks, and every switch wide open all the time, with the switchman sound asleep, and the target-lamp dead out. Get on as you please, and get off when you want to. Don't have to show your tickets, and the conductor isn't expected to do anything but amuse the passengers. No, sir; I was offered a pass, but I don't like the line. . . ."

"Did you try the Methodist?" I said.

"Now you are shouting," he said, with some enthusiasm. "Nice road, eh? Fast time and plenty of passengers. Engineers carry a power of steam, and don't you forget it; steam gauge shows 100, and enough all the time. Lively road; when the conductor shouts 'all aboard!' you can hear him to the next station. . . . No passes, every passenger pays full traffic rates for his ticket. Wesleyanhouse air-brakes on all trains, too; pretty safe road, but I didn't ride over it yesterday."

"Maybe you went to the Congregational church," I said.

". . . Good road bed and comfortable cars. Well managed road, too; Directors don't interfere with Division Superintendents and train orders. Road's might popular, but it's pretty independent too. . . ."

"Perhaps you tried the Baptist?" I guessed once more.

"Ah, ha!" said the brakeman, "she's a daisy, isn't she? River road, beautiful curves; sweep around anything to keep close to the river, but it's all steel rail and rock ballast, single track all the way and not a side track from the roundhouse to the terminus. Takes a heap of water to run it, though; double tanks at every station, and there isn't an engine in the shops that can pull a pound or run a mile with less than two gauges. . . . And yesterday, when the conductor came around for the tickets with a little basket punch, I didn't ask him to pass me, but paid my fare like a little man—25 cents for an hour's run, and a little concert by the passengers throwed in. I tell you, Pilgrim, you take the river road when you want—"

But just here the long whistle from the engine announced a station, and a brakeman hurried to the door, shouting:

"Zionsville! This train makes no stop between here and Indianapolis."

The misogynic tendencies of our humor also become more explicit and forceful in this first uncompromising period of American humor. Artemus Ward declares open warfare against the early suffragettes. Billings jokes about "A man out at the elbows, and his wife out tew a woman's rites convenshun." In *His Sayings* he devotes several essays to woman, although his sharp skepticism puts our predicate in question.

. . . i kant see why she shud be histed up into a posishun, where men has got to cease luving her, jest in proporshun as tha are asked to wonder at her.

If you hav got a real good wife, kepe perfectly still, and thank God evry twenty minitts for it.

Women will sumtimes confess her sins, but i never knu one tu confess her faults.

Or his imputations of feminine sexual psychology are reminiscent of Sut Lovingood.

If yu want tew katch yure bo, run rite ruther wa and skream a smallsized skream, and dont look bak till you katch him.

Even Harriet Stowe's Sam Lawson, in *Sam Lawson's Fireside Stories* (1871), is allowed to speak his acerbic mind on local matronly conduct and counsel.

". . . and took 'em all over the house; and they went peekin' and pokin', openin' cupboard-doors, and lookin' into drawers; and they couldn't find so much as a thread out o' the way, from garret to cellar, and so they went off quite discontented. . . ."

" 'Wal dear,' says she, 'I think it's a shame; but they say you're tryin' to catch him, and that it's so bold and improper for you . . .—

you know folks will talk,—I thought I'd tell you 'cause I think so
much of you,' says she."

Lowell, in "The Courtin'," seizes the clichés.

> To say why gals act so and so,
>   Or don't 'would be presumin';
> Mebby to mean *yes* an say *no*
>   Comes nateral to women.

But even familiar jeremiads fit the growing criticism and increased
hostility. And in *The Tribune Primer* (Denver *Tribune*, 1882),
Eugene Field intensifies feeling, pushing it toward the niggling
sadism of Bierce in the intercentury period.

> The Mud is in the Street. The Lady has on a pair of Red Stock-
> ings. She is Trying to Cross the Street. Let us all give Three cheers
> for the Mud.

All together, the rising shibboleths of American society—
Business, Politics, Christianity, Woman—become open subjects
for assault. The motive of comic skepticism and truthtelling would
have reached maximum proportions in this era had not a counter-
influence played its part. This was the force of professionalization,
one of the great threats to comic integrity in the United States.
Overt and mounting critical attack by comedians on the
Chautauqua circuit had to soften itself even more than was necessary in print. (Bill Nye, for instance, regularly teamed with James
Whitcomb Riley on their circuit, Riley's sentimental readings
taking the curse off what Nye was doing on any given evening.)
And certain internal restraints governed the comedian the closer
he approached celebrityhood, a kind of heroic niche for himself.
Indeed, in a later period, the pell-mell force and intelligence of
another comedian in this mold, Will Rogers, would be thoroughly
blunted by his rise to professional estate and a literally monumental heroism (his granite statue watches over Colorado
Springs). Nonetheless, the crucially antithetic function of American humor is decisively clarified in this period, no matter what
the contemporary softenings or later defections.

Accordingly, it is no surprise to find that a certain amount of
comic animus spills over into misanthropy. Indeed, misogyny
alone is the great step toward comprehensive contempt: the
trouble with women is—men. What women get away with or

what they become is what their men allow or instigate. The explanation for a Dame Van Winkle is Rip Van Winkle, at least as much as the other way around; and if Walter Mitty later has a problem on his hands with his wife, she has her hands full with another powerless and fantasizing husband. These muddled deeps commence to clarify themselves in time, like a process of sedimentation going on right before our eyes. We are enabled to see, further, that attacks on women and religion inevitably become attacks on human nature. And the antagonisms to the new ethos of business and politics eventuate in a broad negative philosophy of society. Smith and Joel Chandler Harris come by their appalling moments of utter disillusion quite naturally in the defeated south. But the others are drawn just as naturally by a dark logic of their primary function in the American setting. And so the background for Twain's whole development, including "Pudd'nhead Wilson's Calendar," is already laid firm for him, as by Henry Shaw's astringent epigrams provided for *Josh Billings, His Sayings*.

. . . some peoples are fond ov bragging about their ansesstors, and their grate descent, when in fack, their *grate descent* iz jist what's the matter ov them.

We often hear ov men, who hav cum within an inch ov dieing, and i haint enny dout thare iz sum, that evry boddy wuld lik tew hear had cum within an inch ov bein born.

"Gra hares are honarabil," but I kno ov a grate menny gra *heds* that the devil will keep under a glas kase, tu sho the curous in theze matters.

Man was kreated a little lower than the angells and has bin gittin a little lower ever sinse.

By this stage of our speculations the literary comedians help us to understand further the presence of cruelty and grotesquerie as well as amorality in American humor. Like the covert southwestern motive, their impulse is to redress our prettified or self-deceiving view of reality, never more falsified than in a gilded age. Unconscious or overt, this effort is a constant one in native American humor, a perennial adjunct of our comic realism. But, in addition, two other factors operate infallibly. The very energy of antithesis and resistance necessary for comic exposé occasions an antagonism that, once called upon as motive force, seeks to

satisfy or exhaust itself to a full measure. Just *that* is the necessary
evil of comedy, over and above its true functions of redressment
and deflation in America especially. Furthermore, the nature of
what it reveals as the truth under all appearances and made-up
myths feeds back upon the process of comic exposure. The ruth-
lessness and cynicism that are the actual rules of conduct in time
of war, reconstruction, and robber barons affect the comic re-
porter sometimes in direct transference. They affect him by
heightening his skepticism, which, like a weapon of protection, he
tends to use first in some crucial battle of life he knows is going
on. These consequences of an antithetic comedy are inescapable.

In light of matters so implicit in our study, Jeannette Tandy's
critical flight from certain questions is poignant. Restive in her
glimpses of the remorselessness, cruelty, and grotesquerie that
prevailed in the period, the early commentator preferred to make
for herself a clever but ingenuous distinction. She phrased a
scholar's epigram, which she wore like smoked glasses. These
humorists displayed "leniency to persons and critical severity to
actions." And having said that, she need not linger over the
notorious and vicious attacks made upon Lincoln, for instance,
by his enemies. The fact of the matter is that there were consistent
lampoons of the President, quite personal and fantastically
virulent. The cruelty of even comparatively late anti-Lincoln
cartoons, up north, was severe and direct in the extreme. And,
sectionally, Smith's Bill Arp, in addition to G. W. Harris' Sut
Lovingood, made pitiful capital out of the President's person.

Locke's Petroleum Nasby is the very distillation of cruelty.
His vulgar white supremacy and his savage comic heart characterize him to the core. Almost anywhere in the Nasby letters,
as collected in *Swingin' Round the Cirkle* (1867), we discover
the sickly-sweet essence of poison.

> The bells rung, and for an hour or two the Corners wuz in the
> wildest stait uv eggsitement. The citizens congratoolated each other
> on the certainty uv the acceshun uv the President to the Dimocrisy,
> and in their enthoosiasm five nigger families were cleaned out, two
> uv em, one a male and the tother a female, wuz killed. Then a per-
> ceshun wuz organized as follers:—. . . .
> ME, with my commishun pinned onto a banner, and under it
> written, "In this Sign we Conker. . . ."

Wagon with a tabloo onto it: A nigger on the bottom boards, Bascom, the grocery keeper, with one foot onto him, holdin a banner inscribed, "The Nigger where he oughter be. . . ."

Citizen with bottle. . . .

Deekin Pogrom's daughter Mirandy in a attitood uv wallopin a wench. Banner: "We've Regained our Rites. . . ."

Citizens, two and two, with bottles. . . .

Wagons loaded with the books and furnitur uv a nigger skool in a stait uv wreck, with a ded nigger layin on top uv it, wich hed bin captoored within the hour. Banner: "My Policy. . . ."

Concurrent with grueling political cartoons and the heartless flamboyance of mutual reproach is an element of grotesquerie. Reserved New England gives us Lowell's indecorous Birdofredum Sawin, whose comedy has its share of violent gallows or battlefield humor.

> The cons'quence is, thet I shall take, wen I'm allowed to leave here,
> One piece o' propaty along, an' thet 's the shakin' fever;
> It's reggilar employment, though, an' thet aint thought to harm one,
> Nor 't aint so tiresome ez it wuz with t'other leg an' arm on;
> An' it's a consolation, tu, although it does n't pay,
> To hev it said you're some gret shakes in any kin' o' way.
>
>   ("A Second Letter from B. Sawin, Esq.")

And in noncombatant subjects, Mrs. Stowe provides other moments of strained comic charm, in *Oldtown Folks*.

> "Why, ye see, Horace, I ben up with 'em pretty much all night; and I laid yer father out myself, and I never see a better-lookin' corpse. It's a 'mazin' pity your daddy hed such feelin's 'bout havin' people come to look at him, 'cause he does look beautiful, and it's been a long time since we've had a funeral, anyway, and everybody was expectin' to come to his'n, and they'll all be dissipinted if the corpse ain't show'd; but then, lordy massy, folks oughtn't to think hard on't ef folks hes their own way 'bout their own funeral. . . . and Aunt Sally, she asked who made his shroud, and when she heerd there wasn't to be none, he was laid out in his clothes, she said she never heerd such unchristian doin's, —that she always had heerd he had strange opinions, but she never thought it would come to that."

". . . I kind o' spoke up to 'em about it. I wasn't a'goin' to hear
no sich jaw; and says I, 'I think ef there is anybody that knows
what's what about funerals I'm the man, for I don't s'pose there's a
man in the country that's laid out more folks, and set up with
more corpses, . . . Ef a man has n't a right to have the say about
his own body, what hes he a right to?' Wal, they said that it was
putty well of me to talk so, when I had the privilege of sittin'
up with him, and seein' all that was to be seen. 'Lordy massy,' says
I, 'I don't see why ye need envi me; 't ain't my fault that folks thinks
it's agreeable to have me round.'"

Out west, writing for the Denver *Tribune,* Eugene Field penned
comic pieces interlarded with grotesque and mischievous sadism,
much of it directed, for its first appearance antecedent to Bierce,
Benchley, W. C. Fields, and Thurber, against children.

Is this a Chignon? No, it is a Plate of Hash. But where are the
Brush and Comb? We cannot serve the Hash unless we have a
Brush and Comb. The Comb is in the Butter, and the Baby has
put the Brush in the Coffee-Pot. Don't cry, Children, we will Give
you some nice Molasses with Pretty, green Flies in it.[2]

[2] Field would renege later in the most sentimental apostasy on record,
his oleomargarine verse. One may be fortified against the early grotesquerie,
but is helpless before the rancid "Little Boy Blue."

> Time was when the little toy dog was new
>   And the soldier was passing fair,
> And that was the time when our Little Boy Blue
>   Kissed them and put them there.
>
> "Now don't you go till I come," he said,
>   "And don't you make any noise!"
> So toddling off to his trundle-bed
>   He dreamt of the pretty toys.
>
> And, as he was dreaming, an angel song
>   Awakened our Little Boy Blue,—
> Oh, the years are many, the years are long,
>   But the little toy friends are true.
>
> Ay, faithful to Little Boy Blue they stand,
>   Each in the same old place,
> Awaiting the touch of a little hand,
>   The smile of a little face. . . .

Against such regression and child-ism, however, Ambrose Bierce, W. C.
Fields, and Charles Addams will be fiendish proof in later, post-Victorian
days.

And we may advert topically again to Joel Chandler Harris. The instances of reciprocal cruelty and incessant grotesque revenge that accompany the tactics of witting and outwitting in the fables are legion. In a gleeful cannibalistic climax Brer Rabbit brings home the fox's head to Mrs. Rabbit for a triumphant broth. And everyone knows the catalogue of inexpressible deaths that the captive rabbit guesses is on the fox's mind in "The Wonderful Tar-Baby Story."

" 'En who stuck you up dar whar you iz? Nobody in de roun' worril. You des tuck en jam yo'se'f on dat Tar-Baby widout waitin' fer enny invite,' ses Brer Fox, sezee, 'en dar you is, en dar' you'll stay twel I fixes up a bresh-pile and fires her up, kaze I'm gwineter bobbycue you dis day, sho,' sez Brer Fox, sezee.

"Den Brer Rabbit talk mighty 'umble.

" 'I don't keer w'at you do wid me, Brer Fox,' sezee, 'so you don't fling me in dat brier-patch. Roas' me, Brer Fox,' sezee, 'but don't fling me in dat brier-patch,' sezee.

" 'Hit's so much trouble fer ter kindle a fier,' sez Brer Fox, sezee, 'dat I speck I'll hatter hang you,' sezee.

" 'Hang me des ez high as you please, Brer Fox,' sez Brer Rabbit, sezee, 'but do fer de Lord's sake don't fling me in dat brier-patch,' sezee.

" 'I ain't got no string,' sez Brer Fox, sezee, 'en now I speck I'll hatter drown you,' sezee.

" 'Drown me dez ez deep ez you please, Brer Fox,' sez Brer Rabbit, sezee, 'but don't fling me in dat brier-patch,' sezee.

" 'Dey ain't no water nigh,' sez Brer Fox, sezee, 'en now I speck I'll hatter skin you,' sezee.

" 'Skin me, Brer Fox,' sez Brer Rabbit, sezee, 'snatch out my eyeballs, t'ar out my years by de roots, en cut off my legs,' sezee, 'but do please, Brer Fox, don't fling me in dat brier-patch,' sezee."

And the possible roasting, hanging, drowning, skinning, and dismemberment all make Brer Rabbit's blows, kicks and head-buttings on the stubbornly reticent Tar-Baby look like positively gentle assaults—assaults (which the fox had counted on in the nature of things) for the Tar-Baby's not saying good morning at the start of the tale. In a still later work, "Brother Rabbit's Laughing Place," Brer Fox is led to a secret grove that happens to contain a hidden hornet's nest. From judiciously chosen sidelines

the rabbit laughs "fit to kill" at the fox's yowling among those
thickets and vines and hornets. He explains at the last that all he
had promised was to show *"my* laughing place."

There is, unmistakably, a high quantum of aggression, gratuitous
and personal, that informs all the levels and regional settings of
the humor of the period. There is no coyness, and there are few
indirections when it occurs. The thrusts of cruelty are naked, the
revelations of sadism frank, and the grotesquerie of violent or
morbid action insistent.

The conspiracy of cruelty and the fantasy of amoralism
intimately shared by the little plantation white boy and Uncle
Remus light up a subsidiary question in American literature and
race relations. Critics whose unorthodoxy has become standard
by now have seen piquant suggestions of homosexuality and
expiation in relationships similar to that of Harris' framework
characters, in Twain's Huck and Jim and Faulkner's Chick and
Lucius Beauchamps or Lucius Priest and Uncle Ned later on, or
indeed Cooper's Leatherstocking and Chingochook and Melville's
Ishmael and Queequeg in classic American literature before Joel
Chandler Harris. But from our vantage point, we are not so sure
of the accuracy or exclusive relevance of such factors, as particularly expounded by the literary critic, Leslie Fiedler. Kenneth
Lynn's insight, especially into the comic pairs of racial protagonists, gives another dimension to the issue. He infers a
theme of common alienation, in which the white hero joins the
colored in voluntary rejection of prevailing injustices or absurdities. Quite operative, then, is a democratic inclination toward
a broader human solidarity of the oppressed and disaffected, a
comic and rebellious companionship. It is no accident that most of
these relationships have something of an extravagant minstrel
unity and revelry as their basis. Furthermore, at least half of
Melville's, Twain's, and Faulkner's juxtapositions are conceived as
comic characterizations in themselves as well as indirect and
humane criticisms of society. To suggest that the power of Eros,
especially in companionable revolt, can transcend the usual
psychoanalytic classifications may strike an old-fashioned note
nowadays. But it is no more vulnerable as an explanation than
to suggest that Nigger Jim's address of "honey" to Huck Finn
was no regional southernism, natural in their fugitive camaraderie,

but a sort of pre-Freudian slip of the tongue.[3] We need not argue the fact that in the famous relationship portrayed by Twain, Jim, who is much older than Huck, was separated from his own children and that he naturally displaced, but did not misplace, his paternal affections on the fourteen-year-old boy. In these matters rigorous psychoanalysts will not necessarily accept paternal regard as an irreducible emotion. How they might dispose of the relation (other than to ignore it very hard, as they have done) between decrepit Uncle Remus and his young interlocutor, between a manifest grandfather figure and a boy in the classic stage of latency, remains a puzzle.

Clearly there is another factor involved, and the comic pairing of the races which Harris gives us is a significant clue. First of all, the conjunction of the two suggests, as in other standard cases, that the very pairing of the races is a renunciation of the culture's artificial separation of them and is comic reduction of arbitrary superiority. It is true that some American comedians, from Browne to W. C. Fields, are touched by racial prejudice, and even Twain had his blindness about Indians. We cannot avoid human variety and bias even among comedians. But in those cases where sympathetic racial pairing does exist, the gross antithetical function of the humor in our WASP culture is obvious. We overlook it only because our infatuation with subtlety intervenes. Moreover, as in the minstrel background of such pairings, the very mixture itself is broadly comic, as well as blasphemous, by virtue of unlikely contrast and of the outlandish comic harmony unexpectedly derived from it. These are factors that must be put together with whatever is tenable theory about homosexual undercurrent and expiation, especially with respect to clearly comic intentions and to those relationships, like Joel Chandler Harris', which are purged of all sexuality and inferred guilt.

In such a relationship as Harris depicts, the second infancy of Uncle Remus and the primary one of the lad conspire, in an in-

[3] At the 1966 Senate Committee Hearings on the plight of the urban Negro, Senator Ribicoff was addressed by the New York Negro writer, Claude Brown, who was responding to Ribicoff's unfeigned sympathy, in this manner: ". . . you are beautiful, Baby." Harlemese is a repository of the older southernisms and, in fact, is the chief contemporary means for reinfusing comic, and therefore unabashed, affectionate expression into our slang, song lyrics, and everyday speech.

sulated free fantasy, to give us parables of the purest comic amorality, rising from the deepest wishes of the new south and of the author himself. We may be taught that the superego is as devious and as manifold as the id. And we are reminded to frame our judgments in the widest and most appropriate cultural settings as well as in nether regions of the hidden heart.

There is no set way to rationalize the continuing emergence of democratic types through this period. At the same time as the humor is turning more negative and even acerbic, the democratic origin of comic characters and creators is more and more evident. Half the time the humor of these democratic literary comedians validates common sense as the prime means of exposing sham or delusion; the rest of the time it turns its skepticism back upon some of its own assumptions. That is as it should be, for comedy is unformulaic and nothing is permanently sacred to it, not even its own voice or most precious prototypes. Later on, even its well of pure realism will be defiled. And writers of the second quarter of the twentieth century will make neurotic victims of their surrogate characters, while later comic novelists will seek an admittedly narrowed interest from "antihero" types.

This is the period, however, when, for the first time, the ambiguities of comic butt and critic fall decisively away, when the question of identity between creator and character becomes fairly clear, and the role of the common man as wise man is ascendant. The latter development corresponds to the rising estate of the democratic comedian himself. (Our terminology is even significant. He is precisely the democratic comedian now; not so long ago, in western history, he was perennially the king's Fool.) It corresponds, also, to the massive dependence of the nation, both halves of it, on the anonymous soldiers of civil war. And it corresponds to the humble origins and manner of the log-cabin President.

Lincoln could be an out-and-out democratic jokester. He would have an instinctive reply to the British diplomat who was scandalized that the President polished his own footwear and was moved to arch commentary:

"English gentlemen never black their own boots."

"Well," said Lincoln, "whose boots do you black?"

Generally, however, we remember him for culminating the popular tradition of comic proverbialism, in which he was frequently as wise as he was wry. "Shooting him," he would speculate about the sleeping sentry he pardoned, "won't do him any good." This humaneness, especially after martyred assassination, contributed to his sainthood in American history, which is our democratic substitute for a true national religion. He was ultimately the common man deified, and it is fitting that from himself came the seriocomic aphorism, "God must have loved the common people, He made so many of them."

While Henry Shaw's Josh Billings turns just as readily to negative as well as positive proverbs, he, too, is often cast as the wise common man, for all his illiteracy. In this cause, he frequently sounds the note of straightforward if slightly antique Jeffersonianism.

> Thare aint no sich thing az a munny aristokrat in this free American land ov freedum. If a man knows more than anuther man, he has got a rite tew throw his hed bak and brag onto it a little. But if a man haint got only munny, he haint got no more rite tu brag onto it then he wud hav tu brag onto a big pile ov manure that wanted spreading.

His bias, in either straight or ironic moods, is clear. And by and large Smith's Bill Arp is the wise southern commoner, drafted to war and to a philosophic self-defense that is even more winning than his forgivable Confederate enthusiasms; he is never a fool. For all of the inversions of traditional values practiced by Joel Chandler Harris, the successes of Brer Rabbit are humble though strong medicine. His hero may be the butt of misfortune and malign enemies at the beginning of various exempla, but he rarely is at the end, when either folk wisdom (all the way back to Africa) or spontaneous ingenuity get him by.

Lowell's technique was to separate butt and wise man into two different leading characters, Birdofredum Sawin and Bigelow, respectively, and to add rascality to the first. Most of the problem of the con man, Sawin, is resolved by splitting the subject this way, and Lowell can serve him the contretemps coming to a fool and the punishment due a fraud. As to the fantastically popular comic ruffian, Petroleum Nasby, David Ross Locke had his own solution. He added to the northern white supremacy of his character a functional illiteracy, so that his audience could feel unmistakably superior both on moral and educational grounds. He also reminded us that a lack of education did not guarantee either wisdom or virtue. It was a grateful complication. There was never any element of doubt, however, in Locke's portrayal or judgment.

Only in Artemus Ward did Charles Farrar Browne deliberately mix roles. But he is more like our best modern figures than his predecessors, for he knew exactly what kind of confusion he was after. When he makes himself his own comic butt, especially as a lecturer—"The highest part of this mountain," earnestly he uses an actual pointer, "is the top."—he is engaged in a parody of Lyceum experts and Chautauqua impostors. He will simply and handily use himself at such times. But more and more, with an avowed debt to Seba Smith's Jack Downing, Browne was becoming a direct political and social commentator in the last years before he died. As our first incarnation of the comic cultural hero in his own right, he had to gentle down some of his harsh comic criticisms. But his role as self-controlled democratic gadfly was becoming clearer and clearer.

Browne's influence on Henry Shaw and David Ross Locke was patent, and there are indications that even Smith's Bill Arp in the south took much from him. Lincoln was buoyed by him,[4] on one celebrated occasion delaying the reading of his Gettysburg Address to the Cabinet while he first read to them from Artemus Ward. Indeed, in his popularity and influence and even in his death at thirty-three, after practically inaugurating our Elizabethan period of American humor, Browne stands as our comic Marlowe in relation to Mark Twain.

These relationships are not tangential to our discussion. All of the literary comedians, especially Browne and Twain, showed a common background. Instead of a shared stage experience, though they had that in common later, too, they were united by an almost universal apprenticeship in tramp printing and itinerant journalism. These men rose famously out of a common democratic mass life, and progressively they found a new clarity of role along with substance and esteem.

[4] The President was also enthusiastic about Locke and Newell.

The most striking technique of the comedians of this period is the utter seizure of democratic style. That style will shortly become a chief instrument of American literature in the hands of Mark Twain, but the triumph of realistic and colloquial expression in comedy per se is completed in this period. Only Eggleston of Indiana hesitated in rendering Hoosier dialect, because he felt that comic dialect had been discredited by the underground and roisterous southwestern humorists. Still, he overcame his scruples. Elsewhere, in the north, Artemus Ward and Josh Billings spoke in highly recognizable accents . . . with just a little too much concession to illiteracy for the sake of newly educated mass readers who hugely enjoyed the spelling mistakes. We are now put off somewhat by the orthographic humor, especially when it is inconsistent, as in Henry Shaw's alternatives of "to": "tu," "too," and "tew," etc. Locke is better; Nasby's border speech is less meretricious than usual and, as we have noticed, more functional for the character anyway. Of them all, it was the versifier, Lowell, who won most plaudits in this matter, Joel Chandler Harris and Mark Twain being particular admirers. He had the canniest of techniques with colloquial expression at the verge of provincial dialect; it was never really inaccessible, as in "The Courtin'":

> Says he, "I'd better call agin";
> Says she, "Think likely, Mister";
> Thet last word pricked him like a pin,
> An' . . . Wal, he up an' kist her.
>
> . . . . .
>
> The blood clost roun' her heart felt glued
> Too tight for all expressin',
> Tell mother see how metters stood,
> An' gin 'em both her blessin'.
>
> . . . . .
>
> Then her red come back like the tide
> Down to the Bay o' Fundy,
> An' all I know is they was cried
> In meetin' come nex' Sunday.

In the south Smith was always dexterous and careful with Arp's speech. And the incredible accuracy of Joel Chandler Harris' Negro dialect withstands all tests.

The comic penchant for realistic and concrete expression is

part of the overwhelmingly verbal cast of American humor, as particularly revealed in the period of literary comedians. This is no claim but description. I do not mean to suggest that punning, malapropism, *jeux-de-mots* and *double-entendres*, for instance, are not features of all languages. But the American enthusiasm seems to exceed the British in this respect, perhaps as some South American proclivities, as in Chile, surpass continental Spanish. Either language becomes more fixated in the New World, a function of conservatism, or it regresses in order to serve elemental conditions. In either case a certain primitive factor of competitive comic play inheres at least in American English, strongly incorporated in the work of the comedians who cater to our first mass self-consciousness of literacy.

It accounts for the tenacious hold of punning in the period. At the lowest level it is represented by the predictable Yankee battlefield interpretation of the B. C. initials on Brigade Commissary rations: Before Christ. Slightly higher but not unexpected either is Smith's Confederate punning on proper names: "Madame Harriet Beecher's toe," "the Lee side of any shore am onhealthy fer your population," and "Chickohominy! what a job you have undertook" in getting over Longstreets, Hills, and Stonewalls. But Browne's Artemus Ward asserts himself surpassingly in these regards: Africa has "the white rose, red rose, and Negroes." In the same tenor he could observe on his western jaunt: "Utah girls mostly marry Young." Or as the infallible ancestor of Groucho Marx, he could expand his quipping: "Our [Indian] brethren drink with impunity . . . and anyone else that will ask them." This was the kind of advanced American punstering for the time that particularly captivated his audiences in Britain, where he had a phenomenal success. Lowell has his incurable tendencies, too: not merely predictable political gibes as in "What Mr. Robinson Thinks" ("He's been true to *one* party—and thet is himself") but neologistic puns like "eye-dollar-try's" for "idolotries" in "A Fable for Critics."[5] And David Ross Locke is indulgent, but with greater

[5] This work appears to be a source-field for Lowell's fellow Harvardian in the next century, Ogden Nash. The manufactured and stigmatical pun-words, like "iceolation" (to describe Bryant), and the outlandish rhymes—from relative simplicities like "English" and "jinglish" to radical complications like "you furl at, if" and "superlative"—seem incontestable inspiration for Nash's later career.

political subtlety, remorselessly misspelling the suffix of "Democrisy" so that it suggests hypocrisy. And although he is circumscribed in rendering Negro patois, Joel Chandler Harris puns whenever he can and to any purpose, for instance, in describing his hero as "stuck up" while the rabbit is glued to the tar-baby. Part of the reason that Henry Shaw gave Billings the name Josh lay in his frank presentation of Josh's addictions. "I hav known folks whose *calibre* was very small, but whose *bore* was very big." Probably the best punned pen name of the time is that of Robert H. Newell, "Orpheus C. Kerr," office seeker. But there is no greater triumph in the play on a proper name or in any kind of pun than Lincoln's own gratuity, on a Washington stroll with Stanton. They had just crossed a corner in front of a grocery store beneath the proprietor's sign, "T. R. Strong," and the President observed, under the influence of Artemus Ward or under his own power, or both: "But . . . Coffee Are Stronger."

A great deal of the pun play was orthographic. It tickled most primitively when derived from mispronunciation, as in Bill Arp's "Linkhorn" or "Mack C. Million." Or Uncle Remus' fetching extensions of vocabulary: "dar wuz dish nice-lookin' gal a-pommynadin' up en down. . . ." The delight in spelling or mispelling was a clear indication of the newly acquired character of mass literacy, accelerative but unsure of itself yet and needing to laugh at the next lowest level from which most of the population were just barely lifting themselves. Such interest bears also on the neologisms of the period: Lowell's "kerwoosh" and Smith's alliterative tricolons, like "kulmination, konsummation and koruskation." The technique is pervasive in Smith, Harris, Shaw, Lowell, and the rest, but it provides something other than low-level appeal when functionally employed by Browne and Locke. Artemus Ward's epithetical adjective of criticism, "absurb," is more self-caricature than anything, and Nasby's slips of the pen are deviations into the wittiest sense: "My political daze is well-nigh over."

The verbal jocosity of the period works best when providing matching techniques for the antithetic content of the humor. It signifies, for instance, that Locke's orthography constitutes in itself an anticliché that devastates Nasby's oratorical flights: "dorrin the fratrisidle struggle which drenched this happy land in goar." It is safe enough to say that the Civil War and its aftermath maimed our rhetorical, cliché-ridden tradition, especially up north, as World War I all but killed it later. Almost all the humorists of the postbellum period were "literary comedians" because, in great part, they were precisely aware of the cliché as used by "literary" writers and appropriated by politicians. To them, clichés were more than mere accidents of worn-out style; they were hypocritical modes of thought. Therefore, when Bret Harte directs his best parodies to the wholesale destruction of the clichéd mind, we understand that a demolition of past mentality, not just of some previous author's weaknesses, is his comic aim. He attacks, for example, Fenimore Cooper's whole concept of highminded character and aristocratic disposition when he attacks Cooper's language in "Muck-A-Muck, a modern Indian novel after Cooper."

> The Judge was the first to break the silence.
> "Genevra, the logs which compose yonder fire seem to have been incautiously chosen. The sibilation produced by the sap, which exudes copiously therefrom, is not conducive to composition."
> "True, father, but I thought it would be preferable to the constant crepitation which is apt to attend the combustion of more seasoned ligneous fragments."

Indeed Bret Harte's parodies are vastly underrated, considering how much they attempt. The fact is that his obliterations of Cooper's narrative tricks and falsifying dialogue are sometimes more effective than Twain's more famous expository attack and diatribe.

> ". . . Delicious are the grasshoppers that sport on the hillside,— are they better than the dried apples of the Pale Faces? Pleasant is the gurgle of the torrent, Kish-Kish, but is it better than the cluck-cluck of old Bourbon from the old stone bottle?"
> "Ugh!" said the Indian,—"ugh! good. The White Rabbit is wise. Her words fall as the snow on Tootoonolo, and the rocky heart of Muck-a-Muck is hidden. What says my brother the Gray Gopher of Dutch Flat?"

                              · · · · ·

The well-aimed bullet had done its work. Entering the open throat of the grizzly, it had traversed his body only to enter the throat of the California lion, and in like manner the catamount, until it passed through into the respective foreheads of the bull and the buffalo, and finally fell flattened from the rocky hillside.

Genevra turned quickly. "My preserver!" she shrieked, and fell into the arms of Natty Bumppo, the celebrated Pike Ranger of Donner Lake.

The strategy of parody and the discrediting of the cliché strongly reinforce the deflationary realism of the humor. Another reinforcement is comic repetition, as practiced by Artemus Ward.

"Base man, leave us, oh leave us."
And I left them, oh I left them.

Still another contribution is simple concreteness of expression, a repudiation of abstractness and camouflage through literalistic comedy. "Be still my sole," says Artemus Ward, "And you, heart, stop cuttin' up." Here is Josh Billings:

"Truth is mitey and will prevail"; so iz cider mitey, but yu hav got tew tap the barrell before it will prevale.

There is 2 things in this life for which we are never fully prepared, and that iz twins.

Comic pertinence serves the same purpose.

We dont question a persons rite tew be a fule, but if he klaims wisdom, we kompare it with our own.

In Locke's exposé of Nasby's "remorse" for Lincoln, in "The Assassination," comic pertinence is even more explicit, concrete, and revealing.

He hed ended the war uv oppression—he hed subjoogatid a free and brave people, who were strugglin for their rites, and hed em under his feet; but I, in common with all Dimecrats, mourn his death!

Hed it happened in 1862, when it wood hev been uv some use to us, we wood not be so bowed down with woe and anguish. It wood hev throwd the guverment into confusion, and probably hev sekoored the independence uv the South.

But alas! the tragedy cum at the wrong time!

Now, we are saddled with the damnin crime, when it will produce no results.

The animus, then, was against hypocrisy and misrepresentation,
against all lies. Through style especially, the brunt of the attack
was on false expression, oracular, literary, clichéd, and abstract.
These comedians set themselves to oppose received modes and
values, and they pressed a great variety of miscellaneous techniques into the service of comic destruction. It is for this overarching reason that meaningless nonsense was also effective and
tremendously popular. In Browne's full exploitation of the *non
sequitur* the destruction is of all conventional sense, part of a
virtual campaign of discrediting not only what we think but how
we think. That accounts for the uproarious reception of such lines
as, "I knew a man in Oregon once that didn't have a tooth in his
head, but that man could play the drums better than anyone I
ever knew." It also accounts for Henry Shaw's popular circularities.

Yure inquiry stumps me, the darndest. . . . Much mite be ced
both ways, and neether wa be rite. Upon the whole i rather reckon
i wud, or i wuddent, jist az i thought best, or otherwise.

The same impulse accounts for the device of semireversal and
contradiction, notably in Shaw.

Lastly—i am violently opposed tu arden speerits as a bevridge,
but for manufaktering purposes, i think a leetle of it tastes good.

The tactic anticipates what Groucho Marx will do more blatantly
and shamelessly in another era.

The spirit of denial and the mood of exception are also apparent in the antiproverbialism practiced in the period. This
technique does not yet overwhelm positive proverbialism, which
indeed receives a kind of religiopolitical apotheosis in Lincoln.
Fittingly the savior of the union speaks in parables, his phrasing a
culmination of epigrammatic wisdom touched by original genius:
"switching horses in mid-stream," not "fooling all the people all
the time," having "malice toward none," etc. And Smith's Bill Arp,
another forebear of Faulkner, has his positivism: "Some things
pay in the short run, but honesty, truth and diligence pay in the
long run, and that is the one we have to live by." But Henry Shaw

is more representative. He is also more whimsical and less sententious, even while experimenting with only the slightest bent "afferism."

> Thar iz only one good substitute for the endearments of a sister and that iz the endearments of some other fellow's sister.

But the chief successes of Shaw's Josh Billings are clearly antiproverbial, in larger harmony with the time.

> "Large bodys move slo," this ere proverb dont apply tu lies, for the bigger tha ar, the faster tha go.
>
> Piety iz a good kind ov dissease for a man tew hav, but when he has so mutch ov it that he has tew go behind the door on Sunday to drink his whiskee, it will dew tew watch him the rest of the week.
>
> We are told that a contented man is happy, and we mite hav bin told, at the same, that a mudturkle could fly if it onla had wings.
>
> It is tru that welth won't maik a man vartuous, but i notis thare ain't ennyboddy who wants tew be poor jist for the purpiss ov being good.
>
> I hav herd a grate deal ced about "broken hartes," and thare may be a fu ov them, but mi experiense is that nex tew the gizzard, the harte is the tuffest peace ov meat in the whole critter.
>
> Rize arly, work hard, and late, live on what you kant sell, giv nothing awa, and if you dont die ritch, and go tu the devil, you ma sue me for damages.
>
> "Giv the devil hiz due," reads wel enuff in a proverb, but mi friend what will bekum ov you and me if this arrangement iz carried out?

It is, then, from this period of the literary comedians that we may unmistakably date the steady rise of the antiproverb, locate our first sure reflexes of parody, nonsense, and reversal, define our comic onslaught on the cliché, and fix our tactical subversion of rhetoric and the pieties that support it. Close antecedents of our modern period must include just these literary comedians. Parallels are often extremely apparent, as between Frank Sullivan, Benchley, Perelman, and Browne. Or in quoting Shaw on right expression—

> The power . . . lays more in the manner, than in the matter; you cant reduse it tew writing, enny more than yu kan pla a streak of lightning on a hand organ.

—we might, but for the spelling, be quoting Thurber or E.B. White. Which is a way of saying, perhaps, that native American humor, once risen, is of one topographical piece, with some peaks but all recognizably of the same range and tone. Our comedy exists on a high plateau of coterminous performance, steeply falling off only on either side.

Or we may observe that our comic tradition, defined as a usable past, has been much more available and actively consulted by modern practitioners than previously thought. To the fact that Twain read his southwestern forebears and comic contemporaries closely and that Faulkner relied on both the southwesterners and Twain, we can add the educated guess that a host of twentieth century humorists regularly put themselves in debt to these literary comedians. And in the triumph of academia since World War II, we detect spoofs that are conjunctions of modern topicality and Wardean technique. Thus "The Gettysburg Address" is corrected for rewrite. Mencken had once playfully revised it, as he had the Declaration of Independence, in the baldest and worst "American" English. But in the fifties new translations were undertaken (some of them eventually printed in journals like *Word Study* and *The New Republic*). These were designed as special attacks upon infelicities of Eisenhower prose and Madison Avenue-ese. They also constituted an attack on the original inflations of Lincoln, whose break with oratorical tradition, we see now, was in his astounding brevity, not actually in his phraseology.

This is a simultaneous assault. Half of it is a delayed attack derived from the antirhetorical impulses of the literary comedians, who feed directly into the modern period themselves because they have become subjects of study in the universities.

Similarly, precisely in proportion as Charles Farrar Browne is researched, there are academic bagatelles under Wardean influence, like the nonsense transliterations currently popular in higher education, notably of "Little Red Riding Hood."

> Wants pawn term, dare worsted ladle gull hoe lift wetter murder inner ladle cordage honor itch offer lodge dock florist. . . . "Tick disc ladle basking tudor cordage offer groin murder hoe lifts honor udder site." . . . "Ho-cake, murder," resplendent ladle rat rotten hut, and tickle ladle basking an stuttered oft. Honor wrote

Mr. Lincoln:

I am sorry, but this simply won't do. You don't seem to be able to get the idea across in plain, forceful language. Try again. Let's get this out— it is three weeks old now.

LINCOLN'S GETTYSBURG ADDRESS

CORRECTED FOR REWRITE

Say "Eightyseven"

"Founded" would be better.

Sounds awkward. Say "with the idea of freedom."

Four score and seven years ago our fathers brought forth on this continent a new nation, conceived in liberty, and dedicated to the proposition that all men are created equal.

Get the name in there Big!

How about women?

Now we are engaged in a great civil war, testing whether that nation, or any nation so conceived and so dedicated can long endure. We are met on

we have

Make this the first paragraph. We're taking too long to get into our story!

"Endure" what? make it last

a great battlefield of that war. We have come to dedicate a portion of that field, as a final resting-place for those who here gave their lives that that nation might live.

Put in name.

Don't beat around the bush—say "cemetery."

tudor cordage offer groin murder, ladle rat rotten hut mitten anomalous woof.

"Wail, wail, wail," set disk wicket woof, "evanescent ladle rat rotten hut! Wares or putty ladle gull goring wizard ladle basking?" . . . Oil offer sodden throne offer carvers an sprinkling otter bet, disc curl am bloat Thursday woof ceased pore ladle rat rotten hut and garbled erupt.

We need not, by the way, stress the modern penchant for the unhappy ending, *that* supreme anticliché, or theorize here upon comedy's joy in difficulty. The issue is the use of nonsense style, rationalized only by familiar background rhythm; it is a linguistic tool for the analysis of speech patterns, but the tool is provided through no sheer coincidence at the time we restudied the literary comedians and Browne in particular. The same influence is at work, and the same antiproverbialism is the motive, when we elaborate long involved stories of Polynesians who hide their bejeweled royal chair of state in the attic of the chief's straw hut, fearful of the greed of visiting Americans. But when, just before the Americans leave, the chair falls through, they are foiled. Moral: "People who live in grass houses shouldn't stow thrones." That, too, is delayed academical inheritance, directly descending from an overflowing period still spilling down to us,[6] through arcane passages as well as by more usual cross-influences. We derive from the watershed of the literary comedians a great deal of our fluid nonsense, our model of antirhetorical delights and energetic confusionism, and our inspiration to force language itself to the service of the most outlandish reversalisms.

The importance of Browne's Wardean model cannot be exaggerated. Thurber's "who-whom" confusions, standard orthographic jokes confusing "defectives on the police force" with "detectives on the police farce," etc., and Victor Borgean verbal play on "wonderful" and "two-derful," etc., are traceable in part to the original examples of helpless self-correction and mocked progressive logic in Browne.

[6] There is the recent exercise, really elongated neologism or transliterated punning again, about a man who loses his billfold in a pool of fish, who proceed to pass it back and forth between themselves: a rare instance of "carp-to-carp walleting." The inventive American tall tale, of course, continues as a basic element also.

As a singer, I was not a success. As a singster, I was a failure. Why is this thus? Why is this thusly? Why thus this thusness?

Browne also best illustrates the growing versatility of the literary comedians. He is an adept at the pure thing as well as at subsequent combinations. His literalism is not only the safe and sound "Henry the Three," but his renowned answer to the sponsors' telegraph, "What will you take for forty nights in California?" when he wired back succinctly, "Brandy and water." His reversalism—

I was so blessed with the girl's brightness that I could have kissed the dear child, and I would if she'd been six years older.

—is the abrupt change from paternalism to sexuality, so reflexive by now in popular jokes. His use of the anticlimax not only descends clearly to Finley Peter Dunne's practice but retains comic force purely on its own.

There's one king in the [museum] who is mounted onto a foamin steed, his right hand graspin a barber's pole.

Browne had his competitors, of course, although they were inclined to consider themselves admirers and followers. After Ward's example, Henry Shaw seized upon the device of literalism gratefully (as he avowedly took Browne's advice on colloquial language). Not averse to raiding Thoreau for his figure either, he puts both influences together, as a model of the period's rampant eclecticism, to produce his effect, as in his essay, "On Dogs."

Tha kant talk, but tha kan lick yure hand, this shows that their hearts iz in the plase where uther folks' tungs iz. Dogs in the lump are useful, but tha are not always profittable in the lump. The Nufoundlin dog is useful tew saive children from drowning, but yu hav got tew hav a pond or water, and children running around kareless, or else the dog aint profittable.

His talent at reversalism is equally certain in *His Sayings.*

Fust appearances are ced tu be everything. I don't put all mi fathe into this saying; i think oysters and klams, for instanze, will bear looking into.

And he is a strict pupil of anticlimax.

> Perhaps it iz best i shud state sum good advise tew yung men,
> who are about tew court with a final view to matrimony, az it was.
> . . . After the fust year yu will begin to be well ackquainted and
> will begin tew like the bizzness. Thare is one thing I alwus advise,
> and that iz not to swop fotograffs oftener than onse in 10 daze,
> unless yu forgit how the gal looks.

> an auctioneer told me ov it, and I never knew an auctioneer tu
> lie unless it was absolutely convenient.

In the *Nasby Papers* Locke also is an apt technician, especially
in anticlimax.

> I see in the papers las nite that the Government hez institooted
> a draft, and that in a few weeks sum hundreds uv thousands uv
> peeceable citizens will be dragged to the tented field. I know not
> wat uthers may do, but ez for me I cant go.

> owin to my foot becomin entangled into the lock uv my gun,
> wich was acksidentally across the muzzle thereof. . . .

And Bill Nye constantly exercises himself in the same recognizable mode, as in "A Resign."

> I need not say that I herewith transmit my resignation with great
> sorrow and genuine regret. We have toiled on together month after
> month, asking for no reward except the innate consciousness of
> rectitude and the salary as fixed by law.

But the admired pacesetter was Browne.

Browne was also in the vanguard in the use of multiple and
simultaneous devices for his effects. To a certain extent, of course,
at least a minimal combination of devices characterizes humor
most of the time. But Americans, even in the more venturesome
southwesterners a generation before, had been inclined toward a
more concentrated if sharp effect. The literary comedians, however, as often as not choose not to limit themselves. The employment of combined devices, stylistic and otherwise, becomes a
standard practice in this time; single and even doubled techniques
will become harder to identify and the isolation of them more
academic after this period. Browne, for instance, mixes anti-
climactic deflation with a piquant contrast of the highfalutin and

the colloquial styles and then adds orthographic humor in misspelling a key word on each side: "The Sunny South is makin'
an egrejus mutten-hed of herself." So does Smith unite several
comic eccentricities of Bill Arp—"As General Byron said at the
Battle of Waterloo, I ain't now what I used to was"—combining
misquotation and mispronunciation with comic redundancy.
Smith, we know, borrowed content as well as technique from
Browne.[7] But Browne would have felt complimented on both
scores. As he would also have been pleased if he knew how much
he influenced as well as consoled Lincoln. The chances are that
Lincoln's later humor, though he always had a gift of his own
in sudden comic pertinence, was affected by Browne's literalisms;
for example, the President's description of the reluctant Army of
the Potomac as "McClellan's bodyguard."

Browne's leadership in the experimental combinative technique
extended to a mixing of genres. At certain "historical" lantern-
slide lectures, as on the Indian question, he called for "Tenting
Tonight" as background music for scalping scenes. Both the contrast and the mixture became perennial devices of comic stage
practice.

Just about the best example of the combinative technique in
literary comedy of the period, however, occurs in George Horatio
Derby, better known as "Phoenix." In "Musical Review Extraordinary," he writes a memorable music review of a visiting soprano or, rather, *two* reviews ahead of time, raving and damning
notices in case she turns out one way or the other; this is an early
instance of that blatant and easy self-contradiction that Chaplin
and Groucho Marx later solidify as a technique. Then Derby con-
centrates on a review of a symphony composed for the western
plains. It is here that he combines extended literalism, constant
stylistic deflation, the antirhetorical mode, parody, and anticlimax
all carried to extravagant but imperturbable length.

    . . . The solos were rendered by Herr Tuden Links, the recitations
    by Herr Von Hyden Schnapps, both performers being assisted by

[7] In Artemus Ward's piece on "The Tower of London," traitors are
defined for Smith's subsequent use: they "conspire to bust up a country—
they fail, and they're traters. They bust her, and they become statesmen and
heroes." Smith, in fact, addressed some of his letters to Ward as well as to
Lincoln.

Messrs. John Smith and Joseph Brown, who held their coats, fanned
them, and furnished water during the more overpowering passages.
. . . The symphonie opens upon the wide and boundless plains, in
longitude 115° 21′ 03″ N., and about sixty miles from the west bank
of Pitt River. These data are beautifully and clearly expressed by
a long (topographically) drawn note from an E flat clarinet. The
sandy nature of the soil, sparsely dotted with bunches of cactus and
artemisia, the extended view, flat and unbroken to the horizon, save
by the rising smoke in the extreme verge, denoting the vicinity of
a Pi Utah Village, are represented by the bass drum. A few notes
on the piccolo [call] the attention to a solitary antelope, picking up
mescal beans in the foreground. The sun having an altitude of 36°
27′, blazes down upon the scene in indescribable majesty. "Gradually the sounds roll forth in a song" of rejoicing to the God of Day.

> "Of thy intensity
> And great immensity
>   Now then we sing;
> Beholding in gratitude
> Thee in this latitude,
>   Curious thing."

Which swells out into "Hey Jim along, Jim along Josey," then
decrescendo, mas o menos, poco-pocita, dies away and dries up.

The question of parody in the period deserves further comment. Where it is obvious, in Derby's dissection of cultured absurdity[8] or in Bret Harte's necessary destruction of the all too
recent literary past (Cooper, Poe, Whittier, etc.), it calls sufficient
attention to itself. But in other ways the technique was so tho-
roughgoing as to be almost subtle and undetectable or so implicitly
topical that we may overlook its governance. Browne's Ward was
constantly parodying the Lyceum and those lantern slide pan-
orama entertainments so popular during the period in all their
sentimental and didactic appeal. His fecklessness in public speaking ("I don't know nothin about no ded languages and am a little
shaky on livin ones"), for example, and his generally self-defeating mis-corrections of himself (". . . my first perfeshernal tower of

---

[8] The newspaperman and part-time humorist, George T. Lannigan, also
chose to deflate and parody cultural expression, music performances in
particular. Studiously he described a violin concert as the drawing of a bow
consisting of "the hair of a noble horse," across "the intestine of an alley
cat."

New Englan, causes me to feel—to feel—I may say it causes me to *feel*.") have added point in this regard. In this vein also Josh Billings lectures on "Milk," never once alluding to it, though there is a glass of milk prominently placed on the lectern throughout his discourse. Later he would answer the inevitable question from the floor by readily confessing that he had drunk a full quart of milk before he mounted the platform: "Of course I have been lecturing on milk."

For his part, David Ross Locke takes off on the Psalms and the whole Bible in *Swingin' Round the Cirkle*, editing scripture for a slavocracy that believed, as some believe yet, in the base blunt truths he revises: "God created a White Man in his own image." The old plantation owner, in "Abolition in Kentucky," emancipates his Negroes with inexorable Biblical lamentation.

> "Wunst I hed a hundred niggers, and the men were fat and healthy, and the wenches wuz strong, and sum uv em wuz fair to look upon.
>
> "They worked in my house, and my fields, from the rising uv the sun to the goin down uv the same.
>
> "Wuz they lazy? I catted them till they wuz cured thereof; for lo! they wuz ez a child under my care.
>
> "Did they run away? From Kentucky they run North, and lo! the Locofoco Marshals caught them for me, and brought them back, and delivered them into my hand, without cost, sayin, lo! here is thy nigger—do with him ez thou wilt. . . .
>
> "Farewell, Looizer, my daughter, farewell! I loved your mother ez never man loved nigger. She wuz the solace uv my leisure hours —the companion uv my yooth. She I sold to pay orf a mortgage on the place—she and yoor older sisters. Farewell! I hed hoped to hev sold yoo this winter (for yoo are still young), and bought out Jinkins; but wo is me! Curses on the tirent who thus severs all the tender ties uv nachur. Oh! it is hard for father to part with child, even when the market's high; . . . .

In his comprehensive monograph, *American Humorists*, Professor Thorp has indicated also the immense amount of spoof reporting in the comic literature. There was a prodigious number of abusive letters to the editor and burlesques of solemn travel sketches, sermons, and orations in contemporary newspapers. When we add to such conscious and prevailing intentions, the several antirhetorical devices of style which we have encountered, Browne's attack on poetic and other highfalutin diction or Locke's demolishment of oratorical splendor, we have a complete view. Almost nothing of entrenched or sacrosanct value in the time escaped a many-sided antithetical attack. Not education, or journalism, piety, literature, oratory, politics, suffragism, prejudice or culture were exempt from comic assault, as especially prosecuted through the varied means of overt and implicit parody available to the literary comedians.

Other devices of humor, mainly clear legacies of comic practice just before the war, deserve notice. The manner of the tall tale continues, together with the extravagant substance. Lincoln describes a thin western soup: "made by bathing the shadow of a pigeon that had starved to death." Shaw devotes an essay to the Erie Canal mule who pulls his barge from underwater—breathing through his long ears. Anonymous jokers of the war report that on eating hardtack they occasionally bite something soft. A worm? "No," goes the reply, "a ten-penny nail." And Locke's Nasby fixes watches in rude bivouac with a bayonet as mainspring and fiddle string as chain. Our critical American ingenuity is still outpaced by our grossest imagination.

The most famous American comic understatement occurs in this period: the subsequent reference to the Civil War as "the late unpleasantness." In the native grain, however, there is so much extravagance involved in the euphemism that the phrase is a kind of miniature and reversed tall tale. The same thing may be said of Bill Nye's western begrudgments of facts, wondrous exercises, as in "He Sees the Navy."

> The guard-house contains a choice collection of manacles, handcuffs, lily irons and other rare gems. . . . With a pair of lily irons on the wrists and another pair on the ankles a man locked in the brig and caught out 2,000 miles at sea in a big gale, with the rudder knocked off the ship and a large litter of kittens in the steam cylinder, would feel almost helpless.

Comic metaphor, while present, is not as strong as in the antebellum period. Lincoln is one of the adepts, quick and concrete, especially in his earlier career: "The rain makes the corn laugh."

He said in his first stump speech: "My politics are short and sweet, like the old woman's dance." There are engaging similes in Josh Billings: "Lov iz like the measles, the older you are the worst it iz" and "Women are like echoes, tha always hav the last word." Joel Chandler Harris has a moment now and then: "right there is where he broke his molasses jug"; i.e., made his big mistake. And we may recover the usual metaphorical derogations of wartime conditions, of battlefield hardtack as "sheetiron crackers," etc. But Bert Harte's, "A Baby no bigger nor a derringer" in "The Luck of Roaring Camp" is, considering the context, probably the best comic figure of speech written in the period.

We cannot leave the subject of techniques without commentary on the device of masquerade, as exemplified particularly in pseudonyms and the creation of alter egos. On every side humorists of the period rise to recognition and even esteem, but still disguised, they take no chances in their own right. As their predecessors were before them and as Samuel Clemens will be for his psychological reasons later, they seem to respond to necessity in splitting their personalities in America. We must acknowledge the use of the nom de plume and assorted disguises in the United States as far more general and insistent than anywhere else. Do these representative comedians throw their voices, like ventriloquists, hiding behind dummies, masks, and names, because they are fearful, not of simple failure, but of too great a success? That is as much their secret motive in this country as is their desire to be two men with a sort of stereoscopic view on things. They seek safety as well as perspective.

The coming of age of our humor in this period is marked not only by sheer performance or lasting influence. In addition, this is the age of our first tentative comic theoreticians, Henry Shaw and Bret Harte particularly. Hypothesis rarely precedes experiment in literature, and theory almost never anticipates accomplishment but follows it. It must give a hostage of good works to any philosophizing. A genre authorizes itself only when it can take for granted a body of material strong enough to call for explanation. For good or ill, the first theories are indications of arrival and maturity, as the last may be of querulous decay. Thus

Shaw speculates a good deal of his aphoristic time on the nature
of comedy, especially the American contribution. It is immaterial
if he is right or wrong; he simply feels secure enough to talk,
as in *Josh Billings on Ice* (1868).

> Amerikans love caustick things; they would prefer turpentine
> tew colone-water, if they had tew drink either.
> So with their relish of humor; they must hav it on the half-shell
> with cayenne.
> If you tickle or convince an Amerikan yu hav got tew do it quick.
> The English are better punsters, but i konsider punning a sort ov
> literary prostitushun in which future happynesz iz swopped oph for
> the plezzure ov the moment.
> Don't forget *one* thing, yu hav got tew be wize before yu kan be
> witty; and don't forget *two* things, a single paragraff haz made sum
> men immortal, while a volume haz bin wuss than a piledriver tew
> others. . . .
> Englishmen all laff at us for our sensashuns, and sum ov them
> fret about it, and spred their feathers in distress for us, az a fond
> and foolish old hen, who haz hatched out a setting ov ducks' eggs,
> will stand on the banks ov a mill pond, wringing her hands in agony
> to see her brood pitch in and take a sail. *She* kant understand,
> but the *Ducks* know awl about it.
> Fitckshun is a kind ov haf wa hous, betwen the temples ov
> Truth and Fallshood, whare the good and the bad meet tu lie a
> little.

On another more sustained level, Bret Harte maintains that it
is not local colorism (essentially realistic, even to a sentimental
corrupter like Harte) that accounts for the rise of American
humor but quite the contrary. And when, with Shaw, he diagnoses
conciseness and general economy of means as the hallmarks of
American humor, Harte opposes Twain with more impartial objectivity than the master could bring to the question.

But that the questions were now formulated at all is significant. This theorization is part and parcel of the whole attitude
of critique the period exemplifies, and it is conclusive certification
of the rise of American humor itself.

From this time on, our humor is never so innocuous or covert as
to constitute a titillating diversion or an underground species

of subliterature. Our humorists themselves, wearing their masks and motley as they may still be and generally suffering pseudonymic schizophrenia, come into estates of public affection and respect and sometimes fortune, trusted custodians of an hilarious but dark conscience of the people. There are softnesses yet in this humor, wry self-deflations and gentle declensions, as in most of Lincoln's humor and in some of the others, like Joel Chandler Harris. And there are even apostasies from cruelty, cynicism, and amorality, as in the later Eugene Field. But by and large the period of the literary comedians signals the first full and overt astringencies of American humor. The antithetical motive of our comedy becomes definitive in this era. And technical versatility is active to the point of explosion.

With the period of southwestern humor before it, the period of the literary comedians provides the preparatory attitudes and devices for the almost predictable appearance of genius, Mark Twain. I do not mean by that observation to cheapen history by discounting the unforeseeable. But if certain historical developments must always surprise us, by the same token certain periods seem to develop mood and means to encourage the highest talent, like an enabling act of Time. If that is what this period did, it is enough, though there is always more to account for genius than genesis.

But the period of the literary comedians, in an even larger perspective, represents clear achievement in its own right. It appears to have come to a rapid maturity of gift on every side, it was national in scope, it continues to astonish us in its comic energies, and in the bulk of its work it remains significantly and durably modern.

IV

Mark Twain

IF MARK TWAIN (1835–1910) had written everything he did write except *Huckleberry Finn*, we would
still think of him in the front rank of American humor.
On the other hand, if he had not written anything but *Huckleberry Finn*, we would still be arguing his greatness. Postponing
consideration of that tenacious comic masterpiece of American
literature until its academic place in a chronological review would
be rigorous but coy methodology. The work is the high point of
Twain's career and a summit in American humor. It looms. We
look to it at once as a culminative and commanding work.

It is an unsettling and dangerous book, as the critic, Lionel
Trilling, has pointed out. Many readers and trustees of public
libraries have instinctively recoiled from it. It has been banned
not merely as an indiscretion but as a desecration in a number of
cities and towns, including that virtual American Sinai, Concord,
Massachusetts. Called "vulgar, rough, inelegant, coarse, trashy,
vicious," it has been ceremoniously indicted for its episodes of
lying, thievery, blasphemy—and poor grammar. Under these
superficial tirades, however, is a perfectly understandable motive
of censure and fear. The book commits a deep crime in its repudiation of social morality. One never fully recovers from reading *Huck Finn*. Its subversion of any comfortable American balance between the individual and society is lasting. Twain spoke
of his agnostical "sermons" in the book, and its work of conver-

sion is insidiously and uproariously devastating. No sooner do we take its essential measure, however, in these our more sophisticated and liberated days, than we feel the force of the very newest joke in the reception of the book. Suburban Negroes of Connecticut protest the inappropriate treatment of Nigger Jim in the story; they object to his very name. The book, then, subverts everything sacred, even civil rights. It undermines everything organized or conspiratorial, including tyrannical righteousness. Everything but our most private rectitude and perspective stands in the way of it. Its hold upon us is all the more appalling, for it speaks to a sort of responsible anarchy in all Americans, who sense its health, respond to its honest characterization, and are convinced by a superlative technical vindication of its themes.

Like the peculiarly American ambitions in the epical *Moby Dick* and in that novelistic tour de force, *The Great Gatsby*, *Huck Finn* is basically inaccessible to foreigners. They may accept other flamboyant performances like the work of Whitman or Poe, but something more fundamental and intimate than a fresh wind or romantic melodrama escapes them in these other works, whose significance they must accept out of critical good sportsmanship. The great American tragic epic takes its own processes of symbolic transference so seriously, beneath all its comic flourishes, that readers abroad cannot believe in Melville's final intentions. Fitzgerald's careful naïveté, as it appears to sophisticated outsiders, must be some sort of joke. And Mark Twain's triumph seems so overt and episodic that they cannot get past its mere effrontery to something less trivial than they see, to some substantive heart of the matter. In fact, no masterwork puzzles them more than *Huck Finn*, for they can take the measure, after a fashion, of the wild investment Melville made in the one classic and the intensity of Fitzgerald in the other, but Twain's manner, unlike Whitman's and Poe's in other contexts, puts them off. It is not a matter of puerility that embarrasses them, for they contend successfully with adolescence in other major writers. Some deep American in-fighting, some basic topicality, so to speak, and some gift of subtlety, screened by the most ingenuous of means, belong to Americans alone in Mark Twain's supreme and obdurate work.

Indigenous and honest controversies about the form of the book we shall treat as we proceed. But for the principal and compelling themes of *Huck Finn* there are no stumbling blocks. Writing retrospectively in the 1880's about the antebellum generation, Twain set himself against two of the most grueling lies of American life. As an erstwhile and halfhearted Confederate (recorded in "A History of a Campaign That Failed"), he assailed the memory of a happy southern society built on human slavery. And as a midwesterner he delivered the classic thematic rebuke to a mid-American social morality displaced from Puritan New England and consequently outworn and hypocritical. Missouri was a confluence of the two most pernicious conducts of life we have ever honored. From directly across the Appalachians came a tide of southern custom that informed the whole border-state structure of life. And down from the Ohio valley came the descendants of Calvinists, who settled the upper midwest and imposed mere pietism upon the conscience of the region. The resultant mores were those of an open-faced duplicity and strong repression. Accordingly, Twain took his stand for a natural individual morality, the governing plea of his work. Safeguarded by the comic and narrative distance of sheer time and by the objective device of a narrator like Huck, Twain's view is incisive and, finally, uncompromising. Against a cheap religiosity no longer viable, against piety that masks inhuman economics, Sunday Schoolism built on slavery that was finally more harrowing psychologically than physically, Twain believed in a common-sensical natural morality that some among us could achieve. The qualification is an adjunct of his realism. It is the outcast, Huck Finn, not Tom Sawyer, who ironically stands the best chance of coming into his own.

Such orientation seems to make the book a kind of Rousseauean romance in the end. But there is no certain telling. The amount of comic but realistic cynicism in the novel is a counterforce. The work slips out of easy classifications. The vagabond hero is, as such, a romantic figure, but in the story he scarcely leads an unthreatened idyllic life—certainly not physically and, even more certainly, not morally. The psychological realism of the book accounts, perhaps, for its greatest triumph to both alert and subliminal American readers. But the realism of the book is not programmatic or comprehensive. Twain missed, for instance, or he deliberately ignored the realism of flagrant Mississippi steamboat prostitution. But even if we answer with the observation that he was after a realism far more significant than mere naturalistic reporting allows, we must face up to his themes. And they involve the individual flight from "sivilization"—always a misspelling, from the functional example of Ward and Locke—and a misconstruction. There is a tight circle of romantic and realistic concerns joined together in what first appears as a loose and largely improvisational scheme. But paradox and equipoise, as never before achieved in his career or quite regained afterward, account for Twain's fullest success in theme and character.

The book contains two epical heroes who seek freedom, freedom from actual servitude for Jim and freedom from psychological slavery for Huck. Alienated and freed from greed to begin with, both characters are progressively freed from all illusion and from personal sham and self-interest. And they are free with one another.[1] Huck plays his joke of disappearance on Jim, and Jim's response is uninhibited.

"... When I got all wore out wid work, en wid de callin' for you, en went to sleep, my heart wuz mos' broke bekase you wuz los', en I didn' k'yer no mo' what become er me en de raf'. En when I wake up en fine you back agin, all safe en soun', de tears come, en I could 'a' got down on my knees en kiss yo' foot, I's so thankful. En all you wuz thinkin' 'bout wuz how you could make a fool uv ole Jim wid a lie. Dat truck dah is *trash;* en trash is what people is dat puts dirt on de head er day fren's en makes 'em ashamed."

And Huck's reaction is 99 per cent liberated.

Then he got up slow and walked to the wigwam, and went in there without saying anything but that. But that was enough. It made me feel so mean I could almost kissed *his* foot to get him to take it back.

It was fifteen minutes before I could work myself up to go and humble myself to a nigger—but I done it and I warn't ever sorry for it afterward, neither. I didn't do him no more mean tricks, and I wouldn't done that one if I'd 'a' knowed it would make him feel that way.

[1] This is one of those reverberations, in the nature of incommunicative American life, not available to European critics.

That clinging if miniscule white supremacy in Huck is the saving realism of his characterization. The prejudice undergoes its complete erosion, too, and that process is one of the chief points of interest in the book, part of the whole theme of freedom, which is most important when fundamentally psychic. It is precisely such a consequential theme that sets this work, a sequel itself to *Tom Sawyer,* against its own inconsequential sequels (*Tom Sawyer, Abroad* and *Tom Sawyer, Detective*).

The theme does more than govern the course of the book. It positively dictates to it. As such, it accounts for the celebrated lapse of narrative realism, the possibility of the characters' escape across the river early in the story. As for the fact that the theme and story become more and more gripping the further *south* Huck and Jim go, that is the central irony and drama of the plot rather than its fault. The dictatorial and symbolic theme of Huck's new life in freedom absolutely determines the downstream motif of the novel, and it obviates mere narrative lapses. Certainly Huck and Jim could have paddled on a log or rafted or swum over to the Illinois shore very early in the book. And their passing of the Ohio River junction at Cairo later on is no real disaster because they never could have powered themselves *up* the Ohio in any event. The story must move downstream, not simply to continue the action but to signal a natural reliance on the great current of Nature and to symbolize, as Professor Lauriat Lane mentions, a type of downward birth process.[2]

The true crises of the story, therefore, are not those of pure action but of the spirit. These, of course, center on Huck. They are the psychologic climaxes of the work. In the first instance, Huck resolves his inner dilemma by weakly deciding to tell on the runaway Jim; simultaneously Twain provides just the ironical thoughts and parallel incidents that will lead Huck to resist himself.

> I tried to make out to myself that I warn't to blame because I didn't run Jim off from his rightful owner, but it warn't no use, conscience up and says, every time, "But you knowed he was running for his freedom, and you could 'a' paddled ashore and told

[2] Hence also, probably, the varied emphases on nakedness, too, throughout the story.

somebody." That was so—I couldn't get around that no way. That was where it pinched. Conscience says to me, "What had poor Miss Watson done to you that you could see her nigger go off right under your eyes and never say one single word? What did that poor old woman do to you that you could treat her so mean? Why, she tried to learn you your book, she tried to learn you your manners, she tried to be good to you every way she knowed how. *That's* what she done."

I got to feeling so mean and so miserable I most wished I was dead. I fidgeted up and down the raft, abusing myself to myself, and Jim was fidgeting up and down past me. . . . He was saying how the first thing he would do when he got to a free state he would go to saving up money and never spend a single cent, and when he got enough he would buy his wife, which was owned on a farm close to where Miss Watson lived, and then they would both work to buy the two children, and if their master wouldn't sell them, they'd get an Ab'litionist to go and steal them.

It most froze me to hear such talk. He wouldn't ever dared to talk such talk in his life before. Just see what a difference it made in him the minute he judged he was about free. It was according to the old saying, "Give a nigger an inch and he'll take an ell." Thinks I, this is what comes of my not thinking. Here was this nigger, which I had as good as helped to run away, coming right out flat-footed and saying he would steal his children—children that belonged to a man I didn't even know; a man that hadn't ever done me no harm.

I was sorry to hear Jim say that, it was such a lowering of him. My conscience got to stirring me up hotter than ever, until at last I says to it, "Let up on me—it ain't too late yet—I'll paddle ashore at the first light and tell." I felt easy and happy and light as a feather right off. All my troubles was gone. I went to looking out sharp for a light, and sort of singing to myself. By and by one showed. Jim sings out:

"We's safe, Huck, we's safe! Jump up and crack yo' heels! Dat's de good ole Cairo at las', I jis knows it!"

I says:

"I'll take the canoe and go see, Jim. It mightn't be, you know."

He jumped and got the canoe ready and put his old coat in the bottom for me to set in and give me the paddle; and as I shoved off, he says:

"Pooty soon I'll be a-shoutin' for joy, en I'll say, it's all on accounts o' Huck; I's a free man, en I couldn't ever ben free ef it hadn' ben for Huck; Huck done it. Jim won't ever forget you, Huck;

you's de bes' fren' Jim's ever had; en you's de *only* fren' ole Jim's got now."

I was paddling off, all in a sweat to tell on him, but when he says this, it seemed to kind of take the tuck all out of me.

Inevitably he reaches the opposite but commensurate decision.

. . . I got aboard the raft, feeling bad and low because I knowed very well I had done wrong, and I see it warn't no use for me to try to learn to do right; a body that don't get *started* right when he's little ain't got no show—when the pinch comes there ain't nothing to back him up and keep him to his work, and so he gets beat. Then I thought a minute and says to myself, hold on; s'pose you'd 'a' done right and give Jim up, would you felt better than what you do now? No, says I, I'd feel bad—I'd feel just the same way I do now. Well, then, says I, what's the use you learning to do right when it's troublesome to do right and ain't no trouble to do wrong, and the wages is just the same? I was stuck. I couldn't answer that.

Relentlessly, as a result of a steamboat collision, Twain separates the two characters just on this note. But reunited with Jim further along, Huck solidifies his decision and resolves to go to hell. The moral inversion, of a right-minded depravity, is a triumph of reversalism.

So I got a piece of paper and a pencil, all glad and excited, and set down and wrote:

Miss Watson, your runaway nigger Jim is down here two mile below Pikesville, and Mr. Phelps has got him and he will give him up for the reward if you send.

HUCK FINN

I felt good and all washed clean of sin for the first time I had ever felt so in my life, and I knowed I could pray now. But I didn't do it straight off but laid the paper down and set there thinking— thinking how good it was all this happened so. . . . And went on thinking. And got to thinking over our trip down the river; and I see Jim before me all the time: in the day and in the night-time, some- times moonlight, sometimes storms, and we a-floating along, talking and singing and laughing. . . . and at last I struck the time I saved him by telling the men we had smallpox aboard, and he was so grate- ful, and said I was the best friend old Jim ever had in the world and the *only* one he's got now; and then I happened to look around and see that paper.

It was a close place. I took it up, and held it my hand. I was a-trembling, because I'd got to decide, forever, betwixt two things, and I knowed it. I studied a minute, sort of holding my breath, and then says to myself:

"All right, then, I'll *go* to hell"—and tore it up.

It was awful thoughts and awful words but they was said. And I let them stay said; and never thought no more about reforming. I shoved the whole thing out of my head and said I would take up wickedness again, which was in my line, being brung up to it, and the other warn't. And for a starter I would go to work and steal Jim out of slavery again; and if I could think up anything worse, I would do that, too; because as long as I was in and in for good, I might as well go the whole hog.

He will risk immortal hell—the greatest of all lies?—for mortal freedom. And there is the suggestion that he does so, finally, on pure impulse, though we must not underestimate the struggle and traumatic price to him, an impulse purified of lingering inner debate and torment, freed from tortured social reason, more righteous and truthful than that almighty guilt instilled not by God but by society. The comic id conquers the superego, the unconscious triumphing over "conscience," though for all his demurrals about the way he was "brung up," the boy is responsibly ready to pay the fullest of costs. In most detailed and harrowing comedy of mind, Twain falsifies nothing, earning his theme, earning his character, and earning the drama which we are bound to acknowledge. *Huckleberry Finn* thereby becomes the most sustained and transcendent comic work in American literature.

Nonetheless, critical exceptions have been taken to the structure of the novel. The incidents are episodic, sometimes loosely organized, usually improvisational. At one point in composition, Twain considered turning his circus episode into slapstick disaster, with wild elephants and outlandish camels romping up and down the Mississippi. Yet he kept the excrescence out of the book and at this high point of his career followed the dictates of an artistic logic more powerful than his own willfulness. As it came out, at the last, there are true circular unities of theme, like that of freedom from "sivilization," which clearly bring the end of the comic novel into accord with its beginnings. And all events in between contribute unfalteringly to the psychological dimensions of the book. Still, in formal critical debates over the "greatness" of the work, there remains the prime controversy over the concluding extravaganza Twain provides. This has to do with the last section of Tom's reintroduction into the story and that self-entertainment of Tom's in "freeing" Jim from the cabin jail on the Phelps plantation. The questions raised about the legitimacy of the conclusion are indeed fundamental and frequently sensitive, and they call for adequate reply.

Professor Leo Marx, for instance, sees a disruptive change of tone from the earlier and dominant sincerity and tenderness, and he indicts Twain's radical shift from serious themes. It seems to him that Twain turns to unalloyed farce. Santayana had put it another way, that Twain's nerve failed him. All the critics with reservations agree that Jim becomes a submissive stage-Negro type and that in Jim's manumission by Widow Watson, Twain at the last vindicates the whole society of its fakery and false gentility. Twain should have shown the remorseless defeat of adjustment and the doom of the central quest for freedom. Indeed, the implicit metaphor of the rudderless raft indicates the human powerlessness and vulnerability that account for the book's true meaning. According to Henry Nash Smith, Twain violates that meaning in his conclusion and presents a burlesque Tom Sawyer, all at once turning the book into an imaginative trifle.

But the master key to the book is just in the change of relationship between Huck Finn and Tom Sawyer. In the wholeness of comic creation, Huck is steadily characterized as growing away from Tom Sawyer's compulsive and play-acting sense of "style." Twain is vitally concerned to show that unmistakably at the very end. All the logic and drift of the narrative is to that purpose. All this Sawyeresque made-up danger, all this manufactured or derivative experience of Tom's romantical and superficial American character must be placed again in conclusive contrast to all that Huck finally stands for. This, indeed, is what forces Huck definitely to leave the whole society. For Huck has been through the real thing, has undergone the true dangers and suffered the deepest education. In his moral immorality he must meet again his closest analogue in Tom, who represents only a basically safe though insensitive mischief, an allowable variation of the society's immoral morality. The subtlety is that Huck *tries* to play along but really cannot. Always a good companion and therefore always somewhat at the mercy of present company, fraudulent Dukes and Dauphins and also Tom Sawyers, he joins in half-heartedly but can't go it anymore. That is the point of the conclusion as Twain has it or as he would have had to arrange some other event to serve the same interior logic of story and characterization. The only course for Huck to take, then, is to "light out for the territories," escaping not only from all that Aunt Polly represents—"I been there," says Huck—but from Tom Sawyer's great American spell—and he's been there, too. He will not allow himself to stay on and lapse, as he has slipped a few times even with Jim during their journey together. He knows now that the only answer to the question of how to adjust to a bad and seductive environment is to get out of it.

This is, in point of cold fact, our American formula—or none of us indeed would be here. *Huck Finn* is the very apotheosis of that meliorative individual escapism inherent in our national character, that final commitment to survivalism and futurism that accounts for original and westward settlement, that distinctive motive we (alone, perhaps) respond to in our depths. Which is to say that our native genius runs to epic or comedy, or both, and not convincingly to tragedy.

At all events, Twain needed something very like the concluding contrast of character which he provides, to motivate Huck's final and typical decision and to resolve thematic structure. In so doing he does not really vindicate any surrogate of the society. The Widow Watson had always been better than the rest, and, anyway, her manumission of Jim functions in another manner, as ironic undercutting of the whole story, a point to which we shall return. As to the general society, Huck knows his people to the hard core. When Mrs. Phelps exclaims at Huck's report of the steamboat accident and hopes no one was hurt, he answers: "No'm. Killed a nigger." This is not Longstreet's deflection at all, in a similar case. This is not even Huck at heart, certainly not any signal of rapport with the Phelpses and the Valley, but only an instance of Huck's self-protective, quick understanding. But there's judgment in it, of course, the searing type that was all Twain's own. And it fits the ensuing conclusion, valid as it is, though probably overdrawn: a defect of comic momentum, not of intention or fundamental art.

There appear to be no critical exceptions whatsoever to Huck's characterization. That is because, manifold as his character may be, it is replete with a comic realism everyone appreciates. A right boy in a wrong environment, as Trilling has noted, he experiences his psychological conversions and his moral reversals, all with perfectly realistic backslidings. His age, for one thing, is just right—and far more rigorously on the author's mind than was Sut Lovingood's for G. W. Harris. In mid-adolescence Huck yearns wholeheartedly to conform, but in his depths is the insurgent candor of boyish independence. His societal position is centered exactly, too. Midway between a respectable and repressive society (Widow Douglas) and the lowest order of unregeneracy (Pap), between hypocritical gentility and brutal bigotry, he convincingly exercises his own natural morality by a law of canceled extremes that helps free him from both sides. Poised between sets of opposite realities, between childhood and manhood, between dry conventionalism and searing revolt, he takes the hint of decency from the one side and the primitivist self-trust from the other, coming of age in the process. If he is fallible and overinfluenced one way or the other at any given instance, we are only mindful of the forces working upon him and of his humanity.

But he has the native, paradoxical stuff of humanness in him in almost any event—and he is living that one time of life that permits an expression of all sides of his nature. He is a reflexive liar, finding the up-and-up an astonishing anomaly.

> . . . here's a case where I'm blest if it don't look to me like a truth is better and actually *safer* than a lie.

But if he is a liar, he is a marvelously quick-witted and basically self-defensive one. At the same time one must grant a certain native joy of improvisation, as when in girl's disguise he keeps fibbing about his assumed name.[3]

[3] Beyond a doubt there is also deeper psychological significance in Huck's assuming so many names and identities throughout his adventures before coming into his own. And we may associate the matter with Twain's own confusions of identity.

"What did you say your name was, honey?"

"M-Mary Williams."

"Honey, I thought you said it was Sarah when you first come in?"

"Oh, yes'm, I did. Sarah Mary Williams. Sarah's my first name. Some calls me Sarah, some calls me Mary."

If Huck is not a fundamental liar, it is because he never deceives himself. His motives, even when confused, are never glossed or denied. And in crises he will not tell himself stories about others. For all of the corners of heartland naïveté within him, the cynicism about human nature on which he realistically operates in the main is put to constant use, as in the triumphant "smallpox" episode.

"What's that yonder?"

"A piece of a raft," I says.

"Do you belong on it?"

"Yes, sir."

"Any men on it?"

"Only one, sir."

"Well, there's five niggers run off to-night up yonder, above the head of the bend. Is your man white or black?"

I didn't answer up prompt. I tried to, but the words wouldn't come. I tried for a second or two to brace up and out with it, but I warn't man enough—hadn't the spunk of a rabbit. I see I was weakening; so I just give up trying, and up and says:

"He's white."

"I reckon we'll go and see for ourselves."

"I wish you would," says I, "because it's pap that's there, and maybe you'd help me tow the raft ashore where the light is. He's sick —and so is mam and Mary Ann."

"Oh, the devil! we're in a hurry, boy. But I s'pose we've got to. Come, buckle to your paddle, and let's get along."

I buckled to my paddle and they laid to their oars. When we had made a stroke or two, I says:

"Pap'll be mighty much obleeged to you, I can tell you. Everybody goes away when I want them to help me tow the raft ashore, and I can't do it by myself."

"Well, that's infernal mean. Odd, too. Say, boy, what's the matter with your father?"

"It's the—a—the—well, it ain't anything much."

They stopped pulling. It warn't but a mightly little ways to the raft now. One says:

"Boy, that's a lie. What *is* the matter with your pap? Answer up square now, and it'll be the better for you."

"I will, sir, I will, honest—but don't leave us please. It's the—the—Gentlemen, if you'll only pull ahead, and let me heave you the headline, you won't have to come a-near the raft—please do."

"Set her back, John, set her back!" says one. They backed water. "Keep away, boy—keep to looard. Confound it, I just expect the wind has blowed it to us. Your pap's got the smallpox and you know it precious well. Why didn't you come out and say so? Do you want to spread it all over?"

"Well," says I, a-blubbering, "I've told everybody before, and they just went away and left us."

"Poor devil, there's something in that. We are right down sorry for you, but we—well, hang it, we don't want the smallpox, you see. Look here, I'll tell you what to do. Don't you try to land by yourself, or you'll smash everything to pieces. You float along down about twenty miles and you'll come to a town on the left-hand side of the river. It will be long after sun-up then, and when you ask for help you tell them your folks are all down with chills and fever. Don't be a fool again and let people guess what is the matter. Now we're trying to do you a kindness; so you just put twenty miles between us, that's a good boy. It wouldn't do any good to land yonder where the light is—it's only a wood-yard. Say, I reckon your father's poor, and I'm bound to say he's in pretty hard luck. Here, I'll put a twenty-dollar gold piece on this board, and you get it when it floats by. I feel mighty mean to leave you, but my kingdom! it won't do to fool with smallpox, don't you see?"

"Hold on, Parker," says the man, "here's a twenty to put on the board for me. Good-by, boy; you do as Mr. Parker told you, and you'll be all right."

Yet Huck is not corroded by the understanding he has. He can still muster compassion even for the prime villains of the piece when they are ridden, tarred and feathered, on a rail out of the story.

Well, it made me sick to see it, and I was sorry for them poor pitiful rascals, it seemed like I couldn't ever feel any hardness against them any more in the world. It was a dreadful thing to see. Human beings *can* be awful cruel to one another.

He knows what frauds they are, but his judgment does not overpower his pity.

These successive layers to his character, these mobile emotions, these live alternatives of feeling serve more than Twain's human and realistic portrait. They suggest, perhaps, the essence of comic characterization. For if the epic or tragic protagonist is presented as a grand but more or less monolithic personality—Ahab, consummately in American literature—then the quintessence of the comic hero is his multifaceted personality. His plural nature, as it were, is an especial reflection of his Americanness. His self-divisions pull and tug at one another in a violent comic psychology tentatively unified only at the end: an apocalyptic prophecy of the nation. And if our insight seems applicable chiefly to comic rogues like Huck Finn, Chaplin's tramp, etc., we may be allowed to guess that just *that* comic hero is the pure thing, especially in the United States.

If Twain's other signal achievement in the book is to contain his animus through comic form, still there is no doubting the antitheticism basic to the work. It pervades the story. A primary target, as we have seen, is our diluted Puritan conventionalism. We register the severity of Twain's attack on the morally hypocritic "kindness" involved in the smallpox incident. But he broadens his attack to include the religious-economic hypocrisy of the society in general.

> And at last, when it hit me all of a sudden that here was the plain hand of Providence slapping me in the face and letting me know my wickedness was being watched all the time from up there in heaven, whilst I was stealing a poor old woman's nigger that hadn't ever done me no harm, and now was showing me there's One that's always on the lookout and ain't a-going to allow no such miserable doings to go only just so fur and no further, I most dropped in my tracks I was so scared. Well, I tried the best I could to kinder soften it up somehow for myself by saying I was brung up wicked so I warn't so much to blame, but something inside of me kept saying, "There was the Sunday school, you could 'a' gone to it; and if you'd 'a' done it they'd 'a' learnt you there that people that acts as I'd been acting about that nigger goes to everlasting fire."

He proceeds to indict the moral equivocations of people like the Grangerfords.

Next Sunday we all went to church, about three miles, every-body a-horseback. The men took their guns along, so did Buck, and kept them between their knees or stood them handy against the wall. The Shepherdsons done the same way. It was pretty ornery preaching—all about brotherly love, and such-like tire-someness; but everybody said it was a good sermon and they all talked it over going home, and had such a powerful lot to say about faith and good works and free grace and preforeordestination, and I don't know what all, that it did seem to me to be one of the rough-est Sundays I had run across yet.

. . . there warn't anybody at the church [later], except maybe a hog or two, for there warn't any lock on the door, and hogs likes a puncheon floor in summer-time because it's cool. If you notice, most folks don't go to church only when they've got to; but a hog is different.

And in his more playful portrait of Emmeline Grangerford, we may also trace the diminution of sincerity and soul struggle from Emily Dickinson, last of the true New England Puritans, to the morbid sentimentalisms of little Emmeline, first of the mere poetasters.[4]

She warn't particular; she could write about anything you choose to give her to write about just so it was sadful. Every time a man died or a woman died or a child died, she would be on hand with her "tribute" before he was cold. . . . the undertaker never got in ahead of Emmeline but once, and then she hung fire on a rhyme for the dead person's name, which was Whistler.

Correlative exposés are Twain's attacks against the ideals of social conformity, cowardice, and a philosophy basically of means. In addition, of course, he inveighs against racial bigotry. His special accomplishment is to show how the virulence of prej-udice clings even to Huck. But he is at pains, naturally, to show Huck redeemed at the end; cleansed, in fact (the river as a baptismal image). Adverse critics of the book forget the subtleties

---

[4] "Emmeline" and "Emily" are accidental convergences, however. Twain had a live model on his mind in the portrait of Emmeline, and he would not have known of Emily Dickinson as an example one way or the other. The similar names constitute one of the great coincidences in American literature. We must set the record straight, although we are under no obligation to give up our critical point of view.

and resolutions of the case when they bring to bear a hyper-sensitivity to concluding issues. We hear a modern objection that Twain does not sufficiently condemn the Phelpses at the end, as they sit to Sunday dinner, like *gemütlich* families of Nazi concentration camp guards, while Jim languishes in his little Buchenwald. We know exactly that Huck himself never meant "No'm'. A nigger killed" and that he is more than restive as Tom seeks to free Jim with grueling complications. It is to Twain's credit that his own indignation is kept under control and that he does not violate Huck's character in making him more than he could have been in the last circumstances. Huck's "lighting out" finally is repudiation enough. The attacks on a Protestant ethic and on southern mores are of a piece. There is no inconsistency, no breakdown of form, no letup of attack.

Furthermore, the assault on Tom Sawyer is at once the central subtlety and explosion in the book. We grant all that we must to that all-American type Twain himself created and devoted three books to. But there were two authors in the same man (the acrostic, mark twain),[5] and if Samuel Clemens loved Tom Sawyer, Mark Twain in his masterpiece had his alternative view of this biggest little con man of them all. For in *Huckleberry Finn* Tom is an ambiguous charmer at best, for all his fetching outlawry. At his worst, which he is in this book, he is a self-deceiver, over-romanticizing and falsifying all experience, bathing in sentimentality, and living a constant lie of style and substance. His characterization represents the ultimate devolution not only of Scott's heroes but of Cervantes' immortal romanticizer. Indeed, Mark Twain's grasp of the situation is what helps to lift this work so far above all others in his career and far and away above his own

[5] Sophisticated literary gamesmanship plays with the possibility that such cryptography could become our own Baconianism. Further acrostical homework along these lines might indicate that "I, Henry Wadsworth Longfellow, wrote these stories." Clemens, like Shakespeare, was an American hostler, or hustler, incapable of writing our greatest work. At the same time, as *Life* columnist, Dora Jane Hamblin, suggests, Longfellow, like Bacon or Raleigh or the Earl of Southampton, was ashamed of his accomplishment. The game, with all its inherent exposé of blue-blood critical prejudice, operates to satirize the original Shakespearean controversy, of course, rather than open a new one. In a less facetious but thoroughly homegrown and convincing work, Justin Kaplan's study, *Mr. Clemens and Mark Twain*, reopens the question of Twain's double personality, with the one side of the man in furious conflict with the other.

nagging middle-class timidities. In *Huck Finn* he not only slays dragons but strikes at bosom serpents. Dragons, however, are hydra-headed, and serpents continue to writhe. Eventually, long afterward, Americans would sentimentalize Tom in ritualized games at Hannibal, Missouri, every year (finding Huck less useful to a false mythology, as he has also been intractable in Hollywood adaptations of the book). What a reincarnated Twain would say, meanwhile, would depend on whether it was the bourgeois Sam or demonic Mark who came back.

There was certainly some devil in the authentic Mark Twain. His diabolism in *Huck Finn* is controlled but thorough. He exposes not only respectable citizenry at large and a respectable deviationist like Tom, but barbaric Pap as well. Also those perennial savages of semicivilization, like the loafers of town.

> There couldn't anything wake them up all over and make them happy all over, like a dog-fight—unless it might be putting turpentine on a stray dog and setting fire to him, or tying a tin pan to his tail and see him run himself to death.

Also the out-and-out con men, the Duke and the Dauphin. With this pair, however, we return to the subject of general misanthropy, a tautology almost in the nature of things. The Duke's billboard reads:

LADIES AND CHILDREN NOT ADMITTED

> "There," says he, "if that line don't fetch them, I don't know Arkansaw!"

The audience won't "tell" on how bad the show of the Duke and Dauphin is, in order not to look silly themselves; that is, almost everyone is finally made into a confidence man.

And, very carefully, Twain extends his objective comic exposé even to Huck and Jim themselves, those democratically good but gullible types, who are, after all, overawed by the suggestion of royalty . . . because they are still somewhat under the spell of Tom Sawyer's romanticism. In one of the funniest of all brief interludes in *Huck Finn*, a consummation of hilarious literalism, Twain exposes that residue of ignorance and false literalistic logic in our provincial types, heroes though they are.

So I went to talking about other things, and let Solomon slide. I told about Louis Sixteenth that got his head cut off in France, long time ago; and about his little boy the dolphin, that would 'a' been a king, but they took and shut him up in jail and some say he died there.

"Po' little chap."

"But some says he got out and got away, and come to America."

"Dat's good! But he'll be pooty lonesome—dey ain' no kings here, is dey, Huck?"

"No."

"Den he cain't git no situation. What he gwyne to do?"

"Well, I don't know. Some of them gets on the police, and some of them learns people how to talk French."

"Why, Huck, doan' de French people talk de same way we does?"

"*No*, Jim; you couldn't understand a word they said—not a single word."

"Well, now, I be ding-busted! How do dat come?"

"I don't know; but it's so. I got some of their jabber out of a book. S'pose a man was to come to you and say Polly-voo-franzy— what would you think?"

"I wouldn' think nuffin; I'd take en bust him over de head—dat is, ef he warn't white. I wouldn't 'low no nigger to call me dat."

"Shucks, it ain't calling you anything. It's only saying, do you know how to talk French?"

"Well, den, why couldn't he say it?"

"Why, he *is* a-saying it. That's a Frenchman's way of saying it."

"Well, it's a blame' ridicklous way, en I doan' want to hear no mo' 'bout it. Dey ain' no sense in it."

"Looky here, Jim; does a cat talk like we do?"

"No, a cat don't."

"Well, does a cow?"

"No, a cow don't, nuther."

"Does a cat talk like a cow, or a cow talk like a cat?"

"No, dey don't."

"It's natural and right for 'em to talk different from each, ain't it?"

"Course."

"And ain't it natural and right for a cat and a cow to talk different from *us?*"

"Why, mos' sholy it is."

"Well, then, why ain't it natural and right for a *Frenchman* to talk different from us? You answer me that."

"Is a cat a man, Huck?"

"No."

"Well, den, dey ain't no sense in a cat talkin' like a man. Is a
cow a man?—er is a cow a cat?"

"No, she ain't either of them."

"Well, den, she ain' got no business to talk like either one er the
yuther of 'em. Is a Frenchman a man?"

"Yes."

"*Well,* den! Dad blame it, why doan' he *talk* like a man? You
answer me *dat!*"

But *Huck Finn* is midway between the early histrionics and
touch of smart aleckism in Twain's canon and the unmitigable
gloom of his late stage. One result of the complex factors of personal and professional equipoise that the book represents is especially significant. Its antithetic comedy does not override all sense
of values. Social morality, for instance, is regarded as a kind of contradiction in terms, but only the first half of the term is ques-
tioned, not the latter. Moreover, the burgeoning misanthropy
in the book is not yet comprehensive, so that Twain's attack is
somewhat topical yet; a particular society is a little more in focus
than society as a whole. The force of generic suggestion, nonetheless, is still very strong, but it is restrained and qualified by
comic hopefulness. Huck lights out, after all, to something better
for himself. Against the fact that the later Twain envisaged an
aged Huck's mental breakdown we may recall the fortune of
Twain's actual-life model for Huckleberry Finn. Blankenship,
the model, became a sheriff in Montana. Heroes are not so individualistic and renunciatory that they do not uphold and even
embody law freely and honestly chosen on their own terms. In
such ways art is prophetic, with more accuracy in it than a later
demoralized mood would dare accept.

Related to his positive thematic values of freedom and individualism is Twain's love of Nature in *Huck Finn.* Huck and Jim
often accommodate themselves to Nature gratefully, almost exquisitely. The influence of Defoe's *Crusoe* on Twain is insistent,
though he modified it in placing the lonesome raft in constant
opposition to all other artifacts and disruptive machinery.

Soon as it was night out we shoved; when we got her out to
about the middle we let her alone and let her float wherever the
current wanted her to; then we lit the pipes and dangled our legs

in the water, and talked about all kinds of things—we was always naked, day and night, whenever the mosquitoes would let us—the new clothes Buck's folks made for me was too good to be comfortable and besides I didn't go much on clothes nohow.

Sometimes we'd have that whole river all to ourselves for the longest time. Yonder was the banks and the islands, across the water; and maybe a spark—which was a candle in a cabin window; and sometimes on the water you could see a spark or two—on a raft or a scow, you know; and maybe you could hear a fiddle or a song coming over from one of them crafts. It's lovely to live on a raft. We had the sky up there, all speckled with stars, and we used to lay on our backs and look up at them. . . .

Once or twice of a night we would see a steamboat slipping along in the dark, and now and then she would belch a whole world of sparks up out of her chimbleys, . . . then she would turn a corner and her lights would wink out and her powwow shut off and leave the river still again; and by and by her waves would get to us a long time after she was gone, and joggle the raft a bit, and after that you wouldn't hear nothing for you couldn't tell how long, except maybe frogs or something.

Over and over again, in the course of the story, Crusoe and Friday return to their floating little island amid threatening social waters, manifest pirates, and even moral cannibals. From the individual's connection with Nature comes his support for innate, natural virtue. That honesty, which society travesties, is still very much a value of conduct to Twain. It is what all the freedom, all the individualism, and all the natural reliances are finally good for.

The humane comic virtues turn out to be the obverse of social practice. They are real nonetheless and veritably preached by the action: humanity over property, a paradoxical dignity emerging from a humble and instinctive sense of justice, and the supreme personal virtue of loyalty. This last implicit recommendation provides us with our truest insight into the comic power that made the book possible. Twain supplements the general victory of western egalitarian values over the southern by adding, preeminently, the undeniable southern virtue that confounds our indictment of *all* southern mores. The great thematic triumph of the ideal western spirit was impossible without salvaging and integrating the supreme southern virtue of loyalty. The comic writer is, at the height of his powers, never so repudiative as to forget that he is essentially liberal rather than radical. He acknowledges and even appropriates worth from what he rejects as a whole. *Huck Finn,* like all infinite comedy, is positivist to this extent. The nth degree of humor, as we have glimpsed before, is unformulaic. Its open-mindedness works against all exclusive theses, even its own intellectual formulae. In this sense, any true comic conjunction of values is always unforeseeable. And sublime.

But there are dark depths as well as sublimity in *Huck Finn,* for the essence of a masterwork is how many dimensions or facets it has. The critic, Philip Young, has counted thirteen separate corpses in the story, the "spill of blood" everywhere. Such statistics underscore, perhaps, the baffled critical sense of foreigners in dealing with this perverse comic masterpiece. But native intuitions plumb even further.

More fearful than the violence and terror in the narrative is the possible subtle nihilism embedded in the story. Jim is really free the whole time of the adventure, having been manumitted by the Widow Watson. Perhaps nothing has meant anything. W. H. Auden, drawn to comment on the book, adds the observation, furthermore, that Huck's search for a true father and Jim's search for a substitute son (hence his southernism, "honey," for Huck, though the word was affectionately and comprehensively in the regional vocabulary anyway) are doomed. The two protagonists are irrevocably parted at the end. The compassionate, symbolic comradeship is inevitably broken asunder. Is this the deepest and most unnerving of jokes in the structure of the book, or does the comic form approach that Alsatian border of tragedy? In any event, the ending is not happy, for all the happified folderol involved in the whole conclusion. Possibly informing the entire story are the subterranean themes of eventual incompatibility and complete futility.

Other American critics point to the keelboat incident to unsettle us further. Stowaway Huck reveals himself, after the keelman's ghost story of a murdered child, as C. W. Albright, Jr., that same dead child, floating down the river in a barrel. It is more than hilarious happenstance that he identifies himself this way. A lonely, frightening past (we remember bloodthirsty Pap) is at the core of his comic prevarication. The Moses myth, together with baptismal themes and the question of moral rebirth downstream, is severely undercut by the terror of death-in-life and possible meaninglessness. Thus, *Huck Finn* strikes that appalling note of nihilistic pessimism heard earlier in American humor, struck all through Twain's career up to the 1880's, belled in his late years, and sounding progressively louder through the next century of his inheritors. It speaks like a carillon for ultimate comic objectivity. But it also peals ominously.

"All of us are his heirs," William Faulkner confessed of Mark Twain's influence. For all his own partisanship for Cooper, Mencken conceded that Twain was "the true father of our national literature." And Ernest Hemingway traced all legitimate modern work to one book, *Huckleberry Finn*. We may even note Hemingway's modeling of his personal career on Huck Finn: the perpetual lighting out to territories, his feeling for native countryside (African highlands remind him of Wyoming), the derivation of his supreme American hero and alter ego, Robert Jordan, in the quasi-mythical Montana of the real and fictional Huck, and his almost composed expiration in the same general area. But even for Hemingway, as for opposite temperaments like Mencken and Faulkner, the greatest impact of Twain was not that of theme or derived character but of style alone. And no book perfected the uses of style as did *Huck Finn*.

In it American humor and realism are exactly wedded. The vernacular expression itself is purged of all affectation, as it is not in our poetic equivalent, Whitman's *Leaves of Grass*. It is the most precise of instruments. The colloquial expression achieves subtlety and careful psychological effects, as T. S. Eliot admitted. In contrast to orthodox stylists like Hawthorne and James and their heavy reliance on modifiers to qualify and abstract as much as possible, Twain valued the noun and especially the verb. "As to the adjective," he announced, "cut it." The tactic led to a triumph of simple and direct prose. The verbs are highlighted for passages of active narration.

> . . . we run nights and laid up and hid daytimes; soon as night was most gone we stopped navigating and tied up—nearly always

in the dead water under a towhead; and then cut young cotton-woods and willows and hid the raft with them. Then we set out the lines. Next we slid into the river and had a swim, so as to freshen up and cool off; then we sat down on the sandy bottom where the water was about knee-deep and watched the daylight come.

The nouns are emphasized during sequences of concrete descrip-tion.

The first thing to see, looking away over the water, was a kind of dull line—that was the woods on t'other side; you couldn't make nothing else out; then a pale place in the sky; then more paleness spreading around; then the river softened up away off, and warn't black any more, but gray; you could see little dark spots drifting along ever so far away—trading-scows, and such things; and long black streaks—rafts; sometimes you could hear a sweep screaking; or jumbled-up voices, it was so still, and sounds come so far; and by and by you could see a streak on the water which you know by the look of the streak that there's a snag there in a swift current which breaks on it and makes that streak look that way; and you see the mist curl up off of the water, and the east reddens up, and the river, and you make out a log cabin in the edge of the woods, away on the bank on t'other side of the river, being a wood-yard, likely. . . .

Hemingway, especially, schooled himself in this studied technique of natural and spoken rhythms, combining the heavy reliance on substantives in a descriptive passage with a stress on verbs for the very action of vision or being. He learned also the device of syntactical progression, the view proceeding in independent and conjunctive spurts or clauses, for the purpose of an expanding view.

Phelps's was one of these little one-horse cotton plantations and they all look alike. A rail fence round a two-acre yard; a stile made out of logs sawed off and upended in steps, like barrels of a dif-ferent length, to climb over the fence with and for the women to stand on when they are going to jump onto a horse; some sickly grass patches in the big yard, but mostly it was bare and smooth like an old hat with the nap rubbed off; big double log house for the white folks—hewed logs with the chinks stopped up with mud or mortar, and these mud-stripes been whitewashed some time or an-other; round-log kitchen with a big broad, open but roofed passage joining it to the house; log smokehouse back of the kitchen; three little log nigger cabins in a row t'other side the smokehouse; one little hut all by itself away down against the back fence, and some outbuildings down a piece the other side; ash-hopper and big kettle to bile soap in by the little hut; bench by the kitchen door, with bucket of water and a gourd; hound asleep there in the sun; more hounds asleep round about; about three shade trees away off in a corner; some currant bushes and gooseberry bushes in one place by the fence; outside of the fence a garden and a watermelon patch; then the cotton-fields begins, and after the fields the woods. (*Huckleberry Finn*)

After a while we came out of the mountains, and there were trees along both sides of the road, and a stream and ripe fields of grain, and the road went on, very white and straight ahead, and then lifted up to a little rise, and off on the left was a hill with an old castle, with buildings close around it and a field of grain going right up to the walls and shifting in the wind. . . . Then we crossed a wide plain, and there was a big river off on the right shining in the sun from between the line of trees, and away off you could see the plateau of Pamplona rising out of the plain, and the walls of the city, and the great brown cathedral, and the broken skyline of the other churches. In back of the plateau were the mountains, and every way you looked there were other mountains, and ahead the road stretched out white across the plain going toward Pamplona.   (*The Sun Also Rises*)

All this, from Twain through Hemingway, is calculated to give us the "heard voice" of spontaneous, unpretentious truth, "the way it was," according to Hemingway's famous codification. *Huckleberry Finn* was the wellspring because the comic realist style in it became a productive means to render the spoken and therefore direct and therefore honest American language.

But no waters are undefilable. The very silt of unintended parody seeps in with Hemingway's own programmatic monosyllabism; one could push simplicity to the far reaches of inarticulateness, though that was always the disciple at his worst and most affected. But the very principle could be sullied in cinematic imitation and corrupted by producers of television advertisements. The studied hesitancy and slurring of speech in television commercials keyed to the common man selling razor blades and soap is the rankest corruption of the heard and "honest" voice.

The steely, efficient radio or TV announcer is replaced by ordinary voices in an intimate pseudodrama of impromptu modest
testimonial, allegedly more convincing as it simply fumbles along.
There is, of course, a further comedy imaginable—and sometimes
indulged during infrequent moments of self-satire on TV—in
unmanageable common types who might undermine or explode
their messages. But the latter-day devaluation of simple realistic
speech on the whole ends an epoch of codified belief in the in-
vulnerable sincerity of the comic and realistic style per se. There
are no infallible instruments of comedy, no absolutes of realism.
The recognition has contributed its full measure to the modern
decline of comic and literary morale.

   That would not have surprised Twain, who plumbed the fullest
pessimism and defeatism. Indeed, we need speak here less and
less of the "later Twain" and plot *Huck Finn* upon a curve of
doubt and hostility, as we graph a developing misanthropy in his
career. Even in hindsight, of course, no work before *Huck Finn*,
not even *Life on the Mississippi*, makes the subsequent masterpiece inevitable. But after *Huck Finn*, an astute contemporaneous reader could have made reasonable guesses about the mood
following such a master work.
   At all events, nowadays we can trace Twain's philosophic
deterioration after *Huck Finn* easily enough, and we tend to place
the book more bravely than we did before in his later stage of disenchantment and despair. Professor Henry Nash Smith interprets
the Mississippi shore as a clear prototype of all society for Twain,
much as it is for the character, Colonel Sherbourne, who opposes
and castigates a lynch mob in the novel. For both the cosmopolitan Sherbourne and Twain, Missouri and Arkansas are not so
local after all but represent the average cowardly and corrupt
human condition. Smith's argument has much to recommend it. It
means that already Twain appreciated the exceptionality of Sherbourne, as he did Huck, and felt perhaps that there was no permanent courageous holding action possible against human nature.
   The tension between his mounting disaffection and wistful
democratic faith was shortly resolved in the favor of increasing
skepticism and apprehension. In his very next book, *A Connecti-*

cut Yankee (1889), he judged that the ultimate democratic strength, technological progress, would be ineffective.[6] And in *Pudd'nhead Wilson* (1894), which we shall consider in its own right, the exceptional figure of Wilson, for all his intelligence, serves only futility, his practical revelations proving ineffectual at the climax. After *Huck Finn, A Connecticut Yankee* and *Pudd'n-head Wilson,* his dark philosophy is a foregone conclusion. The themes of determinism and nihilism become obsessive. The view of man's inferiority, because of his capacity for guilt and cruelty, is insistent. When we reach "The Man that Corrupted Hadley-burg" (1900) and "The Mysterious Stranger" (posthumous), we are quite prepared for all those transcendent characters whose power always operates outside the stories and after the fact, un-availing, as is all comic understanding itself.

It is out of his lack of faith in either style or substance that Twain comes to remark, "There is no humor in heaven," there, where it is not necessary. His corresponding view of this world, as confirmed in the recently released *Letters from the Earth,* was not even a view of vacuous purgatory but of a contemptible hell. It goes without saying that he lost almost all of his comic poise, technical distance, and fertile playfulness in his wholesale derogations. We are left with a proposition that makes us vibrate doubly today. A certain amount of human faith, as in Huck, is a requisite of comedy, to keep it this side of diatribe and filibuster. And no comic sense is durable but that which prevents us from succumbing to any corrosive philosophy—most of all, our own.

Although it is true that Twain's later personal griefs contributed heavily to his stringencies, no critic denies the steady drift of Twain's own impersonal thought. In all truth, the movement of that thought can be plotted on an accelerative curve from his earliest works to his last, with *Huck Finn* as a lucky point of rest

[6] The artist in him was far ahead of the businessman, who lost a fortune on such faith. His basic ambivalence in this matter can be focused very effectively in the earlier work, *A Tramp Abroad* (1880). In the course of that book he parodied sentimental and Romantic legend, on one occasion equipping a Connecticut Yankee type of character with a fire extinguisher against a local dragon. Nonetheless, this scientized, technologic hero is somewhat dehumanized, also a victim of Twain's satire.

along a line of remorseless development. Professor Gerhard Friedrich has described Twain's report of life as moving from "local idiosyncrasies to empty eternities." There was never a basic change of perception in Twain, only an intensification of attitude. Or, put another way, he steadily widened his perception of the same thing. His irreverence was always there, strengthened by the license that had been seized for him by contemporary humorists; it simply became more embittered. His skepticism and misanthropy lay at the core of being, encouraged by the example of his southwestern predecessors; they turned inevitably and fiercely hostile.

Even in his first full-scaled book, the playful *Innocents Abroad* (1869), there are clear signs and portents. For all his frank and somewhat professional provincialism, there is a personal cutting edge turned against all travelers, especially souvenir hunters, guidebook tourists, and those exotical rhapsodizers of all picturesque scenery and historic ruin. A more cosmopolitan Jack Downing, writing letters back home to a whole nation rather than a village, Twain thought he had to expand Seba Smith's method further by making his correspondent more smart-alecky, as if sarcasm meant sophistication. But a man who is determined not to be taken in is a reverse provincial anyway. Still, the decision not to take things at face value was intrinsic, and from the outset irreverence was as much part of the man as his eyes. His antireligiosity, especially at shrines, was at once a consequence of his pose and a deep, developing conviction. The whole book is inclined to be overdirect and too explicit, defects accounted for by his age and his assumed role. But he had a genuine eye for fraud, organized and personal. He would come to see imposture not as an idiosyncrasy of those who took the grand tour but as an inherent trait of human nature. In a number of subsequent works he proceeded to read the lesson back into his western and native experiences.

In *Roughing It* (1872), we can note the sharp twangs of democratic disabusement with western types. Again, he will not be taken in, especially not on his own ground, by any sentimental myths. We come to believe that it was this determination which set him particularly against the Indian—or, more accurately, against the glorification of the noble savage. His anti-

theticism works out to a qualified racism, true enough, but
then his partisanship for the Negro confounds allegations of
that kind. The Indian is a degenerate (and, as such, the villain in
Tom Sawyer). But Twain's prejudice is conveniently taken over
from Artemus Ward, where its original motivation was probably
the same. The intransigent attitude was a counterattack against
romanticizings. If it was particularly fierce, that was also because,
as in the whole subject of James Fenimore Cooper, Twain was
initially attracted, and had to wrench himself away by main force.
(Exactly the same psychology later applies to Mencken in the
matter of antisentimentalism. His earliest work consisted of
execrable saccharine love lyrics, which he was eager to suppress
afterward.) The Indian, unfortunately, became one of Twain's
specific symbols for all the false emotion he came to loathe after
having been seduced by lies. Even toward the end of his career
he projected yet another fictional travelogue, *Tom Sawyer and
Huckleberry Finn among the Indians*, to flay his special target.
It was a preoccupation of his on a par with fraudulent religion
and Christianity. How poorly missionaries fare in *Roughing It*,
too. Both mythicized groups become favorite and enduring targets. Twain's life appears as a continuous voyage through the
world of humanity, which it quite literally and philosophically
was, and he eventually reached unholy generic conclusions. But
those two symbols stayed with him as convenient images of all
fake values, becoming special repositories for his own reverse
intolerance.

When we follow him to the verge of his masterpiece, in *Life on
the Mississippi* (1883), we find him shifting his wrath decisively
to the white man, however, and to the local arena, almost the
microcosm it will become in *Huck Finn*. La Salle's priests are remembered for their "pious consecration" of land thefts, and we
are reminded of the Spaniards' "robbing, slaughtering, enslaving
and converting" of the Indians. The humor of anticlimax and
sharp relevancy broadens out from an attack on mere Catholicism.
Twain assaults all historical, religious and moral pretension and
all Romantic mythicizing. (Sir Walter Scott stands behind even
Fenimore Cooper as prime literary archenemy.) His references,
furthermore, to contemporary WASP cruelties and grotesqueries
assuredly set his mind to finish the novel of *Huck Finn* that he

had been working on for five years; the feuders, the cock fight
spectators, the bullying steamboat pilots are all there in preparatory acerbic view. The Watsons take callous, gleeful pot shots
at the lost Darnell swimming in the River. Sporting members of
the cock-fight audience revive the two fighting birds, tenderly
putting the birds' heads in their warm mouths, to overcome utter
animal exhaustion so they may continue fighting. And meanwhile
cub-pilot Twain is really ragged and bullied unmercifully in his
apprenticeship, more for the hell of it than for training. We are
set up for the misanthropic currents and darkness of *Huck Finn,*
where his control matches his growing force.

Forward of *Huck Finn* we move into declining comic control
right to the end of Twain's career. But one book in this period is
still within the band of comedy, the woefully underrated *Pudd'n-
head Wilson* (1894). It is a constantly mordant novel, which *Huck
Finn,* for all of its reverberant exposures, is not. But it is held
within comic bounds by interest in humorous plot, comic devices
and thematic extravagances that Twain still maintains before
passing in his next works out of the range of comic hearing. In
fact, he seems to have his requirements so well in mind that he
adds excrescences like the totally unnecessary and inexplicable
subplot of the Italian twins. Structure, we may admit, was never
his real forte, and luck had played its part in the construction of
Huck Finn. But in extenuation of structural excess in *Pudd'nhead
Wilson,* two judgments are equally interesting at this stage of his
work. Perhaps he was engaged in a kind of narrative self-mockery.
That is conceivable by this time. Or, more probably, he deliberately sought narrative excess as another technical distraction, understanding but only too well the complex strategy of diversion
in all its basic meaning.

He is impatient, however, as he was not a decade before. The
evidence is everywhere. It is in the obvious and crude narrative
beginning, in the author's willful obtrusions upon the story, in
the heavy-handedness of the false Tom's being too grotesquely
wicked, in the frequently clumsy narrative transitions, and in
several inadvertencies of plot. But he still revels in wild comic
farce, in those madcap vicissitudes of Roxy and her son which he

keeps centered for us. And he can lead us to an antic crescendo in the last third of his story, for he is still interested in story as well as sermon. But foremost is his joy of characterization, giving us in Roxy his most magnificent character after Huck. The force of Twain's morality and environmental determinism is as strong as possible. But the central comic drama and the manifold side issues are all still there, even to the degree that they spill over. And most of all, the protagonist—who, together with Jim in *Huck Finn,* constitutes a case for the superiority of the Negro, as Faulkner later caught up the idea—is presented fully. He gives us Roxy in all her authoritative, energetic, and native glory and in that triumphant indefatigability of her nature.

> "You's gwyne to be safe—if you behaves." She bent an austere eye on him and added, "En you *is* gwyne to behave—does you know dat?"
>
> He laughed and said he was going to try, anyway. She did not unbend. She said gravely:
>
> "Tryin' ain't de thing. You's gwyne to *do* it. You ain't gwyne to steal a pin—'ca'se it ain't safe no mo'; en you ain't gwyne into no bad company—not even once, you understand; en you ain't gwyne to drink a drop—nary single drop; en you ain't gwyne to gamble one single gamble—not one! Dis ain't what you's gwyne to *try* to do, it's what you's gwyne to *do*. En I'll tell you how I knows it. Dis is how. I's gwyne to foller along to Sent Louis my own self; en you's gwyne to come to me every day o' yo' life, en I'll look you over; en if you fails in one single one o'dem things —jist *one*—I take my oath I'll come straight down to dis town en tell de Jedge you's a nigger en a slave—en *prove* it!" She paused to let her words sink home. Then she added, "Chambers, does you b'lieve me when I says dat?"

The controlled rendition of dialect and the objective fidelity to character are as much on Twain's mind as in *Huck Finn.* They help mightily to hold both character and author in comic bounds.

His manipulation of event and his grip on the psychology of inverted relationships represent the firm comic mastery of his middle period. Tom, the false "white," must humble himself to a Negro, his discovered mother, Roxy, just as Huck did to Jim. It is a powerfully ironic moment, and comic momentum carries Twain to the most complicated and excruciating truth. Tom is really

"Chambers," but Chambers is 1/32 Negro anyway. A refinement of lineage, however, to 1/32 of a part is the merest racial pedantry in any case, and so, in Twain's biology and humanism, Chambers is not distinctly or primarily Negro, though it makes no difference to Twain either way. Nonetheless, out of a tragicomedy of fantastic inbred literalism, Roxy subsequently accuses just *that* 1/32 fraction of Chambers for his defect of cowardice.

> "En you refuse' to fight a man dat kicked you, 'stid o' jumpin' at de chance! En you ain't got no mo' feelin' den to come en tell me, dat fetched sich a po'low-down ornery rabbit into de worl'! Pah! it makes me sick! It's de nigger in you, dat's what is it. Thirty-one parts o' you is white, en on'y one part nigger, en dat po' little one part is yo' *soul*."

This is our earliest revelation of the horrendous self-contempt instilled by prejudice, and Twain got to the frightening heart of the matter by virtue of the momentum of comic psychology.

There is no question that, on the whole, Twain despises the general populace of the town he depicts. Professor Fiedler, who has made up for his perverse study of *Huck Finn* in providing us with the only significant critical evaluation we have to date of *Pudd'nhead Wilson*, puts it a familiar way. The townsmen of *Pudd'nhead Wilson* are so far south that there is no hope of western redemption for them. Twain just barely suppresses his own rage at their misnaming[7] of the one intellect (from the north) among them, "Puddn'head" Wilson, who becomes a bona fide detective in order to solve the local intrigue and mysteries.

> "I wish I owned half of that [barking] dog."
> "Why?" somebody asked.
> "Because I would kill my half."
> . . . They fell away from him as from something uncanny. One said: " 'Pears to be a fool."

They misconstrue Wilson because they cannot judge either intelligence or comedy, and they think of him as stupid rather than funny. What they lack, what benighted people in general lack, is, exactly, a sense of humor (which Twain abbreviated and

[7] Generally, off-beat names like "Pudd'nhead"—or "Huckleberry"—are names of individualistic and worthy protagonists. Ordinary names like "Tom," for Driscoll and Sawyer, signal crude heroes or merely insensitive conformists. At a profound level, the distinction reflects upon the names "Mark" Twain and "Sam" Clemens also.

equated to sense). Embedding his attitude in the background and story proper, however, Twain can suppress his own epithetical violence. That objectification is what allows him to hold back his rage also from what he regards as the greatest theft in human history, the robbery of another human being's liberty. But the bigotry of deep-south slavocracy is a transparent symbol, a cesspool image of man's exploitations and oppressions of fellow men. Twain's restraint is a luxury he still affords himself because his symbols are adequate and his form comprehensive. His moral misanthropy was never really in danger of becoming the chaotic immorality or confusion of mind apparent in most of his southwestern forebears; it was susceptible only to the other danger of didactic and hardened disgust. But here he says all he needs through comic plotting, irony, indirection, and understatement.

Still, he needs to do more at this stage, something unmistakably overt and vituperative. Fortunately he hits upon a device that does not interfere with the story. He furnishes headings at the start of each chapter, excerpts from Pudd'nhead Wilson's "calendar." Strongly reflecting the influence of Josh Billings, these are antiproverbialisms by virtue of explicit truthtelling or extreme and devilish reversalism. Whereas half of Henry Shaw's efforts were folksy, positive epigrams, all of Twain's are negative shafts of radical lightning, reflections of hostility and pessimism that will inflame all his work after this. Meanwhile, the device gives him the additional emotional outlet he wants for this novel, which is governed by the April 1st, July 4th, and October 12th entries: we're all perpetual fools, and the chance at a right New World was doomed, for America should have been missed. This is antisentimentalism with a vengeance, misanthropy reinforced by patriotic snub.

What saves these cynical distillations in themselves is comic manner. Concreteness of expression certifies his pertinencies.

> Habit is habit, and not to be flung out of the window by any man, but coaxed downstairs a step at a time.

Tried and true Wardean circularity is combined with anticlimax.

> October. This is one of the peculiarly dangerous months to speculate in stocks in. The others are July, January, September, April, November, May, March, June, December, August, and February.

Reversalism and literalism are joined.

> Behold, the fool saith, "Put not all thine eggs in the one basket"
> —which is but a manner of saying, "Scatter your money and your
> attention"; but the wise man saith, "Put all your eggs in the one
> basket and—WATCH THAT BASKET."

He is still mindful of technique even at his most personal . . .
it is really Twain, not the mild Wilson, who speaks. As a result
his skepticism and antagonism are still under comic control.

In the end, as Fiedler has seen, the book represents what has
become the Faulknerian rather than Cooperesque side of our
American consciousness: the absorption in guilt rather than innocence, particularly in race relationships, and the feeling of a
Calvinistic doom over all. In this work the Mississippi River becomes not an image of rebirth of life but of death; the threat of
being "sold down the River" clangs like an alarm knell through
the book.

Nonetheless, the novel is comic, because of the freedom Twain
still allows himself. He is still interested in comic technique, in
the divagations of his plot, in the comic ironies he pursues for
their own sake and trusts for thematic relevance, in the superlative comic portraiture, in the grip on real speech, and even in the
technical phrasing of his own disenchanted antiproverbialism.
It was his last true performance.

The works that followed *Pudd'nhead Wilson* represented a clear
decline in two ways; they were stories of weak-kneed comedy unworthy of Twain in any stage or recriminatory fusillades. What
he published or hid away in secret lockers was the palest reflection of former work or was out-and-out diatribe.

The two later *Tom Sawyer* books, *Abroad* and *Detective* (1896),
exemplify the one category. On an exotic balloon trip, Tom, Huck,
and Jim engage in dialectical arguments that might have called
forth the old verve but do not. The best comedy Twain is able to
manage is to have Huck on the lookout for "pink" Indiana, in ac-
cordance with maps that don't lie. Its plotting is most arbitrary,
and it proceeds to an ending in no way inevitable. Twainophiles
have tried to rescue it from oblivion, but it is not very humorous.

It has no consequential theme, in or out of the comic tradition, or any unified theme at all. It is, compared to *Huck Finn,* where the trio had been together before, the sharpest of descents.

Its narrative mate bears the same unfavorable relation to *Pudd'nhead Wilson.* In its alleged comedy of mystery and detection, the highest efforts of *Tom Sawyer, Detective* involve simple malapropisms, the "diseased" instead of "deceased," and "witness for the prostitution." There is no real energy as in *Pudd'nhead Wilson,* no gift of portraiture, no true technique.

Following the Equator (1897) is a bridge between the two later modes of Twain. It falls into the episodic, traveloguish mold that he took both from the European picaresque tradition of the novel and travel sketch and from native southwestern practice. He was still doing it in the *Tom Sawyer* dialogues. We may remark here that most of Twain's books can be set in two contextual groups, travels abroad and travels at home. In his late years, he tended to combine the two. Going around that world in *Following the Equator,* he carries Pudd'nhead Wilson's calendar with him. These later entries intensify the misanthropy we have seen before and look forward directly to the utter nihilism of his last works.

"Be good and you'll be lonesome."
"Pity is for the living, envy is for the dead."
"Man is the only animal that blushes—or needs to."

But the headings are not correlated with any particular chapter material in *Following the Equator.* Or, aside from momentary whimsies in the helter-skelter book, they are very generally related to his successive denunciations of all he sees. His frank realism becomes gruesome reporting on the world-wide scene, as he depicts the worst aspects of leprosy, the caste system, etc. His tireless broadsides against missionary zeal are expanded to the fullest antireligiosity, as in his attacks now on Hindooism. With the notably and highly personal exception of misogyny, Twain catches up all the negativity and disaffections of previous literary and subliterary comedians and adds some of his own, but in his vituperation, he forsakes comedy.

In his last two famous or notorious stories, "The Man That Corrupted Hadleyburg" (1900) and "The Mysterious Stranger" (1916), we find him on his last narrative explorations within and abroad. Hadleyburg is an obvious image of the United States, detailed in the central device of a reversed evangelical meeting, led by a pastor, with the concluding reversal of the town's motto, "Lead us into Temptation." It is the story of an untested, artificial honesty thoroughly broken by events. The story embraces total misanthropy; no one is redeemable in it, and doomed self-righteousness is made the essence of the human condition. The narrative proceeds mechanically, the moralism is at a far more sweeping and superficial level than in his mid-stage authentic comedy, and the strategy of oversimplification is self-defeating in any case. We note the familiar irony of the town fool's being the only one with a passable sense of humor, but the story as a whole is too direct, sarcastic, and predictable to succeed as legitimate comedy. Twain was right in one thing, however; cynical or hysterical laughter is all we are left with.

"The Mysterious Stranger" is a culmination of both his misanthropy and bitter antireligiosity. It is almost all very thinly veiled diatribe and demonic invective. There are, in fact, only two genuine instances of comic technique. One is the opening stylistic image, "'upon the top of the precipice frowned a vast castle." The other involves his central device of reversal, i.e., Satan as true angel and God as the Devil. Again mechanical and oversimplified, the story is the merest vehicle for human abuse. Cruelty, we are told, is man's exclusive prerogative in the universe. All man's conception of heaven, its gentle peace, its equality and all the rest, is a removed ideal that leaves him at ease for exactly the reverse practice on earth. This is a theme which Twain strikes even more venomously in the posthumous *Letters from the Earth*. And all, *all* we have been taught is a vicious lie, as Satan concludes in utter nihilism . . . and rather evangelically himself.

> ". . . there is no God, no universe, no human race, no earthly life, no heaven, no hell. It is all a dream—a grotesque and foolish dream. Nothing exists but you. And you are but a *thought*—a vagrant thought, a useless thought, a homeless thought, wandering forlorn among the empty eternities!"

From *Huck Finn* and *Pudd'nhead Wilson* to Twain's last work we trace a steady loss of comic distance particularly. It is the leading critical irony about him that, as he became more universal in his thinking, he moved too close to generalization, the most subjective of all lines of literary pursuit. In the strict logic of the courage he owned, he also became a thorough determinist. In adapting such comprehensive fatalism as he did in his last pieces, he necessarily compounded the loss of comic freedom. True, we may recall the powers and free movement he gives his Satan, but they are superficial powers and unavailing movement, and the Negator's role is fixed rigidly for him. In the end Satan consoles us only with the thought of death as surcease from pain, although he concedes the alternative of happy insanity. Twain's pessimism, propelled by bitter autobiographic event, nonetheless runs its implicit course. His nihilism is complete and unvarying. And with neither the freedom from his own now programmatic despair nor the comic distancing of multiple comic devices, his view is uncomic at the last.

He now speaks, as it were, with a deadly seriousness. The handbills for his later lectures carry "Sam Clemens" rather than "Mark Twain" as the name before the audience. He was not two men anymore, least of all the regionalist entertainer in humor. Or we may say, more consistently, that Mark Twain usurped Sam Clemens and took *his* name. Either way, however, he met his own neatest reversal, for his previous reputation had preceded him and nobody took him at his public word. Prepared to laugh, his audiences consented at least to smile indulgently. Although Pudd'nhead Wilson finally managed to overcome his previous reputation, Twain could never do the same for himself. The bitterest of all jokes his life played upon him was such concluding frustration. Nobody truly heard him. But the very last irony of all is how his later acidity and skepticism have favorably struck the modern audiences of Hal Holbrook's impersonations of Twain, where the later disaffections and vinegar in Holbrook's compendium of Twain's performances are more welcome than the lightheartedness and honey.

We are left, in retrospect, with the task of defining the essential character of the humor Twain reached and then forsook in his career. One conclusion especially forces itself upon us. That is the proposition that technique even more than substance is what bestows comedy. The comedian must be free-minded enough to enjoy the device as well as the point. His techniques represent his salvational investment in life; the containments and restraints of his view are its necessary form. And he must love the form. His comic devices must in themselves outlast his targets. The distance between comic artist and his unholiest intuition or conviction is particularly important to his freedom. When it collapses, he may still be writing something, but it is not comedy anymore. And if that is so, it is also because he has, after all, lost the joy of special undertaking. More than any failure of content, the diminution of technique means infallibly that the humorist has lost heart.

But Twain's career forces us to speculate further on the question and importance of form. It we compare his "Letter to the Gas Company," with his long essay, *What Is Man?* (1917), we discover that the form itself may determine not only the effectiveness of comedy but its very existence and that the consciousness of that form is crucial. Indeed, how fundamentally irreverent the humorist is may come less from what he says, no matter how unholy, than from how he abuses or uses a formal and prevalent social convention.

TO THE GAS COMPANY

Hartford, February 12, 1891

Dear Sirs:

Some day you will move me almost to the verge of irritation by your chuckle-headed Goddamned fashion of shutting your Goddamned gas off without giving any notice to your Goddamned parishioners. Several times you have come within an ace of smothering half of this household in their beds and blowing up the other half by this idiotic, not to say criminal, custom of yours. And it has happened again to-day. Haven't you a telephone?

Ys
S L CLEMENS

This letter triumphantly violates business letter etiquette, the style of it a comic contradiction to the format. In riddling the form, Twain indulges his comic extravagance and literalism, the possibility of willful suffocation and exploding of his family, just as joyfully as he does vengefully. Furthermore, the specificity required of a business letter demands precise content and targets for the epitheticism, a savingly concrete and real problem for even the briefest humor. He must not only subvert or overcome the special form (which also happens to be one of the sacrosanctities of our business intercourse) but must answer to its particularities, meeting two kinds of resistance in the quick process.

What Is Man? fails, however—certainly as humor, but also as effective expression in any event. It is, as we know, didactic and too long and too explicit. Its form presents no genuine resistance. A thinly disguised Socratic dialogue, during which the Old Man sermonizes the Young Man on human depravity and determinism, the piece is, precisely, a sermon. And a sermon is the one form that allows and even demands orthodox invective against sinful humanity. Using it, and consciously so, as Twain really does, deprives him of any force whatsoever of antithesis, irreverence, or reversal. All Sunday churchgoers, even in optimistic and sentimental America, expected as much as he gave them and in the manner he gave it, traditionally. Moreover, the essence of what was said had to be generalized and comprehensive in the nature of things, in order to conform to the convention. For all of Twain's sense of urgency, signaled by his relentless use of italics, there were no resistances at all to overcome, outwit, or subvert. In fact, the stridency of what he says is the only way he can approximate force, comic or otherwise, and his typography proves that he knows as much. There is nothing else that he can objectively do, when he is being *allowed* the kinds of statements he is making by the very form itself. And the longer he might go on, the further he would get from the resistant comedy and effectiveness of that short paragraph of his letter, a piece we tend to include now in almost all anthologies of Twain, as a testament to a later moment when he recovered the joy of special undertaking and momentarily joined his heart and consciousness to the task.

As to his whole technique, excepting those last works of his which are scarcely humorous at all, Twain culminated a whole series of comic devices. We may isolate some of his consummate mastery in minor works and bagatelles of the early and middle periods, quite apart from their rich combination in *Huck Finn* and *Pudd'nhead Wilson.*

From his southwestern forebears comes the employment of dialect to its fullest effect, together with the anecdotal method and the framework device, as in "The Celebrated Jumping Frog." The elongated epithet is another inheritance, perfected by Twain for literary warfare.

> . . . when a personage talks like an illustrated, gilt-edged, tree-calf, hand-tooled, seven-dollar Friendship's Offering in the beginning of a paragraph, he shall not talk like a negro minstrel in the end of it.

Likewise, southern understatement can be enlisted, peerlessly.

> In the matter of intellect, the difference between a Cooper Indian and the Indian that stands in front of a cigar-shop is not spacious.

All tall-tale extravagance and frontier Crockettry he incorporated gleefully. The distinguished Twain scholar, Bernard De-Voto, insists, rightly, that these are culminations, of course, not originations. In this light stand exercises like these in "Frescoes from the Past."

> "I'm a child of sin, *don't* let me get a start! Smoked glass, here for all! Don't attempt to look at me with the naked eye, gentlemen! When I'm playful I use the meridians of longitude and parallels of latitude for a seine and drag the Atlantic Ocean for whales! I scratch my head with the lightning and purr myself to sleep with the thunder! When I'm cold, I bile the Gulf of Mexico and bathe in it; when I'm hot I fan myself with an equinoctial storm; when I'm thirsty I reach up and suck a cloud dry like a sponge; . . . I bite a piece out of the moon and hurry the seasons; I shake myself and crumble the mountains! Contemplate me through leather— *don't* use the naked eye."

Culminative also and in the provincial frontier mode, though somewhat influenced by Wardean confusionism, is the traditional burlesque of Shakespeare. Its monstrous wrenchings become an eclectic shambles, best appreciated by scholars . . . or the cultivated easterners who, like William Dean Howells, were his strictest audience.

To be, or not to be; that is the bare bodkin
That makes calamity of so long life;
For who would fardels bear, till Birnam Wood do come to Dunsinane,
But that the fear of something after death
Murders the innocent sleep,
Great nature's second course,
And makes us rather sling the arrows of outrageous fortune
Than fly to others that we know not of.
There's the respect must give us pause:
Wake Duncan with thy knocking! I would thou couldst;
For who would bear the whips and scorns of time,
The oppressor's wrong, the proud man's contumely,
The law's delay, and the quietus which his pangs might take,
In the dead waste and middle of the night, when churchyards yawn
In customary suits of solemn black,
But that the undiscovered country from whose bourne no traveler
    returns,
Breathes forth contagion on the world,
And thus the native hue of resolution, like the poor cat i' the adage,
Is sicklied o'er with care,
And all the clouds that lowered o'er our housetops,
With this regard their currents turn awry,
And lose the name of action.
'Tis a consummation devoutly to be wished. But soft you, the fair
    Ophelia:
Open not thy ponderous and marble jaws,
But get thee to a nunnery—go!

Twain's frequent leisureliness and digressiveness were prime legacies of Charles Farrar Browne, whose device of satiric dialogue he triumphantly employed in "The Whittier Dinner Speech."

Mr. Holmes was as fat as a balloon; he weighed as much as three hundred, and had double chins all the way down to his stomach. Mr. Longfellow was built like a prize-fighter. His head was cropped and bristly, like as if he had a wig made of hair-brushes. His nose lay straight down his face, like a finger with the end joint tilted up. They had been drinking. . . .

Well, between drinks they'd swell around the cabin and strike attitudes and spout; and pretty soon they got out a greasy old deck and went to playing euchre at ten cents a corner—on trust. I began

to notice some pretty suspicious things. Mr. Emerson dealt, looked
at his hand, shook his head, says:

"I am the doubter and the doubt—"

and ca'mly bunched the hands and went to shuffling for a new lay
out. Says he:

"They reckon ill who leave me out;
They know not well the subtle ways I keep
I pass and deal *again!*"

Hang'd if he didn't go ahead and do it, too! Oh, he was a cool one!

His irreverence, however, for which he personally paid dearly,
was as much his own as any legacy of southern predecessors,
western friends, and colleagues among contemporary literary
comedians.

Certainly some of his special gifts are more his own than inheritance. The discussion of French in *Huck Finn* illustrates his
original talent in literalism, while it is also a monument to comic
circularity, another natural superiority. The arsenal he brings to
bear in the most celebrated demolition we have, on Cooper,
shows his unique combinative technique, literalism, understatement, and cruel sarcasm joined distinctively.

And I do not altogether like the phrase "while those hands which
she had raised." It seems to imply that she had some other ones
which she had put on a shelf a minute so as to give her a better
chance to raise those ones; but it is not true; she had only the one
pair. The phrase is in the last degree misleading. But I like to see
her extend these ones in front of her and work the fingers. I think
that that is a very good effect.

His appropriations of reversal and anticlimax are also an inimitable display in the same piece.

Cooper's eye was splendidly inaccurate.

.   .   .   .   .

A work of art? It has no invention; it has no order, system, sequence, or result; it has no life-likeness, no thrill, no stir, no seeming of reality; its characters are confusedly drawn, and by their
acts and words they prove that they are not the sort of people
the author claims they are; its humor is pathetic; its pathos is funny;
its conversations are—oh! indescribable; its love-scenes odious; its
English a crime against the language.

Counting these out, what is left is Art. I think we must admit that.

On the whole, except for the Whittier piece and minor ex-cruciations in the Sawyer books, Twain does very little punning. Like Lincoln, however, one signal triumph is attributed to him, which ought to be true. Seated at a dinner for his wealthy friend, Rogers, Twain was confidentially accosted by a neighbor: "Your friend Rogers' money is tainted." The reply represents one of the heights of instantaneity and austere pertinence: "It's twice tainted—'taint yours and 'taint mine." That's Mark Twain, all right, if only for his unarguable psychology, a lightning flash of understanding.

A certain feature of grotesque and macabre comedy touches his work, as in "Frescoes."

> "You look at the graveyards; that tells the tale. Trees won't grow worth shucks in a Cincinnati graveyard, but in a Sent Louis grave-yard they grow upwards of eight hundred foot high. It's all on account of the water the people drunk before they laid up. A Cincinnati corpse don't richen a soil any."

He also exercises himself in practical joking, enjoying the out-and-out deflationary hoax. His description of "The Petrified Man" is climaxed by the detail of the man's fingers fanned in rock to his stone nose. We return in such bagatelles to his comic misanthropy. And foregoing the indelicacy of quotations from a surreptitious piece like "1601," we may recall certain urgencies to blasphemy and scatology that are also part of his practical joking, general irreverence, and larger deflationism.

Twain's elevation over all competing regionalists and local colorists was manifest and granted in his time. The western egalitarian and fun-loving spirit in him triumphed over the resi-due of southern violence and venom—until his subsequent sur-render to a black philosophy that asked for a plague on all houses. Up to then, however, he may be properly regarded as a culmi-native figure for the tall tale and all uproarious extravagance, for a fecund comic irreverence and for his characteristic mastery of literalism, reversal, circularity, and anticlimax. Added to that was a genius for superbly realistic speech, despite the fact that the times denied him his bawdry. Like Stephen Crane in an un-profane book about army life, Twain succeeded anyway—or all the better for overcoming resistances. In any event, he was un-

matched, and he remains unmatched even in a more liberalized
age, for his uncanny precision of realistic speech. That techni-
cality alone, placed at the disposal of superb comic characterization, accounts for the transcendence of his two prime works.

Twain theorized on humor in "How to Tell a Story" (1895),
where he formulated his artificial and general categories for the
American humorous story, the English comic story, and the
French witty story. His insight is interesting but quite partial
in both senses of the term. He wanted very much to direct attention to a special manner, American and his own. But his theoretical refinement was arbitrary and false (he had never read,
or he conveniently forgot, the digressive English masterpiece,
Tristram Shandy). If he had ever exclusively followed his own
dictum, it would have meant the loss of his deepest prerogatives
and variety. He was led to such codification in order to focus
that rambling Wardean technique he himself liked to use often.
Like Artemus Ward, he, too, liked to practice the strategy of
elaborated pointlessness, which the tactics of incongruity and
absurdity ultimately lead to. There was, accordingly, a parochial,
professional contest in seeing how close one could come to sense
without actually getting there. It was an in-group game of withheld or broken promise, and in his late years of summing up
Twain overvalued its consequence. There is no doubt that it was
a facet of his written work and raconteur performances, another
means to the utter comic deflation of meaningfulness. But Twain
overrated its distinctiveness for the very good additional reason
that he was so good at it.

Two years later, in the equally theoretical "Platform Readings,"
he spoke again from a professional pride about the value of improvisation, the effect of "unpremeditated talk" and of only apparent plausibility. The point once more was true enough, but
not the whole truth. His demonstration of the point, however, is
welcome, particularly in the outlandish but poker-faced passage,
"You couldn't hit a dog with an Irishman."

". . . one day my Uncle Lem and his dog was downtown, and he
was a-leanin' up against a scaffold—sick or drunk, or somethin'

—and there was an Irishman with a hod of bricks up the ladder along about the third story, and his foot slipped and down he came, bricks and all, and hit a stranger fair and square and knocked the everlasting aspirations out of him; he was ready for the coroner in two minutes. Now then people said it was an accident.

"Accident! there warn't no accident about it; 'twas a special providence, and had a mysterious, noble intention back of it. The idea was to save that Irishman. If the stranger hadn't been there that Irishman would have been killed. The people said 'special providence—sho! the dog was there—why didn't the Irishman fall on the dog? Why warn't the dog app'inted?' Fer a might good reason—the dog would 'a' seen him a-coming; you can't depend on no dog to carry out a special providence. You couldn't hit a dog with an Irishman because—lemme see, what was that dog's name . . . (musing) . . . oh, yes, Jasper—and a mighty good dog too; he wa'n't no common dog, he wa'n't no mongrel; he was a composite. A composite dog is a dog that's made up of all the valuable qualities that's in the dog breed—kind of a syndicate; and a mongrel is made up of the rif-raff that's left over. That Jasper was one of of the most wonderful dogs you ever see. Uncle Lem got him of the Wheelers. I reckon you've heard of the Wheelers; ain't no better blood south of the line than the Wheelers.

"Well, one day Wheeler. . . ."

Wardean and western manner could still make him funny, even in a semiacademical piece, but his career had scarcely been confined to this mode. Even in this very piece, in his straight expository humor, other specialties of Twain, like the comedy of sudden pertinence and explicit truth, are in evidence, as in his reference to Authors' Readings as "that kind of *crime*." His was a wonderfully manifold technique, and he could be forgiven his later partialities of thought.

His theories turn out to be unfortunately less valuable than usual from a practitioner, because he was a very poor critic of himself anyway. He notoriously underrated *Huck Finn* and overrated his ponderous *Joan of Arc*. He was a mother to his works, and his ugly duckling psychology made his pronouncements more subjective than usual. Still, his later willingness to theorize at all, as an act in itself, puts the mark of conclusiveness to his whole performance and confirms again the maturation of American humor.

We return to *Huck Finn* as his indisputably great work. Everything is in it, all compact: the best devices and combinations, the healthiest point of view, the grandest conception.[8] Despite Aristotle's surmise that tragedy is closer to epic cast than comedy is, *Huck Finn* exactly fits the mold of comic epic, and even more properly—that is, heroically—than those other western works that the great critic would not have predicted, *Don Quixote, Candide,* and *Tom Jones.* (He anticipated what he did on the basis of the pragmatic evidence available to him then. If he had consented to the great amount of comic conception in Homer's *Odyssey,* he would have guessed much more.) But Aristotle's concession about the proximity of high comedy to tragedy is accurate and germane. *Huck Finn* frequently hits the indefinable line between them. Chaplin will later do the same thing in a few of his finest films. A cruel and unpretty cosmos evokes pity and terror as much as comic effect. In Twain's book there is the added and native balance of pathos with comic wisdom, the Lincolnesque quality.

One of the accomplishments of *Huck Finn* is the suitable compassion in it, the saving mean between Bret Harte's sentimentalism on the one side and Bierce's bitterness on the other. The deep-layered cynicism and heartsoreness are controlled or encased by the comic technique. The result is a work rising straight out of the cosmic genre either to a realm of simultaneous classifications that even the formal Greeks allowed for or to a realm of the unclassifiable. As to Twain's reputed casualness in his left-handed composition of the book, perhaps the seven years he finally spent on it guaranteed the necessary distance for its *juste* creation. His need to get it right, to weigh the structural or thematic correctness of one improvisation against another, forced him to take it slow for the greatest success at that precise midpoint and high point of his career. As a result, the work combined the maximum force with the maximum form. As such, in all its lasting and sometimes overwhelming influence, it remains the major achievement in American humor and the landmark it is in our literature.

[8] Including the resistances presented by a children's story form, which he marvelously turned to his own greater purposes, as he could not or dared not yet do in *Tom Sawyer.*

V

Intercentury Humor

OF TWAIN's later contemporaries and successors, Ambrose Bierce (1842–1914?) is surpassing heir to the fullest negativity possible. Unquestionably he schooled himself in the gothicism of Poe. His macabre stories, like those of *In the Midst of Life* (1898), fulfill the Poe-etics of classic American shock; they are also very close, as the innovator's work was, to the blackest humor. But in *The Cynic's Word Book* (1881–1906), renamed *The Devil's Dictionary* (1911), Bierce also subscribed to the explicit Satanism of Twain's concluding stage. In such work his mordancy even exceeds Twain's. The only factor that alleviates what has been called his Puritanism of hate is the luxury of sophisticated verbal play.

His misanthropy is particularly insistent in the *Dictionary*, although it permeates all his work.

> MAGPIE, n. A bird whose thievish disposition suggested to someone that it might be taught to talk.
> NEIGHBOR, n. One whom we are commanded to love as ourselves, and who does all he knows how to make us disobedient.

This is the same general antagonism he looses in *Tangential Views* (1911) when inveighing against a favorite subject like Christmas celebrations:

. . . teaching them by means of the Santa Claus deception that exceedingly hard liars may be good mothers and fathers and miscellaneous relatives—thus habituating the infant mind to charitable judgment and establishing an elastic standard of truth that will be useful in their later life.

His nihilism, or what Professor Walter Blair with whimsical euphemism has elsewhere termed "futilitarianism," comes into sudden blinding focus under any entry. The more intimidating his problem, the better.

MIND, n. A mysterious form of matter secreted by the brain. Its chief activity consists in the endeavor to ascertain its own nature, the futility of the attempt being due to the fact that it has nothing but itself to know itself with.

This is the typical diabolism also of his swift deflationary fables, *Aesopus Emendatus,* some of which are remarkable anticipations of the later James Thurber, when Thurber confronted utter human vacuity.

"See these valuable golden eggs," said a Man that owned a Goose. "Surely a Goose that can lay such eggs must have a gold mine inside her."

So he killed the Goose and cut her open, but found that she was just like any other goose. Moreover, on examining the eggs that she had laid he found they were just like any other eggs.

Bierce's comprehensive pessimism is for all seasons, although the wintry mood suits him best.

NOVEMBER, n. The eleventh twelfth of a weariness.

And his cynicism lurks in unanswerable offerings anywhere in the alphabet.

SELFISH, adj. Devoid of consideration for the selfishness of others.

Bierce is the naked model of antitheticism in American humor, the bare thing itself in all the social antagonism and painstaking comic fury he embodies. Only Charles Addams, in later American humor, is an adequate rival. Bierce misses few opportunities of fierce antipatriotism, a kind of compounded blasphemy when it takes the familiar semihymnal form.

A RATIONAL ANTHEM

My country, 'tis of thee,
Sweet land of felony,
    Of thee I sing—
Land where my fathers fried
Young witches and applied
Whips to the Quaker's hide
    And made him spring.

My knavish country, thee,
Land where the thief is free,
    Thy laws I love;
I love thy thieving bills
That tap the people's tills;
I love thy mob whose will's
    All laws above.

Let Federal employees
And rings rob all they please,
    The whole year long.
Let office-holders make
Their piles and judges rake
Our coin. For Jesus' sake
    Let's *all* go wrong!

His antidemocracy, like Poe's, is a means of aristocratic self-identification and therefore pervades his work, an adjunct to his misanthropy. His essay on *Disintroductions,* begins: "The devil is a citizen of every country but only in our own are we in constant peril of an introduction to him." The final pronoun is generic, accounting for every companionable, social, affable democratic type one is in danger of meeting in our streets. His definition of republic settles the point, as are all his definitions, worked over for twenty-five years and refurbished for another five years, meant to define and settle his long-lasting individual quarrels with the shibboleths all about him in America.

REPUBLIC, n. A nation in which, the thing governing and the thing governed being the same, there is only permitted authority to enforce an optional obedience. . . . There are as many kinds of republics as there are gradations between the despotism whence they came and the anarchy whither they lead.

Living through our most infamous period of rampant capitalism, he sets himself virulently against the hallowed economic system. Predictably, he inveighs against the practice of inscribing "The Lord's Prayer on a Coin," although he curiously misses the opportunity of setting "In God We Trust" against "In Gold We Trust" as a fair measure of native hypocrisy and the minted lie. But he proceeds to broader things. Here is his quick definition of

PIRACY, n. Commerce without the folly-swaddles, just as God made it.

And from *The Scrap Heap* (1910) a typical syllogism of verse:

> A defrauded of his land by B,
> Who's driven from the premises by C.
> D buys the place with coin of plundered E.
> "That A's an Anarchist!" says F to G.

His animosity leads him also to his attacks on science and technology as the handmaidens of the system, rapes which he commits and recommits upon vestal virgins.

GRAVITATION, n. The tendency of all bodies to approach one another with a strength proportioned to the quantity of matter they contain—the quantity of matter they contain being ascertained by the strength of their tendency to approach one another. . . .
TELEPHONE, n. An invention of the devil which abrogates some of the advantages of making a disagreeable person keep his distance.
TELESCOPE, n. A device having a relation to the eye similar to that of the telephone to the ear, enabling distant objects to plague us with a multitude of needless details. Luckily it is unprovided with a bell summoning us to the sacrifice.

Among his *Fantastic Fables* (1899), "The Flying Machine" is in the same tenor, though reversalism rather than circularity is his device.

An Ingenious Man who had built a flying-machine invited a great concourse of people to see it go up. At the appointed moment, everything being ready, he boarded the car and turned on the power. The machine immediately broke through the massive substructure upon which it was builded, and sank out of sight into the earth, the aeronaut springing out barely in time to save himself.

"Well," said he, "I have done enough to demonstrate the correctness of my details. The defects," he added, with a look at the ruined brick-work, "are merely basic and fundamental."

Like the other comedians of the intercentury period, Bierce is also mightily disabused of warfare. The costly Civil War and the blatantly imperialist Spanish-American War were particular sources of revulsion. But, as many were coming to see, those instances were only two in a series of constant American imbroglios. Seizing the country from the redman, wresting militant independence from the mother country, fighting the English in 1812 and the Mexicans in 1846, periodically thrusting back the diminishing Indians out west, torn asunder in civil war when for once our domestic compromises failed in spectacular violence, righteously aggressive against the Spanish, we could already be characterized as a warlike democracy. And always heroics stood between us and accurate self-appraisal, even undercutting Stephen Crane's exposé, *The Red Badge of Courage.* Meanwhile, Bierce's tales of warfare were attacks upon romantic combat, his best-known contributions to realistic deflation. But his humorous verse had its thematic point, too. In it, he enlisted satire in his opposition to that military impulse[1] we have always mantled in patriotism and glory. "Polyphemus," in *Shapes of Clay* (1903), is a representative broadside, with our vocabulary for Bierce's pacificism tending to flagrant paradox.

POLYPHEMUS

'Twas a sick young man with face ungay
And an eye that was all alone;
And he shook his head in a hopeless way
As he sat on a roadside stone.

---

[1] On the other hand, just a little too much can be made out of such criticism. We have not been unqualified militarists and conquerors. No other victor would have demobilized so precipitously after World War II or been so ambivalent about prosecuting Asian wars in the last seventeen years. And there was plenty of contemporary criticism from our midst against the immoral Mexican and Spanish-American wars, not to mention the powerful cartoons against our adventitious entry into World War I. The self-criticism of our use of the Bomb in World War II, for all of the objective comic dimensions of a debate about what constitutes ethical mass bombing, is another instance of a basic pacifism that has characterized us almost as much as our solemn militancy.

"O, ailing youth, what untoward fate
  Has made the sun to set
On your mirth and eye?" "I'm constrained to state
  I'm an ex-West Point cadet.

" 'Twas at cannon-practice I got my hurt
  And my present frame of mind;
For the gun went off with a double spurt—
  Before it, and also behind!"

. . . . .

" 'Twas O for a breach of the peace—'twas O
  For an international brawl!
But a piece of the breech—ah, no, ah no,
  I didn't want that at all."

If in the subject of native pietism and religiosity, other comedians of the period turn predictably incandescent now and then,
Bierce is an arsonist.

REPROBATION, n. In theology, the state of a luckless mortal pre-
natally damned. The doctrine of reprobation was taught by Calvin,
whose joy in it was somewhat marred by the sad sincerity of his conviction that although some are foredoomed to perdition, others
are predestined to salvation.

He is influenced, as we have seen, against the transparent commercialism and sentimentalism of Christmas,[2] and he employs
the most extreme reversalism in his work of destruction. From
his poem, "An Unmerry Christmas," come the typical lines:

. . . my stocking's tied,
My pocket buttoned—with my soul inside.
I save my money and I save my pride.

Dinner? Yes; thank you—just a baby's body
Done to a nutty brown, and a tear toddy
To give me appetite; and as to drink,
About a half a jug of blood, I think,

[2] The Christmas holiday began to overtake the Fourth of July in importance during the last quarter of the nineteenth century. In fact, Cady,
in *The American Poets, 1810–1900,* remarks that sentimental American
Christmas poems, subsequently set to music as carols, largely invented
Christmas as we know it. Bierce's anti-poetry on the subject is, in part, a
special reaction to the surge of pietistic verse of the period.

Nothing releases his misanthropy like the hypocritical annual ritual, and in *Tangential Views* he gets his consolation as he can in his essay on the subject.

> It is affirmed by some that persons deliberately and with malice aforethought put themselves in the way of being killed, in order to avert the tiresome iteration of Christmas greetings. If this is correct, the annual Christmas "holocaust" is not an evil demanding abatement, but a blessing to be received in a spirit of devout and pious gratitude.

But the question is part of the whole obsessive subject of contemporary American Christianity, and Bierce is tireless in setting fires at every flammable juncture, as in his short sardonic poem, "The Lord's Prayer on a Coin." In addition to linking consistently the business ethos and modern Christianity and indicting our religious hypocrisy, he illuminates the core of self-interest in the pseudoreligiosity practiced all about him.

> Preachers he will see who teach
>   That it is divine to preach—
> That they fan a sacred fire
> And are worthy of their hire.
>   ("Visions of Sin" in *Shapes of Clay*)

He quotes Governor Stoneman's Thanksgiving Proclamation—"Especially should we be thankful for having escaped the ravages of the yellow scourge by which our neighbors have been so sorely afflicted"—and proceeds in his poem, "Matter for Gratitude," in *Black Beetles in Amber* (1892), to excoriate the seamy propitiation of all prayer.

> An earthquake here rolls harmless through the land,
> And Thou are good because the chimneys stand—
> There templed cities sink into the sea,
> And damp survivors, shrieking as they flee,
> Skip to the hills and hold a celebration
> In honor of Thy wise discrimination.

The same treatment, combining irreverence and comic pertinence, is accorded to "The Farmer's Prayer" in the same collection.

> Our neighbors all about have copious rains
>   That fall on them like manna.
> Send *us* the showers, Lord, and parch the plains
>   of Indiana.
>
> . . . . .
>
> We ask but justice: treat us not with scorn;
>   Our comfort make less chilly;
> And those who pray for an advance in corn—
>   O smite them silly!

Even in a country of markedly increased hostility between the sexes, Bierce's misogyny is strong, his venom mitigated only by wit.

BELLADONNA, n. In Italian a beautiful lady; in English a deadly poison. A striking example of the essential identity of the two tongues.

In his works, a special antagonism is directed at feminine deceitfulness, his favorite target being the false widow. Here is the representative piece, "The Crimson Candle" from *Fantastic Fables*.

A Man lying at the point of death called his wife to his bedside and said:

"I am about to leave you forever; give me, therefore, one last proof of your affection and fidelity. In my desk you will find a crimson candle, which has been blessed by the High Priest and has a peculiar mystical significance. Swear to me that while it is in existence you will not remarry."

The Woman swore and the Man died. At the funeral the Woman stood at the head of the bier, holding a lighted crimson candle till it was wasted entirely away.

Now and then the highest pitch of mordancy occurs for the topic, as in "The Inconsolable Widow" in the same work.

A woman in widow's weeds was weeping upon a grave.

"Console yourself, madam," said a Sympathetic Stranger. "Heaven's mercies are infinite. There is another man somewhere, besides your husband, with whom you can still be happy."

"There was," she sobbed—"there was, but this is his grave."

Three other subjects, of very particular American valuation, appear in Bierce's work with the strangest and most grotesque treatment. They are special sanctities he is out to violate no matter what: the maudlin sentimentalisms about parents, children, and dogs. Accordingly, parenticide, infanticide, and canine agglutination, all compacted in his story, "Oil of Dog," are recurrent themes of horrific private comedy in Bierce. The son in "Oil of Dog" becomes a dogsnatcher for his father, who boils the dogs in his vats for pharmaceutical purposes, and a kidnapper for his mother, who "disposes of unwelcome babes" for a fee. Both parents are willing to accept surpluses of precious as well as cast-out dogs and children. The comic momentum of events naturally reaches that complication in plot where an interchange occurs. Trapped by circumstances one night, the son substitutes a baby for a dog in the vats. The incident is attended by the greatest pharmaceutical success. The parents flexibly combine their pursuits into a common enterprise, and Bierce brings together the influences of Swift and Defoe in his satanic portrait of commercial fanaticism, adding to his sources his own tactic of macabre understatement.

> Finding a double profit in her business, my mother now devoted herself to it with a new assiduity. She removed not only superfluous and unwelcome babes to order, but went out into the highways and byways, gathering in children of a larger growth, and even such adults as she could entice to the oilery. . . .
>
> So enterprising had they now become that a public meeting was held and resolutions passed severely censuring them. It was intimated by the chairman that any further raids upon the population would be met in a spirit of hostility.

Balked in their zeal at last, the parents see in each another victim, and in their concluding struggle both collapse into one of the vats, leaving behind their son, who is stricken with "remorse for a heedless act entailing so dismal a commercial disaster."

Tawdry violence and wanton cruelty[3] in all the pieces of

[3] A Chinaman is incidentally but lavishly shot in "My Favorite Murder." And Bierce's fable about the cat and the king rests on the concluding cruelty as if it were the height of comic climax.

A Cat was looking at a King, as permitted by the proverb.

"Well," said the monarch, observing her inspection of the royal person, "how do you like me?"

"I can imagine a King," said the Cat, "whom I should like better."

"For example?"

Bierce's "The Parenticide Club" constitute something more than
the ruling influence of Poe on Bierce's mind. ("The Cask of
Amontillado," however, weighs heavily, with many verbal echoes,
on "My Favorite Murder.") The question of literary influence,
after all, is always answered by susceptibilities. One is never
tyrannized by an influence, but subjects himself to it, for his own
reasons. Like the French, Bierce took Poe as the supreme repudi-
ator of prevailing values and master nihilist that he himself
wished to be. If in "My Favorite Murder" Bierce's narrator can
add "insubordination and treachery" to the killing of his uncle,
the crime would be as "reasonless as I could wish." The black or
sick humor is a measure of Bierce's recoil from a whole cultural
system of sentimentality and falsification, and the key word is
"treachery." His mistake is not in unmasking society, for that is
a prime function of comedy, particularly in America. His error
is to fall in love with the death's head revealed. But that act
shows his fundamental passion . . . to love, practically at any cost.

The proper humorist is less compulsive. He is basically more
disengaged, more dispassionate, in order precisely to bestow a
more discriminate love where it is deserved. He is paradoxically
more strict and credulous. And he has trained himself to look
things in the face with less revulsion when, stripped, they do not
conform to subjective ideal. Which is to say that black or sick
humorists, like Bierce, are infallibly romantic and that in a
realistic age they are necessarily more and more prone to the dark
expression . . . of themselves, primarily. They are, in the end,
lyricists; the beauty or perversity of what they say depends on
the material and tenor of the age. Their need is to express rather
than to report or truly dramatize.

In all his haughty severities, Bierce thus reveals himself. He
had no middle stage like Twain; he was a lifelong versifier and
prose poet of black humor who could never really objectify his
themes in another character outside of himself. There was no
Huck Finn, no Wilson, and certainly no Jim or Roxy for him to
imagine. He could not, like his contemporary, Finley Peter
Dunne, project either a Dooley or a Hennessey. And we never

"The King of Mice."
The sovereign was so pleased with the wit of the reply that he gave
her permission to scratch his Prime Minister's eyes out.

hear the slightest change of voice throughout his entire work. A strident subjectivist, he provides the essential clue to black humor in any day: his relentless abuses are reverse rhapsodies. Black subjectivist humorists are disenchanted poets. This point distinguishes them from authentic comedians, who have not been particularly enchanted to begin with or who register, at least, a prolonged period of objective disengagement sometime in their career.

But in the complication of all psychology, we cannot deny a man like Bierce his insights. Prototypical black humorist, he was especially capable, by a law of intimate attraction and then repulsion, to fix upon the weaknesses of what we may term white or garish romanticism, upon cultural sentimentalities most of all. These have been almost conspiratorially manifest in the United States. There they superlatively were all around Bierce, as in the period's sentimental fiction, which particularly revolted him. Dark and reactionary romantics are always capable of the kind of satanic deflationism animating Bierce's literary parodies, which appear like last chapters of insufferable romances, employing anticlimax for special effect. Here is "A Demising Love" from *The Sample Counter.*

James endeavored ineffectually to ascertain the trend of her affections; her expression remained a blank. He erroneously attributed his failure to poor skill in physiognomy and inwardly bewailed his youthful neglect of the advantages of education. While so engaged he fancies he detected in her look something significant of an interest in his personality. Could he be mistaken? No, there it was again! . . .

"Mabel," he inquired, "do you not experience the promptings of a dawning tenderness for one to whom you are much?"

Receiving no negative answer he kissed her simultaneously on both cheeks, and falling rapidly upon one knee, poured out his soul in beautiful language, mostly devoted to commendation of her fine character and disposition.

Mabel did not at once respond. She was deceased.

He is on the lookout for the highfalutin' style, as in "Her Diplodocus" in the same collection. We surmise that his efforts here are a form of self-mockery as much as anything else, for he too ran risks of affected stylistics.

"Sir!" Miss Athylton drew herself up to her full height and looked her interlocutor squarely in the visage. For an instant he returned her scrutiny; then his eyes fell to the earth, stammering apologies. With a sweeping curtsey she passed out of the room, hand over hand.

In this vein, he likes to take off on Jamesian prose, with a grand attack on high triviality in "March Hares."

> Mrs. Rorqual deposited her embroidery on the sofa by her side and, slightly changing color, said, "No, my ideals are not unchangeable; they have undergone memorable alteration within the last hour."
>
> "Let us hope," said D'Anchovi, uncrossing his hands, and putting one forefinger into a buttonhole of his coat, "that they are still high."
>
> She resumed her embroidery and, looking at a painting of the martyrdom of St. Denis over the mantel, replied, "Would it matter?"
>
> "Surely," said he, lightly beating the carpet with the heel of his well-fitting shoe; "for ideals are more than thoughts. I sometimes think they are things—that *we* are their *thoughts*."
>
> She did not immediately reply. A curtain at an open window moved audibly. A sunbeam crept through the lattice of the piazza outside and fell upon the window-ledge. The fly previously mentioned now walked indolently along the top of the Japanese screen, then fearlessly descended the face of it to within an inch of the mouth of a painted frog. D'Anchovi, with a lifting of his eyebrows, maintained a determined silence.
>
> "I should think that an uncomfortable creed," Mrs. Rorqual said at last, withdrawing the tip of her shoe, which had been visible beneath the edge of her gown, and shifting her gaze from St. Denis to one of the crystal ornaments of the candelabrum pendent from the ceiling.
>
> He passed the fingers of his right hand through his hair, slightly shifted his position on his chair and said: "Mrs. Rorqual, I have to thank you for a most agreeable hour. Shall I see you on the golf-links to-morrow?"
>
> So they parted, but when he was gone she toyed thoughtfully with a spray of heliotrope growing in a jardiniere and then ran her forefinger along a part of the pattern of the wallpaper.

The pernicious influence of Cooper is still current, technically as inflated vocabulary and thematically as romantic heroism of the field, and Bierce makes his contribution to the now standard depreciation.

"Clifford," said Isabel, earnestly yet softly, "are you sure that you truly love me?"

Clifford presented such testimony and evidence as he could command, and requested her decision on the sufficiency of what he had advanced.

"Oh, Clifford," she said, laying her two little hands in one of his comparatively large ones, "you have extirpated my ultimate uncertainty." ("The Recrudescence of Squollander")

Plympton arrived at the scene of action just as the commanding general ordered an advance along the entire front. Spurring his steed to the centre of the line he rang out his voice in accents of defiance and was promoted for gallantry.

Bertram, who was an eye-witness, immediately withdrew his objection to the marriage. This took place shortly afterward and was attended with the happiest results. ("Lance and Lute")

But he is at his best in more individualistic performances, as in his deflation of the whole popular tradition of the melodramatic, sentimental romance novel.

A misstep precipitated her into the stream, from which with no small difficulty she was taken in a dying condition, a half-mile below. The person that drew her forth from the waters was Paul's aged uncle.

"Tell Paul Dessard," she said with her last breath, "that I love him, die for him! Tell him how I strove successfully to hide my love from him lest he think me unmaidenly; but it cannot matter now if he know it. Tell him all, I pray you tell him all, and add that in that Better Land whither I go my spirit will await him with impatience, prepared to explain all."

The good old man bent over her, placed his open hand behind his ear and ejaculated:

"Hay?"

Of all the comic techniques Bierce used throughout his work, anticlimax was a favored device, prosecuted with a special economy. And with witty vindictiveness, as in his denigrative ode, "A Trencher-Knight."

> . . . and Fame
> Inscribes in gravy his immortal name.

His own use of the heightened style that plummets is a signature of his expression, as in *To Elevate the Stage.*

. . . the long desired "elevation of the stage" to such a plane that even the pulpit need not be ashamed to work with it in elicitation of the human snore. . . .

His epigrammatical gifts he put in service to antiproverbialism, which fills his *Dictionary*. His entry and examples under "saw" are typical.

SAW, n. A trite popular saying, or proverb. (Figurative and colloquial.) So called because it makes its way into a wooden head. Following are examples of old saws fitted with new teeth.
A man is known by the company that he organizes.
Think twice before you speak to a friend in need.
What is worth doing is worth the trouble of asking somebody to do it.
Where there's a will there's a won't.

All of which is a noteworthy subclass of reversalism, to which he is devoted all through his humor.

REVELATION, n. A famous book in which St. John the Divine concealed all that he knew.
BORE, n. A person who talks when you wish him to listen.

He regularly combines the device with personal epithet but to no greater effect than in his quatrain on "Elihu Root" in *The Scrap Heap*.

> Stoop to a dirty trick or low misdeed?
> What, bend him from his moral skies to it?
> No, no, not he! To serve his nature's need
> He may upon occasion rise to it.

And his essay on *Disintroductions* is a *locus classicus* for the technique as an expression of his misanthropy.

MR. WHITE—Mr. Black, knowing the low esteem in which you hold each other, I have the honor to disintroduce you from Mr. Green.
MR. BLACK (bowing)—Sir, I have long desired the advantage of your unacquaintance.
MR. GREEN (bowing)—Charmed to unmeet you, sir. Our acquaintance (the work of a most inconsiderate and unworthy person) has distressed me beyond expression. We are greatly indebted to our good friend here for his tact in repairing the mischance.
MR. WHITE—Thank you. I'm sure you will become very good strangers.

The approach of taking things the other way around is, of course, fundamental to the antithetic character of comedy and may become just as much a habit of convenience as straight conformism is, just as automatic and just as easy. But Bierce frequently strikes comic wisdom in the technique, which is its essential reason for being.

> It is unknown to me why a Christmas should be always merry but never happy, and why the happiness appropriate to the New Year should not be expressed in merriment. (*Christmas and the New Year* in *Tangential Views*)

He is prone to comic literalism only slightly less than reversalism. We therefore anticipate the tentative but sardonic helpfulness of his literal cannibalistic suggestions at the end of *Did We Eat One Another?*

> Observe the significance of the phrase "sweet sixteen." What a world of meaning lurks in the expression "she is as sweet as a peach," and how suggestive of luncheon are the words "tender youth." A kiss is but a modified bite, and a fond mother, when she says her babe is "almost good enough to eat," merely shows that she is herself only a trifle too good to eat it.

And one of his most sharply sustained entries in the *Dictionary* employs literalism almost exclusively.

> GOOSE, n. A bird that supplies quills for writing. These, by some occult process of nature, are penetrated and suffused with various degrees of the bird's intellectual energies and emotional character, so that when inked and drawn mechanically across paper by a person called an "author," there results a very fair and accurate transcript of the fowl's thought and feeling. The difference in geese, as discovered by this ingenious method, is considerable: many are found to have only trivial and insignificant powers, but some are seen to be very great geese indeed.

The pun on "fowl" is not exceptional, though it is more subtle than usual. For as a particular brand of literalism, the flagrant pun seduces Bierce frequently from superior heights of expression. He has his weakness for this most American of temptations, though he tries his wit every chance he gets.

> ORTHODOX, n. An ox wearing the popular religious yoke.

Still, he can devote a whole miniature fable to the simplest play on words.

> A Public Treasury, feeling Two Arms lifting out its contents, exclaimed:
> "Mr. Shareman, I move for a division."
> "You seem to know something about parliamentary forms of speech," said the Two Arms.
> "Yes," replied the Public Treasury, "I am familiar with the hauls of legislation." ("Treasury and Arms" in *Fantastic Fables*.)

In the varied techniques of verbal comedy, Bierce was no maverick. He has his adeptness with native comic metaphor, illustrating his own concept of "platitude."

> A thought that snores in words that smoke. . . . A fossil sentiment in artificial rock. A moral without the fable. . . . A jelly-fish withering on the shore of the sea of thought. . . . A desiccated epigram.

His association or circularity of expression is another indulgence, which may have influenced Benchley and other figures.

> HIPPOGRIFF, n. An animal (now extinct) which was half horse and half griffin. The griffin was itself a compound creature, half lion and half eagle. The hippogriff was actually, therefore, only one-quarter eagle, which is two dollars and fifty cents in gold. The study of zoology is full of surprises.

He was, however, firmly opposed to realistic, colloquial speech, and therefore avoided the humor of slang, on one occasion attacking George Ade's "laminated kidney-suet trade." He thought the practice unliterary, commercial, and cheap, and would have nothing to do with it. The principle is related to his antidemocratic beliefs as a whole and to his scorn of local color, which focused on low, ignorant characters. Still, he descended to popular practice in a number of other ways, including understatements so extreme that they fit squarely into the native mode of all-out extravagance, as in "An Imperfect Conflagration."

> That afternoon I went to the chief of police, told him [I had killed my father] and asked his advice. It would be very painful to me if the facts became publicly known. My conduct would be generally condemned; the newspapers would bring it up against me if I should ever run for office.

As a matter of fact, the technique is an element of farce, and Bierce often drops out of sight to the nethermost regions of comedy, or just beneath it, in this practice. He can be too explicit—though he has rare successes, as in city names, like "South Asphyxia"—and he goes too far unnecessarily, particularly in "My Favorite Murder."

> The customary oath having been administered, I made the following statement [of avuncular murder], which impressed the judge with so strong a sense of the comparative triviality of the [matricide] for which I was on trial that he made no further search for mitigating circumstances, but simply instructed the jury to acquit, and I left the court, without a stain on my reputation.

Added to his unvarying subjectivism and tone are this penchant for farce and the whole strategy of explicitness in his humor, a crucial disadvantage because it makes the comedy too readily exhaustible. Bierce preferred to think of himself as a wit and farcicist rather than mere humorist, vastly appreciating his own directness and devaluating the techniques of indirectness and objectification. But, in addition to the excesses of his own point of view, his technique becomes far too predictable and heavy.

Up to now, in fact, enough of Bierce went a long way with most readers, due as much to the technical load as anything else. His renewed popularity, as in the recent reissues of his *Dictionary* and George Barkin's new paperback collection, occurs despite these considerations. In a time of almost epidemical sick humor, Bierce is recognized as a source or old spore, the more virulent the better.

There is a story about Finley Peter Dunne (1867–1936) meeting Mark Twain one noon hour at 42nd Street and Fifth Avenue. The aged Twain was a familiar figure in his mustache'd white-haired austerity and his immaculate linen suit, so that as he talked with Dunne a crowd of wellwishers and gapers gathered about them. Presently Dunne said, "Maybe all these people looking at me make you uncomfortable—let's go over to the Century Club for private talk and lunch." If the anecdote isn't true, it ought to be. It dots the i's and, as Dooley would say, crosses the t of Chicago "irrivirents," where Dunne was champion.

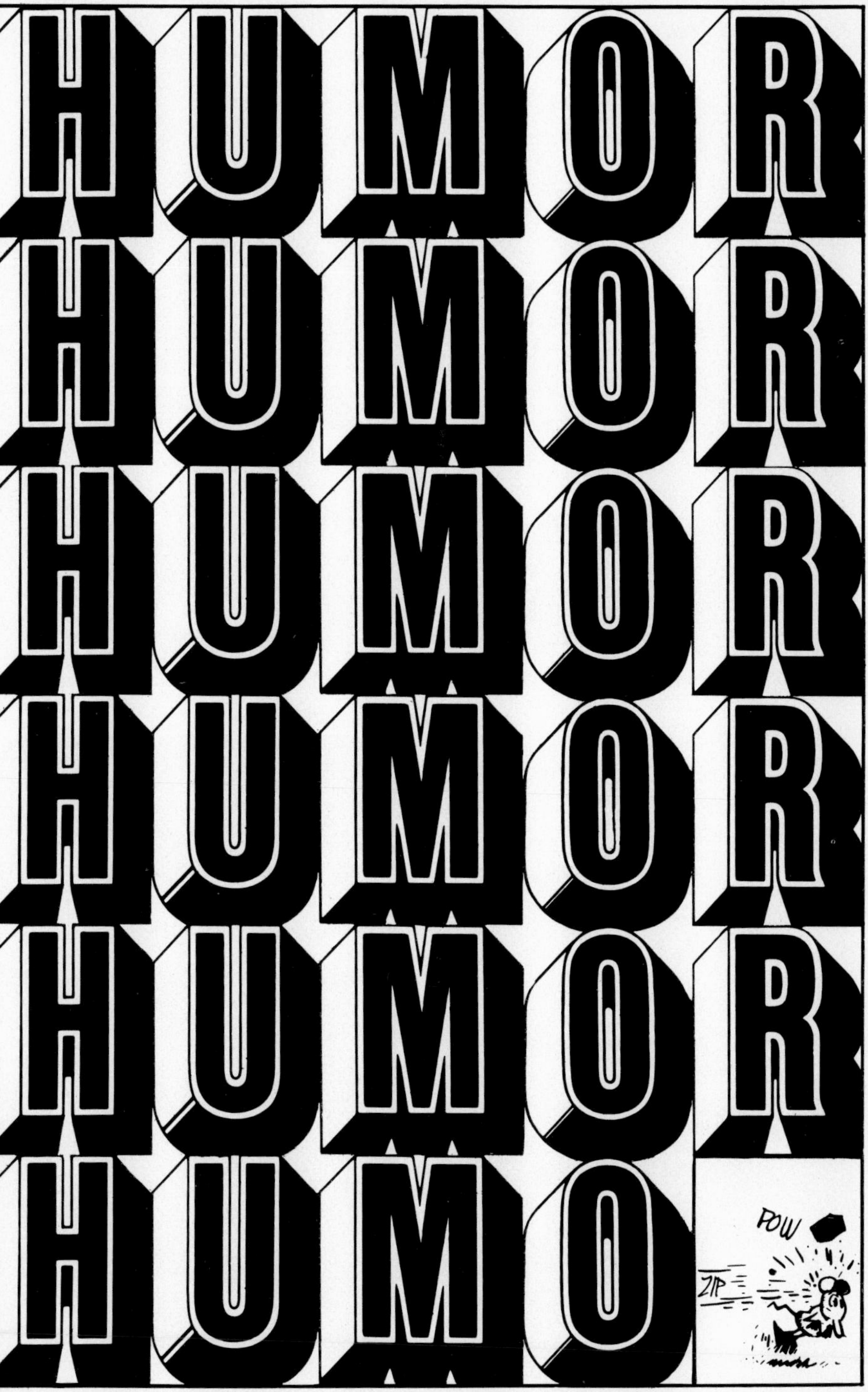
HUMOR
HUMOR
HUMOR
HUMOR
HUMOR
HUMO
POW
ZIP

1

2

3

1. War is bosh! — for W. C. Fields, Louise Fazenda, and Chester Conklin
2. "Pack Up Your Troubles" — with Laurel and Hardy
3. Buster Keaton in "No Man's Land" sans rose.
4. Pomp and Circumstance. W. C. Fields in "If I Had A Million."
5. Keystone Cops. Stop motion.
6. Nonplused Harold Lloyd.

4

5

1. Harry Langdon. The hat was the hand.
2. Lou Costello. The hat was the hand.
3. W. C. Fields. The hat was the hand.
4. Buster Keaton. The hat was the hand.
5. A resigned? Chaplin in "City Lights."
6. Buster Keaton in "Battling Butler." 6

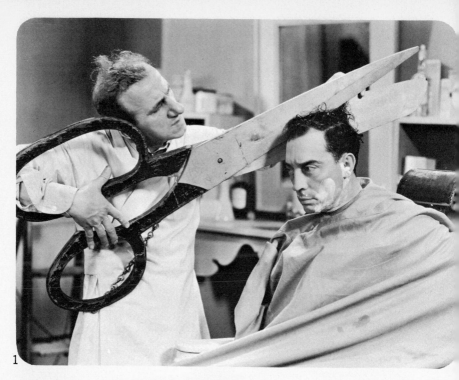

3

1. Jimmy Durante and Buster Keaton cutting up in "What-No-Beer."
2. Harold Bisonette (W. C. Fields) tells Mr. Muckle (Charles Sellon) it's all right to cross the street.
3. "Now make him play, Ollie!"
4. Baby Leroy and sidekick. W. C. Fields and sidekick.

4

When dey found dat delicious drink dey... "Just laffed at de sun"

Drink
Coca-Cola
Delicious and Refreshing

FOLD FORWARD

UNCLE REMUS and the happy ANIMALS

1

2

1. "Uncle Remus," and an early
Madison Avenue client adaptation.
2. Thomas Nast's "What I Know About
Swallowing." Greeley and Tammany.
1872 campaign.
3. 1812. "The Gerry-Mander!"
A new political word and the defeat
of Massachusetts Governor
Gerry for re-election.
4. The first American cartoon.
Benjamin Franklin in his
Pennsylvania Gazette May 9, 1754.

3

4

JOIN, or DIE.

1

WHEN GOD MAKES A
BEAUTIFUL WOMAN,
THE DEVIL OPENS A
NEW REGISTER.

WOMEN AND FOXES,
BEING WEAK, ARE
DISTINGUISHED BY
SUPERIOR TACT.

A BAD MARRIAGE IS
LIKE AN ELECTRIC
THRILLING MACHINE:
IT MAKES YOU DANCE,
BUT YOU CAN'T LET GO.

MARRIAGE, *N*. THE
STATE OR CONDITION
OF A COMMUNITY
CONSISTING OF A
MASTER, A MISTRESS
AND TWO SLAVES,
MAKING IN ALL, TWO.

2

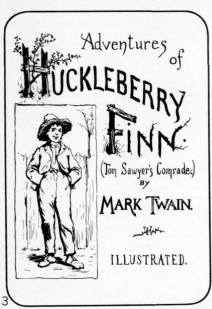

Adventures of

HUCKLEBERRY
FINN.

(Tom Sawyer's Comrade.)
BY
MARK TWAIN.

ILLUSTRATED.

3

4

5

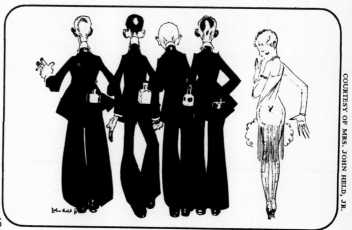

6

1. Bitter Bierce. Ambrose Bierce.
A most uncompromising satirist.
2. Joel Chandler Harris' Uncle Remus.
More than postbellum plantation
literature.
3. Hemingway thought it
began Modern American Literature.
4. Twain's "The Celebrated Jumping
Frog of Calaveras County."
5. Flesh was "in"! Charles Dana Gibson's
drawings set a style for the Gay 90's.
6. John Held Jr.,
"Four Out of Five Have It."
7. H. L. Mencken. The antagonist of
flap and doodle, balder and dash.
By Covarrubias.

7

1

2

3

4

5

6

1. "Another such victory and I
   am undone." Nast created the
   Republican elephant for the close
   Hayes-Tilden election of 1876.
2. Thomas Nast.
   "A thief to catch a thief."
3. Harry Langdon in "One Good Turn
   Deserves Another."
4. Franklin in full regalia wears the
   emblem of the company he
   founded in 1736.
5. "What have you done with
   Dr. Millmoss?" James Thurber.
6. Robert Benchley. The Mayor of All
   Things. Drawings by Gluyas Williams

1

2

3

1. Krazy Kat. The end result of a br
   Kat and Offissa Pup.
2. Peanuts. By Schulz.
3. Archy the Cockroach;
   a former *vers libre* bard.
   Mehitabel the Cat;
   a former demi-monde
   or lively lady.
   Free verse by Don Marquis.
   Illustrated by George Herriman.

Mark Twain

Benjamin Franklin

Robert Benchley

Dorothy Parker

James Thurber

S. J. Perelman

Ring Lardner

Mort Sahl

Buddy Hackett

STAMP HELP OUT!

And other short stories

THE POT SMOKERS

BY LENNY BRUCE

SEE... ACTUAL PHOTOS OF TORTURED MARIJUANA! Tes

SEE... HOOKERS RESORT TO PROSTI--TUTION

SEE... SHAME

SEE... SHAME SELL

SEE... SHAME SELL SEA SHELLS AT THE SHIM SHAM!

Lenny Bruce, Publisher, circa 1960

Just as unillusioned as the man he greeted or as Bierce was, Dunne was always lucky in having an appreciative audience. But more significant, even magical, was his own Irish fun-lovingness, a counterweight to all his acerbities. And his humor, readied to dash anybody or anything, had the great good fortune of the saving, objective form he hit upon, including the character finally of Mr. Dooley.

In our perspective today, Dunne comes almost midway in the American saga between the folly of Brackenridge's Teague O'Regan and the wit and charm of John F. Kennedy, between the immigrant scapegoat and the Irish-American President. Dunne left all obsequiousness and folderol behind him but still took querulous, alienated exception to practically all of the terms of American life. The Dooley papers are filled with insurgency, as they also are with vitality, all of a piece as acidic satires against fraud and American pretense, richly comic exercises in archskepticism.

Dooley sets himself firmly against the economic system and all its patriotic blandishments, as in his report *On the Victorian Era.*

"I have seen America spread out fr'm th' Atlantic to th' Pacific, with a branch office iv the Standard Ile Comp'ny in ivry hamlet."

He mightily loosens the connection between Business and Progress.

"An' th' invintions,—th' steam-injine an' th' printin'-press an' th' cotton-gin an' the gin sour an' th' bicycle an' th' flyin'-machine an' . . . —crownin' wur-ruk iv our civilization—th' cash raygisther."

In *Mr. Dooley in Peace and War* (1898–1899) and in all of his turn-of-the-century fusillades, he fires incessantly and with extra glee upon the imperialism that was the shameful consequence of our aggressively expansionist industrial system at home.

"An' afther awhile, whin he gits tired iv th' game, he'll write home an' say he's got the islands; an' he'll tur'rn thim over to th' gover'mint an' go back to his ship, an' Mark Hanna'll organize th' F'lip-ine Islands Jute an' Cider Comp'ny, an' th' rivolutchinists'll wish they hadn't."

His gibes at American profiteering are constant during the early stages of the Spanish-American War.

"No human bein', Hinnissy, can undherstand what the divvle use it was to sink a ship that cost two hundherd thousan' dollars an' was worth at laste eighty dollars in Sandago Harbar, if we have to keep fourteen ships outside to prevint five Spanish ships fr'm sailin'."

And they are just as sharp and pertinent as time goes on.

"We import juke, hemp, cigar wrappers, sugar, an' fairy tales fr'm th' Ph'lippeens, an' export six-inch shells an' th' like."

But these sallies are part of a whole bombardment of American politics and mentality. In the first matter, he sounds as if he is illustrating Bierce's *Dictionary*: "POLITICS, n. A strife of interests masquerading as a contest of principles. The conduct of public affairs for private advantages." Dooley refuses to go and hear McKinley when the self-serving and ignorant President visits Chicago.

"I may niver see him. I may go to me grave without gettin' an' eye on th' wan man besides meself that don't know what th' furrin' policy iv th' United States is goin' to be."

He gets a report of the rally, however, confirming his worst suspicions.

"Th' proceedin's was opened with a prayer that Providence might r-remain undher th' protection iv th' administrhation."

Behind it all, as he knows, is American self-righteousness at the core of our thinking, as he shows in *On War Preparations*.

"Well," Mr. Hennessy asked, "how goes th' war?"
"Splendid, thank ye," said Mr. Dooley. "Fine, fine. It makes me hear-rt throb with pride that I'm a citizen iv th' Sixth Wa-ard."
"We're a gr-reat people," said Mr. Hennessy, earnestly.
"We ar-re," said Mr. Dooley. "We ar-re that. An' th' best iv it is, we know we ar-re."

He has his minority disabusements to go on. He is against going to Alaska for gold because "Whin I was a young man in th' ol' counthrey, we heerd the same story about all America. . . . But, faith, whin I'd been here a week, I seen that there was nawthin' but mud undher th' pavement . . . an' I came west. Th'

on'y mine I sthruck at Pittsburg was a hole f'r sewer pipe. . . .
Me experience with goold minin' is it's always in the nex county."
Cheated and disaffected, he is not one to be taken in, least of all,
as an Irish Catholic, by the Protestant work-ethos. His essay,
On Our Cuban Allies, reaches profundities of exposé in the
matter.

"D'ye raymimber th' sign th' mob carrid in th' procession las' year?
'Give us wurruk, or we perish,' it said. They had their heads bate
in be polismen because no philan-thropist'd come along an' make
thim shovel coal. Now, in Cubia, whin th' mobs turns out, they carry
a banner with the wurruds, 'Give us nawthin' to do, or we perish. . . .'

"Ye can't make people here undherstand that, an' ye can't make
a Cubian undherstand that freedom means th' same thing as a
pinitinchry sintince. Whin we thry to get him to wurruk, he'll say:
'Why shud I? I haven't committed anny crime.' That's goin' to be
th' throuble. Th' first thing we know we'll have another war in
Cubia whin we begin disthributin' good jobs, twelve hours a day,
wan sivinty-five. Th' Cubians ain't civilized in our way. I sometimes
think I've got a touch iv Cubian blood in me own veins."

It may well be that Dunne's steady opposition to American
business, militarism, politics, and custom is a displacement of
both his Irish and Catholic hostility to the English, who left the
brand of WASP on this new world. For when, in *On the French
Character*, he reviews the record of French and English imperialism wreaked upon darkest Africa and Asia, Dooley sides
with the French as the lesser of two evils because they are partly
Celtic and honest, the two qualities more or less equatable. The
English, like the American come-latelies, are all hypocritical
moralism and religiosity.

" 'What ar-re ye doin' here?' says th' Englishman. 'Robbin' th'
naygurs,' says th' Fr-rinch-man, bein' thruthful as well as polite.
'Wicked man,' says th' Englishman. 'What ar-re ye doin' here?'
says the Fr-rinchman. 'Improvin' the morals iv th' inhabitants,' says
the Englishman. 'Is it not so, Rastus?' he says. 'It is,' says wan iv th'
kings. 'I'm poorer but a better man since ye came,' he says. 'Yes,'
says th' Englishman, 'I propose f'r to thruly ray form this onhappy
counthry,' he says.
". . . ' 'Tis shameful they shud go out with nawthin' to hide their
nakedness,' he says. 'I'll fetch thim clothes; but,' he says, 'I'll

not sell thim annything that'll last long,' he says. 'If it wasn't f'r relligion,' he says, 'I don't know what th' 'ell th' wurruld wud come to,' he says."

But liberated from the dominant pietism of the English-speaking world, Dunne is also alienated from the whole question of religion and is Shavian in observations prompted by the Spanish-American War in *On Prayers for Victory*.

"Th' Lord knows how it'll come out. First wan side prays that th' wrath iv Hiven'll descind on th' other, an' thin th' other side returns th' compliment with inthrest. Th' Spanish bishop says we're a lot iv murdherin', irreligious thieves, an' ought to be swept fr'm th' face iv th' earth. We say his people ar-re th' same, an' manny iv thim. . . . We have a shade th' best iv him, f'r his fleets ar-re all iv th' same class an' ol' style, an' we have some iv th' most modhern prayin' machines in the warruld. . . ."

And so Dooley presides as bartender and critic behind his bar on Archy Road. The great and leading questions suffer reduction to the ward level, but the narrowed scope gives him and some of his customers their telling insights, too. What Dooley doesn't choose for discourse on his own he reports secondhand from somebody else, as Donahue's signal rebuff to rising feminism in his own house, in *On the New Woman*.

" ' 'Tis th' era iv th' new woman,' says Mollie. 'Ye're right,' says th' mother. 'What d'ye mean be the new woman?' says Donahue, holdin' his boot in his hand. 'Th' new woman,' says Mollie, ' 'll be free fr'm th' opprision iv man,' she says. 'She'll wurruk out her own way, without help or hinderance,' she says. 'She'll wear what clothes she wants,' she says, 'an' she'll be no man's slave,' she says. 'They'll be no such thing as givin' a girl in marredge to a clown an' makin' her dipindant on his whims,' she says. 'Th' women'll earn their own livin',' she says; 'an' mebbe,' she says, 'th' men'll stay at home an' dredge in th' house wurruk,' she says. 'A-ho,' says Donahue. 'An' that's th' new woman, is it?' he says. An' he said no more that night.

"But th' nex' mornin' Mrs. Donahue an' Mollie come to his dure. 'Get up,' says Mrs. Donahue, 'an' bring in some coal,' she says. 'Ye drowsy man, ye'll be late f'r ye'er wurruk.' 'Divvle th' bit iv coal I'll fetch,' says Donahue. 'Go away an' lave me alone,' he says. 'Ye're inthruptin' me dreams.' 'What ails ye, man alive?' says Mrs. Donahue. 'Get up.' 'Go away,' says Donahue, 'an lave me

slumber,' he says. 'Th' idee iv a couple iv big strong women like
you makin' me wurruk f'r ye,' he says. 'Mollie 'll bring in th' coal,'
he says. 'An' as f'r you, Honoria, ye'd best see what there is in
th' cupboard an' put it in ye'er dinner-pail,' he says. 'I heerd th' first
whistle blow a minyt ago,' he says; 'an' there's a pile iv slag at
th' mills that has to be wheeled off befure th' sup'rintindint comes
around,' he says. 'Ye know ye can't afford to lose ye'er job with
me in this dilicate condition,' he says. 'I'm going to sleep now,'
he says. 'An' Mollie, do ye bring me in a cup iv cocoa an' a pooched
igg at tin,' he says. 'I ixpect me music-teacher about that time.'. . .
'Th' Lord save us fr'm harm,' says Mrs. Donahue. 'Th' man's
clean crazy.' 'Divvle's th' bit,' says Donahue, wavin' his red flannel
undhershirt in th' air. 'I'm the new man,' he says.

   ". . . Mrs. Donahue got nervous as eight o'clock come around.
'Ye're not goin' to stay in bed all day an' lose ye'er job," she says.
'Th' 'ell with me job,' says Donahue. 'I'm not th' man to take
wurruk whin they'se industhrees women with nawthin' to do,'
he says. 'Show me th' pa-apers,' he says. 'I want to see where I can
get an eighty-cint bonnet f'r two and a half.' He's that stubborn
he'd've stayed in bed all day, but th' good woman weakened.
'Come,' she says, 'don't be foolish,' she says. 'Ye wudden't have
th' ol' woman wurrukin' in th' mills,' she says. ''Twas all a joke,'
she says. 'Oh-ho, th' ol' woman!' he says. 'An' I don't mind tellin'
ye th' mills is closed down today, Honoria.' So he dhressed him-
silf an' wint out; an' says he to Mollie, he says: 'Miss Newwoman,'
says he, 'ye may find wurruk enough around th' house,' he says.
'An' if ye have time, ye might paint th' stoop,' he says. 'Th' ol' man
is goin' to take th' ol' woman down be Halsted Sthreet an' blow
himself f'r a new shawl f'r her.' "

And so Dunne adds a certain misogyny to the rest of his antitheses, colorfully localized as the subject has to be.

All of which prompts the question of provincialism in the
humor of this period and in Dunne peculiarly. On one side in
the matter is George Ade, who proceeds in many of his fables
to expose deep-seated mid-western provincialism; he does so
good-naturedly but unmistakably. On the other side is Will
Rogers, who makes the issue into a personal tenet. Paris, he
defines, as "the Claremont, Oklahoma, of France." It is part of
his charm, though when he slowly but surely became a professional American, he hardened his comic attitudes into serious
values and became too literally an isolationist. Between the two

is Dunne's Dooley, at loose ends. Severely provincial as only some urbanites can be,[4] yet he is ferocious in discountenancing every telltale sign of national imperialist provincialism on a world stage. He is comically and sublimely unaware of the resulting disparity.

Such comic doubleness, duplicity even, stands in contrast to the monolithic integrity, catastrophic perhaps but grand and somewhat superhuman, of the classic tragic figure. Mr. Dooley lives in the Sixth Ward of Chicago but projects a higher self to Washington, Havana, and Manila, split into several comic alter egos. A certain unintegration probably, rather than disintegration, recommends the comic spokesman. Of course Dunne is at pains to create a comic character of some objective fascination. And contradiction, a form of internal conflict, is a prime means to the artistic end. But in doing so, almost by the way, he uses Dooley's provincialism, in contrast to the character's liberating imagination otherwise, in a manner that is profoundly instructive.

It is not primarily that Dunne removes himself from Dooley, though that also is true enough. Dooley's anti-intellectualism, for instance, together with his provincialism, keeps him separate from the author. We find Dooley arguing out the question of books with the parish priest. "What ar' ye goin' to do with thim young wans? We're goin' to make thim near-sighted an' round shouldered." But Dunne has the good priest, with a wild catechistic logic of his own, have rather the best of it. So that once again we feel Dooley's adamant position at variance with his good sense. Dooley is only, but supremely, human, a parvenu with stubborn prejudices that he can voice with the same breath he gives to his amazing perspectives and insights. He is variable enough to be one of the ideal representatives of comic human diversity, which always defies strict formulation—and which has always been dearer to our American experience than its opposite. Which means that, in our depths, we believe that we certainly

[4] Fifty years later we meet the same phenomenon, satirized especially in a "New Yorker's Map of the United States": Manhattan is about 500 miles long, outlying suburbia stretches practically to the Mississippi, with the rest of the eastern seaboard and midwest fit in narrowly; the far west appears as an Outer Mongolia, etc. It remains a more or less accurate psychograph as well as satiric comic literalism.

perish as tragic whole men but that we endure in comic bits and pieces.

In these days of renewed American interventionism and tragical heroic saviorism, Dooley recaptures more and more interest as archcritic and satirist. But his topicality will pass, too, and Dooley must abide on the intrinsic grounds of his comic human nature: paradoxically provincial and broad-minded, anti-intellectual but thoughtful, pugnacious but humanitarian, a marvel of self-division but capable of the most concerted singularities of insight and feeling. Dunne's conception of him is one of the finest creations we have after Twain's Huck and Roxy. His portrayal of Dooley alone, all other characters and themes and techniques aside, is both a clue to the essence of humor and one of the triumphs of American practice.

Still, there was evidently more to Dunne's practice than the characterization of Mr. Dooley. His techniques, predominantly verbal, were varied and expert.[5] Apart from being one of the country's greatest dialecticians, Dunne may still be regarded as one of our most tough-headed but flexible technicians.

He is a specialist in anticlimax.

"Winsdah night a second ar-rmy iv injineers, miners, plumbers, an' lawn tinnis experts, numberin' in all four hundherd an' eighty thousan' men, ar-rmed with death-dealin' canned goods, was hurried to Havana to storm th' city." (*On War Preparations*)

. . . . .

"Sure," said Mr. Hennessy, sadly, "we have a thing or two to larn oursilves."

"But it isn't f'r thim to larn us," said Mr. Dooley. " 'Tis not f'r thim wretched an' degraded crathers, without a mind or a shirt iv their own, f'r to give lessons in politeness an' liberty to a nation that manny-facthers more dhressed beef than anny other imperyal nation in th' wurruld." (*Expansion*)

[5] They seem eminently stageable also. *The New Woman* and other dramatical essays could provide interludes with Dooley not only behind his bar lecturing and bamboozling Hennessy, but out on Archy Road fighting with Dorsey, and one might transpose scenes to actual courtroom settings and Democratic rally halls. Updated international and Asian references might give another topical dimension to the political satire. An Holbrookian impersonation of Dooley and an over-all conception like that of *The Thurber Carnival* suggest an inevitable production in the near future.

He turns the trick devastatingly upon General Garcia:

> "... he marched at th' head iv his tin thousan' men down to Sandago de Cuba an' captured a cigar facthry, ... an', when Gin-ral Shafter arrived, there was Gin'ral Garshy with his gallant band iv fifty Cubians, r-ready to eat at a minyit's notice." (*On Our Cuban Allies*)

The device works for self-satire also, as in Dooley's hierarchical library of "Shakespeare, th' Bible, an' Mike Ahearn's histhry iv Chicago." Dunne uses the twin device of undercutting almost as often in his comedy.

> "... as soon as he can have his pitchers took, he will cr-rush th' Spanish with wan blow." (*On War Preparations*)

> "No sooner had th' conspirators landed thin ... Tynan was shadowed be detectives in citizens' clothes; an' whin he was seen out in his backyard practisin' blowin' up a bar'l that he'd dhressed in a shawl an' a little lace cap, th' suspicions growed." (*On A Plot*)

And his frequent use of the comic catalogue relies either on anti-climax—

> "'... with me trusty rifle shootin' down th' buffalo, th' elk, th' kilt, th' wounded, th' missin', an' th' seryously disturbed." (*On the Anglo-Saxon*)

—or partial undercuttings:

> "'... with me trusty rifle shootin' down th' buffalo, th' elk, th' moose, th' grizzly bear, th' mountain goat,' he says, 'th' silver man, an' other ferocious beasts iv thim parts. ...'" (*A Book Review*)

His antiproverbialism is less active than Bierce's but is apparent. "There's only one thing that would make me allow myself to be a hero to the American people," says Dooley, "and that is it don't last long." We might deduce the tendency from his proud and truculent urban cynicism, but it is also a consequence of general reversalism and opposition, as in every other humorist who tries it. In this light, the inveterate enmity between Dooley and the County Mayo man, Dorsey, is deliberate antithetic reversal of Christian, or Protestant, charity and loving-kindness.

Neither Dooley's nor Dorsey's New Year's resolutions of friend-
ship change anything, but that is all right, as Dooley explains to
Hennessy in *On New Year's Resolutions.*

> "Well, I've been thinkin' it over, an' I've argied it out that life'd
> not be worth livin' if we didn't keep our inimies. I can have all th'
> frinds I need. Anny man can that keeps a liquor sthore. But a rale
> sthrong inimy, specially a May-o inimy,—wan that hates ye ha-ard,
> an' that ye'd take th' coat off yer back to do a bad tur-rn to,—is
> a luxury that I can't go without in me ol' days. Dorsey is th' right
> sort. I can't go by his house without being' in fear he'll spill th'
> chimbly down on me head; an', whin he passes my place, he walks
> in th' middle iv th' sthreet, an' crosses himsilf. I'll swear off on any-
> thing but Dorsey. He's a good man, an' I despise him. Here's long
> life to him."

We may observe, incidentally, the instinctive role of aggression,
as Dunne furnishes it to us. This is the deepest kind of cultural
and philosophic reversal. One can't love well if he does not hate
well, too . . . sane Irish candor made to rectify the simple, if not
hypocritical, midwestern American fairy tales of mutual adora-
tion.

> "Whin England purrishes, th' Irish'll die iv what Hogan calls
> ongwee, which is havin' no wan in the weary wurruld ye don't love."
> (*On the French Character*)

The corrective is a legacy of the brawling Old World, one of
the ways in which America has been vitally dependent on first-
generation immigrants, who will not dissolve readily into the
seething mindlessness and indiscriminate, chummy conformity
of any Melting Pot.

Dunne is weaker at literalism than we would expect, though
he has his moments. He cribs "Dooley the Wanst" from Artemus
Ward, and he puns with unmerciful simplicity. He does not care
if Queen Victoria has reigned or "snowed."[6] Typically, however,
he talks about a young man, another "bum vivant," on the make
for a rich woman as his "financée." He deflects to the easy literalist pun in almost any circumstance, as in a political rally
exchange.

---

[6] The particular pun is also used by Bierce in a quatrain on Napoleon.
But there is the slight extra suggestion in Dunne about the icy-cold nature
of his subject, the high wit of pertinence.

" 'Th' inimies iv our counthry has been cr-rushed,' he says, . . . 'Now,' he says, 'th' question is what shall we do with th' fruits iv vichtry?' he says. [A voice, 'Can thim.']" (*On a Speech by President McKinley*)

His best gibes, however, have to rise out of some difficulty, like an extravagant literal war of mules that he describes in Cuba, during which someone observes, "It can't be an American jackass, or he'd speak."

Dunne's verbal comedy was a compound of the greatest brilliance at dialect we have, after Joel Chandler Harris, and much lower forms of oral technique. Like the earlier Billings and his contemporaries, Dunne sometimes labored his orthographic humor unnecessarily, spelling "foot" as "fut," etc. He is not above simple malapropism, as when he describes Chicago after the fire rising "felix-like" from its ashes. And he seeks out the comedy of the misquote: "he's as thrue as th' needle in th' camel's eye, as Hogan says." But his surprising talent at what we have come to call "Dooleymorphisms" is just as much a special technical gift as it is a matter of over-all characterization. Dooley's anti-imperialism extends to the Boer War as well as to the Spanish-American War, and he takes out his scorn for the Dutch and Germans in his contempt for the Bavarian butchershop owner on Archy Road. But Dooleymorphisms also account for the way Dooley's brain works in sheer comic metaphor, so that his description of the universal drunk is inimitably local.

". . . wanst in a while a mimber iv th' club, comin' home a little late an' thryin' to riconcile a pair iv r-round feet with an embroidered sidewalk. . . ." (*On Reform Candidates*)

Dunne is, of course, a partisan of the talltale, his Irish extravagance making him susceptible to the gross and fanciful exaggeration. His comic catalogues often function exuberantly to this point, climaxing a tale that mixes one part blarney to one part frontier-ism (even if we have to go north to get there now).

"What ta-alk have ye?" Mr. Dooley demanded. "A walrus don't fly, foolish man!"

"What does he do, thin?" asked Mr. Hennessy. "Go 'round on crutches?"

"A walrus," said Mr. Dooley, "is an animal something like a

hor-rse, but more like a balloon. It doesn't walk, swim, or fly. It rowls whin pur-suin' its prey. It whirls 'round an' 'round at a speed akel to a railroad injine, meltin' th' ice in a groove behind it. Tame walruses are used be th' Eskeemoyoos, th' old settlers iv thim parts, as lawnmowers an' to press their clothes. Th' wild walrus is a mos' vicious animal, which feeds on snowballs through th' day, an' thin goes out iv nights afther artic explorers, which for-rms its principal diet. Theyse a gr-reat demand among walruses fr artic explorers, Swedes preferred; an' on account iv th' scarcity iv this food it isn't more than wanst in twinty years that th' walrus gets a square meal. Thin he devours his victim, clothes, collar-buttons, an' all." (*On Nansen*)

Inevitably there are marks of the outré in such interludes.

"To march well, a man's feet have to be mates; an' if he has two left feet both runnin' sideways, he ought to have interference boots to keep him fr'm setting fire to his knees." (*On Political Parades*)

Now and then the outlandish and slightly macabre come together.

" 'Why, man alive,' I says, 'Charter Haitch was assassinated three years ago,' I says. 'Was he?' says Dugan. 'Ah, well, he's lived that down be this time. He was a good man,' he says." (*On Reform Candidates*)

Dunne's greatest departure from Bierce, who is really the exception in the period, lies in his democratic attitudes. Dooley is a triumphant commoner, and all tirades against generals and monarchs and the like are of a piece with his democratic bias and the deflationism it breeds. He is also inclined, as Bierce is not, to self-deprecation (simultaneous with Queen Victoria's Diamond Celebration is Dooley's "rhinestone jubilee"). And quite separate from Bierce's high style, against which Bierce like the southwesterners had to defend himself, is the totally democratic vocabulary, rhythm, and tone of Dunne's language. The Irish American's antirhetorical thrusts are pure and genuine parodies, as when he travesties McKinley's oratory.

" 'We can not tur-rn back,' he says, 'th' hands iv th' clock that, even as I speak,' he says, 'is r-rushin' through th' hear-rts iv men,' he says, 'dashin' its spray against th' star iv liberty an' hope, an' no north, no south, no east, no west, but a steady purpose to do th' best we can, considerin' all th' circumstances iv the case,' he says."

An avowed admirer of Bill Nye, Dunne was probably influenced by the whole deflationary technique of the literary comedians. But there is so much his own in his immigrant, urban, and democratic talent that there is less value than usual in pointing out influences except to indicate the continuity of American humor.

The *Fables in Slang* (1899) and *More Fables in Slang* (1900) of George Ade (1866–1944) are of the same vintage as the best work of Dunne, whom Ade admired and whose colloquial journalistic humor in the Second City stimulated him greatly. Without the extra charge of immigrant disillusion, Ade partakes of the ruling skepticism and even cynicism, though his Indiana softness and total good-naturedness make him deceptive. His hometown settings and hometown snapshots of the big city take the edge off his cynicism, but that cynicism was constantly moralized, and accounted for more than half of his appeal across the nation. "Always count your change," he wrote characteristically; and he added to our growing tradition of negative wisdom, "and if you can't be good, be careful."

His comedy is both gentle and biting, and judgment of no one else in American humor is more slippery and difficult. His way of withholding the force of his antipathies puts off the strong-minded of a later day. As a result his audacities appear often as merely Victorian dares, which not only do not shock us but set us against his courageless bravery.

These are not indefinable feelings we have but arise from defects of his expression, which is frequently too careful for all of the slangy manner. "It is proper," he concludes one of his fables, "to enjoy the Cheaper Grades of Art, but they should not be finally Indorsed." He does not really mean that plebeian and pretentious taste is even "all right," yet he says "proper"; his own ironic exception to it is finally not strong enough to cancel his own partial indorsement, which his phraseology signifies. In addition, a great amount of his moralizing elsewhere is deliberately unpointed or fearfully evasive.

On the other hand, he can be explicit enough on occasion. "Get a good make-up and the part plays itself." Sometimes in between Bierce's thematic antidemocracy, on one side, and Dunne's popular inclinations and democratic warranty of vernacular, on the other, he pushes himself to the sarcasm of the former. "Give the people what they think they want," he writes with eruptive contempt, though, as Bierce implied, Ade gave them just that.

We may phrase our judgment another way. His procedure was not exactly to tread a thin line between involvement and noninvolvement but to jump back and forth between sympathy and castigation. He had no "periods" in so doing but alternated constantly. He is a genialist and a nihilist simultaneously. At the risk of offending a small band of intense loyalists, which includes such modern aseptics as Jean Shepherd and S. J. Perelman, we may conclude that he missed greatness in his careerlong strategy of such alternation. He did not seek—in fact, he avoided—the thematic and tonal synthesis that indicates the courage of genius, with all the hazards it runs. He would not take the supreme compacted chance. His moral, "Don't try to account for everything," is the safest nihilism, the diminuendo of cliché rather than the innuendo of full wit.

His readers tend to fall into two groups, the totally indifferent and the fanatic. The indifference is not wholly a consequence, as his addicts claim, of the topicality we must break through or of much of the dated language; we can recover his allusions and provide our current substitutes for his slang. The indifference is a response to Ade's deeper liabilities: his tentativeness, his withdrawals, his alternations, his safeness. These qualities are displayed in his on-and-off-again misogyny and anti-intellectualism and in his wavering between active antiproverbialism and the simplest bromides.

But if he misses greatness for these reasons, he earns second place to it, and that is very high. It is high enough for him to retain the loyalists he still has, comic writers themselves and lay readers who enjoy endless coterie talk about which of his pieces is the essential Ade. Is it "The Fable of Sister Mae, who Did as Well as Could Be Expected," concerning the more shapely of two sisters who married well and took her hard-working, plain

sister from a Hat Factory at $3 a week and made her an assistant
cook at home for $5? The moral is the purest lemonAde: "Industry
and Perseverance bring a sure Reward." Or is it "The Fable of the
Caddy who Hurt His Head While Thinking," the closest Ade
gets to expressing bitterness about the economic system, The
Way Things Are? Never mind, but his fierce partisans have a
point. It is the idea that in his more antithetical pieces Ade did
discover a singular mode of covert and comprehensive attack.
Which is to say that, at his best, he did the peculiar American
thing again, achieving a certain subtlety for all of his overtness.
"Early to bed, and early to rise is a bad rule for people who
want to get acquainted with our most prominent persons," he
wrote, giving not only the easy lie to Franklin but the more
difficult one to prominent persons and to 90 per cent of the rest
of us who do want their acquaintance.

The closer one looks, the more he is drawn into the coterie,
and commences his own search for the quintessential Ade of the
clever, devious, and committed comedian. Of the restricted but
pulverizing canon of these works, one may choose "The Patient
Toiler Who Got It in the Usual Place."

Once there was an Office Employee with a Copy-Book Education.
He believed it was his Duty to learn to Labor and to Wait.

He read Pamphlets and Magazine Articles on Success and how to
make it a Cinch. He knew that if he made no Changes and never
beefed for more Salary, but just buckled down and put in Extra
Time and pulled for the House, he would Arrive in time.

The Faithful Worker wanted to be Department Manager. The
Hours were short and the Salary large and the Work easy.

He plugged on for many Moons, keeping his Eye on that Roll-
Top Desk, for the Manager was getting into the Has-Been Division
and he knew there would be a Vacancy.

At last the House gave the old Manager the Privilege of retiring
and living on whatever he had saved.

"Ah, this is where Humble Merit gets its Reward," said the
Patient Toiler. "I can see myself counting Money."

That very Day the Main Gazooks led into the Office one of the
handsomest Tennis Players that ever worked on Long Island and
introduced him all around as the new Department Manager.

"I shall expect you to tell Archibald all about the Business," said
the Main Gazooks to the Patient Toiler. "You see he has just gradu-

ated from Yale and he doesn't know a dum Thing about Managing anything except a Cat-Boat, but his Father is one of our principal Stock-Holders and he is engaged to a Young Woman whose Uncle is at the head of the Trust."

"I had been hoping to get his Job for myself," said the Faithful Worker, faintly.

"You are so valuable as a Subordinate and have shown such an Aptitude for Detail Work that it would be a Shame to waste you on a $5,000 Job," said the Main Gazooks. "Besides you are not Equipped. You have not been to Yale. Your Father is not a Stock-Holder. You are not engaged to a Trust. Get back to your High Stool and whatever Archibald wants to know, you tell him."

The expense of satire is on *both* the undeserving beneficiary of the corrupt system and on the Faithful Worker who also wants the short hours, large salary, and easy work. The moral is, "One who wishes to be a Figure-Head should not Overtrain." In his portrait of the self-seeking individual out for spoils. Ade's undoctrinaire point of view finally does achieve the singular compaction of a classless, annihilating attack. In the midst of the caterwauling Progressivist era, which helped along much of the realistic humor of the time, he takes his comic exception to combative reformism and to the Jeffersonianism behind it. In fables like "The Patient Toiler" and "What Our Public Schools and the Primary System Did for a Poor but Ambitious Youth," he brings forward his view of a useless artificial plutocracy and a useless natural plutocracy. This "inside" group of fables is a testament to the processes of Poetic Injustice, and Ade's cynicism and pessimism are under such utter control that we scarcely detect all that is going on.

It is with these pieces on our mind that we can accept his theoretical conclusions about himself. He thought he was more a realist than a humorist. But the comic art is there, too. His aim was to tell the truth, he said, and get some fun out of it. But he did not want to be brutal in the process. His is the first of American theories absolutely commensurate with practice, so long as we select the illustrations for his strongest intentions. One gains enthusiasm for the essential Ade and has only to guard against overreading the rest of him.

Among Ade's techniques none is at once more flamboyant

and understated than his portrayal of people like animals. Just perceptibly his men and women are bumbling bears, little foxes, hungry wolves, or frightened rabbits. There are cheetahs, American bald eagles, sloths, possums, old hens, wild cats, and cunning lynx portrayed in these overgrown glades of American life. His central device constitutes one of the most extreme and subtle technical reversals in our humor.

Ade's extravagant verbal comedy makes use of extended comic metaphor and original Crockettry. A man suffering a hangover feels "like a steamradiator and somebody had gone down the drain to repair it." In addition to conventionalisms of exaggeration like, "a bowie knife as big as a spade," goes the immortal description of the outskirts of an ugly and vicious-minded small town where, from the swamp, "the Bacilli were croaking loudly."

His investment in slang brings diminishing returns, of course, because it dates quickly and leads him also to hackneyed phrases he cannot enliven at every point. By the same token, however, few humorists show so much concreteness of expression, a perquisite of his method. In the course of things, he originates certain popular concrete truisms, himself, in the comedy of absurd and extravagant literalism and the metaphorical wisecrack.

". . . [he] couldn't jump out a Boat and hit the Water. . . ."
". . . he had a Dim Idea that any one wearing a Tuxedo would have to cut out the tan shoes. . . ."

We must also recognize that some of the topical disability of his slang was mitigated even in his own day by amusing cryptological effects, some of them neologistic and ingenious: "moca in feathers" = "coffee in bed." And those unsystematic capital letters,[7] which he hoped would signal to everyone his literate play with slang, sometimes contributed directly to satiric highlighting, as in his grouping of elite social matrons in the "Society of Large Gloomy Ladies." But, most of all, we return to his unyielding specificity of style in general. At a church social, convened to repair the church:

[7] Probably the example of Eugene Field influenced both Ade and Bierce in their fables.

Mr. Frisbie and three other Pillars of the Church devoted $7 worth of valuable Time to unloading Tables and Camp-Stools.

The Women Folks ruined $14 worth of Complexion working in the hot Kitchen to make Angel Food and Fig Cake.

On the Night of the Raspberry Orgy the Public Trampled down $45 worth of shrubbery.

When it came time to check up the Linen and Silverware it was found that $17 worth of Spoons with Blue Thread tied around them had been lost in the Shuffle.

The Drip from the Candles ruined $29 worth of Summer Suits and Percale Shirt-Waists.

. . . . .

After clearing the Wreck, paying the Drayman and settling for the Ice Cream and Berries, it was discovered that the Church was $6.80 to the Good. So everybody said it was a Grand Success. ("The Fable of the Good People Who Rallied to the Support of the Church")

All the vitalizing details and figures are there. And the lesson about self-righteous busy-ness and the superfluous but enormous need for extra self-proof is phrased with immediate and concrete expression: "Anything to avoid dropping it in the Basket." That, too, is the essential Ade, who finds his very wit often in the concrete literalism of the language, as in his moral to "The Fable of the Good Fairy with the Lorgnette . . .": "In uplifting, get underneath."[8]

We are scarcely surprised to find Ade practicing the anti-rhetorical mode very often. He does so most handily in satirizing novelistic and romantic sentimentalism, as Bierce did. In "The Fable of the Girl Who Could Compromise in a Pinch," the over-literary girl thinks over her requirements:

"The Man who wins my Cardiacal Regard must be Tall and Dark with Raven Hair tossed back from a Brow of Alabaster Whiteness.

[8] Nevertheless, it is also true that whole pieces, like "The Fable of How Gertrude Could Keep it Up until Ten O'clock in the Morning," are dedicated to the simple pun: "Any Kind of conversation goes in a clinch."

THE RISE AND FALL OF AMERICAN HUMOR

> . . . He must be Brave yet Gentle . . . a Chesterfield as to Manners.
> . . . Withal . . . Strong and Manly. . . ."

> That evening a Red-Headed Boy wearing striped Flannels . . .
> came to the Front Gate and Whistled. She upset four Flower Pots
> in getting to him.

The phrase "Cardiacal Regard" is affected periphrasis similar to
legalistic inflation. Such travesty occurs by the way in a great
deal of Ade's expression. Once again, as in the southwestern
humorists, lawyers' language is a particular model of rhetoric
coming under attack, as it frequently is in Bierce and in Dunne.
(The latter, in "On Expert Testimony," is most explicit.) Ade is
less sustained on this subject, but it keeps cropping up as an
adjacent interest related to these other rhetorical targets in his
work.

In the final analysis, an addiction to Ade may not be inevitable. But an indifference to him certainly isn't. Basically vulgar
and somewhat contemptible as he appeared to Bierce, he struck
William Dean Howells forcibly as an absolute realist. We may
have our doubts about the comprehensiveness and consistency of
his thematic realism, but, with Howells, none about his subject
matter and character types. We may gauge the great risk he took
with ultracolloquial language, but are more inclined than Bierce
simply to measure rather than condemn it. His two books of
fables qualify and rank him with Bierce and Dunne. And their
mass appeal, along with that of the work of Dunne, Hubbard,
and Rogers, is another indication of the meteoric rise of a
broad, popularly based humor.

Ade's later stage-comedy writing was workmanlike and popular, though not distinguished. But it illustrates his willingness
to go on experimenting out in the open. He accepted and embraced musical comedy and vaudeville competition, as indeed he
had welcomed the newspaper cartoons decorating his daily
fables. The comic strip was coming into its own, the Follies were
catching on. Although the high point of his own career was
well behind him, and insurmountable even if he had turned
around to try again, he moved out of the welter of successful
comic journalism toward an age of moving flickers and radio
static, settling for Broadway. It is a career marked by experiment,

but his work was not deepened by such venturesomeness. For that reason primarily it missed greatness . . . but, in the more valuable *Fables,* not by much.

More and more the period became a time of accelerative mass entertainment. The serialized Sunday supplement stories of William S. Porter ("O. Henry" 1862–1910), were phenomenally successful. Kin Hubbard's popular rural comic philosopher, Abe Martin, with his whiskers and striped trousers in accompanying cartoon drawings, appeared regularly in the newspapers; he was a retrenchment of the American ideal, Downingesque and Lincolnian in his countrified wit and his very appearance as Uncle Sam. And on stage and later in the movies, the man with the lasso, Will Rogers, rose the whole distance in American iconography, reaching the pinnacle of comic idolatry in the late twenties and early thirties.

Fundamental sentimentalists, or vice versa, as they were, these men had nonetheless a touch of potent skepticism in their natures. Porter's technique of the abrupt surprise ending, coupled with a measure of realism, often brought him to the very ledge of sharp irony and nihilistic reversal. Indeed, his influence on early and abiding storylines in American movies needs study. Right through the thirties and into the forties, men like Frank Capra in Hollywood would find themselves directing scripts originally laid out by Porter and imitated endlessly in scenarios. Porter's famous "The Gift of the Magi" is a stunning example of what a remorseless American Maupassant could do in conclusive self-corruption; if we dare discount the happy resolution, the story is a marvel of hard comic reversal, exactly as fifty-five minutes of Capra's best films are later on. Since the conclusions are usually not inevitable, they do not really determine the structure of at least half of Porter's stories. The barely rescued endings are bourgeois denials, more hopeless than hopeful in their last-minute extravagance, of the facts that the comic realist saw quite clearly. His real stories, from an artistic as well as thematic point of view, are the central stories within arbitrary stories, and they are replete with despair (as in the "Magi" piece) or cynicism (as in "Mammon and the Archer").

A local colorist of New York City, Porter willfully made himself into the Bret Harte of Gotham, with devices subsequently elaborated by his successor, Damon Runyon: the picturesque names for eccentric characters who are deliberately robbed of interiority, the Broadway speech (Runyon's later and particular exploitation), and the pervasive sentimentality. Unquestionably Porter made a career of corrupting his vision, all the greater sin because he had the vision. He also had the talent[9] that Ambrose Bierce lacked, being able to objectify and dramatize in an infinitely varied manner. He allows himself occasionally to break through, particularly in stories which his lower middle class could condescend to. "The Cop and the Anthem" is the tale of Soapy, the Chaplinesque reformed tramp who cannot stay out of jail even when he decides truly to make his way in the wintry world. But Porter's major influence is pernicious. There is no greater essential apostasy in American literature than his, Sinclair Lewis' included. His nearly complete commercial and sentimental debasement is an omen of how much the pressures against integrity continue to mount in the twentieth century.

Kin Hubbard (1868–1930) is no apostate, though the case of his friend, Will Rogers, is another matter again. Hubbard's character, Abe Martin, was simply a George Ade who stayed home. He is not very forceful down on the farm, but he takes his modest place in a field of wry. "Some folks get credit for havin' horse sense that ain't ever had enough money to make fools o' themselves." And he has a slight gift at the concrete expression of gentle skepticism: "There's always somebody at any dinner that eats all the celery."

In this period, which includes the muckraking era, there is little surprise in tracing the strong careers of humorists like Bierce, Dunne, and Ade. The surprise is that the mild and rural Hubbard should be popular at all in a time of highly antithetic or ascendant urban comedy. Or that, later in this period and into the next, Will Rogers (1879–1935) should rise to such bland

[9] He had his meretricious stylistic tendencies, as did Bierce. But his polysyllabic vocabulary was a premeditated and effective device rather than a defense mechanism. It was meant, as was the old orthographic technique, for newly educated audiences to savor. He was not strictly culpable in this regard, for we allow a writer any contemporary stylistic means to his end. That end, however, must be inviolably his own.

heights of fame. This stubborn optimist, who "never met a man I didn't like," seemed subsequently unmoved by Al Capones in the Prohibition and Depression years and serenely unaware of imminent evil from Hitlerite gangsters overseas. But his incognizance was a result of his professionalizing himself as a native American, even to an indecent Cherokee pride. In so doing, he appears as the rural counterpart of O. Henry, sublimely and ruthlessly subduing his innate talent and clarity of mind. More and more, he became the occasionally irreverent critic but increasingly genial and harmless western type. Indeed, his reputation is established and even monumentalized in the larger than life sculpture of him at Colorado Springs, that Rocky Mountain resort of the elderly and fond-hearted.

Both the success of Kin Hubbard and the phenomenon of Will Rogers can be explained, however, as the result of nostalgia in a period of accelerated urban growth. It was emphatically the time of the first growth of our cities, when the urban humorist and cosmopolitan satirist were superseding the crackerbox philosophers and all country types. Even O. Henry's citified stories are a clue to the change of taste and public. Bierce operates out of San Francisco (before disappearing over the Mexican border in complete renunciation of all American drab and drivel), heralding the great iconoclast who will by main force root himself in his city on the opposite coast, Baltimore's Mencken. Dunne's Dooley is the archetype of them all; Brackenridge's comic butt became a critical force to be reckoned with down the block. Even the deep-dyed Hoosier, George Ade, moves into the big city. Such profound demographic shifts, however, do not occur at once or without regret for the old crackerbox humor. During transition the public values the fading types, all the more as they become anachronized.

In the case of the Oklahoman, the substitution of the cowboy for the customary rural figure, coincident with early silent movie exploitation of the simple, wise, and mythic cowboy hero, presented an irresistible prototype. Rogers worked cannily at the individualism inhering in his character. To do him justice, he did in fact write and rewrite all his material, happy as a later columnist to get "one good gag a month." He did not lend himself to organization in the subsequent manner of most radio comics, who were actors primarily. He was still, and at least, his own comedian. And Hubbard acknowledged his supersedence: "the only time when having enough rope didn't end disastrously." True to their mutual last stand for the provincial, countrified type, Rogers would set himself explicitly against urban and industrial pressures and that symbol of New America, the Ford car, an image for standardization. All these Fords came like their drivers, with "the same parts, the same upholstery and the same noises." Sophisticated contemporary sociologists would have predicted the emergence of Rogers and succeeding variants of the type, (Hal Kinney, Andy Griffith, Herb Shriner), who diminish in number and force but run true to form. The disappointment we feel is that whatever was genuinely shrewd and sharp in Rogers turned almost willfully antiseptic. The man who wrote, or culled from Thoreau, the definition of America as "a nation that flourished 1900–1942, conceived many odd inventions for getting somewhere, but could think of nothing to do when they got there" had a comic and satiric view which the limelight could only blind. At all events, that is what happened.

If it had not happened, he would have fit himself solidly into the main comedy of the period and not become a sentimental apologist. Bierce, for instance, had spared some of his time to attack pedantic pretensions. "EVERLASTING, adj. Lasting forever." And Dunne lets Dooley swing at what he thinks is a modish intellectualism. "I cud write pomes that'd make Shakespeare an' Mike Scanlan think they were wur-rkin' on a dredge . . . Life, says ye! There's no life in a book." Rogers was with them early, and his phraseology had just the little sting it needed for authenticity.

> "Shucks, I didn't know they was buyin' grammar now. . . . I had a notion it was thoughts and ideas. . . . I'm just an ignorant feller, without any education. . . . but I try to know what I'm talking about."

Later, his self-deprecation was to become much more insulated and rather harmless.

But his authentic irreverence was instant and sharp. If Dunne went after McKinley and even Theodore Roosevelt in national life, Rogers could follow suit. In his Downingesque association with great men he was introduced to President Coolidge and leaned forward to say, "I didn't catch the name." His endless gibes at Congress were traditional and more than a little safe, but he took his place with Dunne when he attacked Republicanism, a state of mind that had grown more than political. Still, there is no doubt that he had joy in the main thing as well as in the overtones. "Ohio claims they are due a President," he remarked on Harding's candidacy. "Look at the United States. They haven't had one since Lincoln." His literalism and comic momentum, like Groucho Marx's later, were most promising. "The nation is prosperous on the whole. But how much prosperity is there in a hole?"

But he moved away from the dangers of epitheticism and chose caution in generalized commentary. His punning could still serve comic pertinence—"The United States never lost a war or won a conference"—but he is carefully not hurting anybody. He might join the Anti-Bunk Party and oppose Prohibition, but he was already dropping the role of a Jack Downing and becoming the Uncle Tom of American humor. He accomplished the change-over mainly by indulging the self-mockery he had always been prone to but that no longer carried the outer criticism he had attached to it. His genuine pertinence and irreverence decreased.[10] He became lovable. The touches even of misogyny, relatively safe and expected by now, were dropped. Whenever he reverted to his role of prankster, it served the purposes of an almost exclusive insulation he was after. His use of an active alarm clock during his appearances on the stage and in the early days of radio was affected self-criticism; he was making secure fun of his garrulousness.

How far he had come from what he might have been in the contemporary mold and in the tradition of American humor is signaled by an illuminating contrast between him and Thoreau, whom he probably read at one time secretly in his dressing room. If he then took the author of *Walden* as a model for his definition of a feckless America, he later used him almost as an antitext. "I never met a man I didn't like" is practically the deliberated

---

[10] He was less and less willing and able to observe in the old manner that we "shot [Mexicans] in the most cordial way possible," wanting "only their good will . . . and oil and coffee."

annulment of Thoreau's expression, "I have never yet met a man who was quite awake."

His complete recantation of antithetical humor and the comic criticism he had imaged in the Ford car is neatly symbolized for us in his later enthusiasm for American aviation, especially after Lindbergh's patriotic flight; he died in a fateful air crash with Wiley Post. But the man who perished then with the adventuring pilot was a man of such inveterate good will and optimistic faith that, it seems now, only the cruelest comic vengeance could have dashed him to earth. At that moment, in truth, we lost a potential America Firster instead of the anti-Bunkist. But we must avoid the mysticism of condemnation, which is as tempting as that of celebration, and merely summon up the first half of his career to counteract his decline and his sentimental enshrinement in Colorado. What is petrified for us there is only the apostate he was durably becoming in his last years, and not the humorist he had been. Thus his violent end remains saddening to two different groups of appreciators for entirely separate and opposed reasons.

The techniques of the masquerade and alter ego continue in this period. The most famous of all apotheoses is already under way in Chaplin's early movie experiments as the tramp. The clown's disguise is protective and operates as a traditional reflex. But certain features of leading comedians in this period indicate another purpose of masquerade. The device appears as a means of doubling the effect of one's comic criticism in reversed consideration of its unlikely source. Even Bierce's masks as a spontaneous lexicographer, as a casual columnist of antietiquette, as a criminal and insouciant murderer are to the point. But I refer mainly to Dunne's not so mere bartender, Mr. Dooley, who presides over Chicago and the world; to George Ade, whose high-flown slang and topicality on occasion barely conceal unsuspected depths; to Kin Hubbard, whose Abe Martin—"The safest way t' double you money is t' fold it over once. . . ."—is not always the dyed-in-the-wool comic patriot he is painted to be; and to Will Rogers as the uneducated cowboy, in the old orthographic mold of comic writing, who is not so inarticulate in print or on stage as his slow drawl at first suggests. They all take the technical risk of putting us off, like every one of Shakespeare's wise fools, in order to put us on. Their low estate, their offhandedness, their self-deprecation, their very speech all function to this purpose, another one of our ties to the past. They even wear their caps or cowboy hats or shabby derbies, and they jingle their bells or drum their bartender's spoon or strum their banjos (and soon, in one notable case, a harp); only the dimensions and complexion of the court are changed. They are all democratic clowns, and their wisdom rather than foolishness is uppermost.

For they are all, at their best, gentle or excoriative critics, not fundamentally comic butts. It is true that Dunne uses the boob, Hennessy, as a foil to Dooley, but that technique highlights the penetrative Dooley all the more as central figure and commentator. Ade has few hesitancies as a broad social critic, and Bierce certainly none at all. Even Hubbard and Rogers are rarely confused as to function, only rather withholding in their astringencies and then, in Rogers, becoming something else entirely. At various times in their careers, whether they admired or carped at one another, they took their places in a democratic chorus of comic and satiric critique of the national scene.

That scene, an outgrowth of the Civil War and its aftermath, particularly our rampant industrial imperialism, became focused for most of the successors of the literary comedians and Twain in McKinleyism. George V. Hobart's character, Dinkelspiel, joins Dooley (and Howells and all the liberals of the period, including immigrant German Socialists) in concerted attack, as on the "Bresident uf der Union Sdades und der Philly-peanuts Islands, mit der exception of dot part vich Nnoggynaldo is using to run avay on." Taken all together, our scandalous international adventurism, our uncontrolled capitalism, our manifest destiny absorbed into the more generalized doctrine of progress, our scientific and technological as well as political mythicism, our pieties, our romantic and matriarchal idolatries, our sentimentalisms, all made for a conglomerate body of false cultural lore, under the aegis of Republicanism, that realistic comedy brought under eager and often vituperative attack.

It is no coincidence that such directness as appears in the

satirical humor of the period was sheltered by its third force in America, the Progressivists. Nor is it a surprise that the general headquarters of most of the urban comedians, like Dunne and Ade, was the biggest city in the Progressivist region of the country, Chicago, also the nexus then for the Realist movement in our literature. What the combined groups had in common, the serious Realistic writers and the Progressivist reformers and the satiric commentators, was a powerful sense of scandal and hypocritical lies. The humorists had not only a tradition of exposé in their own right by now but a heady if localized atmosphere to breathe in.

But the first Roosevelt and Woodrow Wilson worked a change that broke the necessity for their alliance. Only much later would they learn that such reforms and changes as were won strengthened a more subtle adversary in American life than they had uncovered, one that would change shape only to hold on more invidiously than ever. That, plus the World War for "democracy" and national survival, which temporarily canceled out all true third forces, accounted for the loss of Progressivist support in particular. The essential connection between American humor and Realism would continue, often in the same man; but humorists and literary Realists would be unhoused, as it were, to become again minstrels and prophets abroad in the wide land. Had a Bull Moose Roosevelt[11] or an Ickes or a La Follette become President, the course and character of both our humor and literature would have changed abruptly and radically. But so would everything else, for that would have meant a decisive revolution of politics and mores.

William Dean Howells—not an ineffectual humorist himself in his novels, also the prime mover of Realism, and also a Socialist—understood and appreciated what men like Dunne and Ade were doing. He was eager to tell them that they were writing for *cognoscenti* as well as for less sophisticated but also responsive masses. His encouragement was lavish, perhaps a little desperate, but acute. He perceived the incalculable advantage to both courageous literary Realism and regenerative social thought of such allies as the humorists.

[11] During his Republican Presidential Administration, Theodore Roosevelt had, in fact, read Dunne delightedly.

But, as some of us believe, a continuing alliance with a socio-political group in particular would have been disastrous for our humor and probably for the liberal thinkers and activists as well. Programmism is a threat to all individualism, but comic originality and freedom suffer most. The humorist, particularly in America, is in the anomalous position of needing to fight a perpetual fight but never to win it. He feeds on the frustration that may even tire or bore him at last. It is the price he pays as gadfly. This is not to say that the country itself would not have been a more just and happy land had Howells' political and social hopes been fully realized. That is a moot question, outside our provenance. But we may echo Twain in observing simply that there would have been less need for humor after such social victory, since nobody laughs in heaven. That does not rationalize hell, of course. It does not mean that adversity automatically produces humor. After a certain point, affliction is demoralizing. But it is also true to a certain extent that beneficence disarms humor; the Swiss and the Scandinavians are not the funniest people in the world.

Be that as it may, the realistic character of humor in America is another matter entirely. The two strains seem intrinsically connected. That is because Realism, aside from the highly codifiable and determinist Naturalism temporarily attached to it for a certain period in American thought,[12] is also the freest of viewpoints and expressions. It is also individualist; even when it attends "schools," it is not quite tractable or predictable in its varied allegiences to truth telling. It may sell its virtue more easily than humor does, mistress to romantic Expressionists, but such uses do not obscure its blood relationship to humor. As a

[12] There is a variety of seriocomic nihilism, however, among certain Naturalists, like Stephen Crane. That is tonally and thematically evident in much of his fiction (in the greater part of "The Blue Hotel" and in all of "The Bride Comes to Yellow Sky," for example). And it is true for a great deal of his verse, where devices of humor lighten his heavy-laden and sardonic expression of universal indifference.

> A man said to the universe:
> "Sir, I exist!"
> "However," replied the universe,
> "The fact has not created in me
> A sense of obligation."

In such ways Crane is a not-so-distant cousin of Bierce.

purely literary spokesman, Howells was most astute in detecting the bond (as he was perceptive also, very early, about Twain).

The colloquial style, for example, whether flat midwestern or metropolitan, united practically all the humorists of the time in realistic endeavor. Hubbard's restrained use of Indiana dialect and Dunne's high-fidelity reproduction of Chicago Irish speech represent rural and urban agreements on technique. Less strict and local are Will Rogers' westernisms and George Ade's unabashed slang. There is no doubt that Twain and his predecessors gave this group an inherited and ample warrant to practice realistic speech. But they were supported further by the same Howells who encouraged Stephen Crane and Frank Norris and were buoyed by knowing they were no longer practicing an offbeat and peculiar expression.

Moreover, they thought of their own realism as something more than linguistic. It usually is, but their avowals at this juncture are significant. Dunne's Dooley sounds as if he is issuing a minor literary manifesto, which is quite the case.

> " 'Y're goin' to have thim believe that, if they behave thimselves an' lead a virchous life, they'll marry rich an' go to Congress. They'll wake up some day, an' find out that gettin' money an behavin' ye'ersilf don't always go together,' I says. 'Some iv th' wickedest men in th' wur-ruld have marrid rich,' I says. . . . 'Ye're goin' to teach thim that a la-ad with a curlin' black mustache an' smokin' a cigareet is always a villyan, whin he's more often a barber with a lar-rge family. . . . If ye want to show thim what life is, tell thim to look around thim. There's more life on a Saturdah night in th' Ar-rchy Road thin in all th' books fr'm Shakespeare to th' rayport iv th' drainage thrustees.' " (On Books)

Ade openly called himself a Realist, trusting that his attempts at psychology and negative philosophy were really the heart of the matter, his deflationism more characteristic of his better things than his playfulness. And Hubbard's Abe Martin and the more relevant efforts of Rogers are consciously in the mode of skeptical wisdom.

Final validations came naturally from Howells, the custodian of the generic movement. His was the ultimate certification of the real artistry involved. He bestowed it on Ade for Ade's "absolute" portrayal of setting and native types. But he reserved the very highest of his kind of praise for Dunne, acknowledging Dunne's comic maturity in the essential way: Mr. Dooley was always realistically in character, never falsified, never merely an instrument.

Taken together, Bierce, Dunne, and Ade are figures to be reckoned with. They constitute no transition in American humor but the on-going thing itself. With the impetus of post-Civil War humor behind them and with the encouragement for Dunne and Ade of an almost formalized movement of Realism and of an embattled immigrant and Progressivist public as special audience and host, they yet maintained the force of idiosyncrasy that qualifies them most. They contribute full strength to that comic momentum that describes the whole acceleration of American humor, propelling it forward from the single genius, Twain, to the period ahead of them, the most varied and productive of all in American humor. Bierce's infanticide suffers only the slightest diminution in Benchley and W. C. Fields, and his horrific reversalisms have their studied counterpart in Charles Addams; Dunne's wit is metamorphosed in Fred Allen; and Ade's fabulosities re-emerge in Thurber and Thurber's successor, Perelman. Mencken, Lardner, and Chaplin take root in the latter part of the period. The vigor and continuities abound, and the overlap of careers is indicative. From an intercentury period that is a falling off not in talent but only in numbers, we pass to the interwar period of the fullest array of numbers and diversity in our history.

VI

Interwar Humor

NOBODY who accepts a review of the past is apt to sit perfectly still when the material comes within the circle of living memory. There are those who are gifted with a total recall of broadcast interludes, of whole sequences of silent movies, and of some of the sound tracks of the thirties; and they can quote passages of Benchley, Marquis, and Thurber as well. They may accord the evidence that follows all the force of private whimsy. No refuge will serve, especially in these days of mass paperback reprints and film clubs and TV reruns. Only a naïve author dares count on human forgetfulness and inaccuracy about the interwar period. At the same time we are helped by the *cognoscenti*. Their very existence confirms general grounds of belief that the twenties and thirties represent a culmination of American humor. For the uninitiated or unmindful, the task is as it has been, a matter of demonstration. For the knowledgeable and forebearing, the questions of continuity and development may absolve us of haphazard illustration.

Our designation of the interwar era is in itself a convenience, for the period includes figures who rose before and during World War I and careers that continue after World War II. So is the division of the survey into parallel studies of literary humorists and mass-media performers. This is all the more arbitrary for an intrinsic reason, quite apart from instant surmise. I do not refer to the fact that literary humorists were popularly appearing in mass-circulation newspapers, magazines, and collections;

or that intellectuals, then as now, were quick to appreciate Chaplin, W. C. Fields, and the Marx Brothers in the movies or Fred Allen on the radio; or that members of the networks and filmdom, for their part, appreciated the competition of the written word.[1] I mean that some of the literary humorists were actively engaged in more than one medium. Thurber drew his cartoons, Benchley acted in his short subjects, and Perelman and others were employed on movie scenarios; mass entertainers of note, like Chaplin, Fields, Fred Allen, and Goodman Ace, wrote their own scripts, and others, like Groucho Marx and George Burns, had a strong hand in their material. This intramural character of the humor is implicit in our review.

At the outset, we may frame certain overarching generalizations for the whole epoch. In our modern criticism we undoubtedly tend to think too much in epochal terms, having a more and more exquisite sense of time as we move through the twentieth century. That is probably because we feel a certain acceleration of events, perhaps to a final judgment. Nonetheless, the period under present discussion, within the confines of our subject matter, appears well-marked and crucial in the extreme. It does so for three significant reasons.

First, the period fulfills the promise of the southwesterners, of the literary comedians, and of the intercentury group in providing at last the sheer number of forceful humorists all at work at the same time. The result is a veritable collaboration to an extent unmatched in history. The extraordinary energies and diversity of the combined achievement in the period constitute a summation of American humor. Next, one of these individuals, Chaplin, possessed obvious genius; another, James Thurber, came very close; and a few, like Marquis and Benchley, were in the first rank just below. In the most cautious retrospect, the time appears to have been a high point not only for combined though unformalized group activity but for singularity unmatched since the colossus, Twain. And, lastly, the continuities of American humor manifest themselves at every turn, even as they are brought to certain thematic and technical culminations just at

[1] Eventually radio's Henry Morgan would record stories by Ring Lardner on discs, for instance. And Marx's book *Groucho and Me* would be dedicated not only to Benchley, Kaufman and Perelman—adepts in both worlds—but to Lardner, Thurber, and E. B. White as well.

this time and just before some of them collapse in the ensuing period.

So much for the range and heights of comic performance and the line of continuous as well as collective effort which marks our argument. If we slight members of "the Algonquin Group" or avoid a depth analysis of each one of Chaplin's films, we are guided by requirements of proportion peculiarly our own. We shall be principally considering, in the first portion of our survey, such diverse literary humorists as Mencken, Lardner, Nash, Thurber, Benchley, Marquis, and Leo Rosten, with allusions to Clarence Day, Dorothy Parker, E. B. White, Wolcott Gibbs, and Frank M. Colby, and with references to a few major novelists of the period, like Fitzgerald and Nathanael West. The list is not exhaustive. My apologies to partisans of George Jean Nathan, Franklin P. Adams, Heywood Broun, Alexander Woollcott, Phyllis McGinley, and Ruth McKenney on one side, and of Milt Gross or Chic Young on the other, to loyalists of S. N. Behrman's plays or of *Helzapoppin'* slapstick—and of all that lies between. Countless favorite writers and personalities will remain unnoticed and undisturbed. Meanwhile, even disinclinations serve to indicate the further ranges of performance in the period, extensive and diversified on every side.

It was Mencken who thought of the culminative term for comic deflation, "debunking," later picked up by Benchley. It suited Mencken's iconoclasm better than it would have Bierce's, because Mencken was entertained by his view of the country whereas Bierce was corroded and progressively alienated, and the word is more in keeping with Mencken's flamboyant and sometimes slangy disrespect than with consistent fury. He was simply against almost everything that contemporary America stood for and wrote his series of *Prejudices* accordingly. He was particularly opposed to democrats, feminists and women in general, American "uplifters," and sentimentalists. He was also an anticapitalist, though this animus was exceeded by his anti-socialism. All in all, the goings-on in the United States represented "the greatest show on earth," and Mencken chose a box seat. At other times, he preferred to image the country as a

nation of hallowed and hollow sanctuaries, where he flung his
dead cats. There were no real sanctuaries in that circus, he believed, because there was nothing after the exhaustion of Progressivism in which to believe save one's own comprehensive skepticism. If he attacked the materialistic and corrupt capitalistic
system, he did not put easy credence on the other side. He had
no credences at all finally, and in this sense his mockeries and
disengagements are more unsettling than the worst of Poe,
Twain, and Bierce put together. He judged the whole mass of
his countrymen as oppressive or ludicrous self-servers, all politics, reformism, and idealistic belief as now quite irrelevant.
In this way he prefigures the exhaustion of comic philosophy to
come, protected as he was only by his own aristocratic joy in
comic debunkism.

He had two favorite targets. One was Puritanism. He defined
the word in his *Chrestomathy,* a kind of *Devil's Dictionary* once
more, as "the haunting fear that someone, somewhere, may be
happy." His other bête noire, which he hunted down relentlessly
and which inspired his best epithets, was our sentimental, hypocritical democracy. Close to Lardner in this regard, he described
our average stupid citizen as "boobus Americanus," characteristically combining his quasi-scholarly hauteur with vernacular in his
finest stroke. He could not believe in superior do-gooders because
he did not believe in the good of ordinary doers. He felt surrounded by imbeciles and hypocrites. Nobody really pursued
private happiness, and no one was essentially democratic. He
rejected both the terms of life and all pretensions to these terms.
He understood the broadest implication, as he appreciated the
technical felicity, of one of Ring Lardner's literary caricatures:
"first coxcomb at Yale." That was the very height the average
American boob, in Mencken's view, was striving for.

Ultimately, Mencken's co-worker, Lardner, also worked groves
of the bitterest fruit. For if Mencken was more than the haughty
disdainer, so was Lardner more than the "recorder of the great
American bicker." He had more than domestic or marital comedy
on his mind as he set himself to expose the predominant American types. There is more involved in both men than an intense
misogyny or subjective misanthropy. Lardner especially provided
what Mencken did not, the downright focus on specific fictional

characters, the artistic concentration which effectively condemned the class-conscious or egomaniacal *arrivistes* that Americans, as a species, were. Luckily he, too, was saved by his savage delight in technique, or his thought also would have hurled him into limbo.

What Lardner did superbly, in contrast to Ade, was to reveal the cliché-ridden, slipshod mind behind the sloppy garrulity of American speech. For this purpose he had fantastic phonographic powers of expression and was the closest contemporary influence upon the style of Hemingway and O'Hara. But the greatest impact of his work was in his attack on our new folk heroes. His pitiless tales of baseball heroes and Hollywood tycoons and raconteur barbers are exposés of common types elevated to spurious mythic proportions, boobs looked up to by fellow boobs. The accuracy of "for some reason another" or "sick in tired" is a rendition of their lazy American elision and what it essentially stands for: the flaccid ordinary mind, cheap in all processes of thought, slurring all distinctions of feeling, comatose. The verbal technique represents the content perfectly.

The democratic bias of much of our traditional humor was running afoul of a conformist, vast middle-classism reconciled to the success ethos and the entire system of things. In this regard, the half-hearted social comedies of F. Scott Fitzgerald are precise indices of what the genuine comedians were up against. None of Fitzgerald's characters desires to overturn the system, only and desperately to belong. This spectacle of the romantic longing of any one class to join the next highest was, ironically, the most realistic of portrayals, and against this fact of American existence the humorists fought anew in one last collaborative effort. They would not be moved, on the one side, by the pathos of Gatsby's efforts or, on the other, by Babbitt's ineffectual revolt. They took their exception to the whole of middle-classism and to all the shibboleths and heroics of a country deeply interested in the vacuities of a "progressive" sentimental democracy.

For his part, taking his cue perhaps from Dunne, Thurber made frontal assault on the aviator-as-hero. It was an attack on our entire, historical tendency to hero worship, culminating in Lindbergh, who later, indeed, was tempted to the political arena, running true to form as a military figure and frontier type.

Thurber's hero is the thorough rapscallion, Jacky Smurch, whose mother hopes he'll drown during oceanic flight. But he flies his glorified boxkite to successful conclusion, and the problem is what to do with a hero who pares his fingernails while speculating on his potential "loot," just as the President himself enters for an interview. Only a deep-leveled amoralism will get Thurber out of difficulties in "The Greatest Man in the World."

Smurch stood up and walked over to an open window, where he stood staring down into the street, nine floors below. The faint shouting of newboys floated up to him. He made out his name. "Hot dog!" he cried, grinning, ecstatic. He leaned out over the sill. "You tell 'em babies!" he shouted down. "Hot diggity dog!" In the tense little knot of men standing behind him, a quick, mad impulse flared up. An unspoken word of appeal, of command, seemed to ring through the room. Yet it was deadly silent. Charles K. L. Brand, secretary to the Mayor of New York City, happened to be standing nearest Smurch; he looked inquiringly at the President of the United States. The President, pale, grim, nodded shortly. Brand, a tall, powerfully built man, once a tackle at Rutgers, stepped forward, seized the greatest man in the world by his left shoulder and the seat of his pants, and pushed him out the window.

"My God, he's fallen out the window!" cried a quick-witted editor.

"Get me out of here!" cried the President. . . .

The funeral was, as you know, the most elaborate, the finest, the solemnest, and the saddest ever held in the United States of America.

From the comic destruction of contemporary hero types to the siege of that last stronghold of legendary heroism, American history itself, is but a short step for another of the debunkers to take. In a series of pseudohistoric pieces, Robert Benchley mercilessly reduces a large assortment of famous American heroes. Figures like Paul Revere come out less than life size in Benchley's gleeful sketches, which also set the pattern for subsequent radio skits that capitalized either on the triviality or inebriate madness that "really" lay under heroic action.

Just before I hit Medford I saw a man standing out in his nightshirt in front of his house looking up the road. I asked him if he had seen anybody who looked like Mr. Revere. He seemed pretty sore and said that some crazy coot had just ridden by and knocked at his door and yelled something that he couldn't understand and that if he caught him he'd break his back. . . .

A lot of people in Medford Town were up and standing in front of their houses, cursing like the one I had just seen. . . .

"Some god-dam drunk," said one of the Medfordites, and they all went back to bed. ("Paul Revere's Ride")

Benchley not only raked legendary heroes in our history but, carried forward by the momentum of comic logic, he assaulted American history itself.[2] In his famous essay, *Political Parties and Their Growth,* he tries to master the difficulties of the case calmly once and for all but is characteristically and completely overcome by the subject, in which his fanciful confusionism is only an addition to the central confusion of the situation itself.

> During the early years of our political history the Republican Party was the Democratic Party, or if you choose, the Democratic Party was the Republican Party. This led naturally to a lot of confusion, especially in the Democratic Party's getting the Republican Party's mail; so it was decided to call the Republicans "Democrats" and be done with it. The Federalist Party . . . became, through the process of Natural Selection and a gradual dropping-off of its rudimentary tail, the Republican Party as we know it today. This makes, as prophesied earlier in this article, *two* parties, the Republicans and the Democrats. As a general rule, Republicans are more blonde than Democrats.

We are prepared amid such comprehensive nay saying for the fullest antiproverbialism. The mockery of existing theses of communal wisdom is as unmistakable as it is inevitable. It proceeds from a satire of crackerbox cleverness to a complete rejection of our most revered proverbialists. Benchley's circularities are designed frequently for the express annihilation of favored voices in comic aphorism. Types like Josh Billings and Kin

---

[2] A series of durable popular jokes deflating patriotic hoopla takes rise in this period, although we cannot attribute them directly to Benchley. They may be typically set in a classroom, where the teacher asks for the famous last words of historic figures. "Nathan Hale said, 'I regret that I have only one life to give for my country.'" "Fine. And Patrick Henry?" "'Give me liberty or give me death.'" "That's right. And General Custer?" A lax class plumbs its depths and finally a hand shoots up. "Yes, Johnny?" "That was in Montana. Custer said, 'Where the hell did all those goddamn Indians come from?'"

Hubbard, in their proverbialist mood, seem to have come directly to his mind, all that wise epigrammatic humor that Professor Blair treats in *Horse Sense in American Humor*. The horse sense turns fractious in Benchley, bolting to wild anarchy.

> How it is true that opposites attract each other. It is nature's way, I guess, of making her wishes known.
> How it is true that opposites repel each other. I suppose it is nature's way of making her wishes known.
> It isn't so much what you put *into* a pudding as it is when you trip yourself up.
> I could go on looking at life like this forever, just a-sittin' and a-dreamin', with only an occasional attack of nausea.

The modern topsy-turvy technique mocks all superficial, simple-minded, complacent understanding. The intervention of mixed and irrelevant clichés is the special device of the sudden, treasonable, cosmopolitan attack on cozy, homespun witlessness.

At this stage of our experience, events and national maturity had done this violence to epigrammatical wisdom; they had revealed the exceptions that riddle it. In an Einsteinian, Freudian, and geopolitical world, without a faith in palpable mass or conscious thought or the sureties of international entente or prosperity, nothing could be trusted in its simplicity anymore. All codified received wisdom was unavailing, and comic realists gave themselves utterly to the lesson. Their long-standing comic belief in the unholy complication and unblinkable non-sense which life provides was now supported by the shattering implications of new ideas and by the failure of both progressivism and Wilsonianism. As pragmatic as ever but more sophisticated than before, they are vengeful but high-spirited instructors of skepticism. They teach the ineffectuality of past wisdom under any guise. Marquis puts it succinctly in *Archy and Mehitabel*.

> an optimist is a guy
> that has never had
> much experience.

Verging on the brink of nihilism, they are safeguarded only by their joy in manipulative and inventive techniques.

> if you get gloomy just
> take an hour off and sit

> and think how
> much better this world
> is than hell
> of course it won t cheer
> you much if
> you expect to go there

Thurber's early fables, playful but nonetheless circular and resourceful qualifications of proverbial wit and wisdom, are the most pertinent examples of skepticism and antithesis in the period. The short piece, "The Bear Who Let It Alone," is typical of his dogged reversalism.

In the woods of the Far West there once lived a brown bear who could take it or let it alone. He would go into a bar where they sold mead, a fermented drink made of honey, and he would have just two drinks. Then he would put some money on the bar and say, "See what the bears in the back room will have," and he would go home. But finally he took to drinking by himself most of the day. He would reel home at night, kick over the umbrella stand, knock down the bridge lamps, and ram his elbows through the windows. Then he would collapse on the floor and lie there until he went to sleep. His wife was greatly distressed and his children were very frightened.

At length the bear saw the error of his ways and began to reform. In the end he became a famous teetotaller and a persistent temperance lecturer. He would tell everybody that came to his house about the awful effects of drink, and he would boast about how strong and well he had become since he gave up touching the stuff. To demonstrate this, he would stand on his head and on his hands and he would turn cartwheels in the house, kicking over the umbrella stand, knocking down the bridge lamps, and ramming his elbows through the windows. Then he would lie down on the floor, tired by his healthful exercise, and go to sleep. His wife was greatly distressed and his children were very frightened.

Moral: You might as well fall flat on your face as lean over too far backward.

Finally, a veritable curriculum of cynicism is pronounced in the teeth of the standard, even sacred, figures of the old and presumably safe wisdom. In "The Owl Who Was God," Thurber directly challenges the American giant, Lincoln. His invention attains a sort of heretical grandeur against our truest American pedagogue.

The Owl seems to answer all questions with mysterious precision, and most of the animals of the forest adopt and worship him as God. Then:

> . . . they followed him wherever he went and when he began to bump into things they began to bump into things, too. Finally he came to a concrete highway and he started up the middle of it and all the other creatures followed him. Presently a hawk, who was acting as outrider, observed a truck coming toward them at fifty miles an hour, and he reported to the secretary bird and the secretary bird reported to the owl. "There's danger ahead," said the secretary bird. "To wit?" said the owl. The secretary bird told him. "Aren't you afraid?" he asked. "Who?" said the owl calmly, for he could not see the truck. "He's God!" cried all the creatures again, and they were still crying "He's God!" when the truck hit them and ran them down. Some of the animals were merely injured, but most of them, including the owl, were killed.
>
> *Moral: You can fool too many of the people too much of the time.*

Other Thurber fables, especially later in the thirties, are obviously keyed to topical international matters. We see in them Thurber's barely controlled rage at democratic stupidities and cowardice, as in the face of Hitler in "The Rabbits and the Wolves," where the wolves finally devour the betrayed rabbits and the affair ends, like Czechoslovakia, as a "purely internal matter." Quite in contrast to Will Rogers, he was anything but a provincial or isolationist, and he indicted the culpabilities of his own countrymen as well as of Englishmen and Frenchmen. But his prime purpose was to attack our whole national mentality, our very habits of self-deception and oversimplification, habits fundamental to our political expediences and naïveté. It was basic to his aims to discredit our patron saints of easy sense. His fantastic reversals of political or domestic epigram force us to see things the other way around and, in discrediting cherished formulae, educate us in humorous but real complexity.

In "The Shrike and the Chipmunks" the female chipmunk leaves the male to his artistic designs with nuts. Unknowingly she also escapes the ravages of a certain shrike who has devastated the local chipmunk population and then been accidentally killed in nighttime pursuit of her very mate.

A few days later the female chipmunk returned and saw the awful mess the house was in. She went to the bed and shook her husband. "What would you do without me" she demanded. "Just go on living, I guess," he said. "You wouldn't last five days," she told him. She swept the house and did the dishes and sent out the laundry, and then she made the chipmunk get up and wash and dress. "You can't be healthy if you lie in bed all day and never get any exercise," she told him. So she took him for a walk in the bright sunlight and they were both caught and killed by the shrike's brother, a shrike named Stoop.

Moral: Early to rise and early to bed makes a male healthy and wealthy and dead.

While it is true that Thurber's misogyny is given full play in this fable, the moralized demolition of Franklin is the other motive behind it. For such a specific target he had his allies, like Ogden Nash: "A penny saved is—impossible." The mode of antiproverbialism was rampant in the period and chose all models and belief for demolition.

Neither was this group disinclined to attack that religiosity of ours, which we have seen frequently displaced as our sense of venerated history, in and of itself. There are clear touches in Thurber's work, culminating in the post-World War II fable, "The Bat Who Got the Hell Out." In the fourth series of *Prejudices*, Mencken declares his aim as the ridicule not only of our cheap chauvinism, stupidity, and false moralizing but of "American piety." In both *Life With Father* and *God and My Father*, Clarence Day struck delicately but unerringly at the last fifty years of merest pietism in the United States. But by all odds Don Marquis led the way in the most explicit and, for him, an exceptionally murderous attack, in the humor of the "the robin and the worm."

> a robin said to an
> angleworm as he ate him
> i am sorry but a bird
> has to live somehow the
> worm being slow witted could
> not gather his
> dissent into a wise crack
> and retort he was
> effectually swallowed

before he could turn
a phrase
. . . . .
and this comfortable situation
in his midst
so affected the marauding
robin that he perched
upon a blooming twig
and sang until the
blossoms shook with ecstasy
he sang
i have a good digestion
and there is a god after all
which i was wicked
enough to doubt
yesterday when it rained
breakfast breakfast
i am full of breakfast
and they are at breakfast
in heaven
they breakfast in heaven
all s well with the world
so intent was this pious and
murderous robin
on his own sweet song
that he did not notice
mehitabel the cat
sneaking toward him
she pounced just as he
had extended his larynx
in a melodious burst of
thanksgiving and
he went the way of all
flesh fish and good red herring
a ha purred mehitabel
licking the last
feather from her whiskers
was not that a beautiful
song he was singing
just before i took him to
my bosom
and even yet his song
echoes in the haunted

> woodland of my midriff
> peace and joy in the world
> and over all the
> provident skies
> how beautiful is the universe
> when something digestible meets
> with an eager digestion. . . .
> well well boss there is
> something to be said
> for the lyric and imperial
> attitude
> believe that everything is for
> you until you discover
> that you are for it

Such cosmic dubiety is matched by some concrete Biercean animus against Christmas. Mencken guffaws over the commercialized and sentimentalized holiday. For him, it functions like one of those enlarging mirrors at the Fun House, magnifying our two basic and gross defects. One of his last published works for *The New Yorker* was called "A Christmas Story," and it showed how much phony evangelism had warped the very bums it was practiced on. And no one needs instruction in the famous spoof that Benchley provides in "Christmas Afternoon," turning a reversed Dickens loose on modern suburbia.

> What an afternoon! Mr. Gummidge said that, in his estimation, there never had *been* such an afternoon since the world began, a sentiment which was heartily endorsed by Mrs. Gummidge and all the little Gummidges, not to mention the relatives who had come over from Jersey for the day.
> In the first place, there was the *ennui*. And such *ennui* as it was! A heavy, overpowering *ennui*, a dragging, devitalizing *ennui*, which left its victims strewn about the living-room in various attitudes of prostration suggestive of those of the petrified occupants in a newly unearthed Pompeiian dwelling; an *ennui* which carried with it a retinue of yawns, snarls and thinly veiled insults, and which ended in ruptures in the clan spirit serious enough to last throughout the glad new year.

. . . . .

Luther Gummidge said that he must be starting along home soon, anyway, bringing forth the acid query from Mrs. Gummidge as to whether or not he was bored. Lillian said that she felt a cold coming on, and added that something they had had for dinner must have been undercooked. And so it went, back and forth, forth and back, up and down, and in and out, until Mr. Gummidge's suggestion of a walk in the air was reduced to a tattered impossibility and the entire company glowed with ill-feeling.

In the meantime, we must not forget the children. No one else could. Aunt Libbie said that she didn't think there was anything like children to make a Christmas; to which Uncle Ray, the one with the Masonic fob, said, "No, thank God!"

. . . . .

Then came hurried scramblings in the coat-closet for overshoes. There were the rasping sounds made by cross parents when putting wraps on children. There were insincere exhortations to "come and see us soon" and to "get together for lunch some time." And, finally, there were slammings of doors and the silence of utter exhaustion, while Mrs. Gummidge went about picking up stray sheets of wrapping paper.

And, as Tiny Tim might say in speaking of Chrismas afternoon as an institution, "God help us, every one."

Those carefully embedded notations about the children are germane. Childism was one of the last preserves of both Christian and Rousseauistic sentimentalism, jealously guarded by the public from any affront. But if it was one thing to dismiss the Swiftian motif of infanticide in an extremist like Bierce, it was another and more difficult matter to withstand the persistence of Benchley and others. At any rate, the preserve was overrun. The relation between Christmas and children has always been obvious, so that the standard attack on the one led inevitably to the attack on the other. Moreover, Benchley's career of debunking bourgeois American family life, early "togetherness," practically forced him to concentrate his fire on child devotion sometime. In vignette after vignette, reality functions like a quiet comic diabolism to disrupt the rituals of museum excursions, trips, vacations, family visits. And the villain is the child (rather than the father of later TV mythologies), for whom he has the frankest hostility. So ends "Museum Feet."

. . . on the pretext of locating the section of the building in question you lead the boys down stairs and out the back way.

"Over here, I guess," you say. "No, I guess over there."

By this time, you are at the street and within hailing distance of a taxi. It is but the work of a minute to hit Herbert over the head until he is quiet and to yank Arthur into the cab along with you.

Kiddie-Kar Travel opens definitively—

In America there are two classes of travel—first class, and with children. Traveling with children corresponds roughly to traveling third-class in Bulgaria. They tell me there is nothing lower in the world than third-class Bulgarian travel.

—and closes decisively with an overheated parent dropping his three incalculable nuisances off the back platform. "He reached Boston alone and never explained what had become of the tiny tots."

The selection of childism as object of attack was natural. But also apt, for children have represented the most obdurate sanctification in American values and mores. That is probably due slightly less to the status of children themselves than to the regressive tendencies in adults, signalled notoriously in Elizabeth A. Allen's poetic apotheosis, "Rock Me to Sleep," as early as 1860:

> Backward, turn backward, O Time, in your flight,
> Make me a child again just for tonight!
>
> . . . . .
>
> Mother, dear mother, the years have been long
> Since I last listened your lullaby song . . .

Such puling fixation on the child becomes even stronger than that on Mother, who is always somebody else's wife or mother-in-law. The ultimate sentimental valuation of children disappears, however, in the sketches of Benchley, dissolved by an insouciant but utter comic directness. The theme occurs in others as well, but never better focused than in Benchley. Nash, however, on the side of educated gentility, was a Benchleyite once upon his uncompromising time.

TO A SMALL BOY STANDING ON MY SHOES WHILE I AM WEARING THEM

> Let's straighten this out, my little man,
> And reach an agreement if we can.

I entered your door as an honored guest.
My shoes are shined and my trousers are pressed,
And I won't stretch out and read you the funnies
And I won't pretend that we're Easter bunnies.
If you must get somebody down on the floor,
What in the hell are your parents for?
I do not like the things that you say
And I hate the games that you want to play.
No matter how frightfully hard you try,
We've little in common, you and I.
The interest I take in my neighbor's nursery
Would have to grow, to be even cursory,
And I would that performing sons and nephews
Were carted away with the daily refuse,
And I hold that frolicsome daughters and nieces
Are ample excuse for breaking leases.
You may take a sock at your daddy's tummy
Or climb all over your doting mummy,
But keep your attentions to me in check
Or, sonny boy, I will wring your neck.
A happier man today I'd be
Had someone wrung it ahead of me.

But more than the new folk heroes or the legendary historical
ones or proverbialists or pietists or children, women were the
supreme target. American misogyny receives absolute apotheosis
in James Thurber, as everyone knows. The theme is obsessive in
his cartoons, as in that house shaped in the presiding image of
a harridan for the homecoming husband. There is even a sequence
of cartoon work entitled "The Battle Between the Sexes," *the* civil
war of all time; it takes the most militant assertion for men to
win back their prerogatives. Fables like "The Shrike and the
Chipmunk" exploit the male's superior sensitivity, and "The Unicorn in the Garden" stands now as every man's vicarious classic
victory over cynical, hostile, crass bitchery. The separate, quick
delineations of the female reveal her instant and instinctive
hostility, her cynicism, her coldness, her aggression, her deceit,
and her excited sadism.

"There's a unicorn in the garden" he said. "Eating roses." She
opened one unfriendly eye and looked at him. "The unicorn is a
mythical beast," she said, and turned her back on him. . . . "The

unicorn," he said, "ate a lily." His wife sat up in bed and looked at him, coldly. "You are a booby," she said, "and I am going to have you put in the booby-hatch."

As soon as the husband had gone out of the house, the wife got up and dressed as fast as she could. She was very excited and there was a gloat in her eyes. She telephoned the police and she telephoned a psychiatrist; she told them to hurry to her house and bring a strait-jacket.

Her defeat is a manifestation of sublime Poetic Justice:

At a solemn signal from the psychiatrist, the police leaped from their chairs and seized the wife. . . .

"Did you tell your wife you saw a unicorn?" asked the police. "Of course not," said the husband. "The unicorn is a mythical beast." "That's all I wanted to know," said the psychiatrist. "Take her away. I'm sorry, sir, but your wife is as crazy as a jay bird." So they took her away, cursing and screaming, and shut her up in an institution. The husband lived happily ever after.

Moral: Don't count your boobies until they are hatched.

If among Thurber's short stories "The Secret Life of Walter Mitty" is a masterful lament for henpecked mankind, "The Catbird Seat" represents the ultimate victory of put-upon man over matriarchism. Thurber's work is a joyfully vengeful and tireless attack on womanhood. His female antagonists are domineering, calculating, insensitive, trivial, overorganized and relentless—but, at the very last, conquered or supremely outwitted. Thurber's stories, with his fables, are the very acme in our literature of controlled wish fulfillment and triumphant, sustained opposition to everything that Woman, especially the aggressive American woman,[3] stands for.

Although he casts all contemporaries in the vast shadow of his practice, Thurber is not alone in the subject. Lardner chooses many female types for his loudmouths and inebriates. Mencken's misogyny is part of his antifeminism, sometimes expressed in oblique but arch epigram. "Love at first sight," he defined as "a labor-saving device." His antifeminism is often a feature of his antidemocracy, so that it is difficult to tell one from the other. But

[3] They were witch-like and generally older women. He felt differently about pretty girls and confessed in a late interview with Alistair Cooke that, if he could no longer see one pass by, he could still *hear* one, though.

they are joined in comic and unholy wedlock; he was "for" women's suffrage because "it would more quickly reduce democracy to its obvious absurdity." Of the stalwart literary figures in the period, Sinclair Lewis in his major phase becomes animated in the subject. He wisecracks more about minor women characters than men: "She sat down as if it were a gymnasium exercise." And whole stories are dedicated to the theme, as "You Know How Women Are" in *The Man Who Knew Coolidge* (1927). Fitzgerald's *The Great Gatsby*, which may be considered as a bitter comedy, shows a rock-bottom misogyny. One or two of Hemingway's pieces, like "Mr. and Mrs. Eliot," though tonally difficult to classify, nevertheless display the hostile misogyny which was the other side of the sexually fantasied female in his serious works.

Benchley contributes forthrightly to the subject in "Ask that Man."

The man's dread [of asking directions] is probably that of making himself appear a pest or ridiculously uninformed. The woman's insistence is based probably on experience which has taught her that *any* one, no matter who, knows more about things in general than her husband.

From Arkansas, we went into Mexico, and once, guided by what I told her had been the directions given me by the man at the newsstand in Vera Cruz, we made a sally into the swamps of Central America, in whatever that first republic is on the way south. After that, Doris began to lose faith in what strange men could tell us. One day, at a little station in Mavicos, I said: "Wait a minute, till I ask that man what is the best way to get back into America," and she said, sobbing: "Don't ask anybody. Just do what you think is best." Then I knew that the fight was over. In ten days I had her limp form back in New York and from that day to this she hasn't once suggested that I ask questions of a stranger.

The funny part of it is, I constantly find myself asking them. I guess the humiliation came in being told to ask.

And Marquis joins in.

                    something i won t stand for in a
                    gentleman friend
                    is jealousy of every other
                    person who may be attracted to me
                    by my gaiety and

aristocratic manner
and if i hear another word
out of you
i will can you first
and kill you afterwards
and then i will ignore you
archy a gentleman
with any real spirit
would have swung on me
when i said that
but this quitter let me
get away with it
i clawed him a little archy
just to show him i could
and the goof stood for it. . . .

He who gets clawed is as much to blame, of course, as is the transmogrified (and eternal) Mehitabel. And it is only fair to say that Mitty's neurasthenic escapism in Thurber's famous story is just as prominent as Mrs. Mitty's domination. Nonetheless, *in toto*, the burden of the period's elaborations upon this theme falls heavily upon the woman.

The conclusive and most penetrating proof lies in the work of Dorothy Parker. Her misandry is actually counteracted by the strongest misogyny in her stories. "Big Blonde," for instance, is a portrait of a stupid and superficial woman, who becomes an alcoholic call girl; her very attempt at suicide is comic-pathetical, and she goes on her feckless way. In such stories Dorothy Parker's alleged reciprocal hatred for men is overcome by her helpless contempt for her stupid or weak female characters. She tries to turn calumnies back upon the male but fails because the portraits of her women are cribbed from the opposition.[4] Her work is the sexual equivalent of the racial irony we detected in Twain's portrait of Roxy; she subscribes unconsciously to the terms of argument set up by the other side. She corroborates all she tries

4 Significantly, her objective drama criticism is most barbed when directed at actresses rather than actors. Her famous remark that Katharine Hepburn ran the gamut of emotions from A to B is representative. Similarly, her famous couplet—

Men seldom make passes
At girls who wear glasses.
—is an exercise in oblique misogyny as well as in comic realism.

to repudiate, joining Thurber, Lardner, Mencken, Lewis, Benchley, Marquis, and others.

Still, even without such corroborations and surrender, the example of Thurber would suffice as an epitomization of the theme in American humor and literature. His treatments are consummate and culminative in themselves. And with half the species thus accounted for, the literary humorists move inexorably into a qualified misanthropy, drawing also toward nihilism. They are negativists on the verge of complete blackness, into which they do not quite plunge yet.

Thurber quips about the supposed power of "abstract reasoning" that has made man one of the great cosmic failures "this side of the ladybug." Clarence Day in *This Simian World* wisecracks, "There is a strong streak of triviality in [simians], which you don't see in cats," and hints strongly about the inferiority of the superrace accidentally spawned by the generic species. Marquis also appropriates a certain biological perspective, looking through the other side of a fanciful microscope:

> germs are very
> objectionable to man
> but a germ
> thinks of a man
> as only the swamp
> in which he has to live

Lardner and Mencken, meanwhile, take dim social views. Lardner's American comes to be a type of talky, shallow, selfrighteous *arriviste* of the whole world, the New World only giving him his superlative chance to show what universal man truly and freely is. Mencken's antidemocracy is rooted, as it was in his model, Cooper, in aristocratic disdain for most men's capacity. His onslaughts are not only on hypocrisy but on thirdratism, an innate disability of mankind.

Don Marquis' attitude is the most poised of all, his emotions suspended in a unique stoicism. But he is utterly candid in his views of human pride and fraud in *Archy and Mehitabel*.

> the cockroach who had been to hell
>
> listen to me i have
> been mobbed almost

there s an old simp cockroach
here who thinks he has
been to hell and all
the young cockroaches make a
hero out of him and admire
him he sits and runs his front
feet through his long white
beard and tells the story one
day he says he crawled into a yawning
cavern and suddenly came on a
vast abyss full of whirling
smoke there was a light
at the bottom billows
and billows of yellow smoke
swirled up at him and
through the horrid gloom he
saw things with wings flying
and dropping and dying they veered
and fluttered like damned
spirits through that sulphuric mist

listen i says to him
old man you ve never been to hell
at all there isn t any hell
transmigration is the game i
used to be a human vers libre
poet and i died and went
into a cockroach s body if
there was a hell i d know
it wouldn t i you re
irreligious says the old simp
combing his whiskers excitedly

ancient one i says to him
while all those other
cockroaches gathered into a
ring around us what you
beheld was not hell all that
was natural some one was fumigating
a room and you blundered
into it through a crack
in the wall atheist he cries
and all those young

cockroaches cried atheist
and made for me if it
had not been for freddy
the rat i would now be
on my way once more i mean
killed as a cockroach and transmigrating
into something else well
that old whitebearded devil is
laying for me with his
gang he is jealous
because i took his glory away
from him don t ever tell me
insects are any more liberal
than humans

He expresses comic futility, philosophically and apologetically in "unjust."

i think it would have been
only justice
if i had been sent to inhabit
a butterfly
but there is very little
justice in the universe
what is the use of being the universe
if you have to be just
interrogation point
and i suppose the universe
had so much really important
business on hand
that it finds it impossible
to look after the details
it is rushed
perhaps it has private
knowledge to the effect
that eternity is brief
after all
and it wants to get the big
jobs finished in a hurry
i find it possible to forgive
the universe
i meet it in a give and take spirit
although i do wish

that it would consult me at times
please forgive
the profundity of these
meditations
whenever i have nothing
particular to say
i find myself always
always plunging into cosmic
philosophy
or something

Given to nihilism, he is unmistakable though matter-of-fact, as in
"the flattered lightning bug."

he said all i
need is a harbor
under me to be a
statue of liberty and
he got so vain of
himself i had to take
him down a peg you ve
made lightning for two hours
little bug i told him
but i don t hear
any claps of thunder
yet there are some men
like that when he wore
himself out mehitabel
the cat ate him

The diametric extreme from him in tone and corrosive force is
Nathanael West, whose *Miss Lonelyhearts* (1933) and *The Day
of the Locust* (1939) are searing exposés of futile conduct and
of a Californian world of ennui and violence about to become
standard in the western world. He gives us back the grim acerbity
of Bierce in both works. His mockery and deflationism qualify
the books as bitter comedies, just over the line from the comic
surrealism practiced by his brother-in-law, Perelman. His vision
of all those Los Angeles crowds coming to the airport hopefully
to see a crash is the soul of misanthropy and nihilism, to say
nothing of the riot that concludes *Locust*, a prophecy of Watts
without the faintest aura of civil rights protest. It is Death and
not Eros that he portrays. Still, there is a kind of controlled

repugnance in these works. He himself will not slide over into sadistic enjoyment of his material. And when he seems to do so elsewhere in *A Cool Million* (1934), he is extravagant, as Professor Douglas Shepard has shown, only because of his comic opposition to Horatio Alger, a model (in *Andy Grant's Pluck*) that he is bound to reverse in every instance, his point-for-point corrective carrying him away. But in *Lonelyhearts* and *Locust*, West is mostly the strong comic realist, portraying malaise without indulging extremity or sickness himself. That is what sets him apart from the post-World War II sickniks who refer to him as their immediate predecessor. But then they would have made books like *Lonelyhearts* and Steinbeck's *Of Mice and Men* into uproarious sick comedy, whereas he knew the gray from the black and the difference between auctorial power and masochism.

Indeed, Marquis' "Fable of the Iron Dogs" shows how far he too could extend himself, like West, in judgment of modern man.

> Once there were two iron dogs on the front lawn of a Pennsylvania millionaire.
>
> One of them said, "I do not believe in a future for iron dogs. When I lose another leg, I will go to the scrap heap, and that will be the end of me."
>
> The other one said, "I have the utmost faith in some noble destiny for iron dogs; though I should be broken to bits, yet will I live again somehow, somewhere, somewhen, to some excellent purpose."
>
> The millionaire just then came along and directed a workman to remove the iron dogs, for his daughter had come home from a select school and told him they were a Mistake.
>
> The first iron dog was thrown upon the junk heap as he had predicted, and became rust, doing no one any good.
>
> But the second one, who had believed in his own destiny, was melted down and made into munitions with which to kill Germans.
> *Moral: You don't have to have a soul unless you want one.*

But *Archy and Mehitabel* illustrates his usual stance, the stoical elevation and resigned patience typical of him.

> i once heard the survivors
> of a colony of ants

that had been partially
obliterated by a cow s foot
seriously debating
the intention of the gods
towards their civilization

the bees got their
governmental system settled
millions of years ago
but the human race is still
groping

Between West and the more usual Marquis, at any rate, falls the typical philosophic negativity of the rest.

We may also note that a certain amoralism characterizes this humor. It is bolstered by a wry and wishful concept of poetic justice and is not the immoralism that informs the next period's black humor. To a certain degree, the lightning bug gets what he deserves when the cat eats him. And Thurber's woman who wants to put her husband in the booby hatch is carried off to one herself, the end seeming to justify the means. Mrs. Ulgine Barrows in "The Catbird Seat" exits from that story also in a hysterical fit of frustration suited to her megalomania. And even Smurch in "The Greatest Man in the World" asks to be shoved out of a skyscraper, no matter how satisfied we are that he is a meet obscenity for the ceremonialists and officials of the land. There is no immoral or sick visitation of punishment upon the merely naïve or unfortunate, as there will be in a veritable movement after mid-century. But the amoralism matches anything that has gone before, in Poe or Joel Chandler Harris or Bierce; and in the insect world of Marquis and the human one of Thurber it reaches a certain culmination even more unsettling because it is less strident.

We must not confuse the place of cruelty in the humor with the foregoing, however. It assumes its old function—and risks—as rectification. When Grandmother is run over casually by the Model T in *Tobacco Road*, Caldwell means that power in the hands of such modern primitives leads inevitably to that driveway scene, and we had better not forget it in our enthusiasms for modern production and generous licensing; more deeply, he means that there is no net progress or that, simply, these things happen, no matter what the pretty advertisements picture. His technique was excessive, but so was the rotogravure ad. That is also why Nathanael West, in reversing Horatio Alger, not only has his hero fail in paying off the mortgage in *A Cool Million* but has him lose his teeth, one eye, a thumb, a leg, and his scalp before he is assassinated. And that is why Nash writes an exuberant poem on "Malice." In an unfalsifying, unexploitive, unsentimental civilization, dedicated to an honest view of difficulties and things as they are even as it seeks to improve them somewhat, there would be no comic need to insist on or to reinstate the cruelty of Nature and human nature. But in a society only pretending to civilization and therefore overidealizing and sentimentalizing existence, the need is preternaturally great. It accounts for the hard realism, harder and harder, in our literature, as in Hemingway's virtual program. The same mechanism is at work in comedy.

We must remember that for all the buoyancy and renewed national vigor provided inspirationally by Franklin Roosevelt, this period, by and large, follows the inhuman breakdown of putative civilization in World War I and the subsequent collapse of universal economy. All New Deal confidence was an overlay, genuine enough in itself, upon a yet crustier pessimism and deeper foreboding. All the more, perhaps, we tried to tell ourselves the old stories and resurrect sensible Progress as our myth, but our doubts now had parity with our illusions, and the uses of amoralism and cruelty a clearer warrant.

And so also was there renewed point in the confusionism of our humor, in all the contravention of supposed sense that it meant—always a perceptible theme under all the ingenious and joyful mayhem. In the age of shaggy-dog stories (given the greatest impetus by Prohibition, as speakeasy revolt drunkenly elaborated antithetical nonsense), comic masters of renewed confusionism and helpless nonsense had a broad popular mode to contend with. The competition, like our earlier verbal extravagance, made for the championship of the fittest: Benchley and Thurber.

Benchley spends at least half his time in the matter. His favorite tack is to bumble into but never quite through every sort of expertise and then, pell-mell, to give himself up to absurd comic momentum. His merest annotations of Shakespeare are typical.

6. *Ho!* In conjunction with the preceding word doubtless means "What ho!" changed by Clarke to "what hoo!" In the original MS. it reads "What hi!" but this has been accredited to the tendency of the time to write "What hi" when "what ho" was meant. Techner alone maintains that it should read "What humpf!" Cf. Ham. 5:0, "High-ho!"

And his associational and mixed "charts," probably a Wardean heritage, are prime examples, like the one illustrating his essay on *The Lost Language*.

One could imagine his expert definition of our entire subject with the use of a chart (see p. 235). He would apologize for the small size of the chart. "I would have blown it up—except that's what I did the first time and haven't found the pieces yet." And then he might laugh self-indulgently at discovering his next error, having held the chart upside down. The imperturbability would be slightly nervous but brave, and the nonsense absolute.

The successive mayhem and unnecessary catastrophe of Thurber's stories, like "The Night the Bed Fell" and "The Day the Dam Broke," are supreme culminations of the mode in American humor. There is no suitable, sure explanation for why everyone starts running one morning in the latter story, but panic and flight are soon city-wide. And it does not help that the announcement of an army sound truck blaring the news, "The dam has *not* broken," is heard as, "The dam has *now* broken," sending everyone more panic-stricken than ever to high ground. The fact, at last, that there is no dam at all near Columbus, Ohio, seems the sheerest irrelevancy to the confused hysteria.

Such storytelling prefigures the reasonless nonsense and completest disruption we will have to live with shortly in all actuality. Thurber's comic momentum was counterpart of another momentum of real events. Everyone living at the time experienced the accelerative current of oncoming, violent madness. And their anticipations were instant. Not long after "The Day the Dam Broke," Orson Welles capitalized on not so latent public hysteria in his radio version of "The War of the Worlds." Thurber was to live to see his strategy of hell-bent confusion outmoded and out-

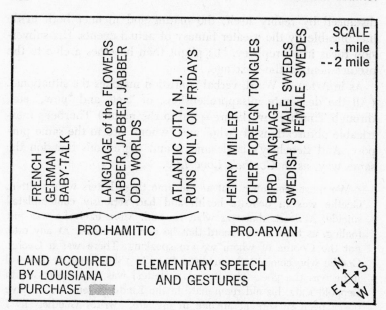

FRENCH
GERMAN
BABY-TALK

LANGUAGE of the FLOWERS
JABBER, JABBER, JABBER
ODD WORLDS

ATLANTIC CITY, N.J.
RUNS ONLY ON FRIDAYS

HENRY MILLER
OTHER FOREIGN TONGUES
BIRD LANGUAGE
SWEDISH } MALE SWEDES
           FEMALE SWEDES

SCALE
-1 mile
--2 mile

PRO-HAMITIC   PRO-ARYAN

LAND ACQUIRED   ELEMENTARY SPEECH
BY LOUISIANA   AND GESTURES
PURCHASE

N
E   S
  W

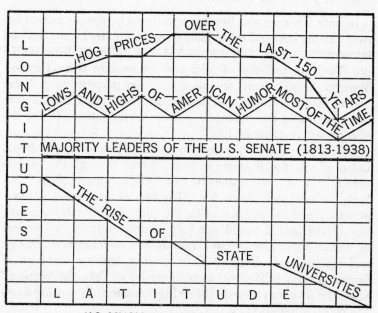

L
O   HOG   PRICES   OVER THE   LAST 150
N
G   LOWS AND HIGHS OF AMER ICAN HUMOR MOST OF THE TIME YE ARS
I
T   MAJORITY LEADERS OF THE U.S. SENATE (1813-1938)
U
D   THE RISE
E
S   OF
              STATE
                         UNIVERSITIES
      L   A   T   I   T   U   D   E

(AS MUCH AS YOU WANT TO TAKE)

distanced by reality itself, the matter and manner both made inapplicable by the greater fantasy of actual events. His subversion turns into prophecy. His plight then becomes a clue to the predicament of the next age.

As in Artemus Ward, verbal confusion matches the situational. (All the desperate misapprehensions, of "not" and "now," etc., through Thurber's works are quite to the point.) Thurber's inextricable obfuscations of "who" and "whom" are to the same purpose. And Benchley's irrelevancies and digressions function the same way, as in *Goethe's Love Life*.

> We must remember that at the time these letters were written, Goethe was in delicate health and had seriously contemplated suicide. At least, that was what he said. More likely he was just fooling, as there is no record that he ever succeeded. At any rate, not the Goethe of whom we are speaking. There was a George Goethe who committed suicide in Paris in 1886, but it is doubtful if he was the poet. The first . . . [letter] was . . . addressed to Leopold Katz, his old room-mate in the Kindergarten. ". . . I have never been so sore at anyone in my life," writes Goethe, "as I was at Martha last Friday."

In both Thurber and Benchley particularly, the distinction between comic butt and critic, gained by the literary comedians and intercentury group, is once again lost. The difference between the pre-Wardean confusion of roles and the modern is a difference, however, between early fumbling and later purposiveness. There was no madness earlier, and no sure method; there is a method to the madness in the twentieth-century manipulations, to the deliberate alternations of role.

Still, a certain clarity is necessarily sacrificed, a fact we should not overlook. For if comic criticism works through the foolishness now, it is more apologetic and self-deprecatory than it has been for over two generations. The loss of communal wisdom, as we have noted in considering the consummate antiproverbialism of the period, could not help undercutting comic wisdom as well. This wisdom often comes as wisecrackism now, though welcome as such. Even at that, it often assumes the form of fantasied wish fulfillment, as in Benchley's "Take the Witness!" where he imagines himself (like Mitty) masterfully putting down the prosecuting attorney.

Q: Perhaps you would rather that I conducted this inquiry in baby talk?
A: If it will make it any easier for you. (*Pandemonium, which the Court feels that it has to quell, although enjoying it obviously as much as the spectators.*)
Q (*furious*): I see. Well, here is a question that I think will be simple enough to elicit an honest answer: Just how did you happen to know that it was eleven-fifteen when you saw the defendant?
A: Because I looked at my watch.
Q: And just why did you look at your watch at this particular time?
A: To see what time it was.
Q: Are you accustomed to looking at your watch often?
A: That is one of the uses to which I often put my watch.
Q: I see. Now, it couldn't by any chance, have been ten-fifteen instead of eleven-fifteen when you looked at your watch this time, could it?
A: Yes, sir. It could.
Q: Oh, it *could* have been ten-fifteen?
A: Yes, sir—if I had been in Chicago.

Over and over again the alter egos of Thurber, Benchley, and Perelman have their moments, but only to face the fact of their sheer daydreaming in the end and conclusive ineffectuality most of the time.

There is something touching in that, a form of self-honesty that prompts all sorts of commentators to make the distinction here between warm humor and cooler comedy. These humorists appear to turn comic deflation willingly upon themselves. Thurber would confess to Alistair Cooke his helplessness in cartooning, "the only thing I can do badly enough to make it good." He judged his own imagination as the plaything of the most vagrant but irresistible associationism.

> . . . I got the seal on the rock but the rock looked like a bedstead. It looked as if he were on the head of a bed, so I drew a man and his wife in the bed; and the shrewish wife is saying to her husband, "All right, have it your way—you heard a seal bark!"

They confess themselves as victims. This victimization is frequently demonstrated with gadgets and machines. One dang-fangled machine, appliance, or device after another, from microscopes and ironing boards to automobiles and conveyor belts, is the instrument of a malign destiny, as Thurber makes clear in *University Days*.

> So we tried it with every adjustment of the microscope known to man. With only one of them did I see anything but blackness or the familiar lacteal opacity, and that time I saw, to my pleasure and amazement, a variegated constellation of flecks, specks, and dots. These I hastily drew. The instructor, . . . came back from an adjoining desk, a smile on his lips and his eyebrows high in hope. He looked at my cell drawing. "What's that?" he demanded, . . . and he bent over and squinted into the microscope. His head snapped up. "That's your eye!" he shouted. "You've fixed the lens so that it reflects! You've drawn your eye!"

E. B. White is the purest Thoreauean in his exception to the world of gadgetry, and he also briefly retires from it. But Benchley continues to fumble with his tripods and maps and screens, harassed by the simplest contraption. They are all more or less hopelessly unmanned by cars and more sophisticated machinery.

This almost fashionable victimization, however, is related to another significant trait, the heightened self-consciousness of demeanor among the literary humorists, half disguise but half truth also. Benchley sooner or later abandons himself knowingly to his own incompetence. Ogden Nash makes his career out of verbal gymnastics, in which the author has deliberately tied himself into linguistic knots for the effect of his Houdini-like escape. He is bold whereas Benchley is ultimately resigned, but both manifest an acute self-consciousness of means. Thurber is the prime case, never even starting, as Benchley might, in manful exposition but confessing himself hopelessly from the beginning. In fact, he was personally and painfully aware of his own frailties, admitting that his simple cartoons were compensatory products of his actually weak eyesight and, toward the end of his life, frankly regretting that he had never had the "good mind," say, of a Mencken. The gentle as well as the loud comics are afflicted with an unremitting consciousness of themselves, speaking in their own person or identified with their narrators, perpetually caught in the acts and reveries of being inescapably what they are. Marquis quips "there is always some/little thing that is too/big for us," and we feel that such impotent self-consciousness now qualifies both their sense of victimization and whatever is left of their wisdom.

Ultimately, they still function in part as wise critics, critics of what victimizes them and forces them inward. They are set against the composite life of absurd, high-pressured, organized machine living of the century, individuals in rearguard action against overwhelming mass politics and mass technology. They are candid about their neurosis, which, in comic reversal, seems to become delicate health. If Thurber speaks of "the ludicrous reflexes of the maladjusted," he is representatively a little proud of the maladjustment. It is as if the slightly awry or neurotic response is the only human one left in a dehumanizing age, and in their self-conscious defeatism these comics protest against accelerative and complex modern existence as part of their general antithetic critique of society. They attempt to be wise comic butts, keeping us off balance. But they are necessarily unsteady themselves. If they lose equilibrium, however, their deliberate uncertainty of the antihero has honest charm, whereas the future treatment of the novelistic antihero fails in proportion to its arrogance.

The threat is quite the contrary in this period. There are striking retrenchments resulting from doubt in this group, notorious apostasies or exhaustions. Sinclair Lewis betrays all he has stood for, not only recanting special details, like misogyny, but his whole hypercritical view. He becomes an apologist, though there were signs of infirmity, even in *Babbitt* (in the plotting and in the conclusion of the book, not in the representative sallies, American businessmen as "corporals of industry," throughout the work). Lardner more and more qualifies his trenchant irony, dilutes his misanthropy, softens his ferocity. Mencken becomes a lexicographer of the American language, finding something worthy of study in democratic Americana he had made a career of despising. Ogden Nash, mixing utter nonsense and satiric common sense, eventually becomes a sophisticated Edgar Guest; in the next period he finally writes blurb poems for Merrill Lynch. Benchley turns increasingly cute and easygoing in his writing, perhaps succumbing to a cinematic personalization of himself. Others go on, Thurber moving to a later strong disillusion and Perelman continuing as the most resilient of exceptions in all our humor. But the apostasies are significant (including Leo Rosten's consent, a generation later, to write tired and commercial comedy of remembrance for *Look*). We are reminded about how difficult it is for any age to maintain comic tension, which may be snapped by overstrain on one side or suddenly relaxed from lost grip on the other.

But under the tension that ruled most of the time, everything contributed to surpassing techniques. Even self-consciousness helped in the exquisitudes of verbal comedy, as in the precious punning of the period. Lardner's solemn anti-Prohibitionism is addressed to our "deeper drinkers," especially down "souse." Marquis stoops to conquer in his insect parables, writing about worms who turn phrases and gather their wits into wisecracks. Nash's stock in trade is the extreme, preferably outlandish pun, often the essential rather than incidental device; customers in a department store search for a "bargain dog," and lawyers debate "who the king affadavit was" in the Bible. Thurber is everywhere addicted to the pun, not able to miss the opportunity of treating a political fable about the "Proper Gander"; in fact, his post-World War II introversion will be signaled most clearly by his rampant fascination with words become a private and ingrown obsessiveness.

Literalism was a richly favored device. It was Benchley's forte, because it helped him so much in his circular associationism.

So when I say "Republicans under Jefferson" I *mean* "Republicans under Jefferson" and no more back talk out of you, either. If you devoted half the time to reading one, or both, of the introductions to this history that you devote to jazz and petting-parties you would know something about the political history of your country instead of being such a nimcompoop. (There is a political party named the "Nimcompoops" a little later on, . . .)

He turned to it more usually than to reversal; indeed, in his work sometimes literalism may be described as the reversal of reversal.

Lillian Walf was three years older than Bodney, but had the mind of a child of eight. This she retained all her life. Commentators have referred to this as feeble minded, but she was not feeble minded. Her mind was vigorous. It was the mind of a vigorous child of eight.

He is also adept in putting literalism to the service of sudden comic relevance, as in his four-point program of "How to Sleep."

1. Go to bed.
2. Close your eyes.
3. Go to sleep.
   and
4. Wake up—that's *very* important.

Others use literalism less systematically and less playfully, as we see in Marquis' drunken version of *Innocents Abroad, The Old Soak.*

> . . . it orter be a great comfort to the Negro to realize he is getting burned in a free country and not in one of them old countries where they was kings and tireants all ways burning people.

Although we may detect the fullest significance in the technical supersedence of reversalism by literalism, nonetheless the practice of reversal is still widespread. It is not pervasively a tactic anymore, but as a strategy it underlies a great bulk of all that Mencken, Lardner, Marquis, Benchley, and Thurber do. They fundamentally reverse attitudes, heroic portraits, middle-class self-adulation, anthropocentrism, proverbial wisdom, and sentimental myth. In a more limited way, they use reversal narrowly sometimes, too. Lardner's title in professionalese really means, *How [Not] To Write a Short Story.* And Nash plays a sophisticated game of double reversal in his light verse, turning sense into a rhymed nonsense that makes its own sense at last; in this way the outlandish length of his lines is a necessity rather than extra comic consideration, for it allows him to rescue his meanings in this manner.

The leading means of confusionism was circularity. We have noted the heavy dependence on literalism for associational pattern, as in Benchley.

> Edny was arrested [for murder] and the trial took place in the Court of Domestic Relations, since she was a domestic and there had evidently been relations, albeit unfriendly. (*Fascinating Crimes: The Missing Floor.*)

But Thurber frequently adopted the device not only for verbal effects (more and more heavy-handedly later on) but for basic situation as in "The Bear Who Let It Alone." And things come together in circular fashion, only with characters or victims reversed in fable after fable or story after story in his work. For their part, short-story writers like Sinclair Lewis and Fitzgerald and others frequently depict a kind of social La Ronde operating in the United States, writing involved ironic stories on how everyone's grass or apartment or job is greener to someone else. Or whole lives wind up where they start after a triumphant expenditure of energy; as Marquis phrases it, the boy goes to the city, where he works forty years in order to retire to the country again.

There is some use of anticlimax: Benchley does best with it.

. . . you have a little dream-picture of how glad the boys will be to see you. "Weekins, 1914" you will say, and there will be a big demonstration, with fire-works and retchings.   (*Back to the Game*)

But there is not much of it. Its radical de-emphasis, like the moderate but sure decrease of reversalism, is a consequence of the shortened distance between events and comedians, a factor we shall examine shortly.

But the virtual elimination of the comic metaphor has no such logical explanation. The device occurs yet, as in Marquis—

> to be bumped
> off the running board of existence

—but only rarely. Given the concreteness of American expression and this period's obvious investment in verbal devices and in style as a whole, we have no suitable way to explain its invisibility. Everything seems favorable for it, suggesting rich elaboration at this time. Its disappearance remains one of the unaccountable mysteries in the technical development of American humor.

On other fronts our expectations are not thwarted. Native outlandishness continues apace. Nash's rhymes are, in part, exercises in the outré, as in "Bankers Are Just Like Anybody Else, Except Richer."

> Most bankers dwell in marble halls,
> Which they get to dwell in because they encourage
>   deposits and discourage withdralls,
>   .   .   .   .   .
> Yes, if they request fifty dollars to pay for a baby you

> must look at them like Tarzan looking at an uppity
> ape in the jungle,
> And tell them what do they think a bank is, anyhow,
> they had better go get the money from their wife's
> aunt or ungle.

But the mode is more than verbal. In *Fascinating Crimes: The Missing Floor*, Benchley's mechanical man, Ajeeb, provides a case in point . . . and a fetching contradiction of Bergson's simple thesis of mechanicality in humor.

> Max Sorgossen worked in the Eden Musée, which was situated on Twenty-third Street just below the Fifth Avenue Hotel. His job was to put fresh cuffs on the wax figure of Chester A. Arthur in the Presidential Group. At five o'clock every afternoon he also took "Ajeeb," the mechanical chess player, out in the back yard for his exercise.

The manner is unruffled, superlatively matter-of-fact. The reportorial imperturbability is in fit contrast to the bizarre matter. Other factors thicken our interest in this technique elsewhere. Marquis' idea of a gymnastic, typing cockroach who has not the strength or leg spread enough for the capital letters suits exactly. We understand how this period's mastery of extra complication provides more than half the humor of the original far-outness of conception.[5] And, of course, the nature of fabulism, especially in Marquis and Thurber, called upon maximum invention of bizarre happenstance. Not any of their predecessors in American humor, not Ade, not Bierce, surpasses them in imaginative gift. The variety of setting and basic conception, in Thurber, for instance, is what distinguishes the talent. And the ability to develop the initial conception is no less striking as in a representative example from *Fables of Our Time*.

The Glass in the Field

> A short time ago some builders, working on a studio in Connecticut, left a huge square of plate glass standing upright in a field one day. A goldfinch flying swiftly across the field struck the glass and was knocked cold. When he came to he hastened to his club, where an attendant bandaged his head and gave him a stiff drink. "What the hell happened?" asked a sea gull. "I was flying across a meadow

[5] In all probability, Rube Goldberg's tortuous cartoons were a contributing influence.

when all of a sudden the air crystallized on me," said the goldfinch. The sea gull and a hawk and an eagle all laughed heartily. A swallow listened gravely. "For fiften years, fledgling and bird, I've flown this country," said the eagle, "and I assure you there is no such thing as air crystallizing. Water, yes; air, no." "You were probably struck by a hailstone," the hawk told the goldfinch. "Or he may have had a stroke," said the sea gull. "What do you think, swallow?" "Why, I—I think maybe the air crystallized on him," said the swallow. The large birds laughed so loudly that the goldfinch became annoyed and bet them each a dozen worms that they couldn't follow the course he had flown across the field without encountering the hardened atmosphere. They all took his bet; the swallow went along to watch. The sea gull, the eagle, and the hawk decided to fly together over the route the goldfinch indicated. "You come, too," they said to the swallow. "I—I—well, no," said the swallow. "I don't think I will." So the three large birds took off together and they hit the glass together and they were all knocked cold.

Moral: He who hesitates is sometimes saved.

It is difficult to decide whether the hallmark of the period is a realism put to the service of fantasy, or vice versa. That is true outside of the pure fable also, as constantly in the work of S. J. Perelman.

We are not unprepared for modern varieties of the tall tale. It is not only implicit in the exaggerative devices and outlandish constructions of the time but is there in its native form, braggadocio, hyperbole and all, as in Marquis' transmogrified roarer in "freddy the rat perishes."

> well we found out this fellow
> was a tarantula he had come up from
> south america in a bunch of bananas
> for days he bossed us life
> was not worth living he would stand in
> the middle of the floor and taunt
> us ha ha he would say where i
> step a weed dies do
> you want any of my game i was
> raised on red pepper and blood i am
> so hot if you scratch me i will light
> like a match you better
> dodge me when i m feeling mean and
> i don t feel any other way i was nursed

on a tabasco bottle if i was to slap
your wrist in kindness you
would boil over like job and heaven
help you if i get angry give me
room i feel a wicked spell coming on

Certainly Leo Rosten's H*Y*M*A*N K*A*P*L*A*N is
relevant in any discussion of these techniques. But not the
least pertinency in Rosten's characterization of a latter-day Jewish
immigrant, or refugee, is the element of the tall tale, complete
with defensive braggadocio. The apearance of Kaplan represents again a fading type, like the rural comedian previously
examined, centered once more for us (as in Milt Gross's cartoons
of the Bronx type) just as he is becoming a nostalgic character,
though the Jewish immigrant was topical once again as an es-
capee from the latest European persecution. Rosten is quite
capable of sentimentalities at large, but his signal victory is to
resist the temptation to sentimentalize just such a character. The
result is that Kaplan thereby becomes one of the significant minor
creations in the comic literature. Kaplan's complicated ingenuity
in getting fantastically in and out of his mental difficulties is
exceeded only by his defensive but massive egotism. His mistakes
are literalistic, malapropistic, and orthographic[6] blunders but also
much more . . . a product of his own queer logic,[7] in which he
preserves the most untutored pride. His conceit, as shown in his
star-spangled spelling of his name, is marvelously unmovable.
Here, at any rate, is the closest thing to the pure comic butt of
the period. There is still an element of *sub-rosa* critique of the
New World, however. Kaplanisms like "Abram Lincohen" or
"Judge Vashington" work in part as delicate deflations of the new
land, which, like the old, could conceivably turn bad. In such
humor the alien accomplishes two things; he defends himself
against his inadequacies and fears and also covertly satirizes the
cause of his difficulties. The root Jewish immigrant joke, from the
turn of the century, is the story of the Chicago-bound woman who

[6] Only Marquis, going back to Artemus Ward's example, is a match
for Rosten's talents and occasional wit. "Henry IV" is referred to by the
Old Soak as "The Ornery Cat."

[7] His comparison of adjectives is no simple linguistic matter but the
product of deep-seated private psychology: "good, better" and "high-cless."
Later he renders the plural of "sandwich" as "delicatessen."

gets off the train momentarily at Pittsburgh, reboards the wrong one, and strikes up a conversation with another woman across the aisle who announces that she is traveling to Brooklyn. "Such a marvelous country!" the first exclaims. "You're sitting over there going to New York City, and I'm over here going to Chicago." It is Kaplanesque logic, but it also makes the land of progress a little *less* marvelous.

Most of Rosten consists in an elaboration of such jokes, which simultaneously allow him to characterize. To this end he seizes on the defensive psychology of his protagonist, whose conceit becomes a little miracle of sustained error. Kaplan is redeemed only by his extravagance and sublime self-confidence, which proceeds through Shakespearean interpretations of "Julius Scissor" and all the rest under power of unstoppable comic momentum. His celebration of Washington and Lincoln is climaxed by his tribute to Jake Popper, a local confectioner; the conclusion of Kaplan's headlong Whitmanisms is a particular rebuff to the Puritan work ethos of his adopted country, though how much he secretly knows that, deep in all his own mad compulsions, is a question.

Mr. Kaplan took a piece of paper out of an inner vest pocket, drew his head up high, and, as Mr. Parkhill held his breath, read:
>   "O hot! hot! hot!
>   O de bliddink drops rad!
>   Dere on de dack
>   Jake Popper lies,
>   Fallink cold an' dad!"

Celestial wings fluttered over the beginners' grade of the American Night Preparatory School for Adults, whispering of the grandeur that was Popper.

"Isn't dat beauriful?" Mr. Kaplan mused softly, with the detachment of the true artist. "My!"

Mr. Parkhill was just about to call for corrections when Mr. Kaplan said, "Vun ting more I should say, so de cless shouldn't fill *too* bed abot Jake Popper. It's awreddy nine yiss since he pest away!"

Mrs. Moskowitz shot Mr. Kaplan a furious look: her tender emotions had been cruelly exploited.

"An' *I* didn't go to de funeral!" On this strange note, Mr. Kaplan took his seat.

· · · · ·

"*Why you didn't?*" cried Mr. Bloom, with a knowing nod to the Misses Mitnick and Caravello.

Mr. Kaplan's face was a study in sufferance. "Becawss de funeral vas in de meedle of de veek," he sighed. "An' I said to minesalf, 'Keplen, you in America, so tink like de *Americans* tink!' So I tought, an' I didn't go. Becawss I tought of dat *dip* American idea, 'Business bafore pleasure!' "

In the inevitable combativeness of the most extravagant classroom in all our humor, the epithetical mode has a new, albeit strange, lease on life. "Maybe isn't 'Heng yourself in resaption hall' altogadder a mistake," Kaplan justifies himself against his archenemies, Mrs. Moskowitz, Miss Mitnik, and Mr. Bloom. "If *som* pipple come to mine house dat vould maybe be exactel vot I should say."

Epitheticism is not absent from the other humorists of the period either. It could scarcely be subdued in a time when Mencken wrote, with his pen like a hammer, as in *The Husbandman.*

> Let the farmer, so far as I am concerned, be damned forevermore. . . . He is a tedious fraud and ignoramus, a cheap rogue and hypocrite, the eternal Jack of the human pack. . . .
>
> No more grasping, selfish and dishonest mammal, indeed, is known to students of the Anthropoidea. . . . Greenbackism, free silver, the government guarantee of prices, bonuses, all the complex fiscal imbecilities of the Cow State John Baptists—these are the contributions of the virtuous husbandmen to American political theory. . . .
>
> Yet we are asked to venerate this prehensile moron as the *Ur*burgher, the citizen *par excellence,* the foundation-stone of the state! And why? Because he produces something that all of us must have—that we must get somehow on penalty of death. And how do we get it from him? By submitting helplessly to his unconscionable blackmailing—by paying him, not under any rule of reason, but in proportion to his roguery and incompetence. . . .
>
> It was among country Methodists, practitioners of a theology degraded almost to the level of voodooism, that Prohibition was invented, and it was by country Methodists, nine-tenths of them actual followers of the plow, that it was fastened upon the rest of us, to the damage of our bank accounts, our dignity and our viscera. What lay under it, and under all the other crazy enactments of its category, was no more and no less than the yokel's congenital and

incurable hatred of the city man—his simian rage against everyone who, as he sees it, is having a better time than he is. . . .

Such are the sweet-smelling and altruistic agronomists whose sorrows are the *Leitmotiv* of our politics, ...

And there is an epithetical rapier as well as sledgehammer, in the hands of the literateur Frank M. Colby, in *The Loeb Classics*.

Take this latest eulogist for example. He says Dr. A. S. Way's translation of Euripides "is uninspiring but close to the Greek," . . . Patience with Way's Euripides is almost a proof of illiteracy. I suppose no man outside a government bureau at Washington ever wrote worse English than Professor A. S. Way, and he wrote it out of sheer love of bad English, for page after page of it has not the slightest excuse in the Greek. . . .

Another instance of this writer's apathy is his mildness toward Professor H. E. Butler's version of Quintillian. . . . Loquacity is a native quality in Professor Butler. He had rather use sixty-eight words than thirty-five, and he will say the same thing twice over in order to do so. This is shown on page after page, when the thought is simple and the way to brevity perfectly open. Professor Butler takes the longest way because he likes it. . . . Quintillian likes to pack things into small space, skip an explanation, leave a little to inference. Professor Butler hates that kind of thing—thinks it selfish, and secretive. He dislikes Quintillian for it and thwarts him when he can. If there is any man in the world that I should hate to resemble, said Professor Butler, when he began this version, it's Quintillian, and his whole text is a demonstration of this incompatibility. . . . I confess I never liked Quintillian at college. I thought him a man of mean outlook and low morality with a vile habit of saying things I knew already, but I did give him credit for putting a platitude into a nutshell, and I should never have dreamed of this long merciless revenge.

Rosten, Mencken, and Colby call up the question of style again in the period, a time that witnessed the most comprehensive and varied approach to comic and literary expression in our history. To link these three constitutes almost enough proof alone for diversity, but to regroup Marquis and Lardner and Lewis and West and Benchley and Thurber and E. B. White with them is to make a case for the most flexible collective style ever attained in our comic prose.

The contrast between high and low styles, in Lardner and

Lewis especially and in Mencken, Marquis, and Rosten[8] only
a little less notably, exceeds the efforts of any other age. The sheer
control of comic style—and attitude, thereby held from sick rage
—is epitomized in the precision of E. B. White, as in *One Man's
Meat*.

> In the kitchen cabinet is a bag of oranges for morning juice. Each
> orange is stamped "Color Added." The dyeing of an orange, to
> make it orange, is Man's most impudent gesture to date. It is really
> an appalling piece of effrontery, carrying the clear implication that
> Nature doesn't know what she is up to. I think an orange, dyed
> orange, is as repulsive as a pine cone painted green. I think it
> is about as ugly a thing as I have ever seen, and it seems hard
> to believe that here, within ten miles, probably, of the trees which
> bore the fruit, I can't buy an orange which somebody hasn't smeared
> with paint. But I doubt that there are many who feel that way
> about it, because fraudulence has become a national virtue and is
> well thought of in many circles. . . .
> I have to laugh when I think about the sheer inconsistency of
> the Southern attitude about color: the Negro barred from the movie
> house because of color, the orange with "color added" for its
> ultimate triumph. Some of the cities in this part of the State have
> fête days to commemorate the past and advertise the future, and in
> my mind I have been designing a float which I would like to enter
> in the parades. It would contain a beautiful Negro woman riding
> with the other bathing beauties and stamped with the magical words,
> Color Added.

And Mencken was saved from the virulence of his own prejudices,
as the later Twain and Bierce were not quite, by his technical
interest in language; it was not stupid American in his private
comic lexicon, but "boobus Americanus." When he ran out of
vituperation, he still maintained his interest in the basic technical
tool, expression itself, and assembled the quasi-academic and

---

[8] The mixture of high and low style in Rosten's expository manner
always makes his highfalutin style serve satiric purposes; the comedy does
not derive from the mere function of contrast but from the deflationary
effect one half of his vocabulary has upon the other: "Mr. Pinsky was com-
pleting an *epistle* to 'Zig Zag Zippers, Inc.'" (my italics). If future theatric
or television producers turn their attention to dramatizing Rosten as well
as Dunne, they would of course lose the force of the expository satire,
though their other gains might be worth the effort.

popular book, *The American Language*. Even here his own vital style continues decisive; indeed, there are energetic moments of the old comic joy of assault. At one point he flings the deadest cat of all into our deepest sanctuary, even upon the sacred altar of American devil worship:

But *darn* and *doggone* are hardly more than proofs that profanity is not an American art. The chief national reliances are still *hell* and *damn*, both of them badly shop-worn. To support them we have nothing properly describable as a vocabulary of indecency. Our maid-of-all-work in that department is *son-of-a-bitch*, which seems as pale and ineffectual to a Slav or a Latin as *fudge* does to us. There is simply no lift in it, no shock, no sis-boom-ah. The dumbest policeman in Palermo thinks of a dozen better ones between breakfast and the noon whistle. The term, indeed, is so flat, stale and unprofitable that, when uttered with a wink or a dig in the ribs, it is actually a kind of endearment, and has been applied with every evidence of respect by one United States Senator to another. Put the second person pronoun and the adjective *old* in front of it, and scarcely enough bounce is left in it to shake up an archdeacon. Worse, it is frequently toned down to s.o.b., or transmogrified into the childish *son-of-a-gun*. The latter is so lacking in punch that the Italians among us have borrowed it as a satirical name for an American: *la sanemagogna* is what they call him, and by it they indicate their contempt for his backwardness in the art that is one of their great glories. In Standard Italian there are no less than forty congeners of *son-of-a-bitch*, and each and every one of them is more opprobrious, more brilliant, more effective. In the Neapolitan dialect there are thousands.

Lofty and erudite Mencken, unlike Bierce, is capable himself of relaxations of style, of regular colloquial and realistic leavening. The combination of literate with down-to-earth expression, as epitomized by both Mencken and E. B. White, is a hallmark of the entire period. These literary humorists are never far away from realistic tone, no matter how high their flights are.

In the transcription of vernacular itself, writers like Lardner and Marquis may even exceed Twain and the Harrises and Dunne because they try for a harder thing than dialect: the rendering of our native, standard speech with bewitching fidelity. They not only caught that element of repetition in American expression,

as Lewis often captures it; or comic redundancy ("most men of
your sex") as Lardner brilliantly reproduces it; or refrain, as
Marquis understands those little signature phrases of ours, meant
forlornly to individualize ourselves (Mehitabel's "toujours gai").
But they captured the whole range of flat, cliché-ridden and inarticulate speech and also the frequent American misrepresenta-
tions of self in language. *Gullible's Travels* was the indicative
title of one of Lardner's books. "I just listen hard," Lardner
explained his practice, but there was, as Hemingway and others
knew, an element of penetrative genius involved, as in "Alibi
Ike" and "The Love Nest." It was Lardner's example that reinforced the Twainian influence upon a continuously viable and
realistic prose.

Under the aegis of Realist expression, the antiproverbial and
antirhetorical efforts of the period could expand all the more.
That accounts doubly for Thurber and Benchley. It also accounts
for Sullivan's Cliché Expert, who mercilessly reproduces the
clichés from every walk of life, including sports and new scientism as well as politics. Most sharply of all it accounts for informal and implicit parody as much as for out-and-out travesty.
Marquis, for instance, gives us one long spoof of free verse in
Archy and Mehitabel. And everything with the hint of fashionable academicism, in an age of now consolidated literacy,[9] is
under the same bombardment of realistic exposé. Sullivan does
it, almost classically for us, in "A Garland of Ibids." And Benchley
is always at it, as in his mock defense of Einstein ("We're in
the same field—writing.") in pseudo-academic style. In one
memorable line Lardner thrust through the new rhetoric of all
how-to pretension. "How to begin—or, as we professionals would
say—how to commence." All pedantry suffers, from the university
to the courtroom (always the setting of the Cliché Expert's
testimony) or to strongholds of pop academicism and authority
anywhere else. Two particular citadels of cultural awe and
literary fashion came under attack by the unintimidated humorists of the era. As a symbol, Cooper had been pulverized, and
Dickens was being toppled, and now the Elizabethans and the
Naturalists, both inviolable in their way, were next. Marquis is the

[9] And of expanding higher education, which insured the success of
The New Yorker.

most distinctive of irreverent realistic deflators, in his Mermaid
Tavern eavesdropping in "pete the parrot and Shakespeare."

here i am ben says bill
nothing but a lousy playwright
and with anything like luck
in the breaks i might have been
a fairly decent sonnet writer
i might have been a poet. . . .

yes says ben i ve often
thought of that bill
but one consolation is
you are making pretty good money. . . .

money money says bill what the hell
is money what i want is to be
a poet not a business man. . . .
the only compensation is that i get
a chance now and then
to stick in a little poetry
when nobody is looking. . . .

well says frankie beaumont
why don t you cut it bill
i can t says bill
i need the money i ve got
a family to support down in
the country. . . .

well says ben jonson
don t blubber into the drink
brace up like a man
and quit the rotten business
i can t i can t says bill
i ve been at it too long i ve got to
the place now where i can t
write anything else. . . .

the manager hands me some mouldy old
manuscript and says
bill here s a plot for you
this is the third of the month
by the tenth i want a good
script out of this that we

can start rehearsals on
not too big a cast
and not too much of your
damned poetry either
you know your old
familiar line of hokum
they eat up that falstaff stuff
of yours ring him in again
and give them a good ghost
or two and remember we gotta
have something dick burbage can get
his teeth into and be sure
and stick in a speech
somewhere the queen will take
for a personal compliment and if
you get in a line or two somewhere
about the honest english yeoman
it s always good stuff
and it s a pretty good stunt
bill to have the heavy villain
a moor or a dago or a jew
or something like that and say
i want another
comic welshman in this
but i don t need to tell
you bill you know this game
just some of your ordinary
hokum and maybe you could
kill a little kid or two a prince
or something they like
a little pathos along with
the dirt now you better see burbage
tonight and see what he wants
in that part oh says bill
to think i am
debasing my talents with junk
like that oh god what i wanted
was to be a poet
and write sonnet serials
like a gentleman should. . . .

Wolcott Gibbs deflates Hemingway's mannerisms in more orthodox parody in his "Death in the Rumble Seat."

Most people don't like the pedestrian part, and it is best not to look at that if you can help it. But if you can't help seeing them, long-legged and their faces white, and then the shock and the car lifting up a little on one side, then it is best to think of it as something very unimportant but beautiful and necessary artistically. It is unimportant because the people who are pedestrians are not very important, and if they were not being *cogido* by automobiles it would just be something else. And it is beautiful and necessary because, without the possibility of somebody getting *cogido*, driving a car would be just like anything else.

And in "Requiem for a Noun," Peter De Vries takes after Faulkner.

"So instead of losing the shooter which would have been a mercy you had to lose the ball," I said, fixing with a stern eye what I had fathered out of all sentient and biding dust; remembering with that retroactive memory by which we count chimes seconds and even minutes after they have struck (recapitulate, even, the very grinding of the bowels of the clock before and during and after) the cunning furtive click, clicks rather, which perception should have told me then already were not the trigger plied but the icebox opened. "Even a boy of five going on six should have more respect for his father if not for food," I said, now picking the cold Brussels sprout out of my lap and setting it—not dropping it, setting it—in an ashtray; thinking how across the wax bland treachery of the kitchen linoleum were now in all likelihood distributed the remnants of string beans and cold potatoes and maybe even tapioca. "You're no son of mine."

But if realistic deflation and predictable literary parody are marvelously expressive and refined instruments in the period, technique still has limits. Indeed, what Marquis guessed or knew about the Elizabethans was being frankly taught in major universities by now, adulatory appreciation of the Bard replaced by realistic understanding; Marquis was beating a dying horse. The whole age was so realistic and skeptical in spirit that even academia was changing.

And something else, momentous for comedy, catches our attention in all the sophisticated fun that is teetering over a void. Here is Benchley taking off on Caldwellian naturalism in "Family Life in America."

The living-room in the Twillys' house was so damp that thick, soppy moss grew all over the walls. It dripped on the picture of

Grandfather Twilly that hung over the melodeon, making streaks
down the dirty glass like sweat on the old man's face. It was a
mean face. Grandfather Twilly had been a mean man and had little
spots of soup on the lapel of his coat. All his children were mean
and had soup spots on their clothes. . . .

"Hasn't the undertaker come yet, Ma?" asked young Mrs. Wilbur
Twilly petulantly. She was boiling water on the oil-heater and every
now and again would spill a little of the steaming liquid on the
baby who was playing on the floor. She hated the baby because
it looked like her father. The hot water raised little white blisters
on the baby's red neck and Mabel Twilly felt short, sharp twinges
of pleasure at the sight. It was the only pleasure she had had for
four months.

"Why don't you kill yourself, Ma?" she continued. . . .

In the dining room of the Twillys' house everything was very
quiet. . . . Grandma Twilly lay with her head in the baked potatoes,
poisoned by Mabel, who, in her turn had been poisoned by her
husband and sprawled in an odd posture over the china-closet.
Wilbur and his sister Bernice had just finished choking each other
to death and between them completely covered the carpet in that
corner of the room where the worn spot showed the bare boards
beneath, like ribs on a chicken carcass.

Only the baby survived. She had a mean face and had great
spillings of Imperial Granum down her bib. As she looked about her
at her family, a great hate surged through her tiny body and her
eyes snapped viciously. She wanted to get down from her high-chair
and show them all how much she hated them.

Bernice's husband, the man who came after the waste paper,
staggered into the room. The tips were off both his shoe-lacings.
The baby experienced a voluptuous sense of futility at the sight
of the tipless-lacings and leered suggestively at her uncle-in-law.

"We must get the roof fixed," said the man, very quietly. "It
lets the sun in."

Unfortunately, however, the excesses of the original were too
close to reality, as many discomfited readers who had read the
documentary Agee and Steinbeck or just the newspapers knew.
Benchley always tried hard to avoid anything topically serious,
but had found he had difficulties even in treating distant American history. The record of reversals and circularities and confusions
in our American past was at least a subliminal part of everyone's
remembered curriculum and did not afford him quite the neces-

sary distance he wanted. His pure literary parody was no more secure, it turned out, for both he and his victim were perilously close to the hard truths of actual Tobacco Roads, truths that were not exaggerated or comic, no matter what manner the humorist assumed. Here, though written at a later date, is factual reporting for *Life Magazine* by the American Negro, Gordon Parks, on Rio de Janeiro poverty, very close to the naturalistic and actual conditions of fellow Negroes of the United States in the thirties.

April 4

It was unbearably hot today. José, looking more dead than alive, lay shivering and feverish underneath a crusty blanket. He squirmed beneath the covers groaning, "God, what's to become of me? What's to become of me?" A huge black spider crawled over his leg and little Isabel, standing nearby, watched until it reached his knee, then doubling her fist, she smashed it. José shrieked and his hand shot out and landed against Isabel's face. She stood crying beside the bed until Flavio took her to the stove, dunked some crusts in coffee and pushed it between her lips. This quieted her but then she started crying again. Suddenly, for no apparent reason, she walked over to Zacarias, the baby, and kicked him in the head. Then Luzia, in defense of Zacarias, shoved Isabel to the floor. Flavio stopped sweeping to intervene. In Mario's haste to get away he plunged headlong into his mother who was entering the door. She grabbed him and cuffed him about the head and he fell to the ground screaming, "What'n hell you hit me for?" The mother picked up Zacarias and placed him on the table where she sat down, buried her head in her arms. Isabel, her wet sullen eyes on Luzia, sat gloomily in a corner. "Bitch! Bitch! Dirty Bitch!" she muttered. After cleaning her feet with cold coffee, Luzia went outside, doubled herself up and began sucking her thumb.

Too many people knew the unlaughable, grotesque truth to laugh at the slight comic convenience of intraliterary spoof. Benchley and others could still get away with it, especially for ultrasophisticates, but the margin of safety was decreasing rapidly. Less and less material is comically secure as modern conditions and events, especially communicated through mass journalism, radio, and newsreels as well as fiction, bring home their impact upon the public at large. In the widest of contexts the grinding and violent non-sense of the real world tends to rob much comedy of its subject matter, even its antithetical force, and especially its perspective.

And that is why the devices of reversalism and anticlimax undergo radical de-emphasis. For it becomes much more difficult to reverse publicized and massive scandals of national and international life, in themselves a repudiation of advertised myths and standard sociopolitical propaganda. And in an age getting accustomed to living from crisis to crisis and climax to climax, the serviceability of comic anticlimax falls in doubt. All these factors are not yet fully operative in the interwar period, but they emerge, and will be passed as dire heritage to the next period.

Meanwhile, we note a slackening of theory. It is as if most of the humorists are too busy to sustain speculation. Later, after World War II, both Thurber and E. B. White will make a series of pronouncements on humor, especially about its being "perilously" close to Truth, and they will get perilously close themselves to casual pontification. During the thirties, Benchley waives the issue of definitions and general description derisively for the group. "We must understand that all sentences which begin with W are funny." He also suggested that laughter was a substitute for sneezing. Aside from that, all we have is Mencken's almost doctrinaire antitheticism and whatever we can glean from inexplicit hints and backstage remarks. We shall descend sheer cliffs of palaver just the other side of eminence in the next generation, in all our books, articles, and even academical conferences about humor during the fifties and sixties. But all technical and thematic speculation in the interwar period is translated almost at once into reflexive practice, even by Mencken during his lexicographic stage. It is as if they were all increasingly conscious of a last precious application, worth volumes. They more than sensed that the oncoming war would finish off their epoch. One or two were even funereal in feeling. Dorothy Parker was one of the few who ventured an overview, and her remark in 1939 is indeed a kind of epitaph. "Today, humorists are whistling past worse graveyards toward worse tombs."

At least their "whistling" work represented a certain joy in technique. They gave themselves to a concrete comic expression, for and of itself, as the night gathered. It was one of the things

Mencken implied was the prime function of humor when he theorized against "the love of the absolute." And when Archy wails, Marquis gives the *Weltschmerz* a conclusive expression which is the very essence of our comedy.

> damned be this transmigration
> doubledamned be the boob pythagoras
> the gink that went and invented it
> i hope that his soul for a thousand
> turns of the wheel of existence
> bides in the shell of a louse
> dodging a fine toothed comb

When we say that radio and the movies gave two new dimensions to entertainment, we acknowledge the massive outlets presented to humor in particular. And a great array of talent took full, consistent advantage of the mass media.

The proportion of radio time allotted to competent and sometimes transcendent humor was more than plentiful. Regular fifteen-minute broadcasts, five nights a week, presented the broadly popular "Amos and Andy" and "Myrt and Marge" programs, the more restricted but clever "Easy Aces," and the first of the relaxed iconoclasts, Henry Morgan. The weekly half-hour programs, concentrated on Sunday evenings mostly and then Tuesday, included Jack Benny, Fibber McGee and Mollie, Burns and Allen, Bob Hope, Red Skelton, and Ed Gardner in the front rank; Eddie Cantor, Joe Penner, Jack Pearl, and Al Pierce on lower levels; and periodic programs like "Can You Top This?" Ezra Stone's "Henry Aldrich," and other seasonals or competent serials as further support. Sustained hour-long programs included the fertile and enormously talented Edgar Bergen, abetted later by W. C. Fields's radio appearances; Fred Allen's "Town Hall Tonight," the closest radio ever came to sponsoring a single genius of comic enterprise, since Allen wrote, acted in, and presided over a week-in, week-out program year after year with unflagging invention and wit; and "The Circle" (with Cary Grant, Basil Rathbone, Groucho and Chico Marx, and Madeleine Carroll), a less long-lived but superlative collaboration. One insists upon the volume of work: 39 weeks each season, with eight or nine continuous sea-

sons (1934-42) of high-level achievement before the war damp-
ened spirits and postwar television effectively terminated radio
entertainment.

In the movies Chaplin reached his zenith in full-length productions, the Marx Brothers moved with inexorable gradation up
to the masterpiece, *Duck Soup*, and back down to their more
usual first-rate farces afterward; and W. C. Fields emerged and
conquered. These comic giants were seconded by minor lights
with major moments, like Buster Keaton, the Keystone Cops,
and eventually Laurel and Hardy; a third rank, consisting of
Lowe and McGlaglan, Wheeler and Woolsey, Leon Errol and
others appeared below. And a host of supporting comedians like
Hugh Herbert, Charles Ruggles, Edward Everett Horton, Franklin Pangborn, Edgar Kennedy, Zasu Pitts, Margaret Dumont,
Mary Boland, and Edna Mae Oliver were on hand in film after
film. Meanwhile, Hope's and Crosby's formula *Road* movies aside,
a whole movie colony of expert leading men and comediennes appeared in countless romantic comedies, like *It Happened One
Night, The Awful Truth, His Favorite Wife, True Confessions,
His Girl Friday* (a remake of *The Front Page* and the fastest-talk-
ing movie ever made), *Nothing Sacred, Mr. Deeds Goes to Town,
Ninotchka, Here Comes Mr. Jordan, The Talk of the Town,* and
so on. These actors became consummate performers in a type of
American lighthearted but well-plotted movie popular the world
over. Such films bestowed as much stardom as American gangster
and epic movies gave to Cagney, Bogart, Muni, Tracy, and
Davis. The roster includes Clark Gable, Cary Grant, Fred Mac-
Murray, Gary Cooper, William Powell, Robert Montgomery, Ray
Milland, James Stewart, and numerous other men, and women
like Claudette Colbert, Irene Dunne, Carole Lombard, Rosalind
Russell, Jean Arthur, Loretta Young, Katharine Hepburn, Myrna
Loy, and a considerable number of others. But numbers for once
do mean something. With double features and a change of bill
at least twice a week, the vehicles for these stars were meeting
a volume of eventual demand, in the thirties, that was nothing
short of prodigious. All of which did not prevent capable directors like Capra, Lubitsch, McCarey, Sturges, and their colleagues
from turning out consistently high-level work. When we add the
range of funny B and even C films, amusing detective mysteries,

and assorted bagatelles, the proportions of comic production appear staggering.

This is the background for our succeeding remarks. It does not include the other mass media, magazine cartooning (Addams, Capp, *et al.*); popular and sophisticated song lyrics (Ira Gershwin, Cole Porter, and others who outdo Ogden Nash more than occasionally); Borscht circuit and night-club comedians of note (Milton Berle, Lou Holz, Henny Youngman, the early Danny Kaye, the emergent Danny Thomas,[10] Myron Cohen and others), legitimate theater comedy (*You Can't Take It with You*, *The Man Who Came to Dinner*, etc.), and remnant vaudeville (Ed Wynn, Bobby Clark). Such an outline indicates a scope of activity that even surpasses the diversity and energy of the literary humorists of the period, reaching crescendo proportions by the mid and late thirties. We may only advert to the scale of that comic enterprise and turn to selected examples of subject and techniques in the two prestigious mass media headquartered in New York and Hollywood. In both cases, we are struck by the reiteration and forthright extension of themes and devices of the literary humor in the period.

"Whatever it is," Groucho Marx sings for a theme song, "I'm against it!" Since he frequently plays the role of a university or governmental president, the zany diabolism is officialized. His antitheticism is instinctive, comprehensive, and wild.

Chaplin's is only a little less wild. His tramp is the perennial outsider instead of the impudent saboteur. He is more complicated in his humanity. *The Immigrant* is the essential model for all of Chaplin's later performances as alienated man in *The Gold Rush*, *City Lights*, and *Modern Times*. As the boatload of passengers crowds to the railing to glimpse the Statue of Liberty, captain and mates quickly and punitively rope them back to the bulkhead for processing. The satirical deflation of leading mythic pretenses informs all of Chaplin's best work in the same way; the American

---

[10] A Lebanese among Jews, he originally assumed a Jewish role, turning unabashedly Lebanese and ultra-American only after TV success in the next generation. The competition of Jewish comedians in all media was so overwhelming that one had to join them.

promise somehow becomes brutalism in practice. More systematically and bravely than anyone in the movies he criticized
phony democracy (whereas all phoniness and all idealism together were dissolved in the anarchy of the Marx Brothers).
Only Fred Allen, on radio, consistently provided an analogue.
"Allen's Alley" was a democratic cross section of boobs as well as
wiseacres. And Allen had a penchant for comic documentary
"interviews" with nonentities: somebody who held the coat of
somebody who held the coat of a great man's retainer's secretary,
or someone who stations himself overnight at Yankee Stadium to
count the overnight crowd for this year's opening game of the
World Series, pitiful exceptionalisms that disastrously cut the
ground from beneath sentimental democracy.

And the economic criticism implicit in the tramp goes without
saying. Chaplin's creation is a constant parody of the American
work ethos and a running exposé of everyday capitalistic exploitation and absurdities. Groucho Marx, for his part, destroys the rags-
to-riches mythology in his memorable comic pronouncement:
"When I came to this country, I didn't have a nickel in my
pocket. Now I have a nickel in my pocket."

Nonheroism and antiheroism are inherent in almost all screen
characterization and caricature. In the sound-track narration
Chaplin later supplied for *The Gold Rush*, he referred to his
protagonist insistently as "the *little* fellow." W. C. Fields's quick
abnegations and the instant cowardices of the Marx Brothers
("Don't shoot!" they cry in a siege during *The Big Store* after
some electric bulbs have popped, and they mean to surrender at
once) are signs of the times, diminishments even from Buster
Keaton and Harold Lloyd. And the common man as the victim as
well as critic of technology informs short and long subjects alike.
Benchley cannot manage his simplest exhibits, even an optometric
replica of the eye, and is foiled by upsidedown charts and spring
mechanisms on all maps and screens. Fields has famous trouble
with cue sticks, golf clubs, and even his cane. Chaplin's auto-
mated factory is an incessant nightmare in *Modern Times*, where
machinery overcomes the little fellow's best will and determination.[11]

[11] In *Modern Times* he consummated a theme he had begun very early,
as in the memorable escalator scene in *The Floorwalker*.

The attack upon other special and familiar targets is unmistakable. On the air, Henry Morgan urges little tots to get their mothers out of the room so they can steal the dime or quarter the sponsor wants them to inclose with box tops; he appeals to their tiny but corrupted hearts. And infanticide is never far from W. C. Fields's mind. He displays violent, instant antagonism to any child, who reciprocates. They are natural enemies, and no soft sentimentalism of the American way of life is going to stand in the way. In *The Bank Dick* Fields's gesture to an eight-year-old, whose mother is momentarily turned the other way, is back-of-the-hand hatred (more than likely coming after a Universal Newsreel featuring a Baby Parade . . . he could almost have counted on the contrast). The upsurge of response from buried depths in his audience, particularly the adult male, signaled a vast Freudian return of the repressed. Such frank comic violence and specific hostility outdid even the literary humorists. Indeed, Fields feigned nothing and in actuality spiked Baby Leroy's[12] orange juice on set. "Any man who hates children," he said, "can't be all bad"; and, according to Wallace Markfield, he was richly profane with young autograph seekers. For such unmitigated candor, Fields was and remains the ugly darling of legions, men mostly, if not exclusively.

Fields was, of course, an active misogynist, too. His answer to the question about the usefulness of clubs for women was that they were all right if all other forms of persuasion failed. He gleefully carried over his prejudices to the screen, where his protagonist is often equipped with a harridan for a wife, with whom he fights in scandalous, low-brow fashion. Even his climactic film with Mae West, *My Little Chickadee*, crackles with acerbities, only his lechery controlling his *ripostes* to the frontier belle she impersonates.

On the radio George Burns and Goodman Ace deal with the malapropistic female as standard fare. Goodman Ace is usually left in stark incredulity at fantastic feminine illogic, and Burns always gives up hopelessly. Such radio portraits coincide with

[12] It was the heyday of Shirley Temple, too. In view of the crass exploitation of children in movies and their corrupt commercial impressment for radio advertisements, it was a puzzle which violence upon them was worse, the obscenity of their prostitution or frank comic response to our hypocrisies.

the "dumb blonde" image, which became traditional on the screen.

Even in her fullest charm, sexual woman is not altogether ascendant. Groucho and Harpo Marx see to that in their reassertion of rapacious male dominance. As Hackenbush or Rufus T. Firefly, Groucho is a shameless lecher, and through lobbies and halls in film after film Harpo is in irrepressible pursuit of all girls who flee his wild-eyed frenzy. It may be objected that Harpo is always focused some moment or other during each film in cinematic arrestment before a harp, embodying then the tender feminine principle himself. This is a unique instance of bisexuality, the result of which is that Harpo completely interiorizes all respect for delicate and accomplished woman and is thereafter free to see pretty girls as merely serviceable. Fields's desexualized roles permit him a high Menckenite annoyance with or hostility toward woman. Burns and Ace remind us that her new-won legal and social equalities do not bestow any other qualities, like mind. And with either farce or derision[13] the Marx Brothers will put her in her primitive place.

Meanwhile the plotting of most of the romantic comedies of the period depicts our warfare between the sexes, a struggle exacerbated by the American woman's prerogatives as wife or as implacable adversary in divorce. But, as in Thurber, she loses. All of these movies, featuring the various and talented film beauties opposite Gable or Grant, are resolved in favor of male pride. Even Garbo's Ninotchka comes to terms as well as to life. And the comic relief in violent films, like Cagney's, seems most effective when the manly gangster squishes a grapefruit in some gun moll's face; more than any other scene in *Public Enemy, that* one is memorialized.

Questions of grateful amoralism extended beyond sexual and misogynic concerns. Chaplin's tramp, with none of the pangs of O. Henry's Soapy, is in and out of jail with an insouciant redundancy, as in *City Lights.* The quack and con-man roles of Fields and Marx are played with such naturalized cynicism as to remove moral issues completely from sight. *You Can't Cheat an Honest Man* is the blatantly ironic title of one of Fields's movies.

---

[13] In a famous fade-in scene at a restaurant Groucho as gigolo exclaims at the tab, "Outrageous!" and flings it across the table to Margaret Dumont: "If I were you, I wouldn't pay it!"

Week-in and week-out on the radio program, "The Circle," came an interlude when Groucho once more fended off the janitor, Chico's "Ravalli," who wanted to be paid. The point here, as well as in the Marx Brothers movies, was to pit con men against one another (as in the opening scene of *Go West*), one of the great solutions of the con-man dilemma in American humor. If harmonic vibrations were felt, that was because under the madcap ingenuity was the tableau of a basic social and business process, which American audiences recognized at once.

And any and all means served the comic's end. This was true even in Chaplin's early short masterpiece, *Easy Street,* where he is a keystone cop desperate to tranquilize the huge bully of the block, whom he finally anesthetizes with the gas of the bendable street light.

The question merges with the issue of comic realism. I refer to a deeper issue than set design. When in *The Immigrant* Chaplin surreptitiously slips his dice game winnings into the pretty girl's pocketbook—or is it her dying mother's?—and on second thought retrieves just a few bills for himself, that is the touch of realistic genius which holds the comedy in perfect balance. With such saving candor did the best of cinematic comedy discover a place between maudlinism and callousness.

Indeed, in the related matter of cruelty, a device of the movies answered the old problem with culminative perfection. An American improvisation became the greatest and most satisfying convenience in the annals of humor. I refer to the now classic custard-pie mayhem of both the twenties and thirties. There was still plenty of orthodox cruelty, from Chaplin's *Easy Street* all the way to the Punch-and-Judyism of Laurel and Hardy and other conventional slapstick violence. But the new device was significant, a perfect release of hostility and aggrandizement.[14] It carried the maximum deflation possible in the spectacle of a walloped, cream-dripped face . . . without fundamental injury. Such episodes were also superlative instances of comic momentum; scenes moved from an impromptu beginning to an inevitable

[14] Fields had theorized about the quantum of cruelty needed in comedy, just enough and no more (as, in fact, Aristotle had indicated millennia before). He was thinking of some of the subdued roughhouse passages of his own films, but his remark suits perfectly the custard-pie device.

riotous conclusion. In retrospect, we judge that there was no sheer accident involved in filmdom's discovery of the technique. And the ensuing competition between the Sennett and Roach studios in the matter showed their unending appreciation of a prime device. It was, after all, the one technique that answered most exquisitely their search for all possible means of hostile expression and comic abandon.

In wild chases and general situational humor, it was an age also dedicated to extreme confusionism. Indeed in the midst of it, Chaplin has moments when he is almost completely overcome, and the famous face can register the nihilism to which the action seems to speed (as, later again, in *The Great Dictator*). Where the Marx Brothers are joyfully at home in havoc and Laurel and Hardy appear as light and heavy straws in a comic whirlwind, Chaplin's little man does all he can to win out but sadly doubts the outcome of all his indefatigable survivalism.[15]

These comics could not help being comic butts as well as critics, in much the same way as the literary humorists created their own dilemmas of role by their very investment in confusionism. Abbott and Costello (who Chaplin thought had the greatest comic possibilities) were hopelessly lost in verbal mazes when they appeared on the radio. Abbott can demonstrate that Costello is not even present. ("Are you in St. Louis?" "No." "Are you in Chicago?" "Of course not." "Well, if you're not in St. Louis and you're not in Chicago, you must be somewhere else." "Ye-es." "Well then, if you're somewhere else, you're not *here*.") And Costello traps Abbott and the nation in a labyrinthine baseball dialogue, "Who's on First?" Their failure on the screen was monumental for, despite Chaplin's guess, their forte was vaudeville exchange and not cinematic action at all. Benchley, however, succeeded very well in translating himself from one medium to another; his short subjects on cashing a check or folding an ironing board are little marvels of confusionism, during which he plays the bungling comic butt to exquisite perfection.

[15] Buster Keaton's deadpan is, in fact, a concession to death. There will be victory after the combative confusion, but no true comic joy. Like the custard-pie trick, his typical comic mask was a brilliant improvisation and integration. In such ways does a persistent, technical address to comedy discover answers which, in themselves, clarify central problems, like the relation of survivalism to heroism, and dissolve theory in art.

There is something self-consciously maladroit in much of Chaplin, and in Keaton, Laurel and Hardy, and even in that stalwart American type, Harold Lloyd. The extra added element of self-consciousness is particularly American. Chaplin's sudden little coynesses are prime examples, endearing, perhaps, because we are all being thrown back at such moments upon the frail weight of ourselves. And those other moments of comic hesitation or suspension, just before custard-pie mayhem or in the silent, staring confrontations of Chico and Groucho Marx before they try to do in one another or during disastrous passages of Laurel and Hardy when Laurel will even break down in tears, are most relevant. In these varied postures of self-consciousness either these comedians intensify pathos and helplessness, or they simply double the force of impending hell-bent action.

But they go so far and no further, leaving to the next age that ultimate and disastrous self-consciousness which is expressed by the comedian's good-natured derision of his own material. In the thirties, however, craftsmen never went so far to break comic illusion, still believing in it as they did rather than wasting it. They approached a verge of self-mockery and devaluation but tested their skill in not passing the invisible line. In the end, then, their self-consciousness was as much technical as it was thematic, a way of vindicating rather than cheapening their abilities. In the nature of these things they could not be surpassed later, for excess would carry the comedian, like Red Skelton on television, directly over the line into the rankest and weakest impertinences.

But self-consciousness in the thirties, operating on a thematic as well as technical level, could already lead to mistakes. A man of capacious talent and understanding like Chaplin often pushed his coyness too far. And fully aware in his profound depths of all he was doing, he moved *The Great Dictator* to a statement of the most heroic sentimentalism. He had always appreciated the outlying coordinates of antithetical realism and sentimentality in his career, and against the strong pull of the first even tried identifying himself with his United Artist contemporary star, Mary Pickford, symbol of transcendent sweetness. His absolute masterpiece, however, turned out to be the nihilistic *Monsieur Verdoux* after the war, but his three last films, *Limelight, A King at New*

York, and *A Countess from Hong Kong,* have been conscious and shameful retrenchments on the other side.

Such hyperconsciousness could also lead to a superb comic director's frightened withdrawal from the field. That is the case of Frank Capra, who had one of the most promising careers in hard American comedy of all home-grown directors but who almost deliberately failed to press on. He had pushed pure O. Henry tricksterism and flagrant coincidence as far as possible to rescue his movie plots (written, generally, by Robert Riskin). The darkness and iron-bound defeat logically and realistically indicated by the drift of story were averted by sleight of hand that becomes increasingly flamboyant and desperate in *Mr. Smith Goes to Washington, Mr. Deeds Goes to Town,* and then *Meet John Doe.* He had to subscribe to the hard inevitabilities of his deepest thinking, quit entirely, or turn utterly to froth. The war saved him temporarily from choices, but his official film work for the government, propaganda movies, doomed him. When it was over, he chose the two latter courses alternately. His postwar film, *It's a Wonderful Life,* was like cinnamon toast compared to the force of his previous work and to Josh Billings' old recommendation of cayenne pepper for native comedy. He quit movie making for a long interval after that[16] and then finally returned to do either remakes of former early work or other harmless triviality, in the vein of Damon Runyon's updated O. Henry-ism. But this director, who had time and again provided vehicles for the most representative American types (Clark Gable, Gary Cooper, James Stewart), had had the talent for the most native, searing comedy in American filmdom. Instead, he joined the apostates.

But, in all truth, perhaps the comic tension achieved could not be made more taut than it was, and one had to choose either savagery, not possible at the time, or desperate faith. Capra himself had worked on the famously destructive Laurel and Hardy two-reelers, *Two Tars* and *Big Business,* doubtless aware of leading implications.

---

[16] Preston Sturges, however, quit permanently. A less talented director than Capra, yet he was an even more astringent scenario writer, who simply dared not press on after *The Great McGinty, Sullivan's Travels, Hail the Conquering Hero* (with its attacks on both patriotism and momism), and the tight and superbly mordant *Christmas in July.*

In the latter, two Christmas tree salesmen are so persistent to sell a Scotch householder one of their trees that he finally brings his shears to the door and snips the tree in half, to be rid of them. They reciprocate with a slightly vengeful garden hose prank. He answers with escalated injury, and they answer him, the whole sequence building magnificently to the thorough destruction of his house and their car. Through most of the violence a policeman happens by and takes dutiful notes on his pad. The comic confusion, misapprehension, distrust, and hostility increase to a violent frenzy and complete inanity—the essential image of things to come in the world. We may say that, naturally, with the fullest benefit of hindsight; in no way was the little movie, a masterpiece of comedy, overladen with extrinsic symbolism. Which only means that the work constituted the most potent symbol possible, the implications welling up pure and undefiled from a skepticism and aggression at the bottom of most American comedy of the period.

But there was nothing doctrinaire yet. Or even quite consistent. As the nation itself was lifted out of the slough of depression and anxiety, although the world steadily moved to holocaust, there were transient doubts about what had been glimpsed or understood. An urgent faith wars with unholy knowledge, as in the principal feature films of both Capra and Chaplin. I do not mean at all that these men were or suddenly became naïve. The myth of American innocence has become an academic imposition (among American, not European intellectuals) much too thoroughly overextended to explain our character; we have seen that quite the opposite has been true for American humorists who were always very close to the popular mind with all its ambivalences. In the thirties, for example, more Americans even than Europeans understood the accelerating menace of fascism, abroad and at home. This vision became the content of Capra's harder films. He and Chaplin, along with Thurber and other literary humorists, were not and never became innocents or willful naïfs. They took their wishes for the truth. Implacable power figures portrayed by Claude Rains and Edward Arnold would recant themselves in Capra's movies, and the adulators of Chaplin's Great Dictator would be reformed, one and all, by a great concluding speech of the Jewish barber impersonating him.

In the final analysis another inconsequential movie of Laurel and Hardy highlights the American psychology. A besieged French Legion post hears the cry "Reinforcements!" and flings open the palisade gates upon two lone recruits, absurdly standing there in the desert. The course of the film, however, is a vindication, confused as it must be, of the two reinforcements who do indeed save the fort. A desperate theme underlies the ensuing technique, and even the masters rely on it . . . and with their experienced eyes wide open. Our foolish, outnumbered, beleaguered selves would somehow necessarily win against fully measured odds. It stands to their credit that they never postulated our superhumanity, for they pictured butts even more than heroes. Still our plain, dogged humanity would win out or, at least, survive—when survival itself would be a momentous comic event in the onrushing scheme of things. Experience was not exactly denied, as it often was by literary apostates, only overcome. The war and the Bomb, of course, lay ahead; a much different and more explicit scheme of things would transform such cinematic faith into its opposite, a spurious joy of annihilation, as in *Dr. Strangelove.*

But as we review the radio and movie comedy of the interwar period before it reaches its penultimate stage in 1940 and plummets immediately after, its varied techniques strike us forcibly. Modes and devices tend very much to duplicate what we have noted among the literary humorists and even exceed them. Furthermore, there are certain interchanges that provoke interest; the increased situational comedy of literary humorists (Benchley, Thurber, Perelman, etc.) is counterbalanced by a great deal of verbal capacity in the movies (the spell of broadcasting and the "talkies"?).

Punning, for instance, is more flagrant and often more adroit than on the printed page. And the Marx Brothers are proconsuls of the realm. Secretary of State Chico and President Groucho strike out the budgetary allotment for chairs in *Duck Soup* because they will have a standing army. In the treason trial[17] the President Judge is moved to remark,

[17] Our humor irreverently flouts legal procedure in particular not only because the law is inherently rhetorical and jargonistic but because it is the essential form of civil authority.

"Do you realize we could give you ten years in Leavenworth? Or how about eleven years in Twelveworth?"
CHICO: "I'll settle for five or ten—in Woolworth's."

There is the element of "building" in such exchanges, the addition of a third or fourth extension surmounting the usual two-part joke. That factor is also apparent in the distinctive Marx Brothers literalism and circularity, in which Bert Kalmar, Harry Rubin, S. J. Perelman, Groucho himself, and others collaborated. (Who was responsible for exactly what must be left to some Folio committee of the twenty-first century.)

PROSECUTOR: "The State accuses you of treason."
CHICO: (on the stand): "I object."
PROSECUTOR: "You object? How can *you* object?"
CHICO: "I couldn't think of anything else to say."
GROUCHO (rapping gavel as judge): "Objection sustained!"
PROSECUTOR: "What? How can you sustain that objection?"
GROUCHO: "I couldn't think of anything else to say either."

The judge then climbs down from the bench to act as defense counsel, and there is additional verbal confusion about "abject" defendants.

In rich combination the punning, literalism, and circularity, plus epitheticism, proceed, furthermore, in a spirit of significant and reflexive hostility. In *Monkey Business:*

SHIPBOARD WAITER: "Stewed prunes: Room 118."
GROUCHO (whose back is turned): "Feed them some black coffee, that ought to bring 'em around."

Or in *Go West:*
GROUCHO (to the ticket teller, who has found him short in payment): "I *told* you not to bother counting it. No wonder they've got you behind bars."

He also quips, taking a bandana from someone's mouth, "This is the best gag in the picture," one of the few forgivable times he self-consciously breaks illusion, as Hope and Crosby are already doing plentifully.

When confronting Margaret Dumont, Marx was in champion form, adding the wildest extravagance to epithetical introductions. "That remark covers a lot of territory," he deflates the tall and imposing woman. "As a matter of fact, *you* cover a lot of territory. Is there any truth to the fact that they're going to tear you down and put up an office building?" Or, about a fancied and ill-fated liaison between himself and Madeleine Carroll, he observed on the "Circle" radio program: "It goes way back. There was puppy love between us. But we outgrew one another, and I started wearing glasses and she became a cocker spaniel."

There is finer wit, too, although the combination of literalism,[18] association, and epithet needs no sophisticated warrant. Against medical or scientific expertise, Marx's notable line while taking Chico's pulse is: "Either you're dead—or my watch stopped." We may read back to such performances as Marx's later radio and early TV series, "You Bet Your Life," where the point was not the quiz but his epithetical wit in deflating contestants. The shows were prerecorded, but the editing process in no way detracted from his spontaneous gifts. His originality was always there.

And he was scarcely alone. Fred Allen's punditry rivaled Marx's. "California's climate is all right. Of course, if you're an orange, it's ideal." And his epithet-ridden "feud" with Benny inaugurated a veritable format on radio. Impaled on his own avarice, Benny's riposte to decrepit-looking Allen might be (on a Christmas program): "You look as if Santa Claus slid down your nose and left a bag under each eye." Following Allen's example, Bergen drew W. C. Fields into a series of regular confrontations with Charlie McCarthy, and drunkenness and wooden-headedness became staples of exchange. Hope proceeded to ask the same of his corps of writers for himself and Vera Vague and Jerry Colonna on the air and for himself and Crosby in movies.

The challenge became a basically technical one (as Benny always made it for himself, in the constant characterization of himself as miser): how long and ingeniously could certain signature effects be elaborated? The audience's delight, true also for the regular mayhem of movie cartoons, was readied for yet an-

[18] We may advert to the comic strip once in our canvass and call attention to the occasional transcendence and economy of, say, Frank Willard's "Moon Mullins." In three frames an exchange between Lord Plushbottom and Moon proceeded in some way like this: "Moon! Can I buy you a drink?" Moon answers, "Sure!" and they enter a bar, where Plushbottom orders, "Two doubles, please." In the final frame, zoomed in, like movie technique, on Moon, Mullins quick-wittedly adds, "Same here."

other unforeseen elaboration, for being imaginatively outwitted itself. All of which meant a resurgence of the comic competitiveness that characterized our earliest tall-tale exaggeration and epitheticism.

This verbal combat is unmistakable, and it stands in extreme contrast to the flaccid pleasantries of post-World War II TV introductions and general bonhomie. In addition to obvious Joe Miller vaudevillisms[19]—

> EDDIE CANTOR: "Go away. I can't talk to an idiot."
> THE MAD RUSSIAN: "Come here. I can."

—there were transcendent vindications of audacity. "As a rule," the volatile Marx might refine his insult, "I never forget a face. But in your case I'm willing to make an exception." In correlative night-club entertainment, Milton Berle would be less clever but notably aggressive or snide to his audiences, who paid for the privilege. "Sir," he would complain suddenly from the klieg-lit floor to a bald-headed customer at a front table, "would you mind [covering your head] . . . the light's in my eyes?" Or spontaneously he would interrupt a routine to greet full-dress, late arrivals surreptitiously getting to their table: "Here's a nice party—they brought their own waiters."

The derogation of audience is intimate and mocking, the exchanges between comics rife with mutual epithet and direct calumny.[20] Night after night, week after week, from the night-spot floor, on the air, or in the movies, comedians provided steady release for aggression, acting as a collaborative team in consistent recrimination and disrespect. No doubt they reflected post-Depression irreverence and contempt, and their audiences responded strongly. The proprieties and sanctities of social intercourse were

[19] We were unapologetically low class or low-middle class in the thirties. The present ideograph of ourselves as at least mid-middle class or higher-middle class is an important explanation for the partial decline of humor in the United States.

[20] W. C. Fields, in earnest and in envy, referred to Chaplin as "That goddam ballet-dancer." Markfield has shrewdly called attention to Fields's deliberate attacks on all of Chaplin's objects of sympathy; the maimed and the dispossessed, flower girls and waifs. (And yet Fields endowed an orphanage . . . so long as it did not inculcate religion. He opposed the ruling sentimentalities, then, keeping some of his own sentiment a necessary secret.)

never more vituperatively and freely violated. The satisfactions were enormous.

All exaggerated respect or adulation, for paying audiences and for fellow stars themselves, was exploded by a mocking style. Legal cant came under special attack. And much other cant, as well. Fred Allen at last hit upon the creation of Senator Claghorn, in whom Texan hyperbole and political rhetoric merge. "Ah'm four-square," he declares in stentorian nonsense, "sixteen, that is." And with superlative misemphasis, he booms during an interview: "Ah take a *firm* neutral stand on *all* controversial issues!" Allen never borrowed Dunne's barroom format, as Ed "Archie" Gardner did for "Duffy's Tavern" and as Jackie Gleason appropriated it for TV later, but he was the strict inheritor of Dunne's scathing Irish wit, which Gardner tried to use in a much lower key, but which Gleason, for all his noisy buffoonery, never would attempt at all.

Still, politics is an easy subject. In the thirties a new topic emerges for brave attack, the very commercialism that sponsors the comedians. Nothing was higher than the Capitol or White House except the big business of Radio City, and now that came into range. Henry Morgan began his comic career when, as a honey-voiced announcer, he added to the hallowed falsity of his message about a New Jersey supper club, "Just twenty minutes from Times Square," the words, "by rocket ship!" That began a relentless career of "knocking" the advertisers. And, like audiences of Berle, they were willing to pay for the dubious privilege, simply because Morgan's metropolitan audience, as Jean Shepherd's now, grew huge. The rarest bravery of all succeeded. And Morgan proceeded to the ultimate breach of ethic in making fun of other programs.

> When last we left the Shadow—who is, in reality, Dupont Cranberry—and his lovely female companion, Boo-boo Lane, they were hanging by their thumbs on the upper deck of the Staten Island ferry.

He helped inaugurate one kind of camp humor, a sort of intramural debunking.

These various forms of antirhetorical deflation prompt a reference to Cole Porter, our most sophisticated stylist in song. In his lyrics there is a double attack, on one side upon sentimentalism and prudery and, on the other, upon *avant-garde* snobbery. Realistic verses in an impressive variety of songs, like "Anything Goes," illustrate both motifs.

> In olden days a glimpse of stocking
> Was looked on as something shocking,
> Now heaven knows, Anything goes.
>
> Good authors too who once knew better words
> Now only use four-letter words, writing prose,
> Anything goes.

Comic pertinence is an accentuated feature of this humor. It informs some of the malapropism. "You could have knocked me over with a fender," says Jane Ace, violating old form but living in her times. It has other flagrant uses as well. In the movies Groucho's pertinency in wooing hefty but rich Margaret Dumont is flamboyant: "Oh, I adore you! with all your beauty and money and charm and jewels and goodness and wealth and sweetness and money. . . ." But nothing in either medium surpasses the comic pertinence and concretism of Harpo Marx, who keeps hitching up his leg on the hand of someone to whom he is listening raptly or against whom he has simply sidled for the purpose. Laziness, in the comic's literal use of others, has never been more extravagantly displayed anatomically.

Harpo's trick is a kind of pictorial tall tale. Indeed, most of the slapstick, the Keystone chases, Harold Lloyd hanging from a hook-and-ladder or a clock, the cabin scene in Chaplin's *The Gold Rush,* and countless other episodes, all represent a cinematic extravagance[21] related to our native tall-tale exuberance

---

[21] Never before had comedy such a medium, not even the fast-moving Elizabethan stage plays, in which to translate speed and comic momentum. The acrobatism of Keaton, Chaplin and Douglas Fairbanks (who was often comic in his chase scenes) probably equaled anything Burbage had done in Shakespeare's time, especially since many of these performers had a circus background. But increased scope and movement allowed by *motion* pictures gave their antic and extravagant talents a new dimension.

What is also significant is that movies were *continuously* funny, certainly not stopping to apologize for themselves with serious or moralized moments, as frequently done after the war; furthermore their speed, as in *Duck Soup,* accelerated as the film went on.

and energetic fantasizing. Outlandish verbal techniques, for their part, were worked into our C movies of the period, as Wallace Markfield has noted, though the phenomenon is also related to increasing self-consciousness; on an African safari some guide mixes Yiddish (*"Zei Gesundt"*) with Swahili in talking to a native. (There was also an emporium sign along that Laurel and Hardy street on the Hal Roach set, reading "Ice Cream Cohen.")

The tall tale itself is a vehicle for Jewish humor, or vice versa. The western and immigrant modes at last merge completely. There are many instances of the engagement of the two, usually urbanized, as in Lou Holz's involved joke of a man with a sore throat suddenly thinking of old-fashioned saline solution and quickly entering a druggist's.

"Do I have salt?" responds the druggist and signals him to follow and they descend to the basement, which is lined with bags and bags of salt.
"You must sell plenty of salt," remarks the impromptu customer.
"Oh no," says the druggist, "not really. But the man who sells *me* salt—can *he* sell salt!"

There is a more fetching marriage of the two strains in Myron Cohen's perfect joke, probably derived from Wobbly agitation in our northwest, when western lumbermen, union organizers, and venturesome Jewish socialists came together. This unique mixture inevitably exploded in volatile braggadocio humor.

A lightweight, narrow-shouldered, skinny Jewish man requests lumberjacking work from a camp foreman.
"We don't need any cook," says the foreman.
"I'm *not a* cook, I cut trees," says the visitor.
"Go on, get out of here," the foreman replies.
"But give me a chance," the other says, and his pathetic insistence is so great that the foreman at last agrees.
"Cut that little tree over there."
The unlikely applicant does so at once.
"Not so bad," the burly foreman admits. "But it's a sapling, though you worked fast. Now: cut down that big one."
The giant spruce is felled rapidly.
"That's pretty good!" shouts the foreman scarcely believing his eyes. "Where did you work before?"
"In the Sahara."

"The Sahara! What do you mean, the Sahara? That's a desert!"
"Sure," the other replies: "*now*."

But tall-tale jokes were not confined to this special American conjunction. Prohibition[22] stories of drunks, burgeoning Freudianism in which psychiatric interpretation was often an extravagance in itself, and the very technology of the country fed constant new material to the technique. The jokes of Joe Laurie, Harry Hershfield, and Ed Ford on the radio program, "Can You Top This?" relied heavily on such matter. And on his programs Henry Morgan made up and elaborated stories in the old mode, with particular reliance on punning and literalism: long and ingenious jokes hinging on expressions like "a driving rain" for automotive humor, or his joke about the refusal of the township of Coffee, Wyoming, to pay the second constable they ever hired because they thought they could have their second cop of Coffee free.

Much of this resurgent tall-tale jocularity, punning, and elaborated literalism also illustrate comic momentum in the period. The milliner's joke between Marx and Madeleine Carroll, detailed in the first chapter, is the best instance of runaway verbal momentum. All jokes built to double or treble climaxes are germane here, too.

Momentum also explains much of the general zaniness in the Marx Brothers movies, where even Groucho's walk is a contribution; it is a sign that he will go too far. The element is also a feature of Laurel and Hardy comedy and equally of Chaplin's. As a result of uncontrollable momentum, the tramp's incessant trust in his drunken benefactor keeps getting him thrown out of the rich house all the mornings after in *City Lights*. He simply cannot learn, under the continual force of his own emotions. As to custard-pie sequences and other comic violence in the movies, we have nothing further to say except to instance them again as supreme illustrations of the almost distinctive American abandon to forward inertia. In the end, one guesses that outer impending

[22] A country whose sublimest sense was to eliminate evil at one stroke by prohibiting alcohol invited nonsense humor, shaggy dog-ism, confusionism, impudent punning and outlandish jokes to the nth degree. Melville had detected this incredible American urge to messianic and singular acts of heroic reformism, like Captain Ahab's, and his answer was also, in part, a comic judgment.

events in the world had been preparing subliminal paths in the public brain, smoothing cortical lines of apprehension. Seen in this way, the comedy of unstoppable momentum was not at all any mystic prefiguration of things to come but an appeal to a suppressed but instantaneous understanding.

That may be true of the accelerative speed of our humor also. The pace of movie comedy is a technical implicate of *motion* pictures, naturally, and was to be attempted in any event as a fulfillment of form. But it receives further impetus from our acceptance of speed in itself as an almost formal cultural requirement of art in tune with accelerative current history. The element of speed in the other media seems corroborative, the quickness and deftness of comic stroke in Marquis, Lardner, Benchley, and Thurber; the swift wisecracking and innuendo of night-club performers; and the extraordinary pace of glib radio monologue (Hope) and rapid canvass of comic character ("Allen's Alley").

We have already seen in the literary humorists how closely comedy was approaching the line of contemporary and impending events fraught with the direst significance. Perhaps, at last, the term comic realism must split apart, the one half surrendering to the other. A piece like Thurber's fable, "The Rabbits and the Wolves," gets too unnervingly close to global events, which are absurd but harrowing. On the screen the Marx Brothers, in *Duck Soup*, still make a certain minimal distance do in a wild satire of international events and morality. But the margin of safety is narrowing, soon to disappear entirely, with catastrophic results for even farcical comedy. Already in *The Great Dictator*, Chaplin has not quite enough room, the anti-Semitism and totalitarian nonsense in his material too real and fearful to distance properly, for all the brave comic effort brought to bear. Just as the humor approaches ultimate verges, it operates with intensified and astonishing success; but there are steep, sudden declivities ahead rather than vistas.

We reserve concluding technical observation for the element of masquerade in the period. It, too, manifests a certain flamboyance before it disappears as a time-honored characteristic. It is true that Ed Wynn and Bobby Clark still romp about with incessant disguises and gadgetry on stage (and Wynn once or twice in the movies). But the decisive clues are elsewhere. The mask is

not worn at all anymore by the literary humorists, frankly on their
own as transparently middleclass butts and wits. And in the movies
Chaplin at last changes his famous make-up for one quite close
to it in *The Great Dictator*. But his device is impersonation rather
than disguise or invention now, and he will give up virtually all
masks in *Monsieur Verdoux* and his last films. Finally, Groucho
Marx wears the most flagrantly amateur mustache, the most non-
sensical of disguises. The mask is now so gross it can only disappear utterly. And in one other instance, there is culminative
success followed by eradication. Amos and Andy are the last
of the blackfaced and Negro-voiced entertainers; they will be
superseded by the real thing. In sum, the period ends an epoch
of clowns. It also witnesses the unabashed emergence of owlish-
eyed, bald-headed, barefaced comics on their own. Such figures
are still sufficiently clownish in the person of Jack Benny or
Robert Benchley, but they are devastatingly normal-looking and
normal-sounding in Fred Allen or James Thurber.

The triumphant amalgam of immigrant and second-generation
comic talent with other indigenous strains of humor is the most
heartening indication of pluralism in our cultural history . . . just
as the phenomenon is about to fade. The mixed gifts of varied
strains in the interwar period represent a supreme minstrel show.
From vaudeville through the new mass media to the literary
humor of the time, we have all that true range and colorful diver-
sification which nineteenth-century blackface and frontier types
had strenuously aspired to. Antidemocratic themes certainly informed much of the content of the humor. But the array of comic
spokesmen was powerful argument for democratic vigor and wit,
no matter which way the wit turned. Irish, Jewish, Italian, and
Swedish characters and comedians predominated: Fred Allen
(with his own gallery of types in "Allen's Alley," from Clancy and
Mrs. Nussbaum to the Old Timer and Senator Claghorn[23]);
Jack Benny and Groucho Marx, among spectacularly effective

[23] Perhaps the character of Mr. Moody, the tight-lipped and acerbic
New Englander, provided Allen with his basic idea and program title; he
is modeled on the Town Hall character who sits listening to a rhetorical
political address and, asked by a latecomer, "What's he talking about?" replies, "Can't tell—he don't say."

Jewish comedians; and Chico Marx, Joe Penner, and Edgar
Bergen. There were superlative German and English strains:
Lardner, Mencken, and Chaplin. In addition, heartland Ohioans
like Thurber and Hope contributed strongly. Will Rogers, we recall, was Oklahoman and part Indian. And the patrician President
Roosevelt found it in his heart of hearts to address the DAR in a
memorable comic greeting, "Fellow Immigrants!" The combined
spectacle was a kind of choral American answer to the world, a
comic harmony eventuated out of dissonance and frictions. It occurred as a late cosmopolitan validation of our whole national
experiment.

Such triumph arose, however, not as a presagement of further
cultural enrichment but as, in fact, the last culminative episode in
our free comic expression and fellowship. After it, spurious pieties
of respect and new sanctimonious regard for race, creed, and national origin assert themselves. Vapid egalitarianism has always
been a lie, and is no nearer truth because of a new enthusiasm for
it. A nonjudgmentive, sentimental tolerance prevents us from truly
appreciating and cultivating one another's differences as well as
censoring each other's inanities. Nonjudgmentiveness leads back
to mediocrity and conformism. The soft requirement of postwar
"tolerance" rather than the hard give and take of the thirties
converts the chorus into a solitary echo chamber. Assimilation, tremendously furthered by the military regularization implicit in a
fourteen-million-man armed force during World War II and a
massive GI bill of general higher education afterward, wins the
day. Moreover, certain manifest virtues of social justice in their
very attainment may become excesses of themselves with obliterating liberal force. Our qualified and mere tolerance of one another
(in one great middle class) has worked that way. That development turns out to be one of the most exquisite ironies of our
modern history, saddening our retrospective delight now in the
most rambunctious, sustained, and diversified array of comic
talent we ever had.

We must not summarize this period, however, in a vein of exceptionality that obscures its connections with the past. We have
indicated, in passing, certain continuities not only apparent to us
at a later date but avowed by figures of the time. Benchley and
Perelman publicly admired Ade, and we can see relationships of

language and farcical "set-ups" in their work, as we can trace much of Marquis' and Thurber's technique of fable directly to Joel Chandler Harris[24] and George Ade. Mencken also thought highly of Ade, as he did of his contemporary, Lardner;[25] his estimation of Twain is a matter of open record, and indeed much of his practice is inspired by later Twainian prose. And he, Benchley, Nash, and Charles Addams have inseparable ties with Ambrose Bierce. Radio's Fred Allen and "Archie" Gardner are formally even studiously connected to Dunne's Dooley. And further back yet, Artemus Ward provides schema and sources for Benchley and Marquis. The comic tradition, always defined as a viable, useful past, contributes strongly to the period, which may equal or exceed or transcend the past but never rejects it and never denies it.

Indeed, the interwar period stands as both a resumé and a culmination of the past. That fact has been a burden of our analysis of the literary humor and mass-media comedy in the era. The marked antitheses of our past humor, consciously termed debunking in this period, are given explicit and consummate treatment. Sentimental democracy, proverbialism, factitious hero worship, childism, feminism, and matriarchy,[26] all conveniently expressed in Thurber, are epitomized in the period. Confusionism and amoralism have their apotheosis, as in the work of Benchley and the Marx Brothers. The techniques of punning, literalism, associationism, circularity, and epithetical exchange are pursued to their nth degree. Realistic subject matter and expression are pressed to utter verges still comic, and devices of parody, general comic momentum, speed, masquerade are brought up to a line of ultimate development.

At the same time certain internal developments begin to operate reactively against further progression or, at the moment of essential fulfillment, suggest exhaustion of whole types of humor or

[24] Young Don Marquis was associate editor of the *Uncle Remus Magazine*.
[25] He lauded the characterization particularly, which he believed Ade and Lardner managed in short space; he took his exception to Ward and Nasby because he could detect no comparable achievement by Browne or Locke.
[26] Philip Wylie's *Generation of Vipers* attacks "Momism" so humorlessly that his tract, though indicative, falls into categories of documentary journalism and pure diatribe.

of the genre as a whole. Realistic style is employed not only to deflate all rhetorical hypocrisy and excess in America but, in Lardner and others, to reveal the poverty of common mind. Realistic subject matter in itself is becoming dangerous—because reality is. In this respect, the image we have is of a comic empire along whose borders certain barbaric inroads are being made. They bode collapse at the very moment of optimal sway. The shortened distance of comic perspective, as in Thurber and Chaplin especially, is an omen. The necessary investment in literalism and the corresponding decline of reversalism, because we cannot so easily turn things the other way around anymore in a world becoming increasingly inside out itself, are other technical signs of portent. The high quotient of college-level literacy that gives support to the most phenomenal instance of sophisticated journalism in American humor, *The New Yorker*,[27] turns increasingly faddist in taste. The great magazine begins to harden its formulae;[28] both "Talk of the Town" and longer essays turn steadily more earnest, heavy, and portentous, leaving the original comic intention to cartoons and less and less frequent Perelmanesque satires. Meanwhile, news of war and American involvement (Lend-lease and peace-time conscription) begins to weigh upon the exuberant comedy of the mass media, even before the new medium of television kills radio and cripples the movies decisively. Just as the movies discover perfect devices for cruelty not fundamentally injurious and the networks hit upon formats of epitheticism, the newsreels of Nazi invasions and the Hitlerite and Churchillian exchanges of rhetoric and vituperation capture the whole attention. The combination of internal developments, working themselves out, perhaps even turning upon basic premises,[29]

[27] Dwight MacDonald has called attention to its original slogan: "Not edited for the old lady from Dubuque."

[28] Indeed, almost all magazines, general, humorous, journalistic, harden their American formulaism in these years, relaxing only a generation later, in the sixties. The classic satiric joke on the matter is the gibe against *Reader's Digest* format, a compendium of standard titillation, exotica, sentimentality, and patriotic and religious cliché; the perfect synopsis is "of a man who had sexual intercourse with a bear, inside an iron lung, for the FBI, and found God."

[29] The exhaustion of humor is signaled when, in extreme self-consciousness, comedy mocks its own processes. This happened on the boards with the repetitious vaudevillian use of the chicken-road joke and its variations. At last *only* the surprise of no surprise—a return to the original punch-line,

and of outer events so forcefully competitive and overbearing in their successive trauma, made for the unholiest of prospects.

Nonetheless, the resumés and culminations which the interwar period as a whole represents are the pinnacle of collective comic performance in the United States, a height scaled just before a fall. Whether that falling-off is merely descent or outright plummetry, a slight or precipitous decline, is our next immediate concern. But that the postwar period manifests some kind of decline from these heights seems scarcely debatable.

Why, in the 1930's particularly, was there a total insurgent rise of humor on practically all fronts? The decade came after a crushing Depression and witnessed global mischief that would soon explode horrendously. But the question is not unanswerable. The broad scope of comic achievement in the period is a help to us, since single eruptive genius always falls outside of complete rationalization. Here, however, the general fecundity of comic spirit and enterprise is a potent clue, as was the Jacksonian and southwestern collectivity of effort and that of the Civil War and postbellum literary comedians.

The upsurge cannot be attributed alone to the introduction of mass media like the radio and talking movies. Of course, such stimuli were undeniable. But the later innovation of TV, a stupendous one, was accompanied by no similar comic renaissance (or any other kind), even after a world war that might have released pent-up comic talent and laughter. The explanation for the thirties cannot rest on technological grounds, certainly not exclusively. If once again we are forced to a sociologic and historic understanding, we do so with previous instances in mind and with a belief in pattern that does no violence to the wayward subtleties of the case. A community of talent begs a cultural rationale.

The previous periods of comprehensive and insurgent activity coincided with confidence in national undertaking. The fact of our expansion and growth carried all else before it in the Jacksonian and post-Jacksonian period. The fact of union, incontestable after Appomattox, and the vitalizing impetus of industrialism

---

"To get to the other side"—constituted the final stage of a desperate ingrown comedy. Similar mocking self-consciousness and decadences reemerge in certain developments of the modern period.

and cosmopolitanism thereafter, energized us despite all counter-influences. We are forced to appraise the era of FDR as one of comparable psychic resurgence. There had been manifest odds against manifest destiny; there had been trauma and disillusion in civil dilemma; and there were fears in the nation and convulsions abroad during the New Deal. But for reasons peculiar to each, the mood of the successive eras was intrinsically propitious and un-arguable. We are not concerned with the perversity of history, which should have stimulated native comic and literary genius right after revolution but did not or which should have reinforced Progressivism in the 1890's and at the turn of the century with a greater number of comedians than it did. We are restricted to the facts. All logic, for instance, indicates that our post-World War II period should have been a time of sure national confidence. It was then that America's unquestioned rescue of allies and assumption of free-world leadership took place and an unparalleled economic security and growth occurred. An uncertainty, a deepening mood of frustration, other thralldoms and insecurities, however, in com-bination with internal comic exhaustions, have reduced comic gaiety and enterprise.

In the decade of the thirties, obstinately perhaps, candor, free-dom, and comic potency found their fullest representation. Nor-man Thomas had not won; there was no true revolution of national form, politics or mores. Indeed, Roosevelt's most sweep-ing reforms, the NRA, the packing of the Court, were nullified or blocked; he saved the country for Republicans themselves as well as for anybody else. But only later on would his left-of-centerism be seen as not enough, and his socioeconomic progress appraised as more gradual than it was. But we cannot, from our later vantage point, argue an epoch out of *its* conviction. There was a mood, a feeling, of momentous ádvance. And indeed there were significant changes in the period, and there was undeniable charisma in the image of Roosevelt. The resulting mood cannot be gainsaid or mocked by those with a later perspective but in the throes of an opposite stubborn mood not without cause itself.

Meanwhile we are forced to diagnose the interwar period as a time of increasing ambivalence and tension. These are factors of the highest theoretical significance, along with whatever it was that the *Zeitgeist* had provided. The pull between antidemocratic

cynicism and deflationary devices, on the one side, and the democratic character of an extensive comic choral effort, on the other,
is striking; the ambiguity between skepticism and desperate
faith is clear; the paradox of darkening content and full joyous
technique is indisputable; the disparity of flagrant masquerade
and barefaced presentation is suggestive, as is the seesaw balance
between leisurely tall tales and involved shaggy-dog stories at one
extreme and the astonishingly fast quippery and accelerating
pacing on the other; the conjunctions of realism and surrealism in
all modes are not to be dismissed as curiosities. We borrow a
concept from the New Criticism of poetry to direct attention to
the phenomenon of "tension"; it gives us psychologic as well as
purely technical insight. Not only might this concept be applied,
for instance, to explain the crucial middle stage of Mark Twain's
greatest successes, but it might describe the achievements of this
whole interwar period. Such tension, probably in the nature of
things, cannot be long maintained, although, also in the nature of
things, it describes the accomplishment while the feat lasts.

We judge, in the end, that under the prevailing and unarguable
mood and by virtue of ruling technical considerations, certain
figures achieved transcendent status and others only slightly
less so in the time. Chaplin looms, and Thurber, failing only in
sustaining a long work, rivals Twain in skill and comic invention.
Figures like Lloyd and Keaton in the earlier movies, and Groucho
Marx and Fields in the later ones, bulk large; Fred Allen remains
a most impressive radio talent; and humorists like Mencken,
Benchley, and Marquis could be underestimated in no other
period.

Two prestigious figures of the time, Perelman and Thurber,
move inexorably into the next era. The one is furiously immune
to events and personal depletion. But the other furnishes us with
an inestimable gauge of developments.

VII

Modern
American Humor

WORKING in both the pre-World War II and post-World War II periods and adequately reflecting both sides of that second great watershed of American morale, James Thurber is the logical figure with whom to begin modern judgments. Since the critical question is one of decline or resurgence, we shall proceed accordingly, evaluating themes and techniques as they directly bear upon that discussion and centering Thurber at the outset and conclusion.

Two works of Thurber give us the most convenient measure of his career. Side by side with *Fables for Our Time* (1940) we can place counterparts from *Further Fables for Our Time* (1956). The difference between "The Owl Who Thought He Was God," reversing Lincoln's proverbialism, and the later "The Rose and the Weed" is instructive.

> In a country garden a lovely rose looked down upon a common weed and said, "You are an unwelcome guest, economically useless, and unsightly of appearance. The Devil must love weeds, he made so many of them."
>
> The unwelcome guest looked up at the rose and said, "Lilies that fester smell far worse than weeds, and, one supposes, that goes for roses."

"My name is Dorothy Perkins," the rose said haughtily. "What are you—a beetleweed, a bladderweed, a beggarweed? The names of weeds are ugly." And Dorothy shuddered slightly, but lost none of her pretty petals.

The Rose and the Weed continue their argument, which the Rose wishes to end by citing Shakespearian references to herself.

Just then, and before Miss Perkins could recite, a wind came out of the west, riding low to the ground and swift, like the cavalry of March, and Dorothy Perkins' beautiful disdain suddenly became a scattering of petals, economically useless, and of appearance not especially sightly. The weed stood firm, his head to the wind, armored, or so he thought, in security and strength, but as he was brushing a few rose petals and aphids from his lapels, the hand of the gardener flashed out of the air and pulled him out of the ground by the roots before you could say Dorothy Perkins, or, for that matter, jewelweed.

Moral: Tout, *as the French say, in a philosophy older than ours and an idiom often more succinct,* passe.

The reversal is now compounded and total. There is the momentary though telling subversion of Lincoln, but the point is now incidental to Thurber's complete misanthropy. Even the acidic Ambrose Bierce would have perversely sided with the aristocratic rose, in simple reversalism; Thurber goes the whole distance. And in the barroom fable, "The Truth About Toads," every animal present owns his desperate pride, even the toad, who thinks he has a precious jewel in his head (a "toadpaz," mocks the bartender). When the Woodpecker opens the toad's head, there isn't "anything there, gleaming or lovely or precious." And Thurber's moral is "Open most heads and you will find nothing shining, not even a mind." This new explicitness and hardness exceed even Bierce's fables ("Man and Goose," for instance) and govern Thurber's last work, replete with its accentuated and uncompromising pessimism. The key to a now developed misanthropy lies in the contrast between the excluded, saving minority of some doubters in "The Owl," a red fox, a humble dormouse, and a French poodle, and the general inclusiveness of his attack in the newer fable.

Moreover, punning is almost the only device Thurber is left

with, a noteworthy technical contrast to the greater number of devices used before, even in stringent pieces like "The Owl" and "The Shrike" and "The Unicorn." What distinguished the earlier pieces was a greater playfulness and the joy of variation he had been patient enough to practice. In the later work his repetitions and overextensions are technical counterparts of a moral decline and bitterness.

In his extremism he pushes the antiproverbialist and anti-rhetorical qualities he always had to absolute limits. There is no communication at all possible in the comic misapprehensions of language that he dramatizes. And that leads him to the defeatism figured in the connivance and stupidity of "The Daws" and to the nihilism of his concluding fable, "The Shore and the Sea."

There are still comic attempts at literalism, comic metaphor, and confusionism, to be sure, along with the now obsessive punning. But his disabusement, barely and cannily saved from diatribe by these last comic gestures, is comprehensive and deep —and, at the last, not very funny.

In the last stage of his career, a number of targets that he and his *New Yorker* colleagues had chosen for special assault are recognizable. The misogyny is still active. "I like to do what I can," he confesses to *Life*, "to keep the American woman—my great mortal enemy—in excellent condition for the fight." He shares in comedy's attack on children in *The Saturday Review*.

"The trouble with you is, you just don't like no children," she said coldly.
"You are wrong, madame," I said icily. "I *do* like no children."

He struck at Madison Avenue rhetoric repeatedly. But he also turned more and more to the unparticularized subject of the world's madness. "I think there's been a fallout of powdered fruit-cake—everyone's going nuts." To a large extent he moved away from special concrete subjects of attack, and he turned either to general assault upon humanity or to an ingrown preoccupation with deteriorating language. In his more vehement mood, "The Bat Who Got the Hell Out" stands in clear contrast not only to his own earlier pieces but to a similar fable of George Ade, "The Good People Who Rallied to the Support of the Church."

The contrast is not merely between a modern forcefulness and an earlier gentleness, but between the misanthropic invective of one age and the partial sympathy of an earlier time. Thurber's last stage represents a retreat from humor. And his irritabilities, his explicitness, his animus, his borderline perversities and grotesqueries, his final hopelessness, and his ingrownness are indices to the whole contemporary epoch, not only to his own career.

He touched philosophically on the general matter when he commented once on the unfunniness of fun in our time and, indeed, on the unfunny meanings we now place upon the word "funny," e.g., ominous ("there's a funny sound in the motor"), disturbing, scary. He recognized an age's declension to fright and horrors and the consequent degeneration of our sense of humor.[1] In this regard, he might have remembered how "comic" books became horror comics in the late forties and fifties and how his own humorous *New Yorker* published one of the most horrific pieces of journalism ever printed, John Hersey's *Hiroshima* (as it, still later, published Capote's *In Cold Blood* in its entirety).

C. S. Holmes has made the best case for a continuously vital Thurber. But Holmes's concessions, for example, to Thurber's growing anger and didacticism, have a way of being leading ones. And when the apologist elaborates Thurber's opposition of a masculine fantasy principle, loving and peaceable, to a female reality principle, cold and hostile, the defense disconcerts us. For such misogyny has become indeed too systematized and unhealthy in Thurber; he moved from his attack on certain women, on American women, to an onslaught on women in general and into a war on reality. And in his tightened equation of fantasy with honorific male idiosyncrasy and confusionism, he capitulated not only to a final grandiose oversimplification but to frank neurosis. Comic social criticism is possible on grounds that are more sophisticated and less extreme than that.

But Thurber increasingly withdraws from outer subjects anyway and seeks his comedy in anagrammatical humor and word play. He still enjoys antiproverbialism, getting his effect from

[1] He told his colleague, E. B. White, that a humorist was like a surgeon. His terminology was both ultimate and curative, but he had less and less recourse to such self-characterization as time went on. His own undertakings were more mortuary, as if he understood that the patient was dead and he consented to sign the last certificates.

changing or omitting single letters: "There's no business like shoe business," or "Don, give up the ship." But his efforts are less and less inspired and are largely predictable or flat: "A stitch in time saves none." Becoming blind, he compensates in comedy of over-intricate verbal play and of a predominantly auditory cast, as in the manufactured compounds of his later definitions. "A Fussgrape: 1. . . . a light eater . . . a scornmuffin, a shuncabbage. 2. . . . one who boasts of his knowledge of wines, a smugbottle." This is the intermittent cuteness to which his old sustained ingenuity is reduced. Almost a generation before, in "Ladies' and Gentlemen's Guide to Modern English Usage" (*The Owl in the Attic,* 1931), he had sustained exquisite comedy in the grammatical confusions of "who," "which," the correct use of "the subjunctive," etc. But in every case his demonstrations were actually rescued by his supplying the right and unaffected style to employ and a common-sensical tact. That implicit hopefulness disappears and, with it, his capacity for situational and sustained humor along with the verbal confusion. He is led to strained punning, insistent alliteration, or general intellectual gamesmanship in his last stage. "We battle for the word where the very Oedipus of reason crumbles beneath us." He becomes our comic Joyce, likewise degenerating into a fascination with ingrown verbal resources. It is his final refuge.

In "The Last Clock"[2] he presents a garbled fragment, as Holmes admits, of a second-rate, nineteenth-century poet, Longfellow, celebrating optimism as the world ends . . . again strained and, as it were, fixated. His satire on the exquisite breakdown of communication, itself a leading cause and symptom of a vaster breakdown, is undercut by his use of Longfellow. The disrupted communication is not worth having anyway. And so he finds himself without a true position to take.

Having himself celebrated disorder and illogicality in the face of overorganized modern life, Thurber at the last champions ordered and adult communication. But he loses his own clarity in

---

[2] The word "last" becomes obsessive in his final works (as in "The Last Flower" also). Clocks and all machines, especially sensitive ones, fail us at last. And "flowers," an even more repetitive image of pathetic doom, are plucked or otherwise destroyed at last judgments. Beauty and fragile life are overcome, as vital speech is, and a pensive nihilism informs his whole concluding view.

the process, his own larger, braver coherence. And he loses his revelry. He withdraws to mere cleverness. He is so disaffected or dug in, overgeneralized or introverted, and both together, that it appears as if he has come over that epochal watershed of World War II as in a barrel over a moral Niagara. Both the vehicle and the man are staved through.

Still, Thurber had gone on trying, and there was a certain pertinacity and courage in that. The recognition puts us in an anomalous position about the whole era as well as Thurber. We find ourselves acknowledging talent while we indict it. What is the essence of the matter if we shall be passing such ambiguous but fell judgment on an age as well as a man?

What we have is a highly diversified group working in a period that is itself a kind of historical anticlimax, the long cold war after hot war. How can they attain or maintain heights in a period that is itself a prolonged repercussion to climactic break-down, a sick joke of history? We will discover comic tenacities everywhere, as, indeed, in Thurber, and be prompted to think of resurgence. But the intransigent evidence argues for net decline and even decadence on all sides. The strains and grotesqueries of the later Thurber are also apparent in other contemporary authors, in a host of fellow cartoonists, especially those who treat the outré in full abandon, in the efflorescence of sick humor in this period, our own latter-day Baudelaireism, in comic enfeeble-ments and excesses on the air and on the screen, and in the un-certain position of Jewish humor in this period. If there are ex-ceptions and resurgences, as there clearly are, they appear as yet insufficient to counter the evidence for the decline and even fall of American humor. Such judgment is impersonal and pragmatic. In the material before us corroborations are alternately subtle and notoriously flagrant.

There is the signal career of Vladimir Nabokov, to whom we will return in another critical light later on. But we may note here that he gave a whole work over to the pursuit of morbid anti-

climax in *The Real Life of Sebastian Knight.* Throughout that
early work there were dark jokes upon the audience, logy travesties of emotion. The narrator gratefully arrives at the bedside
of his dying brother only to discover later that his vigil was for
the wrong man (as Sebastian Knight had once paid a prolonged
visit to a chosen hotel of his mother only to find it was not her
spa and that all his sentiment was foolish). And what we are allowed to glimpse of Sebastian Knight's own books makes them
into works of incalculable complexity and unnecessary sophistication, an intensely private systemless system of thought not
worth the plumbing. Time and again in subsequent works Nabokov will deceive both his characters and his readers, playing the
part of an intellectual practical joker. In *Pale Fire,* for example,
he expends fantastic energy in tracing the most introverted self-
consciousness we have seen in the modern novel.

His most notable success, *Lolita,* is a study in abjectness, perversion, and the comic but deadly consciousness of defeat ("Mc-
Fate"). In his willful seizure of coincidence and his other sophisticated "inside" travesties of plot, he both parodies and panders
to popular expectation, an early though arch employment of camp
humor. But there is no joy in original technique, only the uneasy
satire implicit in manipulation. It is like the last dexterity before
an utter paralysis of technique. And the self-conscious grotesquerie
of the violent humor, Quilty's pose during the most persistent
assassination in our literature, "Desist, sir. Oh, that was abom-
inable, sir," sets the seal on the method as well as the substance
of decadence.

But if *The New Yorker* avoided Nabokov's essential work and
published his more harmless and academical whimsies on *Pnin,*
it made up the difference in sponsoring Charles Addams' cartoons. And certainly Addams' technique, for all the world to see,
becomes even more grotesque after the war than before. Well
ahead of the sick humorists who have seen the barbecue pit as
the abyss, he already had grim antithetical cartoons behind him
like the Christmas portrayal of the Monster house from a high
gabled roof of which the domestic ghouls are about to pour a
caldron of boiling oil upon the carolers below. He advances relentlessly to the sedate and captionless grotesquerie of a living
room scene: Mother vampire knits a skull cap, the smirking chil-

dren play carelessly on the carpet with a scorpion and gila monster, and the father succumbs to himself in a corner armchair, while they all listen to music from their phonograph; presently one notices that the tone arm of the record player is a human one. The humor is of violent, tortured reversal, as he steadily pursues his career in the horrification of American bourgeois living. Mother vampire observes, while turning through a family photo album, "And this is your Uncle Casino, a man of whom it may be truly said he left the world a little worse than he found it." And we have this typical exchange in Addams, to stand beside his wordless living-room apotheosis: "Are you unhappy, darling?" "Oh, yes, yes! Completely."

But remorselessly Addams crosses all lines of taste, and his critic, Kenneth Allsop, reminds us of the gathering superabundance of grotesque and necrophilic images: two-headed babies, corpses in ice cubes, etc. And there is that cartoon, alluded to so often in New York that it seems virtually published, though one cannot discover it: the gorilla at a hospital saying to the attendant in the nursery, "Don't bother wrapping it, I'll eat it here." It is, at least, completely in the vein of the rest.

We recognize the animus against children and nice old ladies; over a nursery school playfield an Addams granny sits in a watchtower with a tommy gun. We note the uncompromising hostility to all women, wives especially; a suburban Mike Fink, now looking like Benchley, rakes autumn leaves around his wife, who is tied to a fire stake on the front lawn. And we appreciate the comic principle of disasterism in all his work: anthills erupt as miniature volcanoes, and stickers from the S.S. *Lusitania* and the *Hindenburg* zeppelin are on someone's luggage in a travel agency. These are traditional though strongly depicted targets and themes. But the fixation upon death becomes entrenched, and the psychopathic pranksterism grows increasingly obsessive. Whether or not it is true, the report attributed to O'Hara that Addams confessed how much he enjoyed walking through insane asylums is indicative. The De Sadean fixities and inversions of reality become more exhibitionist than critical.

The cumulative result is that of the mummified Louisiana Swamp Doctor stalking sophisticated editorial offices of our time, enlisting every terrification for effect. It is an ill-effect that indicates macabre dissociation, pathologically invested more in the shock than in the comedy of "comic shock" technique. It is a tactic exhumed from both Poe and H. C. Lewis, as well as Bierce, straining to surpass earlier performances and more and more either repetitive or exceeding all original motive.

But, as we all know, there is a whole popular mode of excess as well in this period. "Black" or "sick" humor, as we have had occasion to note before this time, is not a phenomenon of kind (or place . . . it runs high in contemporary Europe also). But it is assuredly a phenomenon of degree in postwar America. Never before has this strain of humor exhibited itself in so broad and continuous extent. A post-Korean development, it has encouraged and cultured an epidemic of "sick jokes," generally spreading from universities and then high schools and elementary schools to the general public. Although we have had upsurges of shaggy-dog humor in the twenties and of "little-Audrey" or "little-moron" jokes in the thirties, the new popular mode exceeds anything of the kind before.

"Aside from that, Mrs. Lincoln, did you enjoy the play?" This fillip exceeds the milder generic satire of, "Mother is rotten, God is rotten, the flag is rotten." One recalls the conclusion of the film, *Duck Soup,* when Margaret Dumont suddenly starts singing the national anthem of Fredonia and the Marx Brothers turn and instinctively shower her with rotten fruit. In that farcial never-never land, she of course deserved it. The question is whether all actual motherhood and patriotism are as monolithic and deserving targets as that matriarchal film character was.

The point involves a subtler technical consideration. Writer and critic, John Peale Bishop, had this insight into Dickens, highly relevant to our own subject. He suggested that the very taboos of Victorianism made for resistances that served Dickens; his very circumventions, hints, and indirections gave him his force. The resulting portrait of a homosexual Fagin is all the more un-settling not only because of the concessions Dickens made to prevailing taste but because of the stronger effects gained in technically overcoming the resistances of his problem. The dis-advantage of utter freedom is that the complete victory for realistic expression may constitute its summatory defeat; having nothing to overcome and no concessions to make, it loses the cultural resistances necessary to art. In modern humor, Perelman is one writer who rarely forgets that, for all of his extravagance. His comic satire, "The Saucier's Apprentice," for instance, grants the superiority of French cuisine, grants the cliché (in which there is almost always a grain of truth), and then makes high fun of the excessive consciousness of the cliché.

But the issues of discrimination, no less taste, and of resistance give no pause to black humorists. "I've had poor old mama cremated and keep her in that jar. Now every morning I can have a cup of Instant Mother for breakfast." Virulent desanctifications, of saintly Lincolnianism, of feminine idolatry and momism, of sacred American commercialism, we have seen heretofore, but never to the extent of what is virtually a massive campaign and never pursued to such vengeful, frictionless lengths.

To the comedian, Don Adams, during his night-club career, goes the impure credit of one of the most telling and original sallies in this vein. At the *hungry i* just after a local San Francisco airplane crash, he declared: "Sitting over there, I see Mr. G. A. Thompson, who lost his wife and two children in the crash today. Let's give him a great big hand! Stand up and take a bow, Mr. Thompson. Thank you! Don't hog it." The brilliance of the assault on our modern lovelessness and cynical self-indulgence, the comic assumption of Mr. Thompson's very presence there, almost rescues the savage, irresistant callousness of the attack itself.

Probably the difference between black humor and sick humor is that one is an expression of dark rage at miserable conditions or values[3] and the other is a perverse enjoyment of the same. Since the one generally blends with the other, we shall treat them as two sides of the same coin. We might ask if they are not, in fact, counterfeit humor, closer to annihilatory diatribe and in-

---

[3] William Burroughs, for instance, feels that he is competing with banal advice columns, those repositories of hollow American bourgeois wisdom, and that he needs to be shrill and disgusting to be heard at all. In *Naked Lunch* he is particularly strident in his tirades against "control addicts" everywhere. But the line between objective rage and sado-masochism is thin. It is a short step, in all such American pseudo-comedy, from making darkly explicit all the euphemistic hypocrisies and plots of national life to reveling in the exposé itself.

vective than to deflationary comedy, but the mode is so pervasive that it needs the most direct consideration.

In his article, "Those American Sickniks," Kenneth Allsop proposes his alternative explanations for the phenomenon, our release after the self-censorship of the immediate postwar period or our desperate solvent for terror and tension. It is difficult to understand what he means by the allegation of moral or some other censorship at that time. And the alternative he offers, while possible, is glib. He is more penetrating, however, than anyone else on this subject when he refers to the role of new Jewish comedians, fierce heirs perhaps of Groucho Marx and S. J. Perelman, whose tone of rueful debunking and sardonic fantasy is crucial. They may be considered as the tutors of a mortifying candor. (As such, they were rightly chosen by Goebbels as archenemies of a Germany dedicated to the theses of superman-ism and "the holiest matters in national life.") But the Jews have never been alone as minority critics of American life. Their contribution, while immense, cannot be taken as an exclusive or even determining factor at large or in this particular development. Indeed, it has been amateur and variegated youth, *those* heirs of the recent past, who have broken out most violently and decisively with sick humor.

Two major events have occurred that account for the new mode. They may be more properly called governing conditions, and they have had a decisive and special impact on American consciousness. One is the possibility and even realization of defeat, of a no more than qualified victory as our destiny ever since Korea. The other involves the whole modern collapse of comic as well as tragic distance. Neither condition is a peculiarly American matter, but each has had resounding repercussions in the United States, where they have been particularly highlighted by the effect of mass media.

As to the first matter, we are responding to the successive traumas of the twentieth century, the lessons of which are at last being absorbed. The breakdown of western civilization has made itself felt over and over again, in massive, stupid World War I, the thorough and deep Depression, the unimaginable Nazi atrocities, global and repetitive World War II, the continuing Cold War, and a certain official strategy of prevarication. All bewildering and expedient shifts of alliances have made their own mockery of loyalty and even understanding. We have been against Germany and then with it, against Japan and then with it, against Russia and then with it and against her again and, probably soon, with her again.[4] Such matters are not easily dismissed by a people newly arrived to world power and incessantly cudgeled by rhetoric from one messianic goal to another; the letdowns become a final exhaustion of morale. Disabusements have occurred before; our whole history is a continuous record of them. But now, just as comic virtues had culminated themselves in the previous period, thematic liabilities accumulate in this one. Final illusions or myths seem to have been climactically used up, especially for the liberal mind, making outsiders and cataclysmists of us. Indeed, Professor R. J. Kaufmann's observation in analyzing the exhaustion of the dramatic hero is germane: "Outsiders tend to be people in whom memories are too long. . . ." The collapse of idealism appears to have been decisive; if the incredibly wasteful World War I, with the fiasco of Verdun, had not told upon us completely, then World War II, with its Nazi extermination camps on one side and American ultimate weapons on the other, did. Moreover, following the second war, America at last assumed leadership of the free world with none of the advantages of undisputed power and empire but with all the disadvantages of ungrateful police power. And events continue to engineer the grimmest ironies of comic despair; we find ourselves once again supporting a neofascist strong man in Asia (as we did for Chiang Kai-shek in Taiwan and Rhee in Korea) as the final leader of all the nongovernments of South Viet Nam, hoping we can institute a true polity to justify our support of it. Such matters finally outstrip our most inventive capacities.

Far from being an academic matter, the whole condition is a central one, especially for youth. We had, after all, accomplished *some*thing in our foremost nineteenth-century crisis, the preservation of the union. By comparison with the promises of Lincoln, echoes of Wilson have become hollow; and the distance between Stephen Crane's *The Red Badge of Courage* and Ernest Hemingway's *A Farewell to Arms* is a literary measure

[4] Art Buchwald has made satiric capital of such political charades, including the ins and outs of the China fiasco.

of the psychological depletion. In addition, of course, certain leading domestic questions have become insupportable, like the stubborn problem of segregation. Even the Negro humorist, Dick Gregory, can be pushed to desperate extremes in the mood of violence and cynical revenge. About the Ku Klux Klanner whose sheet was on fire, he quips, "We threw water at him, but we missed. So we went back and filled our buckets—with gasoline." The two-part joke can be taken as a symbol of the chronology of the whole civil rights movement; it is an accelerative image of our abandonment of idealism and comic sympathy. But over and beyond such particularities of the American social scene remain larger general questions of integrated living in a nation not yet wholly identified, a problem unknown to other nations.[5] The resultant mood is wearied, resentful, cynical, violently reactive, thriving anew on irreverence and rebellion. Much of this emotion is adolescent but, at this late stage of affairs, there are certain unblinkable objective correlatives.

So much is true but limited as an explanation. Disillusion and disabusement, we have conceded, are constant historical legacies. What is new, however, is the immeasurable force of mass communications in our time. It heightens the effect of—and this is also new and true—the increased calamities, fraudulencies, and deepening disaffections of our age. The experience we have through our movie and TV newsreels is unique because it is constant. Current events become an immediately studied and restudied past. Recent history is endlessly passed before our eyes for constant review. Like it or not, we are simply made aware of enormities. The loss of morale, with adequate newsreels going as far back as World War I, is a doubled and redoubled subtraction, as it were.

With such pressure of events and reality upon the public mind, it has become difficult or impossible to assume any conventional tragic view. The systematic extermination of millions of people, for instance, was a cruel grotesquerie that inevitably surpassed the tragic and general imagination. To individualize tragedy,

[5] "I wasn't always a handyman," goes a joke absolutely inaccessible to foreigners, "I used to be a song-plugger." What English or French commentators cannot understand is not the vocabulary here but the depths of our social confusion, status consciousness we have never fully clarified—and never will.

under such circumstances, has proved all but impossible. Consequently there had been a shift to something else, a mode defined as the grotesque, the absurd, and the comic all together. A great deal, if not most, of the modern drama, of the new novel, of neorealism in motion pictures can be characterized as attempting the shift.

But conditions have shortened comic distance just as decisively as they have the tragic. If our time has trivialized, so to speak, the basis of tragedy, it has by the same token usurped both comic perspective and extravagance. Indeed, one may argue that the spirit of the new age is inimical to all art and literature, the ever-present facts easily overcoming fictions, actuality far outstripping the imagination. In Tokyo, the Japanese celebrate our Christmas; they install not one, not two, but three Santa Clauses, with real beards, in each department store, improving upon us in a matter of cultural grafting that has no indigenous meaning at all for them. It is an anecdote, chosen from thousands; such incessant news robs us of our powers of exaggeration and distancing. In America, radical "Du Bois Clubs of America" are misconstrued as "The Boys' Club of America," and a national headquarters of the latter receives bomb threats. Comic invention is deprived of certain grounds before it can start. And these things take place in a crescendo now, and, especially in the United States, we are made to know of them remorselessly and all at once.

If the two sets of prevailing conditions are joined, we seem bound to get a sardonic, bitter humor that moves along gradations of absurd, black, and sick humor. The rage to make explicit the euphemistic or tenaciously veiled hypocrisies of national life becomes especially strong. And the attempt to gain distance necessarily overreaches conventional satire in questioning all norms themselves. Even Thurber, in "Footnote on the Future," turns his linguistic obsessions to the uses of sick inversions and neologisms: "I Dismember Mama," "They Slew What They Wanted," and "Oklahomosexual." And a profoundly sick joke like the following attempts at one and the same time to strip the old veils of matriarchism and to gain new distance in doing so by revealing the nth degree of violence in reversed Medea-ism:

CHILD: Where's Mama?
FATHER: Shush. Drink your tomato juice.

CHILD: All right. But where's Mama?
FATHER: Never mind, I said! Drink your tomato juice before it clots.

Similarly, throwing hot pennies to children is a practical sick joke designed as a commentary on the more subtle exploitation of children anyway by a commercial culture.

The trouble is twofold, once we grant the traditional antithetical force of such humor. Obviously, there is always a group of pseudomasochists or egomaniacs as crazy as foxes to promote themselves. If under a banner of comic realism they can enjoy themselves out in the open, they will. In this period, a group of intellectuals adopts pseudo-Existentialism as a further rationale for an excess they need to express in any event. There is no question that, in America, these practitioners cast themselves also in a line of literary bohemians from Whitman to Henry Miller and that a sexual motif and fantasy play their role, as they do in the hipsterism of Norman Mailer, the tawdry mayhem of J. P. Donleavy, the destructive dope addiction of Burroughs, the rapism of James Purdy. A great and predictable percentage of literary black humorists welcome all the sanctions of righteous free-speech movements simply in order to claim license at last. And in a country where there is money in establishing a Disestablishment, none of our critical skepticism is unwarranted.

Nevertheless, another percentage, in all their comic rectitude, is also doomed to excess. They seek to be disinvolved from a world of political and economic chicanery, A-bombism, all war, and hypocritical conformity. They want to make their powerlessnesss into a program. Imperceptibly they are led from protest to separation to insulation. But they find their alienation so insupportable that they return full circle to a sick acceptance, where the ferocity of their irony carries down all before it, including the irony. It is as if in the joke—

"Why do Puerto Ricans wear pointed shoes?"
"To get at the roaches in the corners."

—they move inexorably from social protest to a perverse enjoyment of the roaches. The liberal motive is gone.

It is gone for more reasons than the apparent insolubility of all racial questions may suggest, and for more reasons than we may detail. For instance, the new monolithism of Big Labor, that old base, with Populism, of Progessivist and liberal strength, became invested in Big Business through its huge pension funds, thoroughly mitigating our pluralism. And all the Rooseveltian reforms turn out to have been compromises rather than changes. But more fundamental than living in an age of robber executives, who simply circumvent regulatory commissions and laws (including the egalitarian income tax), is the liberal disabusement with its own kind. It is not a question of crooked unionists on the liberal mind but of a whole public of laboring and middle-class con men out to beat the system for their own cynical purposes. Populism, Progressivism, and liberalism based its faith on "the people," and that faith is gone. A vast amount of political, social, and other economic idealism is broken upon this fact of popular unworthiness. That principally accounts for a career like that of the liberal and then radical and then psychopathic Norman Mailer.

In Mailer's *Barbary Shore*, for example, McLeod laughs to protect himself. But the laughter becomes mechanical and finally, as we have noted earlier for Hemingway and O'Hara, completely unavailing. McLeod, like Julian English, commits suicide. Death longing is the enraged comic's final solution. But that, we are told later in *Advertisements of Myself*, is the "square" answer. The new "hip" solution is . . . murder, as indeed we note the homicidal program in Mailer's own biography and latest works. The full rebel and denunciator, the new "barbarian," is opposed to the "square" liberal and "regulator," not only to the defenders of the *status-quo* but to those who take merely cowardly "bohemian" exceptions to the *status quo*. Perversity is opposed to both piety and timidity. Like a *Mein Kampf* of sick humor, Mailer's work is frighteningly explicit and unnervingly prophetic, especially when he at last sets homicide against suicide in his table of reversed virtues. Comic deflation has become annihilation. It is not for nothing that the humor is called "sick," for the risk of psychopathology when we are literally at our wit's end is considerable for all classes of black humorists.

It is not for nothing either that Max Eastman's sick ant joke becomes a model of black humor. The tale is of a convict who has trained an ant over twenty years to do tricks. After release from

prison, he takes him in a match box to a bar, has a drink, releases the ant and calls to the bartender, "Hey, see this ant . . . ?"
"Oh, that," the bartender says, quashing the ant at once, "sorry."
Some last meaning, rescued from suffering and defeat, is destroyed at once in our world of opaque misapprehension and
defensiveness.

The modern period is one of supreme vulnerability, for one set
of reasons or another or all together. Such insecurity hosts either
sentimental or nonexistent humor on one side or exacerbated,
black, sick rage on the other. Sick humor grows in direct proportion to the increased pressure of falsification or disabusement in
the era, and without the true comedian's fullest responsibility,
the sickest response is all we may have. That is all the more likely
because the resistance the culture used to supply against free
realistic expression is the very concession the culture has made in
our time, the single unmanning concession that throws us back
upon ourselves. And the isolation is complete when we note that
Realism itself has reached some ultimate impasse because the
reality which it is free to transcribe is often insane itself. Thus
the question of insanity becomes a prime one in the comic literature of the time, just as the social question of mental illness
bulks large in the community.

Still, the reason that the most principled of black and sick
humorists take their risks is the high distance they may achieve
over events. They seek an objectivity that is disengaged because
it is aloof from the contemporary scene—and that distance is what
they crave to regain. But, in so doing, their basic problems accumulate; theme overpowers technique, all sympathy disappears,
and another kind of oversimplification merely replaces the oversimplified theses American comedy has always declared war on.
In the scatological and obscene blasphemy of the most notorious
night-club comedian of the movement, Lenny Bruce, exaggerations of disrespect and fierce contempt for the sacred and simple
extreme hypocrisies of American life turn inevitably shrill and
extreme themselves. It is radical hysteric humor that screams
instead of laughs, and the four-letter amoralism is no less cheap
than any hypocritical moralism it attacks. Moreover, as Allsop remarks, sick humorists are in danger of making even the horrible
somewhat too palatable, diluting indignation with a snigger. It

is the last thing they want to do, unless they have floated absolutely off from the realities of their case.

We may add the observation that a campaign in unrelenting cruelty and brutal verbal assault is just as easy to pursue as sentimentalization and puffery. Only a comic criticism that is something else than pitiless, with force but a kind of split-second and last-minute restraint, answers to the true difficulties involved. That is very much like classifying humor as an art.

All this must be said in diagnosis and judgment. But the unholy proportions of the modern question make any usual wisdom perilous. In his last years, Finley Peter Dunne, like Thurber, marked out precisely what the later Twain also understood. But in modern times Twain's targets of stupidity, crassness, delusion became a barbarism and bestiality, as in Nazism, that finally overwhelmed the comic and human understanding. Dunne's words are posthumous or, as it were, posthumorous.

> I have been asked why I don't do some Dooleys on Adolf Hitler. The answer is that I cannot. Insanity and racial murder are not fit topics for one who would be considered a humorist. I fear that . . . if I had a gun in my hand and Hitler in front of me, I would use it—provided that I had waiting for me a fast getaway car with one of Al Capone's drivers at the wheel. And that is the real tragedy of our age, that those who live by hate contaminate us all and drag us down to their level.

Chaplin himself struggled heroically with the exact issue in *The Great Dictator*. The little Jewish barber returns home after serving his country in the first war and spending twenty amnesiac years in a hospital. He comes back to his shop to see anti-Semitic slogans on his window. In weak comic pathos he says, "Ridiculous, ridiculous!" and proceeds to wipe them off. But events have outstripped all absurdities. Behind him appears the ridiculous and absurd but real Gauleiter. The barber's corrective and poignant little expostulation is neither wise comic commentary nor adequate defense. He survives only by the most extravagant and lucky means. In the end, Chaplin's own power of ridicule cannot hold the ground, and he turns at last to desperate and serious oratory to conclude the film. That conclusion was a prophecy of a rhetorical Churchill. The gentle, antithetic Chaplinesque clown is no match for the absurd but potent evil of Hitler, himself our sickest clown, complete with comic moustache and puppeteering gesture, turned inside out. The comic protagonist is unavailing, and he gives over the stage to a monumental stalwart. The deference is significant.

Chaplin's fateful film, we may argue, marks the end of an age. Continuously since then, with the world in perpetual, extravagant upheaval, comedy cannot quite regain its place or employ its usual tactics for distancing its subject. Here is a scenario excerpt from an improbable Marx Brothers film that may illustrate the full problem.

> The President of Fredonia invites the Prime Minister of Ruritania, with whom he has been in contention, to visit him for a parlay. "How can I trust you?" asks the Ruritanian. "I give you my word! We *must* get together. I'll be down at the airport, and we'll have the flags out and the band playing." He sounds earnest, "All right!" agrees the Prime Minister of Ruritania. "It's a deal!"
>
> (Cut to airplane in flight. Cut to airfield. Airplane lands. Banners flying in the wind. Band playing. Close-up of President of Fredonia and entourage. Plane stops. Red carpet rolled out. Band plays. Plane door is opened. Prime Minister of Ruritania appears, descends stairs. President of Fredonia and aide approach Prime Minister.)
>
> PRESIDENT: This is my Secretary of State.
>
> Prime Minister turns to shake hands—but receives handcuffs, clasped upon him.
>
> PRESIDENT: He's also my Chief of Secret Police. You're under arrest.
>
> PRIME MINISTER: But you gave me your word!
>
> PRESIDENT: That was yesterday. (*pause*) I *said* we had to get together.

But this scene did not, in fact, occur in *Duck Soup,* though it might have. With the real names of the Congo and Katanga instead of fictional ones, it occurred outside of the imagination, in the world of fact. And having occurred this way in reality, it robs humor and farce of the exaggeration and distancing necessary to them. In a yet more updated script of actual international affairs, it would not be possible for Chaplin or Groucho Marx or W. C. Fields to match the surrealistic extravagance of the President of Guinea saying to the deposed President of Ghana, "All right, come over here! You can be President with me."

When world figures handcuff their rivals and split the presidential chair, we are told that all this is merely nascent Africa going through the comic-opera phase of South American politics. Meanwhile, among the true powers of the period, a Soviet Premier attending a world forum literally takes off his shoe and bangs with it as a gavel, while an unflappable Prime Minister proceeds with his speech; a President of the United States solemnly displays the scars of his recent surgical operation; and a President of France slips from behind a velvet curtain at the Elysée Palace to conduct a news audience in the manner of Louis Quatorze. Of course, the world is no more absurd today than before. (Napoleon called himself "Emperor, according to the Constitution of the Republic.") But mass communications swell the impact of any given situation, bringing us instant and constant reminders without letup. We have the benefit of universal televised coverage now, and accelerated events of the world outside are borne in upon us as never before.

At home, variations of that same theft of the imagined incident by reality occur on every hand. At the rostrum a Birch Society speaker considers himself interrupted by a cough in the audience; he fixes his eye upon the culprit and, as reported by United Press, says steadily, "That's a dirty cheap, communist trick!" And through these years of domestic embattlement, some public officials, including a southern governor, make clear allegations about the most massive campaign for rectitude and human rights in our history by describing the Negro movement as more red than black.

If the world and the nation live a succession of grim and farcical jokes, what is humor to do? Perhaps its task is simply to keep active the general latent sense of humor with which we are finally to laugh both our clowns and silly conditions out of existence. But that, too, is a more and more difficult assignment if, say, Americans have become anesthetized to their environment. Much of laughter, as Twain and Dunne and others have explained, heads off tears and rage. But if the public chooses another defense, an almost practiced insensibility, then we lose habitual laughter for that reason also.

The worst result of all is the loss of comic instinct. One walks down a street in an American town and sees a sign over one of the disappearing neighborhood groceries, expanded somewhat to compete with the chain food stores. The sign reads, so and so's "Superette." In other words, a small huge store. But few people laugh. No scores or hundreds of prospective or steady customers tell the manager how funny or silly it is. And, furthermore, it has never occurred to him; or he thinks that "ette" is the pluperfect of "ate." And in the great chain stores across the land we shop for "giant-size half-quarts" of synthetic grape juice. Or in the department or furniture store we buy rugs of "Virgin Acrylic" fibers, or a picture advertised as "an actual reproduction." The new variety of commercial and Madison Avenue confidence game is not only a P. T. Barnum fraud but the most cynical of jokes. The point is that, aside from some exasperated indignation among a very limited number of progressives, it occasions no reaction at all, no ridiculing laughter, among the general, solemn, single-minded public. No nation with a reflexive sense of humor would be host for very long to everyday phenomena like these.

We had practiced a certain tolerance of absurdity during Prohibition, of course. But we had repealed Prohibition and in many parallel ways had returned to our comic as well as common sense in the thirties. But other, subtler prohibitions, reticences, a helplessness perhaps, and self-consciousness have come to characterize us.

We are in great part humorless as never before. Indeed, that public fund of humor, which the comedian must believe is there, is not quite liquid anymore. In our increased subjectivity, we have frozen our assets. Perhaps we have become necessarily sanctimonious, engaged as we are in a whole series of economic, political, and social enterprises and changes that are terribly earnest. In that case, we are gratefully saved from Germanic seriousness and fanaticism by what remains of our pluralistic constituency. At best, we avoid totalitarianisms; but locked in these present coils of introversion, we do not hold on to full perspective or essential comedy. We go through a financial revolution, completely reversing Franklinesque economics, and now are dedicated to immense borrowing, publicly and privately, in order to guarantee our prosperity. And in this serious and vast and humorless national undertaking, we solemnly call our life of debt a life of "credit." Engaged in living out a sublime reversal of terms[6] and psychology,[7] we are beyond the potency of the essential reversalism practiced by comedy.

In fact, we join Russia in a virtual conspiracy to deny the humor of that celestial circus act we are both putting on. These two powers, *arrivistes* to international leadership, are just as competitive as one another, just as barbarically serious in displays of raw power, just as organized, bureaucratic, mechanical, and dehumanized. They play a mutual game of shooting protozoa, monkeys, dogs, and men in little capsules from the noses of rocket cannon through space into vast nets of ocean or Siberia: a grand finale of evolution, ending in salt wave or wasteland. On each new occasion of this spatial circus performance, designed ultimately perhaps to land their performers on an absolutely empty landscape of moon, responsible leaders and press deliver, as the English critic Michael Wharton remarks, solemn encomia about, after all, the comedy that is inherent in the situation. Furthermore, the implicit spy joke in America, to which no one adverts, is that in all these years of espionage and counterespionage about nuclear energy and rocket thrust we should have deliberately let the Russians have our "secrets," in order to slow them up. But nobody actively laughs at the prevailing situation or detects any potentiality in the comic dimension of Soviet-American fecklessness during the last twenty years.

In such ways have the forces of contemporary humor been

---

[6] A recent automotive ad cozzens you to "Take charge!" of your 1967 model ———, by which you are meant to "Charge your Take" of it. We live in an actual Thurberesque world necessitating constant translations of reality, economic as well as political. And intellectual. The university community, that bastion of strict sense, succumbs equally to the deterioration of language and thought, especially in the social sciences. A recent psychological experiment on the effects of hunger and thirst presented its results under two principal headings: "Food-deprivation" and "Thirst-deprivation." The desire for pretentious parallelism of expression leads to the completest lapse of precision, scientific self-criticism and common sense.

[7] Since the singing commercials of the late thirties and early forties, we hear love lyrics to things; the corruption of romantic pyschology has been so sustained that there is not the vestige of the earlier comic intention at all now. What irreality or profound cynicism this mass practice breeds in successive generations of the young is as inevitable as it is unhealthy. (We may also remark how impossible it seems to be for TV directors to have their American actresses laugh normally, as if the natural act has been lost by now.)

deprived of a ready public sense of humor, of their base of operation. Furthermore, Americans can no longer turn to devices like
dialect, as we have seen Dunne still able to do, in all his sharp
directness and explicit comic criticism. In the new and hardening
social conformism of middle-class America, class and racial tolerance is a shibboleth. An Irish-American and Catholic can become
President and perhaps, in some near future, a Jew and a Negro
also—and these are, rightly, momentous matters. Nonetheless,
modern humorists find themselves thereby cut off from a number
of ordinary devices of the past. Balked also by the reversalisms
of actuality as well as by the subjectivities of modern American
life, they face the alternatives of the merely feeble jocosity of TV
and movie comedy or literary canards. They choose, instead, one
degree or another of black or sick humor. And in so doing, they
institute the only other reversal left to them, the establishment of
their own made-up myths of depravity and meaninglessness.

Having been used to roughly attacking the false morality and
prettified lies of American life, these quarters now substitute the
value of savage immoralism itself for hypocrisy. Extremists are
dedicated ostensibly to telling the simple, brutal truth, but what
they say turns out to be more simple and brutal than true. It is
not all their fault, of course, and they share a certain predicament
now with black humorists elsewhere in the contemporary world.
But with home-grown precedent, they cross or are pushed across
the invisible line into excess. Aristotle acknowledged a certain
deformity as required comic subject matter, and in our day W. C.
Fields stipulated a certain amount of cruelty necessary to humor.
But not too much ugly deformity, Aristotle continued, and not *too*
cruel a cruelty, Fields confessed. Driven over utter verges, however, sickniks tell their black stories and harrowing jokes almost
helplessly, though there are natural psychopaths among them who
welcome the situation.

They choose grim laughter as a homeopathic protection against
total disintegration, but the rewards are meager. They sport a
new cruel insensibility as a badge of objectivity, but the emblem
is merely one of brutal self-satisfaction. "What's black and crawls?"
is the sick joke from a few years back. The answer is not even a
disgusting animalist sadism but the name of a Negro athlete
paralyzed in an accident. More recently, among new auto bumper

and lapel button signs, are such fillips as, "Mary Poppins Is a Junkie" and the even newer and more typical broadside, "Support Mental Health or I'll Kill You." It is homeopathy with a vengeance.

The degree of it as such and the place it has in contemporary novels of John Hawkes, James Purdy, J. P. Donleavy, William Burroughs, Norman Mailer, and even in Joseph Heller and Terry Southern, are not persuasive arguments for high and flourishing comedy. To be sure, events continue stubborn, and in that alliance we have traced between humor and realism one partner is all but overborne by the other. Sick jokes of actual current history supersede the comic imagination. Mrs. Oswald, especially as portrayed in Jean Stafford's *A Mother in History*, overcomes any conventional portraiture of comic creation, like the one in Bruce Jay Friedman's *A Mother's Kisses*. The odds against resurgence of genuine humor continue strong, and a kind of capitulation to them runs apace. When, with full candor, Joseph Heller claims in a *Time* interview that black or any kind of humor is not a goal at all but a means, we have further matter to rue. His impromptu manifesto signals the decline of the philosophic integrity of humor and its vital function as an end in itself.

The full argument for the adverse status of contemporary humor rests on further evidence. The mass media present an almost unmitigable case for decline. First of all, the post-World War II period saw the demise of radio entertainment as a whole. The satirical impersonators, Bob and Ray, enjoyed a vogue after the war but then abandoned sustained programs, content with "spots" for the NBC weekend Monitor. Goodman Ace tried a last revivification of "The Circle" with Tallulah Bankhead as mistress of ceremonies but failed, as he did still later with an ineffectual use of Jane Ace as disc jockey. No experimentation has occurred since. No hour, half-hour or even quarter-hour comic performers are left on the air, with two qualified exceptions. Chicago's Brad Crandall, of WNBC, is a radio commentator and telephone interlocutor, who is often frank, sharp, and realistic, but he is unsteadily comic. The only full-time practicing humorist really left on the air is Jean Shepherd of New York City. Generally septic and consistently irreverent, he is a descendant of the satiric Henry Morgan of the prewar period and the same metropolitan area. Shepherd may be even slightly more acidulous and brave than his model, but his strict lineal descent from another Mutual broadcaster points up the derivativeness of his comedy. He repeats Morgan closely. But because this vein of radio in New York functions like underground humor of old, he is able to get away with more of the same as the very last exponent of what is now, in that pocket of the country, a coterie comedy. It is, however, a ventriloquist effect we hear, as of a voice thrown from 1939. The rest of the medium, given over to pure advertising and rock'n' rollism, is totally underground, interred.

But we must look to the sequent medium, TV, for a lively and fair comparison. There is, however, no schedule on television that matches the evenings of an ordinary radio week of 1939–1941. That, in itself, is our first and leading observation.

There are still the prestigious holdovers on television, Skelton and Hope. And we had Danny Kaye, from the movies, for several seasons. Skelton now works and reworks sheer sight gags, puns depending on the prop man. He steps out of character so often, in deliberate commentary on the absurdity of the goings-on, that all he demonstrates at the last is a fundamental lack of belief in humor.[8] Where a cardinal rule used to restrain the comedian from ever joining the laughter of his own comedy, now old as well as new hands make a point of laughing at or against it. Meanwhile, Hope,[9] at once the most popular and disjointed of the old guard, continues his merest flippancies and the topical association method ("The freeway . . . that reminds me. . . .").

[8] For all of his mild antitheticism, like the antichildism of "The Wittle Kid" episodes, Skelton has become the most duplicitous of the long-run comedians on TV. His sign-off sentimentalities and even drolled religiosity ("May God Bless . . .") conflict with scatological ingredients of his humor. He frequently provides a good, clean, dirty show, absolving himself with a benediction.

[9] Hope's very name signals optimism, we are not liable to forget. We are helped by a later self-satisfaction in the performer even more smug than vapid. Like Will Rogers, one may institutionalize himself right out of his wit or, like Hope, into the most visible comic snobbery. His annual Christmas shows to the troops are not only the rankest self-advertisements replayed back home but the most exploitive charades, since the audience is automatically appreciative of anything at all and the shows become personal appearances rather than true performances.

And Kaye, a superb mimic and natural comedian, the most talented of all, also degenerates shamelessly into rib-poking self-consciousness (in-group laughter at a poor script, superior winking at the audience) or indulges the frankest sentimentality. We have returned basically not to the worst of the thirties but to the worst of the twenties and before, to the weakest vaudeville. All of the overorganization of radio is there (Bob Hope's corporate efforts rather than Fred Allen's bravery), and little of the sustained individual performances and less of originality. Far more than was ever true in radio, television personalities borrow heavily from one another, are parasitical and even incestuous; a new cowboy, doctor, or spy series engenders endlessly sly and monotonous raiding and repetition. There is, moreover, almost none of the epithetical mode of radio comedy and precious little comic asperity. On variety shows much is made of flagrant camaraderie, quick hugs and bussing, all good inane fellowship. The confusion of good-naturedness with humor, or the substitution of it for comedy, occurs miraculously in a television adaptation of Charles Addams' monster family. The series managed to reverse Addams' quintessential point and deviscerate inherent possibilities; the monsters, after all, conform to the bourgeois code and values, only the fixtures and faces are bizarre. The interlude is another gauge of the prevailing superficiality of TV fare, as compared with comic entertainment and satire available during the heyday of radio.

The most striking illustration of the enfeeblement of TV comedy is provided by a program with a duplicate career on radio and television. Alan Funt's "Candid Microphone" of the late forties was centered upon an incredibly pushy interviewer, who brought his subjects to the highest pitch of infuriation. Funt's ability to sustain such an interview placed a premium on virtuosity, his capacity to antagonize, slowly but surely, exceeded only by his own imperturbability. His comic mastery was cut short only by his change of medium. "Candid Camera" gradually but certainly became a vehicle of cute snapshots and ingenious practical jokes which, in the nature of sentimentalism and good sportsmanship, had to be relatively unsustained. Funt became an emcee for a private newsreel, frequently pointless and always innocuous.

Elsewhere there are flamboyant impostures, especially in the late evening. The Jack Paar and Johnny Carson "Tonight" shows have suggested or represented themselves as impromptu performances, though writers and directors have been in the wings until the very moment of telecast. Actually, Paar could turn into an adroit and even honest parodist and interviewer quite on his own, and Carson, much less arrogant than Paar was, has his own ready wit. But the composed literalistic patter—"He asked me if I'd like a dip in the pool, so I said yes, and he threw a cheese fondue into the swimming pool"—is the most hapless punning and wisecrackery. And the attention called to one's failed technique—"I must have 'peaked' there somewhere, a few minutes ago"—is the most blatant rather than sophisticated self-consciousness. Informal spontaneous staff participation in the ensuing laughter is, moreover, the most cynical device of comic extortion. And the courageless undercutting of commercials, with none of Henry Morgan's frontal attack, is timid derision that goes nowhere at all. Stand-up form robs Carson's real gifts especially.

For the rest, TV comedy occurs in three places. There are set interludes for guest comics on variety shows. And there is a frothing sea of domestic comedies[10] that skip over even teenagers to appeal to the subadolescent audience. Apart from these, adult comedy had been attempted here and there in programs like "That Was the Week That Was" (patterned on an English model, in turn derived from the French *chansonniers* school), which did not last long, in the frequently literate Dick Van Dyke programs, and in the career of Jackie Gleason. But "TWTWTW" huffed and puffed and strained for effect at the last. The Dick Van Dyke series was not exactly fecund or consistently exploitive of its stars' talent. And Gleason's best efforts, apart from "The Honeymooners," have come, like Skelton's, from silent movie mimicry

[10] In most series of this type the male figure or father suffers the fullest reduction—except in the perennial "My Three Sons," where there is no mother or wife at all . . . and no threat. The popular antecedents for the devaluation of masculine authority are the prewar comic strips, like "Bringing Up Father" and "Blondie." Why such influences did not quite affect radio as they subsequently affected television ("Henry Aldrich" as opposed to "Dennis the Menace," etc.) is less a result of time-lag than of the obvious decline of firm script-writing. Television producers, like the inferior movie men of the thirties, in arguing that they give the public what it wants, merely make a virtue out of defect.

now and then. His attempt in one area is especially indicative; a bartender "spot" on his 1964–1965 series verged on social commentary but consistently veered away from bite, wit, and revelation. His Joe the Bartender only pretended to be Archy of radio's "Duffy's Tavern" or Finley Peter Dunne's Mr. Dooley. He had no audacity, comic forthrightness, relevancy, or verve. The alleged humor was harmless. And that, at the last, stands for the medium: guaranteed innocuousness or pratfall. It is bland fun, a species of baby food. And it comes in a package, complete with its own seasoned response, canned or prompted laughter, just in case we fail to hiccup after a certain condiment.

In later efforts to circumvent their difficulties, producers have at least graduated to the college audience. They attempt to capitalize on "camp" humor. The truth is probably that the solid appeal of the "Batman" series is still to the children. But even if the quasi-adult audience existed, the inversions of psychology would signal the devaluation of comedy just as readily.[11] For "camp" by definition is the enjoyment of something so badly done or conceived in the first place that the ridiculous or grotesque fraud, in its transparency, is laughable, much as we laugh at an ineffectual insult to our intelligence. Certainly, "camp" functions in part as a comic criticism of the taste and values of the whole previous generation. But we are fundamentally enjoying our own contemptuousness. And in its use of camp humor, television comedy is pandering, at the *highest* level, to that. What was the lowest form of entertainment a generation ago becomes the highest now through a process of desperate pseudosophistication. The mania will end by being taken seriously by the tots rather than archly by youth. But even if it did maintain a hold on its desired

[11] We may extend ourselves as far as we like about the derivation and function of camp humor. It is necessarily outlandish because it emerged from homosexual theatrical types or because it took rise from the Existential view of the absurd world; it enjoys failure or, in pop art, creates failure, in order to accommodate us to an existence of failure. But we cannot halt analysis at the sophisticated intellectual's happy contentment with origins alone. For if camp humor is an answer to the rage implicit in black humor, it has generated its own extremisms of snobbish noninvolvement or the masochistic love of trivia and defeat. It may now be moving into a new involved, deflationary mode, "stoop humor," as Lee Israel believes, but then it will simply serve orthodox purposes with a new vocabulary of slang. Meanwhile, in itself, as I contend, it is a phenomenon of decadence.

audience, the involuted game of self-consciousness would be the surest sign of comedy's exhaustion, not to say decadence.

Similar things may be said of that phenomenal vogue of James Bondism, the ins and outs of which are equally self-defeating but curious to behold. Bondism is itself a spoof of spy thrillers. Frequently subject matter that is already passé is revivified one last time in literature or popular entertainment for the sake of comedy or romance. Medievalism functioned that way for satiric Cervantes, as espionage does for Fleming. Convinced in his depths that there would be no world-wide war or catastrophe again, Fleming even had to manufacture his villains, the SMERSH superstate; his hero was necessarily fighting straw men. Still, the work constituted a new cartoon or burlesque of spies. It engendered, especially in the United States, two subsequent inverted jokes. Its hero was eventually taken not amusingly, as by John Kennedy, for his anachronism and stratospheric high jinks, but seriously as a new fantasial superhero; at least the two apprehensions of Bond existed side by side. And this second effect occasioned subsequent series of spoofs, like "Get Smart," to spoof a Bondism that was more than half the time taking itself somewhat seriously. In other words, in a final effort to get comic distance, we are asked to consider a cartoon of a cartoon. It is no sheer accident that the malign organization in the spoof of a spoof is named KAOS.

Either a kind of tortured decadence or frank exhaustion seems to be television's answer to the excesses of sick humor. The demise of radio has been followed by the ineffectuality and delirium of TV. Certainly much of the weakness of such TV entertainment comes from its weekliness, and only a major change of commercial telecasting policy will affect the situation at all. Meanwhile, in our age of accelerated developments, all we can claim is that whereas radio had a relatively short career, TV, certainly in comedy, has had an even briefer one. It is a distinction, of kinds.

That leaves the movies as a popular last resort. Here and there workmanlike comedies have been made in the prewar mold. There have been a few sporadic comedies of later vintage and a meager handful of major creative effort. And that is about all we can say, except to advert to Doris Day pseudofilms. Chaplin himself fell off catastrophically after *Monsieur Verdoux* in subsequent maudlin films. There have been no successors to the original comic stars of the thirties except for Jerry Lewis, whom American critics judge as a highly stylized humorist given to comic idiocy and overdrawn sentimentality, scarcely in the class of genius.[12] A high number of films have been brazen remakes of prewar successes, e.g., *Move Over, Darling* and *My Favorite Wife*, Axelrod's *Goodbye, Charlie* and *Here Comes Mr. Jordan*, and, at that, they manage to dilute or destroy the comic effect of the originals. And needless to say, there can be no self-originating force to frankly nostalgic imitations of Keystone techniques, as handsome and as expert as *The Great Race* and *Those Magnificent Men in Their Flying Machines* are.

Two other particular approaches of postwar movies have been marvels of ingenious decadence. The film version of William Humphrey's *Home from the Hill,* an involuted novel about the resurgent disasters of a Texas family, accurately preserved the satirico-epical proportions of the book. In doing so, it piled romantic anticliché upon anticliché with comic imperturbability, the happy climax or denouement always superseded by catastrophe. The result was a tonally serious anti-Hollywood production, but with such slavish dependence in its point-for-point reversals of plot as to be almost studiously comic. The wonder was that the public took the film seriously, which it insensitively did, but that was pro-Hollywood's revenge and a commentary on the fundamental poverty of invention in the book and scenario. The trickery of technique was as decadent as it was consistent, but its consistency is what told at the box office. What also has told at the box office is Hitchcockism, the most cynical joke mass entertainment has ever foisted upon a public willing to be conned. The blatant impossibilities of plot (*North by Northwest*) or belabored sick conveniences of characterization and relentless improbabilities of grotesquerie (*Psycho*) have become Hitchcock's

[12] The otherwise stringent French are curiously eager to lavish their highest praise on a variety of Americans, including Edgar Poe, Orson Welles and William Faulkner—infallibly at their worst. Drawn as the French are to the bombast and broader effects in Shakespeare also, one detects more than a simple language factor. What is probably operative is the classical French mind giving way to the impulse of primitivism abroad, where it is safe to do so.

chief exploitation of a public thinking it is getting suspense of
the old sort instead of new, sick comedy solemnly claiming legitimacy. Both Hitchcock here and Clouzot abroad are treated as
"important" figures by film sophisticates and the public at large,
whereas they both elaborate immense jokes upon their audience.
It is a cinematic form of Nabokovian decadence . . . and without
his grace of technique, which Hitchcock progressively gives up
in increasing contempt for sustained nicety over and beyond his
shock scenes.

Moreover, his success has encouraged even brasher experiments
in thematic decadence on the screen. The movie treatment of
Richard Condon's *The Manchurian Candidate* magnified every
absurdity, the central literalistic device of a Bircher working for
the Communists, the romantic side issue and sick joke of an
engaged heroine falling instantly in love with a railroad passenger
and stranger, the near-psychotic hero, etc. The comic writer,
George Axelrod, who did the scenario, willingly compounds the
organic fallacy by making his plot insane in order to expose insanity. That is the very least to say of it; at the worst, like
Hitchcockism, it hoodwinks the audience in the long, extravagant,
cynical joke it perpetrates under the guise of suspense and "message."

For the rest, the amount of out-and-out comic films is pitifully
small in this period. The same is true for the stage, where there
have been no real competitors to effective period pieces like
Life with Father, sentimental but exuberant zaniness and social
critique like *You Can't Take It with You*, and waspish epitheticism
placed in the midst of suburbia as in *The Man Who Came to
Dinner*. A handful of flip, spunout vulgarities, like *The Seven
Year Itch*, and one or two serviceable comedies, like *The Tea
House of the August Moon*, have accounted for Broadway's chief
efforts in legitimate theater. The theater of the absurd has come
into its American own in the work of Edward Albee during this
period, but the man and the question involve the strict legitimacy
of the theatric or literary achievement, judgments we defer for
the moment. Where stage successes have been clear and memorable, in musical comedies of the period, like *Oklahoma!* or
Carousel or *South Pacific* or *The King and I*, there has been more
music than comedy. Jud is a genuinely malignant figure in the

first; unregenerate Liliom is the subject of the second. The young romantic hero is killed in the third, and, in the last case, the king dies. Few of the stage "books" are original, and most derive from material with decidedly somber shadows. "Light comedy" in the postwar productions frequently turns into grotesque or heavy comedy. The lyrics for "Poor Jud is Dead," in *Oklahoma!* might more appropriately have been written by Charles Addams than Oscar Hammerstein. And the specific gravity of "You've Got to Be Carefully Taught [to hate]" in *South Pacific* and "But Is a Puzzlement" in *The King and I* reminds us of how many passages in these productions were conceived as quite uncomic. In other musicals contemporary realism has completely overcome comedy, as in *West Side Story*.

The only other popular mode to refer to, in a desperate attempt to locate joy, comic or otherwise, is the popular song. Indeed we have had our lyricists in the past. But this period brings to a close the careers of Irving Berlin, Oscar Hammerstein, and the superlatively witty and sophisticated Cole Porter. Only Lerner has continued to show a comic and fertile inventiveness at rhyme and lyric to match his predecessors, while other popular lyricists, like Mercer, write steadily less and less. In the field of the lighthearted popular song as a whole, a witlessness and even inarticulateness have generally consummated themselves in rock'n rollism. The cheap seems to have irreversibly driven out the dear in both the esthetics and economics of the situation. We witness either an incalculable hoax, played upon moneyed youth, or utter depletion of resources, or both.

One other factor asks to be placed among the liabilities of recent popular comedy, and that is the new snobbery of Yiddishization. Wallace Markfield has explored the development fairly adequately, though he does not set it in such perspective. But the fact is that the success of Jewish writers and the correlative acceptance of comic Yiddish terms into urban and suburban parlance have robbed Jewish humor of its minority stance. It has lost a certain di-stance as well, from where much of its power and deflation came.

The causes of such ambiguous success are complex. They are,

first of all, literary; Jewish novelists "arrived" in force in the postwar period. There is an argument, too, that late-show TV interludes of more intimate Yiddish "stand-up" comics had an impact on a much vaster audience than anticipated. A more comprehensive analysis, however, simply holds that sooner or later everything is amalgamated into all-inclusive Americana, Negro jazz, Ozark folklore, Creole cuisine, and Jewish humor. Or we observe that, because everybody is frankly alienated in America and now comfortably symbolizes the American Jew as an image of himself, protective Jewish attitudes and humor are being assimilated as never before.

Whatever the reason, its meaning in broad social context is largely to the good, of course. It parallels the acceptance of Catholics fully into our national life, without seeking to convert them necessarily into respectable WASPs. It also foreruns the inevitable and full integration of Negroes, without alluding to them as really white underneath. These are significant changes, worth every related disability. But there are disabilities, especially for the subject of comedy. Such acceptance tends, at least initially, toward sentimentalization. Softenings occur. Forward cutting edges are blunted. A *sub-rosa* humor is lost, and though a whole level of mockery and self-mockery rises to the fore, particular stringencies are abandoned because the resistances that formerly called them into being are gone.

Certainly there are some special gains. "But what have you done for me lately?" pops into general currency. It is comic shorthand that reveals all our overweening self-interest and constant farcical need for approbation and help. But there are enthusiastic excesses, mostly errors of self-consciousness and fashionableness that blunt effect. "How about a drink?" is the old question. "You got maybe a little seltzer?" is the new, repetitive answer. It would reflect what it used to reflect, antisnobbery, execept that now it is merely the thing to say, a new faddism, our latest modish snobbery. Everybody shares the Jewish joke now. If we occasionally heard an inside Yiddish phrase in an old C movie, now we hear it in countless scripts. Markfield's example from TV of the oriental sleuth throwing out dark hints that "things here veddy veddy far from altogether *kosher*" is representative of the new practice (although it stems from Fred Allen's creation, One-Long-Pan, back in radio.) Indeed the essential example of generalization of Yiddish usage and the Jewish view was the play and film, *Majority of One*. Its material also exemplified the extreme dilution and sentimentalization of that view, the final effect one of cuteness instead of acuteness.

Another disability resides in our purchasing certain phrases or jokes from Jewish humor without fundamentally cultivating the humor itself. One literally buys calendars with Christmas and Chanukah labeled "Them" and "Us" or barometers with the legend, "Tomorrow Fair, Maybe Not So Fair." These are fixtures in Christian homes. The question is related to that of humorous sign cards, about which we will speak in a later connection. The problem is this: how much are we absorbing Jewish or any other humor if it is explicitly manufactured for and sold to us?

Still, the primary liability is the softening of such humor as it comes into general acceptance. The whole matter is related, as Mencken might have pointed out, to the fortune of profanity in our country. Nothing, after all, is more socially antithetical than profanity, though comedy runs a close second. We tend, however, to accept "you old son of a bitch" and "bastard" into general expression and then, by virtue of the affectionate and soft absorption, to destroy original pith and even intent. It is true that Americans have been more impressive in their minority humor than in their profanity, but the one is just as vulnerable as the other. And in these matters, nothing apparently fails like success in America.

Certainly there are efforts among some Jewish humorists and writers to refurbish the essential wit. But they are fully aware of the changed conditions. Joey Adams has even adverted to the disappearance of the old breeding grounds for Jewish free-swinging humor, the Borscht Belt; the long training field for relevance and bite has been denied to a new corps of comedians, reducing their number from legions to a finger count. In any event, resurgence under the general prevailing conditions seems all but impossible. Alan Surgal, who wrote the off-beat movie, *Mickey One*, about a Chicago night-club comedian, bravely tries to update the old technique. But his typical astronaut joke—"How would *you* feel if you were sitting up there on seven hundred and fifty separate parts by the lowest bidders?"—may represent old Yiddish deflation but not quite true pertinence. In the nature of things, he must strain somewhat for effect.

On the negative side of our modern record, there are, then, two great liabilities, an enfeebled or nonexistent comedy and a straining and dark excess of pathological dimension. Force and proportion seem irreconcilable.

But there is a positive side of the record, of course. There are straightforward, enviable triumphs in this period also. The evidence on both literary and popular levels requires not only due consideration but, in the interests of true appraisal, the strongest possible representation.

The continued career of S. J. Perelman, heir apparent to Thurber, is a leading case in point. His work spans both prewar and postwar eras. If his achievement necessarily involves a certain amount of repetition, still his prolific record of comic satires and bagatelles is remarkable for the high degree of durable successes that outlast topicality. Pieces like "Genuflexion in the Sun," "You're My Everything, Plus City Sales Tax," and "No Starch in the Dhoti, *S'il Vous Plaît*," in the postwar collection, *The Road to Milltown*, are brilliantly sustained comic inanity and scathing satire together.

If anything, there is an even higher level of literate and sophisticated comedy in the best of his postwar pieces than in his prewar efforts. Related to the comic fantasies of Groucho Marx, whom Perelman knows, and to the grimmer surrealism of his brother-in-law, Nathanael West, Perelman's work goes on its inimitable way, but the continuing energy is a particular cause for celebration. His well-known series of attacks on Hollywood, "Cloudland Revisited," are deeper attacks upon our American sentimentality, to which many of the older films catered. He frankly accepts prevailing cultural forms as an index to general values, and he gains distance on both the exploiter and voluntary exploitee by means of a high but flexible and withering style, one of the technical phenomena of all our literary history.

In "No Starch in the Dhoti, *S'il Vous Plaît*," Perelman imagines an epistolary exchange in 1903 between the elder Nehru in India and Nehru's Parisian laundryman, remarking about their high-flown and mutual recriminations that, "Even if they accomplish nothing else, they would help widen the breach between East and West." Characteristic letters end in sophisticated riposte: "I . . . remain, with the most transitory assurances of my regard," Pandit Motilal Nehru. And correspondence proceeds with the most direct and literate hostility:

MY DEAR M. PLEURNICHE:

You may be interested to learn—though I doubt that anything would stir you out of your vegetable torpor—that your pompous, florid, and illiterate scrawl of the 27th arrived here with insufficient postage, forcing me to disgorge one rupee three annas to the mailman. . . . Not content with impugning the quality of the cambric in my drawers, you contrive to make me *pay* for the insult.

The laundryman's protestations take the form of haughty replies and explanations to his client.

DEAR PANDIT MOTILAL:

I am desolated beyond words at the pique I sense between the lines of your recent letter. . . . You can be sure, however, that if our staff has been guilty of any oversight, it will not be repeated. Between ourselves, we have been zealously weeding out a Socialist element among the employees, malcontents who seek to inflame them with vicious nonsense about an eleven-hour day and compulsory ventilation. Our firm refusal to compromise one iota has borne fruit; we now have a hard core of loyal and spiritless drudges, many of them so lackluster that they do not even pause for lunch, which means a substantial time saving and consequently much speedier service for the customer. . . .

Ineffectual in class-pleading, Pleurniche is finally sued.

After all, when . . . suit for a million francs breaks over you like a thunderclap, when the bailiffs seize your business and you are reduced to sleeping along the *quais* and subsisting on the carrot greens you pick up around Les Halles, you may mistakenly attribute your predicament to my malignity, to voodoo, djinns, etc. . . . What doomed you from the start was the bumbling incompetence, the ingrained slovenliness, that characterizes everyone in your calling.

The ill-concealed or flagrant aggression and contretemps involved in the high-styled exchange are typical of Perelman.

In one respect his antithetical attack is reserved in extra measure for the cultural form as well as for public gullibility.[13] The Madison Avenue elite have replaced P. T. Barnum, all robber barons and McKinley imperialists, and later Big Business as the archcapitalistic targets and supreme confidence men in his work.

Through his very joy of means, mostly stylistic, Perelman has neither soured nor curdled through more than a generation of work, mainly for *The New Yorker*. He manages to find the right phantasmagoric distance with which to back off from an already outlandish American and world scene. In both plot and verbal play he combines a saving literalism, incalculable punning, and general extravagance ("I was reading a copy of *The Skin Around Us*, when . . .") instead of reversal to gain his ends. At all events, his continuously productive career is evidence either that no decline in our later period is inevitable or that he himself is exempt from sociologic rule.

But there are other literary exceptions to the rule, among them James Farl Powers, whose comic short stories are more than delicate transcriptions of unusual misogynic circumstances ("The Valiant Woman") or humorous and careful portrayals of underdog prelates ("The Forks"). All his work is dedicated to the greatest degree of comic openness and flexibility, and his prevailing practice rests on one supreme overturn of standard literary procedure. Instead of showing how a realm of timeless spirit impinges transcendentally upon our workaday lives, Powers' treatment of churchmen shows how the concrete mundane world obtrudes upon all spiritual and abstracted concerns.[14] That

---

[13] Nonetheless he considers women as particularly gullible addressees. Just as women get along better with machines in Thurber, so are they more accepting or willing victims of advertising than men are in Perelman. But the misogyny is no more exclusive in Perelman than in Thurber. Parallel to Thurber's portraits of masculine repression are the episodes of male insanity in Perelman; for every Mitty in the one there is a man who puts a microphone in the refrigerator in the other. On the whole, however, women and children fare more poorly in Perelman, who is a traditionalist in these regards.

[14] Chon Day's procedure in his "Brother Sebastian" cartoons can be characterized in much the same way. In particular, the world's business ethos constantly overcomes the traditional monastic stronghold ("Soul Agents for This District") in Day's gleeful but sharp work.

THE RISE AND FALL OF AMERICAN HUMOR 322

suppleness of mind accounts for Powers' central comic insight and continuous though not prolific talent.

All popular modes and media provide further confirmations for the resiliency or resurgence of American humor. It can be argued, for instance, that Baker's and Mauldin's cartoon work surpass anything done in previous wars, save some bitter, satiric cartooning of pacifists during World War I. Nobody in our combatant history, however, has been as consistent as Mauldin in the Second War. A long American cartoon tradition, from Nast, the "Yellow Kid," and Rube Goldberg culminates in his work, along with a literary comic past rooted in Mark Twain. Willie and Joe are reverse immigrants in the European theater, combative innocents abroad. They are semiliterate, malapropistic, and ingenious American prototypes regenerated for action. They are provincials abroad: "Some of you men may never come back," explains a QM officer to truck drivers of the Red Ball express. "A French convoy has been reported on the road." They are Huckish, self-protective liars: "I coulda swore a coupla krauts wuz usin' that cow for cover, Joe. Go wake up th' cooks." They are cynical comic realists: "Just gimme a coupla aspirin," Willie resigns himself to a medic. "I already got a Purple Heart." Their comedy is replete with native exaggeration and reversal; during frontline bombardment Joe, the unruffled veteran, remarks, "Ever notice th' funny sound these zippers make, Willie?" Their comic literalism is extravagant and picturesque; a top sergeant stands by his jeep with its broken axle, covers his eyes with one hand, and prepares to shoot it in the motor with the other; and in a soaking rain during the merciless Italian campaign, under pitiless natural cover, Joe says, "This damn tree leaks." In the series, Mauldin's democratic bias is forceful: "Beautiful view," comments a major to his captain in French mountain scenery. "Is there one for the enlisted men?" And his antirhetorical gibes, combined with simplicity of drawn line, are highly effective: "Fresh, spirited American troops, flushed with victory," he cribs from the wire services, "are bringing in thousands of hungry, ragged, battle-weary prisoners . . . ," and his portrait of the bone-weary GI escort is eloquent contradiction. In the very midst of fraud and holocaust, Mauldin's work places a premium on technique, especially literalism and reversal, and

seeks the greatest disengagement and objectivity rather than
bitterness. "We are not pontificators," he once explained in
What's Got Your Back Up? (1961), and in that relativism of
comic consciousness he has found his surest motivation.

His career continues vigorous after the war, in his political
cartooning. He succeeded the famous Pulitzer Prize winner,
Fitzpatrick, at the St. Louis *Post-Dispatch* and pursued his way to
a prize of his own. His work goes on, at its best combining all
the overt caricature intrinsic to the genre with the eloquent
subtlety he also communicates. His 1966 cartoon of Johnson and
De Gaulle is to the point; they appear in a captionless duel of
long noses . . . and prides.

Mauldin is not alone, of course. The whole field is still strong.
In this period, Herblock holds his own as a master of effective
wit. His famous cartoon from the McCarthy era of an hysterical
American dashing up a ladder to the torch of the Statue of Liberty to put the fire out is the very height of comic pith and wisdom.
And we recall that the broadly popular comic strips of Al Capp
and Walt Kelly are not without social and political dimensions
in this time. Capp elaborated one particular sequence of the Li'l
Abner series that attacked both business and labor; his all-provi-
dent "schmoo" threatened at last to destroy the profiteering and
strenuous American system. To date, the invention and doubled
antitheticism of that sequence remain unsurpassed in his work.
In broad outline, nonetheless, his skepticism has always been comprehensive, for he has conscientiously pursued all idols—politicos,
businessmen, Hollywood types, city slickers, and yokels themselves. Although he himself has spoken of the funnies as providing
new folk heroes for popular culture, he has, like Lardner, almost
systematically worked at their deflation. His main technical draw-
back has been too close a repetition from frame to frame. But his
fundamental comic imagination has been venturesome in the
extreme, and he has been forthright in theme. And the best of
these themes have not been severely topical either—as in his
series on the "Kigmy," those kick-me flagellants America temporarily enjoys in one memorable series of his cartoon strip that
deals with the release of aggression we particularly crave.

So has Walt Kelly been brave in "Pogo." Moreover, he surpasses Capp in wit. Where Capp's humor is often cruel and gross,

Kelly's comic realism and occasional pessimism are pushed along more gently. Pogo asks how to spell "delighted," and Porky answers, "It's a stickler, and I avoids it—try 'sad.'" Both Capp and Kelly appear to have been influenced by Fred Allen, as in their choices of political names and mocked rhetorical clichés. But in Kelly's fables Allen's literalistic wit has been more telling: "We have met the enemy," Pogo announces, "and they is US." Kelly's use of typography is not without its point and reveals, further, the fundamentally verbal cast of his humor.

Schulz's "Peanuts" is not at all topical satire but is no less disingenuous. Referred to aptly by *Time* as "A Child's Garden of Reverses," the strip alternates its sentimentalities with the most penetrative, allegorical uses of children. In two frames Charlie Brown, after missing a fly ball, confesses to Lucy: "I wanted so much to be the hero. But I always end up being the GOAT! No matter how hard I try, I always end being the GOAT!" Focused in the third frame, Lucy calls after him: "BAAHAHHH!" In addition to capturing the blunt and epithetical modes of humor ("I enjoy being the bearer of bad news," boasts Lucy), Schulz strongly deflates the nascent self-pity in Americans. And in his more rambunctious moods he packs high explosive in a simple four-frame strip. "If I tell you something, Lucy, will you promise not to laugh." "I promise." Charlie continues, "This is very personal, and I don't want you to laugh." "You have my solemn promise." Charlie concludes, "Sometimes I lie awake at night listening for a voice that will say, 'We LIKE you, Charlie Brown-nnn.'" Lucy's final detonating laughter blows away the code of politeness and the vow of loyalty, unable to contain herself at this confession of a sublimely intermixed egotism and conformism. Such work, including the simple draftsmanship, has certain kinship with Thurber's cartooning.

Meanwhile, *The New Yorker* school of cartoonists is the mainstay of whatever comedy is left to that magazine. And there are the diverse postwar phenomena of *Mad*[15] comics and of Jules

[15] It may be argued that the separate existences of *Mad* for the popular satirical market, *Playboy* for perennial college seniors, *The Realist* for the far leftists, and *Satire Newsletter* for academic quarters, plus the comic departments in *The Saturday Evening Post*, *Look* (Leo Rosten), and *The Saturday Review* (Goodman Ace), show a splintering of taste (and the failure of *The New Yorker* to become our national journal of satiric

Feiffer. Moreover, comic cartooning pops up anywhere and on any subject, filling vacuums left by other media. Thus television's relative inability or timidity to attack its commercial sponsorship is met by the cartoon picturing anxious executives and TV crews awaiting the comment of a "realistic" taster of some brewery's magical product; he remarks before the cameras, "Say this 'Brand X' is pretty good beer." A whole range of work in this medium continues vital, expert, and often anything but innocuous, in the postwar period.

There is no evidence that jokes abate in this era of cocktails, conventions, and parties. "I feel a hell of a lot more like I do now than when I came in," is as competent as Woolcott's dry martini joke of the thirties. It resembles Stengelese, which harks back to the Little Audrey circularity of the previous period; in answer to a midnight ring and apology for the hour, Stengel replies, "It's all right, I had to answer the phone anyway." His humor could be original, however. When the manager of the champion Yankees accepted congratulations for a World Series victory, he declared, "Thanks, thanks! I couldn't 've done it without the players." This is direct, instant jocularity in which the notorious malapropist always calculated more than interviewers knew. And allied with circular jokes and Stengelese confusionism is a new brand of collegiate nonsense humor ("What's purple and hums?" "Electric grapes"), a retrenchment at least from sick humor.

It is notoriously difficult to certify the newness of any joke but, on the whole, subjects like abstract modern art and modern psychiatry suggest new material and new uses of literalism and reversal. "I was in that new alcove of the Museum of Modern Art studying their latest acquisition for thirty-five minutes before I realized it was the ventilator." Or there is the story of the Rorschach test given to a man suffering from lecherous sexual obsession.[16] "What does this ink blot remind you of?" asks the

---

humor). But the isolation or specialization of audience cannot be adduced as a factor of unmitigable decline since the very existence of such publications suggest an over-all, eager audience of some proportion.

[16] We acknowledge all the unprintable ribaldry still current. Sexual stories are generally tall tales, often athletically so, and in addition to hyperbole rely on reversalism and the frankest literalism as chief comic devices. The mode is perennial, no less (if no more) inventive now than

psychiatrist. "A naked woman." "And this next one?" "A naked woman." "And this third one?" "Another naked woman." The psychiatrist nods decisively. "Well, that does it. You're suffering from sexual obsession that is deep-rooted and highly fixated." The patient replies, "What the hell do you mean? *You're* the one with the dirty pictures!"

New political developments provide fresh opportunities, and there is little partisanship in such released comedy. The author has heard of a ball hurled toward one of the pins of a split shot in bowling that passed precisely between them described as "an Eisenhower." A leading joke of the Kennedy years involved RFK's suggesting the possibility of Martin Luther King as a future President; with the blitheness imputed to him, JFK is made to reply: "But do you think the country is *ready* for a Baptist?" As for Johnson's most cherished domestic program, literalistic joking exclaims: "Two billion dollars appropriated for the War on Poverty! And the poor people haven't anything to fight back with." And there is the third-force gibe about the Alabama gubernatorial race of 1966: "Bedfellows make strange politics." One of the most telling arguments of all about our resurged sense of humor occurs in this field of political jocularity, since the defeated Democratic candidate, Adlai Stevenson, was strongly given to wit and comic stories; his defeat can scarcely be attributed to his humor, and we are left with the candidacy of the first man since Lincoln who regularly told and enjoyed jokes during his campaigns.

The rising executive class introduces new uses of satiric realism signaled in the joke about the company president's bulletin board poster, "Do It Now!" As a result, the cashier skips out with $14,000, the sales manager elopes with the best secretary, the

---

before, and occurs anywhere from Bangor to Borneo. Still, the mode seems more rampant in Anglo-Saxon than in Latin cultures, a commentary yet on Puritan repression.

Nevertheless, our prevailing realism makes these jokes a little harder to tell nowadays, forcing us to wit in the mode as much as to extravagance. In the joke—"Have you ever smoked after sex?" Girl: "I don't know, I never looked"—there is a combination of retreat and candor, a witty technical appropriation of realism over and beyond literalist punning, which is more difficult than usual. More sophisticated jokes of the same type may make their appearance in the near future.

typists ask for an immediate raise, the union votes a strike, and the IBM computer wins the office pool. Expanding and changing university life allows for new punning, as in the anecdote of students who marry while still in school session; they put the heart before the course. And if television personalities have replaced Hollywood stars by now, still the topic of huge histrionic egos is comparatively modern and allows new jokes. "Now," says a celebrated panelist at a soirée, "let's talk about you. How did *you* like my last show?" Inevitably, the whole realm of civil rights entertains all sorts of possibilities, particularly of reversal. "Governor Faubus is all right," quips the liberal, "but I wouldn't want him to marry my sister." And last but not least, space topics open the way to stories of astral fantasy and down-to-earth realism in equal proportions. "Get your finger out of your ear," says a middle-of-the-night Martian visitor before an empty service station, addressing the middle gas pump, "and take me to your leader." Or, says another wayward and weird Martian, bumbling into a crowded, smoke-filled bar and all unnoticed coming up against the juke box, "What's a nice girl like you doing in a place like this?"[17]

Moreover, jokes leaven the news by explicit design as well as by virtue of that implicitness we have referred to as the built-in

[17] The joke may be pressed to double reversalism, and a bibulous and misogynic Martian could say, "What's a girl like you doing in a nice place like this?"

We may observe that covert jokes are strewn through the more sophisticated science fiction, as in James Blish's *The Triumph of Time*—the mockery of terminological pretension, the spatial tall tale, and imperturbable reversal and nonsense:

"One can't superimpose an entropy gradient at right angles to a reaction which itself involves entropies of opposite sign on each sign of the equation."

"But why can't you?" Dr. Schloss said. "That's what Hilbert space is for: to provide a choice of axes . . . the rest is only a simple exercise in projective geometry."

. . . . .

They were entirely outside of experience in the macroscopic world. Matter was so completely transparent . . . that stopping an average neutrino in flight would require a lead barrier fifty light years thick.

. . . . .

"It may be that we will find ourselves carrying on as we always did but in the anti-matter universe; if so, we would be unable to detect the difference."

comedy of American life. The newsman Brinkley, on NBC, is particularly selective and calculating in his dry effects. And the staffs of all the networks deliberately excerpt interviews for piquant material. "I'm not against progress," says an alderman protesting rezoning for beautification, "I'm just against improvements."

And with American hegemony in the world, new international jokes abound, including the naming of an American spy plane, incidentally, with the witty forethought, U-2. The national sense of humor, day by day and even in the highest public echelons, is not quite dead . . . or buried.

It might be instructive also to remember that whereas other sensational crimes in our history have given material for sick exploitation, the Kennedy assassination did not do that. We have alluded to the example of Lincoln before. The Lizzie Borden ax murders produced numerous sick rhymes like, "Lizzie gave her father forty whacks and when she was done, she gave her mother forty-one." And the Lindbergh kidnapping produced the sick song, "Who put the snatch on Lindy's baby, was it you, was it you, was it *you*?" But although there have been one or two attempts similarly toward Kennedy, there has been nothing like the vogue in each of the other instances—and that is conspicuously persuasive evidence for resurged taste during an epoch of epidemic black humor.

In mass entertainment, deterioration has scarcely been complete either. In fact, a whole new medium of disc humor took rise in the period. Sometimes gross and generally uninhibited, the field was effectively begun by Tom Lehrer records. Lehrer's comedy has always been somewhat indisposed—there are queasy titles ("Poisoning Pigeons in the Park") and emetic verses ("Life is like a sewer, you get out of it what you put into it.")—but his off-color humor is what principally demonstrated the freedom of the medium. Libraries of this humor include the work of Shelley Berman, Mort Sahl, Nichols and May, Jonathan Winters, Bob Newhart, Woody Allen, Bob Cosby and the comic mimicry of Ralph Meader during Kennedy's Presidency and of Fanny Flagg in the Johnson term. They, too, show the influence of European *chansonnier* commentators. Highly irreverent, they withhold their fullest astringencies and antics from the television screen and vent them in record albums and in night-club and auditorium[18] performances, from which many of the albums are made.

There are light and heavy varieties of such humor. In the former are Cosby and the Smothers Brothers, indulging comic reminiscence and good-natured foolishness. Even in them, however, a certain irreverence prevails; Cosby's foxhole medic refuses to make "house calls." And when, in an interlude of the latter pair, George Washington bravely confesses, "It was I," his father, "with tears in his eyes, smashed him in the mouth—because he was in the cherry tree when George chopped it." But weightier humor informs the other disc comedians more consistently. Berman, for instance, employs a virtual format of antagonizing or unsettling his audiences, enlisting their sympathy (for children, frightened airplane travelers, women hanging from window ledges) only to mock them with outspoken devices of comic pertinence and antithesis. Nichols and May are other exponents of deliberately unsentimental humor, mocking romantic and filial love in particular. The extended complication of some of their sketches, for example, a lost last dime in a pay telephone during an emergency call, is another notable feature of the Chicago pair, probably the most gifted team in the period. At this late date, most of the notable performers are in decline from their best days or have turned to other things, but they have left their mark. And they are joined in these years by Hal Holbrook's uncanny renditions of Mark Twain, so that the disc medium as a whole achieves rich dimension in the period.

Holbrook's TV rendition of "Mark Twain Tonight" was a signal event also, and we are reminded, of course, that all television offerings cannot be totally dismissed. We are miffed at the immense missed opportunities of television but forgetful of some good. Future Pay TV may open a floodgate of possibilities in humor as well as drama; meanwhile, commercial television, almost jocularly self-advertised as free TV, has its slight record. For one thing, the phenomenon of American dancing, always

[18] Their one-night stands, before college groups especially, are latter-day Chautauquan performances. In this sense, they remind us forcefully of the nineteenth century literary comedians on the "lecture" circuit.

On disc they may also represent what Stan Frieberg has called "Pay Radio." That seems only half-true, however, since the selectivity and repetitiveness of record playing make for a difference.

joyous and often comic in choreographic inspiration, ought not be slighted; it is pervasive and effective. And there have been memorable instances of comedy proper by Bob Newhart, Louis Nye and Don Adams, among others. Newhart has often applied the techniques of comic momentum in his monologue skits, seeing "what would happen if real situations go a little further than usual." Nye's simple routine of the hostile and intolerant army indoctrination sergeant, mercilessly exposed, is in itself a classic café and television satire. And practically embedded in the American language by now are the comic self-deprecations of Don Adams' lines, "Well, would you believe . . . ?" and that confessional hallmark of incompetence, "Sorry about that . . ." The attempts on the "Get Smart" program at comic pertinency have scored frequently:

> KAOS MAN: You'll get nothing out of me. I can take threats, torture and endless questioning. How about you?
> MAXWELL SMART: Well, I can take threats and endless questioning. But I'm not too crazy about that torture.

And certain situations involving pool room sets and chess games have been clever and fast-paced, particularly during first-year successes.

Among the stalwarts of the medium, Gleason and Carney have perhaps achieved the best moments in TV comedy. Their old and revived series, "The Honeymooners," is modeled somewhat on the comedy of Laurel and Hardy (whom they have impersonated at least once), but it is more earthy as well as more aggressive and misogynistic. And, for all his slapstick disabilities, Skelton is a consummate master of mime, on occasion openly competing with the French mime, Marcel Marceau, and matching him. Indeed, all the old professionals, including even Lucille Ball, are best when they recover their professionalism and are not smug or self-satisfied or superior to their verbal or pantomimic material. Of course, that material is in question. But there has been a record of some achievement, just as there is a slight one of new talent, like Carol Burnett's, in the medium.

Occasionally some filmed TV comedy, as in the Chrysler Theater, has succeeded exactly to the degree that it recaptures prototypes and techniques of romantic comic movies of the thirties. In the 1966 playlet, "Dearly Deductible," Peter Falk, a kind of James Cagney or John Garfield to Janet Leigh's Irene Dunne, regains the deftness of former acting. A huddled story line is still recognizable and effective: the early hostility and funny epitheticism of a couple in an economically convenient and temporary marriage, followed by armistice and true romance and then by confused disruption (the trapped lover discovered going ambiguously in and out of other boudoirs), etc.

Undoubtedly, the most consistent success of the time has been the Dick Van Dyke program, which, at its best, capitalized on an almost perfect format. Risking the involution of being a TV show about a TV writer, it frequently succeeded on two fronts. It alternated an urban, rapid-paced, wisecracking, and high-powered New York scene with suburban situational comedy, always literate in its better episodes of either setting. It was certainly liable to a family type of bathos and occasionally corrupt sentimentality. But its greatest effect occurred in the New York sequences, as when one of the "writers" fired fusillades of epithets upon the bald head of the feckless "producer" of the TV show within the show. This was a vestige of the combatant radio humor of the thirties. In addition to the quick-witted shafts of Maury Amsterdam, which owed something to Groucho Marx and to his own former career as a stand-up comic, there were sporadic appearances of Carl Reiner. These interludes, with Reiner portraying the egomaniac comic TV star, occasioned some of the sharpest comic hostilities met with on TV.

Septic and epithetical humor on the rest of TV appears unexpectedly on informational and news programs. William F. Buckley, Jr., turns Menckenism to good effect on his interview program, "Firing Line," and the audience he loses as a political conservative he regains as an entertainer. But more credit is due David Brinkley, who has certain resistances to overcome in a formal news program and must compose his remarks or short essays with tonal exactitude. Nevertheless, he is forthright in defining the Imperial Wizard of the KKK as the one who wears more expensive sheets than the others in the cow pasture and, upon his podium, has drier feet. His sardonicism is loosed especially upon all varieties of political rhetoric but particularly upon the inflations of Senator Everett McKinley Dirksen. His abrupt pertinence, or im-pertinence, is ready for colleagues also, since his technique is genuine and not of the *parti pris*. His exchange with NBC's own meteorological authority during the Gemini 9 flight is illustrative, as if an unbemused Frank Sullivan took after his Cliché Expert. We abstract it from memory:

BRINKLEY: Is there weather on the moon?

EXPERT: That depends on . . . what you mean . . . by weather.

BRINKLEY: Oh? How about rain, say. Or snow, ice, heat, or cold. That's what's usually meant by weather in the normal lexicon.

EXPERT (triumphantly): Well, how about solar storms of 300 miles an hour?

BRINKLEY (directly to the camera): Now the thing to ask is what a "solar storm" is, I suppose. . . . Isn't it possible for you to. . . . Well, we know there's such a thing as knowing so much you can't give a straight answer to me or eighty-four million ordinary viewers.

In such unlikely moments, the medium comes into both its comic and human estate.

There is some value in comic film work during the period, without our need to force praise. Chaplin's *Monsieur Verdoux* (1947) is a marvel of technique. His misogyny and misanthropy are ingeniously qualified in the story of a bluebeard with a sick wife and child on his hands. Quite impersonally, after sympathy has been laid for him, Verdoux picks only on the most useless older wealthy widows for his victims. He has his ups and downs, and is even defeated once by the Luckiest Woman in France, whose dumb luck at the Loterie Nationale extends to everything else. The film's quick and sharp ending, in which Verdoux denies any extreme unction before the guillotine as cowardly and recognizes only that he "had not been sufficiently organized," like Krupp, thrusts the homicidal world back upon us all. Chaplin manages to give Verdoux sensibility, esthetic and otherwise, carrying his whole film calmly but relentlessly to that exact line between comedy and tragedy. It is a masterpiece from the period, and in its very conception, especially its dogged retention of standards of sympathy and sensibility, is another answer to black humor. And it sacrifices nothing in extravagantly comic detail. It is hard but triumphant comedy, giving way neither to heroic sentimentality nor to utter anarchy of feeling.[19]

This realistic containment of both sentimentality and nihilism informed other films in the United States, like Stanley Kramer's *High Noon,* where Capra's good, saving "people" fail the hero, although the hero does not fail himself at the last. One would have expected more comedy in the same thematic key, perhaps from Kramer himself, but it did not materialize as a vogue or to any extent whatsoever. Later it accounted for the signal and single success of *The Americanization of Emily,*[20] but that was all. Experimentation veered to the dark extravagance of Kubrick's *Dr. Strangelove* instead.

Meanwhile, more orthodox movie comedies occurred, though not plentifully. Fred Allen's *It's in the Bag,* immediately after the war, was in the old manner. Sylvia Fine's clever vehicle for Danny Kaye, *The Court Jester,* and Norman Krasna's expert film, *The Ambassador's Daughter,* were reminiscent. Two of the old style Cary Grant films, *I Was a Male War Bride* and *Operation Petticoat,* showed what could still be done—unpretentiously but sustainedly. Billy Wilder's films, especially *The Apartment* (where Fred MacMurray was used as a reversed American type) have been significant; although his impure gagsterism and refusal to go the distance undercut his mordant satire, he has a feeling for surfaces, his stark and often sordid urban settings and his use of the desert (in *Ace in the Hole* and *Kiss Me, Stupid*) as imagery for moral desolation contributing to his acerbic themes. New stars like Shirley MacLaine and Jack Lemmon, or Judy Holliday and Paul Douglas, and supporting actors like Tony Randall and others meant also that performers of high competence were still available. Only the slowdown of Hollywood itself and the scarcity of writers, perhaps, held back the force of on-going movie comedy.

We must also allude to the conscientious movie transcriptions of Broadway musicals, plus some original work of quality, like

[19] But its antitheticism is clear; it is set in prewar France, just before the whole particular society will go to its own guillotine, and the time and place operate with uninsistent but great retroactive force.

[20] Paddy Chayefsky's other films, including *Marty,* were more in the old vein of Capra, and of Steinbeck, in weighting the sentimentality conclusively rather than the realism.

Seven Brides for Seven Brothers, in contrast to the neo-Ziegfeld fluff and camp in the B and C musical extravaganzas of the thirties. That has been a noteworthy improvement, a consequence of diminished but quality production in Hollywood.

As for the stage musical comedies themselves, positive things may be said of the venturesomeness of many of the lyrics and "books." Hammerstein's experimentation with Nashian rhymes has had its occasional audacity, like the rhyming of the second syllable of "initial" with "wish" in "People Will Say We're in Love." His light skepticism in songs like "I'm Just a Girl Who Can't Say No" and "It's Either All or Nothin'" in *Oklahoma!* deserves notice, as do his comic innuendo and qualified hostility of "The Cowboy and the Farmer Should Be Friends," also in the same play. All the more, then, is he entitled to his brave clichés set against fashionable nihilism in "Cockeyed-Optimist" during *South Pacific.*

But Frank Loesser's lyrics and Abe Burrows' book for *How to Succeed in Business without Really Trying* are special victories of enterprising old hands. The cynical, competitive, antiromantic success ethos and how-to formulaism of the culture are laid bare, and songs of audacious narcissism are triumphs of exposé ("I Believe in You," the hero caterwauls lovingly to himself). The antidemocratic choral number, "There's a Brotherhood of Man," is a tribute to junior executive and mass mediocrity.[21] Burrows' lines about the "bold caution" of corporation presidents and his phrases about the "purity of ambition" in the hero's self-devoted rise in the organizational world are the soul of wit (and close to Bertolt Brecht). The overview of a confidence game played against the nepotism and masked incompetence of Big Business appealed not only to President Kennedy but to a vast audience still hungering for comic deflation. A certain lilt may be sacrificed in the process, but it appears well lost in an otherwise balanced but strong conception.

The special role of minority humor has not altogether disappeared. The recovery of some undisguised Yiddish directness

[21] Not, as Danny Kaye sings it on TV or in personal appearances, a sentimental ballad to humanity.

and dialect and the emergence of unabashed Negro comedy are
the latest developments in this area. Gertrude Berg carried forward from her radio series, "The Goldbergs," to her private
success in *Majority of One,* helping to institutionalize the familiar
and sentimental strain of Jewish humor. But its more characteristic aggression and deflation resurge in the comedy of Alan
King and Jackie Mason. King's ruthless misogyny and relentless attacks on suburbia are to the point. And Mason's assumption
of personal antagonism or snide hostility to arbitrarily selected
members of his audience recalls a former acerbity and freedom
of manner. And attributable to lesser lights is a new sequence of
nonsense proverbs or antiproverbs, in the tradition of extravagant
Jewish deflation of received wisdom.[22] "A sieve can't hold
water, but it can hold another sieve." Or: "Never spit in a man's
face, unless his mustache is on fire." A minor school of Jewish
comedians keeps alive a Jewish contribution to the tall tale, as
in the horse-in-the-bathtub story, elaborated extravagance also
in the service of conclusive deflation. Since the comparative
Yiddishization of American humor is a fact, we must also
acknowledge the refurbishing and revival of standard Jewish
jokes, which now enjoy very wide general currency. Mostly,
these are stories that puncture egotism and are meant to teach
self-deflation. Stories that make fun of the Jewish sense of importance in the world—a famous one ends with the line, "Who's
that [the King or the President or, more usually, the Pope] up
there with Finkelstein?"—have a carryover value now to American grandiosity. And Theodore Bikel's revival of the synagogue
story, about the wealthy Jews of the congregation who join the
rabbi in ritualistic and loud self-revilement, has hidden pertinence;
when a poor tailor also throws himself in the dust, the rich look
up to exclaim, "Look who thinks he's nothing!" The paradox of

---

[22] And the nonsense joke, pushed to utter verges with a Yiddish shrug:
  "What's green and flies?"
  "I give up. What?"
  "A herring!"
  "A herring . . . ?"
  "All right, it isn't green."
  "And what do you mean . . . ?"
  "All right, so it doesn't fly."
Considering the basic Judaic investment in sense, even in antic Jewish
satire, this is fundamentally a counterattack on nonsense humor.

a protested egalitarianism along with a persistent class consciousness makes such standard Jewish humor more and more accessible to a franker and self-critical Christian audience in America.
And in recent years the rise of the Jewish columnist Art Buchwald as a social and political satirist is significant. His typical
purpose, he has announced, is "to treat important things face-
tiously and facetious things very importantly." In practice, he is
often uneven and wholly mechanical, but in his best political
sallies he is the current holy terror. Politics may continue to be the
safest of all targets in America; nonetheless, Buchwald's innuendos
and asperities represent another resurgence. Think of where we'd
be, he writes in 1965, with broad reversalism and literalistic
fury, if Goldwater had gotten in, "we might be bombing Viet
Nam, have our fleet out there, maybe be landing troops!"

And behind this Jewish contingent, in ranks of their own, are
Negro comedians like Dick Gregory and others who can turn their
humor against themselves. "I waited in a sit-down for two weeks
at a restaurant in Jackson, and when they finally integrated . . .
they didn't have any ham sandwiches!"

We must pause in such an argument, however, to acknowledge
the more fearsome and bitter Negro humor also. Indeed, this side
of Negro humor must be counted among the most sardonic we
have ever produced, not without cause, of course. It has a history,
as Joseph Boskin has indicated, in slave humor: "A black hen
laid a white egg, and they hung her." And Professor Richard M.
Dorson updates this kind of comedy, presumably right up to
the early stages of the civil rights movement: Negroes who have
to ask for "a can of *Mister* Prince Albert"; and one Mississippi
Negro's excuse for crossing against the light, "I saw all the white
folks going on the green light, so I thought the red light was for
us colored folks." But progressively the Negro rage at the continued strength of southern racists and the slowness of integration increases in force. The disabusement, especially with rabid
proletarian whites up north, parallels liberal disenchantment with
"the people." And the growing impatience with Johnsonian reform is remarkably similar to the second thoughts of exhausted
liberals on Franklin Roosevelt.

The hardest and most subjective Negro jokes, therefore, come
in our time, even as strenuous efforts are made in more objective

humor. In addition to Dick Gregory's deflection to hard humor, as in his KKK grotesquerie cited previously, there are two searing examples that deserve our focused attention. The first, Boskin's example, quotes a white sheriff commenting on the discovery of a Negro civil rights worker who had been hand-cuffed and leg ironed and who drowned when he tried to escape.

"Look at that damned nigger. He tried to swim across the river with all them chains he stole from the hardware store."

The second tells the story of a white driver who accidentally killed two Negroes and comes up dazed before the bench.

"What can we do?" he asks in genuine despair.
"Now, just a minute," says the white judge, "hold on. Let's see. I've been reading up. Well, we can get the first one that came through the windshield, on breakin' and enterin'. But the best I can do on the second feller, who went sixty feet, is leavin' the scene of the crime."

But Gregory's way out of the eventual cul-de-sac of Klansmen doused with gasoline is to defend himself (from himself ultimately) with more playful literalistic comedy and with self-deflation. "Boy!" three racists threaten him at a restaurant, "anything you do to that chicken we're gonna do to you," whereupon Gregory puts down his knife and fork and kisses the chicken. But over and beyond such obvious tactics, he declared, "I've got to make jokes [on] myself before I can make jokes about them . . . ," and he has been followed by the greatest number of his Negro colleagues in this direction. "Flesh-colored band-aids" didn't have the Negroes in mind, we hear. And against our protest that banning 20,000 Library of Congress volumes with the word "nigger" in them is ridiculous because there are 50,000 volumes with the word "bastard," comes the reply, "We know, but you bastards aren't organized." This is the self-humor that most rescues and recommends modern Negro comedy. Against Black Muslim superiority, the objective Negro comics can tell jokes on themselves which the rest of us wish not to tell; when God was cooking up the universe and was working on the world and human beings, he held up a Negro and said, "Another burnt one!"

This is the kind of self-mockery we may still achieve in our humor. It is held this side of the masochism and sadism of sick humor, where the prevailing joke about the Negro has been not only the tasteless but the vicious gibe on how far Negro rights have come, "The jig is up." The motive of sick humor is to insist on degradation. Where the difference accrues to healthier comedy is in the use of ridicule or self-ridicule for deflation instead of extermination of character. So that a sense of Molièrean proportion is important, after all, in the comedy of human relations, even or especially in extravagant America. And our fastest-rising minority group, the Negroes, are themselves our best and newest teachers of how to avoid the excesses of our blackest humor, all the more when that humor seems most certified by events. They teach the self-resistant tact we may still combine with objectivity in therapeutic comedy.

We arrive at a juncture in our deliberations, however, where the favorable evidence turns back on itself. From southern California has come a plethora of humorous sign cards, which everybody sports on his office desk or service station walls. The humor is irreverent, deflationary, cynical, and hostile. It is apparently inspired by that champion voice of minority skepticism, Hollywood's Groucho Marx, whose acidic quips and comic reductionism are the very model for this humor.[23] These millions of cards have been bought and displayed everywhere by Americans, who thereby demonstrate a supposedly reactivated and broad-based sense of humor.

Some of the cards are almost in the positive aphoristic tradition: "In ulcers, it's not what you eat but what eats you." A few are straightforward personal epigrams, fair warnings of comic relevancy: "I don't get ulcers, I give them." Akin to this type is the incisive bumper sign: "Left: Passing Side. Right: Suicide," where punning and comic pertinence are combined for automotive proverb. But the greatest number of cards and posters are negative in technique, in their devices of reversal, and in their hostile skepticism. "May I help you out? This way, please," Or

[23] Perelman also exerts his influence on satiric birthday and greeting cards which mistitle stills from silent movies; the facetiousness and obloquy derive from his "Cloudland Revisited" series.

there is sheer mockery, as in what was probably the original of these signs:

The best of this whole mode combines the fullest skepticism with antirhetorical deflation. As such, it chooses sentimental optimism, perhaps Kiplingesque, as its subject of reversal. "If you can keep your head while all about you are losing theirs—maybe you just don't understand the situation."

What is the trouble with this massive publication and display of an almost ritualized comic antithesis for all the world to see? It is, indeed, in the manufacture of the fun cards. The cynical wit has become professionalized and commercialized. One is under no obligation to cultivate his individual sense of humor so long as he carries or shows a sign, like a certifying badge. As it were, he has a credit card in American humor. He may defer payment in this respect endlessly. How can he be doubted if the very pasteboard he flashes is, in fact, funny? His choice of it is, at least, a warranty that he can laugh. In this light, he is unabashedly announcing himself.

But, of course, the self-evident rarely needs advertisement. Or, put the other way around, personal advertisement of any trait is a confession, by default of the thing itself, of the basic uncertainty of what we broadcast to others. Furthermore, all claim to originality is forfeited in the standardization and passivity of mere purchase and display. We are effectively turning the matter over to specialists in the sign, bumper-poster, and greeting-card business, as we are also doing when we expect comic prefabrications and "swiftie" puns at the end of intrabusiness releases as well as the bottom of the pages of *Reader's Digest*. In these ways, we are relieved of the burden of origination. Our public avowals turn about and serve the prosecution instead of the defense.

But how can we entertain a conclusive argument for the decline of American humor at the very time in our literature when the novel has turned so clearly in the comic direction? We need not allude to the programmism of the blackest humorists either. Our references are to the work of another group, to Salinger, Malamud, Nabokov, Bellow, Faulkner's last work, Gover, and Barth, to name the most prominent authors of a comprehensive movement. How, the positivists argue, can we dismiss or slight their example? If we have suffered a clear decline in our comic essayists—having virtually no replacements for Lardner, Marquis, Benchley, and Thurber and with the line held only by Perelman and E. B. White, who grow old—still, comic novelists abound as never before.

But, the evidence is scarcely unambiguous. In each case there are basic objections, which are not carping ones. The vast majority, especially of the Jewish novelists, are painfully subjective. For all their gestures of candor and self-mockery, their antiheroes are taken too seriously, even heroically, and the charm of characterization does not mitigate the perversity of it. In the group as a whole, there is the curse of derivativeness, an eager formlessness in some, a willful decadence in others, and riddling sentimentality in most. The situation does not argue a new, fresh access of nerve. In instance after instance we come away from an author or work with nagging reservations and suspect the execution when we approve the conception or suspect the motives when we approve the skill.

Of the prestigious *The Catcher in the Rye*, what is to be said of a work that is such a conscious updating of *Huckleberry Finn*? The boy hero is on a journey again, across and along the banks of a famous river, alienated by his surrounding culture, a self-protective liar, seeking the deepest personal freedom, compassionate and realistic both, and at last escaping west. But at this late date, he escapes not to an open frontier territory but to a sanatorium in the Los Angeles hills, the old themes demographically and psychologically worn down.

There is no question about elements of pure comedy and satire in the book, about the effectiveness of the adolescent deflation of phoniness. Salinger's technical use of anticlimax and inversion of phrase are often consummate. About an unanswered phone, Holden complains: "Nobody kept answering." Or he swears off a night club: "It was a terrible place. . . . I cut out going there entirely, gradually." All devices of circularity and pertinence are skillfully employed. But the trouble is with Holden Caulfield himself. He is a compulsive, guilt-ridden character, who succumbs to his own fantasies, modeled on Bogart movies, just as easily as criticized adults capitulate to their mores. And he has not that soul struggle and health of decision that we have traced in the triumphant characterization of Huck Finn. Holden's realistic speech, furthermore, is neither the flexible nor comprehensive instrument it was for Huck. It breaks down to signature words like "really," which become psychiatric means of defense, a verbal holding action, ultimately unavailing. He is, then, not quite a comic *hero*. The diminution, added to Salinger's close discipleship of Twain and Lardner, rob the book, in lengthening critical perspective, of the full strength and originality it once suggested.

And neither the pseudoreligious Franny nor the suicidal Seymour Glass are fitting comic advances over Holden Caulfield. The later portrayals and means in Salinger's work serve far other purposes than the satiric. The social fraudulencies he attacked in the earlier comic effort become private and earnest orthodoxies of belief and sentimentality in his later work. There are still comic devices, the famous comic catalogue of Mrs. Glass's completely packed medicine cabinet, and comic metaphor, "cruising in a patrol boat down the children's aliamentary canal." But the devices are used more sparingly, and indeed Salinger's comic interest is less and less basic. Still, he must be judged essentially by *The Catcher in the Rye*. And set against its sources and in the on-going stream of American humor, that book suffers remorseless critical reduction.

Malamud's position is the shakiest of the lot. He strains mightily. A work like *A New Life* is too jokey (A child asks Levin to read to him, "Tory?" and Levin answers, "No, Liberal.") Events are too convenient, tricks mar thematic integrity, and one is put off by a confusing mixture of sincerity and parody. Levin himself is more stubborn than mature at the last, but Malamud does not seem to know that. And the conclusion, involving Levin's acquisition of a new, ready-made family, is the rankest sentimentality.

Malamud's strength lies in the intensity he displayed in *The*

Assistant. It does not lie in pixie Yiddish incongruities of character and situation he is also prone to, along with the sentimentality that places him with Eddie Cantor or Harry Golden. He has, in fact, been subverted by the cultism of that softer Jewish tradition. He might have become a gentle and unique Kafka of sorts. Comedy's short gain has been another genre's total loss.

Nabokov's *Lolita* has been related to absurd and black humor. It may be considered in another related context. We detect an exquisite and arch self-consciousness of method that can be described as decadent, all references to the subject matter aside. More is in question than the stylistic tricks, like the parenthetical tactics, which deliberately call attention to themselves. That is also true of Faulkner. In Nabokov we must also note all those manipulations of plot that parody Hollywood convenience but still very much rely on the clichéd incident.[24] The female antagonist, for instance, Lolita's mother, is killed off in her sudden blind rush into the street directly in the way of an on-coming automobile. Nabokov is winking at us, who know what he is up to. Nonetheless, in cold fact, no other invention seems available to him. The matter is as much one of exhausted as well as of sophisticated technique. His strategy is to make snobbish narrative virtue out of defects of comic imagination, and in this respect his very best work continually throws us off.

His heavy reliance on models extends beyond obvious Holly-woodism. We are meant to acknowledge the reversals he manages of Poe's "Annabel Lee" and James's *Daisy Miller.* He plays to the inside knowledge of literary students for their appreciation of the joke. But his indecision, at the last, to elaborate such jokes and parody or to attempt a sociological masterpiece rends his performance. The result is that he lyricizes and snickers, wanting the best of two worlds. Like others, he is wary of being serious but is insufficiently committed to humor. "Had Nabokov been an American born," the critic, Alan Pryce-Jones, has observed, "he would have been wholly serious." It is a moot question. More naïve and less studious, more foolhardy and less

[24] William Humphrey's *Home from the Hill,* as we have seen, is fixed the same way upon Hollywoodism and soap operatics. His imperturbable reversals rather than farcical extensions of clichés mask his designs more effectively. But the narrative fixations or regressions have the same character, fundamentally, as Nabokov's.

well-read, he might have pursued a less self-conscious and more imposing ambition. Instead, he adds Swift's example of *Gulliver's Travels*, as a satire of contemporary travel novels, to his purposes and in part satirizes the modern American sexual novel. But having chosen funny intellectual crutches or stilts, he wants also to step along vigorously, down to earth. On his most subtle level of academic satire, he wishes to make fun of Marie Bonaparte's psychoanalytic study of Poe. But HH, his hero, will not hold still as an instrument to such purposes, but keeps getting in Nabokov's way as a serious character in his own right. As a result, the author is caught in his own joke of cross-purposes. The specter of sincerity haunts the manifold and playful insincerity of the whole conception. These dilemmas, this superiority to one's means but desperate investment in them anyway, this crucial indecision of attitude finally, cannot be discounted. Combined, after all, with the shock value of sexual precocity and perversion, they are not hidden by the brilliances of Nabokov's style but are given a high gloss. His weaknesses appear, in the end, as the very hallmark of a special decadence in the contemporary novel. As we take the measure of his work now, from the vantage of comic art, we are only intermittently bedazzled.

As to Saul Bellow, heir apparent to leadership in both the comic novel and fiction as a whole, a number of critical impieties may be suggested. The paradox of his entire career through *Herzog* is that his is not only a comic method looking for a worthy subject but a manifold technique in search of a form. There is rarely a true conclusion to his stories; I do not mean merely a neat ending but a final placement of his principal character consonant with the hero's supposed development. Augie March, for instance, is as depthless at the end of his recorded adventures as he was at the start. He is a gigolo, thief, and kept husband. He never actually realizes personal independence. Like the eagle he has trained, he resists authority, but he never asserts himself. And Herzog, for all his victorious self-acceptance and busied self-sufficiency at the conclusion of his story, is as dependent on brothers and mistresses for real and emotional support as ever. The trouble is that in each instance a novelistic form, as well as a central theme, is frustrated. In addition, Bellow's episodic method has a way of running down from a key episode, like the Mexican interlude in *Augie March* or the lion sequence in *Henderson, the Rain King,* and he must work manfully against structural anticlimax.

There is no doubt that Bellow has assimilated his numerous sources. They include, for *Augie March,* diverse figures like the English Defoe and Sterne and the American Twain, Faulkner, and Wolfe. The Alculta climax is rather too heavily mortgaged to Hemingway's *The Sun Also Rises,* perhaps, but always Bellow's style is his own achievement. Moreover, there are towering comic portraits, for example, of Grandma Lausch and of Einhorn, which we dare not, in all good faith, attack. But the rogue-like conception is no excuse for the totally unintegrated character of the hero. Nor is it an excuse for the inarticulation of the novel as such, either. The work is more than "open-ended," by which we mean inconclusive. It is formless. The charge is not minor. *Huckleberry Finn* survives intact all our latter-day questioning of its episodic construction and its conclusion. *Augie March* does not.

One is troubled in *Henderson* by Bellow's constant overreaching of himself. It can rightfully be described as an intellectual *Tarzan of the Apes.* Unfortunately, that is not altogether his original intention; but his ambitions swell as the book proceeds, and then they turn ostentatious. At all events, they fatally slow all action. The prototypes are there again; this time Quixote and Candide figure in Henderson, and also Huck Finn again on a primitive, roguish journey. Plus a little of bumbling Benchley; during a drought Henderson makes a feckless gift of his raincoat, and he ruins the cistern explosion as a Benchley pseudoexpert would fumble his dynamite and mis-illustrate Yankee ingenuity. Bellow, like his protagonist, "wants" too much, however; his character is also serious. Henderson, the great white hunter, stalks himself in Africa, and we are meant to take the spiritual quest importantly. Seeking love, the character at last settles for a bear hug at the end of the story. But Bellow himself will settle for nothing less than a philosophic, as well as comic, tour de force. As a result he must change tone too often and too self-consciously, his profundity turns out meretricious, and his action deteriorates. Wanting the best of two narrative worlds, he has half of one.

Both the self-consciousness and the clogging intellectualization also figure in *Herzog,* where at last Bellow makes them frankly central concerns. It is a brave effort. But, as was true for *Augie March*, the character does not withstand his contradictions. We are left, as we were in Nabokov, with a basically stylistic performance meant to dazzle us out of critical surveillance. Herzog is the Yiddish *schlemiel*, heroified. The very attempt at paradoxical comic portrait cannot be underestimated. Bellow wishes to give us a skeptical believer, a middle-aged innocent, a self-effacing egotist, etc. But the attempt as such is not its own warranty, though many critics who see what he is up to proceed to make the equation. Herzog pulls these configurations of himself together into a zero, "the cipher hero," Professor Kaufmann talks about in another connection, "the man in whose fearful instinct for victimization we are supposed to find our identity as social units." There is the trouble, the attempted heroification of the antihero. Thurber's Jacky Smurch, Lardner's Alibi Ike, and Benchley's bungler are what they are, and no thematic mysticism or stylistic wizardry will or should change them. At the heart of the matter, such transcendent portraiture as Bellow attempts is not in the end only unavailing, it is perverse. We cannot finally accept the heightened dimensions of that comic heroism as Bellow insists we do and almost charms us, breathlessly, into believing.

Once again, an excess of means suggests decadence, though it is of a different kind from the arch superiority in Nabokov, who is a sort of literary con man where Bellow is in earnest. What happens in Bellow, most exactly, is that his Jewish eloquence seeks to surpass his sense of realistic comic deflation.[25] This is what allows him candidly to exalt his modern comic butt as hero. But it is a verbal argument, not structural or truly psychological, and we are in a measure hoodwinked.

The comic style is indeed manifold. His native deflation and mockery are quite apparent in *Herzog*.

> It was painful to instincts . . . that his children should be growing up without him. But what could he do about that? To the sea! To the sea!—What sea? It was the bay—between East Chop and West Chop, it wasn't sea; the water was quiet.

[25] As his love of life seeks to overcome his hostilities, which are frequently fierce, like the misogyny not only of *Herzog* but *Augie March, Henderson* (the displacement of "Mummah"), and especially *Seize the Day*.

One of his lines in *Herzog* is a high point of the reversalism we have traced all through American humor: ". . . the story of my life —how I rose from humble origins to complete disaster." He employs extravagance and literalism with a sure hand. His use of comic catalogue, though less exuberant than it was in *Augie March*, is meant to render plural consciousness, the widest sense of life. And over and beyond the use of comic contrasts of vocabulary levels and minor punning ("Lead me not into Penn Station"), he is particularly apt in Jewish comic pertinency throughout the book.

But we cannot forget our dissatisfaction with Herzog's character and Bellow's unsuccessful theme. Certainly we admire the talent at work and the will to keep the work this side of black humor. And it is true that Bellow's intention, unlike Hemingway's and O'Hara's, is to show humor as salvational for his character. But the hero remains incommensurate to the theme. Our reservation is not secondary. The flaw we might overlook is in reality a chasm. We tire, moreover, of the Caulfields and Herzogs who admit they may be out of their minds. We search for prototypical comic characters who may be in their mind—a critical urge so reactionary by now that it may be considered radical— as we also search for culminations of action instead of inaction.

Certainly, Joseph Heller's *Catch-22* deserves our attention. But his work confirms some of Bellow's basic disabilities, particularly the doubleness of theme and the impurity of execution. For both writers, we are in the position of acclaiming robust talent, but are restrained from the highest praise by fundamental rather than incidental considerations. Heller's zaniness, for instance, necessarily exceeds that of the Marx Brothers, an indubitable model for the action.[26] It exceeds the model precisely in proportion as he tries what they never attempt, a serious hero and maximum direct sense. The Marx Brothers never swerved to frontal sense, which accounts for their comic purity. Heller constantly does, and he must turn yet wilder and wilder for his contrasts as his book proceeds, all of which accounts for his successive impurities and the "too muchness" of his work, factors that have worn his readers down. He has given his own

[26] And also a model for the direct self-contradictions and shameless reversalisms in the course of the book.

referent for judging him excessive, which the Marx Brothers never did.

Pure seriousness, on the other hand, succeeded at least once in the period, in Lay and Bartlett's *Twelve O'Clock High*; the contrast makes Heller's mixed comedy on exactly the same subject appear a more ambitious but significant failure at the last. General Savage is neither Yossarian nor Rotarian. His participation in the desperate effort to keep the industrial empire of Germany off balance during our own build-up in Britain is compelling enough, his own combatant role makes him an authentic soldier, and the claims of an impersonal—and Prussian—efficiency against those of American good fellowship make for potent conflict. His world and his heroical undertaking are real enough, even if he cracks under the strain; and, for once, the movie script surpassed the book in avoiding Bartlett and Lay's unfortunate clichés of style and in tightening the drama.

But the heroics and travestied incompetence of *Catch-22*, the alternative realism and surrealism,[27] are not amalgamated, and the work *itself* not sane[28] or, at least, consistent enough—as even the Marx Brothers basically were. Not sufficiently restricted and discriminate, as is also the case in Bellow, the work tries grandly for two worlds and misses. Our regret is all the keener since Heller, treating ultimate themes of reality, having a rich talent for sustained inversion especially, and owning a sharp style, had a potential masterpiece under hand. In the end he, too, shows insufficient resistance, to his inherent grandiosity in particular and makes little or no concession to truths of the other side: *that* pluralism required in the best humor. As a result he loses out, especially in the second half of his book, in the very highest comic art.

We turn hopefully and at some length to the Golden Book or *The Tempest* of William Faulkner, *The Reivers*, for consolation. It is the likeliest work of the whole period to turn to.

Without dilution, Faulkner's realistic skepticism is held under sure control. The mud-hole episode, similar to the incident of the smallpox rescuers in *Huckleberry Finn*, is a clear example of Faulkner's dramatic and comic objectivity.

[27] Also influenced by Nathanael West.
[28] Although his refrain, like "phony" in Salinger's *Catcher*, is "crazy."

The man [who made the mudholes] said, "I forgot to mention it, so maybe I better. Prices have doubled around here since last year."

"Why?" Boon said. "It's the same car, the same mudhole; be damned if I don't believe it's even the same mud."

"That was last year. There's more business now. So much more that I can't afford not to go up."

"All right, goddammit," Boon said. "Go on." So we moved, ignominious, at the pace of the mules, on, into the next mudhole without stopping, on and out again. The bridge was just ahead now; beyond it, we could see the road all the way to the edge of the bottom and safety.

"You're all right now," the man said. "Until you come back." Boon was unhooking the log chain [of the man's tow mules] while Ned freed the traces and handed the doubletree back up to the man on the mule.

"We ain't coming back this way," Boon said.

"I wouldn't neither," the man said. Boon went back to the last puddle and washed some of the mud from his hands and came back and took four dollars from his wallet. The man didn't move.

"It's six dollars," he said.

"Last year it was two dollars," Boon said. "You said it's double now. Double two is four. All right. Here's four dollars."

"I charge a dollar a passenger," the man said. "There was two of you last year. That was two dollars. The price is doubled now. There's three of you. That's six dollars. Maybe you'd rather walk back to Jefferson than pay two dollars, but maybe that boy and that nigger wouldn't."

"And maybe I ain't gone up neither," Boon said. "Suppose I don't pay you six dollars. Suppose in fact I don't pay you nothing."

"You can do that too," the man said. "These mules has had a hard day, but I reckon there's still enough git in them to drag that thing back where they got it from."

But Boon had already quit, given up, surrendered. "God damn it," he said, "this boy ain't nothing but a child! Sholy for just a little child—"

"Walking back to Jefferson might be lighter for him," the man said, "but it won't be no shorter."

"All right," Boon said, "but look at the other one! When he gets that mud washed off, he ain't even white!"

The man looked at distance awhile. Then he looked at Boon. "Son," he said, "both these mules is color-blind."

In addition, the prevalence and force of "Non-Virtue," as Faulkner refers to a light sense of Evil, is a stroke of philosophic comic
genius. He traces its operation through all the human natures in
his story, makes it account for our reiving (not thieving) instincts,
and shows its universal and enthusiastic enlistments.

> . . . who serves Virtue works alone, unaided, in a chilly vacuum of
> reserved judgment; where, pledge yourself to Non-virtue and the
> whole countryside boils with volunteers to help you.

His misanthropy is qualified, genial and restrained, though clear-
eyed. It is this attitude that dictates his original terms of analysis
and narrative as well as his overview in the story.

The comic wisdom matches anything in American humor, as in
the passage on independent and realistic mules.

> "You ever drive a mule to a buggy?"
> "No sir," I said. He handed me the lines. "I don't know how,"
> I said.
> "Then you can learn now. A mule ain't like a horse. When a horse
> gets a wrong notion in his head, all you got to do is swap him an-
> other one for it. Most anything will do—a whip or spur or just
> scare him by hollering at him. A mule is different. He can hold two
> notions at the same time and the way to change one of them is to
> act like you believe he thought of changing it first. He'll know
> different, because mules have got sense. But a mule is a gentleman
> too, and when you act courteous and respectful at him without
> trying to buy him or scare him, he'll act courteous and respectful
> back at you—as long as you don't overstep him. That's why you
> don't pet a mule like you do a horse: he knows you don't love him:
> you're just trying to fool him into doing something he already
> don't aim to do, and it insults him. Handle him like that. He knows
> the way home, and he will know it ain't me holding the lines. So
> all you need to do is tell him with the lines that you know the way
> too but he lives here and you're just a boy so you want him to go
> in front."

Here Faulkner displays that Negro deviousness of thought or reversed psychology that depends on the outwitting second or third
thought. It is a feature that also energizes the plot wherever Ned
is involved. It generally accounts for Negro endurance and, as we
have seen it at work in Joel Chandler Harris, for learned southern
endurance as a whole, too. Such understanding in Faulkner is

joined, furthermore, to an objective but compassionate interest in almost all his characters, a governing nonjudgmentiveness that frees the mind.

> He was the landlord. That was his official even if unwritten title and designation. All places, houses like this, had one, had to have one. In the alien outside world fortunate enough not to have to make a living in this hard and doomed and self-destroying way, he had a harder and more contemptuous name. But here, the lone male not even in a simple household of women but in a hysteria of them, he was not just lord but the unthanked and thankless catalyst, the single frail power wearing the shape of respectability sufficient to compel enough of order on the hysteria to keep the unit solvent or anyway eating—he was the agent who counted down the money and took the receipt for the taxes and utilities, who dealt with the tradesmen . . . paid the blackmail to the law; . . . fought the losing battles with the street- and assessment-commissioners and cursed the newspaper boy the day after the paper wasn't delivered. And of these (I mean, landlords) in this society, Mr Binford was the prince and paragon: a man of principles, impeccable in morals, more faithful than many husbands during the whole five years he had been Miss Reba's lover. . . .

There are two principal modes of comic complication in the work. One involves the piled complexities of plot. The Grandfather's car is "reived" by Lucius and Boon and Ned, given by Ned in Memphis as surety for a race horse, which must win the race at Parsham, where the sheriff is subsequently on the make for Boon's prostitute lover, a fact leading to Boon's eventual violence and arrest, which complicates the forthcoming race . . . and so on through an interlocking crisscrossed series of unholily complex events. In small, Faulkner does just as well, never allowing a character a simple, straightlined thought or motive, even of escape. Lucius thinks of jumping from the car early in the story but second-guesses himself, understanding through dense syllogisms of a dark but unalterable logic how he is bound to an action already begun. In such fashion Faulkner's comic momentum enhances the general complexity of plotting.

The other principal mode of complication involves the digressionary method of intervening detail, especially pronounced at the start of the book but pervasive. There is no other way to account for the deliberate technique except to note Faulkner's highly calculated playfulness with his audience. We shall bring the technique, along with its unexpected source, into critical focus in our review of selected major American writers, for it provides a new and penetrating insight into his total work. But it is never more obviously employed than in *The Reivers,* as if in his last book Faulkner insisted we read the technique back through all his work.

Other comic devices and inventions abound in the book. All of Faulkner's gift of antic wildness, also apparent in "Spotted Horses," occurs in the novel. There is that mad, extravagant second heat of the horse race, with the track rail ultimately *between* the two racing horses. The comic element of the outré is best exemplified by a horse that is lured to the finish line by sardines. Such incidents are manifestations of the tall-tale conception of most of the story, with tall-tale anecdotes occurring all through the text.

> The man set his lantern down and climbed the ladder on to the roof and released the brake wheel and Sam and Boon jammed the ends of the bars between the back wheels and the rails, pinching and nudging in short strokes like pumping and I still didn't believe it: the car looming black and square and high in the moon, solid and rectangular as a black wall inside the narrow silver frame of the moonlight, one high puny figure wrenching at the brake wheel on top and two more puny figures crouching, creeping, nudging the silver-lanced iron bars behind the back wheels; . . . so delicately balanced now in the massive midst of Motion that Sam and Boon dropped the bars and Boon alone pressed the car gently on with his hands as though it were a child's perambulator, up alongside the platform and into position . . .

The ruling comic deviousness of Ned is a principal device, bearing a certain relation to the improvisational Huckish lying of Lucius in the story. There is general verbal fun in the novel, punning and malapropism in particular.

> "[he] walked up to Butch and snatched that pistol outen his hand and reached up and ripped that badge and half his shirt off too and telefoamed to Hardwick to send a automobile to bring them all back to jail, the women too. When it's women, they calls it fragrancy."

"Vagrancy," Uncle Parsham said.

"That's what I said," Ned said. "You call it whatever you want. I calls it jail."

Faulkner is apt at comic metaphor (weak "as a feather in a saucer of sand") and displays his southern talent also in understatement and the epithetical mode. Among a subsidiary range of devices are comic catalogue and anticlimax, reversalism, circular disqualification, and comic contrasts of formal and informal styles of speech.

In light of such expert achievement, what gives us pause? First of all, we note the heavy reliance on Mark Twain. The point of view of the boy follows the lead of *Huckleberry Finn*, that book with its grip rather than mere influence on modern American literature. The very character of the boy, in his fundamental and redeeming candor, his protective fibbing, and his backsliding psychology, is closely modeled on Huck. The Mississippi valley journey itself, with the car as a raft in the world, is pertinent. And the crucial companionship between Lucius and Ned, the white boy and older Negro, which supersedes the relationship between Lucius and Boon, is all-important. Faulkner participates in the era's obsessive raid on Twain's one book, as much a tyranny as a help by now.

But there is something yet deeper in the nature of our reservation. Faulkner largely succeeds where Bellow fails, in thematic paradox; in *The Reivers* innocence is lost but also maintained through knowledge. Yet he fails even more disastrously than Bellow in his bold strategy of sentimentality. He succeeds all too well in his contrived happy ending and, though he knows exactly what chances he is taking, he defeats himself. The race is won; Carrie becomes the reformed prostitute and is married off to Boon and even has a son; love, as the critic J.M. Mellard points out, triumphs over lust, fertility over sterility, stability over chaos. In his last work Faulkner meant to furnish a deliberate contrast to his story, "The Bear," where Boon had also figured. He wished to press home his positive themes of individual integration and social acceptance rather than the themes of defeat and alienation.

The fact remains, however, that the happy ending is piled on and forced. Faulkner becomes self-consciously literary, curiously having something in common with Nabokov this way. There are models on his mind, predominantly. He evens turns classical in trying to work out his comic drama and in living up to a self-predicted "Golden Book." But there is no need for such old conventions and no reality to them in America. Indeed they were never conventions of authentic American comedy and not even, since Mary Pickford movies went out of style, of sentimental melodrama in the United States.

It is no extenuation either to say that he chose conventions, false ones even, of exaggerated, happified circumstance, just to surmount them. He allows us to gauge his risks the better to measure his Shakespearean competence, let us say, in a conclusive, supreme play with convenience. We are meant to think of *The Winter's Tale* and, precisely, of *The Tempest*. But the fact that the work, then, is deliberately soft in upshot does not redeem the softness, no matter what the classical or Shakespearean precedents might be. And, at any rate, we have been in another age for some time now. As a result, one begins to suspect the conception of even "Non-Virtue" as a softening of his skepticism. In a reappraisal of everything in light of his conclusion, all his successes suffer devaluation.

One may argue, of course, that both his originality and audacity lie in his attempt to reactivate the conventions. But, as we have surveyed our tradition, they have never been the strong or distinctive comic conventions in our country, as he himself well knew earlier in his career. He was, then, not being so brave and ingenious in *The Reivers* as he was academic and artificial. The effect is that we have a gathering cloud over the book. Indeed, countless readers find themselves hoping against hope that he will not do what he does finally. In the very reading of the book, the grateful experience is darkened by a disappointment that becomes permanent. We wish him to raise the threats of abnormal and outdated convention in order to circumvent them; instead, he accumulates them. Only sophisticated academical critics praise him for a highly equivocal effort that should never have been conceived or executed as it finally was.

Two other works, outside of sick novelistic comedy, must stand for the further range of fictional humor, Robert Gover's *$100 Misunderstanding* and John Barth's *The Sotweed Factor;* both of which are stylistically audacious. Technical considerations deprive us of the highest criticism once more. The second half of Gover's book scarcely sustains the first. A brilliant comic setup runs down to mere repetitiousness and plot disentanglement. Furthemore, a magnificent confrontation of types is allowed to become mere slapstick and gimmickry. The opportunity, as in *Pudd'nhead Wilson*, for masterful comic portraiture is there, but it is lost; Roxy does not have anything like her match in Kitten. As to Barth, his energy is unarguable. But his feeding upon the eighteenth century in *The Sotweed Factor* is another confession of modern narrative exhaustion. We are left with preciosity, another tour de farce. That was true for *The Floating Opera* as well and is also true of the more recent *Giles Goat Boy*, allegorical satires in the intricate mold of Cabell's *Jurgen*.[29] Admittedly, Barth is better than Cabell, less esoteric and effeminate, but his intellectual fancifulness, which is often a hoax, and his resistless expression, are intrinsic liabilities.

These selected works of contemporary fiction indicate unquestionable talent at work over a broad spectrum of our literature. There are things going on in Salinger, Nabokov, Bellow, Heller, Faulkner, Barth, and others that deserve clear endorsement. We may say that, manifestly, they indicate a renewed surge of explosive comic talent. But our reservations turn out in each case to be crucial ones. Partisans of the printed word, in an age of electronics and McLuhan's dire prophecies about the future of literature, may note the comparative failure of the mass media so far, which partly accounts for literature's staying alive. But the comic effort in that literature, as in the other media, has not to date produced unmistakable giants or that collectivity of first-rate performance of the preceding period. Even should we grant resurgence, it has simply not yet consummated itself or carried the day.

A high degree of derivativeness stigmatizes the general achievement, models dominating all sorts of present-day efforts. Inherited literary capital is one thing, second-mortgaging is another. Moreover, a frequently exquisite and generally embarrassing self-

[29] But not so stupefying as the alleged comic intricacy of William Gaddis's *The Recognitions*, an endlessly involved work about forgery within forgery and another academical favorite for literary cryptographers, who mistake torturesomeness for profundity and coils upon coils of irony for the highest humor.

consciousness of technique, especially of characterization, flaws the new literary comedy. The specters of sentimentality and preciosity haunt it continually. And, at the last, there is too much adolescent psychology involved. There are, for instance, Salinger's Holden Caulfield, Nabokov's Lolita, Faulkner's Lucius, Gover's college boy and subteen prostitute. And there are those young men who are still boys, like Augie March, who trouble us in their retardation. Even a book like Cozzens' *Guard of Honor,* in great part a comic war novel, centers on the boyish and immature General Beal. And we have those older men who are still boys, Malamud's Levin and Bellow's Herzog, and they give us great pause. And what these matters indicate of a general devolution of psychic age in our literary public and comic audience gives us even greater pause.

But what happens when we turn back to full maturity, to, say, Thurber in his last phase? He gives us "The Weaver and the Worm."

A weaver watched in wide-eyed wonder a silkworm spinning its cocoon in a white mulberry tree.

"Where do you get that stuff?" asked the admiring weaver.

"Do you want to make something out of it?" inquired the silkworm eagerly.

Then the weaver and the silkworm went their separate ways, for each thought the other had insulted him. . . .

Moral: A word to the wise is not sufficient if it doesn't make sense.

The mature vision is of total incommunicativeness[30] and sublime misapprehension. That is what stands as the modern mean between the extremes of transcendent sentimentality and brutal black humor.

Or we assume, as perhaps we must, that the latter is our key today. In that case, comedy has run down in the twentieth century from the antics of Keystone Cops to the dubious hilarity of our wild ones and Hell's Angels in and out of our literature. The best

[30] The inexpressive calligraphy of Steinberg's cartoons, shown by the nonwords in his official-looking maps and documents and the flourished indecipherable signatures, will strike readers of *The New Yorker* as further evidence.

alternatives to that would be Bellow and the later Faulkner on one side or the later Thurber on the other; the worst alternatives would be television inanity or nonexistent humor.

However we interchange the coordinates, we must graph a net decline in our comedy. Looming before us especially is a sickly, black pointlessness.

Conspiratorially almost, a reviewer of William Burroughs' recent book, *The Soft Machine*, asks us to believe that "it is the voice" that counts and "what it is saying is in no sense the point." That is the nether extreme of extremism, in which all meaning whatsoever is gloriously abdicated.[31] There is an implicit joke of good-humored humorlessness involved in this judgment, but that is by the way. Just short of this position, however, is the more articulated senselessness we are more familiar with. That includes Mailer's hipster homocidalism, latent or active in almost all his work. It includes, in James Purdy's *Cabot Wright Begins*, a program of rapism.[32] In J. P. Donleavy's work, *The Ginger Man*, modern Whitmania nourished by Henry Miller's influence[33] and fattened by the permissiveness of the day, we have a reflexive and also indiscriminate violence; it is a sort of black-comic fascism.

Into the desk. Locked. He took the poker and smashed it through the smooth veneer. Curled his fingers round the side and ripped off the cover.

[31] It at least coincides with the indiscriminate misogyny of all Burroughs' work, which comes to stand, after *Naked Lunch*, for the indiscriminateness of his general attack on everything.

[32] See also Evan S. Connell's *The Diary of a Rapist*, where the "hero's" victim is a bathing beauty on a festival float: "No shame. No modesty. . . . If she isn't the symbol of American rottenness, what is? . . ." If we look through Connell's thin window-pane style, we see the need to violate, to accelerate one's destructive rage. Both Connell's work and the Purdy book are remarkably unoriginal, *avant-gardism* just sufficiently old fashioned so as to appear modish again. Purdy's sardonicism especially is pseudo-Nathanael West, except that its dime-novel style and technique are extra devaluations. It is possible that as a typical representation of this group, Purdy's derivativeness and his almost deliberate standards of inexcellence are calculated black subversions, in which case the ultimate repudiative act of writing ought to be—not to bother.

[33] But Donleavy's chaotic appetitiveness and desperate grim hedonism are a falling off from Miller's exuberance and self-indulgence. Miller was genuinely uncommitted, but the Ginger Man confuses his career with family responsibilities and that precommitment makes him a spoiled scoundrel whereas Miller was, in his own dangerous way, pure.

And in addition to these and to the notorious, simple shock value exploited by the avant-garde novelist, John Hawkes and others, we have Terry Southern's promoted prurient, sickly-sweet *Candy*, who represents a climax of incest. That superlative comic ego that used to mediate between repression and shibboleth has receded to the infantile unconscious, no instrument for anything at all now in these extreme instances but a self-indulgence of the id, uninteresting with all the rest of its disabilities and just as commercial and easy as the opposite, the equally frictionless obedience to the superego.

There is cause aplenty for such excess, though explanations are not extenuations, particularly in ordered literary and comic craft. But we note, in summation, that all the exaggerated "Hun" stories of World War I came literally true in World War II. What mood could we have expected, other things apart, after the central shattering impact of the Beasts of Belsen? The diabolism of black and sick Hell's Angels, complete with Nazi helmets and crosses, is youth's reveling and revolting response to the colossal failures of the immediate past. Seen this way, there is no literary, artistic, comic or emotional response adequate at all, only the savage mockery implicit in the identification, the only way left to express or indulge one's self, out of consideration of enormities. Even Simone Weil subtly but perversely embraced Nazi conquest in her essay on *The Iliad* and the Trojan War, a monograph actually on the European debacle. The sophisticated and the primitive alike kiss the terrible enemy or become it, in order to live. It is a superficial and easy but predictable reaction, the popular example of which is rampant in the United States.

Illiterate and even psychotic motorcyclists are the merest filings along a magnetic field of moral force. The extent of that field, however, cannot be underestimated. Life has been cheapened by Nazidom, World War II, and the Cold War. None of our violence and none of our raging black humor, for this reason and others previously examined, is unmotivated.

But all the more, not the less, do we look for genius, or at least high talent, to regenerate creatively its own field of force. We recall, for instance, the tramp's endurance rather than rage in Chaplin's best films, often through the most scrofulous, intimidating, and sordid circumstances. The "little fellow" always tried to recover a certain aplomb and even dignity. That is the model to set against the death wish fundamental to our black humor.

And there is nothing like the difficult requirement of art, comic or otherwise, to guarantee us against fraud. One is in constant doubt about the black or sick humorists who take advantage of us. A playwright like Albee makes profound doubters of us; that, too, is a consequence of dethroned Eros. His *Who's Afraid of Virginia Woolf* is not only characteristically filled with the rankest cruelty, self-loathing, mutual sexual hostility, and general sadism, but its suggestions of homosexuality and nymphomania undercut its generic themes, and the central, unbelievable con game of a make-believe son is a fundamental imposition. Its involutions are a joke upon the audience, as is his chinese-box conception[34] of *Tiny Alice*. It is not sickness alone, or pretentiousness even, but the specter of corruption in Albee's conscious practice, and in Barth's and Gaddis's preconscious practice, which we also have to contend with.[35]

Although these forces and figures will continue in the foreseeable future, another comic joy, hardheaded but undespairing, might conceivably reassert itself. We may anticipate its full reassertion in the parody of black humor, which will probably be its first true signal of counterthrust. At all events, no essential humor ever dies the last death, least of all in such a host country as the United States. One relies in the end on an America pressing forward to a future of characteristically open possibilities; on a deeply ingrained spirit of pluralism that can outlive even excess; on a common sense of mockery, mordancy, even iconoclasm, but not annihilation; on that renewed confidence and objectivity which history may allow us once again.

Which is to say that comedy has run down but not out. No sooner did Mencken stigmatize the south as a hopeless "Sahara of Bozart" than it flourished in world literature. It is a lesson we are ill-advised to forget in our strong criticism and, as a people,

[34] John Chapman of the New York *Daily News* paraphrased Tallulah Bankhead in his apt review of the play . . . and of the whole mode of such humor: "there may be less here than meets the eye."

[35] In Albee's case, however, there is every possibility of genuine pretentiousness only. David Merrick's $400,000 conviction that Albee's work on the musical comedy of "Breakfast at Tiffany's" ruined it utterly is a fell and costly verdict on Albee's reputed talents.

are constitutionally incapable of learning anyhow. For their part, after the black humorists strike shale, they may stop boring. For his part, Thurber told Alistair Cooke in a last interview, "I like to think of humor as one of our greatest natural resources." There is no reason, if one prospector or even an age has had its vein run thin, for concluding that all underlying wealth has been permanently depleted.

VIII

Humor in Selected
Major American
Writers

WE ENTER now upon matter that is even more presumptive than the material of the foregoing two chapters. Because of the stature of authors and the extent of ground covered in this chapter, there is every risk of our merely declaring ourselves upon a comprehensive body of literature. And yet the special insights which selected major writers offer are powerful inducements. We are wary of attitudinizing but hopeful of perspective.

All that is necessary is to insist on the tentative rather than the exhaustive nature of such re-view. In any case, themes and techniques and the very development of our subject will be refocused in our references to classic figures of nineteenth century American literature, Cooper, Thoreau, Poe, Hawthorne, Melville, Whitman, James, and Howells; to Cummings and Frost among the modern poets; to Tennessee Williams and Arthur Miller among recent dramatists; to Faulkner again in the twentieth century; and to examples of literary parody pertinent to our survey. The study has reciprocal advantages that may offset the hazards of all broad, opportunistic procedure. Our method is rapid, highly selective, and wholly suggestive, though we try to make the most of it.

We remember that one humorist, Mark Twain, looms as a major writer in everyone's critical canon, so that through him the comic genre, like the tragical (Hawthorne) and epical (Melville), has made its supreme contribution to American fiction and letters. For the rest, standard anthologies of significant American literature increasingly provide space for other prominent comic writers we have mentioned, so that these lesser representatives of comedy seem also to have achieved their due. But their inclusion is in general so obviously decorative as to be condescending still; they are "sources" for the Realistic movement, they contribute to a local colorism which is itself patronized, they account for certain types of short story, or they otherwise grace a comprehensive and liberal compendium. But the pervasiveness of humor in our major figures is seldom focused for us. Indeed, the extent of it is such that in a few notable instances we are called upon to revaluate crucial figures.

At all events, a consideration of comic modes in otherwise serious writers of the first importance indicates how important the uses of comedy itself have been. We are in fact confirmed in our dignification of a comic mode that steadily informed the general American literary performance. We may gauge, at the last, what great force comedy came to exert when we acknowledge that, with other operative factors, it eventually influenced modern fictional practice to the point that our current figures aspire to be comic novelists.

Apart from one factor, James Fenimore Cooper (1789–1851) is a convenient low-level benchmark against which to measure the heightened sophistication of both means and content later on. Any recommendation of him in American humor belongs solely to his influence upon H. L. Mencken, who derived both his lofty and whimsical antagonism to democratic insurgencies in America from Cooper's political philosophy. But on his own, Cooper deserves no more worshipful consideration than we have accorded Washington Irving, even or particularly when Cooper tries hard for comic effect.

The putative humor he attempted for dramatic relief indicates precisely what we have described in our earliest period; it is highly derivative[1] and painfully heavy-handed. Professor Allan Nevins has spoken of the impossibly strained comic characterization, like that of David Gaunt in *The Last of the Mohicans* (a yet weaker portrait of the Yankee butt than Irving's Ichabod Crane). And there are figures like Dr. Battius, modeled either on Shakespeare's Holofernes or Falstaff, a gross infliction upon the novel, *The Prairie*.

Cooper's humor can be completely out of tune with everything else going on, making him irresponsible and forced. He exceeds himself, however, in the inadvertent humor of his artificial dialogue (a failing, though less pervasively so, in Hawthorne, too). In this matter, his work has deserved all the parody it has received, as by Harte and Twain. In a way, his diction is a marvel of comic unearthliness, and it is a distinct minor loss that we cannot conscientiously take it in this vein. Here are punctilios exchanged between husband and wife, in *The Prairie*, as a prairie fire is about to sweep upon the pair, their incognizance surpassed only by their lyrical intimacy:

"See, Middleton," exclaimed Inez, . . . "how lovely is that sky; surely it contains a promise of happier times!"

"It is glorious!" returned her husband. "Glorious and heavenly is that streak of vivid red, and here is a still brighter crimson; rarely have I seen a richer rising of the sun."

Furthermore, Cooper's gift at primitive dialect is a talent his partisans are ill-advised to stress, especially since some success was being achieved by others in the mode through these years. His unintentionally funny infusions of stage-Negro vocabulary in totally imaginary Indian pidgin-English gives us pause or a full stop.

"Nuttin' see farther than Injin! Red man fly high, too. See from salt lake to sweet water. Know ebbery t'ing in wood. Tell him nuttin' he don't know."

[1] And pretentiously so. It is no exaggeration to say that he not only wanted to become the American Scott but the American Shakespeare. Many of his characters and subplots were borrowed from Shakespeare, together with verbal echoes, and prairie or forest settings often function like the Elizabethan stage. The scale of his ambitions and his consciousness of being the greatest American writer betray his deepest aspirations rather than simple emulations. Accordingly, following a momentous pattern for himself, he sought "comic relief" because Shakespeare had done so.

"You do not suppose, Susquesus, that the Huron warriors could find our surveyors at Mooseridge?"

"Why not find him? Find moose; why not find ridge, too? Find Mooseridge, sartain. . . ." (*Satanstoe*)

In short, Cooper is funny only by default of intention. In his calculated attempts at would-be comic relief, the meagerness of his performance is surpassed only by his superb patronization and general clumsiness. Derivative in his effects, overexpository and obvious, he fits the characterizations we have made elsewhere of our earliest inexpert humor.

After the stubborn embarrassments of our initial figures, there is an even greater leap of native wit and humor made among our major writers than was achieved among our *sub-rosa* humorists of the southwest and their contemporaries of the 1840's and 1850's. Two explanations of this phenomenon are available. The one argues that the advance is more graphic among major writers of the "American Renaissance"[2] since the jump is practically from total inanity, as in Cooper, to the fullest instrumentation of a general sense of humor, as in Thoreau (1817–1862). The other argues that the very nature of genius presupposes the sudden and astronomical distance they achieve over predecessors. Both analyses are correct and compatible.

We begin with Thoreau's masterpiece, *Walden*. It appears to have been brought into being with as much basic humor as anything else. Much, if not all of it, is conceived as a comic contrast to Benjamin Franklin's *Autobiography*.

Having emerged from poverty and obscurity in which I was born and bred to a state of affluence and some degree of reputation in the world, and having gone so far through life with a considerable share of felicity, and conducing means I made use of, which with the blessing of God so well succeeded, my posterity may like to

2 Since there had been no previous significant birth of American literature, the critical designation is somewhat comic in itself. But because its source is F. O. Matthiessen's great work in American critical scholarship, the phrase has grown unimpeachable. One guesses, however, that out of the certainty of his achievement Matthiessen inflicted the term upon the scholarly community as a sort of joke he could afford. Either that or, like President-Judge Groucho, he could not think of anything else to say.

know, as they may find some of them suitable to their own situations, and therefore fit to be imitated.

Pointedly and at once, Thoreau strikes his tonal and thematic contrast: straightforward wit against cautious sanctimoniousness, one candor against the other.

I should not talk so much about myself if there were anybody else whom I knew as well.

Moreover, he is committed to profound jokes upon his pragmatical Franklinesque readers, those moral as well as economic ledger keepers[3] of whom he makes quiet but persistent fun in his own "charts" of expenses.

House	$ 28 12 ½
Farm one year	14 72 ½
Food eight months	8 74
Clothing, etc., eight months .	8 40 ¾
Oil, etc., eight months . . .	2 00
In all	$ 61 99 ¾

He gets by with the extravagance of not rounding off his figures to $62.00 because his subtle refinements to quarters of a cent have taken in his latter-day Franklinian readers in preceding charts.

The whole account and testament of American independence is reinforced everywhere by comic device, much of it masterful and sophisticated. Thoreau's objectivity, partly derived from and everywhere enhanced by his sense of humor, is what mitigates all his serious import, which would otherwise overwhelm us. It renders the idea of his staying on indefinitely at Walden impossible, after all. Like the literalist readers of his charts, all those sanctimonious apostles of Thoreau, who by overextended example contrive or even crave a permanent Walden for themselves, are fooled.

His satiric but balanced comedy informs Thoreau's entire book and reveals a considerable range of varied techniques. He

---

[3] This is the essence of Puritan mentality, Max Weber tells us in *The Protestant Ethic and the Spirit of Capitalism*. And so the religious and capitalist motifs become one and the same, and the instinctual and traditional comic attack on the two fronts has its warrant.

can pun, but wittily. He refers to Walden Pond[4] as a "gem of the first water." The name of his town, Concord, provides him with the subtlest ironies in his report of local recruitment for the Mexican War. His plays on words are carefully premeditated.

When there were several bands of musicians, it sounded as if all the village was a vast bellows, and all the buildings expanded and collapsed alternately with a din. But sometimes it was a really noble and inspiring strain that reached these woods, and the trumpet that sings of fame, and I felt as if I could spit a Mexican with a good relish, . . .

This punning is in evidence also when he uses "constitution" not to signify a document in Washington but a particular temperament in Massachusetts—originality in Thoreau that has since became commonplace.

While my townsmen and women are devoted in so many ways to the good of their fellows, I trust that one at least may be spared to other and less humane pursuits. You must have a genius for charity as well as for anything else. As for Doing-good, that is one of the professions which are full. Moreover, I have tried it fairly, and, strange as it may seem, am satisfied that it does not agree with my constitution.

Seldom has thematic individualism been graced with such technical control, the comic poise a lasting success. For a misanthrope, he had the quickest and most genial wit.

The luxuriously rich are not simply kept comfortably warm, but unnaturally hot; as I implied before, they are cooked, of course *à la mode*.

It is obvious that Thoreau's basic strategy was reversalism: "I made no haste in my work, but rather made the most of it." His whole text is a repudiation of prevailing values and cliché. His subtlest of all triumphs, like Emerson's, only more sustained and daring, is to speak constantly in commercial terms ("cost," especially), even as he seeks to undermine the grounds of the ethos. Or we may say that his basic reversalism serves to deepen

---

[4] "Wall-ed in Pond," Professor Sherman Paul has suggested. This would represent the ultrasubtle side of Thoreau, if true, along with his more flagrant *jeux de mots*, like "grossest groceries," etc.

rather than explode language and to stimulate rather than destroy thought. That is also what his antiproverbialism[5] seeks to do, together with all those carefully wrought paragraphs which are mainly exercises in anticlimax and deflation. His whole effort is to draw up a balance sheet of private and spiritual economy. Nowhere else in American literature does a precious investment in technique pay so many dividends to the purpose, and nowhere else is such care more necessary. Turning the culture back upon itself demands the most sane and scrupulous comic art as well as the most serious intentions.

Of his several targets, Thoreau's favorite is the machine (the railroad[6] is prime symbol), then technology in general, and, more deeply, all mechanical standardization of life. An antiprogressivist, he likens the railroad to a medieval dragon and calls for "the country's champion . . . to meet him at the Deep Cut and thrust an avenging lance between the ribs of the bloated pest," lest it thoroughly overcome us. It may come to ride on us, he tells us, though we delude ourselves in thinking that we "will at length ride somewhere in next to no time, and for nothing." In his essential campaign to discriminate ends from means, he also chooses the telegraph as an object lesson. The lines were up between Maine and Texas, but Maine and Texas, he observes with appalling comic pertinence, may "have nothing important to communicate."[7]

In the end, these were highly specialized targets, as even "Odd Fellows" were. It was human or American nature as a whole that he strove against, and his antitheticism and diabolism were potent impulses barely contained by his genialism elsewhere.

The greater part of what my neighbors call good I believe in my soul to be bad, and if I repent of anything, it is very likely

[5] "Only . . . deserters go to the wars, cowards that . . . enlist"; one "hears a different drummer" and is "a majority of one"; "most men lead lives of quiet desperation," as if they "could kill time without injuring eternity," etc.

[6] It figures prominently as a comic vehicle in Hawthorne and Melville as well. It carries heavier freight, of course, in Walt Whitman and Frank Norris and also serves Hemingway and Faulkner.

[7] The later journalist and minor humorist, George T. Lannigan, was Thoreauvian in his satire of inconsequential cable messages: "The Ahkood of Swat is Dead."

to be my good behavior. What demon possessed me that I behaved so well?

He always spoke with special sharpness when he confronted native self-righteousness.

> A man is not a good *man* to me because he will feed me if I should be starving, or warm me if I should be freezing, or pull me out of a ditch if I should ever fall into one. I can find you a Newfoundland dog that will do as much.

What rescued him from both the excoriative and the hortatory modes in his work was just that measure of humor and self-humor he had begun his book with and carried through to save himself. His own exaggerated . . . and transcendent . . . sense of self is deflated often, as in his mock-heroical portrait of himself: an Achilles slaying Trojan weeds . . . and also "levelling whole ranks of one species, [while] sedulously cultivating another." For this intrinsic reason, we may add, it would be much more difficult to parody Thoreau than Emerson.

More humorous than his colleague, Thoreau was also more conscientious in his depths. On one occasion, the originator of civil disobedience went to the local jail for nonpayment of a certain minor but indecent tax. There in the prison house, history —or legend, for the facts indicate another patron—arranges to have Emerson pay the fine for Thoreau. In the anecdote, Emerson is escorted to Thoreau's cell, shakes his proper head at the spectacle and despite his reserve, to say nothing of his failed insight into his friend, exclaims, "Henry! What are you doing in there?" To which Thoreau replies, "Ralph! What are you doing —*out* there?"

This was veritably the same man who practiced both his principles and comic literalism every day of his life. Hawthorne and local citizens complained of his character in this way. He was a man who could not be greeted with a "how d'you do?" lest he wheel about to ask if you *really* wanted a bill of particulars just then. In such ways he appeared infuriatingly antisocial, as he no doubt struck Emerson as extravagantly unsophisticated. His pertinence was an impertinence—or the other way around, which was worse. He was the deepest of comedians to have about, paradoxically frivolous and impassioned.

And yet, as the soul of irreverence, Thoreau gave the most urbane of rebuttals to that great document of sociability and American formulaism, Franklin's *Autobiography*. Fervid as *Walden* is, yet its comic elements are also decisive and comprehensive. For a work keyed to cultural opposition at almost every point and for a man who actively lived in comic antithesis to his teacher and fellow citizens, that is no surprise. The great critical irony, however, is how infrequently we acknowledge the essential comic element in *Walden*, though that is, perforce, another commentary on our own diminished capacities in our later age. The curse of solemnification has been placed upon a great work by ever more serious students of it, by rock-ribbed disciples who have forgotten what it is also to be tickled.

Popularized or corrupted[8] as the Concord movement became, it was soon fair game for counterattack itself. Not all audiences attended the Lyceum with modish enthusiasm or came mistakenly to lectures on Transcendentalism in order to hear the latest reports on oral bridge work. It had explicit comic enemies enough not to need sentimental friends or feckless allies who got more than they bargained for. Writers like Poe, Hawthorne, and Melville trained the weaponry of satire and humor upon it almost as soon as it was certified as a movement.

Poe (1809–1849) was an especially volatile antagonist, who saw Transcendentalism as the summation of the tortuous New England mind.

> We do not, ourselves, think the poem a remarkably good one:— it is not sufficiently transcendental. Still it did well enough for the Boston audience—who evinced characteristic discrimination in understanding, and especially applauding, all those knotty passages which we ourselves have not yet been able to understand. (*Boston and the Bostonians*)

It was humbug, upon which Poe thought he had a correct perspective.

[8] Emerson's "self-reliance" became a convenient tenet of baronial robbery and rugged individualism in American history and of literary cults of personalism like Ayn Rand's.

And that is the curoisity in our adverting to Poe—that he had a perspective on anything, least of all humbug. His own record is highly ambiguous, showing a man of utterly lucid moments and of playfulness that only a clear overview may authorize, and yet a man who also spent the most valuable part of his career in a literary confidence game of his own. His rambunctious essay on *Diddling* shows his awareness of all the resources and subterfuges of the con man. Yet he was a literary diddler himself in many instances, as in the coincidences of plot and the almost jocularly piled conclusion of "The Fall of the House of Usher"; the successive grimaces and deliberate inconclusiveness, a vast joke upon the reader, in "The Narrative of A. Gordon Pym"; the whole *bizarrerie* of "The Pit and the Pendulum" (burlesqued by himself in his prescient story, "A Predicament"), more than half of which seems a nightmarish joke of the unconscious; and the calculated mixing of clownishness and homicide in "The Cask of Amontillado." In view of the deep ambivalences and self-deceptions in his own life, he appears as the essential neurasthenic in our literature, alternately capable of the surest insights into reality and into himself, followed by the utmost confusions of truth and basic intention.

His first Gothic stories, designed for a prospective collection called "The Folio Club," but never collected as such, were meant as out-and-out parodies of absurdities he had been reading in *Blackwood's Magazine*. Accordingly, a Mr. Solomon Seadrift tells the story, a sort of Gothic tall tale, of "The Ms. Found in a Bottle." Poe proceeded to a formal lampoon of the genre in "How To Write a Blackwood Article," where he spoke clearly of the requirements: overelevated tone, somewhat pedantic, perhaps with accompanying footnotes, preferably long and Latin; the use of stylistic and allusive "filler"; and the portentous use of phrases from foreign languages. Such stories of his own as "Loss of Breath" (subtitled, "A Tale Neither in Nor Out of Blackwood's") and the tale of "Hans Pfaall" (an April's Fool joke upon new science fiction) exactly demonstrate his points, especially in their mock erudition.

Moreover, he pursued gross parody in his poetry, a medium he later employed for his highest ambitions. "Al Araaf" is a manifest take-off on Milton's *Paradise Lost,* and only those pro-

foundly invested in Poe esthetically and psychiatrically can miss
the overt humor in the little work. The piece is funny in design,
compressed cosmology. Furthermore, Poe gives us clear indications that he is spoofing the overwhelming Miltonic mode. His
most forceful hints occur in the pedantic notes he supplies to his
own work, complete with spurious mock scholarship and comic
anticlimax.

> I met with this idea in an old English tale, which I am now
> unable to obtain, and quote from memory: "The verie essence, and,
> as it were, springeheade and origine of all musicke is the verie
> pleasaunte sounde which the trees of the forest do make when they
> growe."

Or he practices the comic complication of avoiding the obvious.

> With the Arabians there is a medium between Heaven and Hell,
> where men suffer no punishment, but yet do not attain that tranquil
> and even happiness which they suppose to be characteristic of
> heavenly enjoyment.

By not referring to the Christian concept of Purgatory, he practices the humor of circularity and irrelevance as well. Indeed,
the whole motive of his piece is to make fun of the exotic and
overblown, and his own text demonstrates his antirhetorical purpose. My italics call attention to the false Miltonic and Keatsian
notes in the ornate setpiece that opens "Part II," but the elongated
similes are equally fair game.

> High on a mountain of *enamelléd* head—
> Such as the drowsy shepherd on his bed
> Of giant pasturage lying at his ease,
> Raising his heavy eyelid, starts and sees
> With many a muttered "hope to be forgiven"
> What time the moon is *quadrated* in Heaven—
> Of rosy head, that towering far away
> Into the sunlit ether, caught the ray
> Of sunken suns at eve—at *noon of night,*
> While the moon danced with
> the fair stranger light
> *Upreared* upon such height arose a pile
> Of gorgeous columns on th' *unburthen'd* air,
> Flashing from Parian marble *that twin smile*
> Far down upon the wave that sparkled there,
> And *nursled* the young mountain in its lair.

Detecting such comic motive in Poe may force us to revaluate some of his other works and perhaps shift otherwise indubitable stories and poems into a borderline position in our criticism of him. This would have the effect of complicating an already complex figure and of sophisticating even his psychopathology. His most enthusiastic partisans in America studiously avoid these questions. And critical quarters abroad, as in France, blanch at the tonal and other expressive problems they would face.

Apart from parody and profound spoof, there are other quite accessible and, as it were, inessential comic devices scattered through Poe's work. Lightly symbolic puns upon names abound in his stories. He enjoys literalism, as in the "left-handed flogging" of "Never Bet the Devil Your Head." And he also favors anti-climax, as in his reference to "Mr. John Neal, a great man in a small way."

While we dare not make too much of these ostensible devices, yet we must fit his wholesale comic irreverences into a true con-figuration of Poe's work. Accordingly we fix upon a mid-region of grotesquerie, the outré, in his performances and ask ourselves how often the intention can be considered perfectly serious. The over-all question resolves itself into two specific and perhaps fruitful queries. How often did Poe begin with a comic impulse and then modulate or abandon it? And how often did a comic motif cling stubbornly[9] to his straightforward purposes of shock and suspense? In either case, we must redefine the psychology of perversity and contrariety that Baudelaire and others too hurriedly and programmatically celebrated in him.

Such a critical approach will not seem totally impudent for "A Predicament," "The Imp of the Perverse" or "Never Bet the Devil Your Head," extravaganzas as they are in tone as well as incident; a popped-out eye winks at the heroine in the first story and dog-meat is made of the decapitated head in the last, comic grotesquerie after Bierce's own heart. But we press our view upon *The Murders in the Rue Morgue,* where an orangutan is the actual killer Dupin tracks down.[10] The work borders far

---

[9] We have elsewhere related Poe to dissociated southern sensibility in our speculations on southwestern humor.

[10] Or up . . . it is the acrobatic and aboriginal leap from high shutters to high shutters that sets Dupin going on his ratiocinative and wild trail.

more closely on the humor of the absurd than we have thought, and we have likewise underestimated the quality of imperturbability in Poe. A great deal of Poe's work may be closer to black humor than it is, so to speak, to the seriously irrational. Moreover, in these stories, particularly of Dupin, we ought to be on the lookout for comic traces in the ratiocinative logic itself. Many of the associations of ideas, masked as inevitable reason, that characterize Dupin's mental processes are disguised jokes. They may have been disguised from the author himself. I am saying that, at the least, Poe often worked with a preconscious impulse of self-parody.

A weird comedy is involved to some degree in the fixtures of "The Pit and the Pendulum"[11] and in the madman of "The Tell-Tale Heart." If there was a "Germany of the soul," as Poe said, in order to dignify the Gothic mode, there may also have been what he would not admit after 1837, a Latin Mardi Gras of the heart. Indeed, just the latter carnival setting is used in his most extraordinary story of all, "The Cask of Amontillado." Here a fool, costumed as jester, is led to a grotesque doom, by a trusted friend.[12] After his drunken stupor and during his final laughing hysteria before annihilation he is mured up in a wall by the friend he had momentarily thought belonged to the Order of Masons. The punned names of the victim, Fortunato, and the murderer, Montresor, give us further warrant for insisting upon the prolonged comic accompaniment to the piece, along with that delighted sense of amorality or antithesis that refuses to punish the crime in the end. This is to say nothing of that ferocious insanity of the narrator, who with grim, sick inversion of values opens the very story with the contention that Fortunato had more insulted than injured him.

In the deep realms of Poe's mind the uses of the macabre would be multiple, and parody and depth psychology and jokes upon his audience and auctorial hysteria would be inextricably mixed. No doubt our critical equipment needs new instrumentation for

[11] No *more* weird or risible, however, than the psychoanalysis of the steadily contracting prison cell in the story, interpreted formally as a symbol of the prenatal womb which Poe, a premature baby, remembered out of his long-standing trauma of Caesarian delivery.

[12] The element of treachery that figures in Poe also greatly appealed to Bierce.

untying such strands of motive and double intention, and we may be more intimidated than challenged. Now a story starts in one humorous key but shifts to another, or starts in all seriousness and gives itself over to comic momentum. Or another story of grim but stolid reputation may appear to us ultimately as a late travesty of the Gothic mode. Yet other works, far more appalling to our critical sensibilities and the most formidable of all, exist in two distinct but simultaneous dimensions, unified by a rare intensity that anneals both sides of the author's split personality.

Failures of dissociated sensibility occur too, as in "The Raven." Here Poe's serious, obsessive effort at lamentation is undercut by several comic devices, both intentional and unintentional. There are inane rhymes: "surely, that is" with "window lattice" and "what thereat is" . . . which are triumphs in their way. There is metric absurdity and bathetic overwriting: "What this grim, ungainly, ghastly, gaunt and ominous bird of yore/ Meant in croaking 'Nevermore!'" There is witless alliteration and assonance rather than true punning: "Whether *Tempt*er sent, or whether *tempe*st tossed." And, finally, there is anticlimax that utterly deflates and destroys the best half-line in all his poetry: "Take thy beak from out my heart," he concludes the penultimate stanza but adds, "and take thy form from off my door!"

But we shall be better able to judge the nature of his precise successes and failures in a great body of his work only if we grant the prevailing impulse of parody and general comedy which motivated Poe just as much as his other compulsions: he could not resist the gratuitous mason joke, for instance, in the otherwise structurally perfect "The Cask of Amontillado." If we also directly apply what we so well know about him, his manic depressive character, we cannot help approximating a supple but true critique of the man. Such revaluation may tell us more exactly what he sometimes actually meant to do and what the rest of the time, for good or ill, he did despite himself. In all, a correct measurement of the comic element in Poe may help us diagnose the nature of both his most integrated and disintegrated performances. It may also make him over into an American De Sade improvising his fantastic monodramas in an asylum of his own mind. And for that reason few critics and fewer idolators, no matter what revelations are possible, will be likely to pursue such lines of thought with any alacrity.

With a single and almost incidental exception, there are no significant revelations for American humor afforded by a study of Hawthorne (1804–1864). We are mindful of the whimsical cast of Hawthorne's "Custom House" introduction to *The Scarlet Letter,* incisive but gentle satire, the tone and extent of which were meant to counterbalance the somberness of his novel. In addition there are two stories of comic literalism in his canon, "Feathertop," a slightly misanthropic tale about a humanized scarecrow, and "The Celestial Railroad," a Bunyanesque spoof of Transcendentalism. He may be waggish.

> . . . the Celestial City. There was much pleasant conversation about the news of the day, topics of business and politics, or the lighter matters of amusement; while religion, though indubitably the main thing at heart, was thrown tastefully into the background. Even an infidel would have heard little or nothing to shock his sensibility.

And he may turn to picturesque comic ridicule, especially of the Transcendentalist.

> He is German by birth, and is called Giant Transcendentalist; but as to his form, his features, his substance, and his nature generally, it is the chief peculiarity of this huge miscreant that neither he for himself, nor anybody for him has ever been able to describe them. As we rushed by the cavern's mouth we caught a hasty glimpse of him, looking somewhat like an ill-proportioned figure, but considerably more like a heap of fog and duskiness. He shouted after us, but in so strange a phraseology that we knew not what he meant, nor whether to be encouraged or affrighted.

All of which is to say that the darkest writer in American classicism shades off into other hues now and then. But what humor he had scarcely gave him color. Hawthorne was not partial to comedy, and it was no real factor in his main work. As to Trollope's passing remark that the sinner's consciousness of sin in *The Scarlet Letter* made the tragedy verge on burlesque, we have the merest critical suggestion rather than supported insight.[13] It is not a fruitful line of inquiry.

Hawthorne's most valuable service to our investigations comes in another way. In three particular stories that form a narrative complex in themselves, "My Kinsman, Major Molineux," "Young Goodman Brown," and "The Birthmark," hysterical laughter figures as a climactic psychological reaction. In each instance, the object of the pent-up, uncontrollable derision is a special sacro-sanctity that had governed the protagonist of each story, a belief in youthful prerogative and political connection for Robin Molineux, a proud sense of Puritan rectitude in Goodman Brown, and presumptive intellect and scientism in Aylmer. Their hysterical laughter signals conclusive disillusion in each case and is protective. It functions not only to vent deep-layered resentment toward ruling social values which they had internalized but to prevent utter psychological breakdown. Such laughter appears as the high charge of repressed hostility, released in outward ridicule; the laughter is always explosive . . . and a substitute for physical aggression. It is a vital defense mechanism, antithetical and protective at the same time. It is, then, a stratagem of the ego that mediates between our destructive satisfactions of the id and the absurd but tyrannical impositions of the superego, or society. The insight is crucial and confirmatory, and we are grateful to it. But it comes, as a kind of literary propriety in Hawthorne study, not from that lighter region he sometimes occupied but, appropriately, from his more serious and profound realms of thought.

For Herman Melville (1819–1891) the uses of comedy were neither ambiguous nor incidental, but wholesale and sustained. That does not rule out subtleties in Melville criticism, but it gives us additional means to outline the most extensive and flexible talent in our classic American literature.

There are rampant farcical attacks upon Transcendentalism and Franklinism in "Cock-A-Doodle-Doo," a short story that burlesques Transcendental optimism in particular, and *Israel Potter*, a comic onslaught on Franklinesque proverbialism and the heroic super-

---

[13] Indeed the remark is self-commentary, for it reflects the intent of Trollope's own delicate mock-heroic stories, like *The Warden*.

ficiality behind it. And *The Confidence Man* is an uneven but dedicated exposé of Mississippi River con men, whom Melville stigmatizes as the indigenous American type. In such works he is variously extravagant, playful, and sardonic, clearly antithetical and, by turns and degrees, pessimistic[14] and misanthropic. One may also bring to mind the decidedly comic cast of most parts of the early south-sea novels. And later, we have mordant comic short stories like "The Lightning Rod Man" and others. But more to the point, his comic impulses were so thorough that a case can be made for his initial comic motivations in both the monumental success and the monumental failure of his career, *Moby Dick* and *Pierre*, respectively.

I mean to extend Granville Hicks's perceptive observations on the humorous cast of *Moby Dick* and maintain that the first flippant quarter of the book was probably composed as the start of a comic rather than heroic epic. The long beginning is not, as many readers have rightly felt, in key with the rest of the narrative. It is consonant only with the humorous "cetological" material, which Melville had further reason to sustain throughout the book, until the very climax, in order to carry forward just that comic tone with which he had begun his story. That the start of his great story is humorous seems inescapable, for there is no other interpretation for the manner in which Ishmael, a rogue-like comic narrator, begins his account.

Some years ago—never mind how long precisely—having little or no money in my purse, and nothing particular to interest me on shore, I thought I would sail about a little and see the watery part of the world. It is a way I have of driving off the spleen, and regulating the circulation. Whenever I find myself growing grim about the mouth; whenever it is a damp, drizzly November in my soul; whenever I find myself involuntarily pausing before coffin warehouses, and bringing up the rear of every funeral I meet; and especially whenever my hypos get such an upper hand of me, that it requires a strong moral principle to prevent me from deliberately stepping into the street, and methodically knocking people's hats off—then, I account it high time to get to sea as soon as I can.

[14] He did write, in correspondence to an Englishman, that he was pessimistic by force of reaction or necessary resistance to the prevailing mood. That is in keeping with a standard definition of a pessimist, in the vein of Ambrose Bierce, as a person who lives with an optimist.

He provides an extended, offhand and otherwise humorous admission, as of hostility, and it is not really contrite. To this subtle and paradoxical confession, Ishmael adds the force of universality, a quick and disarming comic defense.

> With a philosophical flourish Cato throws himself upon his sword; I quietly take to the ship. There is nothing surprising in this. If they but knew it, almost all men in their degree, some time or other, cherish very nearly the same feelings towards the ocean with me.

When we add to this opening the famous three-word sentence that introduces it—"Call me Ishmael"—and relate the pseudonym to the whole comic tradition of assumed identity and masquerade, we cannot avoid the calculated effect. We should not labor the obvious for any other book, except that the obvious has a way of disappearing in the welter of serious symbolic interpretation of *Moby Dick*.

Nor would we ordinarily have to emphasize that the very beginning of any work, in theme and tone, is a powerful indication and often the decisive one of the author's intention. In Melville's novel Ishmael is a typically alienated American vagabond hero, with a protective sense of humor, who journeys upon a great waterway, this time lighting out for distant seas. Appropriately enough, he joins up with a partner (of another race again), humorously named Queequeg. In fact, he completely shares his New Bedford experiences with him, even bed and board. Such are the extended circumstances added to the opening and perfectly consistent with the comic tone struck by the narrator.

All of which suggests a comic design for all that was to follow. It is quite elementary narrative practice, except that something changed Melville's mind. But only later, after a prolonged and insistent beginning; meanwhile he elaborates his initial comedy. There is sexual comic innuendo in the two hilariously contrasting companions, settling in at the incongruous boudoir they share at the seamen's inn. Ishmael reflects: "Better sleep with a sober cannibal than a drunken Christian." In addition to a humorous *mésalliance* which will turn to rich camaraderie, Melville indulges religious satire, latitudinarian comedy in which Ishmael fully ratonalizes his complaisant idol worship with Queequeg on circular Presbyterian grounds.

> But what is worship? thought I. Do you suppose now, Ishmael, that the magnanimous God of heaven and earth—pagans and all included—can possibly be jealous of an insignificant bit of black wood? Impossible! But what is worship?—to do the will of God?— that is worship. And what is the will of God?—to do to my fellow man what I would have my fellow man do to me—*that* is the will of God. Now, Queequeg is my fellow man. And what do I wish that this Queequeg would do to me? Why, unite with me in my particular Presbyterian form of worship. Consequently, I must then unite with him in his; ergo, I must turn idolator. So I kindled the shavings; helped prop up the innocent little idol; offered him burnt biscuit with Queequeg; salaamed before him twice or thrice; kissed his nose; . . . at peace with our own consciences and all the world.

Still further on, apart from such domestic comedy, Melville makes fun of the refinements of Quaker conscience and economics in a steadily comic chapter on the owners' apportionment of the shares of the ensuing voyage; in the course of things, the principal owners come to blows.

At this point, we are already at Chapter Sixteen. There is still some slapstick incident and whimsical description to come, before something else definitely intervenes. But in the meantime, or in this initial prime time, what in effect do we have but the setting up of a comic novel *in toto*? The preparation is unmistakable.

But, of course, Melville glimpsed Ahab, that captain who in altogether consistent circumstances would have been a comic grotesque on some unspeakably outlandish and pretentious voyage. At some point just then Melville changed his mind, more or less retaining caricature but hoping now to transcend the risks involved. He took the chance of serious pretension—that is, his own discovered ambition—in following the lead of heroical epic character and narration which had crossed his mind. If the final effect were broad and ambitious *enough*, it might subsume, as in the cetological chapters, the comic and mock-heroical view with which he started. And that is precisely what happened and what gives us the full measure of his astonishing success. It is indeed a roughed-out success, with slipped and absurd extravagances and constantly modulated changes of key, all of which may put off some unaccustomed readers but which are the signal victories that forty years of students accord the work.

He might have gone on writing another seafaring roguish comedy, as a safe enough American Smollett, but he chose instead to take his chances with a serious masterwork as they occurred to him almost a fourth of the way through his book. The decision called upon a certain courage, which is harder than audacity, and it called upon an amazing suppleness of mind. In fact, it called upon enterprising genius, alert and strong enough to grasp the favorable possibilities as well as the risks, a work so comprehensive that it could still include his original comic intentions. Our insight is double. We see those first intentions and that pervading sense of humor which Melville would not subdue but, on the contrary, would raise to some final contributory service. And we see into the sublimest workings of comic mentality; those qualities of freedom, relativity, and flexibility,[15] which comedy both fosters and feeds upon, enable it not to cancel but to transcend itself. The difference we distinguish between Melville and Poe in this regard appears to be one of heightened consciousness, by which I mean that Melville mostly knew what was going on. At all events, the integration was incalculably higher and surer.

All of which is not to say that taking a conscious[16] long chance insures a masterpiece. What we have seen in *Moby Dick* appears to have occurred just afterward, to catastrophic effect, in *Pierre*. How could the book with its beginning be designed as anything but the broadest literary satire of romantic drama and fiction?

As touched and bewitched by the loveliness of this silence, Pierre neared the cottage, and lifted his eyes, he swiftly paused, fixing his glance upon one upper, open casement there. Why now this impassioned, youthful pause? Why this enkindled cheek and

[15] These, in the transformation of the book, turn out to be the very attributes of Melville's deepest philosophical thinking; they make possible his symbolic ambiguities, his "wicked" unorthodoxies, his even more wicked tentativeness, and his whole Existentialist creation.

[16] I do not mean to suggest that there was *nothing* ever unconscious in anything Melville undertook, only that he did, after all, understand more rather than less of what was going on. I mean intellectually as well as artistically. He was in predominant control, in victory or defeat. Using the same terms for Poe, as implied in the earlier discussion, I would say the exact opposite was true for him.

eye? Upon the sill of the casement, a snow-white glossy pillow reposes, and a trailing shrub has softly rested a rich, crimson flower against it.

Well mayst thou seek that pillow, thou odoriferous flower, thought Pierre; not an hour ago, her own cheek must have rested there. "Lucy!"

It is an imperturbable but relentless farce of Romeo-and-Julietry.

As heart rings to heart those voices rang, and for a moment, in the bright hush of the morning, the two stood silently but ardently eying each other, beholding mutual reflections of a boundless admiration and love.

"Nothing but Pierre," laughed the youth, at last; "thou hast forgotten to bid me good morning."

"That would be little. Good mornings, good evenings, good days, weeks, months, and years to thee, Pierre;—bright Pierre!—Pierre!"

Truly, thought the youth, with a still gaze of inexpressible fondness; truly the skies do ope, and this invoking angel looks down . . . .

. . . And shaking the casement shrub, he dislodged the flower, and conspicuously fastened it in his bosom.—"I must away now, Lucy! see! under these colors I march."

"Bravissimo! oh, my only recruit!"

As *Moby Dick* was originally conceived as a comic epic, so *Pierre* was begun as a flagrant literary burlesque. We need not discuss here what subsequently became of it, especially since Dr. Henry A. Murray's pyschoanalysis remains a standard and convincing interpretation, bolstered, for once, by an analyst's esthetic sensitivities. Taking his own ironies seriously, Melville changed his intentions and again his tone and, seduced this time by his philosophic gravity, plunged to narrative and stylistic disaster; his plotting turned overly contrived and melodramatic, and his discursiveness labored too heavily for piled ironies, becoming pretentious. And so his ambitiousness could just as well destroy his sense of humor as utilize it. The precise equipoise or integration of the two in his successful work, therefore, needs greater technical recognition and study than it has strictly received. One conclusion, in any case, is insistent. Melville was not a man who was incidentally humorous. Indeed, the comic sense he owned led him directly to both his monumental success and his huge failure.

In these connections we must advert to Melville's greatest short story, "Bartleby." Even after the catastrophe of *Pierre*, he followed the same creative path we have traced. But now he repeated his earlier success. The long opening of "Bartleby," describing the law office of the narrator and the three law clerks, is high and expert comedy. The appearance of the outlandish Bartleby, from the Dead Letter Office, gave Melville his alternatives of continued slapstick or of profound import, which is technically more hazardous to achieve. But he took his chances once again. And he found deeper comedy in Bartleby's monomaniacal deflation of all the commanding lawyer's manipulative orders and desperate pragmatism, modulating the comedy into the exquisite pathos of his conclusion. He arrived at where he did only because of a ruling comic motive which he did not allow to tyrannize him but which he would not veto. Thoreau's political metaphors are even more applicable to Melville. It was as if an interior government of checks and balances accounted for the man, the initiative unit of which was almost always an insurgent and legislative comedy, at least through *The Confidence Man* (1857).

The range of Melville's devices is considerable, as we might expect. There is the omnipresent pun, generally less witty than associative in *Moby Dick*; in New Bedford Ishmael finds a new bedfellow. There is mischievous and extensive comic literalism: "It tasted something as I should conceive a royal cutlet from the thigh of Louis le Gros might have tasted, supposing him to have been killed the first day after the venison season." He turns with ebullient self-deflation to comic catalogue: "Oh, Time, Strength, Cash and Patience!" We have frontier extravagance, literary Crockettry:[17] "Give me Vesuvius crater for an inkstand!" And there is the devastating use of comic repetition in "Cock-A-Doodle-Doo!"—"The cock crew" and "They were dead"—reverberant and punctuating refrains coming at the end of that satire on indomitable hopefulness and Transcendental optimism.

[17] The native mode was reinforced by a strong influence of Rabelais upon Melville. The famous chapter on the whiteness of the whale is heavily indebted to Rabelaisian play on color. This relation of the extravagant Frenchman and flamboyant American is an early instance of the compatible comic temperament of the two nationalities. It is a conjunction that we do not altogether expect, though the surprise is grateful and we shall have reason to illustrate it further, through modern example, in chapter 9.

"Cock-A-Doodle-Doo!" presented Melville with numerous opportunities, of course, for scatological punning or *double-entendre*. And there are only slightly indirect but notorious instances in *Moby Dick*.

> No wonder that in old times sperm was such a favorite cosmetic. Such a clearer! such a sweetener! such a softener! such a delicious mollifier!

He adds, almost innocuously:

> After having my hands in it for only a few minutes, my fingers felt like eels, and began, as it were, to serpentine and spiralize.

And he sustains his comedy with such impudent moralizing that the moralizing sanctions the impudence.

> I almost began to credit the old Paracelsan superstition that sperm is of rare virtue in allaying the heat of anger: while bathing in that bath, I felt divinely free from all ill-will, or petulance, or malice, of any sort whatsoever. . . .
> I found myself unwittingly squeezing my co-laborers' hands in it, mistaking their hands for the gentle globules. Such an abounding, affectionate, friendly, loving feeling did this avocation beget; that at last I was continually squeezing their hands, and looking up into their eyes sentimentally. . . . Come; let us squeeze hands all round; nay, let us all squeeze ourselves into each other. . . .
>   Would that I could keep squeezing that sperm for ever! For now, since by many prolonged, repeated experiences, I have perceived that in all cases man must eventually lower, or at last shift, his conceit of attainable felicity; not placing it anywhere in the intellect or the fancy; but in the wife, the heart, the bed. . . . In thoughts of the visions of the night, I saw long rows of angels in paradise, each with his hands in a jar of spermaceti.

Moreover, as in his suggestions here, he combines his scatology with the most demonic religious satire, the penis-ology of Chapter 95, "The Cassock," so blasphemous that it attains a kind of theological status of its own, thorough and audacious diabolism. The pelt of "the enigmatical object—that unaccountable cone" is stripped and spread to dry.

> Ere long, it is taken down; when removing some three feet of it towards the pointed extremity, and then cutting two slits for arm-

holes at the other end, he lengthwise slips himself bodily into it. The mincer now stands before you invested in the full canonicals of his calling. . . .

That office consists in mincing . . . blubber for the pots. . . . Arrayed in decent black; occupying a conspicuous pulpit; intent on bible leaves;[18] what a candidate for an archbishopric, what a lad for a Pope were this mincer!

It is the bawdy mode of Melville, at once the most exacting and indecent example in our literature. It was another influence of Rabelais, although Melville went to him willingly for it as he did for support of his general extravagance and rhetorical stylistics.

The whole phenomenon of rhetorical dexterity in *Moby Dick* is illuminating. For there is a certain leading comic function of style per se in the book. The question is not merely a syntactical matter but a generally expressive one. Like the juggler's performance, Melville's writing is always partly humorous in its deliberately extravagant flourishes, its risks of affectation or bathos, the steady possibilities of disaster from which it is constantly rescuing itself. Two other influences aside from literary precedent, like that of Rabelais, were cultivated by Melville in what we may call this inside entertainment. One was Italian opera, where the heightened effect of full-throated expression must be made to contribute to dramatic impact finally and not to a stylized comedy. The other was native American political oratory[19] of the time. To fit each rhetoric to its appropriate subject matter and then to alternate such passages and chapters with those of outright comic stylization and mock heroics constituted the precise challenge he welcomed. It was the riskiest of enterprises. But it gave him the way to modulate key in *Moby Dick*.

One particular target, in addition to Transcendentalism and orthodox religion, con men and hypocrisy, proverbialism and middle-class comfort, sentimentalism and pragmatism, deserves special notice. That is empiricism, together with its offspring, technology. We understand what is meant when Ahab throws away the sextant at last. But that is not an isolated incident or image. Throughout *Moby Dick* Melville scoffs at all empiric ways

18 Thin slices of blubber, in whalers' jargon.
19 Both influences, opera and oratory, were also dear to Whitman, who was not entirely willing to surmount them.

of knowledge, at measurement itself as an adequate means of taking the measure of any whale—or of apprehending reality in any significant way. Even the literal bare bones of leviathan, stretched out and apparently measurable on deck, fail us in our puerile attempts to encompass or know the thing itself.

> The largest of the Tranque ribs, one of the middle ones, occupied that part of the fish which, in life, is greatest in depth. Now, the greatest depth of the invested body of this particular whale must have been at least sixteen feet; whereas, the corresponding rib measured but little more than eight feet. So that this rib only conveyed half of the true notion of the living magnitude of that part. . . .
> Only in the heart of quickest perils; only when within the eddyings of his angry flukes; only on the profound unbounded sea, can the fully invested whale be truly and livingly found out. . . .
> But the spine. . . .
> There are forty and odd vertebrae in all. . . . The largest, a middle one, is in width something less than three feet, and in depth more than four. The smallest, where the spine tapers away into the tail, is only two inches in width, and looks something like a white billiard-ball. I was told that there were still smaller ones, but they had been lost by some little cannibal urchins, the priest's children, who had stolen them to play marbles with. Thus we see how that the spine of even the hugest of living things tapers off at last into simple child's play.

And in his sketches, "The Encantadas," Melville "classifies" bird and animal life of the Galapagos Islands only to make intellectual fun of the whole Darwinian approach.[20] His comedy in these matters was never impromptu but deep in him, for he wished profoundly to discredit a rising empiricism he believed was a new

---

[20] Melville knew his Darwin and had actually read *The Voyage of the Beagle*. In fact Darwin's "tables" served him as Franklin's moral ledgerism had served Thoreau. Indeed, some of Melville's descriptions echo Darwin's in organization as well as in diction, as James R. Corey has shown, and Melville even copied Darwin's tabular schema to satiric effect.

Men	None
Ant-eaters	Unknown
Man-haters	Unknown
. . . .	
Spiders	10,000,000
. . . .	
Making a clear total of	11,000,000

fake mythology. It is significant that he chose comic devices as chief instruments for the task.

Certainly Melville could strike the note of seriocomic nihilism. He does so in *Moby Dick*.

> The Killer [whale] is never hunted. I never heard what sort of oil he has. Exception might be taken to the name bestowed upon this whale, on the ground of its indistinctness. For we are all killers, on land and on sea; Bonapartes and Sharks included.

And the upshot of "Bartleby," as the most cogent instance of all, is quietly shattering. Throughout his works, Melville has his moments of cynicism and full misanthropy, as in his coinage, "snivelization," and a passage like the following from "Cock-A-Doodle-Doo!":

> Ah! there's that twinge of the rheumatics in my right shoulder. I got it one night on the North River, when, in a crowded boat, I gave up my berth to a sick lady, and staid on deck till morning in drizzling weather. There's the thanks one gets for charity! Twinge! Shoot away, ye rheumatics! Ye couldn't lay on worse if I were some villain who had murdered the lady instead of befriending her. Dyspepsia too—I am troubled with that.

In sections of his novels and in his short stories there are basic devices of grotesquerie and grim humor. His range, then, almost covers the spectrum of American comic technique and theme.

That range and his fundamental motive were so extensive and decisive that even a cursory review of them makes a difference in our judgment of him, whereas our interest in Hawthorne remains narrow and clinical. And even more than is true for a review of Poe, the study of Melville thickens by virtue of the man's natural comic impulse and his supple, consciously manipulated gifts.

Walt Whitman (1819–1892) is the one major figure unredeemable to comedy. He remains humorless despite all the partisan critical expenditure upon him, especially since his centennial. We have the anomaly of comic investiture for a man totally devoid of a sense of humor. Even Emily Dickinson, cultural daughter of Emerson, had her pixie share of it. But Whitman was adamant proof against it. What is doubly irreclaimable about his work is that, unlike even Cooper, he saw no need for comic relief whatsoever and, unlike Poe, he had no partial deflationary instincts at all.

But that one of our most American of writers should lack an essential American attribute has been a kind of affront to esthetical and inclusive criticism.[21] The critic, Richard Chase, represents a group of partisans who seek to rescue Whitman for comedy at all costs. Their method is argumentative and abstract but subtle. Chase, for example, characterizes "Song of Myself" as a fundamentally comic poem. But exuberance is in itself not an adequate definition of comedy. Chase knows as much and therefore argues further for Whitman's technique of deliberate incongruities and for the whole energetic force of the work, as if the method of dramatic contrast or the quality of energy does not also underlie tragic and epic power. Finally, he makes a case for a good deal of intentional farce in Whitman's poetry. It is a shame that this is not—and, in the nature of the work, could not be—true. Intentional farce at any one point in such dedicated exhortation would cast doubt on any other point and wreck the entire effort.

That effort, in which incongruities represented plural and comprehensive democracy, was a thoroughly serious celebration of the American experience. For all of the "singing" and for all of the hortatory "joy" and for all of the celebratory purpose in Whitman's work, the poetry was almost monomaniacal in its political and spiritual import, intensely earnest and too fiercely dedicated to its themes to afford comic deflection or even relaxation. Actually, in trying to extend Whitman's credit over the widest fields, Chase and others give up the citadel.

Where Whitman's comic failure is crucial is in his adamant tactlessness, his lack of proportion and, after all, his lapses into

[21] This occurs in other ways in the course of American literature. Franklin, for instance, so durably American in his pragmatism, extroversion, optimism, and sociability, lacked artistic sensibility and a love of nature. But if Franklin should suddenly be elevated to greatness in American literature, he would undoubtedly be given a love of nature, derived probably from his love of *human* nature, an inference itself from his program of social improvement. That would be the process of what I have called esthetical criticism, which supplies what is missing. It is itself humorous technique though not consciously so.

sheer pretension. The effect of these disabilities may suggest a species of unintended comedy, but that is not an argument in his favor. His exclamatory catalogues, for instance, are meant to be taken quite seriously, but, then, they always go on too long and encourage the expectation of deflation.

> Lands where the north-west Columbia winds, and where the south-west Colorado winds!
> Land of the eastern Chesapeake! land of the Delaware!
> Land of Ontario, Erie, Huron, Michigan!
> Land of the Old Thirteen! Massachusetts land! land of Vermont and Connecticut!
> Land of the ocean shores! land of sierras and peaks!
> Land of boatmen and sailors! fishermen's land!
> Inextricable lands! the clutch'd together! the passionate ones!
> The side by side! the elder and younger brothers! the bony-limb'd!
> The great women's land! the feminine! the experienced sisters and the inexperienced sisters!
> Far breath'd land! Arctic braced! Mexican breez'd! the diverse! the compact!
> The Pennsylvanian! the Virginian! the double Carolinian!

We await mock heroics or anticlimax, out of normal common-sensical experience. We judge that the absurd distention of a repetitive verse paragraph has as little reason to stop where it does as it has to go on forever. We hear the extravagant boasting and expect the frontier poke in the ribs, or even a Franklinesque wink now and then. But the braggadocio is without a saving jocular grace, and we are put off by a relentless declamatory subjectivity that is temperamentally incapable of self-laughter.

We lend him attention time and again, through all the Gallicisms, Spanish phrases, Biblical gestures, Quakerisms, self-taught intellectual jargon, and plummeting descents,[22] but he travesties himself without the faintest suspicions that his grammar, his very words, turn ludicrous.

[22] Parody is easy, but a compaction of Whitman's own lines and words is indicative.

> *Eléves* and *commarados!* Allons! Behold, it is Seven-month and I feel omnific,
> The sound of the belch'd words of my voice loosed to the eddies of the wind
> The orbic flex of . . . mouth pouring and filling me full.
> You should have been with us that day around the chowder-kettle.

Blind loving wrestling touch, sheath'd hooded sharp-tooth'd touch!
Did it make you ache so, leaving me?

And there are whole lines so impermeable to sense that we gasp
less at the affront than at the unknown buffoonery.

Not too exclusive to the reachers of my remembrancers,

. . . . .

In me the caresser of life wherever moving, backward as well as
forward sluing,

. . . . .

To niches aside and junior bending . . .
Look in my face while I snuff the sidle of evening,

There are too many instances of sublime incognizance and bathos,
especially in "Song of Myself." And the poet's self-characterization at last, that he is untranslatable in his "barbaric yawp," only
certifies his incredibly humorless instinct for calling attention
exactly to his weakness.

Such is the dross, however, that comes with the gold. The
admission of worth elsewhere goes without saying. But it is no
reason to transmute the dross into comic quicksilver for general
admiration's sake. That is also the laudatory fallacy in criticism,
to be as indiscriminate in our praise as our subject is in his performance.

If we indulge ourselves this way, we imperil our very ability
to recognize what is valuable in Whitman. For that involves our
seeing what is not valuable, which in turn depends, precisely,
on *our* full sense of humor and not his defective sense, as it
depends also on our sophistication rather than his lack of it.
Whitman himself was incapable of any proper distancing, which
may have accounted for his rare but genuine moments of
lyrical power. But it also accounted for his hyperbolic excesses,
which he had no way of checking or even knowing. He was,
simply, wild rather than comic. And when, for a while at mid-
career, he did pay something of himself in return for his easy
all-inclusiveness, he did so with the same subjectivity that was
always in him; he turned to earnest self-castigation rather than
objective self-derision. He mentions "peals of . . . ironical laughter" in "As I Ebb'd with the Ocean of Life," but that is fanciful

poetic statement rather than actual rendition; the autobiographic lines are now self-flagellant where they used to be arrogant. He could never have been the clown that Chase and others wish him to be, or, constituted as he was, he would have collapsed as a poet. And he never attained urbanity, only guilt. The absurdities which he committed were, after all, the price he unwittingly paid for his successes . . . but we ourselves need not make the wholesale purchase.

Europe takes him to its bosom, even more that it does Poe, as one of its democratic and socialistic heroes. He is more an exotic and political symbol to Europeans than anything else. And he is, of course, just as necessary and symbolical to the newer nations, hopefully emerging from colonialism to democracy, as he is to the Old World. For largely extrinsic reasons, he is an unqualified and hallowed inspiration, and once again the language barrier is a help rather than a hindrance. But for Americans, when all is said and done, he is not at this date so necessary to our own literary politics that we can't laugh at his considerable lapses, which are faults of humor as well as taste—or faults of taste because they are faults of humor.

One does not even know if he absolutely had to commit those mistakes of remorseless sanctimoniousness which he did, including eventual self-conversion to prophethood and a most comfortable accommodation to the mask he wore rather than to his own face.[23] But he did, probably because he was a man of intermittent talent rather than genius. One way or the other he stands as a monumental exception to the native sense of humor operative in our major writers. As such, he is the figure most susceptible of all, Cooper, Poe, and James notwithstanding, to literary parody.[24]

But no one who is absolutely devoid of importance is a subject of constant parody. That importance comes from his moments of rare but undeniable success, but it also comes from liberal criticism that dares not brook the subtraction of any part of him, probably because partisans suspect that any loss may be major

[23] He became a sort of literary confidence man, writing interviews of himself as "the good gray poet," which he then presented to newspapermen in cities he toured to save them time. We may remark that his utter humorlessness at this stage of his career coincided with his feeblest poetry.

[24] Almost exclusively by Americans, of course.

rather than minor. And so it is a political matter here, too, and a question of need in the end.

Nonetheless, it is of some interest to us to see that it is just the quality of humor that many critics want to bestow upon Whitman, no matter what. That is a testimonial of how seriously we have come to take comedy.

On a scale of primitivism and sophistication, Henry James (1843–1916) is at the polar extreme from Whitman. If Emerson helped to bring the poet to a boiling froth, Hawthorne helped cool the novelist toward frigidity. But there is more humor in chill sophistication than in fervid ebullience, as James makes clear in a variety of ways in one of his stories, "The Point of View" (1882). He is capable there, precisely as Whitman was not, of self-satiric relief, for instance:

> They've a novelist with pretensions to literature who writes about the chase for the husband and the adventures of the rich Americans in our corrupt old Europe, where their primeval candour puts the Europeans to shame. *C'est proprement écrit,* but it's terribly pale.

James also manages frequent comic anticlimax, as in a representative thrust from the same story.

> I've been extremely interested in my visit to Philadelphia, where I saw several thousand little red houses with white steps, occupied by intelligent artisans and arranged (in streets) on the rectangular system . . . every block of exactly equal length; blocks and houses economically lettered and numbered. There's absolutely no loss of time and no need of looking for, or indeed *at,* anything.

He is as likely as not to employ British paradox even more than native anticlimax. "In this country the people have rights, but the person has none." This is Wildean aphorism, although one is hard put to describe it strictly as proverbialism or antiproverbialism. His weakness is, curiously for him, overexplicitness.

> [America is] very big, very rich, and perfectly ugly. A Frenchman couldn't live here; for life with us, after all, at the worst, is a sort of appreciation. Here one has nothing to appreciate.

The error comes from the fact that overt satire or humor is not his natural bent. All the more, such venturesomeness even in James points up the lack in his opposite number.

James was not, himself, a home-bred American writer, and in certain leading respects he slips out of convenient classification. He does choose some characteristic and antithetic targets, however, machinery and children. In "The Point of View" there is a kind of distinctive comic terror in his treatment of the American speaking tube, for example, with a touch of the outré.

> There's only a strange orifice in the wall, through which the traveller in distress may transmit his appeal. I fill it with incoherent sounds, and sounds more incoherent yet come back to me. I gather at last their meaning; they appear to constitute an awful enquiry. A hollow impersonal voice wishes to know what I want, and the very question paralyses me. I want everything—yet I want nothing, nothing this hard impersonality can give! I want my little corner of Paris; I want the rich, the deep, the dark Old World; I want to be out of this horrible place. Yet I can't confide all this to that mechanical tube; it would be of no use; a barbarous laugh would come up from the office.

And American childism is a satirical target.

> The position of a child is on the whole one of great distinction. There's a popular ballad of which the refrain, if I'm not mistaken, is "Make me a child again just for tonight!" and which seems to express the sentiment of regret for lost privileges. At all events they are a powerful and independent class, and have organs, of immense circulation, in the press.

We recall slightly horrendous portraits of American children elsewhere in his work, like that of Daisy's little brother, Randolph Miller. But, by and large, his comedy is one of general conception rather than of specific effect. Professor Poirier suggests a certain group of free and ironical characters in James who maintain comic relations with all the fixed and melodramatic characters they meet. And there may be a large-minded, uninsistent comedy involved in James's view of our small capacity, however intelligent, to control events.[25]

[25] Henry Adams expands this view to international and historical questions but, like James, avoids mockery at the spectacle of our limited knowledge, even in high places. The tenth chapter of *The Education* is the model of Adams' controlled comic skepticism.

In a thematic class to himself, James is expectedly rife with ambiguity. He is a champion of aristocratic sensibility, but also the defender of democratic types. That defense is not always the standard partisanship for the American in Europe. In *Washington Square*, for instance, the lowly Catherine rises against all local odds, especially against paternal government and sardonicism. James's consistent bias of interest in the higher class seems contradictory to his prejudice for certain frank, ingenuous, bourgeois Americans (Daisy, Newman, Strether); he is probably a subtle Jeffersonian, believing in a natural aristocracy of sensibility and moral courage, qualities which experience can activate in anyone who inherently has them.

Resolving the ambiguity in other matters is not so easy. In "The Point of View," James's technical problem is both to represent American provincialism[26]—

> The meagreness, the stinginess, the perpetual expectation of a sixpence, used to exasperate me.

—and to satirize it:

> . . . mamma hears that in Boston the people only marry their cousins.

He does both equally well because of his own ambivalences: sophisticates and provincials fare unsystematically well and badly in diverse novels like *Washington Square, Daisy Miller, The American, The Ambassadors*, etc. Similarly, there are sallies against women in "The Point of View:"

> the women . . . are fidgety and talk too much. . . .

and

> The men in America absent themselves systematically from this meal, at which ladies assemble in large numbers to discuss religious, political and social topics.

And certain female types like Aunt Livinia in *Washington Square* or Mrs. Walker in *Daisy Miller* are the very archetypes of feminine vacuity and tyrannical self-righteousness. Nonetheless,

---

[26] The provincial but open American set against the experienced but absurdly calculating European is a contrast that Mark Twain also makes in his travel books.

James also portrays and defends most of his female protagonists, Daisy Miller, Catherine Sloper, Mildred Theale, etc., the way few others do. These ambiguities remain impenetrable.

In the end, we grant him his urbanity. The trait enabled him to fashion scores of subtle human comedies. It also allowed him to pun with delicate regularity on names of people and things throughout his work with a refined wit.

> "It may be enchanting, dear child, but it is not the custom here," urged Mrs. Walker, leaning forward in her victoria, with her hands devoutly clasped. (*Daisy Miller*)

And his arch comic pertinence is not to be underestimated.

> Of course [the doctor's] easy domestic situation saved him a good deal of drudgery, and his wife's affiliation to the "best people" brought him a good many of those patients whose symptoms are, if not more interesting in themselves than those of the lower orders, at least more consistently displayed.   (*Washington Square*)

What prevents us from easily remembering these qualities in the earlier James is the runaway style of the later James. It is the overcomplication especially of his late style that becomes unintentionally comic. In a certain respect the ends of our critical scale come together, for during his concluding stage James was not so far from Whitman in his pitilessly involuted expression, also fit for merciless parody.

James's friend, William Dean Howells (1837–1920), had the advantage of him in his full Americanism. He was no less sophisticated, but he had a readier humor and no puzzling ambivalences.

On occasion he could be close to Twain, as in *A Modern Instance*.

> "I guess you call anything a brain food that you happen to like, don't you, Kinney?"
>
> "No sir," said Kinney, soberly; "but I like to see the philosophy of a thing when I get a chance. Now, there's tea, for example," he said, pointing to the great tin pot on the stove. . . . "You look at the tea-drinkers and the coffee-drinkers all the world over! Look at 'em in our own country! All the Northern people and all the go-ahead people drink tea. The Pennsylvanians and the Southerners

drink coffee. Why, our New England folks don't even know how to *make* coffee so it's fit to drink! And it's just so all over Europe. The Russians drink tea, and they'd e't up those coffee-drinkin' Turks long ago, if the tea-drinkin' English hadn't kept 'em from it. Go anywheres you like in the North, and you find 'em drinkin' tea. The Swedes and Norwegians in Aroostook County drink it at home."

"Well, what do you think of the French and Germans? They drink coffee, and they're pretty smart, active people, too."

"French and Germans drink coffee?"

"Yes."

Kinney stopped short in his heated career of generalization, and scratched his shaggy head. "Well," he said, finally, "I guess they're a kind of a missing link, as old Darwin says."

His forte, however, was wit, apparent throughout his work but particularly informing *The Rise of Silas Lapham*. There he perpetrates one of the most flagrant but witty puns we have.

. . . in a Boston society where Middlesexes have married Essexes and produced Suffolks for two hundred and fifty years.

The humor of the entire book is generally less meretricious than this, though consistent and all-informing.

In his less famous but perhaps richest novel, *A Hazard of New Fortunes*, an equally permeating sense of comedy rules his conception, and the controlled wit is even keener.

They lived near Greenwich Village, and March liked strolling through its quaintness toward the waterside on a Sunday, when a hereditary Sabbatarianism kept his wife at home; he made her observe that it even kept her at home from church.

. . . . .

"Why don't you let March go?" Beaton suggested.

"Ah, I couldn't," said [the cynical] Fulkerson. "I got him to break up in Boston and come here; I like him; nobody else could get the hang of the thing like he has; he's—a friend." Fulkerson said this with the nearest approach he could make to seriousness, which was a kind of unhappiness.

The novel contains what is otherwise conspicuous for its absence in American humor and literature, highly competent and often surpassing repartee. It occurs between Alma Leighton and Beaton, the proud and the prejudiced romantic duelists.

"How do you like that?" he asked, whirling round.

"It seems rather a disrespectful little tune, somehow," said Alma, placidly.

Beaton rested his elbow on the corner of the piano and gazed dreamily at her. "Your perceptions are wonderful. It *is* disrespectful. I played it, up there, because I felt disrespectful to them."

"Do you claim that as a merit?"

"No, I state it as a fact. How can you respect such people?"

"You might respect yourself, then," said the girl. "Or perhaps that wouldn't be so easy, either."

"No, it wouldn't. I like to have you say these things to me," said Beaton, impartially.

"Well, I like to say them," Alma returned.

"They do me good."

"Oh, I don't know that that was my motive."

It may be wise to recall that Twain himself acknowledged Howells as a master hand in literature. He was not merely thinking of the momentary extravagances in *A Modern Instance* or of a drunken scene he liked in *Lapham*. He was thinking of the sustained style, comic without being uproarious, and of so many of Howells' stories in which the humor is quiet but implicit and steady. He undoubtedly saw his ideal alter ego in Howells, but in this case his projections corresponded to the truth. Howells has his prominent position in the history of American Realism, but he deserves the fullest recognition for his humor also.

If humor is not everywhere present or equally distributed in our nineteenth century literature, still it appears as a pervasive mode in our major writers, who both repeat and extend themes and techniques of our out-and-out comic writers. For the twentieth century our references elsewhere to Fitzgerald, Sinclair Lewis, Hemingway, O'Hara, West, and others, and our views of present-day comic novelists have already reflected judgment upon the comic elements in modern American fiction. We reserve extra commentary on Faulkner but turn briefly to two different poets and two dramatists of the modern period for the purposes of kaleidoscopic review.

There is no less a danger of critical indiscretion in commentaries on selected modern figures. If we insist again upon the quality of resumé and mere though sometimes radical suggestion in our remarks, we may be—not acquitted—but pardoned, for the sake of expediency. There is no other extenuation to plead.

In all of his extraordinary individualism, e. e. cummings is a capital case of the rebellious romantic poet in modern American literature. His is an individualism, as in his typographical experimentation, of method as well as content. It is no surprise to find plentiful comic and satiric devices among the varied techniques that serve his revolt. He puns ingeniously, using orthographic humor for new political satire. In his short representative piece, "applaws)," his homophonic play upon the phrase, "fellow citizens" is characteristic. He gives a line to a syllable, the poem furnishing its own exegesis: fall, succeeded by exclamatory satirical anguish, followed by the explicit sedentary image with its association of buttocks, concluded by the pluralized contraction for "is not" as a commentary on mass inexistent vitality. There is something comic about a two-word, four-lined stanza in itself, but Cummings saves himself from both the absurdity and meretriciousness of his anagram by virtue of his brevity. At his best, as in this quintessential verse, his brief forms take the curse off his satiric self-consciousness.

On the whole, he chooses a position, thematically, in the anti-rhetorical tradition of American humor, assailing all clichés in the spirit of Finley Peter Dunne, though he himself laughs less. Often he selects and organizes clichés for angry exposé rather than mixes or plays with them, as in "Next to of course God." Or with the traditional comic freedom of all verbal means at his disposal, he expresses his misanthropy, together with his attack on progress, with the most pliable neologisms, semantic reversals, and sudden transitions of vocabulary. In "Pity This Busy Monster, Manunkind," his use of "manunkind" is a typically ingenious combination of antique noun and negative adjective that saves him from affectation, and throughout the poem his decisive turns to the colloquial style are just what rescues him from monotonous solemnity.

But, in all, Cummings labors against three disadvantages that tell against him increasingly through the years, as they may against more recent romanticists who are as formulaic as he became. For one thing, his device of negating or changing meaning by adding prefixes is a simple trick, and it loses force through constant repetition. It is redeemable only by sparing and subtle use. Otherwise, in poem after poem, it becomes ostentatious; as such, it is highly vulnerable, with his other traits, to literary spoofing, like Philip Green's "unessay":

the really

go

go

good

. . . poems are not really very unsame from any other . . . because most of them are not very anything but . . . games of saying unthings.

Secondly, unlike Twain, he fixes upon the weaknesses of the language, the modifiers, rather than substantives and verbs for his predominant effects. That may be in the nature of his doing the negative rather than positive thing. And, finally, Cummings is often unintentionally funny, after all, in many of his unorthodoxies, a Whitmanian in these respects, as later Beatniks are. Furthermore, as Green claims, he does not advance his meanings through his career, burdened as he is with his own signatory formulae and repetitive themes. That means that he is more readily exhaustible than others and that, at the last, a certain humor of nondevelopment and circularity stigmatizes the whole corpus of his work.

For the rival classical school of modern American poetry, Robert Frost stands as example. The light and facile epigrammaticism of his last stage, thought of as his nonage by hostile academics, induces too many critics to see the same thing in his major phase. He was generally more the subversive than "the cheerful critical Yankee," as Professor Irwin calls him. And he exploited his own personality far less than his detractors suggest.

What really disabuses certain critical quarters is, in fact, the relativism in Frost and what goes with it, the comic mischievousness that Frost refuses to make into any kind of settled program. Correctly seeing himself as a "tough Democrat," for instance, he could not even during Depression years give two tramps some work[27] in "Two Tramps in Mudtime," and deny himself a kind of

[27] Even if he approved of governmental WPA programs. He probably did not, however, not fully at all events. Most of his lighter verse-fables, like "Departmental," make irreverent fun of all bureaucracy.

birthright in the process.

> They knew they had but to stay their stay
> And all their logic would fill my head:
> As that I had no right to play
> With what was another man's work for gain.
> My right might be love but theirs was need.

The good-natured, largely comic poem discovers another truth beyond his unfeigned compassion, coming to him through the thematic resistance he willingly sets up.

> But yield who will to their separation,
> My object in living is to unite
> My avocation and my vocation
> As my two eyes make one in sight.
> Only where love and need are one,
> And the work is play for mortal stakes,
> Is the deed ever really done. . . .

His is a free-thinking humor, working against regional and traditional biases as well as his heartfelt own. That is the essence of his renowned "Mending Wall," where he furnishes his skeptical, humorous criticism of the local cliché, "Good fences make good neighbors," employing comic pertinence, literalism, and even punning to his designs.

> Spring is the mischief in me, and I wonder
> If I could put a notion in his head:
> 'Why do they make good neighbours? Isn't it
> Where there are cows? But here there are no cows.
> Before I built a wall I'd ask to know
> What I was walling in or walling out,
> And to whom I was like to give offence.
> Something there is that doesn't love a wall,
> That wants it down.' I could say 'Elves' to him,
> But it's not elves exactly, and I'd rather
> He said it for himself.

And he joins in the undertaking and gives his neighbor the last words, urbane and realistic in acknowledging how much more than comedy it will take to change long social patterns.

> I see him there
> Bringing a stone grasped firmly by the top
> In each hand, like an old-stone savage armed.
> He moves in darkness as it seems to me,
> Not of woods only and the shade of trees.
> He will not go behind his father's saying,
> And he likes having thought of it so well
> He says again, 'Good fences make good neighbours.'

Frost is tolerant himself as well as skeptical.[28] This is not re-actionariness, which is the veiled modern charge against him. Nor is it radicalism, of course. His comedy is an essentially private instrument, in these ways more individualistic than Cummings' rebellious humor and direct satire, and it was put to flexible uses.[29]

In certain ways, poetry like Frost's is in itself comic by virtue of that relativism and pluralism of meaning implicit in it. I do not refer to ambiguity precisely in his poetry but to the simul-taneity of meaning that much of his poetry lightly makes room for. His work has that mixture of "the cosmic and comic" ascribed also to Emily Dickinson. In the lines from "Stopping by Woods on a Snowy Evening"—

> Whose woods these are I think I know.
> His house is in the village though;

—he is referring both to an absentee landlord in town and to God. And the delicate attack upon property in the poem—and busyness—is joined to his criticism of the death instinct that God allows or even encourages. The two terms tend at last to cancel one another out, leaving the poet-narrator free for his own decision to go on through his "miles" of life, but unmechanically and more free than ever of social or divine injunctions.

---

[28] His skepticism is profound, however, as well as swift. He thinks of the neighbor as "an old-stone savage" in a certain light, imagining the primitiveness in him and the latent threat of violence. The norm is brutal. In his comic wisdom rather than discretion even, Frost does not bother answering to the man directly . . . but helps mend the fence to keep his own distance from a possibly bad neighbor.

[29] Not the least of which was his reading of this particular poem, after the Berlin Wall episode, in Moscow during his last trip abroad.

"Stopping by Woods on a Snowy Evening" is a deservedly famous, densely compacted poem, dulled only by curricular recitations, and its success is rooted in Frost's basically comic apprehension of life. Or, since we have suggested the closeness of this kind of poetry to comedy, we may say that his humor is a consequence of his general poetic sensibility. It contained, he once said, "all I ever knew," so that we may think of it as the very model of his whole approach, complete with comic gesture.[30] That it realizes its freedom of idea through so disciplined a technique,[31] and against thematic resistance which Frost welcomes as his challenge, is instructive in the extreme.

In his preoccupation with the overwhelming superego of southern mores, Tennessee Williams appears as a serious dramatist of psychopathological effects. But two comic plays of his fall within the purview of our subject. In *The Rose Tattoo* he believes that some men and women will find their own values outside of social directives and pressures; the play is a comedy of hopeful fulfillment as well as survivalism. But Serafina, the somewhat overwrought but admirable heroine, is not a native American. Her counterpart, Alma, however, in *Summer and Smoke,* is defeated by Puritanic society and ill-timing. (Williams allows her a final cavalier victory in his short story, "The Yellow Bird," however.) One way or the other, Williams' antitheticism leads him to locate individualism, successful or defeated, in the flesh. Our individual victories are personal triumphs of physical love, not family love, not an idealism or abstinent delicacy enforced by class or social mores, and not tawdry and even insane hypocrisies, but a healthy sexuality.

[30] As in the lines of whimsical deflection:
> My little horse must think it queer. . . .
> He gives his harness bells a shake
> To ask if there is some mistake.

The horse is a symbol of faithful but routinized activity in the context of the poem.

[31] Four quatrains, with only four rhyme-endings, carry to an absolute close the nearest thing to perfect versification in the language. In a sense the perfect technique is a sort of trick, poetic sleight of hand, partially comic as dextrous feat.

Such themes also occur in Williams' serious dramas, in which his comedy is only contributory rather than central, where his ideas are given grotesque treatment, his ironies ultimately derived from O'Neill and his Gothicism from Poe.[32] They also inform diverse dramas like *The Glass Menagerie, A Streetcar Named Desire, The Night of the Iguana,* etc.

Considering these repetitive themes (and repetitive characters and setting), we may contend that Williams even writes the same play over and over, now hopefully, now hopelessly, but always obsessively. We are concerned, however, with a single upshot of this material, especially highlighted in his comedies. His point of view seems to bear out those theoreticians who maintain that comedy, in essence, is a presentation of the claims of individual appetite, which motivates survivalism.

This theory is largely true so long as we reserve two exceptions to it. The first one is that American humor has also consistently striven for freedom of mind. It has not only insistently but primarily sought to discredit prevailing political, economic, religious and social tyrannies or falsifications in America . . . for the sake of liberating or explosive truth. Of course, the point we make is not incompatible with Williams' compulsion, for he also must attack and destroy that mythic and inhibitory southern complex of values which fundamentally oppresses his characters.

The second exception we reserve has to do with Williams' fundamental definition of individualism as sexual and private. We turn to Whitman, of all people, for the demonstration of the opposite. That is, we turn to Whitman in his most effective and profound vein.[33] The fact is that Whitman argued quite the opposite tenet from Williams and with great conviction. That which unites us, he suggested, is our common emotional life, including our sexual emotions. And indeed Whitman made a program and career out

[32] As in the cannibalism of *Suddenly Last Summer,* poised on that line between the ludicrous and the horrific.

[33] We recant nothing we have said contextually about him. If Whitman's stature is grossly and, as it were, necessarily exaggerated for the reasons previously indicated, still he is not a literary dwarf. Beyond our moralizing the fact that truth is relative, we may say that it is various, and a figure we have rejected in one context outwits us in another. But when that happens, as in the processes of comedy itself, truths are not canceled but augmented, or, simply, located in the right places.

of the democratic rebellion he called for, in the name of that common life of emotion which humanity shares, against temporary distortions or inhibitions of it by theocratic or other forces. Where Williams sets the individual against society, Whitman sets eternal society against a wrong temporal ethos.

Unashamed gratification of the private or universal id is the result in either case. But the line between healthy vindication and excess or perversion in Williams is unclear, for it is frequently and unsteadily drawn by characters or personae who are themselves deviates from normal emotion. And that irony plagues his comic, grotesque, and serious dramas all together.

Of Arthur Miller's work, we shall limit ourselves to only two observations. First, while comedy is scarcely present everywhere in his plays, it has a very strong function in much of his best work. In fact, Miller's infallible method of portraying or instilling affection in his characters, as in *All My Sons* and *Death of a Salesman*, is to give them a bantering sense of humor with one another (generally within the family group), through which they almost exclusively express their deepest loyalties and love. Miller actually does little with specific comic devices.[34] There are a mere but pervasive jocular tone and an exchange of gibes, as between father and sons.

But in the second place the comedy fails, thereby preparing the tragedy of thwarted, deep-level relationships. The same thing had occurred in Hemingway and O'Hara; Jake Barnes' ordeal, for instance, was not helped by bantering comic exchanges in *The Sun Also Rises*, and Julian English's doom in *Appointment in Samarra* proceeded apace, no matter how much he joked. The American sense of humor becomes unavailing, unsalvational in itself. Or, reflexive and instinctual as such a native sense of humor is shown to be in representative characters, it functions as an inessential quality of superficial Americans. Which of these alternatives is the proper register of the national psyche is a question. An answer one way or the other makes of us either disillu-

[34] In fact, he is quite uninventive. When he deals with a cliché, for example, he updates it rather than twists or reverses it, as in the spilt-milk reference in *Death of a Salesman*: "When a deposit bottle is broken," says Charlie, "you don't get your nickel back." And the fumbling moments of slapstick or the wide-eyed comic innocence of Marilyn Monroe in Miller's film, *The Misfits*, are ineffective.

sioned or unillusioned students of modern humor, the most hapless of distinctions.

Of the two indisputable giants of twentieth-century American fiction and literature, Hemingway and Faulkner, we choose to fasten upon Faulkner because his reputation is clearly higher at the present moment and because he is a richer figure to mine for our purposes. A virtuoso in his effects and expression, both a conservative and an experimentalist, working in melodramatic and epical and comic genres, distilling influences of previous major writers like Thoreau, Hawthorne, Poe and Twain, he promises greater benefits in review. Whatever decline his reputation may suffer because of style and of thought more involuted than profound, a great bulk of his work is bound to endure. Reflections upon his career reveal one more major figure, rightly celebrated for his power and imagination, who had decisive resources over an astonishing comic range.

We may defer to standard encomia and source studies, to begin with. He fits into a regional comic tradition, extending from the southwesterners, G. W. Harris and T. B. Thorpe especially, through Twain. He has all their frontier extravagance, all their distinctive admixture of violence and farce, terror and antic comedy. Like them, he is a latter-day master of speech patterns, some dialect, and southern comic epithet ("Get up, you transmogrified hallucination of . . ."). He plots triumphant comic reversal, employs devices of literalism, circularity, comic catalogue, and momentum, and observes the frankest sexual realism. And he chooses traditional targets out of his antisectarian, probably antireligious, doubtlessly anticapitalist and certainly antitechnological position.

"Spotted Horses" is the essential illustration of this tradition, as Faulkner appropriates it. An exaggerated tall tale, it plunges through the divagations of its plot out of its own wild comic momentum. But it moves not so quickly that Faulkner can't pause for realistic and whimsical detail anywhere; Eck's horse rampages through the house, crashing into the melodeon, with its one sounded note of "deep and sober astonishment." Along with combinative epitheticism and comic metaphor ("You banjo-faced jack rabbit . . .") goes extravagant southern understatement; of the horse's chaotic wildness someone remarks, "I misdoubted that damn [feed] corn all along." Throughout the story Faulkner's outside view, bestowed upon the sewing machine salesman, Ratliff, grants him just sufficient comic distance and no more. And in Flem Snopes, he has that native type, in the mold of Simon Suggs and Sut Lovingood, of exploitive con man. Indeed he fixes his indictment of rampant acquisitive economics upon this representative of the commercial success ethos . . . without any of the confusion of the old southwesterners in this regard.

"Spotted Horses" remains a triumph in the traditional mode. Other stories, like *As I Lay Dying*, fall in between categories of downright melodrama and long sick joke, a species of at least gray humor in Faulkner.

All such observations are true and germane, but they tend to make Faulkner's comedy appear as an exercise of or adjunct to his other abilities. But it is far more than that, as it was for Melville. The comic mode has an essential function in his career and creates transformational effects inside his whole work.

There are two stories in *Go Down, Moses* of preliminary interest to us in this pursuit, "Was" and "Pantaloon in Black." In "Was" the uncles, Buck and Buddy, play an outlandish poker game at the neighboring Beauchamp plantation, either to win the slave girl Tennie from Hubert Beauchamp for their colored boy, Tomey's Turl, or to lose Buck's bachelorhood in marriage to Hubert's sister, Sophonsiba Beauchamp. In "Pantaloon in Black" the grieving Negro, Rider, happens upon a dice game, joins it, and ends up razoring a white-trash antagonist, for which he is eventually lynched. Canted or tipped only slightly, either story could be its opposite; the uproarious poker game could turn understandably homicidal (especially since Tomey's Turl is shuffling and dealing the cards for the uncles to win), and the threatening dice game could become hilarious release. The factor common to both stories is a careering energy or momentum that can go either way.[35] What Faulkner appears to do, from a basic mid-line position he occupies, is to direct that energy, only slightly, to the

[35] Only Steinbeck, among contemporaries, was at all committed to the same practice. The slightest changes, for example, would have made *Of Mice and Men* an out-and-out farcical comedy.

one side or the other. The central line of his thinking is that of a neutralist, initially dispassionate and then trusting to his intelligence and to the innate pull, at a crisis in the story, of the material itself.

These speculations, if true, have two consequences. One is that Faulkner was one of those rare writers for whom the end of a story did *not* come first or even second. Factors of setting, character, situation were operative motives in themselves, and were even elaborated before the ending could suggest itself to him. In the nature of his imaginative position, this unusual though not unheard-of procedure probably characterized his general creative method, perilous or impossible for most other storytellers. Consequently, in the second case, critiques about the element of strong will in Faulkner, of a man passionately forcing his materials into shape, would have to be modified. The close coordinates of his thinking, comic and tragic, farcical and grotesque, do not permit easy allegations about the role of his will. They press right up to a central line of adamant if not sublime patience, where Faulkner himself stood, and we cannot accord his willfulness the arbitrary force often given it by both partisan and adverse critics alike.

But other deeper indications about the essential role of humor in Faulkner may be found in the body of his work. I do not mean to call prolonged attention to the general factor of overcomplication in his characterization, for example, in the devious motivations he traces, which are often either surrealistic or near comic, or both together. The observation is true enough but furnishes no further insight into his procedure. Where that insight may come is in *The Reivers*, about which we have spoken in other connections. But there is yet another factor of complication in that book which we did not fully broach.

That is Faulkner's digressionary tactic, a matter of both style and narrative technique. The interposition of details that all at once carry us far off from present concerns is the essence of much of Faulkner, to the delight of his friends and to the utter frustration of uninitiates. But he had learned that tactic from Laurence Sterne, a source well concealed from us heretofore, because of Faulkner's generally dark and melodramatic employment of the technique. What was not evident to us because it seemed inappropriate is, in *The Reivers*, starkly clear. It is the

Shandyish method of interposing a background that usurps our interest. The technique figures so prominently in the early sections of the book that it appears as if Faulkner were calling deliberate and unmistakable attention to it in his last work.

A few pages into the story, for instance, we learn of a certain pistol in the stable. The gun belongs to an old picturesque retainer, John. Boon is hell-bent for that pistol, but Faulkner elaborately holds up the pell-mell action in his long comic adversion to John himself.

> . . . how he had earned the price of the pistol by doing outside work on his own time, on time apart from helping his father on the farm, time which was his own to spend eating or sleeping, until on his twenty-first birthday he had paid the final coin into his father's hand and received the pistol; telling us how the pistol was the living symbol of his manhood, the ineffaceable proof that he was now twenty-one and a man; . . .

None of these details, plus many other ruminations, will signify. It would be unforgivable technique except that the essence of the book just then is Sternean parody of suspense and dominant foreground. There is no way to account for it except as some kind of clue Faulkner consciously provided us in his dextrous last work. The device occurs most strikingly in an ensuing divagation, comically evasive and monstrously elongated just at the wrong moment (except that it is right to his purposes), involving yet another supernumerary's background, Dan's.

> On even to old Dan Grinnup, a dirty man with a tobacco-stained beard, who was never quite completely drunk, who had no official position in the stable, partly because of the whiskey maybe but mostly because of his name, which was not Grinnup at all but Grenier: one of the oldest names in the county until the family went to seed—the Huguenot Louis Grenier who crossed the mountains from Virginia and Carolina after the Revolution and came down into Mississippi in the seventeen-nineties and established Jefferson and named it—who (old Dan) lived nowhere (and had no family save an idiot nephew or cousin or something still living in a tent in the river jungle beyond Frenchman's Bend which had once been a part of the Grenier plantation) until he (old Dan) would appear, never too drunk to drive it, at the stable in time to take the hack to the depot and meet the 9.30 P.M. and the 3.12 A.M. trains and

deliver the drummers to the hotel, or on duty all night sometimes when there were balls or minstrels or drama shows at the opera house (at times, at some cold and scornful pitch of drink, he would say that once Greniers led Yoknapatawpha society; now Grinnups drove it), holding his job, some said, because Mr. Ballott's first wife had been his daughter. . . .

Where, though somewhat less grossly, has this been seen before, aside from Sterne? In Faulkner himself. He had done this in book after book—*Sartoris* (1929), *The Sound and the Fury* (1929), *Light in August* (1932), *Absalom, Absalom!* (1936), *Go Down, Moses* (1942), etc.—usually transposing the key of *Tristram Shandy* but always heavily in debt to it for his effects of sudden expansion or dense southern relationships, involuted . . . and partly comic . . . as they were. As a matter of fact, the famous stylistic technique of parenthesis itself derives from Sterne, though Faulkner's own practice has always been an inimitable extension of what he learned. In *The Reivers* it is prosecuted more outlandishly than usual.

> Then it was morning, it was tomorrow: THE day on which I would ride my first actual horse race (and by winning it, set Boon and Ned—me too of course, but then I was safe, immune; I was not only just a child, I was kin to them—free to go home again, not with honour perhaps, not even unscathed, but at least they could go back) toward which all the finagling and dodging and manipulating and scrabbling around (what other crimes subsequent to—all right, consequent to—the simple and really spontaneous and in a way innocent stealing of Grandfather's automobile, I didn't even know) had been leading up to; now it was here.
>
> . . . . .
>
> "Time to go," he said. There was nobody with Lightning now but Ned and Uncle Parsham; if they were all up at the track already, it must be even later still. I had expected Boon and Sam and probably Everbe and Miss Reba too. (But not Butch. I hadn't even thought of him; maybe Miss Reba had really got rid of him for good, back up to Hardwick or wherever it was the clerk said last night he really belonged. I had forgotten him; I realized now what the morning's peace actually was.) I said so.

These are only compacted instances of Faulkner's long-standing Sternean technique of interposition and digression. And the whole

break-off narrative method, justified by the havoc Sterne had
played upon novelistic or sequential time, is another inheritance
from the same source.[36]

That source Faulkner seems virtually to have advertised to us
in *The Reivers* in order to compel us to read it back to the rest
of his works, which the last novel consciously crowned. The Sternean technique informed the greatest part of his career. This is so
not only in transformed effects of narrative texture, social dimension, and stylistic density, but in that constant verging on
nervous or absurd comedy we feel all through Faulkner. I refer to
an almost comic surfeit of sense in his serious work and, in his
overt comedy, to the tantalizing excess of non-sense.

One other question in Faulkner, involving subject matter, demands special consideration. There is no concerted or real
misogyny in his work. To the contrary, a case can be made for
a certain uxoriousness. His valuation of women appears in his
serious work, Lena in *Light in August,* as well as in his
comedies. Once again his lavishing of sentiment on a subject
like the reformed prostitute in *The Reivers* seems to be even
more than deliberate. Quite aside from what he is trying to get
away with technically in the last work, his feeling for women's
superiority appears genuine and strong, and he takes time to point
it up.

> She was much too big a girl, there was much too much of her, for
> smugness or coyness. But she was exactly right for serenity.
>
> ·　·　·　·　·
>
> I was hitting, clawing, kicking not at one wizened ten-year-old
> boy, but at Otis and the procuress both: the demon child who
> debased her privacy and the witch who debauched her innocence—
> one flesh to bruise and burst, one set of nerves to wrench and
> anguish; more: not just those two, but all who had participated
> in her debasement: not only the two panders, but the insensitive
> blackguard children and the brutal and shameless men who paid
> their pennies to watch her defenceless and undefended and un-
> avenged degradation.
>
> ·　·　·　·　·
>
> So maybe what I meant by crying looking well on Everbe was that

[36] Indeed many of Faulkner's novels, like Sterne's work, are near parodies
of the form of the novel.

she was big enough to cry as much as she seemed to have to do, and still have room for that many tears to dry off without streaking.

One might guess that the feeling is southern, but so old it sounds new. In effect, Faulkner went back to one myth in disuetude, cavalier idolatry, for his antithesis to a contemporary misogyny which had finally become a cultural thesis itself.

The fact of the matter is that Faulkner is not quite alone among many of our major writers on the question. Despite allegations to the contrary, there are powerful portraits of memorable women in our classic fiction: Hawthorne's Hester in *The Scarlet Letter*, Melville's Chola Woman in "The Encantadas," Twain's Roxy in *Pudd'nhead Wilson*, James's gallery, and Howells'; and for all his defects of portraiture, we have Hemingway's sympathy for Brett in *The Sun Also Rises*, his high intentions toward the heroines of *A Farewell to Arms* and *For Whom the Bell Tolls*, and his own uxoriousness in *Across the River and into the Trees*.

In other major novelists, like Sherwood Anderson, the attitude is highly ambivalent, and in still others, like Fitzgerald, it is basically hostile; women are pitiful neurotics or mannequin bitches. And, indeed, there are some portraits in both Hemingway and Faulkner, Mrs. Macomber and Temple Drake, that are highly charged with contempt.

Which is to say that the question, by and large, is unclear in our major writers, whereas it is quite clear, in that developing misogyny which culminates in Thurber, for the overwhelming majority of our exclusive humorists. What the disparity signifies may be a moot point. But it suggests a greater effort at comprehensiveness, especially in that principal novelistic concern, the relation of men and women, on the part of our major writers of fiction. Probably necessarily so.

American humor has played a far greater, or deeper, part than is usually and casually admitted in both the successes and failures of our chief literary figures. It is to the point, Mark Twain aside, that most of our greatest writers have conceived and worked heavily in the comic mode, as did Thoreau and Poe in their strikingly different ways. This is true quite apart from considerations of the rise of Realism, and it is true even when, as with Melville and Faulkner, our major figures have been also our most serious and ambitious epicists. And other leading writers of utmost diversity, like Cummings and Frost, Williams and Miller, have often had their fundamental comic intentions. When to these we add the major comic lights we have studied, including Twain and Thurber, the conclusion is forceful. Americans have been long committed to comedy as a prime and not incidental or subliterary mode of expression and fundamental thought.

Although we have consistently referred to literary parody in our study, we may center it once again, formally and appropriately here. Parody is ridicule through mimicry; it is a narrower instance of literary burlesque, because its attack is always directed to a specific work or concrete target. It functions in American literary history in three interrelated ways.

It is, first of all, the comic guardian against literary extremism in the masters. It does not restrict its attack to the fraudulent copiers of genius but directs itself to the extravagances of the models themselves. In this way it is the soul of irreverence, a comic mode in itself; it is the chief means of protest for a democratic, iconoclastic, and even anarchic watchdog group in the republic of letters, set against all authority. As such, we may observe that it has been a particularly vocal and consistent force throughout American literature.

In secondary function, parodists constitute an unexpected but indispensable *avant-garde* for experimenters and new voices, since they desanctify whatever has become tyrannical in the past or threatens to become faddist at any given moment. And lastly, because they are generally deflationary realists, they particularly explode romantic affectation and excess.

They are, of course, overwhelmingly inclined to antirhetorical assault. We have noted the convenience that Cooper represented for Harte, Twain, and Bierce. But our literature has been quite capable, in due time, of setting up equally stylized expression and special rhetoric on the opposite side, against which threat parodists remain on guard. Stephen Crane, for instance, is an anti-Cooperite whose warfaring realism can on occasion be just as affected and romantical as his antagonist's, and Frank Norris is his merciless rectifier.

A Mere Boy stood on a pile of blue stones. His attitude was regardant. The day was seal brown. There was a vermilion valley containing a church. The church's steeple aspired strenuously in a direction tangent to the earth's center. A pale wind mentioned tremendous facts under its breath with certain effort at concealment to seven not-dwarfed on an un-distant mauve hilltop.

. . . . .

Certain cannon, like voluble but-non-committal toads with hunched backs, fulminated vast hiccoughs at unimpassioned intervals. Their own invulnerableness was offensive.

An officer of blue serge waved a sword, like a picture in a school history. The non-committal toads pullulated and . . . swiftly relapsed to impassivity.

"Go teh blazes, b'Jimminey," remarked the Mere Boy. "What yeh's shooting fur? They might be people in that field."

. . . . .

A Thing Lay in the little hollow.

The little hollow was green.

The Thing was pulpy white. Its eyes were white. It had blackish-yellow lips. It was beautifully spotted with red, like tomato stains on a rolled napkin.

The yellow sun was dropping on the green plain of the earth, like a twenty-dollar gold piece falling on the baize cloth of a gaming table.

The blue serge officer abruptly discovered the punctured Thing in the Hollow. He was struck with the ir-remediableness of the business.

"Gee," he murmured with interest. "Gee, it's a Mere Boy." ("The Green Stone of Unrest")

Comic literalism is inevitably the next most favored device. C. L. Edson's rendition of Poe's alliterative and meretricious rhyming technique in "The Raven" is one of the clearest examples.

Once upon a midnight dreary, eerie, scary,
I was wary, I was weary, full of worry, thinking of my lost Lenore,
Of my cheery, airy, faery, fiery Dearie—(Nothing more).

I was napping, when a tapping on the overlapping coping, woke me
    grapping, yapping, groping . . . toward the rapping. I went
    hopping, leaping . . . hoping that the rapping on the coping
Was my little lost Lenore.
That on opening the shutter to admit the latter critter, in she'd
    flutter from the gutter with her bitter eyes a-glitter;
So I opened wide the door, what was there? The dark weir and the
    drear moor,—or I'm a liar—the dark mire, the drear moor,
    the mere door and nothing more!

Anti-climax combines with the most direct literalism in what
I think is a characteristic onslaught (of my own) on "Whitman
in Gotham," catching up some typical affectations of the poet in
the process.

O, Kosmos: I think you much better than cosmos, and far heavier.
Absorb'd, I make free use of all apostrophe,
As me, inchoate, a poor Pete, finding myself in Manahatto, strolling,
    content, euphorical,
I open a door, the rondure of a knob turning,
And fall down a shaft, never even hearing my own
Yawp sounding along the new-fangled subways of old New York—
Myself filet'd, but imperturb'd, across the tracks,
A Square Deific below Columbus Circle.

And Kenneth Tynan manages to turn both devices on Thornton
Wilder and William Faulkner at one and the same time.[37]

Well, folks, reckon that's about it. End of another day in the
city of Jefferson, Yoknapatawpha County, Mississippi. Nothin' much
happened. Couple of people got raped, couple more got their teeth
kicked in, but way up there those far-away old stars are still doing
their old cosmic criss-cross, and there ain't a thing we can do about
it. It's pretty quiet now. Folk hereabouts get to bed early, those that
can still walk. Down behind the morgue a few of the young people
are roastin' a nigger over an open fire, but I guess every town has
its night-owls, and afore long they'll be tucked up asleep like anybody else. Nothin' stirring down at the big old plantation house—

[37] Not the least function of the parodist, though it is a rarer one, is to
perceive ignored relationships, like this one between native sentimentalism
and grotesquerie (for which he puts together *Our Town* and *Requiem for
a Nun*).

you can't even hear the hummin' of that electrified barbed-wire fence, 'cause last night some drunk ran slap into it and fused the whole works. That's where Mr. Faulkner lives.

Other familiar procedures involve confusionism, runaway association, heavy laboring of the obvious, and punning. They are weapons naturally trained upon the greater figures, a man of second rank achieving the elevation of parodied target only if he has set a temporary but pernicious vogue or otherwise become a much publicized sentimental boor. Beatnik novels and poetry are modern exemplifications of the first sort of exception, and Edgar Guest, like Longfellow and Whittier, except that they were certified by an age and a half, illustrates the second category.

Accordingly, the leading nineteenth-century major figures and targets of parody have been Cooper, Poe, and Whitman first and foremost, and James and Crane just after. In the twentieth century, Hemingway and Faulkner are the prime figures and victims. Since a distinctive style is the natural vulnerability of such writers, one would have expected Melville's inclusion, except that he was not considered a major figure until relatively recent date. The ordeal of the others, as it might have been for Melville also, is a consequence of their importance; it is certainly a consequence of their appeal to vast segments of the reading population. At the same time and for these same reasons their parodists perform essential service; they stand between merit and its excesses, between the possible tyranny of greatness and our susceptibilities to it. This is the one manner in which the democratic character of comedy, especially in the United States, is unambiguous and persistent.[38]

It may be that the grip of black pseudohumor will be loosened by parodists, as Updike helped to relax the grasp of Kerouac-ism at the end of the fifties in "On the Sidewalk."

I was just thinking around in my sad backyard, looking at those little drab careless starshaped clumps of crabgrass and beautiful chunk of some old bicycle crying out without words of the Ameri-

[38] And also truthful. Parody often functions as comic exposé to reveal what is latent; Lummis's parody of Poe, "Cannibalee," ferrets out the essential Poe under the sentimentality.

can Noon and half a newspaper with an ad about a lotion for people with dry skins and dry souls, when my mother opened our frantic banging screendoor and shouted, "Gogi Himmelman's here." . . . "Let's go, Lee," he sang out, and I could see he looked sadder than ever, his nose all rubbed raw by a cheap handkerchief and a dreary Bandaid unravelling off his thumb. "I know the WAY!" That was Gogi's inimitable unintellectual method of putting it that he was on fire with the esoteric paradoxical Tao and there was no holding him when he was in that mood. I said, "I'm going, Mom," and she said, "O.K.," and when I looked back at her hesitant in the pearly mystical UnitedStateshome light I felt absolutely sad, thinking of all the times she had vacuumed the same carpets. . . .

Gogi and I went limp at the corner under a sign saying ELM STREET. . . .

In landsend despair I stood there stranded. Across the asphalt that was sufficiently semifluid to receive and embalm millions of star-sharp stones and bravely gay candywrappers a drugstore twinkled artificial enticement. But I was not allowed to cross the street. I stood on the gray curb thinking, They said I could cross it when I grew up, but what do they mean grow up? I'm thirty-nine now, and felt sad.

This augurs a victory of literary democrats over themselves, the most virtuous, often most comical, and always most helpful kind.

IX

American
and Foreign Humor

WHAT WE SAY here in the interests of broadness, that potent excuse for all wrongdoing, may only add miniature international affront to our other transgressions. Nothing is worse than innocence abroad except a little bit of knowledge. Nevertheless, a certain critical inertia carries us forward,[1] not altogether unnaturally as we approach concluding perspectives.

No overview of any kind, however, the most tentative or the most presumptive, will clarify stubborn opacities between peoples. We have elsewhere considered certain standard American works, comic and otherwise, which are essentially impenetrable to most foreigners. There are jokes like that, too. An Ozark son bursts upon his father to report that the fifteen-year-old bride he abducted from the McCoys is a virgin. "Wa-ll," says his old man, "g'wan and give her back then. If she ain't good enough for her own kinfolk, she ain't good enough for us." Too much background is required. Quite aside from topicality even, the implicit and long background in such a matter and the sub-

---

[1] ". . . because as long as I was in and in for good, I might as well go the whole hog."—Mark Twain.

tleties of intimate, national psychology in others, as in the contrast of Huck Finn and Tom Sawyer, thwart alien understanding. And so it is for Americans, for whom a master like Molière seems overnice and more often than not irrelevant and quaint.

Nonetheless there is reason as well as sentiment urging us to emphasize the more and more accessible and even shared characteristics of international humor. That is because mass communication, uninterrupted cultural exchanges, a closer international literary community, and joint film ventures have reduced barriers as never before. In a sense, there *is* a western community of nations by now and a mutual comedy, both conventional and black, available to all. For that reason, our report, brief surveys on English and French humor, briefer yet on the German and the swiftest reference to Italian and Russian traits, moves from a discussion of historical differences to a view of similarities, influences, and even amalgamations.

Influences and cross-influences have always been at work. We have not concealed the early influence of the British mock-heroical style, for example, on Washington Irving or on our southwesterners, of Munchausen exaggeration and perhaps Voltairean extravagances upon our tall tales, or the impact of Shakespeare and Rabelais on Melville. Nor have we ignored the direct transference to the American scene of immigrant comic views and devices, as in the Irish humor of Dunne. If the eventual configuration in general became distinctively American, still Americans have always had their indebtedness, which they have in fact repaid with compounded interest, to the old world. That is to say nothing of their own rich influence on immediate neighbors —Twain's importance for Stephen Leacock and Eric Nicol in Canada, and Chaplin's for Catinflas in Mexico. One way or another, nothing is more certain than the increasing connections we may draw in the modern era and the reciprocity of means and ends.

We proceed to our closest relatives, in language if not always in spirit, the British. But, indeed, among the factors that continue to separate us is an important question of language and the purpose of class differentiation for which it operates in England.

Lower class British humor, as Jonathan Miller has pointed out, leans heavily on spoken accent for its effects and is far less accessible to Americans than our regionalisms are to the English. All Americans can do is overhear a vast in-group humor and witness the fierce comic pride in the implicit Cockney satire upon the monotony of standard British diction. Whatever profound divisions of psyche exist in the United States are common property, so to speak, but there have been two Britains, with two different class tastes.[2]

In the upper reaches of English humor, where Meredith formulated his theories, comedy has functioned as a social instrument, a corrective against false individual eccentricity, all the way from the foppery attacked in Restoration plays to the deviant individualism and modernism attacked in conventional novelistic satire like Evelyn Waugh's. This has never been the American aim. Very early, in Paulding's *The Lion of the West,* Nimrod Wildfire comically deflates and defeats the superior socialite, "Mrs. Wallope" (i.e., Mrs. Trollope, who had recently put down the uncouth Americans in a travel book). Misogyny and Anglophobia play a role in Paulding's motivation, but so does his American motive to attack any representative of normative society. If in the twentieth century we go on to compare Waugh's *Vile Bodies* (1930) with Nathanael West's *A Cool Million* (1934), we note the English preservation of a religio-social norm, Catholicism in this case; West's attack is normless, for it is society and all its ruling values to which the American takes exception. Moreover, even where flagrant caricature has animated high British satire, from Dickens to Waugh, a certain reformist belief—and faith— has been the leading motive. But the comprehensiveness of American spoofing and wild caricature, all the way down to the Marx Brothers and Joseph Heller, has been too broad, hopeless, and generally misanthropic to show a comparable motive.

Furthermore, this literate British humor has always been more deft and sophisticated than the general American example. Waugh's sly implications, for instance, are a world away from the extravagances necessary to West's gross parody. Innuendo

2 Until very recently, that is. The red-brick universities are already making a difference, forming an educated third class between East End and Oxford and assuredly coming into its own power.

underlies the suggestion of homosexuality in Waugh's book: "It's not like you, Chastity, to go riding in a motor car with a woman." West's explicitness and exaggeration are recognizably American even as spoofery: ". . . he turned pale with horror. He looked again at the Maharajah and what he saw of lust . . . made him almost swoon."

The element of sophistication has accounted for a great deal of the most brilliant English successes in comedy, from Chaucer and Shakespeare, master performers who mix it evenly with outright farce, through the Restoration playwrights, and superlative versifiers like Alexander Pope, to the delicate but ironical Jane Austen. A certain psychological complication and large-minded cogency even informed a spate of post-World War II British film comedies, starring either Alec Guinness or Peter Sellers (*Heavens Above!*), allowing their movies in those years to surpass American counterparts.

There are two thematic consequences of this large-minded corrective strain in literate and sophisticated British humor. One of them is exemplified by the wartime BBC broadcasts to occupied Europe, always signaled by the opening notes of Beethoven's Fifth Symphony. The device represented much more than whimsical British irony. It was a constant corrective of German extremism by another and legitimate German example of power. It subverted as well as opposed, and it meant that the enemies of Nazidom were more capable of appreciating civilized German culture than contemporary Germans were, that the British were still sane enough, in the relativism of their sophisticated humor, to appeal to Europe (and Germany) as the best of defenders.

The other consequence has been the lack of misogyny in the higher English humor and literature. Most of what we note here is true also for established religion as a target, toward which the British, including Sterne and Shaw, are often satiric but not vindictive. Women ought to stay in their place, according to Shakespeare, but it was a richly appreciated place, and no amount of rebellion even (*The Taming of the Shrew*) produced a jaundiced view of them. As a matter of fact, spirited heroines capable of equal wit with men (*Much Ado about Nothing*) or even of superior wit (*As You Like It*) are dear to Shakespeare's heart. The same is true of Congreve in *The Way of the World*. And

Shaw's *Pygmalion* makes a case for the utterly transformed and engaging woman. In contrast, the most lively lyrics in two American musical adaptations of the English, *Kiss Me, Kate* and *My Fair Lady,* pick up the misogynic lines of interest most emphatically. All told the quality of sophisticated large-mindedness in high English comedy and satire has safeguarded British irony, kept its corrective function viable, and has withstood obsessive thematic concentrations.

Our median democratic style, with certain exceptions,[3] has never aspired to the consistently literate manner of the British high comic style from Lyly and Shakespeare[4] to the more prosaical Dickens, Beerbohm, Saki, and others. Certainly no one in the United States, least of all our Hudibrastic "Connecticut wits" of the post-Revolutionary period, has ever approached the versified epigrammatical wit of Alexander Pope. Nor have we been capable or willing students of lofty and aphoristical Johnsonian wit in prose. And on only a slightly lower level we must mark as distinctive the lighter epigrammatical wit of Gilbert and Sullivan, the high humor of paradox in the work of Oscar Wilde, and the fanciful sophistication of the lyricist, Noel Coward. Nor have Americans been representatively prone to the humor of British understatement, another consequence of high style and urbanity.

Gauging one success against another, in terms of style and general approach, we tend to a far greater concreteness than the British. The Lend-lease locomotive whimsically named "Austerity" by the English was rechristened, as we have noted once before, "Gypsy Rose Lee" by Americans. And Wilde's witty epigram of anticlimax—"I can resist anything but temptation"— has a pointed American western analogue—"Opportunity knocks

---

[3] We have referred to Mencken, White, and Perelman elsewhere in these connections and have noted their strong intermixture of colloquial vocabulary with elevated diction. Only Bierce, among post-Civil War Americans, harks back to the earlier unadulterated high style of Irving, Cooper, Hawthorne, and Poe. We exempt our southwestern Thackerays because of their twin styles, a phenomenon we have analyzed previously.

[4] Actually the euphuistic style of Lyly has had its modern Baroque counterparts in the American prose of James Branch Cabell and somewhat in the work of the current John Barth. Only the Shakespearean grace of expression (for Viola, Rosalind, et al), the miraculous dignification that presides over all wit and fanfare, is impossible to duplicate on either side of the Atlantic.

only once, but temptation keeps banging on the door for years."
The abstractness of the one, which aids compaction, is met by
the concreteness of the other, which serves immediacy.[5]

Granted that distinction, one would have guessed that both
bawdy humor and lower scatology would be concrete American
tendencies rather than British qualities. But quite the opposite
is true, at least in our printed humor. Certainly we have had
our share of sexual realism, as in the southwesterners, Erskine
Caldwell, and modernists, and we have had our instances of
overpowering suggestiveness, as in Melville. But we do not match
the long and consistent record of British bawdry from Chaucer
through Shakespeare to latter-day works of the angry young men.
We have no gross comic stories like "The Miller's Tale," nor
such relentless exchanges of bawdry as occur in Shakespearean
plays, nor the infinite variations on the cuckold joke in Restoration drama, nor such sustained sexual innuendo as in Pope's
"Rape of the Lock" or in passages of Sterne, certainly not in our
analogous early and "Renaissance" stages of literature.

Moreover, our mass entertainment, even when frankly vulgar
in burlesque humor or stage revues or television analogues like
Skelton's, does not approach the coarseness of the English. No
doubt the breathless inanity, heavy-handed slapstick, and rank
scatology of lower-class British humor functions as another rebuff, like the linguistic one, to prevailing higher modes and tends
almost inevitably to excess. A host of grade-Z British movies,
like the *Carry On* series, illustrates the point mildly. But the
music-hall variety of comedy in Britain is coarse and infantile[6]
beyond even American burlesque humor or other subcomedy
anywhere in the United States. Perhaps the steam is still being
let off from Victorian repressions, in which case it is the lower-
middle class rather than the earthier working class we overhear
in this type of literalistic British comedy.[7]

At all events, one of the most civilized and urbane countries

[5] Compare also Samuel Johnson's "Patriotism is the last refuge of the
scoundrel," with Thoreau's, ". . . cowards that run away and enlist."

[6] It is also proximate rather than direct; it deals with undergarments
rather than sexual organs, flirtations rather than confrontations, etc. But
these features, all the more cheap perhaps, are insistent and rampant.

[7] A Canadian analogue is the joke of a Tampax factory employee: "We
make Tampax for those bloody women."

has produced a level of startlingly puerile humor along with its comedy of distinctive sophistication and understatement. In these respects, American humor has been less schizoid than the British, its explicit popular sexual jokes, for instance, neither downright regressive nor delicately suggestive but in between the two extremes.

But the points of contact between the two nations, now on one level and now on the other, are even more significant than the differences. They result from early imitativeness, from broadly similar functions, from later shared comic response to modern conditions, and from present and powerful American influence.

From Chaucer's example ("The Nun Priest's Tale") and the doggerel verse of John Skelton through Butler's and Pope's poetic lampoons to the novelistic practice of the eighteenth century, the British have provided models of mock-heroic satire that Americans appropriated in both genres, viz., Freneau and the Connecticut wits and Poe, Lowell, and even Bierce in verse; and Brackenridge, Irving, the southwesterners, Thoreau occasionally, and Melville frequently in prose. Indeed, whole modern works like Steinbeck's *Tortilla Flat*, some of West's books, certain strains in Faulkner, and all of Barth's[8] writing hark back to the mode.

These examples may serve as indications of early and specific British instruction in comedy, lessons we domesticated in time and continue to practice somewhat, inevitable early influences which we just as inevitably pay back in other ways later on. It is more fruitful in the long run, however, to consider a generic background of coincidental development, which we cannot everywhere detail with exactitude. It is not possible, for example, to say that the role of the Fool in Shakespeare's plays was the model for democratic comedians later on in both England and the United States. That would be a kind of inspired fatuosity of criticism prompting us always to trace exclusive influences or give up the concept of similar function entirely. It is that function, however, which explains a network of influences and idolatries, and not the other way around.

We have commented before on the role of the wise clown in American humor. That role is certainly similar to the function of

---

[8] The genres come full circle in Barth, who gives pseudohistorical novelistic treatment to the eighteenth-century verse, "The Sotweed Factor."

the Fool in Shakespeare, and the similarity confirms insights we have discussed before and forces yet another conclusion upon us. The purpose of the Fool, given his greatest licence in *King Lear*,[9] where he wittily and remorselessly attacks the infatuated monarch, is simply to tell the truth. It is derogatory truth, and he is allowed to speak it semiofficially. Moreover, as Hazlitt has told us, he reconciles both the King and ourselves to inevitable consequences of character and ensuing action. The court jester and democratic comedian alike exist to tell the full truth, and in them comedy is therefore prophetical and mithridatic. It is also protective, which, once again, explains the disguise or masquerade of cap and bells.[10] But when in the course of time either the monarch or the society loses its authority, both the necessity for disguise and the disguise itself disappear. By and large, that happens at last in *King Lear*, as it is happening in comedy today.[11]

Other standard techniques of comedy like slapstick and confusion are quite evident, as again in Shakespeare. He enjoyed all the high jinks and mixups which were themselves derived from classical Roman sources (*The Comedy of Errors*, etc.). His genius in his episodes of Falstaffian action and throughout his best comedies, *A Midsummer Night's Dream, Twelfth Night, As You Like It*, was to bestow so much charm upon situational humor as to redeem the farce in a way no one else has been able to do . . . and, in so doing, to appeal to the élite as well as to the pit. But quite aside from Shakespeare's distinctive gifts, such basic comedy has been resorted to by diverse English figures, Chaucer, Sheridan, Carroll, in and out of drama. Later English writers are curiously less inclined to the mode than Americans, however; there are no splendid confusionists in England contemporary with Benchley, Thurber, and Perelman.

The same thing is true for verbal nonsense. It occurs in Shake-

[9] He has the profoundest as well as the quickest mind in Shakespeare's greatest play. So has "Pudd'nhead" Wilson in Twain's story.

[10] ". . . if I should . . . sometimes put on a fool's cap with a bell to it . . . don't fly off,—but rather courteously give me credit for a little more wisdom than appears upon my outside . . . ," writes Sterne in *Tristram Shandy*.

[11] We may also point out that Lear himself goes through a period of neurasthenic breakdown, characterized by equal parts of comic understanding and insanity, before he arrives to mature wisdom. That also may be an analogue for the democratic world body.

speare, from the earliest phase (*Love's Labor's Lost*) to the latest (*The Tempest*), and it is epitomized in English literature by Lewis Carroll[12] and Edward Lear. And the British have been consistently ecstatic over American example, from Artemus Ward's devices to Danny Kaye's lyrical gibberish. But they tend not to rely so much on it themselves in the twentieth century as American writers and performers more than occasionally do. There is no question, however, that their previous record makes a case for the peculiar susceptibilities of English, a mixed and compendious language, to jabberwockian playfulness, neologism, punning, ready nonsense, and easy verbal confusion. A generation ago, the scholar, Harry Morgan Ayres, tried to locate the peculiarity of English and define its hospitality to non-sense; he found it in the extraordinary richness of homophones in the English language. Whatever the reason, we may observe for our purposes that New World English had a running start on South American Spanish in further combinations of its legacies.

We take note of misanthropic and allied strains of comedy in the British as well as the Americans, but we do not mean to focus the attitude as exceptional in western literature, though one or two English instances of it and the long American involvement in it are heightened developments. We need only glance at Aristophanes to remember its classic force.[13] Its universal appearance, during various ages, certifies rather than detracts from its operation in the United States. Its British eruptions occur, on the whole, outside of the main purpose of social orientation in English comedy. But that fact corroborates the aggressive rather than corrective function that cannot be ruled out of comedy.

Shakespeare's "dark comedies," for example, *Measure for Measure, All's Well That Ends Well, Troilus and Cressida,* form a puzzling group of plays for Shakespearean scholars to account for. Although Shakespeare is heavily ransomed to his predetermin-

[12] Collaborators for the Marx Brothers' films often seem to have been heavily influenced by Carroll's Looking Glass techniques, especially in courtroom scenes and all "official" reversalisms.

[13] The reactive force of Aristophanic comedy was in response to the Socratic idolators of the day, including honest followers of Socrates and pretenders, both of whom created a kind of philosophic tyranny in Athens. Comedy had its antithetical force long before Americans put it to new strategic uses.

ing sources in attempting a mode of tragical farce, something else consistently intervenes in these plays. That seems to be a basic aversion to his own characters. And critics do not instance the scurrilous character of Thersites in *Troilus and Cressida* alone as their evidence but point to a veritable population of leading and subsidiary characters for whom the playwright has no great love. The comedies are "dark"—the way *As You Like It*, for all the prominence given to the misanthropic Jacques, is not—exactly because there is a general contempt without any redemptive action or technique. Whole plays of Ben Jonson, while less puzzling, are misanthropic in spirit, though the hustling action (*Bartholomew Fair*) or tight structure (*Volpone*) are great technical compensations. But Jonson's view of a conning humanity is so comprehensive that only critics of the severest *parti pris* could argue for social corrective as motive.

Much might be said about the inevitable and fierce epitheticism in such works,[14] and assuredly neoclassical poetic exchange, even in the decorous Pope, was a marvel of invective. Confidence men, dunces, and rivals were never being primarily corrected but excoriated, with astonishing virtuosity, and their sheer numbers suggest a strong hostility beyond any easy mitigation by the Meredithan school. There are enough tendentious modern sallies as well, such as Churchill's Popean swipe at Attlee ("a humble man who had a great deal to be humble about") and such contemporary literary backbiting as we have overheard in the Snow-Leavis dispute. And we must not omit the controversial work of Swift, including the Fourth Book of *Gulliver's Travels* and "A Modest Proposal," where the combinations of bitter humor, brilliantly conceived but splenetic misanthropy, and invective are monuments in literature. If one argues that they are also corollaries of Swift's orthodox Christianity, that is only to push back the question to theology, where we may well concede the

14 Indeed, investigators may trace specific Shakespearean influence upon our southwestern humorists in this regard. It is hard to believe that Shakespeare, a whole curriculum to many American writers, especially in the nineteenth century, would not have influenced them in special devices which they elaborate or crib. We detect barely disguised Falstaffian humor as late as Dunne; Garcia's band of 10,000 men in "On Our Cuban Allies" diminishes to three the way Falstaff's report of his numerous antagonists suffers powerful reduction during his interview with Hal. But these are details for literary detectives.

dim patristic view of man.[15] And even sweet Dickens had his appreciation for flamboyant skepticism and protective insensitivity, pictured within the Jaggers law office in *Great Expectations.*

> "What are you about?" demanded Wemmick, with the utmost indignation. "What do you come snivelling here for?"
>
> "I didn't go to do it, Mr. Wemmick."
>
> "You did," said Wemmick.
>
> "A man can't help his feelings, Mr. Wemmick," pleaded Mike.
>
> "His what?" demanded Wemmick, quite savagely. "Say that again!"
>
> "Now look here, my man," said Mr. Jaggers, advancing a step, and pointing to the door. "Get out of this office. I'll have no feelings here. Get out."
>
> "It serves you right," said Wemmick. "Get out."
>
> So the unfortunate Mike very humbly withdrew, and Mr. Jaggers and Wemmick appeared to have re-established their good understanding, and went to work again with an air of refreshment upon them as if they had just had lunch.

In the matter of parody and literary satire, however, the English are generally less violent than Americans and are animated by corrective waggery as well as by wholesale demolishment: we see that all the way from Fielding (*Shamela*) and Sterne to Malcolm Muggeridge. At that latter end of the scale, however, it is difficult nowadays to distinguish the English acerbic tone from the American: *The New Yorker* reviewers, Dwight Mac-Donald, and others,[16] might just as well be writing for the London *Times Literary Supplement.*

If we carry down other lines of development to the modern period—the macabre humor of Lord Dunsany ("Two Bottles of Relish"), Saki, and Waugh; the satirical cartooning of Searle and the antithetic themes of Joyce Cary; the sick light verse of Auden between his period of reformism and his Anglican con-

---

[15] Swift's distaste and disgust for gross corporeality represents the other side of ribald comedy in English humor or satire . . . and they unsettle those theories of the universal appetitive nature of humor. There is great difficulty about "placing" him at all in traditional genres of humor unless, of course, we acknowledge him as an overflowing fountain of black humor for the French as well as ourselves. Which he is, all the more since he is read studiously by European writers nowadays as well as by Americans.

[16] Note the current Tom Wolfe, however; certain stylistic extravagances, combinations of hipsterism and acid intellectuality, are still all-American.

version; and the darkening humor of the younger novelists and dramatists—the concluding note is not of correction, waggery, or affirmation but of either the outré or the sordid, fortified by anger. There is a postwar rage, in fact, of individual disabusement. It culminates in two signals. One is the ruling epithet, "I'm all right, Jack." The other is the rich British enjoyment of vicarious lawlessness, as in their *Lavender Hill Mob* movies and bona fide robberies of the Queen's mail train. Both the blasphemy and antitheticism have their obvious American counterparts.

Indeed, aside from its vulnerabilities to American influence, current British humor duplicates the American in two ways. Either it degenerates into a tawdry humor of black exposé, where it takes itself with utter seriousness (*The Entertainer*), or it suffers clear enfeeblement on its own, quite apart from its subjection to American example. In the latter case, the decline from the genuinely whimsical humor of A. A. Milne to the long-winded pretentiousness of J. R. R. Tolkien is a perfect gauge.

It is only fair to say that, by and large, the British have problems of shortened distance also nowadays. Many Englishmen have made a public and moral case, for instance, against allowing Commonwealth coloreds into Britain, because that will stimulate hatred. Their prejudice ahead of time is a form of Christian charity. When such immodest proposals are so candidly put forth, it appears just as difficult to achieve proper comic distance in Britain as in America.

As to particular American influences, we need only make one observation. Whereas the Americans finally did not succumb to nineteenth-century British influence, the danger is that the British may do so to the modern American. Everyone is aware of how much *The New Yorker*, for instance, has influenced *Punch* rather than the other way around. Our speed has carried the day in almost all British cartoons, music-hall comedy, and movies. The packed captions and overcrowded draftsmanship in cartooning have given way to American economy and simplicity. Stand-up comics on stage and TV employ the slicker, faster, sharper techniques of American associational method;[17] that is, when they are not part of superentertainments that repeat American stage,

[17] And they copy our historical irreverence, as in Charlie Chester's elaborate spoofing of Sir Walter Raleigh, etc.

screen, and radio extravaganzas of the thirties. And the postwar British film comedies discovered the faster pace of American movies, mostly just at the time television had overpowered American filmdom. There was nothing for Americans to do then but to raid British talent (Guinness, Sellers) and bestow our television fare instead, supplemented by command appearances of Danny Kaye at the Palladium.

And so there are disadvantages in trans-Atlantic influence and exchange. The upper level of British humor appears less and less in evidence as a bulwark. And the popular and darker modes of English comedy appear increasingly vulnerable and undistinctive in the postwar period. But as the red-brick universities grow and a new interclass comes to power, there may develop another sense of humor,[18] resurgent as the American might be and responsive to but not overcome by either American or universal pressures.

The subtle and mercurial French performance would baffle all judgment except that all things French evoke a sense of discrimination even when it is not a native gift. If one sees at all into the law of opposites that operates everywhere, to that extent he has already been Gallicized. There is no rule without an exception of equal force. And yet there is no duplicity, no vagary anywhere, few people being more direct and clear-headed than

[18] Reginald Smythe's comic strip, "Andy Capp," vastly popular in England (and now also in the United States), seems to represent such "interclass" humor. It attacks the Establishment but also the low-class exploitive lush. Andy Capp is an epithetical, irreverent exception-taker, but an indefatigable egotist (like Hyman Kaplan) and professional Laborite bum.

Meanwhile, resurgence may occur without benefit of such background, too. The downright musical fraudulence, derivativeness, and cynicism of the Beatles are being superseded by their joint and individual comic irreverence and candor. And it becomes apparent that the whole mode of costumery and medieval hair style engendered by Beatle-ism has all along been a commentary on the second Dark Ages through which we may be passing . . . not protective masquerade but literalistic comic symbol. Since medieval page boys and doubtful troubadours are being currently replaced by outlandish dandies, the resume of sartorial and comic history has at least reached the seventeenth century, suggesting that the English are coming back out of their unique regression. Before they are through, like Virginia Woolf's Orlando, the Beatles will find themselves in the twentieth century and quite unrecognizable unless they resort exactly to direct, explicit comedy.

the French. There is only a fine-lined multifariousness that would appall the stranger except that the subject itself instructs him in an objectivity almost sufficient to the case.

Molière, for example, ostensibly practices comedy on the assumption of a normative code of conduct. In *Tartuffe*, after being monstrously taken in by the devout hypocrite, Tartuffe, Orgon cries that he renounces all devotionists and would now visit them all with frightening horrors. Molière's spokesman, Cléante, seizes the opportunity to lecture his brother-in-law about his manifest extremism.

> But to correct yourself, what reason demands
> that you pass to a greater error . . . ?

Disengage yourself from appearances to begin with, he argues, and you won't shuttle from one extreme of self-deceit to another. It is an appropriate neoclassical argument, embedded in a perfect play by both the most reasonable and felicitous craftsman who ever wrote comic drama . . . *les mots justes* from the most exacting and tutorial of playwrights. But the paradox of such a mind, to which other famous words of Cléante in the same play are the infallible index, is that balanced with Molière's tutorial faith is the profoundest cynicism about both Cléante's and his own audience.

> *Les hommes, la plupart, sont etrangement faits!*
> *Dans la juste nature on ne les voit jamais*
> *La raison a pour eux des bornes trop petites.*
> *En chaque caractère ils passent ses limites;*

Most men, he exclaims, are strangely made, incapable of median conduct, because their common sense is inadequate. And from this hopeless estimate of the majority of men he passes to the axiom that people simply exceed their limits, which is, in fact, what the sumptuous power figure in the play, Orgon, does right to the end. Molière can conceive of normative conduct, but he suggests that few or next to none have it. It is a conclusion that disqualifies his assumption. In play after play, no class, least of all the bourgeoisie, no vocational estate, no age group is intrinsically wise, balanced, or otherwise normative. In fact, Molière's skepticism is enormous. And yet a patronized brother-in-law or an indulged maid here and there, or Molière himself, grasps the norm that is not normal—but grasps it convincingly. What he alleges as possible and what he shows us as improbable strike us with equal validity and force. Both his idealism and realism carry equal weight; he is the quintessential Frenchman.

Moreover, as the controlled and relativistic humorist, par excellence, and the model of precise, dispassionate French thinking, he expresses himself in an absolute joy of superbly versified wit, exuberant in all the means at his disposal. His is as variegated a comic achievement as western culture has produced.[19]

And from comedy as basically independent and courageous[20] as Molière's, Bergson draws conclusions, as he does from other sources also, of the social *derivation* as well as function of comedy (as Meredith had also used Molière). But the whole of Bergson is faulted splendor. In his essay *On Laughter* we have the most comprehensive, prejudicial, perspicuous, and wrong-minded analysis ever attempted. Any other theoretician so mortgaged to his own philosophy, so expedient in selective illustration, would long ago have been dismissed. Comedy, he declares, is the weapon of society and of the *élan vital* which works through society, operating to ridicule mechanical and primitive individual conduct, to bring deviant and temporary absurdity into line with open progressive human development. But no one is more rigid and mechanical than Bergson is in formulating his views. Comic distance, he avers further, is a product of our suspended emotion and intellectual superiority. And yet, time after time, he shows that any given comic effect involves the spectacle of fallible human reason . . . with, we infer, the vengeful release of the spectator's emotions.

And yet all the things Bergson declares about the function of humiliation in comedy are patently correct, no matter what

[19]Until recently his effect upon Americans has been miniscule, though his themes, basic temperamental extremism in *Tartuffe* and an honest misanthropy in *The Misanthrope,* grow more and more cogent for us, and his technical control in itself becomes an imperative lesson. Perhaps for both reasons the poet, Richard Wilbur, has translated Molière anew in the United States. In so doing he has probably given the English-speaking world the very next thing to the French original, naturalizing the couplets so that they are accessible to us as never before.

[20] He was beset by the religious zealots and superpatriots of his own day, who waited for his slightest mistake and were ready to pounce upon *Tartuffe* especially.

philosophic conveniences he makes them serve, and this insistence on the basic deflationism in humor is worth all his errors. He places us in the position of having to deny his rationalized mysticism on one side and his logical systemizations on the other but of welcoming a supreme insight in between. His views are impressed upon French humor by main force, a procedure which betrays his own native sense of subtlety; in any event, those views are largely inapplicable to the generally antithetic and antisocial function of American practice, to say nothing of the depths in Molière and other Frenchmen. And yet we welcome those processes of elucidation that serve a supreme argument Bergson grants at once and then leaves to the ages. We take our long exceptions, simultaneously unconvinced and dazzled, disbelieving and yet grateful.[21]

French wit, itself, defies any easy formulation. It even overturns standard and obvious definitions of wit in English critical scholarship. Basically Lockean, these definitions have characterized the function of imaginative wit as the perceiving of connections between things. But the famous eighteenth century critic, Samuel Johnson, was the first to see, although he also deplored, the Metaphysicals' wit in yoking opposites. Since Johnson, we have come to accept all the unities that Donne and his Metaphysical school of poets wittily perceived under disparate appearances, and so we remain in countenance. But what the excellent nineteenth century essayist, William Hazlitt, upsettingly remarked, which we have wanted to forget, is that the French regularly practice a wit of distinctions rather than connections. All our cherished theories of the unifying imagination, comic or otherwise, are challenged by the equally imaginative act of witful discrimination among the French. Which is to say that the French are perfectly at home with multiple reality as well as multiple politics, and are not at all inclined to Anglo-American artistic and philosophic monomanias, like Coleridge's, or even to dualisms of thought or of political form.

[21] For all his labored system it is Bergson's brilliant idiosyncrasies, similar to the insights of Lucien Fabre, Mélinaud and Pagnol, that holds us. Likewise, Figaro's admission "I urge myself to laugh at everything lest I weep at it all," is the pithy exactitude that answers to our experience. We respond to the triumphs of French intuition rather than to the more celebrated logic.

Their very language lends itself to careful discrimination and phraseology, the refinements and precisions of which are often enjoyed for their own sake. Rostand is frequently like that, beautifully creating distinctions from the language itself, as in *Cyrano de Bergerac*. But at their best the French discriminate a manifold reality which is really out there. So the wit operates in Voltaire, who is ready to take advantage of every sudden contretemps and turn of experience for pertinency and witful commentary. Such processes are a great advance over simple punning, and are almost always rooted in intellectual acuity.

The result is a certain instantaneity of French wit, often quite transferable to other languages. A bilingual Frenchman determinedly follows a pretty American girl in Paris, who at last turns on her heel and confronts him: "Are you trying to pick me up?" Challenged all at once, but French, he replies: "*Mais non!* I am peeking you *out!*" The anecdote is likely enough.

There is a real enough basis also for the French last word in a whole series of international stories that redound to the credit of climactic Gallic wit. The stories generally contain sexual humor as well, a subject on which we have one or two doubts in its own right, but they demonstrate primarily the force of intellectual and quick French wit.

> An Englishman, an American, and a Frenchman try to define *savoir-faire.*
>
> "If," ventures the Englishman, "one arrives home and discovers one's friend making love to one's wife, he has *savoir-faire* if he can say: 'Excuse me.' "
>
> The American nods but adds, "Well, it's really *savoir-faire* if he says, 'Excuse me—continue.' "
>
> "*S'il vous plaît,*" interjects the Frenchman. "Only if the other one *does* continue—that's *savoir-faire!*"[22]

John Weightman contends furthermore that celebrated and reflexive French wit is a necessary weapon of defense, especially to protect one's class status, for which spoken accent is insufficient. That makes the French as class conscious as the English, for all that the Revolution meant; but without other means of

---

[22] We may add the archetypical joke that defines French tact and instantaneity; a Frenchman walks inadvertently into a *salle de bain*, where a woman is in the tub, and turns immediately about face, leaving with the remark, "I beg your pardon, sir."

clarifying social distinctions, they rely on cultivated wit. Thus Talleyrand replies to a beggar's supplication, *"Il faut que je vive!"* (I must live!), with *"Je n'en vois pas la nécéssite."* (I don't see the necessity for it.) But French education and cultivation have steadily become the prerogatives of a natural aristocracy in France, and anyway, the average Frenchman has been trained sufficiently in his language and is a far less class conscious person than he is an intensely and jealously independent one. He is hyper-reactive to any claims whatsoever upon him. A fierce and private individualist, his hostilities are as instantly roused in him as they are, for different reasons, in Americans.[23] He will not be imposed upon, and, élitism aside, he is the most sensitive of people.

Furthermore, he will not allow a false chivalry or something like our American conspiracy of manners to mitigate his sense of reality. His reflexive objectivity, so often expressed in comic epitheticism, prevents him from either telling himself gray lies or joining others in gentle delusion. Such a passage of experience as occurs in Sarah Orne Jewett's nineteenth century story, "The Dulham Ladies," could never be French. Two old maid sisters, in second childhood, purchase false bangs in a neighboring town (from a French-American wigmaker who had despaired of ever selling his ridiculous and outdated *frisettes*), and then they board the train for home.

> It was the ladies' nature to be girlish and they found it impossible not to be grateful to the flimsy, ineffectual disguise . . . The old conductor . . . looked hard at them as he took their tickets, and, being a man of humor and compassion . . . [said], "You ladies never mean to grow old, like the rest of us. . . ."

Let us suppose the wig-maker had been the conductor; had he said anything at all, it would have been to recall his passengers to the world in an effort to preserve mutual sanity as well as his own integrity. "Why don't you sit in the reverse seats, *mes petites*, since you're going backwards anyway?" Faced with any

[23] We tend to fisticuffs rather than verbal exchange in a crisis. Essentially as argumentative as the French, we are more physical and boorish. Longstreet's "The Fight" could never have been French, unless epithets were exchanged. In French, "Ridicule kills." Still, there is volatile aggression in each.

overt playacting, he would not allow himself at least to be imposed upon; he would never permit gallantry to overcome his intelligence, especially if the occasion invited instant and witful observation.

Of course, what is also apparent is a certain joy in one's means. Those means are educated means. A great number of Frenchmen, who are especially well schooled in language if nothing else, are capable of on-the-spot epigram and pithy, literate rejoinder. No orthographic comedian and no Will Rogers are possible in France.

The roster of classic French humorists therefore includes such names in literary purity and high style as La Bruyère, Madame de Sévigne, Beaumarchais, La Rochefoucauld, Saint-Simon, and La Fontaine. The *Maxims* of La Rochefoucauld (which influenced Swift) bear interesting relation to Josh Billings' Americana. Where the later American is purposefully semiliterate and sometimes coarse in his thrusts at native egotism, the Frenchman is refined . . . though always uncompromising in his exposés of universal self-interest. He calls a spade a spade, but always elegantly and, if anything, it is a blacker spade than Billings sees. But he is unmoved,[24] rested in his style and technique.

The same thing is true of the more fearsome Saint-Simon (like our Bierce perhaps) and of the immortal La Fontaine, whose fully considered misanthropy ("To live happily, you have to hide yourself") is restrained from scurrility only by the abiding French interest in proper expression. The French Aesop and Alexander Pope put together, La Fontaine leads us to one conclusion. His steady performance suggests that frequently all that safeguards the French from their own abyss is an objective, impersonal, and sustained exercise of style in itself. Perhaps comic distance for the French derives exclusively from style. Perhaps it is style which is normative for Molière as well as for La Fontaine, their measured couplets, like the carefully balanced sentence structure of La Rochefoucauld and others, determining the very form of their thought,[25] which then settles upon moderate values.

[24] Except to a rare misogyny.
[25] Speculations in "linguistic relativity"—including the early concepts of Humboldt and the later ideas of his disciple, Cassirer, and ranging from Salvador de Madariaga's naïve differentiations of national character on the

And so the question of elevated style, *in toto,* appears central in French humor, as it does in French literature. For a people of esthetical sensibility, with all the rest we concede to them, that is not unexpected. One of their principal means of such elevation and distance is erudition, which informs equally the early extravagances of Rabelais and the educated allusiveness of Anatole France.

Part of the famous French sophistication, then, comes from their knowledge, which they do not hide under a bushel, stylistic or otherwise. *Their* concept of affectation, almost the exact opposite of ours, is an assumed ignorance or naïveté. Nonetheless, this sophistication allows the French their share of—not sentimentality, except in Daudet and Pagnol—but comic mercy. The pungent aphoristic tendency of French wit and comic exchange may carry other messages than those of jealous attack. *"Tout comprendre, c'est tout pardonner"*—to understand everything is to forgive everything—is American in neither phraseology nor lofty judgment. Our westernism, "Shoot first and then ask questions," reveals our even greater comic hostility.[26] The French can be withering and brutally cynical, but their elevation and urbane abstraction allow them indulgences, sometimes, which are almost never seen in authentic American humor.

A free-minded, ultrasophisticated, and articulate people, the French are also proud, too proud to engage in self-humor. They rarely use themselves as comic butts, certainly not in literary comedy. In this sense Americans are more free and, we might argue, fundamentally more humorous. Moreover, the Americans set no limits to subject and always make free room for political irreverence. Here the French are curiously more timid, creating a number of taboos, at least in entertainment, for themselves.

---

basis of language to Benjamin Whorf's modern and sophisticated theories—declare the formative influences of language on conceptual thought. But, at a more profound level, Noam Chomsky indicates that we are in a pre-Newtonian stage of the field and dare not generalize about "deep" or "generative" grammar. French *littérateurs,* incidentally, give precedence to thought before language. "What is conceived well," says Boileau, "announces itself well, the words for saying it arriving easily." But linguistic scientists, like Chomsky, would view the observation as a mere gratuity, an epigram about "surface" grammar.

[26] And, as in our contrast to the British, our greater concreteness.

Weightman indicates the French refusal to blur distinctions; they will not regard official circumstances as unimportant or otherwise suitable to comic treatment. But officialdom as well as official circumstance is at issue. The French are also afraid as well as puristic. They take chances in cabaret satire but do so rarely if ever in the more permanent forms of books or film, in which they never dare ridicule the police or the army, or authority as such. A satiric comic book on their President's *Grande Société* or a theatric gratuity called "MacGaulle" would be unthinkable. One speculates on how much more rather than less anarchic the French are than we, to require such censoring, lest nothing withstand their comic frenzy.

Nonetheless, the French have their own audacities. Having imported American strip tease, for instance, as at the Mayol Theater in Paris, they daringly introduce a nude who puts *on* rather than takes off her costume. This witty reversal of American burlesque produces startling results. As the French do it, a woman dressing has higher sexual voltage than the opposite, especially considering the hesitancies involved. It represents the utmost audacity, especially to touring and nostalgic Americans, but it is successful. It may also show that postwar experimental French comedians are willing to take the ultimate Gallic chance of mixing things up.

At this juncture we pay our respects to the risqué element in French comedy. It may be slightly less positive or all-informing than the rest of the titillated world expects it to be, but there it distinctly is, as far back as Rabelais, whose explicit lustiness and lewdness are part and parcel of his whole work. We trace it through the brashest episodes of Voltaire and his profanest subtleties ("Cunégonde" as heroine) and into the modern period, where it motivates boudoir film comedy and all allusive or explicit French jokes.

The trouble is, however, that we tend to fabricate stories and anecdotes about the French, and afterward we cannot tell the difference between the original and the imposed. Neither can the French, perhaps. It is next to impossible to determine the precise national origin, for instance, of the old representative international joke about essays on elephants: the Germans write a 500-page tome on the morphology of the elephant's toenail;

the British compose a monograph on "The Elephant and the British Empire"; Americans busy themselves on the work, "Bigger and Better Elephants"; and the French dedicate themselves to "The Love Life of the Elephant." Is the story a compliment to everybody's favorite second country, or is it French chauvinism, its effect premeditated for outsiders? In a more liberated and explicit vein, we hear of the attempted mating of an impassioned ant and an elephant, interrupted by the elephant's cry as he steps on a thorn, followed by the ant's commiseration: "*Chérie*, did I hurt you?" This is an extravagant *histoire de fou*, but the sexual motif is there as expected. How much might the French be advertising themselves, gladly contributing to a vast conspiracy about themselves out of a need it would be indiscreet of us to probe further?[27] We may add here only the reflection that the cuckold joke or the broad situational humor of traditional French stage comedy and cinematic bedroom farce—that is, the preoccupation with sexual distrust and betrayal, however it is converted to laughter—gives us additional pause.

But we only pause, taking no full stop or absolute exception. Because for all our demurral, there still remains an unabashed and totally unserious and unself-conscious side to risqué French humor. And we see this thoroughly in unpremeditated French conversations among themselves, where sexual innuendo is swift, regular, but not meretricious. And we note it throughout the insulate publication, *Le Canard Enchaîné*, a sophisticated *Mad* comics journal where the risqué cartoon and pun are everywhere present for nobody else's benefit but themselves. It is also apparent and unstrained in intragroup punstering, like the renaming of "St. Tropez," that liberated and exhibitionist bathing center on the Riviera, "*St. Trop de fesses*," "St. Too Much Buttocks."

More indicative yet are those lilting popular songs, like those of Maurice Chevalier, which are sung with great charm but whose lyrics are fantastically indecent and explicit. "Valentine" is an example, a favorite for Americans who do not know exactly what they are hearing. We do not even have a comic and melo-

[27] In the comic film *Casanova 70*, the Italians at last suggest impotency at the root of their own Casanova complex. That which is flaunted, any prowess at all, is suspect, because it generally functions to conceal its opposite, a principle that has helped clarify the braggadocio of the American tall tale.

dious imperturbability that masks the effects in song, only an incredible naturalness.

> *En avant regiment des jambes Louis Quinze.*
> *On est (entre parenthèse) bien a l'aise.*

These gay lyrics, which do not actually sound suggestive in the French, are—

> Onward, bow-legged troops of Louis Fifteenth.
> We are (between parenthesis) quite at ease.

Neither the comic typography of print nor the intonation of song can be mistaken; yet they are scarcely noticeable as devices. So that, in the end, we must concede to distinctive French characteristics. Our demurrals notwithstanding, sex is taken at once more pervasively and also less seriously in France than anywhere else.

In present-day America the risqué and scatological matter and cartoons of *Playboy* and *The Realist* do not yet approximate the French attitude. We still tend to use our freedoms too eagerly. We are still self-conscious and not quite as naturally light and inconsequential as the French are.[28]

Differences between Americans and French are apparent in wholesale artistic judgment as well as in certain subject matter. We have had occasion to remark elsewhere on that curious French taste in English and American literature that leads them to unique evaluations, such as their hyperbolical view of Poe. Nowadays, for film comedy, they exceed themselves again in viewing the American comedian, Jerry Lewis, as a cinematic genius. They accept his most uninspired and fumbled slapstick as grand buffoonery. It comes again from that French necessity to admire the primitive, if only to keep themselves in countenance as cosmopolitans. By the same token, perhaps, the French recognized the worth of Faulkner long before we did. And only a French

[28] We are getting there, however, and our concreteness is a help. There is a recent American variation of a famous French witticism, occurring during a national assembly debate over equality between the sexes: There is little difference between men and women, shouts one member, immediately and immortally answered, *"Vive la différence!"* The newest of New World counterparts is the reply to a query in a newspaper etiquette or informational column, "What is the difference between *mademoiselle* and *madame*?" Answer: *"Monsieur."*

film company, not an American one, has thought of doing *Pudd'n-head Wilson,* with all its acerbism and irony intact, for the movies.[29]

But points of contact, certain important similarities of function, and mounting cross-influences, especially exerted by Americans upon the French, are more significant than the divergences and differences that have struck us. Indeed, in certain respects, no other humor or people are closer to us than the French.

We may admit that frequently the French thrust is personal. Responding to a comment on how tall his trees grew, Voltaire replied that they had nothing else to do. But he not only employed nonsense humor to deflate somebody in particular, he also famously indicted the nonsense of his whole age (the philosophy that "all is for the best"); his was a comedy of total deflationism serving social antithesis in *Candide,* where the conclusion urges the individual to cultivate his own garden. The individualistic, skeptic, and hostile bases of both French and American humor are unmistakable. And what binds the French closest to the American is the unapologetic, judgmentive tone common to each. The hypothetical French conductor on the train with the Dulham ladies might also have been W. C. Fields, Groucho Marx, or a character in S. J. Perelman, all as comically subversive as the French.

The drift from social antitheticism to misanthropy in American humor is also apparent in the French . . . in Molière, for all his relativism, and in the classicists, La Rochefoucauld, Saint-Simon, and La Fontaine, as we have mentioned before. They too seek to disengage hypocritical appearance from reality, and what they are left with frequently challenges all their faith. Their resulting cynicism takes two forms. One is La Rochefoucauld's relentless suspicion of all motives: "Self-interest . . . plays all sorts of roles, even that of disinterest." The other form cynicism takes is a utilitarian one, pressed into the service of a stubborn comic good will by those determined to outwit stupidity. The celebrated anecdote of Parmentier, who introduced potatoes into famine-stricken France by placing a military guard around a plot of the new crop, with orders to turn their back on French peasants

[29] On the other hand, we filmed Pierre Boulle's *Kwai* story, a long study in comic irony as well as suspenseful action.

thus encouraged to steal something precious, speaks to us with the same comic pragmatism as Franklin did.[30]

Among similar, much used verbal devices in the two literatures are punning, neologisms, and comic catalogue, most apparent in Rabelais, Rostand, and Anatole France.[31] Epitheticism is a matter of mutual appreciation; it is one of the French *fortes* which Americans richly appreciate in translation, as in passages of Jean Anouilh's plays.

But by all odds the most striking connection between the two is that of extravagance, especially of the tall tale. It occurs in Rabelais, Daudet (*Tartarin de Tarascon*) and others, but its steady existence in popular French *Méridional* (southern) humor is uncannily close to the American, a unique conjunction of national comic forms. (And, as in America, it is not a product of landscape or magnifying light but a means of defense, in this case against feelings of inferiority bred by the rest of France.) Updated but representative *Méridional* stories are counterparts of our whoppers, from Twain on.

> Two passengers strike up acquaintance on a French train. "What business are you in?" the Parisian at last asks the Marseillais. "We manufacture *coffre-forts*, safes." The Parisian is interested, perhaps even commercially. "How good are they really?"
>
> The southerner strikes his thigh in expostulation. "*Eh bien*. Before I left, just now, we conducted an experiment. We put a rabbit inside the safe, locked the door, and placed the safe in a gigantic bonfire that raged for five hours. Then we immediately brushed away the ashes and debris, opened the door, and what did we find?"
>
> "A roasted rabbit?"
>
> "*Mais non*, not at all: *il était gélé*—he was frozen!"

Indeed, one cannot be sure of the origin of a whole series of trans-Atlantic tall stories and cartoon captions. We need only

---

[30] It speaks also of the French appreciation of magnificently devious human psychology, which would lead them to their admiration of the labyrinthine human comedy as well as tragedy in Faulkner.

[31] Anatole France is not only a compendium of previous devices and influences but a source himself, especially for reversalism and literalism. Probably Marcel Pagnol is directly indebted to him for most of his technical reversals (like "seminaries in anticlericalism"). And, through direct reading or by osmosis, our Steinbeck reveals the Gallic influence in his Gallic book *The Short Reign of Pippin IV*, as in the political literalism of center parties, the "Christian Communists" and the "Communist Christians."

preface the line, "I was so sick I would have had to get better to die," with *Alors* to make it French; in fact, we cannot trace this particular sally to its origination on either shore. It is a grateful failure of doubtful scholarship since our point is the equal hospitality each gives to practically identical extravagance. We must recall in these connections those incredible conversations in Raimu movies of Marcel Pagnol, like that in *César* where, waiting for a friend to pass away, the neighbors speculate about what, after all, if the Moslems are right and we all pass to *their* heaven? The elaborations are those of slightly reflective French Marx Brothers, equally given to extravagant comic momentum.[32]

In the modern era, both nations are inclined to speed in their comedy, as demonstrated in their movies particularly. By and large, this is not a matter of coincidence but of American influence. As far back as René Clair, a number of French moviemakers have modeled their work closely on the gags, wild chases, agile transitions, and fast pacing of early American comedy. Later on the Keystone influence was supplemented by musical-comedy devices and the satirical mayhem of the Marx Brothers. And still later their most accomplished director-actor, Jacques Tati, molded a character in a clear Chaplinesque tradition, in both the acrobatics and general conception of his comedy, although he managed to retain some independence also. Even more recently French experimentation, in films like *Jules et Jim*, harks back to the oldest jiggly style of American comic films for regenerative effects.

French cartooning preserves less independence, however, because here the French have been frankly overwhelmed by more venturesome American experiment and pacesetting. Thurber and Addams have had a particularly strong impact upon them, as on the work of Chaval and Ami. Steinberg and Partsch are also favorite models, affecting the skewered draftsmanship and phantasmagoric content of Siné and Mose.

The American commentator, Philippe Halsman, has observed

---

[32] French understatement, on the other hand, tends to be more sedate than the American. One thing is one thing, and another device is another to the French. Compare the comic French understatement—"The trout is the only fish to grow after it dies"—with Thoreau's remark—"Some evidence is highly circumstantial, like a trout in the milk"—where even our New Englander expands with a sudden broadness of image.

how much postwar French cartooning became the precinct of nonsense and grotesquerie, forsaking the native tradition of Daumier. It moves from sociopolitical caricature to *"l'esprit loufoque."* That is a direct consequence of their taking to American traditions instead. Sometimes they outdo us, too, as in their shaggy-dog cartoons; there is the captionless masterpiece of a cat waiting at the end of a railroad tunnel, hunched patiently to spring upon the absolutely biggest mouse one can imagine coming from such a hole in the wall. Perhaps the ingenious device of a shaggy cat is also a means of restoring independence. Nonetheless the French are in thralldom to most of our themes as well as techniques . . . in their misogyny (Siné), menace and sadism (Chaval and Bosc), and grotesquerie (Edme). Their capitulation in cartoon work during the forties and fifties heralded their imitativeness of slick American commercial advertising in the sixties as well. Occasionally ingenious reversals and variations occur, as we have noted in strip-tease burlesque. But a more effective resistance to wholesale importation would be a guarantee of popular French contributions to what is fast becoming communal international humor.

The opposite exchange has occurred, too, though without the pervasive or deep imprint which American forms have made on France. There has been a certain influence on a type of American comedy by the French *chansonniers*,[33] impromptu Parisian café comics who make up spontaneous skits and songs to poke fun at French life. They have had a succession of influences on our nightclub entertainment (Julius Monk's Plaza Nine group in New York), on our disc comedians, on a Chicago school (Nichols and May, and the entire Second City experiment), and even briefly on TV ("That Was The Week That Was"). The gain for Americans has been one of sophistication. But we cannot yet gauge long-term effects.

Actually, developments of contemporary French humor, quite apart from the question of cross-influences, are astonishingly like our own recent polarizations. Their state television entertainment

[33] The French practice is part of a whole European tradition of cabaret humor, also found in Berlin, Vienna, Budapest, etc. But American travelers, entertainers, and producers have been almost exclusively influenced by the Paris example.

reveals the extremes. There is the "Thirty-Six Candles" variety program, an insipid, hackneyed, and sentimental enfeeblement, pandering not even to the lowest taste, as in England, but to a neutralized tastelessness very much like the Ed Sullivan show in the United States. Opposed to it is a noon-hour interview program, given to Huntley-Brinkley dryness, asperity, and barely controlled epitheticism.

France also has its share of inadvertent comedy, which works there as well as elsewhere to collapse comic distance. It results from a species of solemn commercialism that we have noted in America, or it is an effect of pseudosophistication. Bergen Evans reports on the first; the Hotel of Seven Agonies at the Lourdes Shrine advertises "All the Modern Conveniences." And Jean-Paul Sartre and Simone de Beauvoir provide us with public play-acting that would be quite funny except for the dissimulation that both they and their public seriously take to heart; liberated, they refuse to marry—but they carry on an interminable bourgeois liaison anyway.

Deeper matter than that which lies behind these examples of failing humor is evident in the whole French decline of comedy. That decline is clearly represented by a steady erosion of the René Clair and Raimu-Fernandel traditions of movie comedy, by helplessly vulnerable journalistic modes, by unfulfilled TV possibilities, by a thorough subsidence of literary humor, and by the vogue of *"humeur noir,"* with its attendant fraudulencies. No country, perhaps, has a greater right to disenchantment and bitterness. All that we have traced as the overpowering impact of modern events on the American scene applies doubly to the French because, in addition to everything else, they lost. We do not need to push back French depletion of manpower, prestige, and morale to the Franco-Prussian War or to the Napoleonic fiasco of still earlier date. More immediately decisive was the inglorious fall of France in World War II and before that the Pyrrhic victory of Verdun and the entire obscenity of World War I. It is improbable that a massive burden of disillusion and defeat will be lightened by the merely palatial *grandeur* of these recent years.

The deepest issue is one of comic decadence, most clearly exhibited in postwar movies. In Clouzot, as in Hitchcock, grossly improbable coincidences and an impossible central mechanism of homicide are foisted upon us, not only at the last minute but everywhere in the construction. What is done is done solemnly, in the manner of an imperturbable cinematic tall tale, an immense joke, as cynical as it is grim, upon audiences who, for their part, now welcome the dissimulation of means. For the rest, there is the comic exhaustion of the Bardot films, which deliberately play with clichés (like our *Home from the Hill*), and the pretense rather than experiment of most New Wave productions (Robbe-Grillet's *Last Year at Marienbad*). Meanwhile, as in the United States, the amount of total comic production has fallen off drastically in French filmdom, and what is notably left often turns itself thematically inside out, as in the seriocomic *Le Bonheur*.

The question of black humor, whether in a farcicist like Ionesco or in a serious student of *le néant* like Camus,[34] seems at first glance quite indigenous or at least European. Baudelaireism and Existential practice suggest an insulated Continental mode. Similarly, the native sources for dark American expression, from the southwesterners, and even Irving and Shillaber, through Poe, Twain, and Bierce to Thurber, Addams, and Albee are also clear. Yet it is also obvious that the European postwar practice, especially in drama, greatly influenced American writers. Less clear but also true is the fundamental American inspiration of Baudelaire by Poe and of French fiction by the nihilism of early Hemingway and by the Gothicism of Faulkner.

We may choose to see other developmental lines behind present Gallic culminations, but they too are eventually crossed or knotted with strategic American examples. A long history of antithetical reaction to the clergy and the bourgeoisie and a neo-Romantic campaign against rationalist pretensions inform modern French literature. That history includes a range of figures from Baudelaire and even Flaubert through Mallarmé, Rimbaud, and Gide to Sartre, Camus, Beckett, Ionesco, Robbe-Grillet and Saporta. And we know that the Existentialist influence on the novel has rein-

[34] On the whole, French dramatists and novelists have been arrested by the philosophical vision of the absurd in Existentialism rather than committed one stage higher, as the formal philosophers of the movement are, to the belief in self-creative and open possibilities. This is true even for Camus, from *The Stranger* to *Caligula*.

forced the modern school of intellectual mockery and helped produce ferocious parodies of communication, right down to the binding of books, as Davis has pointed out. Saporta invites us to shuffle his pages into any order we desire. But all the same, certain latter-day American influences tell also. The influence of Chaplin upon the characterization and action in the drama of the absurd remains a factor, too. Perelmanesque scenes of Groucho Marx rushing in and out of Thelma Todd's apartment with an umbrella he keeps opening and then folding up for no reason at all are the kind of abstract nonsense and wild surrealist pointlessness that told on playwrights like Ionesco in the thirties. His *The Bald Soprano* is a case in point.

All of which is to say that we share a reciprocally influential set of values impinging on our comedy. In addition, the language barrier slips, especially with rising American tourism and lingual education. Hammerstein can write lyrics for *"Dites-moi pour-quoi"* in *South Pacific*, where a Frenchman is hero in an American war story, and have them understood by his American audience. And Danny Kaye can recount a story about four out of five drowned French kittens—*"un, deux, trois, quatre, sank,"* catching up old Shillaber with newer grotesquerie by adding modern and extravagant bilingual punning. This is not the same at all as Lou Holz's old vaudevillian confusions (*"Je t'adore"* and "Shut the door"). Kaye's conjunctive wit, as in his tall French fairy tales in English (in Paris you can be "three bear" but not "two bare"), is far more versatile and, in its overall structuring, relies upon a more sophisticated level of understanding than we have had previously.

We are closer to one another than ever before. If we can influence rather than overwhelm one another, expand subject matter and add to each other's forms, that gain in itself may contribute to mutual and comprehensive resurgence.

Perhaps the international presence in postwar West Germany, particularly of the Americans since Nuremberg, has forced some Germans to a dark comic perspective on themselves. That development, whatever the cause, is at least an improvement over the past. The Germans have been almost completely devoid of a

sense of humor. Not of laughter, which may be a symptom of
hysteria or, as with the Bavarians, a meaningless reflex of an
endogamous society. German comedy has long been miniscule,
and that in itself has contributed to the modern catastrophe of
the German spirit. This development has been in marked contrast
to the American situation, especially since there are also pronounced similarities of depth psychology between Germans and
Americans, like the elements of self-pity[35] and superiority and
the more alarming recent signs of self-seriousness and a practiced
comic insensibility.

We have had our nativism as well as populism, our lynchings
along with our liberalisms, our war-time concentration barracks,
our practitioners of the Big Lie. But we have not had Our
Leader, and we have not had our ovens. Of all other nations,
the latent paranoia and evangelism and hostility in the American
character, together with the presence of scapegoat minorities all
about, have made the United States the closest of analogues to
Germany. And yet we have laughed our demagogues out of
contention. Is that not what happened to McCarthy, when Eisenhower played his Hindenburg? Counsel Welch not only drowned
proceedings in tears but resorted to laughter, and a key episode
in the climactic Senate hearings was the withering but hilarious
evidence of the cropped photograph, set before the nation as
mass entertainment.

Tiresome as the contrast is, we have never been as monolithic
in our self-dedication as the Germans. To every unrighteous war
we have fought there have been vocal and moral objections, to
every kind of slavery an eventually victorious abolition, to every
malice encountered (even Nazidom) a charity, to every neurotic
Prohibition an ultimate repeal. We have never yet gone the whole
distance in tragical or heroic self-investiture. Even when we were
indirectly but clearly under the influence of German Transcendental "profundity," it is to the point that the movement here
produced a Thoreau as well as an Emerson. When we at last
claimed our own cultural identity, we produced Twain and Whitman, the national *Geist* discovered as comic or otherwise exuber-

[35] In this trait, the French are incomparably healthier than anyone in the
world. Made in France, the Emil Jannings film, *The Last Laugh*, would have
been a Molièrean satire instead of a stunning whimper.

ant. And these things are true, for all their self-recommendation, and they allow us to judge.

Moreover, our own insulated German populations, like the "Pennyslvania Dutch," allow the infiltration of American playfulness, irreverence, and crucial self-satire. Pennsylvania Germans of the Lancaster Valley make their own fun of traditional parental wisdom. "I saw a spook," cries the child to his all-knowing guardian. "No," says the parent, "it was a dog, without a head, carrying a lantern in his mouth." And to all the gibes the rest of us offer at the inverted word order of Pennsylvania Germans, they themselves make all-important fun of their absurd English syntax: "When goes by the little red house, the train is all, hain't, Ma?" Their punning works two ways, but it is self-deflationary as well as defensive.

"Give me a noun—the name of a person, place, or thing."
"Organ-grinder."
"How's that?"
"Is a person plays a thing."

Such humor may not long be proof against commercialization (on sign posters and tourist souvenirs everywhere in the area) or against the Pennsylvania German Society's campaign to refine it and make it "literary." But the original frontier-farmer humor of such Germans in America, with its special feature of self-criticism, is in pointed contrast to the incapabilities or willessness of continental German.

We are left with the old proposition that fanaticism and humor are mortal enemies. The deepest polarizations are those of an authoritarianism based on the need for absolute certainty on the one side and a free individualism based on relativism and an accepted principle of uncertainty on the other. Indeed, one of the signal elements of the humorless[36] and horrendous Nazi regime was their pursuit of "an *ultimate* solution" to the "Jewish problem," the philosophic motive of which was absolutism.

And yet there was that qualified German attraction toward

[36] Not *altogether* so; there were black fascist jokes among concentration camp guards. Children were allowed to play preparatory "games" in the courtyards outside the injection rooms and oven barracks, just before they were led inside.

cabaret humor, mostly performed by Berlin or Viennese Jews. There is, after all, no other reasonable way to account for its swift and fearful suppression. It is significant that the most brutal violence was at Nazi disposal only after a planned repression of humor. There was a perfect logic, as we have had previous occasion to observe, in the ruthless, urgent, totalitarian extirpation of it in Germany; unholy humor, practiced by its mocking Jewish disciples (and the savagely irreverent cartoonist, George Grosz), had a fatal appeal to the more sophisticated Germans at least.

But, today, as John Mander has shown, the Germans have joined the west in skeptical and dark comedy. Brecht, so much revived after the war, and Frisch and Dürrenmatt and Weiss have become forces themselves in international humor. The Brechtian theory that human nature is pathetical rather than tragical (itself a decisive break with German mood) and is best revealed in varieties of farce, is a fundamental motive. Moreover, a certain literary subjectivism is being overcome in drama and fiction.[37] Novelists like Günter Grass appear with a striking comic objectivity and gift of both savage realism and symbolism. How much he himself has been influenced by American literary example, through the early years of the Occupation, remains to be confessed.

All sorts of genies are escaping from a black ink bottle, in fact. The author of *Marat/Sade*, Peter Weiss, turns his attention from German subject matter to an indictment of latter-day Americans, *gauleiters* of Viet Nam. We may predict that a whole American record, including old genocide (the Indians) and new genocide (Hiroshima), will also come under attack after Weiss's lead. So long as that is a consequence of comic perspective, however dark, and is not a disguised self-vindication, that, too, is legitimate. Weiss, himself, chooses to live in Sweden, just outside the pull of Germany proper but not too far away. It is like Hemingway's pre-Castro residence in Cuba, not so near to be whelmed, not so far to be remote. Such calculation may furnish Weiss an exact perspective and comic distance, a peripheral

---

[37] Though not yet in movies. They have made one or two Brechtian films, with pronounced "gratitude" to the Adenauer regime, and then abandoned the effort. Movies are too immediate, perhaps, and broadly appealing for them to use significantly yet.

view upon developments in Asia, tendencies in America, and neo-Nazi resurgences in Hesse and Bavaria as well. Meanwhile, any contributions such new authors make to a supranational literature and humor will be the greatest gain since *Till Eulenspiegel*. On the whole, considering the new German openness to foreign influence, we may make the most hopeful rather than sardonic predictions.

We make no extended observations upon Italian comedy except to draw attention to the astonishing vogue and success of Italian comic films, comprising the work of De Sica, Fellini, Antonioni and a host of other director-writers. The Italian defect is pacing, but forthrightness is their strong point. Connections with postwar Italian realism are obvious and significant. The Italians tend to slide their comedy into social commentary, now socialist and now nihilist in inspiration.[38] Their most frequent inclination is toward the tragicalcomic or bleakly pathetic effect. Their successes, however, raise an objection that threatens our whole line of inquiry.

They prompt us to consider the possibility that a people project their alter egos instead of their basic character. Have the Italians come to produce ultrarealistic and tragical-pathetic cinema (*The Bicycle Thief, The Nights of Cabiria*, etc.) in a way that had thrust them to tragic opera before, simply to maintain equilibrium? Are they really a people of bright and comic disposition who project the opposite image of themselves for psychic balance? That would mean that others, like Americans, who are adept at light musical comedy, for example, are basically not humorous. Should we not interpret the forms and content of a nation's entertainment as clues to reversed temperament?

On the whole, it would seem incredibly perverse for a whole people to express their negative character primarily throughout their history . . . and impossible, furthermore, to simulate what they do not possess, like an artistic or musical capacity. People are inclined to expression or lack of expression, to begin with, on the basis of fundamental resource. And having the resource,

[38] They have even come to do so in the same film, as in the masterful work, *The Organizer*.

they are generally inclined to express it positively. The formal difficulties for such expression, after all, are great enough in themselves without a people's having to burden that expression with what they do not consciously believe. To say that is not to rule out the unconscious but to claim that it, too, makes itself felt from underneath through pressure on the ego. It does that rather than create alter egos . . . unless the culture is hopelessly schizophrenic, in which case all of its performers would be Edgar Poes.

We recall two things about the Italians. First, they *are* inclined to straight Mastroianni and Sordi comedy in their films. And secondly, they *are* a lyrical and musical people, which predisposes them to opera in any event. And they are an impassioned people, predictably choosing melodramatic forms of declaration and gesture. The fact is that they have never been true tragedians but either passionate or joy-ridden melodramatists. And the passionate melodrama and the lyricism (often expressed in photography) and the joy, all together, are forces that mix and contend with one another in their modern films. On the whole, out of their own historic complication of character, they now strike their balance for social melodrama and realistic comedy.[39]

The fact is that Americans, more complicated than any other single people because all peoples are in them, have until now struck for epical and comic expression. That is what the positive evidence allows us to say. All art and cultural forms, including the comic, are registers of what *is* there, not of what basically is not. If all the Italian performance has forced us to do is to clarify the grounds of analysis, that is almost enough to ask. But we are all the more indebted to the achievements, especially cinematic, that have raised the question.[40]

[39] In fact, the Italians have signaled a whole European mood, from the Mediterranean to the Baltic, just as much as they have set patterns or pace. Some particular sensitivity at this time has allowed them the initial and continuing expression of a whole continent's malaise, regardless of politics. The Communist film, like the Polish *"Knife in the Water,"* a kind of withering domestic and social comedy, responds to the same mood, and is probably indebted to the later and more handsomely set films of Antonioni.

[40] The American historian, Daniel Boorstin, has complained of literary-critical myopia in these regards. He is quite right if we consistently over-generalize on the basis of isolated examples. His own example is the

We are less sure of what to say about the contemporary Russian performance, and so we treat it more summarily than the others, even the Italian. First of all, there is a Soviet humor, including sharply comic satire and even self-satire. The humor and cartoon work in *Krokodil* reveal a measure of free expression and, what must be more disappointing to professional Americans, a sufficient confidence in the system to allow such comedy. There is no other conclusion we can accept. And in proportion as party fanaticism relaxes, confidence and comedy will increase rather than decrease. Moreover, buried in the Russian psyche is a long record of subjugation to czars and politburos. Like America, it has always been a multiracial country, but, unlike America, it has not been truly plural in social psychology. What the full release of repressed comedy and antitheticism would mean might be surprising.

Up to this point, their humor has appeared heavy-handed and chiefly sarcastic. In the modern era most of it has been directed at the capitalist world, especially at America, during these years of Cold War rivalry. It is propagandistic gibe they practice, and they are entitled to what they are after. And we are free to stigmatize it not merely as propaganda (which can still be funny), but as the heaviest of forced labor sometimes. A recent Soviet book recording the American scene concludes at great length with the observation that our Statue of Liberty has her back turned upon the Land of the Free; the Russians take to the most weighty symbolism and obvious reversalism as if these devices were the most incisive and original strokes of subtlety . . . and, at that, they insist upon calling prolonged attention to the technique itself. But, of course, their sole-shaking premier had officially done the same thing.

We must acknowledge that all we have said throughout our surveys about the antisocial function of American humor is sus-

---

inappropriate image of America that a study of Faulkner provides. One hopes, however, that Boorstin would grant the pertinence of a larger-minded, configural criticism and the sometimes shocking relevance of literary portrayal. Certainly the Gothicism of Faulkner does not portray an all-American mood. But not to include Faulkner's import (the themes of guilt, the philosophic naturalism, etc.) is also to falsify American character, and we dare not venture physically into the real Mississippi without reading him or the newspapers or both.

ceptible to Marxist construction. Our only answer to communist theorizers, who can say they might have told us as much about our antitheticism, is to believe that the imposition of a communist mythology (and religion) would have occasioned the same thing. Or it would have stimulated even greater irreverence, subversion, and destruction than the nonsystem of quasi-capitalism in America has called for. Which is to say that *our* Krokodils, the most dangerous of pets, have always had longer teeth than theirs—and no tears at all.

Yet, heavy-handed and utilitarian as it is, current Russian self-satire is an unmistakable relief. One wishes that the best of international Russian jokes, the Moscow subway anecdote, were actually a Soviet story in this mold.

> An American tourist in the Russian capital is climactically escorted through a Moscow subway station. For some minutes he admires the décor—the tiled and marble walls, the mosaic designs. For another ten minutes of inspection, he proceeds to take in the cleanliness and the modernism of the station. But after a half-hour he turns to his Russian guide and asks, "Where's the train?"
>
> Given to Leninist attack as the best defense, the Russian wheels around to exclaim, "And what about your Negro problem down south?"

Our wisest guess, however, is that this is a Franco-American collaboration. For one thing, we hear it only here and in France. For another, the overview upon the pragmatical American suggests French perspective,[41] but the climactic stigma seems originally American, or American-in-Paris. It is one or the other or quite possibly both—but in all probability not Russian. I mean, not yet Russian.

The current version of the Elephant Essay joke is the international satire accounting for the high accident rate of Western Europe; the average German driver can't stand having anyone pass him, the Italian perpetually looks at himself in the rear-view mirror, the Frenchman must have his last word with the abused

[41] Placed between the two raw barbarian powers, prior at least to De Gaullist magnification, the French would be inclined to such neutral but acerbic exposé, slightly tilted to American favoritism.

pedestrian he has just knocked down, etc. Nowhere is there even a reference to American drivers, who also swarm over Europe, many of whose license stickers are quite recognizable. The American is left out because, among other reasons, his longer experience, his defensive driving, and his greater automotive sanity exempt him from the particular satire involved. It is not he who is the innocent or the *arriviste*. The comparatively brief but accelerative history of the United States has put him ahead in certain ways.

But these ways are not merely technological. What may have appeared as presumption, in comparing the American performance in literature and humor to that of much older cultures, is not really so. Enough has happened in American history, compassable though it is, to warrant broad comparisons and judgments.

Our humor tends to greater concreteness and comic imagery than European. Its wit is not as discriminatory as the French. Its sexual component is less scatological than the English but not as instinctive or light as the French. And yet the irreverence of American humor is more comprehensive and consistent than French, English, or other Continental examples, without any powerful circumscriptions of subject matter or office—in this sense the freest of all. Our strong point is not intellectualism or sophistication, but our base in realism is formidable. And our classlessness, though it forever breeds self-consciousness, also accounts for liberal self-humor and expansive techniques.

Indeed, our movement, almost instinctually, has been into the international scene, as we seek new material and setting as well as devices. Newer American movies are indicative, in their placement of the new romantic comedy stars, Jack Lemmon, James Garner, Kim Novak, Shirley MacLaine, and others, in England and France,[42] for example, *The Notorious Landlady, The Americanization of Emily, Irma La Douce, A Shot in the Dark*, etc. The use of foreign comedians, like Sellers in the latter film, and even the improvement of the foreign script (by Blake Edwards) are indicative. From *Around the World in 80 Days* to *Those Magnificent Men in their Flying Machines* the major American

[42] And Germany inevitably, for Billy Wilder's *A Foreign Affair* and *One, Two, Three*.

effort, in fact, has been in characterization of international types. Furthermore, in *The Russians Are Coming, The Russians Are Coming*, the American venturesomeness was honest as it was opportunistic in psychology; it caught the hectic comic desperations and temperament of both the Russian and American characters (portrayed by Alan Arkin and Carl Reiner), plus that sentimentalization of children by both nationalities in the convenient but correct conclusion.[43]

No curtains, walls, or resurgent nationalisms can put off the interchange that is already underway. The development will have its disadvantages as well as advantages and will proceed not so swiftly as some believe but no less certainly for all that.

There have always been interconnections, as we have seen, so that we shall be returning to broad origins and common humanity at the last. Subject matter will be wider in scope, modern characters less provincial. The task will be to maintain particular strengths as others are gained. As Americans learn greater sophistication, for example, they ought not to abandon their concreteness. Nor should the French, in appropriating American economy, as in cartoons, abandon their own flourishes of wit nor submerge their social satiric impulses as they copy our grotesquerie.

With as much talent . . . and genius . . . now on earth as has ever lived in the past and with a whole world of opening, shared possibilities and pluralism, the chances are good for a general transition from comic despair to comic joy and to renewed technical experiment. Indeed, the chances under present and probable future conditions are better for comedy than for tragedy.

[43] We may think of Soviet-American coproductions of films in the near future as inevitable.

X

Conclusion

99 WE ARE TOLD that in the Alexandrian period of critical
scholarship Lycophron wrote a treatise of eleven books
On Comedy. Eratosthenes devoted twelve volumes to
The Old Attic Comedy.[1] We ourselves may have already entered
upon a new age of creative decline signaled by our own critical
preoccupations. We are also now writing our tomes, including
this one, on comedy, and, what is more, we are writing volumes,
like René Wellek's series, of criticism of criticism. Our very effort
at encompassment may be really part of a general embalmment.
We appear to be modern Hellenists in Egypt.

Perhaps even Professor McLuhan is correct in speaking of the
decline of literature and literacy, his own prose not the least
evidence for his thesis. He instances *Don Quixote* as an illustration of men's obsession with the immediate past, feudalism for
Cervantes' audience, once we know it is truly gone. He believes
that is true for our modern subjects and themes; the power that
the American west exercises upon us is an illustration, and perhaps
spy subjects would also suit his purposes. Furthermore, he sug-

[1] Wimsatt and Brooks, in *Literary Criticism: A Short History*, rightly
single out the age as one of the most belletristic and antiquarian in western
history.

gests that literary expression itself is now a preoccupation with a dead or dying form of communication and even consciousness. Any interest, such as ours, in a whole genre of expression will be taken as further proof of the eager autopsies going on now. The argument is a comprehensive and closed one. We are either guilty of burying our dead or of leaving them, with a brutal incognizance of what is happening in this new age, to rot. We are damned if we do and damned if we don't.

McLuhan's thesis, however, has its own stillborn absurdities. It would force us to view Aristotle's monumental *Poetics* as marking an end to Greek and, by the same token, western tragedy. Deviously, it suggests an equation between dead subject matter and post-mortem treatment, so that we tend to forget that the work, *Don Quixote,* is a vital masterpiece and endures. And, lastly, it makes us overlook the written scripts that have accounted not only for Shakespearean drama but our movies and television as well. As the mass media develop, the printed word will become more, not less important. And since the camera has not surrendered its sound track, literate human exchange, including the comic, has a greater lease on life than ever.

We may well admit that we are in a hypercritical period and that the mass media threaten books as such. But nothing, least of all a whole means of expression, is permanently superseded or interred.[2] There is always the real prospect of decline and dormancy in anything, but arguments about the absolute mummification of cultural forms and modes, as the death of literature or of comedy, either serve someone's cynical self-interest or are honest poppycock. We proceed to concluding speculations without the fear of placing another miniature stone upon a tomb.

We have spoken of the strategy of antithesis and the tactics of literalism or reversal; of assaults on themes and attacks on ruling values; of collaborative comic onslaughts, individual campaigns, battles, technical weaponry; of the deflationary force of comedy and the need for formal discipline; of hostility and the need of self-command. Our descriptive vocabulary has been un-

---

[2] Painting has not disappeared since the introduction of photography.

mistakably military, an inevitable consequence of the subject.[3]

For this reason as much as for any other, Koestler's theory of bisociation, humor as the result of the sudden intersection of one idea by another, is partial and unavailing. In fact, the psychologist, Gordon Allport, has criticized Koestler's ingenious formulations as crucially lacking all social dimension. In any case, Koestler curiously ignores Freudian and post-Freudian postulates of normal human aggression.

By now the biological experiments of Konrad Lorenz, summarized in his work, *On Aggression* (1963), seem conclusive. Lorenz is unequivocal in declaring that the function of humor in the highest biological species is the expression and release of the nervous, muscular and, at base, psychic reflexes of aggression. Long before Lorenz's laboratory work and those anthropological studies among the Eskimos by Jean Charcot, of the French Ethnographic Museum, describing the song and joke duels in the North, the humorist Stephen B. Leacock had his insights into the primitive aggressive nature of humor. At its root, the Canadian theorized, laughter was a savage's triumphant expression over a defeated enemy, and no subsequent evolutionary development is entirely devoid of original and gratifying violence. Furthermore, semantic study, such as Eric Partridge's, has put us in possession for a long time now of certain distinct clues, especially for American vernacular. It is no accident that the words for utter comic enjoyment, a "riot," "hysterical," etc., are also words describing mass violence. The processes of civilized humor constitute a vast sublimation. And so we return to Freud.

We need not subscribe, however, to all Freudian conclusions, many of which are interesting and germane, though others are highly mechanistic or merely terminological. Comic techniques of reversal, circularity, associationism and literalism resemble the processes of "displacement" and "condensation" in the dream work. These equations seem to identify humorous expression more closely than tragic expression with the Unconscious. But although the Unconscious often makes use of punning and other comic devices, its processes are rarely subtle and almost always

[3] There is always the possibility, of course, that style is the man. I believe, however, that imagery inheres in content. At all events, there is no necessary contradiction between the two principles.

gross and crude in verbal and other symbolic activity; too strict an identification of humor with the Unconscious deprives us of the highest workings of comedy. A broader and more useful concept may serve: in dreams, as in humor, almost all techniques are placed at the disposal of forces at war with a principle of social reality. This view, including the concept of a return of the repressed, is not only true but frequently central. There is a leading exception we shall take for American humor to these psychoanalytic discoveries, but they remain, on the whole, among our soundest theories, despite the overnice distinctions Freudians often contrive. The main thing is that Freudian analysis dispenses with the idea of social corrective. It studies the way humor expresses itself against external authority.

But an extraordinary cathexis qualifies American humor, which may be satisfactorily described only by the most flexible of psychological approaches. Obviously, antitheticism in American humor, more comprehensive, consistent and highly charged than anywhere else, is a result of clear antagonisms and contempts. But our mordant, destructive, and even most violent humorists are always a hairsbreadth away from love, as indeed they also are from sentimentalism. We are left with the proposition that Americans are more bound up than others with the fiercest kind of love and hate. And that is so for a reason we have glimpsed frequently. It is so because no other people is so much less of a people than Americans. Without the comfort of homogeneousness, they are without the security of national identity, on which concept therefore they are always fixated. They cannot take for granted what other people can, and, therefore, as a social body, they more willfully impose shibboleths and ideals; at the same time, they need the rectifications humorists vengefully supply. The necessary impositions and the grateful exceptions taken are two sides of the same thing; tyranny and freedom are uniquely wedded. And so fury is bound with regard.

We must recover the human note and our ordinary wisdom in these matters of definition. Only indifference, we remember then, is a true sign of disengagement in cultural and personal relationships. We know that the hostility of epitheticists can turn easily to love. That is the lesson of Shakespeare's epithetical pair, Beatrice and Benedict, in *Much Ado* and of all antagonists who become lovers in romantic stage comedies and films. We accept the device because it represents true human psychology. People who are hostile to one another are paying sufficient attention to one another. It is attention which can turn to love quickly, because it is a partly engaged love to begin with.

The record of deepening misanthropies and of equally notorious apostasies in American humor bear on the point. Mark Twain's later repulsions are in direct proportion to initial attractions. He came to resist false idealizations, of the south, of the Indian, of religion, etc., in order desperately not to be taken in. He had wanted to be taken in at the start. His later resistance carried him too far, but almost necessarily. Other figures, like Sinclair Lewis or Will Rogers or Frank Capra, had to give in all the way to sentimentalism, needing more to love at any cost than to maintain opposition. The comedians' love-hate relationship to America is resolved either for sentimentalism or contempt, with only infrequent genuine love matches, because of the character of the national experience.

Basically, however, even contemptuous humor functions to redress false love. That is the deepest service of antithetical comedy. So much is clear in American humor. What is not so clear is that varieties of love may restrain antithesis and save it from itself.

I mean two things by this observation. The first has to do with an ancient Chinese proverb: "Hypocrisy is the first step to proper conduct." Somewhere the line must be redrawn, no doubt, between hypocritical first steps toward true morality and hardened fanatical moralism. But an increased philosophic tolerance might make American humor more elastic than it has become and grant it, in fact, the extra distance it urgently needs.

The other point I wish to make is yet more subtle but fundamental. It involves our profoundest exception to Freudian perspective on the human condition. I contend that any attempt at form, especially artistic, is an act of conservative and conserving love. It is at least an act of respect for something outside of ourselves, a dedication and, in some cases, a devotion. Such attitudes are motivations of love. While men *are* actuated by aggressive instincts, the essence of being human is to be nonetheless and uniquely capable of a mediative and transmuted expression of our needs and ourselves. Man is also the artistic animal. Form itself, as we see it in the best of Twain, Chaplin, and Thurber, serves to contain the most effective antithesis. It is what holds skepticism from the fullest misanthropy or nihilism and yet keeps it from becoming sentimental vindication or apology. It is our human prerogative and our artistic and comic responsibility.

But let us make no mistake about the prime antithetical function of humor in America. All specific devices are ruled by deflationism in order to serve our comedy. The fairy tale of "Little Red Riding Hood," for example, has its measure of absurd complication (the wolf does not devour the girl in the woods but unaccountably goes to grandma's house); it has its appetitive notes (the lunch basket) and its happy ending after climactic difficulties; and it has a certain brief but mad momentum of events. But it is not comic, because these devices are not directed by a deflationary aim. When that happens, as in Thurber's fable of the new Red Riding Hood or as in the anagrammatical "Ladle Rat Rotten Hut" discussed earlier, we have varieties of humor. The antithetical humor must be formed . . . but what is formed is unmistakable.

We confront another theory of comedy, touched upon in our considerations of Walt Whitman and Tennessee Williams but advanced comprehensively by the literary critic and formulator, Northrop Frye. His is "the green world" theory, whereby comedy is an ultimate manifestation of the mythos of spring, as tragedy is of winter. As Frye applies his Spenglerian and Jungian methodology,[4] he traces the successive periods of comedy and its amalgamations with religion. In the earlier stages, gladsome rites of nature and appetitiveness become affirmative worship. In their mature stages of western development, both comedy, which, somehow, keeps its separate identity, and Christianity are characterized by motifs of appeasement and redemption. In the

[4] Spenglerian and Jungian methodology, but the Freudian pleasure principle. These are united to anthropological precedents, traceable ultimately to James Frazer's *Golden Bough* (1890) and, afterward, to Francis Macdonald Cornford's *The Origin of Attic Comedy* (1914), an erudite but Procrustean monument.

last stage of each, there is a collapse of social morale and then a mood, probably like the modern, of intense introversion and irony.[5]

Professor Thorp has referred to Frye's ambitious categories as a "Mendeleev's table of [literary] elements." In subtilizing various gradations of comedy and distinguishing minutely and arbitrarily the many kinds of corresponding comic heroes, Frye's categories are overrefined, pedantic, and almost humorous themselves. Among comic protagonists he lists in *The Anatomy of Criticism*, for instance, are "the high neumatic hero," "the low neumatic hero," and "the ironic neumatic hero." Furthermore, where the connections between comedy, myth, and religion are not merely uselessly broad, they are inaccurate. Thorp himself once characterized myth as "fairy tale on the way to becoming religious belief," and the hard evidence is that realistic comedy has regularly opposed itself to all three, certainly in America.

It is only fair to Northrop Frye to say that he has little concern with the modern case and draws his perspective and categories largely from the classical period.[6] For all his super-refinements and tabular schema, however, he makes one significant point, chiefly in his discussion of *Lysistrata*, which we need to face. That point is that there is a "green world" of joy and physical vitality essential to most humor.

There is an American joke about three mice who discover a leaky barrel of wine in the cellar, lap up the contents, and become

[5] Frye's theories have already influenced practical literary criticism in a most narrow manner. We have alluded to Mellard's use of Frye's schema to rescue Faulkner's *The Reivers* as a comedy of the "mature" rather than "late" stage. Mellard does not once refer to Faulkner's indebtedness to *Huckleberry Finn*, whose upshot is renunciation. Nor does he dare allude to Frye's early article, *The Argument of Comedy*, where Frye himself referred ill-advisedly to the idyllic "green world" content of Twain's book, ignoring the realism, the spill of blood, the ultimate lighting out, and the undercurrent of nihilism in the work. Since Faulkner's departures from his native tradition account for his weakness, Mellard is probably quite right in keeping perfectly still.

[6] He also disguises his jargon by neologisms from the Greek. "Eirons" are "sympathetic" characters; "alezons" are "blocking" characters; "bomolochi" are "buffoons," and "agroichos" are "churlish, rural" characters. This practice might almost be taken as a New Critical and academic confidence game, but we are too much intimidated to judge. One admits that the terminology for comedy is, at the least, amusing.

drunk. "If I was the—hic—President," says the first mouse, "I'd
do—" such and such. "I'd tell you what *I'd* do," says the second
. . . "Never mind this small talk," says the third, "let's go upstairs
and rape the cat." The motifs of sex and power may indeed be
characteristics of a great deal of humor. In this way, precisely,
critics may rescue Whitman for the genre, and Tennessee Williams even more easily. Bellow's principal theme in all his work,
as well as in *Herzog*, may be just his characters' ultimate comic
joy in being alive, although he also pointedly elaborates sexual
episodes and dinner scenes.

Teaching in western universities, Professor Warren Carrier
has lectured on just such differences between tragedy and comedy. His distinctions are more cogent than Frye's. He maintains
that tragedy invariably deals with the cosmological, with the
relationship between man and the gods, and with transcendent
sense. Just as invariably comedy, which may be either serious
or humorous, according to Carrier, deals with the earthy and the
appetitive (especially money and sex), with man and man (for
or against society but always *in* it), and with common sense. In
this way, Aristophanes remains the model comic author; he brings
Socrates back down to the stage, insisting that the stratospheric
intellectual figure come back to the world of common-sensical and
appetitive reality.[7] Transposing Carrier's observations to American literature, we must therefore emphasize the intervention
of sexual realism in the comedy of the southwesterners, the
physical raft life of Huck and Jim, the Burguete Mountain and
fishing interlude in Hemingway's *The Sun Also Rises*, the worm
and the robin and Mehitabel the hungry cat in Marquis, etc.[8]

The argument has force, and it has the merit of reconciling
itself with clear evidence. But it is not sufficiently comprehensive.

[7] According to this view, the third mouse's delusion of grandeur in our
anecdote is nonetheless a clear deflation of abstract, exalted ambitions of
the first two.

[8] The Gershwins' *Porgy and Bess* is another striking instance of values,
especially as a conjunction of two of our most vital minorities, Jews and
Negroes. Comic lyrics from "It Ain't Necessarily So" are representative.

> Methusla lived nine hundred years,
> Methusla lived nine hundred years,
> But who calls dat livin'
> When no gal'll give in
> To no man what's nine hundred years?

Or it is at one and the same time too general and not comprehensive enough. Themes of sex and power and money and fame give us a tragical or melodramatic *Carmen* as well as humor. And physicality and appetitiveness do not, in American literature, make humorists out of Walt Whitman or Thomas Wolfe. But more importantly, such a view does not take into consideration the powerful ideational component, as we saw even in Tennessee Williams, actuating most or all of American humor. The full potency of *Huckleberry Finn*, Twain's masterwork, resides in its psychology. The regular and powerful attempt that comedy makes to gain freedom of mind, *that* pleasure, is the predominant motive of American humor.

But there is no necessary contradiction between the two comic motives. Both of them may obtain, as they probably do even for Molière.[9] The question is one of priority. In our subject that priority is established by the insistence with which governing considerations of comic antithesis are made through all the subperiods of American humor. Nonetheless, Frye's central point, absurdly burdened though it is by academic paraphernalia, and Carrier's insights are scarcely irrelevant. For one thing, they counteract a certain specific gravity of analytical criticism and save us from our own worst judgments.

We have generally opposed comic reduction to tragic heightening. But there are reductions more complete than the comic and heightenings more elevated than the tragic. Beneath comic deflation is the utter destructiveness of invective and diatribe, and above tragic grandeur is religious exaltation. Set against a four-part rather than tripartite grid, comedy and tragedy are yet closer to one another than each is to the opposite extreme. Genuine comedy may be antithetic and reductionist, but it retains

[9] They may also apply to the earliest comic epic we have, Homer's *Odyssey*, where feasting and dallying play their part but where, at the last, the hero returns home to destroy the society that has usurped his interests during his absence. In addition, we may note that the greatest of all survivalists constantly provokes semicomic incidents and catastrophes (his bragging insults to Cyclops, etc.). Moreover, his trip is one of such long and difficult frustration that it has become proverbial for comic-epic endurance.

some sympathy, some vestige of human worth, and a partial sense. Great tragedy may be exalted and inspiring, but it reserves some limitation of human will and fulfillment.

As a matter of fact, this contiguity which we now emphasize serves in meeting a special objection to assumptions we have appropriated from L. J. Potts. If, for example, comic treatment is primarily deflative, why are there some comic heroes, like Huck Finn and Chaplin's characters in *The Great Dictator* and *Monsieur Verdoux*, who are set apart and even elevated? And why have there been tragic protagonists, like Shakespeare's Hamlet and King Lear, who are a good deal less than exalted personages? The answer must be that there is something courageous and ennobling about such comic heroes and something comically absurd about such tragic protagonists. The German theorist, Jean Paul, referred to comedy as "a laughable form of the sublime." A consequence is that sometimes a work is partly sublime and still mainly comic, and sometimes it is partly comic and still mainly sublime. The mixture will naturally affect characterization.

I do not hesitate to exchange our ruling topographic concept for another in emphasizing here the compatibility of tragedy and comedy. In this world of changing appearances, wrote that aesthetician of life, Santayana, the role of contingency makes all experience inherently comic. A proper perspective will remind us of the perpetual "accident" of existence. For that philosophic purpose, Santayana thought, comedy suits us better than tragedy. But we need not become formal Platonists ourselves in order to validate the true basis of comedy, making it the expression of vital "existence" as tragedy is of abstract "essence."

In more pragmatic terms, we may say that one is importantly reminded of his possible grandeur by tragedy, of his capacity for extraordinary supernatural transcendence of himself. But he is realistically brought back to his nature by comedy. These are complementary rather than rival views. The most divergent extreme from tragic heightening is the destructiveness of black or sick comedy and diatribic satire. Comedy proper, as Congreve and Goldsmith maintained, is not annihilatory. It simply does not glorify human nature but sees it as it ordinarily or realistically is. It is skeptical, deflationary, and truthful, but not necessarily splenetic or obliterating. The furthest divergence from it is either ecstatic religion or sentimentality and pathos. It is, ideally, the twin lens with tragedy for a stereoscopic view of the human condition. In American humor particularly, the best examples of both Twain and Chaplin remind us of the blended perspective necessary for the truest vision.

Nonetheless, only rarely has a poised comedy been achieved in American humor. The dominant thrust has been away from the heightened view. We may admit theoretically that such a direction is not inevitable but is only the way matters have worked out in the United States as a response to the false myths and artificial theses of national life. But have we selected the most boisterous voices as our evidence? Have we simply ignored a less reactive tradition of quiet humorists who have striven for a lower but no less real synthesis than that achieved in *Huckleberry Finn* or *Monsieur Verdoux*? I do not believe that such a tradition exists; that is to say, not if we are considering figures of recognized stature or significance.

I do not think that our omissions in the nineteenth century of Anna Cora Mowatt, N. P. Willis, Oliver Wendell Holmes, C. G. Halpine, Edmund Stedman, John Saxe, Henry Van Dyke, and others have been crucial. In any event, most of their work is perfectly consonant with themes and techniques we have traced, though infinitely more withholding and genteel. Mowatt's play, *Fashion* (1845–50), is a native but delicate attack on the socialite world; Holmes's *Autocrat* (1858) shows comic independence although quite respectably, and his poetic fable of the same year, "The Deacon's Masterpiece," is a whimsical spoof of outdated Calvinist orthodoxy; Stedman's insouciance, "Pan on Wall Street" (1869), criticizes finance-minded and busied New Yorkers in the lightest manner; and Saxe's "The Blind Men and the Elephant" (1884), the height of his talents in whimsical verse, represents a fanciful and fashionable skepticism.

In the twentieth century we have ignored the thoroughly middle-class counterpart of Mark Twain, Booth Tarkington (*Penrod, Seventeen,* etc.). There are no others to consider at all, except panderers like William S. Porter, whom we have grievously lamented, and sentimental renegades like Will Rogers, whom we have mourned for our own reasons. To add Eddie Cantor as a decisive entry from the days of radio, to think of Jerry Lewis in hyperbolic terms on the screen, or to raise H. Allen Smith, Max Shulman, William Saroyan or Harry Golden[10] to literary pinnacle would be to enmass further nonevidence in nonsupport of a nonexistent case.

There has been little or no effective humor to demonstrate a standard comedy of social norms, to defend religion or politics or business or woman or children, to support uplift or promulgate kindliness. There have been apostasies and rank declensions to sentimentality, but few commentators will instance them as genuine humor or anything else. Theoretical possibilities are not, prima facie, unacceptable; indeed, we want a positive thrust to pull us away from the current ill humor of pathological despair and sadism. But there can be no appeal from the facts that have overwhelmingly characterized the history of American humor up to this point.

What might that history suggest to save itself from its own excesses and still insure force? Several possible answers come to light as we recapitulate our study and give our pragmatism a somewhat ameliorative turn. But there is a practical joke implicit in such a review. Since we have regularly admitted the hard determinants in the long case, how can there be lessons of any avail? Nevertheless, if we refuse to prescribe rigorously, there may be no inconsistency in our position and no harm done.

We learn most obviously from the earliest period of American humor that if foreign influence is one thing, subjection is another. Subjection to British models deprived us of technical bravery, decisive theme and characterization, and our own style. Of course, the colonists scarcely regarded English models as foreign. National identity had to wait until the Revolution. But it took us a long time, up to Emerson's *The American Scholar* (1837), and then some, until we thought of independence in terms other

10 One of Golden's books, *Enjoy! Enjoy!*, was greeted by the most trenchant and probably the shortest literary and comic review on record: "Enough! Enough!"

THE RISE AND FALL OF AMERICAN HUMOR

than the political. That has had two consequences for us. Our comic as well as general preoccupation with militant politics, from Freneau, Irving and Seba Smith through the southwesterners, the literary comedians, and Dunne, to Norman Mailer and Art Buchwald, is both inheritance and original sin. The subject is too easy and external and, by now, too stereotypical to engage the deepest comic interest. On the other hand, the basic irreverence partly bred in us by such political creations as Jack Downing is a long-term strength of our humor.

Covert as southwestern humor was, its seizures of native realism, in "low" speech and in content, are lasting examples. Unpretty, hard, even cruel, its repudiative features gave our humor initial force. Providing our first wild rectification of idealized society, nonetheless it also demonstrated the superiority of something very like artistic control in the best work of George Washington Harris and H. C. Lewis. Furthermore, its venturesomeness, carrying it frequently beyond the preconceptions of its authors (Baldwin and Harris, especially), is a valuable reminder.

For their part, the literary comedians plead the great effect of brave experimentation for any age, although we can do nothing about manufacturing a comparable morale for it if we do not have it. In addition, the verbal dexterity of this period was the first great, concerted prospecting of mother-lode in America. Moreover, the special antithesis against rhetoric, which would become our reflex of inherent parody, continues to be instructive.

As to Mark Twain's *Huckleberry Finn*, we need only recall how he joined subtlety with the most overt of means. Beyond that indisputable American distinction and his manifest triumphs of subversion and realism in the work, we confine our didacticism to three salient points. First, the form of the work restrained his comic improvisations at the same time that it contained his comic animus. Secondly, in the course of the book, Twain achieved a certain balance between cynicism and compassion. His attack on social morality or hypocritical moralism never became an attack on natural morality; in fact, the latter was thematic. Furthermore, Twain's open-mindedness allowed him to combine southern and western values for his own overview; as a result, his comedy lost nothing in power for having been relativistic. In the same way his comic objectivity carried over to the deflation of his protagonists, who are enhanced as characters and human beings rather than essentially undercut. The conclusions we reached about Twain's subsequent career, certainly after *Pudd'n-head Wilson,* about the swelling determinism and misanthropy he no longer restrained by comic form are the most dire lessons. They particularly remind us of the crucial significance of objectivity in comedy, infallibly expressed through manifold and organic techniques but basically a matter of controlled philosophy.

In the intercentury period, Bierce's techniques almost mitigate his shock, his relentless misanthropy, and his dark subjectivism. Dunne's objectivity, in the characterization of Dooley especially, makes a pointed contrast, particularly since there is no loss of antithetic force or aggressivity. And Ade's forms, when he is not withholding his fullest thematic implications, show again the strong possibilities of uniting subtlety and overtness in American comedy.

Continued "debunking" informs the interwar period, a fiendish and inventive delight to tell the truths that upset our sentimental democracy, hagiarchies, and shibboleths of all kinds. And yet a marked amoralism, while emphatic, is not sick immoralism; and the grimmest revelations, as provided by West, are not masochistic. Nonetheless, the shadow of the truths to which the literary and mass-media humorists are faithful begins to darken their comedy. The formed comic confusion and nonsense which they elaborate, in order to mock the alleged sense of the world, become less and less sufficient to the purpose; the world's manifest confusion and broadcast non-sense begin to rob them of distance. Culminative as the leading figures are, they fulfill themselves precariously. Nonetheless, they are aided by the mood of the time and by ruling technical tensions, factors which seem short-termed in the nature of their influence and operation. But perhaps the latter factor may be more subject to the will than we believe.

Of the modern, post-World War II period, evidence of decline or fall is far more persuasive than that of resurgence. Thurber's surrender to noncommunication and pessimism is a particular gauge among many. A manipulative or psychopathic technique, as in Nabokov or Charles Addams, predominates; and the triumph of indiscriminate black humor in sick jokes and literature is unmistakable. Such excess is a symptom of defeatist morale and the collapse of comic distance; it is also a result of remorselessly devaluated liberalism and of a technical realism now licensed to go too far for its own best effects. Enfeebled humor of the mass media and commercial fraudulence complete the preliminary argument for decline. Against this evidence appear the positive phenomena of S. J. Perelman's career, the continuing vitality of cartooning, new disc humor, and the rise of Negro humor working to contain its rage. But a second case for the falling off of our comedy appears conclusive. The vogue of Yiddish humor is modish, "sign-card" humor is an insidious surrender of originality and a confession of bankruptcy, and the supposed ascendancy of comic novelists is everywhere undercut by sentimentality, self-consciousness, regressive characterization, derivativeness, and perversity.

Having reached a nadir or even still heading for it, we are not, however, beyond the aid of our own precedents, especially of the immediate past. Those miniscule but insistent dignifications of character in Chaplin, for example, may be pertinent to a genuine resurgence from the antiheroism we have come to practice. Indeed a restudy of the themes and techniques of our most successful humor of the interwar period and a refamiliarization with the best tradition before it may be all the stimulus needed for a resumption of our prerogatives and fullest powers.

To that end, reminders of those exercises of humor in our major writers may be relevant also. The subtle uses of wit and self-humor,[11] as in Thoreau, may be especially valuable now. The enormous flexibility of Melville's practice may be instructive in the widest sense. Frost's combinations of tolerance and skepticism and his relativism serve as reminders of basic attitude. On the other hand, Whitman's remorseless subjectivity and the undevelopmental quality of E. E. Cummings mark historical dangers. And the spectacle of Poe, taking his self-parodies seriously, has its special meaning for us. So does the worth of ortho-

[11] It is significant for our comic character that we quickly appropriated the name, "Yankee," a British derogation, for ourselves. Later, the northern derogation for the southerners, "Reb," was also instinctively taken to heart by the south. We are founded in self-humor and branded in self-epithet.

dox parody itself, which may be turned against our prevailing pseudo-modes.[12]

Breaking outside of our own history, we may profit from foreign example. The French wit of discrimination may have a conceivable import for us. Their antitheticism supports us, their failure at self-humor warns us, and their recourse to style alone for an irreducible comic distance is most suggestive. Across from them the German humorlessness and alternative fanaticism are negative examples with the greatest weight for Americans.

At this date, the possibilities of international enrichment, through mutual cross-influences, are most hopeful. Whatever distance has been shortened by the steady impact of events, whatever resistances have disappeared before permissive realism, whatever we have lost to comprehensive black humor may be redressed in whole or in part. Our gains may come in the broadened area of characterization, where international types will predominate, in new resources and sophistications of theme, and in renewed experimentation. There will be no full American resurgence, probably, apart from what occurs in the cultural context of the Atlantic community.

The concept of tension and resistance, to which we have several times alluded, calls for extra consideration. When Twain abandoned it, he slid to diatribe. When Chaplin gave it up, he floated off to the utmost maudlinisms. Of course, Twain had his lifelong tendencies to nihilistic pessimism and Chaplin his constant proclivities for sentimentalism. The fault is not entirely in the stars or in our times, then, but in ourselves. It is not merely fortuitous that we echo Shakespeare on the point, for his own progressions through various popular genres, histories, comedies, tragedies, tragicomedies, suggest that he moved from one to another out of fear of having overcome final resistances in each

[12] Albee, for instance, may be another Poe, ending by taking himself with utmost seriousness. The gross improbabilities of . . . *Virginia Woolf*, everybody baring himself to everybody else so quickly, intimacies of sex life exchanged on first meeting, fantasies of invisible children, etc., are exactly the solemn impostures of sick comedy that healthy comedy can make new capital of, especially through elaborated parody.

and needing to move on for his own good; the point is not inconsistent with whatever theatric demands were being made of him at the same time. A resistless medium is not triumph for an author but disaster.

Part of our contemporary trouble, for instance, is not that we have a licentious realism but that we have a licensed realism, where ease of subject has become ease of technique. Eventually a total indiscriminateness characterizes subject and technique together.

A little old crippled lady, perhaps blind also, trips on a banana peel and breaks her hip. That is extremely funny in insane asylums and the inner circles of sick humor. If we recreate a man, a large man, with no disabilities, then make him pompous, sticking his nose high in the air, so that he is as much responsible as he is deserving for his fall, and contrive at last to land him on his asinine buttocks, we infallibly return to comedy. That venerable pratfall has its proper thematic subject at least, and its discriminated technique. Shlomo Zemach has remarked upon the superiority of the old banana-peel device to that of the falling brick, because in comedy, as in all literature, accident and outside instrument are never fully satisfying.[13] The conscious sadism of sick humorists, who are more delighted if they themselves have placed the peel before the little old lady than if it were there by accident, is their very last contact with reality—tense human agency, at least, is still there, and that is not a requirement for laughter inside asylum walls. But if our black or sick humorists can discriminate *that* far, why not further . . . all the way back to the sanest humor, in which they resist themselves if nothing else?

What the concepts of resistance, tension, and discrimination ideally imply is fitting the means to the end. And what that, in turn, implies is choosing the proper end. Even the most aggressive comedy must suit the punishment to the crime. And so there is a comic justice to serve. It is the oldest of all concepts and prob-

[13] Zemach also calls attention to the triviality of the banana peel. Comedy, however, does not necessarily increase as we diminish the size or importance of the instrument . . . but it does if we increase the size and importance of the human subject. The illustration is a critical instance of deflationism operating at the root of the most elementary comedy.

ably the most radical at the present stage. It is also the most interesting. If the contemporary humorist can lead us back to that, it is enough—it is all—we can ask.

Nonetheless, it is clear that almost systematic American lies and pretenses exacerbate the situation of black or sick humor in the United States. In their earliest schooling American children are taught that Columbus was the only one of his time who believed the earth was round, a largely unnecessary and an absolutely apocryphal story. It is an anecdote out of our elementary mentality, but indicative. Real life and history are difficult enough to come to terms with, but willful delusions intervene in America, as in a virtual schooled campaign. At the end of a long semi-official educational process, there is enough warrant for *The Realist* to indict our public vocabulary now of prevaricated obscenity: violent "pacification," "clean bombs," etc.

One may simply construct any number of legitimate arguments on behalf of dark social critics and leftist comics in America. The psychology of extremists is understandable as never before. But it is no less regrettable. A healthy skepticism, bred by liberalism, has become in turn an anti-liberal force, frictionless and psychotic. Without self-resistance, attitudes deepen at last to what, in another context, Kenneth Burke has named "the drastic irony of paranoia." In their hopelessness black satirists at last turn to their own conspiratorial delusions. If, according to Rightists, Marshall and Eisenhower were tools of the communists, then according to realists and comics of the Left, Johnson is Hitler.[14] Even valid frustration leads to indiscriminate fury. There may be nothing to interpose but self now. And that is an act of mind as well as feeling.

Having no adequate outlet for an excess of feeling, we resort to that "buffoonery of emotion" T. S. Eliot detected in Hamlet's character. It does not matter that we have more objective correlatives than Hamlet had. Or, rather, it does precisely matter and calls for a greater rather than diminished exercise of the comic intelligence.

[14] *The Realist* magazine at least provides deflation of the tendency in its satirically put query, "Who killed Adlai Stevenson?"

Once again we suspect an actual craving of antagonism among a host of black humorists, Romantics[15] feeding on dark emotion for its own sake. Much of that impulse, we judged, was in Bierce, whom we considered a reverse lyricist and sentimentalist. Or we suspect varieties of psychic compensation, like the fetish of youthful rebellion in black humorists, including Mailer and others, men of forty plus who are tirelessly young, virile, and reactive. Their psychological needs are converted to philosophical terms, and we are hoaxed.

At all events, comedy must outwit those friends of it who are its own worst enemies. It needs all of its intelligence and all of its own force to counteract the extremism and growing indiscriminate violence of the black humorist. For he has become a psychotic and self-righteous bully by now, or a fraud, and the cruelty we visit upon him is meet. We must become Chaplin's Keystone cop and by all means domesticate that huge loathsome ruffian on Easy Street.

But we must defeat and not simply loathe him in our turn. For loathing, in any case, as Joyce pointed out, is an improper artistic emotion. It is a moving away from the subject, a repulsion, after all. Having drowned Shillaber's kittens in warmed water, we have proceeded to allow extremists to drown too many cats in deliberately iced cold water . . . and in vats like Bierce's. Our own freezing fingers and creeping paralysis ought to have warned us that we had to resist ourselves at some point, before the work became loathsome reflex. The nature and survival of

[15] Perhaps, in the sense that almost all American humor takes the part of individualism and antithetic revolt, it has a core of Romanticism. For this reason, furthermore, it may thrust itself to Realism, in order to resist its own deepest inclinations. Certainly it gravitates to literary Realism for its down-to-earth subject matter and is attracted also by the antitheticism of most Realistic movements (although these movements, like Ibsenism, are essentially uncomic themselves, because they take their own programmism and heroes too seriously). But the Realistic attempt at objectivity may be more compelling for humor, more necessary to it, than anything else.

At the furthest depths of the subject, one is baffled. When we consider that a great part of formal Realism is pseudorealistic and, at bottom, bleakly romantic in its portrayals of squalor and victimization, we are at the limits of our theories. The only recourse is to say, then, that it is black comedy that is basic, the thing in itself. If that is so, our topographical explanations become desperate imprecisions. But the concept of self-resistance becomes even more significant than ever.

the genre, to say nothing of scarce kittens and fully human custodians, depend upon it.

We all know that humor can be playful and serious at the
same time . . . the best of it always is. In emphasizing the element
of play now, I mean only that the serious antitheticism or specific
thematic purpose of comedy must not, after all, overwhelm the
humor. In particular, a comedian must never take himself too
seriously; least of all should he become messianic. A certain
element of caprice is even the essential exercise of irreverence
and comic freedom. At any rate, he must not ever take himself,
or his positions, which he may confuse with himself, too dog-
matically. There is a prophetic role in comedy,[16] but the
humorist must not fully become the prophet. He may have
ample warrant, and indeed his modern subjects may force the
function a little more upon him than usual, but he must resist
the full role.

Mr. Dooley, for instance, might have slid into some such role
in regard to the Far East and China especially. The west's
cavalier imposition of the opium trade upon the Chinese, its
almost jocular sphering of influences, its varied geopolitical
exuberances at the rotting Empire's expense, all might have
tempted Dunne, as it did a little, to sermonize on how much we
would have to pay for the amusement eventually. But he
restrained himself. He knew, both for Dooley's sake and his own,
that in comedy truth must not make us evangelists.

With similar knowledge aforethought, Chaplin sets *Monsieur
Verdoux* against a world of munitions makers and imminent mass
bombing. But he resists his own evangelism, restricting his themes
and ironies very carefully. Furthermore, he makes the most of all
the absurdities that assail his Bluebeard protagonist. At the end
of the film story, facing the guillotine, Verdoux concludes that he
was simply not "organized enough." The powerful social indict-
ments are all there, but *Monsieur Verdoux* is neither Camus' *The
Stranger* nor a sordid work of sick humor. That is because Chaplin's comic liberalities and, above all, his self-resistances are
paramount.

[16] As in all art. It is not, however, mystical foresight; it is insight into
present things before the rest of us see what is already here.

A certain modesty inheres in Chaplin and his character. And a certain kindliness, too (Verdoux lets one willing victim go and even encourages her "to live"). But both qualities have historical warrant, at least as far back as *Don Quixote*. For although Cervantes constantly deflated his hero's romantical and anachronistic idealism, when he at last brought him back to reality he did so not unkindly. He could afford to, of course, considering what he had done. But all comedy must so conceive and form itself that it can afford to.

That is probably why the French can raise themselves to levels of magnanimity, an otherwise puzzling characteristic in them which we have noted. They have such a habit of telling one another off wittily that they can afford an occasional but significant generosity, too. Their prevailing objectivity allows them their large-minded indulgences.

In the fullest latitude of speculation, we must allow for the insight of the psychologist, William McDougall. Without actually refuting the aggressive nature of comedy, he suggested that laughter is basically a substitution for sympathy that in itself would overwhelm or unman us. The fullest implications of his thought slip beneath the ground of empiricists like Lorenz or even depth-psychologists like Freud, for they pose an insoluble question of priority. Does a projective sympathy precede aggression in the recesses of even the most primitive psychology; or is there a feeling, immediately following self-assertion, of intolerable identification with one's victim, which is then converted to more complex but still aboriginal hostility? The factors of empathy and defensiveness seem to mitigate concepts of pure aggression, as it were. Whatever our answer, McDougall's clinical formulation certifies a whole line of our thought, which might otherwise be taken as essentially verbal argument.

We are left with the proposition that comedy must balance its aggression and love. It may on occasion be deadly, but never deathly ill. It is made ill when its hostility or contempt, even for righteousness' sake or for reality's, utterly consumes it. That is an especial threat in America. We have to remember that if comedy must be cruel to be kind, it ought never be cruel . . . to be cruel. Humor can avoid that error only if it does not take itself with absolute seriousness, if it affords itself a saving doubt about what it is doing. That is an effective concession to the world, another exercise of love.

The danger of comedy is not the political and social subversion that Plato feared for his republic of philosophic kings. Not in the United States at any rate. The danger for us is closer to what Sir Phillip Sidney glimpsed: laughter may lead us to enjoy sin.

Sidney was moralizing Aristotle. Remembering that, we may further interpret his remark as meaning that there can be too much of a good thing. Of all that Aristotle said, nothing is more viable and wise than his relativistic philosophy of the golden mean. It applies to comedy as to general conduct. He habitually located his median ideal qualities between defects and excesses on either side. These relative placements were his definitions. Courage, for example, was defined as that quality placed midway between craven cowardice and foolhardiness. That much can be said for comic bravery as well. And so might a range of comic qualities or ideal functions be viewed: comic truthtelling fixed between high social idealization and furious personal antagonism; comic portrayal of men-as-they-are coming between the urge to deify and the compulsion to annihilate; and comic control setting itself between the defects of sanctimoniousness and sentimentality and the excesses of black scorn and sick invective.

In the end we ask indeed for the sense of complication and relativism that humor can provide. That is why we do not rule Koestler's theories out of consideration, for the simplest bisociative function of a joke is gratifying to us if only because we come to see another point of view. The "Knock, Knock" comic anagrams of the thirties rose to that purpose chiefly.[17] They are joking parables of comic tentativeness and psychologic expansion. All comic reversalisms operate in the same elementary way; we are consistently led to see as much truth in the opposite contention;

[17] "Who's there?" *"Formaldehyde!"* *"Formaldehyde* who?" *"Formaldehyden* places the Indians came running." Phrases like *"evanescent* ladle rat rotten hut," in those postwar transliterations which we considered legacies of Artemus Ward, function the same way. And Bennett Cerf's inventions operate similarly; the piano tuner, Mr. Oppornockety, never repeats his work, because Oppornockety tunes only once.

the opposite is made apposite. Humor qua humor must always look at things the other way round.

Humorists exist by virtue of their own plural consciousness. That is why they cannot ever commit themselves to a narrow absolutism about anything. For this reason, Ed Fisher's modern cartoon, which reverses the already reversed humor of current novelists and *their* Disestablishment norms, is effective. "I'm sorry," pleads a young man in modern courtship, "I'm not cowardly, cynical, effeminate, uninvolved . . . we can't *all* be anti-Heroes!"

We in America have always had the broadest advantages as well as disadvantages of our pluralism. Significantly, ours is the only country in the world without a consolidated capital. Washington has always been merely our political seat. The cultural capitals are decentralized, New York sharing power with Chicago especially, but also with New Orleans and St. Louis sometimes and perhaps more and more with San Francisco.[18] There has never been a compaction of cultural, literary, or comic consciousness in the United States. The dispersion has always encouraged the multiple approaches that are basic to regenerative humor. Hazlitt once theorized that comedy would flourish best in a mixed, plural society, and though he was only speculating freely at the time, the observation has become a true prediction about the American scene.

And yet even our pluralism can lead us too far, to chaos or to nowhere. We must oppose one principle to another, like that of complexity to extreme relativism, in order to strike our median way. As we have seen, even hypocrisy may be a means to proper conduct; the strong antisocial force of American humor must take factors like that into account, the resulting complication holding it from ultimate nihilism. The final comic antithesis of all is having no thesis whatsoever, a direction in which the majority of our nethermost humorists are heading. The furthest reaches of such comedy are psychotic; we hear a continual, hollow laugh, as in asylums, about nothing, an intensely, terribly simplified

[18] Minneapolis is on its way to a hegemony of its own, Boston has never exactly disappeared as a cultural seat, and other centers like Seattle-Portland make a contemporary place for themselves. And now even Los Angeles, after the cinematic decline of Hollywood, advances certain claims.

private joke with no public or social contacts whatever. This represents a sense of humor no more than driveling sentimentalization does a sense of tragedy. We are brought back to the theoretical importance of resistance. Life is sufficiently complex after all that there is even some sense or order in it, too. That makes for the most welcome complication of all, for the great philosophers and master humorists both.

Pathologic laughter tends to a rising tone of explosion, hysteria, the madness of delight. Grievous tears tend to a lower tone of implosion, strangulation, the madness of collapse. Comedy and tragedy are our sane alternatives to manic depression. Each of them, however, demands an element of operative will. We may admit, for reasons we have touched upon, that tragedy is now less susceptible to our will than ever before. That places the burden doubly upon the comic mode today. The enterprise, bound as it is to mental health, is an enormous challenge.

We turn again to statistical probabilities for hope. With as many human beings alive now as have ever lived on earth before, we trust in resurgence. Genius may be exercising itself in nuclear physics and biochemistry, but there will be enough left over for the arts, including comedy. Men of comic intelligence and imagination will find their way back to the motives and resources we have spoken of. The talented and inspired are all about us, and will arrive at first principles either on the basis of present-day critical imperatives or, which is more likely, on their own. They will make decline or fall temporary.

They always have.

BIBLIOGRAPHY

Adams, Henry, *The Education of Henry Adams*. Boston: Houghton Mifflin Co., 1961.

Addams, Charles, *Addams and Evil*. New York: Random House, Inc., 1947.

——, *Dear Dead Days; A Family Album*. New York: Putnam's Sons, Inc., 1959.

——, *Drawn and Quartered*. New York: Random House, Inc., 1942.

——, *Homebodies*. New York: Simon & Schuster, Inc., 1954.

——, *Monster Rally*. New York: Simon & Schuster, Inc., 1950.

——, *Nightcrawlers*. New York: Simon & Schuster, Inc., 1957.

Ade, George, *The America of George Ade*. Edited by Jean Shepherd. New York: Capricorn Books, 1962.

——, *Fables In Slang*. Chicago: H. S. Stone & Co., 1900.

——, *Forty Modern Fables*. New York: R. H. Russell, 1901.

——, *Hand-made Fables*. New York: Doubleday, Page & Co., 1920.

——, *More Fables*. Chicago: H. S. Stone & Co., 1900.

Allport, Gordon W., "Like an Apollo Amok," *Contemporary Psychology*, XI (Feb., 1966), 49–51.

Allsop, Kenneth, "Those American Sickniks," *The Twentieth Century*, CLXX (July, 1961) 97–106.

"American Humor: Hardly a Laughing Matter," *Time*, LXXXVII (March 4, 1966), 46–47.

Anderson, John Q., ed., *The Louisiana Swamp Doctor*. Baton Rouge: Louisiana State University Press, 1962.

Aswell, James R., ed., *Native American Humor*. New York: Harper and Brothers, 1947.

Auerbach, Erich, *Mimesis*. Translated by Willard R. Trask. Princeton, New Jersey: Princeton University Press, 1953.

Ayres, Harry Morgan, *Carroll's Alice*. New York: Columbia University Press, 1936.

Baldwin, Joseph G., *The Flush Times of Alabama & Mississippi*. New York: Sagamore Press, Inc., 1957.

Barth, John, *Giles Goat-Boy*. New York: Doubleday and Company, Inc., 1966.

——, *The Sotweed Factor*. New York: Doubleday and Company, Inc., 1960.

Bate, Walter Jackson, *Criticism: The Major Texts*. New York: Harcourt, Brace & World, Inc., 1952.

Becker, Stephen D., *Comic Art in America*. New York: Simon & Schuster, Inc., 1959.

Beerbohm, Max, *The Incomparable Max*. New York: Dodd, Mead & Company, Inc., 1962.

Bellow, Saul, *The Adventures of Augie March*. New York: Popular Library, 1955.

——, *Henderson, the Rain King*. New York: Popular Library, 1960.

——, *Herzog*. New York: Fawcett Publications, Inc., 1965.

——, *Seize the Day*. New York: Popular Library, 1958.

Benchley, Robert, *The Benchley Roundup*. New York: Harper & Brothers, 1954.

——, *Inside Benchley*. New York:

Universal Library, Grosset & Dunlap, 1942.

Bergson, Henri, *Laughter.* Translated by C. Brereton & F. Rothwell. New York: The Macmillan Co., 1911.

Bierce, Ambrose, *The Devil's Dictionary.* New York: Sagamore Press, Inc., 1957.

———, *The Collected Works of Ambrose Bierce.* New York: Neale Publishing Co., 1909–1912.

———, *The Sardonic Humor of Ambrose Bierce.* Edited by George Barkin. New York: Dover Publications, Inc., 1963.

Bishop, John Peale, *The Collected Essays of John Peale Bishop.* Edited by Edmund Wilson. New York: Charles Scribner's Sons, 1948.

Blair, Walter, *Native American Humor.* San Francisco: Chandler Publishing Co., Inc., 1960.

———, *Horse Sense in American Humor, From Benjamin Franklin to Ogden Nash.* Chicago: The University of Chicago Press, 1942.

Blish, James, *The Triumph of Time.* New York: Avon Publications, Inc., 1958.

Blistein, Elmer, *Comedy in Action.* Durham, N. C.: Duke University Press, 1964.

Boatright, Mody C., *Folk Laughter on the American Frontier.* New York: The Macmillan Company, 1949.

Bonaparte, Marie, *The Life and Works of Edgar Allan Poe, a Psycho-Analytic Interpretation.* Translated by John Rodker. London: Imago Publications Co., 1949.

Boskin, Joseph, "Good-by, Mr. Bones," *New York Times Magazine* (May 1, 1966), 30, 31, 84, 86, 88, 90, 92.

Brackenridge, Hugh Henry, *Modern Chivalry* 1792–1815 (Part I: Vol. I and II–1792; Vol. III–1793; Vol. IV–1797; Part II: [Volume I] 1804; Vol. II–1805; Vol. IV–

1815). Edited by Claude M. Newlin. New York: American Book Company, 1937.

Bradley, A. C., *Shakespearean Tragedy.* Second Edition. London: Macmillan & Co., 1956.

Brooks, Cleanth and Robert Penn Warren, *Understanding Fiction.* Second Edition. New York: Appleton-Century-Crofts, Inc., 1959.

Browne, Charles Farrar, *Artemus Ward, His Book.* New York: Carleton, 1862.

———, *Artemus Ward; His Travels.* New York: Carleton, 1865.

———, *Artemus Ward in London, and Other Papers.* New York: Carleton & Co., 1867.

Burke, Kenneth, *Attitudes Toward History.* Second Edition, Rev. Los Altos, California: Hermes Publications, 1959.

———, *Counter-Statement.* Second Edition. Los Altos, California: Hermes Publications, 1953.

———, *A Grammar of Motives.* New York: Prentice-Hall, Inc., 1945.

———, *The Philosophy of Literary Form; Studies in Symbolic Action.* Baton Rouge: Louisiana State University Press, 1941.

Burroughs, William, *Naked Lunch.* New York: Grove Press, 1962.

Cady, Edwin H., ed., *The American Poets, 1800–1900.* Glenview, Illinois: Scott, Foresman and Company, 1966.

Caldwell, Erskine, *Tobacco Road.* New York: Random House, Inc., 1940.

Carlisle, Henry C., *American Satire in Prose and Verse.* New York: Random House, Inc., 1962.

Carroll, John B., "Linguistic Relativity, Contrastive Linguistics, and Language Learning," *International Review of Applied Linguistics in Language Teaching*, I (1963), 1–20.

Cassirer, Ernst, *An Essay on Man.* Garden City, New York: Doubleday Anchor Books, Inc., 1953.

Cazamian, Louis F., *The Development of English Humor.* Durham, North Carolina: Duke University Press, 1952.

Chase, Richard, *Walt Whitman Reconsidered.* New York: William Sloane Associates, 1955.

Chaucer, Geoffrey, *The Poetical Works of Chaucer.* Edited by F. N. Robinson. Boston: Houghton Mifflin Company, 1933.

Chomsky, Noam, *Aspects of the Theory of Syntax.* Cambridge, Mass.: The M. I. T. Press, 1965.

———, *Cartesian Linguistics: A Chapter in the History of Rationalist Thought.* New York: Harper & Row, 1966.

———, "The Current Scene in Linguistics: Present Directions," *College English,* XXVII (May, 1966), 587–595.

Clark, Thomas D., "Humor in the Stream of Southern History," *The Mississippi Quarterly,* XIII (Fall, 1960), 176–188.

Clemens, Samuel, *Adventures of Huckleberry Finn.* New York: Charles L. Webster & Company, 1885.

———, *A Connecticut Yankee in King Arthur's Court.* New York: Charles L. Webster and Company, 1889.

———, *Following the Equator.* Hartford, Connecticut: American Publishing Company, 1897.

———, *Letters from the Earth.* Edited by Bernard DeVoto. New York: Harper & Row, 1962.

———, *Pudd'nhead Wilson.* New York: Bantam Books, 1959.

Cohen, Hennig and William B. Dillingham, eds., *Humor of the Old Southwest.* Boston: Houghton Mifflin Company, 1964.

Colby, Frank M., *The Colby Essays.* Selected and edited by Clarence

Day, Jr. New York: Harper & Brothers, 1926.

Connell, Evan S., *The Diary of a Rapist.* New York: Simon & Schuster, Inc., 1966.

Cook, Albert, *The Dark Voyage and the Golden Mean; A Philosophy of Comedy.* Cambridge, Mass.: Harvard University Press, 1949.

Cooke, Alistair, ed., "James Thurber in Conversation with Alistair Cooke," *Atlantic Monthly,* CXCVIII (August, 1956), 36–40.

Cooper, James Fenimore, *The Last of the Mohicans.* New York: E. P. Dutton & Co., Inc., 1951.

———, *The Leatherstocking Saga.* Edited by Allan Nevins. New York: Pantheon Books, 1954.

———, *The Prairie.* New York: Rinehart & Co., 1954.

———, *Satanstoe.* Lincoln Nebraska: University of Nebraska Press, 1962.

Corey, James R., "Darwin's *The Voyage of the Beagle* and Melville's "The Encantadas," (unpublished Master's Thesis, University of Montana, Missoula, Montana, 1963).

Cornford, Francis Macdonald, *The Origin of Attic Comedy.* Edited by Theodore H. Gaster. Garden City, New York: Doubleday Anchor Books, Inc., 1961.

Cox, James M., "Remarks on the Sad Initiation of Huckleberry Finn," *Sewanee Review,* LXII (Summer, 1954), 389–405.

Crane, Stephen, *The Red Badge of Courage, & Other Stories.* New York: Harper & Bros., 1957.

———, *Selected Prose & Poetry.* Edited by William M. Gibson. New York: Rinehart & Co., 1950.

Crews, Frederick C., *The Pooh Perplex.* New York: Dutton & Co., Inc., 1963.

Croy, Homer, *What Grandpa Laughed At.* New York: Duell, Sloan & Pearce, 1948.

Cummings, E. E., *Poems, 1923–54.* New York: Harcourt, Brace & Co., 1954.

Dahl, Curtis, "Artemus Ward: Comic Panoramist," *New England Quarterly,* XXXII (Dec., 1959), 476–485.
———, "Mark Twain and the Moving Panoramas," *American Quarterly,* XIII (Spring, 1961), 20–32.
Day, Clarence, *God and My Father.* New York: A. A. Knopf, Inc., 1932.
———, *Life With Father.* New York: A. A. Knopf, Inc., 1935.
———, *This Simian World.* New York: A. A. Knopf, 1920.
Davis, Douglas M., "Black Humor," *Freelance* (August, 1965).
DeMott, Benjamin, "The New Irony: Sickniks and Others," *The American Scholar,* XXXI (Winter, 1961–62), 108–119.
DeVoto, Bernard, ed., *The Portable Mark Twain.* New York: The Viking Press, Inc., 1946.
Dickens, Charles, *Great Expectations.* New York: Rinehart & Co., 1951.
Dobrée, Bonamy, *Restoration Tragedy.* Oxford: Clarendon Press, 1929.
Dodgson, Charles L., *The Annotated Alice: Alice's Adventures in Wonderland and Through the Looking Glass.* New York: C. N. Potter, 1960.
Donleavy, J. P., *The Ginger Man.* New York: Berkeley Publishing Corp., 1951.
Dorson, Richard M., *Negro Tales from Pine Bluff, Arkansas, and Calvin, Michigan.* Indiana University Publications, Folklore Series No. 12, Bloomington, Indiana, 1958.
Dudden, A. P., *The Assault of Laughter, A Treasury of American Political Humor.* New York: T. Yoseloff, 1962.

Dunne, Finley Peter, *Mr. Dooley At His Best.* Edited by Elmer Ellis. New York: Charles Scribner's Sons, 1938.
———, *Mr. Dooley In Peace and in War.* Boston: Small, Maynard & Co., 1899.
———, "Mr. Dooley's Friends: Teddy Roosevelt & Mark Twain," *The Atlantic Monthly,* CCXII (Sept., 1963), 77–99.

Eastman, Max, *The Enjoyment of Laughter.* New York: Simon & Schuster, Inc., 1936.
Eliot, T. S., "Hamlet and His Problems," *Selected Essays, 1917–32.* New York: Harcourt, Brace & Co., Inc., 1932.
Elliott, George P., "Wonder for *Huckleberry Finn,*" *Twelve Original Essays on Great American Novels.* Edited by Charles Shapiro. Detroit, Michigan: Wayne State University Press, 1958.
Enck, John J. et al, eds., *The Comic in Theory and Practice.* New York: Appleton - Century - Crofts, Inc., 1960.
Esar, Evan, *Esar's Comic Dictionary.* New York: Harvest House, 1943.
———, *The Humor of Humor.* New York: Horizon Press, 1952.

Falk, Robert P., *The Antic Muse.* New York: Grove Press, 1955.
Faulkner, William, *As I Lay Dying.* New York: Random House, Inc., 1957.
———, *Go Down, Moses.* New York: Random House, Inc., 1955.
———, *The Reivers.* New York: Vintage Books, Inc., 1966.
Feibelman, James K., *In Praise of Comedy.* New York: Russell and Russell, 1962.
Fiedler, Leslie, "'As Free As Any Cretur . . . ,'" *The New Republic,* CXXXIII (August 15, 1955), 17–18 and (August 22, 1955), 16–18.

———, "Come Back to the Raft Ag'in, Huck Honey!" *Partisan Review*, XV (June, 1948), 664–671.

Field, Eugene, *The Tribune Primer*. Boston, Mass.: H. A. Dickerman & Sons, 1900.

Fielding, Henry, *The History of the Adventures of Joseph Andrews and of His Friend, Mr. Abraham Adams*. New York: Rinehart & Co., Inc., 1949.

Fitzgerald, F. Scott, *The Great Gatsby*. New York: C. Scribner's Sons, 1953.

Flanagan, Bud, "Knowing Your Audience," *The Twentieth Century*, CLXX (July, 1961), 35–39.

Foster, Edward F., "A Study of Grim Humor in the Works of Poe, Melville, and Twain," *Dissertation Abstracts*. XVII (August, 1957), 1761–2.

Franklin, Benjamin, *The Autobiography of Benjamin Franklin*. Edited by Leonard W. Labaree, et al. New Haven: Yale University Press, 1964.

Freud, Sigmund, *The Basic Writings of Sigmund Freud*. Translated and edited by A. A. Brill. New York: Random House, Inc., 1938.

———, *Wit and Its Relation to the Unconscious*. Translated by A. A. Brill. New York: Moffat, Yard, & Co., 1916.

Friedman, Bruce J., *Black Humor*. New York: Bantam Books, 1965.

———, *A Mother's Kisses*. New York: Simon and Schuster, Inc., 1964.

Friedrich, Gerhard, "Erosion of Values in Twain's Humor," *The CEA Critic*, XXII (Sept., 1960), 1, 7, 8.

Fromm, Erich, *The Art of Loving*. New York: Harper & Brothers, 1956.

Frost, Robert, *Complete Poems of Robert Frost*. New York: H. Holt & Co., Inc., 1949.

Frye, Northrop, *Anatomy of Criticism*. Princeton, New Jersey: Princeton University Press, 1957.

———, "The Argument of Comedy," *English Institute Essays*. New York: Columbia University Press, 1949.

———, *Fables of Identity*. New York: Harcourt, Brace & World, Inc., 1963.

Gaddis, William, *The Recognitions*. New York: Harcourt, Brace & Co., 1955.

Gibbs, Wolcott, *A Bed of Neuroses*. New York: Dodd, Mead & Co., 1937.

Gilbert, Allan H., ed., *Literary Criticism: Plato to Dryden*. New York: American Book Company, 1940.

Goldsmith, Oliver, *The Works of Oliver Goldsmith*. Edited by Peter Cunningham. London: John Murray, 1854.

Gover, Robert, *One Hundred Dollar Misunderstanding*. New York: Ballantine Books, Inc., 1961.

Grattan, C. Hartley, *Bitter Bierce*. Garden City, New York: Doubleday, Doran & Co., Inc., 1929.

Green, Philip, "unessay on ee cuMming S," *The New Republic*, CXXXVIII (May 19, 1958), 24–26.

Grotjahn, Martin, *Beyond Laughter*. New York: McGraw Hill Co., 1957.

Halsman, Philippe, *Best Cartoons from France*. New York: Simon & Schuster, Inc., 1953.

Hamblin, Dora Jane, "Mark (Ye) (The) Twain," *Life*, LVII (July 10, 1964), 13.

Harris, Joel Chandler, *Nights With Uncle Remus*. Boston: Houghton Mifflin & Co., 1883.

———, *Told by Uncle Remus*. New York: McClure, Philips & Co., 1905.

———, *Uncle Remus and His Friends*. Boston: Houghton Mifflin & Co., 1892.

————, *Uncle Remus, His Songs and Sayings.* New York: D. Appleton & Co., 1895.

Hart, Fred H., *The Sazerac Lying Club.* San Francsico: H. Keller & Co., 1878.

Harte, Bret, "The Rise of the 'Short Story,'" *Cornhill Magazine,* VII (July, 1899), 1–8.

Hašek, Jaroslov, *The Good Soldier: Schweik.* Translated by Paul Selver. New York: The New American Library of World Literature, Inc., 1963.

Hawthorne, Nathaniel, *Hawthorne's Short Stories.* Edited by Newton Arvin. New York: Alfred A. Knopf, 1950.

————, *The Portable Hawthorne.* Edited by Malcolm Cowley. New York: The Viking Press, 1955.

Hazlitt, William, *Lectures on the English Comic Writers.* Edited by William Carew Hazlitt. London: George Bell & Sons, 1903.

Hemingway, Ernest, *For Whom the Bell Tolls.* New York: C. Scribner's Sons, 1940.

————, *Green Hills of Africa.* New York: C. Scribner's Sons, 1935.

————, *The Sun Also Rises.* New York: C. Scribner's Sons, 1926.

Hicks, Granville, "A Re-Reading of *Moby Dick,*" *Twelve Original Essays on Great American Novels.* Edited by Charles Shapiro. Detroit: Wayne State University Press, 1958.

Highet, Gilbert, *The Anatomy of Satire.* Princeton, New Jersey: Princeton University Press, 1962.

Hill, Hamlin, "Modern American Humor: The Janus Laugh," *College English* XXV (December, 1963), 170–176.

Hobart, George V., *D. Dinkelspiel, His Gonversationings.* New York: New Amsterdam Book Co., 1900.

Holliday, Carl, *The Wit and Humor of Colonial Days.* New York: F. Ungar Publishing Co., 1960.

Holmes, C. S., "James Thurber and the Art of Fantasy," *Yale Review,* LV (October, 1965), 17–33.

Hopkins, Robert, "Simon Suggs: A Burlesque Campaign Biography," *American Quarterly,* XV (Fall, 1963), 459–463.

Howells, William Dean, *A Hazard of New Fortunes.* New York: Bantam Books, 1960.

————, *The Rise of Silas Lapham.* New York: Rinehart & Co., Inc., 1949.

Humphrey, William, *Home from the Hill.* New York: A. A. Knopf, Inc., 1958.

Irwin, W. R., "Robert Frost and the Comic Spirit," *American Literature,* XXXV (Nov., 1963), 299–310.

Israel, Lee, "Notes on Stoop," *Esquire,* LXVI (Aug., 1966), 90–91.

James, Henry, *Washington Square, and Daisy Miller.* New York: Harper & Brothers, 1956.

Jewett, Sarah Orne, *Tales of New England.* Boston: Houghton, Mifflin & Co., 1894.

Joyce, James, *The Portable James Joyce.* Edited by Harry Levin. New York: The Viking Press, Inc., 1949.

Kapplan, Justin, *Mr. Clemens and Mark Twain.* New York: Simon & Schuster, Inc., 1966.

Kaufmann, R. J., "On the Supersession of the Modern Classic Style," *Modern Drama,* V (Feb., 1960), 358–369.

Koestler, Arthur, *Insight and Outlook.* New York: The Macmillan Co., 1949.

Krutch, Joseph Wood, *The Modern Temper.* New York: Harcourt, Brace & Co., 1929.

"Ladle Rat Rotten Hut," *Word Study,* XXVIII (May, 1953), 4.

La Fontaine, Jean de, *Fables,* Edited by V.-L. Saulnier. Paris: Editions de Cluny, 1950.

Lait, Jack, *Our Will Rogers.* New York: Greenberg Publisher, Inc., 1935.

Lane, Lauriat, Jr., "Why *Huckleberry Finn* Is a Great World Novel," *College English,* XVII (October, 1955), 1–5.

Lauter, Paul, ed., *Theories of Comedy.* Garden City, New York: Doubleday Anchor Books, Inc., 1964.

Lay, Bierne, Jr. and Sy Bartlett, *Twelve O'Clock High.* New York: Harper & Brothers, 1948.

Leacock, Stephen B., *The Greatest Pages of American Humor.* New York: The Sun Dial Press, 1916.

———, *Humor and Humanity.* New York: Henry Holt & Co., Inc., 1938.

Levine, Jacob and Frederick C. Redlich, "Failure to Understand Humor," *Psychoanalytic Quarterly,* XXIV (1955), 560–572.

Lewis, Sinclair, *Babbitt.* New York: Harcourt, Brace & Co., 1922.

———, *The Man Who Knew Coolidge.* New York: Harcourt, Brace & Co., 1928.

Locke, David Ross, *Swingin Round the Cirkle.* Boston: Lee and Shepard, 1867.

Longstreet, Augustus B., *Georgia Scenes.* New York: Sagamore Press, Inc., 1957.

Lorenz, Konrad, *On Aggression.* Translated by Marjorie K. Wilson. New York: Harcourt, Brace and World, Inc., 1966.

Lynn, Kenneth, *The Comic Tradition in America.* Garden City, New York: Doubleday Anchor Books, Inc., 1958.

MacDonald, Dwight, ed., *Parodies: An Anthology from Chaucer to Beerbohm—and After.* New York: Random House, Inc., 1960.

Maclachlan, John M., "Southern Humor As a Vehicle of Social Evolution," *The Mississippi Quarterly,* XIII (Fall, 1960), 157–162.

Mailer, Norman, *Advertisements For Myself.* New York: G. P. Putnam's Sons, Inc., 1959.

Malamud, Bernard, *A New Life.* New York: Farrar, Strauss & Cudahy, 1961.

Mander, John, "Germany: A Renaissance of Comedy?" *The Twentieth Century,* CLXX (July, 1961), 107–115.

Mann, Thomas, *Confessions of Felix Krull, Confidence Man.* Translated by Denver Lindley. New York: A. A. Knopf, Inc., 1955.

Markfield, Wallace, "The Dark Geography of W. C. Fields," *The New York Times Magazine* (April 24, 1966), 32, 33, 110, 112, 114, 116, 119, 120.

———, "Yiddishization of American Humor," *Esquire,* LXIV (October, 1965), 114, 115, 136.

Marquis, Don, *The Almost Perfect State.* New York: Doubleday, Page & Co., 1927.

———, *Archy and Mehitabel.* New York: Doubleday, Doran & Co., Inc., 1930.

———, *The Old Soak.* New York: S. French, Inc., 1926.

Marx, Groucho, *The Groucho Letters.* New York: Simon & Schuster, Inc., 1967.

———, *Groucho & Me.* New York: B. Geis Associates; distributed by Random House, 1959.

Marx, Leo, "Mr. Eliot, Mr. Trilling, and *Huckleberry Finn,*" *American Scholar,* XXII (Autumn, 1953) 423–40.

Masson, T. L., *Our American Humorists.* New York: Moffat, Yard & Co., 1922.

Matthiessen, F. O., *The American Renaissance.* New York: Oxford University Press, 1941.

Mauldin, William, *Up Front.* New York: Henry Holt & Co., 1945.

McClary, Ben Harris, ed., *The Lovingood Papers.* Athens, Tennessee: The Sut Society, 1962.

McClure, Alexander K., *"Abe" Lincoln's Yarns and Stories.* Chicago: Educational Company, 1904.

McDougall, William, *The Group Mind.* New York: G. P. Putnam's Sons, 1920.

McElderry, Bruce R., Jr., ed., *The Realistic Movement in American Writing.* New York: The Odyssey Press, Inc., 1965.

McLuhan, Marshall, *The Guttenberg Galaxy; The Making of Typographic Man.* Toronto, Canada: University of Toronto Press, 1962.

———, *Understanding Media; The Extension of Man.* New York: McGraw-Hill Book Co., Inc., 1964.

Mellard, J. M., "Faulkner's 'Golden Book': *The Reivers* as Romantic Comedy," *Bucknell Review*, XIII (Dec., 1965), 19–31.

Melville, Herman, *The Complete Stories of Herman Melville.* Edited by Jay Leyda. New York: Random House, Inc., 1949.

———, *Moby Dick.* Edited by Willard Thorp. New York: Oxford University Press, 1947.

———, *Pierre.* Edited by Henry A. Murray. New York: Hendricks House-Farrar, Straus, 1949.

Meredith, George, *An Essay On Comedy, and the Uses of the Comic Spirit.* New York: Charles Scribner's Sons, 1897.

Miller, Arthur, *Death of a Salesman.* New York: Bantam Books, 1955.

Miller, Henry, *Tropic of Cancer.* New York: Grove Press, Inc., 1961.

Miller, Jonathan, "A Bit of a Giggle," *The Twentieth Century*, CLXX (July, 1961), 39–45.

Miller, Perry, ed., *Major Writers of America.* New York: Harcourt, Brace & World, Inc., 1962.

Milne, A. A., *The World of Pooh.* New York: E. P. Dutton & Company, Inc., American Book-Stratford Press, Inc., 1957.

Molière, Jean-Baptiste, *The Misanthrope.* Translated by Richard Wilbur. New York: Harcourt, Brace & Co., 1955.

———, *Théatre Choisi.* Edited by E. Boully. Paris: Belin Frères, n.d.

Morton, J. B., "The Laughing-Stock," *The Twentieth Century*, CLXX (July, 1961), 7–9.

Murdock, George P., *Social Structure.* New York: Macmillan & Co., 1949.

Nabokov, Vladimir, *Lolita.* New York: G. P. Putnam's Sons, Inc., 1958.

———, *Pale Fire.* New York: G. P. Putnam's Sons, Inc., 1962.

———, *Pnin.* New York: Doubleday & Co., Inc., 1957.

———, *The Real Life of Sebastian Knight.* Norfolk, Conn.: *New Directions*, 1959.

Nash, Ogden, *The Face is Familiar.* Boston: Little, Brown & Co., 1940.

Nietzsche, Friedrich, "The Birth of Tragedy," *Complete Works*, I. Translated by W. A. Haussmann. London: George Allen & Unwin, Ltd., 1910.

O'Connell, W. E., "Multidimensional Investigation of Freudian Humor," *The Psychiatric Quarterly*, XXVII (Jan., 1964) 97–108.

O'Hara, John, *Appointment in Samarra.* New York: Random House, Inc., 1953.

Orel, Harold, *The World of Victorian Humor.* New York: Appleton-Century-Crofts, Inc., 1961.

Ostrom, John Ward, ed., *The Letters of Edgar Allan Poe.* Cambridge, Mass.: Harvard University Press, 1948.

Parker, Dorothy, *Death and Taxes.* New York: The Viking Press, Inc., 1931.

———, *Here Lies.* New York: The Viking Press, Inc., 1939.

Parks, Edd Winfield, "The Intent of the Ante-Bellum Southern Humorists," *The Mississippi Quarterly,* XIII (Fall, 1960), 163–68.

Parks, Gordon, "Freedom's Fearful Foe: Poverty," *Life,* L (June 16, 1961), 86–98.

Parrington, Vernon Louis, ed., *The Connecticut Wits.* New York: Harcourt, Brace & Company, 1926.

Partridge, Eric, *The "Shaggy Dog" Story; Its Origin, Development and Nature.* London: Faber & Faber, Ltd., 1953.

———, *Slang To-Day and Yesterday.* New York: The Macmillan Co., 1934.

Perelman, S. J., *The Road to Miltown.* New York: Simon & Schuster, Inc., 1957.

Poe, Edgar Allan, *Poe's Poems and Essays.* London: J. M. Dent & Sons, Ltd., 1955.

———, *Selected Prose and Poetry.* New York: Rinehart & Co., Inc., 1954.

Poirier, William R., *The Comic Sense of Henry James; A Study of the Early Novels.* London: Chatto & Windus, Ltd., 1960.

Pope, Alexander, *The Best of Pope.* Edited by George Sherburn. New York: The Ronald Press Company, 1940.

Potts, L. J., *Comedy.* London: Hutchinson & Co., Ltd., 1948.

Purdy, James, *Cabot Wright Begins.* New York: Avon Books, 1965.

Rexroth, Kenneth, "Humor in a Tough Age," *The Nation,* CLXXVIII (March 7, 1959), 211–213.

Richter, Jean Paul, "Vorschule der Asthetik," No. 28, *Werke* (I, ii). Weimar: Historisch-Kritisiche Ausgabe, 1935.

Rickels, Milton, *Thomas Bangs Thorpe, Humorist of the Old Southwest.* Baton Rouge, La.: Louisiana State University Press, 1962.

———, "The Imagery of George Washington Harris," *American Literature,* XXXI (May, 1959), 173–187.

Robacker, E. F., *Pennsylvania German Literature; Changing Trends from 1683 to 1942.* Philadelphia: University of Pennsylvania Press, 1943.

Rosenberry, Edward H., *Melville and the Comic Spirit.* Cambridge, Mass.: Harvard University Press, 1955.

Ross, John F., "The Character of Poor Richard: Its Source and Alteration," *PMLA,* LV (Sept., 1940), 785–94.

Rosten, Leo C., *The Education of Hyman Kaplan.* New York: Harcourt, Brace & World, Inc., 1937.

———, *The Return of Hyman Kaplan.* New York: Harper & Row, 1963.

Rourke, Constance, *American Humor,* Garden City, New York: Doubleday Anchor Books, Inc., 1955.

Salinger, J. D., *The Catcher in the Rye.* New York: New American Library of World Literature, Inc., 1957.

Santayana, George, "Carnival," *Soliloquies in England and Later Soliloquies.* London: Constable & Co., Ltd., 1922.

Seelye, John D., "The American Tramp: A Version of the Picaresque," *American Quarterly,* XV (Winter, 1963), 535–553.

Seitz, Don C., *Artemus Ward.* New York: Harper & Brothers, 1919.

Shakespeare, William, *The Complete Works of Shakespeare.* Edited by George Lyman Kittredge. Boston: Ginn and Company, 1936.

Shaw, Henry W., *Josh Billings, Hiz Sayings*. New York: Carleton, 1866.

———, *Josh Billings on Ice, and Other Things*. New York: G. W. Carleton & Co., 1868.

Shepard, Douglas, "Nathanael West Rewrites Horatio Alger, Jr.," *Satire Newsletter*, III (Fall, 1965), 13–28.

Shillaber, B. P., *Life and Sayings of Mrs. Partington, and Others of the Family*. New York: J. C. Derby, 1854.

Smith, Charles Henry, *Bill Arp, So Called*. New York: Metropolitan Record Office, 1866.

Smith, Henry Nash, *Mark Twain: The Development of a Writer*. Cambridge, Mass.: Belknap Press of Harvard University Press, 1962.

Smith, Seba, *The Life and Writings of Major Jack Downing of Downingville, Away Down East in the State of Maine*. Boston: Lilly, Wait, Colman, & Holden, 1833.

Sontag, Susan, "Notes on 'Camp,'" *Partisan Review*, XXXI (Fall, 1964), 515-530.

Speaight, George, "Puppets over Europe," *The Twentieth Century*, CLXX (July, 1961), 59-64.

Spiller, Robert E. et al, ed., *Literary History of the United States*. New York: The Macmillan Company, 1949.

Stafford, William T., ed., *Twentieth Century American Writing*. New York: The Odyssey Press, Inc., 1965.

Steinbeck, John, *Of Mice and Men*. New York: Convici-Friede, 1937.

———, *The Short Reign of Pippin IV, a Fabrication*. New York: The Viking Press, Inc., 1957.

———, *Tortilla Flat*. New York: Random House, Inc., 1937.

Sterne, Laurence, *The Life and Opinions of Tristram Shandy, Gentleman*. Edited by James Aiken Work. New York: The Odyssey Press, Inc., 1940.

Stowe, Harriet Beecher, *Oldtown Folks and Sam Lawson's Oldtown Fireside Stories*. Boston: Houghton, Mifflin & Co., 1896.

Styan, J. L., *Dark Comedy: Development of Modern Comic Tragedy*. New York: Cambridge University Press, 1962.

Swift, Jonathan, *Gulliver's Travels, A Tale of a Tub, Battle of the Books, Etc.* Edited by William Alfred Eddy. New York: Oxford University Press, 1933.

———, *Satires and Personal Writings*. Edited by William Alfred Eddy. London: Oxford University Press, 1949.

Sypher, Wylie, ed., *Comedy*. Garden City, New York: Doubleday Anchor Books, Inc., 1956.

Tallman, Marjorie, *Dictionary of American Folklore*. New York: Philosophical Library, Inc., 1960.

Tandy, Jennette, *Crackerbox Philosophers in American Humor and Satire*. New York: Columbia University Press, 1925.

Thoreau, Henry David, *Walden; On the Duty of Civil Disobedience*. New York: Rinehart & Co., Inc., 1948.

Thorp, Willard, *American Humorists*. (University of Minnesota Pamphlets on American Writers, #42) Minneapolis: University of Minnesota Press, 1964.

———, "The Literary Scholar as Chameleon," *Literary Views*. Houston, Texas: Semi-Centennial Publications, Rice University, 1962.

———, "Suggs and Sut in Modern Dress: The Latest Chapter in Southern Humor," *The Mississippi Quarterly*, XIII (Fall, 1960), 169-175.

Thurber, James, "Come Across With the Facts," *Saturday Review*, XLIII (June 18, 1960), 6.

———, *Further Fables for Our*

Time. New York: Simon & Schuster, Inc., 1956.

———, "The Future, if any, of Comedy or, Where do we non-go from here?" *Harper's Magazine,* CCXXIII (Dec., 1961), 40–45.

———, *The Thurber Carnival.* New York: Harper & Bros., 1945.

Tocqueville, Alexis, de., *Democracy in America.* Edited by Phillips Bradley. Translated by Henry Reeve and revised by Francis Bowen. New York: Vintage Books, Inc., 1954.

Tolkien, J. R. R., *The Hobbit.* New York: Ballantine Books, 1965.

———, *The Fellowship of the Ring.* New York: Ballantine Books, 1965.

Trilling, Lionel. *The Liberal Imagination, Essays on Literature and Society.* Garden City, New York: Doubleday Anchor Books, Inc., 1954.

Trollope, Anthony, *The Warden, and Barchester Towers.* New York: Random House, Inc., 1936.

Turner, Arlin, "The Many Sides of Southern Humor," *The Mississippi Quarterly,* XIII (Fall, 1960), 155–156.

Updike, John, "On the Sidewalk," *The New Yorker,* XXXV (February 21, 1959), 32.

Van O'Connor, William, "Why *Huckleberry Finn* Is Not the Great American Novel," *College English,* XVII (Oct., 1955), 6–10.

Voltaire, *Candide.* Périgueux: Editions Fontas, 1944.

Wade, John Donald, *Augustus Baldwin Longstreet.* New York: The Macmillan Co., 1924.

Waugh, Evelyn, *Vile Bodies.* London: Chapman & Hall, Ltd., 1930.

Weber, Brom, *An Anthology of American Humor.* New York: Thomas Y. Crowell Co., 1962.

Weightman, John, "Humour and the French," *The Twentieth Century,* CLXX (July, 1961), 117–126.

———, "Ionesco: The Absurd and Beyond," *New York Times Magazine,* (May 1, 1960), 24, 25, 113, 114, 115, 116, 117.

Weil, Simone, "The Iliad or, The Poem of Force," translated by Mary McCarthy, *Politics,* II (November, 1945), 321–331.

Wellek, René and Austin Warren, *Theory of Literature.* New York: Harcourt, Brace and World, Inc., 1956.

Wells, Carolyn, *A Nonsense Anthology.* New York: Charles Scribner's Sons, 1902.

West, Nathanael, *The Complete Works of Nathanael West.* New York: Farrar, Straus & Cudahy, Inc., 1957.

Wharton, Michael, "Beyond a Joke," *The Twentieth Century,* CLXX (July, 1961), 10–15.

White, E. B., *One Man's Meat.* New York: Harper & Brothers, 1950.

———, *The Second Tree from the Corner.* New York: Harper & Brothers, 1954.

White, E. B., and Katherine S., eds., *A Subtreasury of American Humor.* New York: Random House, Inc., 1941.

Whitman, Walt, *Leaves of Grass, and Selected Prose.* Edited by Sculley Bradley. New York: Holt, Rinehart and Winston, 1966.

Whorf, Benjamin Lee, *Language, Thought & Reality.* Edited by John B. Carroll. Cambridge, Mass.: M. I. T. Press, 1964.

Wilson, Edmund, "Poisoned!", *The New Yorker,* XXXI (May 7, 1955), 150–159.

Wimsatt, William K., Jr., and Cleanth Brooks, *Literary Criticism: A Short History.* New York: Alfred A. Knopf, 1964.

Yates, Norris W., *The American Humorist: Conscience of the Twentieth Century*. Ames, Iowa: Iowa State University Press, 1964.

Yeats, William Butler, *The Collected Poems of W. B. Yeats*. New York: The Macmillan Company, 1959.

Young, Philip, *Ernest Hemingway*. New York: Rinehart & Co., Inc., 1952.

Zall, P. M., ed., *A Hundred Merry Tales, and Other English Jestbooks of the Fifteenth and Sixteenth Centuries*. Lincoln, Nebraska: University of Nebraska Press, 1963.

Zemach, Shlomo, "A Theory of Laughter," *The Journal of Aesthetics & Art Criticism*, XVII (March, 1959), 311–329.

INDEX

Abbott and Costello, 265
"Abe Martin," 197, 198, 202, 206
absurd, theater of the, 444
Ace, Goodman, 209, 262, 263, 308, 324n
Ace, Jane, 274, 308
Adams, Don, 294, 330
Adams, Franklin P., 210
Adams, Joey, 318
Addams, Charles, 91n, 260, 291-93, 316, 443, 468; antecedents, 163, 207, 280; influence, 440; television, 310
Addison, Joseph, 34, 51, 72
Ade, George, 6n, 8, 177, 190-97, 198, 199, 202-4 *passim*, 467; provincialism, 183; realism, 201, 206; quoted, 192-96 *passim;* successors, 207, 212, 243, 279, 287
adolescence, preoccupation with, 355
adventurism, U. S., 83, 203
advertising, 262n, 321n, 441
advice columns, 294n
Aesopus Emendatus, 163
Agee, James, 255
aggression, humor and, 6, 16, 36, 62, 80, 93, 187, 268, 271-73, 321, 323, 335, 423, 456, 458, 474
Alaska, "Mr. Dooley" on, 180
Albee, Edward, 315, 358, 443, 469n
Algonquin Group, 210
alienation, 93, 179, 182, 210, 260, 299, 317
Allen, Elizabeth A., 222
Allen, Fred, 2, 70, 209, 258, 261, 273, 278, 284,

333; antecedents, 207, 280; influence, 318, 324; quoted, 271
Allen, Gracie, 258
Allen, Woody, 328
Allsop, Kenneth, 292, 295, 301
American Language, The, 239, 250
amoralism, 25, 26, 78, 82, 88-89, 95, 213, 232, 280, 301, 372, 467
"Amos and Andy," 258, 278
Amsterdam, Maury, 331
Anderson, Sherwood, 409
"Andy Capp," 427n
anger, humor and, 9, 24, 217, 249, 288, 294, 301, 304, 336, 357, 426, 468
"Annabel Lee," 342, 411
anticapitalism. See capitalism
anticliché, 101, 107, 314
anticlimax, comic, 8, 19-20, 30, 71-72, 110, 412; Benchley, 242; Bierce, 172, 174; Browne, 108; decline of, 257; Dunne, 185, 186; Faulkner, 352; James, 390; Locke, 109; Poe, 371; Salinger, 340-341; Shillaber, 36; Thoreau, 366; Twain, 144, 158
antidemocracy, 57, 164, 177, 191, 211, 225-26, 227, 278, 283, 361
antihero, comic, 95, 239, 261, 340, 345, 468, 476
anti-imperialism. See imperialism
anti-intellectualism, 38, 184, 191
antipatriotism, 163-64

antiproverbialism, 8, 20, 30, 103, 148, 149, 175, 186, 191, 214, 218, 236, 251, 366; Thurber, 285-286, 288
antireligiosity, 131, 143, 150, 151, 167, 181-82, 218-20
antirhetorical humor, 8, 72-73, 105, 110, 113, 189, 251, 273, 281, 287, 322, 324, 339, 396, 410
anti-Semitism, 3, 277, 302
antisentimentalism. See sentimentalism
antitheticism, 2, 25, 30, 69, 82, 88-89, 116, 130, 143-44, 163, 176, 257, 323, 329, 333, 426, 438, 455, 457, 459
aphorism, comic, 75, 81, 96, 214, 390, 434
Appointment in Samarra, 19, 26, 402
Archy and Mehitabel, 215-216, 226, 227-30, 231-232, 251
Aristophanes, 423, 461
Aristotle, 455, 475; on comedy, 12, 161, 264n, 307
Arnold, Edward, 268
"Artemus Ward," xi, 2, 24, 80, 81-84 *passim,* 86, 97, 98, 110; comic devices, 18, 99, 102; influence, 105, 159, 160, 187, 234, 236, 280, 475n
As I Lay Dying, 404
astronaut joke, 318
Attlee, Clement, 424
Auden, W. H., 137, 425
Auerbach, Erich, 12n
"Augie March," 26, 343-346 *passim,* 355

Austen, Jane, 418
aviation, 202, 212-13
Axelrod, George, 314, 315
Ayres, Harry Morgan, 423

Babbitt, 212, 239
Baby Leroy, 262
Baldwin, Joseph, 22, 25, 52, 56, 61, 65, 68, 75, 466; quoted, 66, 67, 72. *See also* "Simon Suggs, Jr."
Ball, Lucille, 330
banana-peel joke, 10, 470
Bankhead, Tallulah, 308, 358n
banks, architecture of, 7-8
baptism, 131, 138
Barkin, George, 178
Barnum, P. T., 24, 47, 305, 321
"Baron Munchausen," 39, 416
Barth, John, 340, 353-54, 358, 419n, 421
"Bartleby," 381, 385
Bartlett, Sy, 347
"Batman," 312
Baudelaire, Charles, 62, 290, 371, 443
bawdy humor. *See* ribaldry
"Bear Who Let It Alone, The," 216, 242
Beatles, 427n
beatniks, 397, 413
Behrman, S. N., 210
Bellow, Saul, xi, 26, 340, 343-46, 347, 352, 354, 355, 356, 461; quoted, 345, 346
Benchley, Robert, 17, 27, 208-10 *passim*, 213-15, 227, 233-34, 236-39 *passim*, 251, 284, 340; antecedents, 91, 104, 177, 207, 279, 280; humor, 20, 26, 51, 261, 269, 277, 278, 345; influence, 344; movie career, 265; quoted, 213-214, 215, 220-21, 225,

234, 236, 237, 240, 241, 242, 243, 255, 257
Benny, Jack, 70, 258, 278; quoted, 271
Berg, Gertrude, 335
Bergen, Edgar, 258, 271, 279
Bergson, Henri, 15-16, 29n, 243, 429-30
Berle, Milton, 260, 272, 273
Berman, Shelley, 328, 329
Bible, 12n, 20, 186, 240; takeoff on, 112
Bier, Jesse: quoted, 412
Bierce, Ambrose, xi, 12, 17, 161, 162-78, 191, 196, 198, 202, 203, 205n, 210, 286, 376n, 410, 421, 467; antichildism, 91, 221; black humor and, 443, 472; disappearance, 27, 199; misogyny, 22, 87, 169; Poe and, 371, 372n; prejudices, 249; quoted, 24, 162-70 *passim*, 172-178 *passim*, 180, 200; style, 419n, 433; successors, 230, 243, 280, 293
Big Business, 267-69
Big Store, The, 26, 261
bigotry, 21, 131, 148
Bikel, Theodore, 335
"Bill Arp," 78, 80, 82, 89, 96, 100, 103, 110
"Birdofredum Sawin," 83, 90, 96
bisociation, 7, 456, 476
black humor, 3, 24-25, 293, 298-300, 307, 308, 328, 340, 416, 463, 468-75 *passim;* Bierce and, 162, 171-72; education and, 470; fascism and, 357, 446n; France and, 442, 443; fraud in, 25, 299, 358; Nabokov and, 342; Nathanael West and, 231; Negroes and, 338; Poe and, 372;

sick humor and, x, 294; sources, 443; Swift and, 425n
blackface comedy, 37-38, 44, 48, 278, 279
Blair, Walter, 67, 163, 215
Blish, James, 327n
Bob and Ray, 308
Boer War, 188
Boland, Mary, 259
Bonaparte, Marie, 62, 343
Boorstin, Daniel, 449-50n
Borge, Victor, 107
Borscht circuit, 260, 318
Boskin, Joseph, 336, 337
Brackenridge, Hugh, 34, 37, 179, 421
Bradley, A. C., 14
braggadocio, comic, 41, 244, 245, 275, 436n
Brando, Marlon, 17
Brecht, Bertolt, 13, 14, 334, 447
"Brer Rabbit," 92-93, 96
Brinkley, David, 328, 331-332, 442
British humor, 17, 20, 34, 115, 159, 417-27, 465
Broun, Heywood, 210
Browne, Charles Farrar, 78, 82, 94, 97, 100, 104, 105, 107, 109-10, 156, 280n; quoted, 81-82, 99, 108, 110, 111-12. *See also* "Artemus Ward"
Bruce, Lenny, 301
Bryant, William Cullen, 99n
Buchwald, Art, 296n, 336, 466
Buckley, William F., Jr., 331
Burdette, R. J., 78; quoted, 84-86
bureaucracy as comic target, 18, 397n
burlesque: literary, 380; stage, 70, 420, 435, 441
Burnett, Carol, 330

Burns, George, 209, 258, 262, 263

Burroughs, William, 294n, 299, 308, 356

Burrows, Abe, 334

Butler, Samuel, 421

cabaret humor, 3, 435, 441n, 447.
    See also chansonnier; night-club comedy

Cabell, James Branch, 354, 419n

Cady, Edwin H., 167n

Cagney, James, 259, 263

Caldwell, Erskine, 2, 68, 232, 420

California, comic aspects, 83, 230, 271, 338

Calvinism, 119, 149, 167, 464

"camp" humor, 273, 291, 312

camp meetings, 57-58, 68

Camus, Albert, 443, 473

"Can You Top This?" 258, 276

Canada, humor of, 416, 420n, 456

Candide, 161, 344, 438

cannibalism, 176, 401n, 413

Cantinflas, 416

Cantor, Eddie, 258, 272, 342, 465

capitalism, 24, 79, 82-83, 165, 203, 210, 211, 261, 321, 403, 450

Capote, Truman, 288

Capp, Al, 260, 323-24; quoted, 28-29

Capra, Frank, 27, 197, 259, 267, 268, 333, 458

caricature, 83n, 211, 378, 417, 441

Carney, Art, 330

Carousel, 315-16

Carrier, Warren, xii, 461, 462

Carroll, Lewis, 422, 423

Carroll, Madeleine, 6-7, 258, 271, 276

Carson, Johnny, 311

cartooning, 2, 17, 197, 245, 260, 281, 291-92, 322-23, 476; anti-Lincoln, 89; British, 425, 426; French, 440-41; political, 83n, 90; risqué, 437.
    See also names of cartoonists, e.g., Addams, Mauldin, Thurber

cartoons, movie, 6, 58, 271, 325

Cary, Joyce, 425

"Catbird Seat, The," 22, 25, 224, 232

Catch-22, 346-7

Catcher in the Rye, The, 340-41, 347n

Catholicism: as social norm, 417; attacks on, 144; "Mr. Dooley" and, 181

"Celebrated Jumping Frog, The," 155

Cervantes, Miguel, 12n, 132, 313, 454, 474

chansonnier, influence of, 311, 328, 441

Chaplin, Charlie, 21, 207, 279, 281, 284, 302-3, 464; black humor, 472-473; comic protagonist, 25, 26, 202, 463, 468; genius of, 209, 357-58, 472-73; influence, 416, 440, 444, 459; movie career, 202, 259, 260-61, 263-66 *passim,* 268, 274, 276, 278, 313-14, 332-333; sentimentality, 27, 272n, 469; tragicomedy, 12, 13, 161

"Charlie McCarthy," 70, 271

Chase, Richard, 386, 389

Chaucer, Geoffrey, 418, 420, 421, 422

Chautauqua circuit, 87, 97, 329n

Chayefsky, Paddy, 333n

Chevalier, Maurice, 436

Chicago humorists, 178, 183, 190, 204, 308, 441

children as comic target, 91, 170, 207, 220-22, 262, 280, 287, 298-99, 309n, 321n, 391

Christianity, 84, 87, 144, 168, 186, 424, 426, 459.
    See also Catholicism; religion; sectarianism

Christmas, 162-63, 167-78, 176, 220-21, 291, 298, 318

Churchill, Winston, 281, 302; quoted, 424

"Circle, The," 6, 258, 264, 271, 308

circularity, comic, 2, 148, 157, 177, 241-42, 270, 280, 325, 370, 403

City Lights, 26, 260, 263, 276

civil rights movement 118, 230, 297, 327, 336-38

Civil War, 9, 28, 77-78, 101, 113, 166, 203

Clair, René, 440

Clark, Bobby, 260, 277

Clemens, Samuel L., 114, 132, 147n, 152.
    See also Twain, Mark

cliché: American mentality and, 3, 101, 212, 251, 281n, 342n, 396, 402; comic use, 215, 294, 398, 443; *South Pacific,* 334.
    See also anticliché

Cliché Expert, 251, 332

"Cloudland Revisited," 319, 338n

clown, 421-22; circus, 3; disappearance of, 278; Hitler as, 303; tramp, 202; "Uncle Sam" as, 33

Cohen, Myron, 260, 275-76

Colby, Frank M., 210, 248

Cold War, 29, 290, 295, 357, 450
Coleridge, Samuel Taylor, 430
comedy: "corrective" function of, 9, 12, 417, 418, 429-30, 457, 465; "dark," 423-24; theories of, 10-12, 401, 454, 459-464, 474
comedy, American. *See* humor, American; movie comedy; musical comedy
"comic" books, 288, 435
comic butt and critic, distinction between, 32-33, 73-74, 95-97, 203, 236, 265
comic catalogue, 186, 188, 341, 346, 352, 381, 403, 439
comic distance, 433, 447; collapse of, 281, 295-296, 298, 302-4, 308, 426, 442, 468
comic hero, 95-97, 130, 345, 460, 463.
See also antihero
comic instinct, loss of, 304-5
comic pairs, interracial, 93-95, 352, 377
comic relief, 362n, 386
comic strip, 196, 271n, 311n, 323-24, 427n
comic technique, 98-114, 153-59, 161, 215, 240, 257-58, 269-71, 280, 284, 340-57 *passim*, 381, 455-56, 467-68.
See also deflation; devices, comic; dialect; fantasy; grotesquerie; momentum; monologue; nonsense; reductionism; wisecrack; wit
commercialism, 167, 170, 220, 262n, 273, 294, 305, 339, 442

commercials, broadcast, 140-41, 306n, 311
comparative humor, 17, 20, 415-53
compensation, humor as, 16
complication, comic, 3-5, 19-20, 215, 243, 350, 370
concreteness, comic, 49-50, 53, 102, 194, 242, 419, 434n, 452
Condon, Richard, 315
confidence man, 21, 22-25, 47, 65-68, 263-64, 300; Big Business and, 334; Faulkner, 404; Longstreet, 73; Lowell, 96; Madison Avenue and, 321; Melville, 376, 381; Poe, 369; Twain, 132, 133; "Uncle Remus," 80, 81
conformism, 1, 21, 30, 131, 212, 279, 299, 307, 324
confusionism, comic, 8, 107, 155-56, 214, 233, 241, 265, 276n, 280, 287, 288, 325, 413, 422
Congreve, William, 418, 463
"Connecticut wits," 419, 421
Cooke, Alistair, 224n, 237, 359
Cool Million, A, 231, 233, 417
Cooper, Gary, 259, 267
Cooper, James Fenimore, 36, 93, 144, 149, 227, 251, 360, 386, 419n; humor, 361-63; parodied, 101, 111, 173-74, 410, 413; quoted, 362-363; Twain on, 157
Cosby, Bob, 328, 329
Coward, Noel, 419
Cozzens, James Gould, 355
Crandall, Brad, 308
Crane, Stephen, 79, 158,

166, 205n, 296; parodied, 410-11, 413
Crockett, Davy, 6, 37, 38, 41, 49-50
Crosby, Bing, 259, 270, 271
cruelty, humor and, 1, 2-3, 25, 29, 58-59, 63, 88, 89, 232, 307; Bierce, 170; Capp, 323; black humor, 358, 472, 474; G. W. Harris, 8; movie comedy, 264, 281; tall tale, 45; "Uncle Remus," 92-93
Cuba, 447; "Mr. Dooley" on, 20, 181, 186, 188, 424n
Cummings, E. E., 360, 396-97, 399, 410, 468
custard-pie comedy, 7, 264-265, 266, 276
cynicism, 9, 33, 79-81, 263, 284; Ade, 190; Bierce, 163; commercialism and, 306n, 338; Dunne, 186; French, 438; Melville, 428; Molière, 428; snobbery and, 44; Thurber, 216; Twain, 161
Cynic's Word Book, The, 162

Daisy Miller, 342, 391, 392, 393
dancing, comic inspiration of, 329-30
DAR, 279
Darwinism as comic target, 384
Daudet, Alphonse, 434, 439
Davis, C.A., 38, 48, 65
Day, Clarence, 210, 218; quoted, 227
Day of the Locust, The, 230-31
deadpan comedy, 265n
"debunking," 210, 221, 273, 280, 295, 467.
See also deflation
deflation, comic, 5, 20, 45,

253-54, 417; Ade, 206;
Bierce, 172; comic strip,
323, 334; Derby, 110;
Dunne, 189; Jewish, 335,
345; Mailer, 300; Marquis, 230; Twain, 158;
Thoreau, 366; Voltaire,
438
Defoe, Daniel, 135, 170,
344
De Gaulle, Charles, 304,
323, 435, 451n
democracy, satire on, 260-
261; 280.
  See also antidemocracy
Democratic Party, 51, 79,
214
denominationalism, Protestant, 84-86
Depression, 24, 199, 233,
268, 282, 397
Derby, George Horatio,
78, quoted, 110-11
determinism, 142, 151,
467
devices, comic, 155-59.
  See also comic technique; anticliché; circularity; complication;
confusionism; epithet;
exaggeration; malapropism; masquerade;
metaphor; neologism;
nom de plume; punning; self-contradiction; undercutting;
understatement
Devil's Dictionary, The,
162, 175, 176, 178, 180
De Vries, Peter: quoted,
254
diabolism, 151-52, 162,
163, 250, 260, 357, 366,
382
dialect, comic use of, 8, 50,
98, 155, 188, 206, 403;
Chicago Irish, 185; Negro, 80, 146, 362; New
England, 38-39; pseudo-
Indian, 362-63; taboo
on, 307

diatribe, 11, 26, 151, 280n,
294n, 462, 463, 469
Dickens, Charles, 220, 251,
293, 417, 419; quoted,
425
Dickinson, Emily, 131, 385,
399
"Dinkelspiel," 203
Dirksen, Everett McKinley,
332
disaster, comic, 5, 30, 234
disc comedians, 328-29,
441, 468
Dr. Strangelove, 19, 269,
333
dogs, sentimentalizing of,
108, 147, 170
Don Quixote, 161, 344,
454, 455, 474
Donleavy, J. P., 299, 308,
356
Dorson, Richard M., 336
double-entendre, 99, 382
draft, military, 79, 109
dreams, humor and, 456-
457
Dreiser, Theodore, 8
Du Bois Clubs, 298
Duck Soup, 259, 269-70,
274n, 277, 293, 303
"Duffy's Tavern," 273, 312
"Duke and Dauphin," 23,
24, 126, 133
Dumont, Margaret, 259,
263n, 270-71, 274, 293
Dunne, Finley Peter, 8, 9,
17, 22, 24, 178-90, 199,
202, 203, 204, 207, 212,
249n, 251, 416, 467, 473;
antecedents, 108, 424n;
Bierce and, 171; quoted,
19, 178-90 passim, 200,
206, 302; successors,
207, 273, 280, 132, 396
Dürrenmatt, Friedrich, 13,
447
Dutch, "Mr. Dooley" on,
188

Eastman, Max, 10, 39, 300
"Easy Aces," 258

Easy Street, 264, 472
Edson, C. D., 411
egalitarianism, 136, 158,
279, 336
Eggleston, Edward, 84, 98
egotism as comic target,
245, 324, 327, 331, 335,
427n, 433
Eisenhower, Dwight D.,
105, 326, 471
Eliot, T. S., 138, 471
Emerson, Ralph Waldo, 36,
157, 365, 367, 368n,
385, 390, 445, 465
empiricism as comic target,
383-84
epic, comic, 161, 380, 462n
epithet, comic, 18, 36, 70,
155, 247-48, 270, 271,
280, 281, 331, 403, 424,
432, 439, 457-58
escalation, 268
escapism, humor and, 16,
126, 226
espionage, 306, 313
Evans, Bergen, 442
exaggeration, comic, 39,
43-44, 153
expansionism, U.S., 28, 76,
77, 179, 282
exposé, comic, 23, 67, 82,
88, 131, 133, 181, 204,
212, 230, 261, 413n,
426

"Fable of the Iron Dogs,"
231
Fables for Our Time, 243,
285
Fables in Slang, 190
Fabre, Lucien, 14, 430n
Fairbanks, Douglas, 274n
fairy tales, 14, 459, 460
Falk, Peter, 331
"Falstaff," 422, 424n
family life as comic target,
221, 254-56
fanaticism, humor and, 29,
446-47, 450, 469
Fantastic Fables, 165, 169

fantasy, 39, 43, 244, 288, 295, 327
farce, 10, 11; Bierce, 178, British, 418; Faulkner, 403; French, 436, 443; international, 447; Melville, 380; movie, 259, 436; Shakespeare, 418, 424; Twain, 145; Whitman's alleged, 386
farmer as comic target, 247-48
Fascinating Crimes: The Missing Floor, 241, 243
fascism: black-comic, 356; movie treatment, 268
Faulkner, William, 340, 347-56 *passim,* 360, 366n, 410, 450n; antecedents, 47, 65, 68, 74, 103, 105, 149, 421; comic technique, 404-9; French and, 314n, 437, 439, 443; influence, 344; Negroes in, 81, 93, 146; parodied, 254, 412-13; quoted, 348-51 *passim,* 406-9 *passim;* style, 342; women in, 408-9
Federalist Party, 51n, 214
Feiffer, Jules, 20, 324-25
feminism, 21n, 182, 210, 225-26, 280
"feuds," comic, 70, 271
"Fibber McGee and Mollie," 258
Fiedler, Leslie, 93, 147, 149
Field, Eugene, 116, 195n; quoted, 87, 91
Fielding, Henry, 425
Fields, W.C., 4n, 91, 94, 272n, 303, 438; antecedents, 207; movies, 209, 259, 261, 284; quoted, 262; radio, 70, 258, 271; theories of humor, 16, 264n, 307; women and, 262, 263
film comedy. *See* movie comedy

Fine, Sylvia, 333
Fink, Mike, 46, 292
Fisher, Ed, 476
Fitzgerald, F. Scott, 118, 210, 212, 225, 242, 395, 409
Fitzpatrick, D. R., 323
"Flem Snopes," 74, 404
Fleming, Ian, 313
folk heroes, 212, 323
folklore, American, 45, 317.
    See also Crockett; "Paul Bunyan"; tall tale
"Following the Equator," 150
fools, Shakespearean, 95, 203, 421-22
Ford car, 2, 200, 202, 232
France, 333n; and U.S., 171, 314n, 371; Franklin and, 37; humor, 159, 427-44, 445n, 451, 453, 469; imperialism, 181; language, 134-35, 431, 444
France, Anatole, 439
Franklin, Benjamin, 9, 32, 34, 37, 39, 72, 439; character, 47-49, 51, 386n; comic attacks on, 192, 218, 305, 363-364, 368, 375, 384n; quoted, 35, 50
fraud, comic exposure of, 179, 227
freedom, comic, 5-7, 12, 30, 152, 462
Freneau, Philip, 51, 421, 466
Freud, Sigmund: psychology, 62, 276, 456, 458, 474; theories of humor, 15, 16, 29
Frieberg, Stan, 329n
Friedman, Bruce Jay, 308
Friedrich, Gerhard, 143
frontier humor, 6, 10, 51, 75, 155, 188, 446.
    See also Crockett;

"Paul Bunyan"; tall tale
Frost, Robert, 360, 397-400, 410, 468
Frye, Northrop, 14, 459-460, 461, 462
"funnies." *See* comic strip
Funt, Alan, 310

Gable, Clark, 259, 263, 267
Gaddis, William, 354n, 358
gangster films, comic relief in, 263
Garbo, Greta, 263
Gardner, Ed ("Archie"), 258, 273, 280
Garvin, Harry, xii
gentility, Southern, 63, 82
Germans, immigrant, 203; "Mr. Dooley" on, 188
Germany, 298, 469; humor, 444-48; Nazi, 3, 295, 357, 418; postwar, 444
"Get Smart," 313, 330
Gettysburg Address, 97; comic revision of, 105
giantism, theory of, 41-42, 45n
Gibbs, Wolcott, 210, 253; quoted, 254
Gilbert and Sullivan, 419
Ginger Man, The, 11, 356
Gleason, Jackie, 273, 311-312, 350
Gold Rush, The, 260, 261, 274
Goldberg, Rube, 4, 232
Golden, Harry, 342, 465
Goldsmith, Oliver, 463
Goldwater, Senator Barry, 336
good "bad" boy, 74
gothicism, 47, 64, 162, 369, 401, 443, 450n
Gover, Robert, xi, 340, 353-54, 355

Grand Central Station joke, 42-43, 45
Grant, Cary, 258, 259, 263, 333
Grass, Günter, 447
Great Dictator, The, 13, 265, 266, 268, 277, 278, 302-3, 463
Great Gatsby, The, 118, 212
"Greatest Man in the World, The," 25, 213, 232
Greece, ancient, 13, 39, 40, 56, 161; comedy, 423n
Green, Philip, 397
greeting cards, satiric, 338n, 339
Gregory, Dick; quoted, 297, 336, 337
Griffith, Andy, 200
Gross, Milt, 210, 245
grotesquerie, comic, 1, 25, 39, 46-47, 88-89, 90, 91, 92, 93, 288, 290, 291, 297, 314, 371, 412, 441
Guest, Edgar, 239, 413

Haliburton, Richard, 23, 32-33, 36, 50; quoted, 35.
See also "Sam Slick"
Halsman, Philippe, 440-441
Hamilton, Alexander, 51
Hamlet, 463, 471
Hammerstein, Oscar, 316, 334, 444
Hannibal, Missouri, 133
Harding, Warren G., 201
Hardy, Thomas, 68n
Harlemese, 94n
Harris, George Washington, 8, 22, 52, 57, 59, 64, 65, 66, 72, 75, 89, 403, 466; quoted, 17, 19, 58, 61-62, 68-69, 70, 71.

See also "Sut Lovingood"
Harris, Joel Chandler, 23, 47, 78, 80-81, 88, 93-95, 96, 98, 116, 188, 232; quoted, 82, 92-93, 100, 114; successors, 280, 349
Harte, Bret, 8, 16, 75, 78, 111, 114, 115, 161, 410; quoted, 101-2, 114
Hašek, Jaroslav, 23
Hawkes, John, 308, 357
Hawthorne, Nathaniel, 57, 84, 138, 360, 361, 362, 366n, 367, 374-75, 385, 390, 403, 409; laughter in, 375; style, 419n
Hazlitt, William, 12, 28, 422, 430, 476
Heller, Joseph, xi, 308, 346-47, 354, 417
Hell's Angels, 355, 357
Helzapoppin, 210
Hemingway, Ernest, 233, 296, 366n, 395, 447, 461; antecedents, 138, 140, 212, 251; characters, 17, 26, 409; French and, 443; humor, failure of, 300, 346, 402; influence, 344; misogyny, 225; parodied, 253-54; quoted, 4, 140
Henderson, the Rain King, 344, 345n
"Henry Aldrich," 258, 311n
Hepburn, Katharine, 226n
Herblock, 323
Here Comes Mr. Jordan, 259, 314
hero worship, 212-13, 280
Hersey, John, 288
Hershfield, Harry, 276
Herzog, 343, 344-46, 461
Hicks, Granville, 376
High Noon, 333
high style, 73, 172-73,

189, 248-49, 319, 419, 433
history, lampooning of, 51n, 213-14, 255-56, 426n
Hitchcock, Alfred, 314-15, 442
Hitler, Adolf, 199, 217, 281; as sick clown, 302-3; Johnson as, 470
Hobart, George V., 203
Holbrook, Hal, 152, 329
"Holden Caulfield," 340-341, 346, 355
Holmes, C. S., 288, 289
Holmes, Oliver Wendell, 156, 464
Holz, Lou, 260, 275, 444
Home from the Hill, 314, 342n, 443
Homer, comedy in, 161, 462n
homosexuality, 93, 293, 358, 418
Hooper, Johnson J., 52, 61, 68; quoted, 53-54, 57, 71.
See also "Simon Suggs"
Hooter, Mike: quoted, 17
Hope, Bob, 258, 259, 270, 271, 277, 309, 310
"Horatio Alger," 3, 15, 231, 233
horror "comics," 288
horse sense, 198, 215
horse-trading, 60, 65
hostility, humor and, 18, 30, 63, 83, 264, 268, 270, 331, 334, 338, 434, 455
Howells, William Dean, 9, 155, 196, 203-7 *passim,* 360, 409; humor, 393-95
How to Succeed in Business Without Really Trying, 334
Hubbard, Kin, 9, 197, 198, 199, 200, 202, 203, 206, 214-15

Huckleberry Finn, 9, 93, 117-41, 142, 145, 151, 157, 160, 161, 344, 416, 461, 464, 466; comic hero, 463; Faulkner and, 347, 352, 460n; Salinger and, 340-41; psychology, 462
humor: comedy and, x; decline of, 25-27, 29, 141, 272n, 280-81, 287-288, 290, 339-40, 355-359, 368, 442, 468; inadvertent, 4; seriousness of, xi; theories of, 2, 16, 28-29, 41-42, 115, 159-60, 257, 264n, 456. *See also* comedy; comparative humor
humor, American: as antisocial force, 10-11, 25-26, 476; British influence, 34, 51, 421; character, 1-10, 14-21, 25-31, 62-63, 78-79, 115-116, 207, 232-33, 267, 279, 280-84, 401, 445, 452-53, 457-58, 465-468; commercialization of, 338-39, 446; conventions, 352-53; democratic bias, 37-38, 95, 189, 212, 278-79, 322, 392, 413, 414; early, 32-51; literary importance, 204-7, 409-10; targets, 21-25, 82-87, 113, 130, 203, 210-11, 217, 280; tradition, 53, 58-59, 105; urbanization, 198-99; verbal cast, 17, 30, 98-100, 185, 238, 240, 242, 249-50, 269-72, 275-276, 288-89, 324, 351
humor, sense of: commercialized, 338-39; Melville, 379, 380; Thoreau, 363, 364; Twain, 147-48, 151. *See also* humorlessness

humorlessness, 305-6, 339, 356, 402-3, 475-76; German, 444-46, 469; repression and, 29n; Whitman, 20, 385-90, 462
humors, Medieval concept of, 11
Humphrey, William, 314, 342n
hungry i, 294
H*Y*M*A*N* K*A*P*-L*A*N, 245-47, 427n
hypocrisy: as comic target, 130, 165, 168, 204, 227, 281, 298, 301, 384; proper conduct and, 458, 476

"Ichabod Crane," 33, 362
iconoclasm, 10-11, 30, 210, 258
idealism, 296, 297, 300
Immigrant, The, 260, 263
immigrant as scapegoat, 179
immigrant humor, 8, 275, 279; German, 203; Irish, 416; Jewish, 245-47
immoralism, 25, 68, 307
imperialism, 24, 83, 166, 179, 181, 184, 188, 203, 321
incommunicativeness, 120n, 355, 444, 467
Indian, American, 43-45, 94, 99, 143-44, 166, 458; Cooper, 362-63
innocence, American myth of, 149, 268, 352
Innocents Abroad, 143
international humor, 416, 435-36, 441, 444, 447, 451, 452-53, 469
invective, 10, 83n, 151, 154, 288, 424, 462, 475. *See also* diatribe
Ionesco, Eugene, 443, 444
Irish, 79, 181; humor, 37, 179, 273

irony, British, 418, 419
irreverence, comic, 38, 51, 63, 73, 83, 272, 452; Bierce, 168; British, 426n; Poe, 371; political, 200-201, 328, 434-435; Thoreau, 368; Twain, 143, 157, 158
Irving, Washington, 12, 22, 33, 34, 36, 46, 48, 361, 416, 419, 421, 443, 466; quoted, 35, 47
Irvin, W. R., 397
isolationism, 183, 217
It Happened One Night, 27, 259
Italian comedy, 436n, 448-449
Italian opera, 383, 448-49

"Jack Downing," 33, 38, 48, 50, 66, 97, 143, 200, 466
Jackson, Andrew, 28, 37, 38, 65, 66
James, Henry, 360, 409; comedy in, 390-93; Nabokov and, 342; parodied, 173, 413; style, 138, 393
"James Bond," 18, 313
Japan, U. S. and, 296, 298
Jewett, Sarah Orne: quoted, 432
Jewish humor, ix, 3, 245-247, 260n, 275, 290, 295, 316-19, 334-36, 345-46, 447
John Birch Society, 304, 315
Johnson, Lyndon, 304, 323, 326, 328, 336, 471
Johnson, Samuel 419, 420n, 430
jokes: astronaut, 318; banana-peel, 10, 470; Jewish, 245-6, 275-6, 317, 335; "Knock, knock," 475; "Little

Audrey," 293, 325; Martian, 327; Negro, 336-37; nonsense, 107; off-color, 325-26, 328; optimist-pessimist, 15; psychological theory of, 16

Jonson, Ben, 424

"Josh Billings," ix, 7, 16, 22, 79, 82, 84, 86, 88, 96, 98, 100, 102, 104, 112, 114, 115, 188, 214, 267, 433

journalism, 52-53, 281, 288, 324n, 436

joy, comedy and, 78, 233, 284, 386, 449, 460-61

Kallen, Horace, 16

Kalmar, Bert, 270

Kant, Immanuel, 15n

Kaplan, Justin, 132n

Kaufman, George S., 209n

Kaufmann, R. J.: quoted, 296, 345

Kaye, Danny, 260, 309, 310, 333, 334n, 423, 427, 444

Keaton, Buster, 259, 261, 265n, 266, 274n, 284

Keats, John, 370

Kelly, Walt, 323-24

Kennedy, John F., 179, 313, 326, 334; assassination, 29, 328

Kerouac, Jack: parodied, 413-14

Keystone comedies, 259, 274, 314, 355, 440, 472

Khrushchev, Nikita, 304, 450

Kiddie-Kar Travel, 222

King, Alan, 22, 335

King, Martin Luther, 326

King and I, The, 315-16

King Lear, 422, 463

"knock, knock" jokes, 475

Koestler, Arthur, 7, 11, 15, 456, 475

Korean War, 295-96

Kramer, Stanley, 333

Kubrick, Stanley, 333

Ku Klux Klan, 297, 331

Lamb, Charles, 12, 15

language, theories of, 433-434n

Lannigan, George T., 111n, 366n

lapel button humor, 308

La Rochefoucauld, François de, 433, 438

Lardner, Ring, 12, 23, 27, 207, 209n, 210, 279, 323, 340, 345; characters, 211-12, 224, 227, 280; comic devices, 240, 241, 277; influence, 341; style, 248-49, 250-51, 281

laughter, psychological theories of, 15-16, 257, 375, 429, 445, 476-77

Laurel and Hardy, 4, 21, 259, 264, 265, 266, 267-269, 275, 276, 330

Leacock, Stephen, 416, 456

legal procedure, humor and, 67, 269n, 273, 381

Lehrer, Tom, 328

Lerner, Alan Jay, 316

"Letter to the Gas Company," 153

Letters from the Earth, 142, 151

Letters to Dwight, 38

Lewis, H. C., 52, 64-65, 74, 75, 292-93, 466. See also "Madison Tensas"

Lewis, Jerry, 314, 437, 465

Lewis, Sinclair, 8, 23, 27, 47, 198, 225, 227, 242, 248-49, 395; apostasy, 239, 458

Life on the Mississippi, 141, 144-45

Life With Father, 218, 315

"L'il Abner," 323

Lincoln, Abraham, 28, 66,

105, 296; "Artemus Ward" and, 97; assassination, 293, 328; comic attacks on, 89, 216, 245, 285, 286; humor, 78, 95-96, 100, 110, 113, 116, 158, 326; "Petroleum V. Nasby" on, 102-3

Lindbergh, Charles A., 202, 212, 328

literalism, comic, 2, 3, 19, 276, 280-81, 325, 411, 456; Ade, 194, 195; Benchley, 240; Bierce, 176; Browne, 108, 110; Faulkner, 403; Franklin, 34; Groucho Marx, 270; Hawthorne, 374; Mauldin, 322; Melville, 381; Perelman, 321; Rosten, 245; Thoreau, 367; Twain, 133, 153, 157; Thurber, 287

"literary comedians," 9, 28, 75, 77-116, 190, 203, 236, 422, 466

"Little Audrey" jokes, 293, 325

"Little Red Riding Hood," comic versions of, 105-106, 459

Lloyd, Harold, 261, 266, 274, 284

loathing, humor and, 472

local colorism, 8, 115, 158, 177, 198, 361

Locke, David Ross, 25, 78, 97, 99-100, 280n; quoted, 88-89, 100-101, 102-3, 109, 112. See also "Petroleum V. Nasby"

Loeb Classics, The, 248

logic, comic, 245, 246

Lolita, 291, 342, 355

Longfellow, Henry W., 156, 289, 413

Longstreet, A. B., 25, 52, 61, 63, 64, 65, 68n, 69 74, 126, 432n; quoted,

54, 55, 56, 59-60, 70, 72-73
Lorenz, Konrad, 456, 474
"Louisiana Swamp Doctor"; *see* Lewis, H. C.
Lowell, James Russell, 22, 47, 78, 96-97, 100, 421; quoted, 83, 87, 90, 98, 99
Lubitsch, Ernst, 259
Lyceum circuit, 97, 111
Lyly, John, 419
Lynn, Kenneth, 48, 57, 93; quoted, 58-59

McCarey, Leo, 259
McCarthy, Senator Joseph, 29, 323, 445
MacDonald, Dwight, 281n, 425
McDougall, William, 474
McKinley, William, 180, 189, 200, 203, 321
McLuhan, Marshall, 354, 454-55
MacMurray, Fred, 259, 333
Mad magazine, 324, 436
Madison Avenue, 105, 287, 305, 321
"Madison Tensas," 64, 71, 74
Mailer, Norman, 299, 300, 308, 356, 466, 472
Malamud, Bernard, 340, 341-42, 355
malapropism, 19, 188, 245, 262, 274, 325, 351
Manchurian Candidate, The, 315
Mander, John, 3, 447
manifest destiny, 82, 203, 283
Mann, Thomas, 23
"Man That Corrupted Hadleyburg, The," 150-151
Marceau, Marcel, 330
Markfield, Wallace, 262, 272n, 275, 316, 317
Marquis, Don, 208, 209, 210, 227, 240, 243,

245n, 248, 250-51, 254, 277, 284, 340, 461; antecedents, 280; quoted, 215-16, 218-20, 225-26, 227-30, 231-32, 241, 242, 244-45, 252-53, 258
Martian jokes, 327
Marx, Chico, 258, 264, 266, 269-70, 271, 279
Marx, Groucho, 3, 6-7, 18, 209, 266, 269-71, 276, 284, 363n, 438; antecedents, 47, 99, 103, 110, 201, 295; influence, 331, 338, 444; mustache, 278; quoted, 18, 260, 261, 272, 274; radio career, 258, 264, 271, 276; women and, 263
Marx, Harpo 25, 263, 274
Marx, Karl, 13
Marx, Leo, 9, 125
Marx Brothers, 21, 26, 209, 259, 261, 265, 276, 280, 293, 303, 346-47, 417, 423n, 440
Mason, Jackie, 335
masquerade, comic, 48, 75, 80, 114, 202-3, 277-78, 377, 422
mass media, 280-82, 354, 455, 468.
    See also radio; television
matriarchy, 21, 203, 280, 293, 298
Mauldin, Bill, 322-23
Meader, Ralph, 328
Meet John Doe, 27, 259, 267
Mellard, J. M., 352, 460n
Melville, Herman, 93, 118, 276n, 360, 361, 366n, 368, 409, 410, 413, 416, 421; comedy in, 375-85, 420, 468; quoted, 376-380, 382-85 *passim*
Mencken, Henry L., 6n, 9, 11, 105, 144, 199, 207, 210-11, 220, 241, 279,

284, 318; antidemocracy, 227, 361; influence, 331; lexicography, 12, 239, 257; misogyny, 224-25; quoted, 247-48, 358; style, 248-49, 280, 419n
"Mending Wall," 398-99
Mercer, Johnny, 316
Meredith, George, 417, 424
"Myrt and Marge," 258
metaphor, comic, 17, 31, 70-71, 113-14, 177, 188, 194, 242, 287, 341, 352
Mexican War, 18, 166n, 365
militarism, 166, 181
Miller, Arthur, 360, 402, 409
Miller, Henry, 299, 356
Miller, Jonathan, 417
Milne, A. A., 426
Milton, John, 369-70
minority humor, 334-38, 461n.
    See also immigrant humor; Jewish humor; Negroes
minstrel comedy, 37-38, 50, 94
misanthropy, comic, 30, 87-88, 227; Bierce, 162, 168, 175; Chaplin, 332; Cummings, 396; Faulkner, 349; French, 429n, 438; Melville, 385; Mencken, 211; Shakespeare, 423-24; Thurber, 286; Twain, 133, 135, 143, 148, 150, 158
misogyny, 21-25, 69, 86-87, 211, 223-26, 262-63, 409; Bellow, 345n; Bierce, 169; British lack of, 418-19; Burroughs, 356; Chaplin, 332; Dunne, 183; Faulkner, lack of, 408-9; Franklin, 48; French, 441; Alan King, 335; Paulding, 417; Perelman, 321n

Miss Lonelyhearts, 230, 231

Mr. Deeds Goes to Town, 27, 259, 267

"Mr. Dooley," 20, 179-90, 199, 202, 203, 206, 207, 280, 312, 467, 473

Moby Dick, 118, 376-79, 381, 382-84, 385

mockery, humor as, 3, 10, 30, 214, 272-73, 329, 339

Modern Times, 260, 261

Molière, Jean-Baptiste, 6, 16, 338, 416, 428-29, 430, 433, 438, 445, 462

momentum, comic, 6-7, 18, 30, 170, 207, 246, 264, 274n, 276-77, 330, 350, 403, 404, 440

momism, 21n, 267n, 280n, 294.
  See also matriarchy

Monkey Business, 270

monologue, comic, 17, 22, 31, 277

Monsieur Verdoux, 13, 266, 278, 314, 332-33, 463, 473

morality, social, 119, 121-124, 135

Morgan, Henry, 209n, 258, 262, 273, 276, 309, 311

Mother in History, A, 308

movie comedy, 3, 4, 7, 17, 21, 27, 259-71 *passim,* 274, 276-78, 284, 313-315, 332-34, 347, 437-438, 452-53; British, 418, 426, 427; conventions, 353; French, 435, 440, 442-43; Italian, 436n, 448-49; O. Henry and, 197; television, 330-31

Muggeridge, Malcolm, 425

Murray, Henry A., 380

music: popular, 260, 316; "witty," 1

music hall comedy, 420, 426

musical comedy, 196, 315-316, 333-34, 358n, 419, 448

"My Favorite Murder," 170n, 171, 178

My Little Chickadee, 262

"Mysterious Stranger, The," 150-51

Nabokov, Vladimir, 290-291, 315, 340, 342-43, 345, 352, 354, 355, 467

names, significance of, 147n, 152

Nash, Ogden, 99n, 210, 218, 233, 238, 239, 241, 260; antecedents, 280; quoted, 222-23, 242-43

Nast, Thomas, 84, 322

Nathan, George Jean, 210

Naturalism, literary, 205, 254-56

nature, love of, 134-35

Nazism, 281, 296, 302, 357

Negroes, 55-56, 60, 61, 89-90, 93-95, 112, 126, 241, 249, 256, 317; Faulkner, 146, 349-50, 352; J. C. Harris, 80-81, 100; humor of, 297, 335-38, 468; Twain, 118, 120, 125, 126, 132, 144, 146-47, 354

neologisms: comic, 17, 49, 100, 107n, 194, 298, 396, 423, 439; critics', 460n

neurosis, humor and, 59, 63, 239, 288

New Criticism, 284, 460n

New Deal, 233, 283

New England humor, 38, 46, 50, 90, 278n.
  See also Lowell; Shillaber

Newell, Robert H., 78, 100

Newhart, Bob, 328, 330

newsreels, 281, 297

New York City, 198; provincialism of, 184

New Yorker, The, 220, 251, 281, 287, 288, 291, 321, 324, 355n, 425, 426

Nichols and May, 328, 329, 441

Nietzsche, Friedrich, 14

night-club comedy, 260, 272, 277, 294, 318, 328, 441

nihilism, comic, 25, 30, 63, 227, 476; Bierce, 163; Chaplin, 265, 266; Crane 205n; Hemingway, 443; Italian, 448; Longstreet, 61; Marquis, 215, 230; Melville, 385; opposed, 334; tall tale, 45; Thurber, 287; Twain, 137, 142, 151-52

Ninotchka, 259, 263

nom de plume, comic use of, 74, 100, 114

noncommunication. *See* incommunicativeness

nonsense humor, 1, 8, 103, 105, 107, 233, 234, 241, 276n, 325 335n, 422-23, 438, 441

non sequitur, 5, 103

Norris, Frank, 366n; quoted, 411

novel, comedy in, 339-54, 444, 447, 468

Nye, Bill, 78, 87, 109, 190; quoted, 113

Nye, Louis, 330

"O. Henry," 197-98, 199, 267

Odyssey, comedy in, 161, 462n

Of Mice and Men, 231, 404n

off-color humor, 325-26, 328.
  See also ribaldry

O'Hara, John, 19, 26, 212, 292, 300, 346, 395, 402

Oklahoma!, 315-16, 334

Oliver, Edna Mae, 259

One Man's Meat, 249

optimism as comic target, 15, 80, 215, 289, 339, 375, 381
optimist-pessimist joke, 15
oratory, humor and, 189, 383
orthography, comic, 98, 100, 101, 110, 188, 245, 396
Oswald, Mrs., 308
"Owl Who Was God, The," 216-17, 285, 286, 287

Paar, Jack, 311
pacifism, 166, 445
Pagnol, Marcel, 434, 439n, 440
pantomime, 330
Paradise Lost, parody of, 369-70
Parker, Dorothy, 210, 226-227; quoted, 257
Parks, Gordon: quoted, 256
parody, 38, 82, 101-2, 104, 172-74, 251, 253-55, 342, 410-14, 417, 468-469; British, 425; Cooper, 101-2, 111, 362; Crane, 411; Cummings, 397; Poe, 369-70, 411-412, 413n, 468; Whitman, 387n, 412
Partridge, Eric, 456
patriotism, 214n, 267n, 293
Paul, Sherman, 365n
"Paul Bunyan," 6, 45n
Paulding, James Kirke, 417; quoted, 41
"Peanuts," 324
Pearl, Jack, 258
pedantry, 251, 369
pen names. See nom de plume
Penner, Joe, 258, 279
"Pennsylvania Dutch" humor, 446
Perelman, S. J., 209, 230, 237, 239, 244, 269, 270, 281, 284, 294, 319-21,

340, 438, 468; antecedents, 104, 191, 207, 279; influence, 295, 338n, 444; quoted, 320; style, 419n
pertinence, comic, 7, 30, 51, 338; Berman, 329; Bierce, 168; Brinkley, 332; Dunne, 187n, 201; James, 393; Jewish humor, 335; "Josh Billings," 102; Groucho Marx, 274; Thoreau, 366, 367; Twain, 158
pessimism, 78, 79, 138, 152, 163, 233, 286, 324, 376, 467-68, 469
"Petroleum V. Nasby," 25, 78, 88-89, 97, 98, 100-101, 102-3, 113, 280n
"Phoenix," 78, 110-11
Pickford, Mary, 266, 353
Pierre, 379-80
Plato, 11, 475
Playboy, 324n, 437
pluralism, 1, 3, 30, 278, 300, 305, 346, 347, 358, 399, 453, 476
Poe, Edgar Allan, xi, 59, 62-65, 118, 211, 232, 360, 385, 421; comic aspects, 368-74, 386, 409; con man, 23, 47, 369; French and, 314n, 437, 443; influence, 164, 170, 293, 342, 343, 401, 403; parodied, 111, 389, 411-12, 413; quoted, 368, 370-71; self-parody, 372-73, 468-69; style, 419n
poetry: metaphysical, 430; symbolist, 62.
See also Cummings; Frost; Poe; Whitman
"Pogo," 323-24
Poirier, William R., 391
political parties, U. S., 51n, 214.
See also Democratic; Federalist; Progressiv-

ism; Republican; Whig
politics as comic target, 83, 87, 180, 181, 273, 326, 336, 434-35, 466
"Polyphemus," 166-67
"Poor Richard," 32, 35, 37, 48
Pope, Alexander, 418, 419, 420, 421, 424, 433
popular song lyrics, 260, 273-74, 316, 436-37, 444
Porter, Cole, 260, 273-74, 316
Porter, W. T., 52
Porter, William S., 197-98, 464
Potts, L. J., 10, 463
Powers, J. F., 321-22
prejudice, racial, 94, 131, 143-44, 147, 249, 336-37
Prentice, G. P.: quoted, 17
profanity, 54, 250, 318
progress, humor and, 179, 203, 233
Progressivism, 24, 29, 204, 211, 215, 283
Prohibition, 199, 201, 233, 240, 247, 276, 305, 445
proportion, comic, 6, 16, 338, 386
proverbialism, 35-36, 96, 103, 214-15, 223, 280, 285, 375, 383
provincialism, 134-35, 143, 183-84, 392
Pryce-Jones, Alan, 342
pseudo-comedy, 294n, 413
pseudonyms, 114, 116, 377
psychology: feminine, 68-69, 86; Freudian, 16, 456-57; Negro, 81
psychopathology, humor and, 26, 30, 59, 300, 307, 371, 476-77.
See also neurosis; sick humor
"Pudd'nhead Wilson," 88, 142, 145-49, 150, 151, 152, 354, 409, 422n, 438
Punch, 17, 426

"Punch and Judy," 264
punning, 18, 29n, 99, 115, 276, 280, 326n, 327, 338, 413, 456; Bellow, 346; Bierce, 76-77; bilingual, 444; Dunne, 187; Faulkner, 351; French, 436, 439; James, 393; H. C. Lewis, 74n; Marx Brothers, 269-70; Melville, 381; Pennsylvania Dutch, 446; Perelman, 321; Poe, 371, 372; Will Rogers, 201; Thurber, 286, 287; Twain, 158
Purdy, James, 299, 308, 356
Puritanism, 130, 131, 162, 211, 346n; and ribaldry, 326n

Rabelais, François, 381n, 383, 416, 435, 439
racism. See prejudice, racial
radio comedy, 70, 258-59, 261, 262-63, 265, 271-273, 276, 280, 284, 331, 465; decline of, 308-9
Rains, Claude, 268
Rathbone, Basil, 258
"Rational Anthem, A," 164
"Raven, The," 373, 411-12
realism, comic, 8-9, 15, 51, 233; and literary Realism, 8, 138, 204, 251, 361, 395, 410, 472n; Chaplin, 264; cruelty in, 88; exhaustion of, 277, 280-81, 284, 301, 347; fantasy and, 244; in Nathanael West, 230-31; parody and, 410; sex, 57, 68-69, 326n, 403, 420, 461; style of, 138-141, 250
Realist, The, 324n, 437, 471
recordings, comic, 328-29
Red Badge of Courage, The, 79, 166, 296
reductionism, comic, 10, 11, 39, 338

reformism, 193, 211, 276n
Reiner, Carl, 331, 453
Reivers, The, 347-53, 405-408, 460n
religion as comic target, 21, 51, 83-86, 182, 377-78, 403, 418
  See also antireligiosity
repartee, comic, 394-95
repetition, comic, 102
Republican Party, 201, 203, 204n, 214, 240, 283
Restoration comedy, 12, 417, 418, 420
Revere, Paul, 213-14
reversalism, comic, 8, 15, 19, 30, 107, 325n, 327n, 475; Benchley, 240; Bierce, 165, 167, 175, 207; Browne, 108; Buchwald, 336; comic novel, 346; decline of, 242, 257, 281, 306; Faulkner, 403; French, 439n; Marx Brothers, 26, 423n; Nash, 241; Thoreau, 365-66; Thurber, 216, 286; Twain, 123, 149, 157
ribaldry, 325-26n, 382-83, 420, 425n, 435
Riley, James Whitcomb, 87
"Rip Van Winkle," 22, 33, 48, 88
Roach, Hal, 265, 275
Road to Miltown, The, 319
Robb, John S., 75; quoted, 69
Robbe-Grillet, Alain, 443
Rogers, Will, 2, 9, 17, 24, 87, 183, 197, 198-203, 206, 217, 279, 309n, 433, 458, 465
rogue, comic, 34, 56, 65, 74, 344, 376
romanticism: black humor and, 171-72, 472; corruption of, 306n; parody and, 410; "Tom Sawyer" and, 132-33
Roosevelt, Franklin, 28, 204,

233, 283, 300, 336; quoted, 279
Roosevelt, Theodore, 20, 200
"Rose and the Weed, The," 285-86
Rostand, Edmond, 431, 439
Rosten, Leo, 210, 240, 245-247, 248, 249, 324n; quoted, 246-47, 249n
Roughing It, 143-44
Rourke, Constance, 42, 44, 74
Rubin, Harry, 270
Ruggles, Charles, 259
Runyon, Damon, 198
rural humor, 197, 198-200
Russia: humor, 450-51; U. S. and, 296, 306, 453

sadism, 10n, 46, 58-59, 61, 91, 93, 223, 307, 358, 441, 465, 470.
  See also cruelty
Sahl, Mort, 328
Saint-Simon, Claude Henri de, 433
Saki, 419, 425
Salinger, J. D., xi, 340-41, 347n, 354, 355
"Sam Slick," 33, 47, 50
Santa Claus, 18, 163, 271, 298
Santayana, George, 125, 463
Saroyan, William, 465
Sartre, Jean-Paul, 442, 443
satire, 10, 11, 203-4, 245-246, 249n, 281, 284, 324n, 326-27, 463; Bierce, 166-167; black, 471; British, 417-18; Chaplin, 260-61; Franklin, 34; international, 451-52, mock-heroic, 421; Nabokov, 343-44; political, 8, 185, 277; religious, 376-77, 382-83; rhetorical, 72-73, Russian, 450; social, 45, 47, 247; Twain, 156

Schulz, Charles M., 324
science and technology as comic targets, 165
science fiction, humor in, 327n, 369
Scott, Sir Walter, 132, 144, 362n
Scrap Heap, The, 165, 175
sectarianism, religious, 84-86, 403
segregation, racial, 297
self-consciousness, comic, 20-21, 238, 240, 266, 282n, 310, 313, 342
self-contradiction, comic, 103, 110, 346n
self-mockery, 145, 172, 317, 337-38, 367, 450
self-pity as comic target, 324, 445
self-righteousness, 180, 195, 367, 392
"Senator Claghorn," 2, 273, 278
Sennett, Mack, 265
sentimentalism, 25, 30, 87, 281n, 310, 314, 453, 457, 458, 465; Chaplin, 266-67; comic attack on, 131, 167, 170, 171, 172, 195, 203, 210, 220-21, 274, 319, 331, 383; comic novel, 340-42 *passim,* 352, 355, 468; comic strip, 324; Harte, 161; O. Henry, 197-98; parodied, 412; Rosten, 245
sexes, battle of, 22, 48, 223-226, 263.
   See also misogyny
sexuality, humor and, 8, 299, 325-26, 377, 431, 436-37, 461
shaggy-dog stories, 10, 233, 276n, 284, 293, 441
Shakespeare, William, 18, 70, 132n, 206, 254, 286, 314n, 353, 362n, 421-24, 455, 463, 469-70; burlesqued, 38, 155-56, 246, 252-53; comedies, 418,

419, 420, 422, 423-24, 457; comic annotation of, 234
Shaw, Bernard, 418-19
Shaw, Henry W., 78, 82, 97, 98, 100, 113, 114; quoted, 79, 88, 96, 103, 104, 108-9, 115.
   See also "Josh Billings"
Shepherd, Jean, 191, 273, 308-9
Sheridan, Richard Brinsley, 422
Shillaber, Benjamin, 2, 46, 48n, 443, 444, 472; quoted, 1, 36, 50
Shriner, Herb, 200
Shulman, Max, 465
sick humor, x, 10n, 290, 293-95, 298-301, 307, 314-15, 328, 463, 470; Albee, 469n; antecedents, 25, 62, 171, 178, 231, 404; Nabokov, 291.
   See also black humor
Sidney, Philip, 475
sign-card humor, 318, 338-339, 468
"Simon Suggs," 22, 53-54, 57, 61, 65, 68, 74, 404
"Simon Suggs, Jr.," 65, 66
simplification, humor as, 3
Skelton, John, 421
Skelton, Red, 258, 266, 309, 311, 330, 420
skepticism, comic, 30, 35, 78, 79, 87, 95, 143, 152, 198, 215, 268, 284, 323, 391n, 399, 428
slang, 94n, 194, 206
slapstick humor, 56, 210, 274, 354, 378, 381, 402n, 420, 422
slavery, 56, 75, 81, 119, 148, 445
smart aleckism, 35, 135, 143
Smith, Charles Henry, 78, 80, 82, 88, 89, 96, 98; quoted, 99, 103, 110
   See also "Bill Arp"

Smith, Henry Nash, 125, 141
Smith, Seba, 8, 33, 38, 48, 50, 65, 97, 143, 466.
   See also "Jack Downing"
Smollett, Tobias, 34, 379
Smothers Brothers, 329
social class, comedy and, 11-12, 272n, 279, 335-336, 417, 431-32
social constraints, humor and, 12
social criticism, humor as, 203-4, 232-35, 239, 260-261, 288, 448, 476
Socialism, 203, 204, 210, 275, 448
South Pacific, 315-16, 334, 444
Southern, Terry, 19, 308, 357
"southwestern" humorists, 8, 47, 52-76, 155, 196, 371n, 404, 419n, 421, 424n, 443, 466
space race, humor of, 306
Spanish-American War, 166, 180, 182, 188
Spanish Sephardic humor, 23
speech, American, 8, 38-39, 53, 212, 250-51, 341, 352.
   See also dialect; vernacular
speed, comic, 17, 30, 70-71, 265, 274n, 277, 284, 426, 427, 440
Spencer, Herbert, 12, 15
"Spotted Horses," 403-4
Steinbeck, John, 231, 255, 404n, 421, 439n
Steinberg, Sol, 355n, 440
Stengel, Casey, 325
Sterne, Laurence, 344, 405-408, 418, 420, 422n, 425
Stevenson, Adlai, 326, 471n
stoicism, comic, 227, 231
Stone, Ezra, 258

"Stopping by Woods on a Snowy Evening," 399-400

Stowe, Harriet Beecher, 78; quoted, 86-87, 90-91

Sturges, Preston, 27, 259, 267n

style, comic, 12, 138-41, 248-49, 281, 383, 433-434.
See also high style

suburbia, comic attacks on, 220-21, 292, 315, 331, 335

success, ethos of, 80, 212, 404

Sullivan, Ed, 442

Sullivan, Frank, 104, 251, 332

surrealism, comic, 230, 284, 303, 319, 347, 444

"Sut Lovingood," 19, 58, 61, 66, 71, 74, 80, 86, 89, 127, 404

Swift, Jonathan, 34, 72, 170, 343, 424-25, 433

tall tale, 17, 39-46, 71, 113, 284, 416, 436n; Dunne, 188-89; Faulkner, 351, 403-4; French, 439-40, 442; Jewish, 335; Marquis, 244; movie, 274-276; sex, 325n; space, 327n; Twain, 155

Tallman, Marjorie, 42n

Tandy, Jeanette, 56, 73-74, 89

Tangential Views, 162-3, 168, 176

Tarkington, Booth, 464

Tati, Jacques, 440

"Teague O'Regan," 37, 179

technology as comic target, 261, 366, 383-84, 391, 403

television comedy, 266, 273, 281, 282, 309-13, 325, 327, 329-30, 426, 441; French, 441-42

Temple, Shirley, 262n

tension, humor as discharge of, 2, 6, 469-70

"That Was the Week That Was," 311, 441

theater, comic, 260, 315-16

This Simian World, 227

Thomas, Danny, 260

Thompson, W. T., 52, 64

Thoreau, Henry David, 18, 108, 200, 201-2, 360, 363-68, 384n, 403, 409, 421, 445, 468; quoted, 363-68 passim, 420n, 440n

Thorp, Willard, 39, 50, 460

Thorpe, T. B., 41, 52, 69, 403; quoted, 54, 61, 71

Thurber, James, 16, 20, 25, 91, 208-13 passim, 232-34, 236, 241-42, 268, 269, 277, 284, 319, 340, 410, 459; antecedents, 105, 107, 163, 207, 280; antihero, 345; as clown, 278; black humor, 443; cartoons, 29n, 223, 237, 238, 324, 440; maladjustment, 239; misogyny, 22, 48, 218, 223-24, 227, 263, 321n; quoted, 213, 216-18 passim, 237, 238, 243-44, 285-86, 287, 355, 359; post-World War II, 257, 285-90; verbal obsession, 240, 288-89, 298

Tobacco Road, 232

Tocqueville, Alexis de: quoted, 63

tolerance, shibboleth of, 279, 307

Tolkien, J. R. R., 426

Tolstoy, Leo, 56

"Tom and Jerry," 6

Tom Jones, 161

"Tom Sawyer," 119, 124-126, 132, 133, 149-50, 161n, 416

"Town Hall Tonight," 258, 278n

tragedy, comedy and, 10-11, 12, 13, 14, 137, 161, 402, 404-5, 461, 462-64, 477

tragicomedy, 13, 147, 469

tramp, comic, 25-26, 198, 202, 260, 261, 357

Transcendentalism, 445; satire on, 368, 374, 375, 381

Trilling, Lionel, 117, 127

Tristram Shandy, 159, 407, 422n

Troilus and Cressida, 423-424

Trollope, Anthony, 374-75

Trollope, Mrs., 417

Twain, Mark, 7, 8, 9, 12, 27, 116, 117-61, 392n, 395, 410, 445, 459, 464; antecedents, 53, 56, 67-68, 74, 75, 88, 97-98; Bierce and, 171; black humor and, 443; comic technique, 17; con man, 23; Dunne and, 178; Faulkner and, 352; Holbrook, 329; humor, 153-159, 466-67; misanthropy, 458; pessimism, 469; quoted, 9, 120, 121-124 passim, 127-40 passim, 146-60 passim, 205, 415n; racial protagonists, 93-94; 226; style, 98; successors, 203, 209, 249, 280, 284, 302, 340-41, 344, 393, 403; theories of humor, 16, 159; women, 409

Twelve O'Clock High, 347

Tyler, Royall, 33

Tynan, Kenneth: quoted, 412-13

U-2 incident, 328

ultrapropriety, comic use of, 74-75

"Uncle Remus," 80, 93-94, 100, 280n.
See also Harris, Joel Chandler

"Uncle Sam," 33, 197
undercutting, comic, 19, 33, 72, 186
understatement, comic, 71, 113, 155, 157, 170, 177, 352, 404, 419, 440n
"Unicorn in the Garden, The," 223-24, 287
University Days, 238
Updike, John: quoted, 413-414

Vague, Vera, 271
Van Dyke, Dick, 311, 331
vaudeville humor, 10, 70, 196, 265, 272, 278, 281n, 310, 444
vernacular, comic use of, 12, 98, 211, 250-51
victimization, humor and, 237-39, 261, 345
Victoria, Queen of England, 187, 189
Victorianism, 16, 293, 420
Viet Nam, 296, 336, 447
violence, humor and, 59-62, 68, 262, 268, 276, 403, 456
virtues, comic, 74, 136-37, 296
Voltaire, 416, 431, 435, 438.
    See also Candide

Walden, 363-68
"Walter Mitty," 22, 88, 224, 226, 236, 321n
war and wartime conditions, 79-80, 113, 114, 166, 179-80, 322.
    See also specific wars, e.g., Mexican War

Washington, George, 51, 245, 246, 329
Washington Square, 392, 393
WASP culture, 94, 144, 181, 317
Waugh, Evelyn, 417-18, 425
"Weaver and the Worm, The," 355
Weightman, John, 15, 431, 435
Weiss, Peter, 447
Welles, Orson, 234, 314n
West, Mae, 262
West, Nathanael, 210, 230-231, 232, 233, 319, 347n, 356n, 395, 417-18, 421
West Side Story, 316
Wharton, Michael, 11, 306
What Is Man?, 153, 154
Wheeler and Woolsey, 259
Whig Party, 38
Whitcher, Frances, 48n
White, E. B., 16, 105, 209n, 210, 238, 250, 257, 288n, 340, 419n; quoted, 249
white supremacy, 81, 89-90, 121
Whitman, Walt, 118, 138, 299, 356, 360, 366n, 383n, 401-2, 445, 459, 461, 468; humorlessness, 20, 386-90, 462; parodied, 412, 413; quoted, 387-88
Whittier, John Greenleaf, 111, 413
Who's Afraid of Virginia Woolf?, 358, 469n
Wilde, Oscar, 419
Wilder, Billy, 333, 452n

Wilder, Thornton: parodied, 412-13
Wilkes, George, 52
Willard, Frank, 271
Williams, Tennessee, 360, 400-402, 459, 461
Willis, N. P., 464; quoted, 17
Wilson, Woodrow, 204, 215, 296
Winters, Jonathan, 328
wisdom, comic, 96, 161, 206, 236, 349
wisecrack, 35-36, 194, 225, 236, 277
wit, 11, 16, 18, 271; British, 418-19; French, 429, 430, 431, 435, 469; Howells, 394; Thoreau, 365
Wolfe, Thomas, 344, 462
women: as comic target, 21-25, 86-87, 210, 223-226, 288, 321n, 392-93; fictional portraits, 408-9; in British humor, 418-19.
    See also matriarchy; misogyny; psychology
Woollcott, Alexander, 210
work-ethos, satire on, 181, 246-47, 261
World War I, 101, 204, 233, 295, 296, 357, 442
World War II, 166n, 295, 296, 357, 442
Wynn, Ed, 260, 277

Yeats, W. B., 14
Yiddish. *See* Jewish humor
Youngman, Henny, 260

Zemach, Shlomo, 470